ZAGAT®

San Francisco Bay Area Restaurants

2011

LOCAL EDITOR
Meesha Halm
STAFF EDITOR
Karen Hudes

Published and distributed by
Zagat Survey, LLC
4 Columbus Circle
New York, NY 10019
T: 212.977.6000
E: sanfran@zagat.com
www.zagat.com

ACKNOWLEDGMENTS

We thank Jon, Olive and Jude Fox, Randi Gollin, Gayle Keck, Katie Robbins, Becky Ruthenburg and Sharron Wood, as well as the following members of our staff: Josh Rogers (senior associate editor), Brian Albert, Sean Beachell, Maryanne Bertollo, Jane Chang, Sandy Cheng, Reni Chin, Larry Cohn, John Deiner, Alison Flick, Jeff Freier, Matthew Hamm, Justin Hartung, Garth Johnston, Natalie Lebert, Mike Liao, Jacqueline Wasilczyk, Art Yaghci, Sharon Yates, Anna Zappia and Kyle Zolner.

The reviews in this guide are based on public opinion surveys. The ratings reflect the average scores given by the survey participants who voted on each establishment. The text is based on quotes from, or paraphrasings of, the surveyors' comments. Phone numbers, addresses and other factual data were correct to the best of our knowledge when published in this guide.

Our guides are printed using environmentally preferable inks containing 20%, by weight, renewable resources on papers sourced from well-managed forests. Deluxe editions are covered with Skivertex Recover® Double containing a minimum of 30% post-consumer waste fiber.

SUSTAINABLE FORESTRY INITIATIVE	Certified Chain of Custody Promoting Sustainable Forest Management www.sfiprogram.org

PWC-SFICOC-260

ENVIROINK™

The inks used to print the body of this publication contain a minimum of 20%, by weight, renewable resources.

Maps © Antenna Audio

Contents

Ratings & Symbols

Zagat Top Spot	Name	Symbols		Cuisine	Zagat Ratings			
					FOOD	DECOR	SERVICE	COST

Area, Address & Contact	**Z** **Tim & Nina's** ● *Seafood*

	∇ 23	9	13	$15

Embarcadero | 999 Mission St. (The Embarcadero) | 415-555-7233 | www.zagat.com

Review, surveyor comments in quotes	Open "more or less when T and N feel like it", this bit of unembellished Embarcadero ectoplasm excels at seafood with Asian-Argentinean-Albanian accents; the staff seems "fresh off the boat", and while the view of the garbage barges is "a drag", no one balks at the "beneficent" "bottom-feeder prices."

Ratings   **Food, Decor** and **Service** are rated on the Zagat 0 to 30 scale.

0	-	9	poor to fair
10	-	15	fair to good
16	-	19	good to very good
20	-	25	very good to excellent
26	-	30	extraordinary to perfection
	∇		low response	less reliable

Cost   Our surveyors' estimated price of a dinner with one drink and tip. Lunch is usually 25 to 30% less. For unrated **newcomers** or **write-ins,** the price range is shown as follows:

I	$25 and below	**E**	$41 to $65
M	$26 to $40	**VE**	$66 or above

Symbols

Z	highest ratings, popularity and importance
●	serves after 11 PM
Ƨ	closed on Sunday
M	closed on Monday
⊄	no credit cards accepted

Maps   Index maps show restaurants with the highest Food ratings in those areas.

About This Survey

Here are the results of our **2011 San Francisco Bay Area Restaurants Survey,** covering 1,373 eateries in the greater San Francisco Bay Area, including the Monterey Peninsula, Silicon Valley, Wine Country and Lake Tahoe. Like all our guides, this one is based on input from avid local consumers – 10,118 all told. Our editors have synopsized this feedback and highlighted representative comments (in quotation marks within each review). You can read full surveyor comments – and share your own opinions – on **ZAGAT.com,** where you'll also find the latest restaurant news plus menus, photos and lots more, all for free.

OUR PHILOSOPHY: Three simple premises underlie our ratings and reviews. First, we've long believed that the collective opinions of large numbers of consumers are more accurate than the opinions of a single critic. (Consider that, as a group, our surveyors bring some 1.5 million annual meals' worth of experience to this Survey. They also visit restaurants year-round, anonymously – and on their own dime.) Second, food quality is only part of the equation when choosing a restaurant, thus we ask surveyors to separately rate food, decor and service and report on cost. Third, since people need reliable information in a fast, easy-to-digest format, we strive to be concise and to offer our content on every platform. Our Top Ratings lists (pages 10–17) and indexes (starting on page 255) are also designed to help you quickly choose the best place for any occasion.

ABOUT ZAGAT: In 1979, we started asking friends to rate and review restaurants purely for fun. The term "user-generated content" had not yet been coined. That hobby grew into Zagat Survey; 31 years later, we have over 375,000 surveyors and cover airlines, bars, dining, fast food, entertaining, golf, hotels, movies, music, resorts, shopping, spas, theater and tourist attractions in over 100 countries. Along the way, we evolved from being a print publisher to a digital content provider, e.g. **ZAGAT.com, ZAGAT.mobi** (for web-enabled mobile devices), **ZAGAT TO GO** (for smartphones) and **nru** (for Android phones). We also produce customized gifts and marketing tools for a wide range of corporate clients. And you can find us on Twitter (twitter.com/zagatbuzz), Facebook and other social media networks.

JOIN IN: To improve our guides, we solicit your comments; it's vital that we hear your opinions. Just contact us at **nina-tim@zagat.com.** We also invite you to join our surveys at **ZAGAT.com.** Do so and you'll receive a choice of rewards in exchange.

THANKS: We're grateful to our local editor, Meesha Halm, who is a Bay Area restaurant critic, cookbook author and dedicated momnivore. We also sincerely thank the thousands of surveyors who participated – this guide is really "theirs."

New York, NY
September 21, 2010

Nina and Tim Zagat

What's New

Despite the recession and, with it, the closures of such bubble-era stalwarts as **Aqua** and **Bacar,** Bay Area openings have kept up a brisk pace. Vets from higher-end ventures reinvented themselves by launching everything from approachable prix-fixeries to superb sandwich shops, making the quality of everyday eating that much better. Our surveyors, too, are seizing opportunities afforded by the downturn – 36% say they're now landing tables at hard-to-get-into places and 50% are finding better dining deals. Since the average cost per meal has gone down from $39.40 to $38.78, never has so little bought so much.

FARM-FRESH FEASTS: NYC's David Chang may have stirred up a "lipstick on a pig"–style controversy with his "figs on a plate" characterization of SF cuisine, but locally sourced, pristine ingredients, from produce to whole beasts, remain the driving force behind the year's biggest debuts, from the celeb-powered **Wayfare Tavern** (**Tyler Florence**) and **Morimoto Napa** to more casual, yet no less impressive, arrivals, i.e. the Castro's **Frances** – voted No. 1 newcomer – as well as SoMa's **Benu** and **Boulevard**-offshoot **Prospect.**

SAMMY I AM: Sandwiches unlike anything your mom ever packed in your lunchbox – from handmade bologna to banh mi – are storming the food scene, rewarding desk jockeys with gourmet eats at (relatively) affordable prices. Prime purveyors include SoMa's **Spice Kit** and **American Grilled Cheese Kitchen,** North Beach's **Naked Lunch,** Dogpatch's **Kitchenette SF** and **Boccalone Salumeria** on the Embarcadero.

TAVERNS ON THE GREEN: While viticulture dominates Downtown's new **Barbacco** and the Mission's **Heirloom Cafe,** beer took a gulp out of wine's market share this year with the help of cicerones (beer sommeliers) at the Marina's **Delarosa,** the Castro's **Starbelly** and Sunset's **Social Kitchen & Brewery.** Meanwhile, startenders at the Barbary Coast–style **Comstock Saloon,** Cow Hollow's **Café des Amis** and Healdsburg's **Spoonbar** are finding inspiration in both past and present, slinging old-timey drinks and farm-to-table cocktails (expect SoMa's **Bar Agricole** to follow suit).

CHART TOPPERS: Again voted No. 1 for Food and Service as well as Most Popular, the Wharf's **Gary Danko** retains its lead on the high-end scene. Big Sur's **Sierra Mar** repeats as tops for Decor and also shows it's more than just a pretty face, landing the No. 4 spot for Food (following the **French Laundry** and **Cyrus**). Meanwhile, the taco truck fleet **El Tonayense,** which was hawking street food long before it became fashionable, snags the title of Best Bang for the Buck.

GASTRO TECH: Eating out has never been easier thanks to social media sites and other technologies: 60% of surveyors book reservations online (up from 52% last year), 85% check a restaurant's website before dining and 23% track food trucks and other eateries via Twitter and Facebook. Still, while 91% think it's ok to snap photos at the table, 63% denounce TWI (texting while ingesting) or talking on the phone.

San Francisco, CA
September 21, 2010

Meesha Halm

Most Popular

These restaurants are plotted on the map at the back of this book. Places outside of San Francisco are marked as: E=East of SF; N=North; and S=South. When a restaurant has locations both inside and out of the city limits, we include the notation SF as well.

1. Gary Danko | *American*
2. Boulevard | *American*
3. Slanted Door | *Vietnamese*
4. French Laundry/N | *Amer./Fr.*
5. Cyrus/N | *French*
6. Chez Panisse/E | *Cal./Med.*
7. Zuni Café | *Mediterranean*
8. Kokkari Estiatorio | *Greek*
9. Chez Panisse Café/E | *Cal.*
10. A16 | *Italian*
11. Delfina | *Italian*
12. Bouchon/N | *French*
13. Fleur de Lys | *Cal./French*
14. Acquerello | *Italian*
15. Quince | *French/Italian*
16. Yank Sing | *Chinese*
17. Tadich Grill | *Seafood*
18. Ad Hoc/N | *American*
19. Perbacco | *Italian*
20. Chapeau! | *French*
21. Absinthe | *French/Med.*
22. Jardinière | *Cal./French*
23. La Folie | *French*
24. In-N-Out/E/N/S/SF | *Burgers*
25. Auberge du Soleil/N | *Cal./Fr.*
26. Ritz-Carlton Din. Rm.| *Fr.*
27. Bottega/N | *Italian*
28. Redd/N | *Californian*
29. House of Prime Rib | *Amer.*
30. Evvia/S | *Greek*
31. Bistro Jeanty/N | *French*
32. Mustards Grill/N | *Amer./Cal.*
33. Aziza | *Moroccan*
34. Buckeye*/N | *Amer./BBQ*
35. Tartine Bakery | *Bakery*
36. Spruce | *American*
37. Chow/Park Chow/E/SF | *Amer.*
38. Manresa/S | *American*
39. Scoma's/N/SF | *Seafood*
40. Nopa | *Californian*
41. Burma Super/E/SF | *Burmese*
42. Farallon | *Seafood*
43. Amber India/S/SF | *Indian*
44. Zachary's Pizza/E | *Pizza*
45. Village Pub/S | *American*
46. Greens | *Vegetarian*
47. Range | *American*
48. Coi | *Californian/French*
49. Hog Island/N/SF | *Seafood*
50. Bix | *American/French*

Many of the above restaurants are among the San Francisco area's most expensive, but if popularity were calibrated to price, a number of other restaurants would surely join their ranks. To illustrate this, we have added lists of Best Buys and Prix Fixe Bargains on pages 15-17.

* Indicates a tie with restaurant above

KEY NEWCOMERS

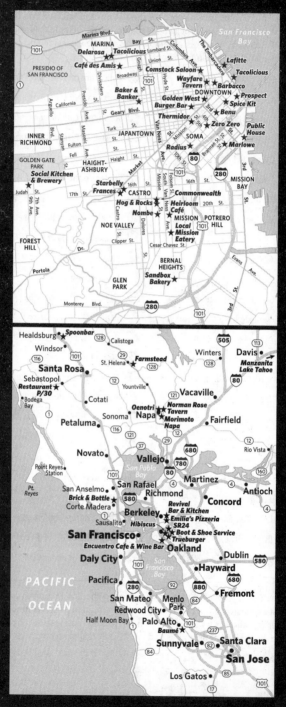

Menus, photos, voting and more - free at ZAGAT.com

Key Newcomers

Our editors' take on the year's top arrivals. See page 312 for a full list.

HOT CHEFS & OPENINGS

Barbacco
Baumé/S
Benu
Burger Bar
Café des Amis
Frances
Manzanita/E
Morimoto Napa/N
Prospect
Public House
Wayfare Tavern

LOCAVORE/VEG.

Encuentro/E
Farmstead/N
Local Mission Eatery
Radius
Revival Bar & Kitchen/E
Spoonbar/M
SR24/E

PIZZA

Boot & Shoe Service/E
Emilia's Pizzeria/E
Zero Zero

SANDWICHES/BITES

Golden West
Sandbox Bakery
Spice Kit
Tacolicious
Trueburger/E

SMALL WONDERS

Baker & Banker
Commonwealth
Hibiscus/E
Hog & Rocks
Lafitte
Marlowe
Oenotri/N
Restaurant P/30/N
Thermidor

WINE/SPIRITS/BEER

Brick & Bottle/N
Comstock Saloon
Delarosa
Heirloom Café
Nombe
Norman Rose Tavern/N
Social Kitchen
Starbelly

Big changes are afoot in the **Michael Mina** empire this October: the chef's new **Bourbon Steak** is taking over the longtime digs of his eponymous flagship restaurant, which, in turn, is moving to the former **Aqua** space and shifting to a lower price point. Also heeding the more casual trend, Survey champ **Gary Danko** is slated to open a breezy brasserie in Ghirardelli Square come early 2011.

Meanwhile, a parade of pizzaioli hits town this fall, including Anthony Mangieri's SoMa incarnation of NYC's shuttered **Una Pizza Napoletana**, **Gialina**'s Western Addition offshoot **Ragazza,** and in the Mission, **Farina**'s spin-off **Antica Pizzeria Napoletana** and **Pizza del Populo** (its working name) by Jon Darsky (ex **Flour + Water**). Other ventures set to launch in the Mission are **Delfina**'s forthcoming Roman osteria **Locanda,** and an ambitious complex whose tenants will include **Central Kitchen** and **Salumeria** (both from the **Flour + Water** gang); **The Parlour by Henry Slocombe,** a cafe from the cult creamery; and the late-night drink kitchen **Trick Dog.** On the food-cart front, additional hubs like the one at the Ferry Building's popular Thursday farmer's market are ready to roll into Justin Herman Plaza, Dolores Park and Golden Gate Park.

Outside the city, Daniel Patterson (**Coi**) is planting the Californian **Plum** in Oakland, and **Plate Shop** will dish up its ingredient-driven cuisine in Sausalito. Farther North, Napa's recently renovated Riverfront is poised to hit full tilt with the fall arrival of sustainable seafooder **Fish Story**, joining the just-launched **Morimoto Napa** and imminently opening **Tyler Florence Rotisserie & Wine.**

Top Food Overall

29 Gary Danko | *American*	Pizzetta 211 | *Pizza*
French Laundry/N | *Amer./Fr.*	House | *Asian*
28 Cyrus/N | *French*	Kokkari Estiatorio | *Greek*
Sierra Mar/S | *Cal./Eclectic*	Farmhouse Inn/N | *Cal.*
Acquerello | *Italian*	Swan Oyster | *Seafood*
La Folie | *French*	Frances | *Cal./Med.*
Erna's Elderberry/E | *Cal./Fr.*	Ad Hoc/N | *American*
Hana Japanese/N | *Japanese*	Rivoli/E | *Cal./Med.*
Chez Panisse/E | *Cal./Med.*	Zushi Puzzle | *Japanese*
27 Kaygetsu/S | *Japanese*	Cafe Gibraltar/S | *Med.*
La Toque/N | *French*	Range | *American*
Marinus/S | *French*	Cheese Board/E | *Bakery/Pizza*
Sushi Zone | *Japanese*	Evvia/S | *Greek*
Canteen | *Californian*	Tartine Bakery | *Bakery*
Chez Panisse Café/E | *Cal.*	**26** Auberge du Soleil/N | *Cal./Fr.*
Masa's | *French*	Cafe La Haye/N | *Amer./Cal.*
Ritz-Carlton Din. Rm.| *Fr.*	La Forêt/S | *Continental/Fr.*
Boulevard | *American*	Le Papillon/S | *French*
Sushi Ran/N | *Japanese*	Terra/N | *American*
Manresa/S | *American*	Coi | *Californian/French*
Commis/E | *American*	Alexander's/S | *Japanese*
Kiss Seafood | *Japanese*	Kabuto | *Japanese*
Sebo* | *Japanese*	Aziza | *Moroccan*
Fleur de Lys | *Cal./French*	Bakesale Betty/E | *Bakery*
Redd/N | *Californian*	Rosso | *Italian/Pizza*

BY CUISINE

AMERICAN (NEW)

29 Gary Danko
French Laundry/N
27 Boulevard
Manresa/S
Commis/E

AMERICAN (TRAD.)

27 Ad Hoc/N
25 Mama's on Wash.
House of Prime Rib
24 Press/N
Maverick

ASIAN

27 House
24 Flying Fish Grill/S (Carmel)
23 Koo
Eos
22 Bushi-tei

BARBECUE

23 Buckeye Roadhouse/N
22 Wexler's

BarBersQ/N
Bo's Barbecue/E
21 Memphis Minnie's

BURGERS

23 Joe's Cable Car
22 In-N-Out/E/N/S/SF
21 Gott's Roadside/N/SF
20 BurgerMeister/E/S/SF
19 Barney's/E/N/SF

CAJUN/CREOLE/SOUL

24 Brenda's
23 Brown Sugar Kitchen/E
1300 on Fillmore
22 Chenery Park
21 Picán/E

CALIFORNIAN

28 Chez Panisse/E
27 Canteen
Chez Panisse Café/E
Redd/N
Farmhouse Inn/N

Excludes places with low votes, unless otherwise indicated

Menus, photos, voting and more – free at ZAGAT.com

CHINESE

25 Yank Sing
24 Great China/E
    R&G Lounge
    Ton Kiang
    Tommy Toy's

CONTINENTAL

26 La Forêt/S
25 Anton & Michel/S
24 Ecco∇
22 Bella Vista/S

DIM SUM

25 Yank Sing
24 Ton Kiang
23 Koi Garden/E/S
20 Harmony/N
    Gold Mountain

ECLECTIC

28 Sierra Mar/S
    Willi's Wine Bar/N
24 Firefly
    Va de Vi/E
    Willow Wood Mkt./N

FRENCH

28 Cyrus/N
    La Folie
    Erna's Elderberry/E
27 La Toque/N
    Marinus/S

FRENCH (BISTRO)

26 Chapeau!
    Bouchon/N
25 Bistro Jeanty/N
    Chez Spencer
    Syrah/N

INDIAN

25 Ajanta/E
24 Amber India/S/SF
    Shalimar/E/S/SF
23 Lotus/Anokha/N
    Sakoon/S

ITALIAN

28 Acquerello
26 Rosso Pizzeria/N
    Delfina
    Quince
    La Ciccia

JAPANESE

28 Hana Japanese/N
27 Kaygetsu/S
    Sushi Zone
    Sushi Ran/N
    Kiss Seafood

MED./GREEK

27 Kokkari Estiatorio
    Rivoli/E
    Cafe Gibraltar/S
    Evvia/S
26 BayWolf/E

MEXICAN

25 Tamarindo Antojeria/E
    La Taqueria
24 El Tonayense
23 Nopalito
    Tacolicious

MIDDLE EASTERN

26 Truly Mediterranean
23 Kabul/S
    Troya
    A La Turca
    Helmand Palace*

PERUVIAN

24 La Mar Cebicheria
23 Limón
    Mochica
22 Fresca

PIZZA

27 Pizzetta 211
    Cheese Board/E
26 Rosso Pizzeria/N
    Tony's Pizza
25 Pizzeria Picco/N

SANDWICHES

26 Bakesale Betty/E
24 Boccalone Salumeria
    Sentinel
    Saigon Sandwiches
22 Il Cane Rosso

SEAFOOD

27 Swan Oyster Depot
25 Bar Crudo
    Fish/N
    Passionfish/S
    Hog Island Oyster/N/SF

SPANISH/BASQUE

25 Piperade
24 ZuZu/N
    Contigo
    Fringale
    Zarzuela

STEAK

26 Alexander's Steak/S
   Seasons
25 Harris'
   House of Prime Rib
24 Press/N

THAI

24 Soi4/E
23 Thai House
   Marnee Thai
   Manora's Thai
   Thep Phanom

VEGETARIAN

26 Ubuntu/N
25 Millennium
24 Greens
23 Cha-Ya Vegetarian/E/SF
20 Udupi Palace/E/S/SF

VIETNAMESE

26 Slanted Door
25 Tamarine/S
   Crustacean
24 Xyclo/E
   Thanh Long

BY SPECIAL FEATURE

BREAKFAST

27 Tartine Bakery
25 Mama's on Wash.
   Dottie's True Blue
   Boulette's Larder
23 Café Fanny/E

BRUNCH

27 Canteen
25 Zuni Café
   Mission Beach Café
24 Navio/S
23 Foreign Cinema

CHILD-FRIENDLY

26 Tony's Pizza
22 Chenery Park
21 Gott's Roadside Tray/N/SF
   Pizza Antica/E/N/SF
20 Chow/Park Chow/E/SF

HOTEL DINING

28 Sierra Mar/S (Post Ranch)
   Erna's/E (Château/Sureau)
27 La Toque/N (Westin Verasa)
   Marinus/S (Bernardus)
   Masa's (Hotel Vintage Ct.)

NEWCOMERS (RATED)

27 Frances
25 Baker & Banker
   Barbacco
24 Boot & Shoe Service/E
23 Tacolicious

OPEN LATE

25 Nopa
24 Flour + Water

23 Beretta
22 Absinthe
21 Globe

SMALL PLATES

25 Tamarine/S
   Picco/N
   Isa
   Willi's Wine Bar/N
24 À Côté/E

TRENDY

25 Nopa
   A16
24 Flour + Water
23 Beretta
21 Gitane

WINE BARS

26 Martini House/N
23 Eos
22 RN74
21 Uva Enoteca
20 Cav Wine Bar

WINNING WINE LISTS

29 Gary Danko
   French Laundry/N
28 Cyrus/N
   Acquerello
27 La Toque/N

WORTH A TRIP

29 French Laundry/N
28 Cyrus/N
   Sierra Mar/S
   Erna's Elderberry/E
   Chez Panisse/E

Top Decor Overall

29 Sierra Mar/S
Garden Court
Ahwahnee Din. Rm./E

28 Pacific's Edge/S
Auberge du Soleil/N
Cyrus/N

27 Navio/S
Erna's Elderberry/E
French Laundry/N
Farallon
Ritz-Carlton Din. Rm.
Gary Danko
Farm/N
Marinus/S
Meadowood Rest./N

26 Roy's/S
Fleur de Lys
Bix
Big 4
Jardinière
Rotunda

Étoile/N
Spruce
Nepenthe/S
Press/N
Waterbar
Madrona Manor/N
Kokkari Estiatorio
John Ash & Co./N
Quince
Ana Mandara

25 Madera/S
Boulevard
Epic Roasthouse
Acquerello
Sutro's at Cliff Hse.
La Toque/N
Lake Chalet/E
Martini House/N
Anton & Michel/S
Seasons*
Shadowbrook*/S

OUTDOORS

29 Sierra Mar
28 Auberge du Soleil/N
26 Étoile/N
Nepenthe/S
Waterbar
25 Epic Roasthouse

Lake Chalet/E
Martini House/N
Murray Circle/N
24 Tra Vigne/N
23 Foreign Cinema
La Mar Cebicheria

ROMANCE

27 Marinus/S
26 Fleur de Lys
Madrona Manor/N
25 Shadowbrook/S
24 Terra/N
Casanova/S

La Forêt/S
23 Aziza
Bella Vista/S
22 Supperclub
21 Chez Papa Resto
19 Cafe Jacqueline

ROOMS

29 Garden Court
Ahwahnee Din. Rm./E
27 Farallon
26 Fleur de Lys
Bix
Jardinière
Spruce

Quince
25 Boulevard
Plumed Horse/S
24 RN74
Grand Cafe
Gitane
23 Five/E

29	Sierra Mar/S		Greens
28	Pacific's Edge/S	22	Slanted Door
27	Navio/S		Wolfdale's/E
25	Sutro's at Cliff Hse.	21	Beach Chalet
24	Caprice/N	20	Guaymas/N
	Albion River Inn/N	19	Sam's Chowder Hse./S

Top Service Overall

28	Gary Danko		Étoile/N
	French Laundry/N		Kaygetsu/S
	Cyrus/N		Boulevard
	Acquerello		Le Papillon/S
27	Erna's Elderberry/E		Madrona Manor/N
	Coi		Quince
	La Toque/N	25	Fifth Floor
	Ritz-Carlton Din. Rm.		Chez Panisse Café/E
	Seasons		Albion River Inn/N
	Commis/E		Bistro des Copains/N
	Marinus/S		Silks
	Masa's		Ad Hoc/N
	Sierra Mar/S		Aubergine/S
	Meadowood Rest./N		Kokkari Estiatorio
	Manresa/S		Jardinière
26	La Folie		Rivoli/E
	Fleur de Lys		Ame
	Chez Panisse/E		Lalime's/E
	Auberge du Soleil/N		BayWolf/E
	Farmhouse Inn/N		La Forêt/S

Best Buys Overall

BAKERIES

27| Cheese Board/E
     Tartine Bakery
26| Bakesale Betty/E
25| Della Fattoria/N
24| Gayle's Bakery/S
     Downtown Bakery/N
     Emporio Rulli/N/SF
     La Boulange/N/SF

DINERS

25| Dottie's True Blue
23| Bette's Oceanview/E
     Joe's Cable Car
21| Gott's Roadside Tray/N/SF
20| Sears Fine Food
19| St. Francis
     Jimmy Beans/E
     Fog City Diner

EARLY-BIRD

27| Cafe Gibraltar/S ($25)
26| Chapeau! ($28)
25| Anton & Michel/S ($25)
23| Chez Papa ($25)
     Marica/E ($21)
22| Boca/N ($22)
21| Tarpy's Roadhouse/S ($12)
20| Sardine Factory/S ($20)
     Alamo Square ($15)

HOLE-IN-THE-WALL

24| Shalimar/E/S/SF
     Saigon Sandwiches
23| A La Turca
     Shanghai Dumpling
22| Katana-Ya
     Brother's Korean
21| Tu Lan
     Yamo▽
20| Yuet Lee

FOOD STANDS/TRUCKS

28| 4505 Meats▽
25| RoliRoti▽
     Chez/Spencer on the Go!
24| Boccalone Salumeria
     El Tonayense
23| Namu
22| Kitchenette SF▽
19| Let's Be Frank

NO CORKAGE FEE

25| Fig Cafe & Winebar/N
24| Tra Vigne/N

23| Rutherford Grill/N
     Cafe Citti/N
21| Pizzeria Tra Vigne/N
20| Uva Trattoria/N▽
19| Healdsburg B&G/N
     Indigo

NOODLE SHOPS

23| San Tung
     O Chamé/E
22| Katana-Ya
21| Citrus Club
20| Hotaru/S
     Hotei
18| King of Thai

PRIX FIXE LUNCH

27| Chez Panisse Café/E ($29)
26| Spruce ($30)
25| Ajanta/E ($12)
24| Bix ($22)
     Jin Sho*/S ($16)
     Tommy Toy's ($23)
23| One Market ($23)
     Chez Papa ($18/24)

PRIX FIXE DINNER

27| Chez Panisse Café/E ($29)
     Cafe Gibraltar/S ($25)
25| Bistro des Copains/N ($30)
     Chantilly/S ($30)
     Ajanta/E ($17)
     Isa ($28)
     Esin/E ($28)
24| Great China/E ($15)

TAQUERIAS

23| Nopalito
     Tacolicious
     Tacubaya/E
22| Mamacita
     El Metate
     Pancho Villa/S/SF
     Papalote

TOP CHEF BARGAINS

27| Chez Panisse Café/E
26| Pizzeria Delfina
24| Sentinel
23| Bocadillos
22| Il Cane Rosso
     Out the Door
21| Mijita
19| Burger Bar

BEST BUYS: BANG FOR THE BUCK

In order of Bang for the Buck rating.

1. El Tonayense
2. In-N-Out/E/N/S/SF
3. Saigon Sandwiches
4. Arinell Pizza/E/SF
5. Caspers Hot Dogs/E
6. Bakesale Betty/E
7. Let's Be Frank
8. Rosamunde
9. Taqueria Can-Cun
10. El Metate
11. Cheese Board Collective/E
12. Mixt Greens
13. Sentinel
14. Cheese Steak Shop/E/N/S/SF
15. Jay's Cheesesteak
16. La Cumbre Taqueria/S/SF
17. Truly Mediterranean
18. Boccalone Salumeria
19. Gioia Pizzeria/E
20. Pancho Villa/S/SF
21. La Corneta/S/SF
22. La Taqueria
23. Papalote Mexican
24. Blue Barn Gourmet
25. Cactus Taqueria/E
26. Tartine Bakery
27. Showdogs
28. Burger Joint/S/SF
29. Downtown Bakery/N
30. Nick's Crispy Tacos
31. Green Chile Kitchen
32. Red's Java House
33. La Boulange/N/SF
34. Pluto's Fresh Food/S/SF
35. Good Luck Dim Sum
36. Sol Food/N
37. Vik's Chaat Corner/E
38. Zeitgeist
39. Model Bakery/N
40. BurgerMeister/E/S/SF

BEST BUYS: OTHER GOOD VALUES

Alamo Square
American Grilled Cheese
Avatar's/N
Bodega Bistro
Bovolo/N
Brenda's
Brown Sugar Kitchen/E
Burma Superstar/E/SF
Cafe Citti/N
Chapeau!
Charanga
Cha-Ya Vegetarian/E/SF
DeLessio
Emilia's Pizzeria/E
Emmy's Spaghetti
Fig Cafe & Winebar/N
Firefly
Giordano Bros.
Golden West
Gott's Roadside Tray/N/SF
Il Cane Rosso
Jimtown Store/N
Kasa Indian
Kitchenette SF
Lahore Karahi
Le Cheval/E
Limón Rotisserie
Little Star Pizza/E/SF
Mario's Bohemian
Muracci's/S/SF
Naked Lunch
Nopalito
Outerlands
Out the Door
Pagolac
Pakwan/E/SF
Parada 22
Pica Pica Maize/N/SF
Prime Rib Shabu
Roam Artisan Burgers
Spice Kit
Super Duper
Table Café/N
Tacubaya/E
Ti Couz
Trueburger/E
Underdog Hot Dog
Yumma's

PRIX FIXE BARGAINS

Since hours may be limited and prices can change, please call ahead to confirm.

DINNER ($30 & UNDER)

Ajanta/E	$17	Eve/E	25
Alamo Square	15	Esin/E	28
Amber Bistro/E	30	Garibaldis/E/SF	30
Axum Cafe	17	Grasing's Coastal/S	30
Baker St. Bistro	17	Hyde St. Bistro	28
Basque Cultural Ctr./S	20	Isa	28
Bistro Aix	25	Jimmy Beans/E	15
Bistro Central Parc	18	Jin Sho/S	16
Bistro des Copains/N	30	La Terrasse	22
Bistro Liaison/E	28	Lavanda/S	25
Bistro St. Germain	20	Ledford House/N	25
Bridges/E	27	Le P'tit Laurent	22
Cafe Bastille	25	Mantra/S	29
Cafe Gibraltar/S	25	Mezza/E	23
Caffe Delle Stelle	26	MoMo's	29
Capannina	25	Palio d'Asti	29
Chantilly/S	30	Plouf	25
Chapeau!	28	Rick & Ann's/E	20
Charcuterie/N	20	Tarpy's Roadhouse/S	12
Chez Panisse Café/E	29	Town's End	23
Cliff House Bistro	25	Unicorn Pan Asian	25
Digs Bistro/E	25	Zazie	24
Duck Club/E	20	Zucca/S	18

LUNCH ($25 & UNDER)

Ajanta/E	12	One Market	23
Ana Mandara	25	Parcel 104/S	22
Bistro Liaison/E	17	Plouf	19
Bix	22	Ribisi/N	15
Chez Papa Bistrot	18	Scala's Bistro	19
Garibaldis/E	19	Scoma's	24
Grand Cafe	20	Sens	20
Grand Pu Bah	20	Sino/S	19
Hurley's/N	18	Tarpy's Roadhouse/S	9
Isobune/S	9	Tommy Toy's	23
Jin Sho/S	16	Vik's Chaat Corner/E	6
Junnoon/S	12	Waterbar	24
MarketBar	24	Waterfront Restaurant	18
Midi	19	Zibibbo/S	16

CITY OF SAN FRANCISCO

Top Food

29 Gary Danko | *American*

28 Acquerello | *Italian*
    La Folie | *French*

27 Sushi Zone | *Japanese*
    Canteen | *Californian*
    Masa's | *French*
    Ritz-Carlton Din. Rm. | *French*
    Boulevard | *American*
    Kiss Seafood | *Japanese*
    Sebo* | *Japanese*
    Fleur de Lys | *Cal./French*
    Pizzetta 211 | *Pizza*
    House | *Asian*
    Kokkari Estiatorio | *Greek*
    Swan Oyster Depot | *Seafood*

Frances | *Californian/Med.*
Zushi Puzzle | *Japanese*
Range | *American*
Tartine Bakery | *Bakery*

26 Coi | *Californian/French*
    Kabuto | *Japanese*
    Aziza | *Moroccan*
    Delfina | *Italian*
    Chapeau! | *French*
    Seasons | *Seafood/Steak*
    Truly Mediterranean* | *Med.*
    Quince | *French/Italian*
    Ame | *American*
    La Ciccia* | *Italian*
    Jardinière | *Cal./French*

BY CUISINE

AMERICAN (NEW)

29 Gary Danko
27 Boulevard
    Range
26 Ame
    Spruce

AMERICAN (TRAD.)

25 Mama's on Wash.
    House of Prime Rib
24 Maverick
    Bix
23 Chloe's Cafe

ASIAN FUSION

27 House
23 Koo
    Eos
22 Bushi-tei
    Café Kati

BAKERIES

27 Tartine Bakery
22 Liberty Cafe
    DeLessio
21 Emporio Rulli
    La Boulange

BURGERS

23 Joe's Cable Car
22 In-N-Out

21 Gott's Roadside Tray
20 BurgerMeister
19 Barney's

CALIFORNIAN

27 Canteen
    Frances
26 Coi
    Jardinière
25 Silks

CHINESE

25 Yank Sing
24 R&G Lounge
    Ton Kiang
    Tommy Toy's
23 San Tung

FRENCH

28 La Folie
27 Masa's
    Ritz-Carlton Din. Rm.
    Fleur de Lys
25 Cafe Jacqueline

FRENCH (BISTRO)

26 Chapeau!
25 Chez Spencer
24 Fringale
23 Chez Papa
    Le P'tit Laurent*

Excludes places with low votes; *indicates a tie with restaurant above

INDIAN/PAKISTANI

24 Amber India
Shalimar
22 Indian Oven
Roti Indian Bistro
Dosa

ITALIAN

28 Acquerello
26 Delfina
Quince
La Ciccia
25 Perbacco

JAPANESE

27 Sushi Zone
Kiss Seafood
Sebo*
Zushi Puzzle
26 Kabuto

MED./GREEK

27 Kokkari Estiatorio
26 Truly Mediterranean
25 Frascati
Zuni Café
23 Bar Tartine

MEXICAN

25 La Taqueria
24 El Tonayense
23 Nopalito
Tacolicious
22 Mamacita

MIDDLE EASTERN

26 Truly Mediterranean
23 Troya
A La Turca
Helmand Palace*
21 Bursa Kebab

NOODLES

23 San Tung
22 Katana-Ya

21 Citrus Club
20 Osha Thai
Hotei

PERUVIAN

24 La Mar Cebicheria
23 Limón
Mochica
22 Fresca

PIZZA

27 Pizzetta 211
26 Tony's Pizza
25 Gialina
Pizzeria Delfina
24 Tommaso's

SEAFOOD

27 Swan Oyster Depot
26 Seasons
25 Bar Crudo
Hog Island Oyster
24 Farallon

SPANISH/BASQUE

25 Piperade
24 Contigo
Zarzuela
23 Esperpento
Bocadillos

STEAK

26 Seasons
25 Harris'
House of Prime Rib
24 Morton's Steak
Ruth's Chris

VIETNAMESE

26 Slanted Door
25 Crustacean
24 Thanh Long
Bodega Bistro
Saigon Sandwiches

BY SPECIAL FEATURE

BREAKFAST

27 Tartine Bakery
25 Mama's on Wash.
Dottie's True Blue
Boulette's Larder
Campton Place

BRUNCH

25 Mission Beach Café
24 Brenda's

23 Foreign Cinema
Universal Cafe
1300 on Fillmore

CHILD-FRIENDLY

26 Tony's Pizza
25 Yank Sing
24 Tommaso's
22 Chenery Park
17 Pasta Pomodoro

NEWCOMERS (RATED)

27 Frances
25 Baker & Banker
Barbacco
23 Tacolicious
22 Delarosa

OPEN LATE

25 Nopa
24 Flour + Water
Shalimar
23 Beretta
Thai House

OUTDOOR SEATING

24 La Mar Cebicheria
23 Sociale
Foreign Cinema
21 Epic Roasthouse
20 Waterbar

PEOPLE-WATCHING

27 Boulevard
26 Jardinière
25 Zuni Café
24 Bix
19 Orson

POWER SCENES

26 Spruce
25 Perbacco

23 One Market
Town Hall
20 Le Central Bistro

ROMANCE

28 Acquerello
27 Fleur de Lys
26 Aziza
25 Cafe Jacqueline
21 Gitane

SMALL PLATES

25 Isa
23 Charanga
Oyaji
Eos
Terzo

TRENDY

25 Nopa
23 Beretta
22 5A5 Steak Lounge
21 Gitane
19 Orson

WINNING WINE LISTS

28 Acquerello
27 Boulevard
26 Quince
25 A16
22 RN74

BY LOCATION

CASTRO/NOE VALLEY

27 Sushi Zone
Frances
26 La Ciccia
25 Eiji
24 Firefly

CHINATOWN

24 R & G Lounge
21 House of Nanking
Hunan Home/Garden
Oriental Pearl
20 Yuet Lee

COW HOLLOW/ MARINA

27 Zushi Puzzle
25 Isa
A16
Capannina
24 Greens

DOWNTOWN

27 Masa's
Fleur de Lys
Kokkari Estiatorio
26 Seasons
Quince

EMBARCADERO

27 Boulevard
26 Slanted Door
25 Boulette's Larder
Hog Island Oyster
24 Boccalone Salumeria

FISHERMAN'S WHARF

29 Gary Danko
22 Scoma's
Ana Mandara
In-N-Out
20 McCormick/Kuleto

HAIGHT-ASHBURY/ COLE VALLEY

23 Eos
22 Alembic
 Zazie
21 Citrus Club
 La Boulange

HAYES VALLEY

27 Sebo
25 Zuni Café
 Bar Jules
23 Hayes St. Grill
 Espetus Churrascaria

LOWER HAIGHT

25 Rosamunde
23 Thep Phanom Thai
22 Indian Oven
21 Uva Enoteca
 Memphis Minnie's

MISSION

27 Range
 Tartine Bakery
26 Delfina
 Truly Mediterranean
25 Chez Spencer

NOB HILL/ RUSSIAN HILL

28 La Folie
27 Ritz-Carlton Din. Rm.
25 Frascati
 Rist. Milano
24 Zarzuela

NORTH BEACH

27 House
26 Coi
 Tony's Pizza
25 Mama's on Wash.
 Cafe Jacqueline

PACIFIC HEIGHTS/ JAPANTOWN

27 Kiss Seafood
25 Pizzeria Delfina
24 SPQR
22 Eliza's
 Bushi-tei

RICHMOND

27 Pizzetta 211
26 Kabuto
 Aziza
 Chapeau!
25 Richmond Restaurant

SOMA

26 Ame
25 Yank Sing
 Fifth Floor
24 Sentinel
 Fringale

SUNSET/W. PORTAL

24 Thanh Long
23 San Tung
 Marnee Thai
 Koo
 Ebisu

Top Decor

29	Garden Court
27	Farallon
	Ritz-Carlton Din. Rm.
	Gary Danko
26	Fleur de Lys
	Bix
	Big 4
	Jardinière
	Rotunda
	Spruce

	Waterbar
	Kokkari Estiatorio
	Quince
	Ana Mandara
25	Boulevard
	Epic Roasthouse
	Acquerello
	Sutro's at Cliff Hse.
	Seasons
	Campton Place

Top Service

28	Gary Danko
	Acquerello
27	Coi
	Ritz-Carlton Din. Rm.
	Seasons
	Masa's
26	La Folie
	Fleur de Lys
	Boulevard
	Quince

25	Fifth Floor
	Silks
	Kokkari Estiatorio
	Jardinière
	Ame
	Chapeau!
	La Ciccia
	Frances
24	Big 4
	Campton Place

Best Buys

In order of Bang for the Buck rating.

1. El Tonayense
2. In-N-Out
3. Saigon Sandwiches
4. Arinell Pizza
5. Let's Be Frank
6. Rosamunde
7. Taqueria Can-Cun
8. El Metate
9. Mixt Greens
10. Sentinel
11. Cheese Steak Shop
12. Jay's Cheesesteak
13. La Cumbre Taqueria
14. Truly Mediterranean
15. Boccalone Salumeria
16. Pancho Villa
17. La Corneta
18. La Taqueria
19. Papalote
20. Blue Barn Gourmet

OTHER GOOD VALUES

American Grilled Cheese
Boccalone Salumeria
DeLessio
Emmy's Spaghetti
4505 Meats
Kasa Indian
King of Thai
Limón Rotisserie

Naked Lunch
Out the Door
Prime Rib Shabu
Showdogs
Super Duper
Tacolicious
Ti Couz
Tu Lan

Menus, photos, voting and more – free at ZAGAT.com

City of San Francisco

☑ Absinthe ❶Ⓜ *French/Mediterranean* | 22 | 23 | 21 | $47 |

Hayes Valley | 398 Hayes St. (Gough St.) | 415-551-1590 |
www.absinthe.com

"Parisian" "panache" and "mean", "marvelous" cocktails fuel a "sensational scene" at this "sumptuous" Hayes Valley brasserie that gets "jam-packed with the arty set" "during the pre-symphony and -opera rush"; "well-executed" French-Med "classics" are served by a "thoughtful" staff, so while the atmosphere and the tabs are "too much" for some, many feel everything's just "right"; P.S. a post-Survey chef change is not reflected in the Food score.

Academy Cafe *Eclectic* | 19 | 15 | 14 | $20 |

Inner Richmond | California Academy of Sciences | 55 Music Concourse Dr. (bet. Fulton St. & Lincoln Way) | 415-876-6121 | www.academycafesf.com

"If only all museums had food like this!" exclaim fans of this "world-cuisine cafeteria" in the California Academy of Sciences offering a "remarkably diverse", slightly "pricey" selection of "well-prepared" eats by chef Charles Phan (The Slanted Door), from "organic" Vietnamese fare to tacos and "slow-cooked" meats; despite a "chaotic" interior, there's an "awesome aquarium" and "nice outside dining" – but "too bad you can't go there without paying the entrance fee."

Ace Wasabi's | 20 | 16 | 18 | $33 |
Rock-N-Roll Sushi *Japanese*

Marina | 3339 Steiner St. (bet. Chestnut & Lombard Sts.) |
415-567-4903

"Still a social scene after all these years", this "gimmicky", "Americanized" sushi bar is "more about the party" and "the best pick-up line than the best maki", drawing a "very young, very Marina-esque" crowd" that "screams to be heard" over music that "peps you up and makes you want to down a sake bomb"; for "discerning sushi lovers", though, it's "not worth the wait or the 'tude."

NEW Acme Burgerhaus ❶ *Burgers* | ▽ 18 | 15 | 17 | $20 |

Western Addition | 559 Divisadero St. (Hayes St.) | 415-346-3212

This new Western Addition joint offers an "interesting menu of burgers" – from "veggie to ostrich" to Kobe – that are customized with mix-in ingredients and served till late (2 AM on the weekends); despite an appealing "toppings bar", detractors beef the "pricey" patties are "not particularly memorable", suggesting its "saving grace" is its happy hour, which lasts from 3-10 PM.

☑ Acquerello ⌦Ⓜ *Italian* | 28 | 25 | 28 | $84 |

Polk Gulch | 1722 Sacramento St. (bet. Polk St. & Van Ness Ave.) |
415-567-5432 | www.acquerello.com

Ever "elegant", this "enchanting" Italian in a "tranquil" converted chapel off Polk presents "glorious", "masterfully prepared" prix fixe dinners complemented by a "daunting" but "extraordinary" wine list; "impeccable maitre d' oversight" and "outstanding" "choreographed service" complete the picture, so even if it feels a bit "stodgy" to some – and "only the Medicis can afford" the bill – it offers an "exquisite" dining experience that remains "unequaled in the city"; P.S. jacket suggested.

	FOOD	DECOR	SERVICE	COST

Alamo Square Seafood Grill *French/Seafood* | 20 | 16 | 20 | $34 |

Western Addition | 803 Fillmore St. (Grove St.) | 415-440-2828 | www.alamosquareseafoodgrill.com

Surveyors spy "a steal" at this "few-frills" French bistro whose "commendable" fish, "prepared how you like it with a choice of several sauces", is part of the three-course "bargain" until 7 PM, and still "cheap" after that; some feel it's just "ok", but Western Additioners who like its "quiet", "mellow vibe" "will definitely return."

A La Turca *Turkish* | 23 | 11 | 17 | $19 |

Tenderloin | 869 Geary St. (Larkin St.) | 415-345-1011 | www.alaturcasf.com

"A small slice of Turkey" in the "sketchy" Tenderloin, this "authentic" joint dishes up "beautifully presented" appetizer plates, "fresh-baked pides" and "lots of yummy things on skewers"; even though "Turkish soap operas on TV provide the atmosphere", the "large", shareable platters for "light-on-your-pocketbook" prices mean most "leave feeling stuffed and happy."

Albona Ristorante Istriano 🗷 Ⓜ *Italian* | 23 | 17 | 24 | $45 |

North Beach | 545 Francisco St. (bet. Mason & Taylor Sts.) | 415-441-1040 | www.albonarestaurant.com

Despite the retirement of the original "garrulous" owner, this "charming", "out-of-the-way" North Beach Italian with a "distinctive", slightly expensive Istrian menu (combining Venetian, Croatian and Slovenian influences) has maintained the same "standout" food and "warm, unassuming" service; "don't expect to be wowed by the decor", but it's a "real adventure" nonetheless.

Alegrias, Food From Spain *Spanish* | 20 | 17 | 21 | $35 |

Marina | 2018 Lombard St. (Webster St.) | 415-929-8888 | www.alegriassf.com

Beyond its "unlikely" setting on Lombard Street, this "quaint" Spanish "gem" in the Marina makes you feel "like you're in someone's home" as you sup on "enjoyable", "affordable" paella and tapas with a "jug of sangria"; though a few claim it's "inconsistent" and could use an "update", most appreciate the "family-run" "hospitality"; P.S. closed Tuesdays.

Alembic, The ☻ *Eclectic* | 22 | 20 | 18 | $33 |

Haight-Ashbury | 1725 Haight St. (bet. Cole & Shrader Sts.) | 415-666-0822 | www.alembicbar.com

"If this is bar food, save me a stool" order advocates of the "haute" Eclectic gastropub grub at this lunch-to-late-night "jewel in the Haight", whose "seasonal" menu complements "unique" "artisan cocktails" and an "extensive" whiskey selection; the tin-ceilinged space has "lots of personality" (with a little "attitude") and can be a "mob scene at night", but it's an "oasis on Sunday afternoons."

Alfred's Steakhouse 🗷 Ⓜ *Steak* | 22 | 21 | 22 | $56 |

Downtown | 659 Merchant St. (bet. Kearny & Montgomery Sts.) | 415-781-7058 | www.alfredssteakhouse.com

"If you've got a hankering" for a "huge" slab of "well-aged" beef and a "single-malt scotch", take a "step back in time" and settle into a "red leather booth" at this Downtown "throwback", the kind of place where the "Mad Men would go"; nostalgics note it "never disappoints" with its "perfectly cooked" meat and "old-fashioned sides" for "reasonable" (though "high") tabs, even if modernists maintain there are "better steakhouses" around; P.S. lunch on Thursdays only.

Alice's *Chinese*
20 | 14 | 18 | $22

Noe Valley | 1599 Sanchez St. (29th St.) | 415-282-8999

"Spot-on" renditions of "fresh, simple" Chinese dishes cater to the "too-tired-to-cook" crowd at this "inexpensive" outer Noe Valley "staple"; even if there's "nothing terribly imaginative" on the menu, the "airy" surroundings are "peaceful" and service is "efficient" (especially for takeout).

Alioto's *Italian*
18 | 17 | 18 | $46

Fisherman's Wharf | 8 Fisherman's Wharf (Taylor St.) | 415-673-0183 | www.aliotos.com

When locals want to "play tourist", they head to this "Fisherman's Wharf classic" whose "memorable" waterside vistas set the scene for "simply prepared" seafood with a Sicilian touch; though the menu is fairly "ho-hum" and "overpriced", and the "crowded" dining room "dated", "as the sun begins to set behind the Golden Gate Bridge", the "spectacular view" is "worth the effort."

❷ Amber India *Indian*
24 | 20 | 20 | $38

SoMa | 25 Yerba Buena Ln. (bet. Market & Mission Sts.) | 415-777-0500 | www.amber-india.com

See review in South of San Francisco Directory.

Ame *American*
26 | 25 | 25 | $74

SoMa | St. Regis | 689 Mission St. (3rd St.) | 415-284-4040 | www.amerestaurant.com

"Brilliant" New American cooking (with a "haute Japanese" streak) in the St. Regis offers a "delicious coda to a day of sightseeing", or simply an "ame-zing", "adventurous" "date-night" dinner, at Hiro Sone and Lissa Doumani's "swanky" SoMa sib to St. Helena's Terra; replete with "Eastern"-style, "polished" service in the "immaculately designed" main room and "choreographed action" behind the sushi bar, it's a "steep" but "memorable" "Zen gourmet dining experience."

NEW American Cupcake Ⓜ *American/Bakery*
- | - | - | I

Cow Hollow | 1919 Union St. (Laguna St.) | 415-896-4217 | www.americancupcake.com

At this stylish Cow Hollow dessert lounge, ditch the diet with the titular treat, plus made-to-order cotton candy, fried Oreos and a menu of savory American small plates (think pulled pork sliders and tater tots with wasabi aïoli), accompanied by beer, wine and 'candy cocktails'; the Vegas-style glam storefront is outfitted with pastel-colored glass light fixtures and tufted white pleather booths.

NEW American Grilled
Cheese Kitchen Ⓢ *American/Sandwiches*
- | - | - | I

SoMa | 1 South Park Ave. (2nd St.) | 415-243-0107 | www.theamericansf.com

Reigning Grilled Cheese Invitational champion Heidi Gibson goes legit at this airy arrival in SoMa, where she griddles up over seven different pressed fromage sandwiches along with other traditional American salads and fixin's (including the requisite smoky tomato soup); the gooey goodness can be washed down with wine and beer or more wholesome quenchers such as housemade sodas and seasonal lemonade in the industrial-chic-meets-retro-kitchenette setting; P.S. open for breakfast and lunch only.

Americano *Californian*

| 18 | 21 | 17 | $43 |

Embarcadero | Hotel Vitale | 8 Mission St. (The Embarcadero) | 415-278-3777 | www.americanorestaurant.com

"It's all about the view, and I'm not talking about the Bay Bridge right outside" josh habitués of this "hip" Embarcadero hang serving "solid but not spectacular" Californian fare for "leisurely outdoor lunches" and "post-work" bites; at night the sprawling patio becomes more of a "meat market" for "unemployed i-bankers to pick up their next conquest", but somehow the "staff is slow no matter what size the crowd."

Amici's East Coast Pizzeria *Pizza*

| 19 | 14 | 17 | $21 |

AT&T Park | 216 King St. (3rd St.) | 415-546-6666
Marina | 2200 Lombard St. (Steiner St.) | 415-885-4500
www.amicis.com

NYC expats who need their pizza "thin and foldable" flock to this local chain for "slightly charred", "chewy" pies with "dynamite" toppings, dished up in "no-frills" "family joints" where "kids love to watch the pizza dough fly"; while critics call the combos "Californicated" and "too expensive", many are hooked on the "speedy delivery."

Ana Mandara *Vietnamese*

| 22 | 26 | 21 | $51 |

Fisherman's Wharf | Ghirardelli Sq. | 891 Beach St. (Polk St.) | 415-771-6800 | www.anamandara.com

Locals and their "out-of-town guests" feel like "tourists on a trip to Asia" (or perhaps "French colonists") as they dine on "upscale", "beautifully prepared" Vietnamese dishes at this "enchanting" Wharf destination accented with "plantation"-style "dark woods and huge plants everywhere"; those who find the "theatrical" setting a bit too "Disneyland" (and the food too "Americanized") can escape to the "sexy" upstairs lounge for "excellent jazz" on the weekends.

Anchor & Hope *Seafood*

| 21 | 20 | 20 | $44 |

SoMa | 83 Minna St. (2nd St.) | 415-501-9100 | www.anchorandhopesf.com

"Former East Coasters" "get their lobster-roll fix" at this "cool", "playful" re-creation of a "clam shack" by the "guys from Town Hall" (and Salt House, too), "hidden down an alley" in a "revamped" SoMa warehouse; the "inventive" seafood, served by a "warm, helpful" staff, "pairs perfectly with an insane list of beers", but a few critics carp about the "noise" and wonder whether it's "really worth the price."

Anchor Oyster Bar *Seafood*

| 23 | 15 | 20 | $33 |

Castro | 579 Castro St. (bet. 18th & 19th Sts.) | 415-431-3990

"Aw, shucks" – this "old-school" seafood joint in the Castro is "a catch" swear regulars who drop anchor for its "simple but expertly prepared" "daily specials", "excellent" oysters "from either coast" and the "best chowder this side of Boston", "paired with a well-priced white wine"; "you really can't go wrong, except to arrive late", as the place is tighter "than a submarine" (and "doesn't take reservations"), but the "happy" staff is "accommodating."

Andalu *Eclectic*

20 | 17 | 18 | $35

Mission | 3198 16th St. (Guerrero St.) | 415-621-2211 | www.andalusf.com

"First dates" and "large groups" "doing the communal dinner thing" are both in evidence at this "loud" tapas place in the Mission, whose "reasonably priced" Eclectic small plates "really bring the flavor", washed down with pitchers of "awesome sangria"; still, a minority maintains "the magic is gone", citing a "dated" style that's "not special enough" for a big night out.

Angkor Borei *Cambodian*

23 | 16 | 24 | $22

Bernal Heights | 3471 Mission St. (Cortland Ave.) | 415-550-8417 | www.cambodiankitchen.com

"Those who want to relive their visit to Siem Reap" or simply crave "something different for a change" "can't stop raving" about this "mom-and-pop" "neighborhood surprise" in Bernal Heights, serving "delicate", "mildly exotic" Cambodian curries, "outstanding vegetarian choices" and other dishes that "engage the palate"; with simple decor and "kind" service, it's an "understated" place whose "price is right" for the times.

Antica Trattoria Ⓜ *Italian*

23 | 18 | 22 | $39

Russian Hill | 2400 Polk St. (Union St.) | 415-928-5797 | www.anticasf.com

It's "like being in Milan at Polk" at this "reasonably priced" Russian Hill trattoria where chef Ruggero Gadaldi (Beretta, Delarosa) rewards both "regulars and tourists" with "absolutely delicious" cooking and "excellent" wines by the glass in a "neighborhood atmosphere" that's "noisy in a nice Italian way"; so while a few guests remark the "chairs are not too comfortable", the "warm welcome" and "pleasant" service keep it "homey."

Anzu *Japanese*

22 | 21 | 21 | $51

Downtown | Hotel Nikko | 222 Mason St. (O'Farrell St.) | 415-394-1100 | www.restaurantanzu.com

"Beautiful" sushi and "unique" Japanese fusion dishes "deliver" at this "underappreciated" Downtowner, an "oasis" in the Hotel Nikko; it's "perfect for a bite before a show" in the Rrazz Room downstairs (where "the hostess will save your seats") or during the Sunday jazz brunch ("a treat"), but a few find the "Zen-like" den a bit "boring" and the meal unsatisfying for the "dollars spent."

Aperto *Italian*

24 | 16 | 22 | $34

Potrero Hill | 1434 18th St. (bet. Connecticut & Missouri Sts.) | 415-252-1625 | www.apertosf.com

"Relaxed" and "inviting", this "neighborhood favorite" on Potrero Hill is "everything a small Italian restaurant should be", serving "beautiful pasta dishes" and "intriguing daily specials" among other "moderately priced" plates; servers who "could not be nicer" take the sting out of tables that are "a bit too close together", and impatient patrons are pleased they "now take reservations" for parties of any size.

Ariake Japanese ⓩ *Japanese*

23 | 14 | 21 | $35

Outer Richmond | 5041 Geary Blvd. (bet. 14th & 15th Aves.) | 415-221-6210 | www.sfariake.com

"Superb omakase service" performed to "exacting standards" sets apart this "plain" but "cozy" sushi place in the Outer Richmond

FOOD | DECOR | SERVICE | COST

dubbed "Tsukiji by the Bay"; purists are partial to the "pristine" cuts of fish, served "without unnecessary embellishment", but the "charming" chef-owner also concocts "creative" rolls for a "fair price."

Arinell Pizza ⊄ *Pizza*   21 | 5 | 12 | $8

Mission | 509 Valencia St. (16th St.) | 415-255-1303
"Just the right amount of grease" drips off the "legit", "floppy" slices at these "cheap" counters in the Mission and Berkeley, satisfying the "hankering" of "homesick New Yorkers", students and pizza "snobs"; there's "no delivery" and "no froufrou toppings", just a "long-haired metalhead" staff playing "awful music" amid digs you might "need a Hazmat shower after visiting", so plan to "get your slice on a piece of wax paper and eat it on the street"; P.S. the Valencia branch now serves till 3 AM Friday–Saturday.

Arlequin To Go ⊠ *Mediterranean*   18 | 15 | 14 | $20

Hayes Valley | 384B Hayes St. (bet. Franklin & Gough Sts.) | 415-626-1211 | www.arlequinwinemerchant.com
"An offshoot of Absinthe" and Arlequin Wine Merchant (right next door), this "lovely" Hayes Valley cafe is a "lunchtime standby" for "delicious, creative" Med bites (eaten here or to-go) and a "best bet" for a "pre-concert" dinner; it's also "virtually self-service" and "can be slow", but all is "forgiven" when sitting on the "gorgeous", "not so secret" back patio replete with free WiFi and "pitchers of lemony water."

AsiaSF ⊠ *Asian/Californian*   17 | 19 | 21 | $47

SoMa | 201 Ninth St. (Howard St.) | 415-255-2742 | www.asiasf.com
The "faux-togenic girls" at this "gender-bending" SoMa venue "flirt" quite a bit, serving small Cal-Asian plates and drinks before jumping on the bar to perform their "best Donna Summer" for "bachelorette parties", "out-of-towners" and "tempted" fellas looking for a "slice of SF's other side"; while the food is "tasty" enough, some say "eat before you go" to avoid "over"-paying for a "wild night out" that's "all about the show"; P.S. prix fixe required Friday-Saturday, closed Monday-Tuesday in the winter.

⊠ A16 *Italian*   25 | 20 | 21 | $45

Marina | 2355 Chestnut St. (bet. Divisadero & Scott Sts.) | 415-771-2216 | www.a16sf.com
"If you can make it through" the "racy" bar crowd and "crushing" "noise that reminds you of an Italian speedway" at this "hot" Marina trattoria, you're in for a "sublime" time "nibbling on the house-cured meats", "stellar" pastas and "incredible", "wood-fired" Neapolitan pies while watching the "pizza chefs" at work; the "hip, knowledge-able" staff can get "overwhelmed" but ultimately offers "lots of help" navigating the "obscure" but "outstanding" wine list; P.S. lunch is available Wednesday–Friday.

Asqew Grill *Californian*   16 | 11 | 14 | $17

Haight-Ashbury | 1607 Haight St. (Clayton St.) | 415-701-9301
Laurel Heights | 3415 California St. (bet. Laurel & Locust Sts.) | 415-386-5608
Marina | 3348 Steiner St. (bet. Chestnut & Lombard Sts.) | 415-931-9201
www.asqewgrill.com
It's "skewers galore" at this "quick", "cheap" local Californian chain where fans make a "healthy" "protein stop" for "marinated and

grilled" "meat on a stick" (plus veggie options) served with "tasty" sides; while "sparse" settings are part of the package, those who cite "dull" offerings and "small portions" call it "disappointing, even for a fast-food joint."

Axum Cafe *Ethiopian*

▽ 21 | 11 | 17 | $20

Lower Haight | 698 Haight St. (Pierce St.) | 415-252-7912 | www.axumcafe.com

"Get ready to get messy" as you "pick up morsels" of "delicious", "interestingly spiced" Ethiopian food with "spongy" injera bread at this Lower Haight "standby"; the "low-key" interior is "nothing to look at", but the "hospitality" and "filling", "inexpensive" platters easily suit a "midweek meal with friends."

⚡ Aziza *Moroccan*

26 | 23 | 24 | $50

Outer Richmond | 5800 Geary Blvd. (22nd Ave.) | 415-752-2222 | www.aziza-sf.com

"Rising star" chef Mourad Lahlou "brings Moroccan food into the 21st century" at this "unexpected" Outer Richmonder, highlighting "locally sourced" ingredients, "dynamic flavors" and a "not-to-be-missed" tasting menu that's "extravagant" but still "costs considerably less" than comparable meals elsewhere; with "complex, savory" cocktails, a "sultry" setting lined with "snug, romantic booths" and service that "accommodates your every whim", it's ideal for a "long, leisurely dinner"; P.S. closed Tuesdays.

Baby Blues BBQ *BBQ/Southern*

20 | 14 | 18 | $25

Mission | 3149 Mission St. (Precita Ave.) | 415-896-4250 | www.babybluessf.com

"In a city that's in desperate need of some BBQ", this Mission joint (by way of LA) largely "does it right", doling out "killer ribs" among other "solid" "smoked meats", "homey" sides and "scrumptious" desserts; the "funky roadhouse decor" and "sit-down-at-your-table casual service" don't quite match the "prices", and some say the 'cue "wouldn't cut it" in Memphis, but it's still "good eating", plus "they deliver."

Bacco Ristorante *Italian*

22 | 20 | 22 | $43

Noe Valley | 737 Diamond St. (bet. Elizabeth & 24th Sts.) | 415-282-4969 | www.baccosf.com

"Way off the tourist circuit in residential Noe Valley", this "cozy" neighborhood trattoria serves housemade pastas prepared "with love", the "best risotto" and other "no-fuss" "classics" that are "better than you're likely to find in North Beach"; "the staff is largely Italian" to boot, which adds to the "convivial" atmosphere, as does the selection of "modestly priced Italian wines."

NEW Baker & Banker Ⓜ *American*

25 | 23 | 24 | $54

Upper Fillmore | 1701 Octavia St. (Bush St.) | 415-351-2500 | www.bakerandbanker.com

Run by a "dedicated" couple – chef Jeff Banker and pastry chef Lori Baker – this Upper Fillmore newcomer "hits on all cylinders", proffering "simple" but "artfully presented" New American "comfort food" and "exceptional" desserts along with "personal" service; the "small" storefront space (former home to Quince) adorned with "dark woodwork" and a chalkboard displaying "esoteric beers and wines" gets "noisy" but ultimately delivers a "fine-dining experience at a fair price"; P.S. the owners just opened a bakery and sandwich shop next door.

Baker Street Bistro Ⓜ *French*

| 22 | 18 | 21 | $34 |

Marina | 2953 Baker St. (bet. Greenwich & Lombard Sts.) | 415-931-1475 | www.bakerstreetbistro.com

Now boarding, a "nonstop flight to Paris" courtesy of the "quintessential French bistro fare" at this "intimate" Marina mainstay; with "heated outdoor seating", it's easy to pretend you're dining alfresco "on the Left Bank" while saying *mais oui* to an "excellent brunch" or "awesome" prix fixe dinner, so while it's "not quite perfect" (and some say "not the same" since changing owners), it's "very good for the price"; P.S. prix fixe offered till 7 PM Friday–Saturday, till closing other nights.

Balboa Cafe *American*

| 19 | 18 | 19 | $36 |

Cow Hollow | 3199 Fillmore St. (Greenwich St.) | 415-921-3944 | www.plumpjack.com

For a "peek at the city's power-brokers", linger over lunch at this "legendary" Cow Hollow "institution", where the burger is "tops" on the "simple, satisfying" American menu; at night it's an "obvious singles scene", "crazy crowded" with "cougars" and "rowdy" "frat boys", all tended to by "personable bartenders" who make it "feel like home" (and pour a "great Bloody Mary" at brunch); P.S. the Marin outpost is "one of the livelier places in Mill Valley."

NEW Bar Agricole ◑ *Californian*

| - | - | - | M |

SoMa | 355 11th St. (bet. Folsom & Harrison Sts.) | 415-355-9400 | www.baragricole.com

This agro-chic tavern that startender Thad Vogler (Beretta, Jardinière) and chef Brandon Jew (Magnolia Brewery) are opening in SoMa will feature seasonal Californian cuisine sourced from local biodynamic farms, served till 1 AM; the LEED-certified space is clad floor-to-ceiling with barrel staves, and an herb-lined garden patio features communal tables, but all eyes will be trained on the 15-seat bar where the beverage boys will be pouring natural wines, farmhouse spirits and handcrafted farm-to-table cocktails.

NEW Barbacco Ⓢ *Italian*

| 25 | 23 | 23 | $34 |

Downtown | 220 California St. (Front St.) | 415-955-1919 | www.barbaccosf.com

Let the "CEOs go to Perbacco" while FiDi "workers" gamely "nosh" at its "hip" new little sib turning out "high-quality" house-cured salumi, "perfect" *polpette* (Sicilian meatballs) and other "terrific", "clean-tasting" Italian small plates for "decent" tabs; the "gleaming" marble counter, "prompt" service and dozens of wines by the "taste, glass and quarto" are additional pluses, though cocktailers kvetch "it'd be nice to have a full bar."

Bar Bambino *Italian*

| 23 | 21 | 21 | $41 |

Mission | 2931 16th St. (Mission St.) | 415-701-8466 | www.barbambino.com

This "postage stamp"–sized enoteca "hidden" on a somewhat "sketchy" stretch of the Mission lures "young twentysomethings" with its "exciting" selection of "super-tasty" salumi and cheese platters, "delicately prepared" pastas and "eccentric Italian wines"; though "scoring a table" on the weekend can be "as difficult as finding a parking space", and the bill can "add up quickly", its "upbeat" service and appealing patio make it "enjoyable" all around.

Bar Crudo 🗹 Seafood
25 | 17 | 19 | $49

Western Addition | 655 Divisadero St. (Grove St.) | 415-409-0679 | www.barcrudo.com

"If you're a fan of sushi or seafood", join the "young hip crowd" hooked on this "quirky" relocated raw bar in the Western Addition known for its "refreshing" "Mediterranean takes on sashimi", plus some "perfectly cooked" dishes including "out-of-this-world" chowder; the "lengthy list" of Belgian ales is "tops" too, and the "stark" new digs benefit from "added elbow room" – just watch out for "lacking" service, and "don't go too hungry", as the portions are "crazy-small and expensive."

Bar Jules 🗹 American
25 | 18 | 21 | $41

Hayes Valley | 609 Hayes St. (Laguna St.) | 415-621-5482 | www.barjules.com

"The heart and commitment" of the "young" chef-owner are "evident" at this New American "bright star in Hayes Valley", where a "slim", "handwritten menu" announces the "fresh-from-the-farmer's-market" daily offerings and a "knowledgeable" staff works the "ador-able", "super-tiny" space; since reservations are taken only for big groups, be sure to "get there right when the doors open, because it gets slammed"; P.S. no lunch Tuesdays, brunch-only Sundays.

Barney's Gourmet Hamburgers Burgers
19 | 12 | 16 | $17

Marina | 3344 Steiner St. (bet. Chestnut & Lombard Sts.) | 415-563-0307
Noe Valley | 4138 24th St. (Castro St.) | 415-282-7770
www.barneyshamburgers.com

There's a "burger for everyone", from "pure carnivores to vegans", at this "sprouty" "microchain" purveying "big", "standout" patties with a "cornucopia of toppings", "addictive" curly fries and "swoon-worthy" milkshakes; though some critics cite "hefty prices" and "middling" service, at least the "noisy", "cramped quarters" can be skipped at most branches by heading for the "sweet outdoor patio."

Bar Tartine 🗹 Mediterranean
23 | 20 | 20 | $41

Mission | 561 Valencia St. (bet. 16th & 17th Sts.) | 415-487-1600 | www.tartinebakery.com

"Out-of-the-ordinary" Med dinners (on a "compact" menu), "stellar" brunches and "heavenly" desserts stand out at this unmarked Mission hangout that's "sceney" but still "calmer than its frantic bakery sister"; with "chic", "comfortable" digs capped off by an "antler chandelier", "relaxed" yet largely "accommodating" service and prices that "won't break the bank", it's the "personal favorite" of many.

Basil Thai Restaurant & Bar Thai
23 | 18 | 20 | $27

SoMa | 1175 Folsom St. (bet. 7th & 8th Sts.) | 415-552-8999 | www.basilthai.com

Basil Canteen Thai

SoMa | 1489 Folsom St. (11th St.) | 415-552-3963 | www.basilcanteen.com

SoMa's "urban grit gives way to urban chic" at these "gourmet" Thais where a "zippy" staff serves up "delectable" dishes (with a "small-plate" focus at the Canteen branch) that are "frequent stars in foodie daydreams"; the "modern" settings and "reasonable cost, particularly

	FOOD	DECOR	SERVICE	COST

for lunch", help ensure "return visits", so "avoid peak hours" or try "takeout" to beat the rush.

Beach Chalet Brewery *American*   14 | 21 | 15 | $32

Outer Sunset | 1000 Great Hwy. (bet. Fulton St. & Lincoln Way) | 415-386-8439 | www.beachchalet.com

"Try to get a window seat" advise vista-ficionados of this Outer Sunset "treasure", who trek to the edge of Golden Gate Park to "watch the waves crash over Ocean Beach" while imbibing "exceptional" "micro-brewed beer made on-site"; the "gorgeous sunset" views and "terrific Depression-era murals" on the first floor are bonuses when "bringing out-of-town visitors", but the New American fare is "forgettable" fuss foodies, who are also frustrated by the "slow" service.

Beautifull *Health Food*   17 | 11 | 16 | $19

NEW **Inner Sunset** | 816 Irving St. (bet. 9th & 10th Aves.) | 415-664-2033
Presidio Heights | 3401 California St. (bet. Laurel & Locust Sts.) | 415-728-9080
www.beautifull.com

"Virtuous" eaters eager for "wholesome" meals that are both "good and good for you" patronize these prepared health-food havens in Presidio Heights and the Inner Sunset; more popular "for takeout than eating in", they "quickly" fill orders for those who "don't feel like cooking", but a number of noshers note there's "nothing beautiful about the price", dubbing the food "decent" "but not delicious."

Bella Trattoria *Italian*   22 | 19 | 24 | $36

Inner Richmond | 3854 Geary Blvd. (3rd Ave.) | 415-221-0305 | www.bellatrattoriasf.com

"Go once and you're an old friend forever" with the "nice folks trying hard and succeeding" at this "intimate" Inner Richmond trattoria, providing "fresh pastas" and other "solid" Southern Italian cuisine; decorated with a mural of Venice, it's a "cute" but not fancy, "good-value" choice.

Benihana *Japanese*   17 | 16 | 19 | $40

Japantown | 1737 Post St. (Webster St.) | 415-563-4844 | www.benihana.com

"Bring on the onion volcano" clamor customers who count on an "entertaining" "show" for "all ages" (even "jaded teenagers") at this Japanese steakhouse chain where teppanyaki chefs perform tableside feats while delivering "reliable" eats, including sushi and other "updated" items; critics call it "tired", "tacky" and "overpriced", but it works as a place to "take the kids and still have an edible meal."

NEW Benu 🅂🅼 *American*   - | - | - | E

SoMa | 22 Hawthorne St. (bet. Folsom & Howard Sts.) | 415-685-4860 | www.benusf.com

Rising from the ashes where the now-shuttered Two and Hawthorne Lane stood in SoMa, this contemporary American arrival named after the Egyptian version of the mythical phoenix showcases the cuisine of French Laundry protégé Corey Lee, who crafts elaborate multicourse tasting menus as well as more accessible à la carte dishes; the small but sleek dining room keeps the focus on the food, which is served on custom-made porcelain plates and reclaimed-wood petit-four boxes, while the secluded courtyard provides a peaceful perch for apéritifs.

	FOOD	DECOR	SERVICE	COST

Beretta ◐ *Italian* ⬛ 23 | 19 | 19 | $38

Mission | 1199 Valencia St. (23rd St.) | 415-695-1199 |
www.berettasf.com

"Like its namesake pistol", this "raucous" Mission "hipster haven"
with a "vibrant bar" and a "sea of singles" "packs a huge punch", pouring "handcrafted" drinks as "delicious" as its "devilishly thin pizzas"
and "rustic" Italian plates; the "goth-y" "no-res" room "gets insanely
crowded" "during evening or brunch" (when "you're dining practically
on top of your neighbors"), but "despite the crush" it's a "welcome"
"late-night" option.

Betelnut Pejiu Wu *Asian* ⬛ 23 | 21 | 20 | $40

Cow Hollow | 2030 Union St. (Buchanan St.) | 415-929-8855 |
www.betelnutrestaurant.com

"Trendy" Cow Hollow "fashionistas" and the "out-of-town visitors"
they want to "impress" are wu-ed by this still-"happening", red-hued
hub that combines "superior Americanized" Pan-Asian fare ("love the
spicy green beans") with "exciting cocktails and a festive vibe"; "go
with a group" so you can "try different things" or "sit at the kitchen
counter for dining entertainment", but remember there's usually "a bit
of a wait."

B44 *Spanish* ⬛ 21 | 18 | 19 | $38

Downtown | 44 Belden Pl. (bet. Bush & Pine Sts.) | 415-986-6287 |
www.b44sf.com

"Inventive", "enjoyable" paellas and "Catalan-style tapas" come with
a "street-party vibe" at this moderately priced cafe on Belden Place
that feels very "European" on a "warm night under the awnings";
though some say the food "doesn't sparkle" – nor does the "dark"
interior – and service is "merely adequate", many "love" it for the
outdoor "atmosphere" alone.

☑ Big 4 *American* ⬛ 23 | 26 | 24 | $61

Nob Hill | Huntington Hotel | 1075 California St. (Taylor St.) |
415-771-1140 | www.big4restaurant.com

"If you love American standards" and a "late-1800s ambiance" hark-
ing back to "when big railroad money ruled Nob Hill", this "classic"
"gentlemen's club" filled with "socialites", "celebs" and "cougars"
rates "more like a big 100"; so knock back a "mean Manhattan" at the
bar "while the piano player rattles off" another tune, or chow down on
"excellent" "red-meat, red-wine" fare in the "dark" "wood-paneled"
dining room, known for its "old-school" service and "annual wild game
dinners" in which "you eat half of Africa"; P.S. no longer serving lunch.

Bissap Baobab Ⓜ *Senegalese* ∇ 22 | 18 | 19 | $23

Mission | 2323 Mission St. (bet. 19th & 20th Sts.) | 415-826-9287 |
www.bissapbaobab.com

The "exceptionally flavorful" food is seasoned with "spices you've
never heard of" (and probably "can't pronounce") at this "super-
fun" Mission Senegalese, whose "exotic" drinks lend it extra appeal for "birthday celebrations"; though there's often a "wait for a
table" in the "dark" dining room, it's still a "real treat for cheap";
P.S. "eclectic live music" and DJs are the draw at Little Baobab, its sister spot around the corner.

	FOOD	DECOR	SERVICE	COST

Bistro Aix ⓜ *Californian/French* — | - | - | M

Marina | 3340 Steiner St. (bet. Chestnut & Lombard Sts.) | 415-202-0100 | www.bistroaix.com

After an extensive renovation, this Marina bistro has reopened with a new midpriced Cal-Provençal menu (much of it prepared on a wood-burning fireplace grill), but kept its Sunday–Thursday $25 prix fixe (5:30–7 PM); the rustic revamp includes furniture made from old-growth redwood wine barrels, while the patio has been completely transformed as a glassed-in atrium centered around an 80-year-old olive tree.

Bistro Boudin *Californian* 20 | 18 | 16 | $28

Fisherman's Wharf | 160 Jefferson St. (near Pier 43½) | 415-928-1849 | www.boudinbakery.com

"Touristy, yes", but the "trick is to go upstairs away from the crowds" at this "easygoing", "reasonable" Californian bistro that's a choice place for "sightseers to crash, regroup" and refuel on "creamy" clam-chowder bread bowls while taking in the "spectacular" views; all in all, the food is a "cut above the Wharf traps", and after the meal it's "fun to watch them" make those sour loaves at the downstairs bakery.

NEW Bistro Central Parc ⓜ *French* — | - | - | M

Western Addition | 560 Central Ave. (Grove St.) | 415-931-7272

Tucked away in a residential neighborhood just a few blocks from Golden Gate Park, this NoPa newcomer (from the former owners of the popular Baker Street Bistro) woos well-heeled locals with a slate of midpriced textbook Gallic plates, served in a snug corner storefront with a long wooden bar stocked with spirits and *vins de pays*; it's open for dinner Wednesday–Sunday, with a $17.50 early-bird prix fixe (served till 7 PM), and brunch on the weekends.

Bistro St. Germain *French* ▽ 20 | 16 | 21 | $36

Lower Haight | 518 Haight St. (Fillmore St.) | 415-626-6262

The owners of Le P'tit Laurent "bring affordable", "tasty" French bites "to yet another neighborhood in need" affirm *amis* of this "happening" Lower Haight hangout; most appreciate the "enthusiasm" of the "charming" staff, though the barely-there decor and somewhat "basic" cooking keep it from being a "destination."

ⓩ Bix *American/French* 24 | 26 | 23 | $57

Downtown | 56 Gold St. (bet. Montgomery & Sansome Sts.) | 415-433-6300 | www.bixrestaurant.com

"Come dressed" and "step into the swing" at this "glamorous" Downtown supper club whose "retro" touches like "live jazz", "waiters in white waistcoats shaking" "snazzy cocktails" and an "alley entry that makes you feel like Dick Powell and Myrna Loy" "set it apart"; dishing up American-French "classics done well", it's "still the coolest place in the city" for "three-martini power lunches" (served Fridays only) and "very adult" "date nights" on the "romantic" balcony overlooking the bar scene.

Blowfish Sushi To Die For *Japanese* 21 | 20 | 18 | $44

Mission | 2170 Bryant St. (20th St.) | 415-285-3848 | www.blowfishsushi.com

"Flashier" than your neighborhood Japanese joint, this "over-the-top" twosome in the Mission and San Jose provides "clever", "cutting-edge rolls" with "killer" cocktails amid "pounding techno music" and "sometimes sexually charged" "nonstop anime"; servers "with lots of tats and piercings" add to the "hip vibe", but those daunted by the "deafening" noise opine it's "overhyped" and "not worth the price."

Blue Barn Gourmet *Californian*   21 | 15 | 16 | $15

Marina | 2105 Chestnut St. (Steiner St.) | 415-441-3232 | www.bluebarngourmet.com

Marina "worker bees" and "health-conscious twentysomethings" "adore" the "creative" salads and "top-of-the-line" sandwiches made with "fresh, scrumptious" ingredients at this slightly "pricey" (but "worth it") Californian run by the family behind Oak Hill Farm; since it can be "crowded", "slow" and "tough to score a table", "calling ahead for pickup" is often the best bet.

☑ Blue Bottle Café *Californian/Coffeehouse*   23 | 14 | 18 | $9

Embarcadero | 1 Ferry Bldg. (The Embarcadero) | 510-653-3394
SoMa | Mint Plaza | 66 Mint St. (Mission St.) | 510-653-3394

☑ Blue Bottle Kiosk 🍴 *Californian/Coffeehouse*

Hayes Valley | 315 Linden St. (Gough St.) | 510-653-3394

☑ Rooftop Garden Blue
Bottle Coffee Bar *Californian/Coffeehouse*

SoMa | SFMOMA | 151 Third St. (bet. Howard & Mission Sts.) | 415-243-0455
www.bluebottlecoffee.net

"Baristas consider each drink a work of art" at this "champion" cult coffee chain – an SF "rite of passage" – producing "amazingly vivid", "drip-to-order" brews (with "beautiful foam filigrees") that attract "massive lines" out the door of the "industrial chic" settings; "addicts", who also find "bliss" in the "simple" Californian breakfast and lunch fare, assure that one sip will make you "forget how annoyed you were" by the wait; P.S. the Hayes Valley kiosk and SFMOMA rooftop garden serve java and pastries only.

Blue Plate, The *American*   23 | 18 | 20 | $39

Mission | 3218 Mission St. (bet. 29th & Valencia Sts.) | 415-282-6777 | www.blueplatesf.com

"Just plain finger-lickin'" New American eats are a "throwback to mom's cooking" (but fit for "foodies") at this "satisfying", "quirky" and moderately priced Mission "favorite" staffed by a "hip" but "courteous" crew; the "small", "rustic" and "charming" space "makes you feel like you're dining at a friend's house", but lovebirds looking to "invite romance" "request a patio table" to "put a cherry on top of the entire experience."

Bocadillos ⑤ *Spanish*   23 | 18 | 19 | $35

North Beach | 710 Montgomery St. (bet. Jackson & Washington Sts.) | 415-982-2622 | www.bocasf.com

The "unusual", "well-crafted" Basque tapas and "varied" "little sandwiches" for which this "chic" "baby sis to Piperade" is named are "delightful" for a "quick snack", "casual lunch" or "after-work" nibble in North Beach; while the "communal" seating can be "a bit of a squeeze", admirers assure that "once you get a table" or a perch at the bar you're treated to "gracious" service by a staff with a talent for "pairing wines with plates."

	FOOD	DECOR	SERVICE	COST

Boccalone Salumeria *Sandwiches* | 24 | 13 | 20 | $15 |

Embarcadero | Ferry Plaza Mkt. | 1 Ferry Bldg. (The Embarcadero) | 415-433-6500 | www.boccalone.com

This pig-powered outpost of the "offal empire" ruled by Chris Cosentino (Incanto) at the Ferry Plaza is basically "just a ham and chorizo" stand (with only four seats) hawking artisanal sausage sandwiches that are a "treat and a half", along with other "tasty pork products"; it charges "crazy prices" and closes by nightfall, but cured-meat mavens confess it's impossible "not to skip around like a little girl on a spring day while clutching a salumi cone."

Bodega Bistro *Vietnamese* | 24 | 13 | 19 | $27 |

Tenderloin | 607 Larkin St. (Eddy St.) | 415-921-1218 | www.bodegabistrosf.com

Chef-owner "Jimmy is a gem" gush groupies who find their "fix" of "Hanoi street food" – like "slurpin' good pho" and "number-one green papaya salad" – at this Tenderloin "go-to"; some are "surprised" given the "dicey" locale, but most are just pleased to have a "basic" joint in "Little Saigon" for "fresh" Franco-Vietnamese fare "served in a simple manner" – and for "half the price" of peers elsewhere.

Boogaloos *Southwestern* | 18 | 14 | 17 | $17 |

Mission | 3296 22nd St. (Valencia St.) | 415-824-4088 | www.boogaloossf.com

Arguably "the most hipster breakfast place on the planet", this day-time diner churning out "cheap", "satisfying" Southwestern eats (with lots of "vegetarian variations") in a vintage drugstore is packed with the Mission's "young couples and their kids when it opens up", followed by "the hungover" and "their dogs"; still, cynics are "unclear" why they all "stand on the corner" waiting for "contagiously bored" service, except to check out the "interesting tattoos" and "artwork."

Boulette's Larder *American* | 25 | 17 | 20 | $34 |

Embarcadero | Ferry Plaza Mkt. | 1 Ferry Bldg. (The Embarcadero) | 415-399-1155 | www.bouletteslarder.com

While this "microscopic" shop in the Ferry Building is prime for picking up "special spices" and "prepared foods", its in-demand seats draw devotees to "sit outside" amid "smashing" "bayfront" views or by the "working kitchen", savoring "outstanding", "daring" and "immensely satisfying" New American midday fare or Sunday brunch with a "dreadlocked dog snoozing under the communal table"; some sniff the "smug" attitude and "absence of all fine-dining amenities" "make the price a bit absurd", but most declare "if this is Slow Food, I'll decelerate!"

☒ Boulevard *American* | 27 | 25 | 26 | $69 |

Embarcadero | Audiffred Bldg. | 1 Mission St. (Steuart St.) | 415-543-6084 | www.boulevardrestaurant.com

"One of the few 'sure thing' restaurants" (for "business or pleasure"), Nancy Oakes' "pricey" yet "recession-proof" "belle epoque"-meets-"Barbary Coast" "institution" boasting "knockout views" of the Embarcadero delivers the "total package", with her "phenomenal", "delectable" New American dishes, a "wine list from Bacchus" and "gorgeous design"; the "high-energy crowd" never quits, so it's "tough to land a table", but once you're inside the "staff lives to please."

	FOOD	DECOR	SERVICE	COST

Brandy Ho's *Chinese* | 19 | 13 | 16 | $24 | M

Castro | 4068 18th St. (bet. Castro & Hartford Sts.) | 415-252-8000
Chinatown | 217 Columbus Ave. (bet. Broadway & Pacific Ave.) |
415-788-7527
www.brandyhos.com

Fans with "fireproof taste buds" order their "superb smoked meats"
and other "classic Hunan" chow "hot, hot, hot" at this "always-
crowded" Chinatown "hole-in-the-wall" and its "trendier"-looking
(but some say less "tasty") Castro spin-off; sure, the "curt waitresses"
"are not going to win any awards", and there's "no ambiance" to speak
of, but it's "fun" to "watch the flames fly from the wok-tossing chefs."

Brazen Head, The ●⇄ *American* | 21 | 20 | 22 | $40 |

Cow Hollow | 3166 Buchanan St. (Greenwich St.) | 415-921-7600 |
www.brazenheadsf.com

Maybe it's because it's "hard to find" (there's "no sign"), or perhaps
it's the "dark" dining room "that makes everyone look that much better", but "you feel like you're an exclusive club member" at this "romantic" "late-night" pub in Cow Hollow; "great steak" is a standout on
the "old-school, meat-heavy" American menu, and the "delightful"
bartenders shake up "bad-ass martinis" – just remember to "bring
cash" and "be prepared for a wait" (there are "no reservations").

Brenda's French Soul Food *Creole/Southern* | 24 | 12 | 19 | $20 |

Civic Center | 652 Polk St. (bet. Eddy & Turk Sts.) | 415-345-8100 |
www.frenchsoulfood.com

"Take everyone's word for it" – the "heavenly" Creole eats are "the real
deal" at this "tiny" Civic Center "brunch mecca", from "the most
amazing grits outside the deep south" to "can't-miss" po' boys to "fat
molten chocolate-filled beignets"; despite "quick" service, waits for
one of the "back-to-back tables" can be "interminable", but lovers say
"lordy" it's "so worth it"; P.S. closes at 3 PM.

Broken Record ●⇄ *Soul Food* ▽ | 22 | 10 | 11 | $17 |

Excelsior | 1166 Geneva Ave. (Naples St.) | 415-963-1713 |
www.brokenrecordsf.com

Slinging 300 types of whiskeys and "fancied-up" Southern soul eats
from the back of a "classic dive bar", this under-the-radar watering
hole in a "sketchy" Excelsior locale draws late-night lines that "tell you
something about how good the food really is"; though the original
"brains in the kitchen" left, it ain't broke, since ex-Firefly chefs con-
tinue to spin the most "amazing" combinations, tastier still when
scarfed down on the back patio.

Brother's Korean Restaurant *Korean* | 22 | 7 | 14 | $30 |

Inner Richmond | 4014 Geary Blvd. (bet. 4th & 5th Aves.) | 415-668-2028 M
Inner Richmond | 4128 Geary Blvd. (bet. 5th & 6th Aves.) | 415-387-7991 ●

"Heat your meat" "on charcoal" (and "leave smelling like smoke") at
these Korean BBQ joints in the Inner Richmond catering to the DIY
"carnivorous crowd"; there's rarely enough room in the "cafeteria"-
like digs, and the servers are "spread too thin", but the "wonderful
quality" of the grilled goods and "accompanying dishes" help "justify
the price" and the "wait"; P.S. the 4014 Geary location serves dinners
only, Friday-Sunday.

	FOOD	DECOR	SERVICE	COST

B Star Bar *Asian*
22 | 16 | 19 | $27

Inner Richmond | 127 Clement St. (bet. 2nd & 3rd Aves.) | 415-933-9900 | www.bstarbar.com

Generating "less hype" and a "fraction of the lines" compared with "its progenitor down the street", this "spunky little brother to Superstar" in the Inner Richmond "steals the show" with Pan-Asian fusion "flavors that never cease to delight"; if a few B-moan that it's Burma "lite", loyalists find the "ambiance way better, with "outdoor tent seating" perfect "for weekend brunch" and, oh yeah, it "takes reservations besides."

Buca di Beppo *Italian*
15 | 16 | 17 | $28

SoMa | 855 Howard St. (bet. 4th & 5th Sts.) | 415-543-1209 | www.bucadibeppo.com

"Loads of red-sauced pastas" fuel the "merry" "gluttony" at this family-style Italian chain that's always "loud" and "crowded with groups" indulging in "monster portions" amid "kitschy", "over-the-top" decor (including "wacky photos"); despite "average" fare, the "ridiculously perky" crew, relatively "cheap" tabs and "Dean Martin songs" make it a staple for big "get-togethers" in a "Mamma Leone's" vein.

NEW Burger Bar *Burgers*
19 | 17 | 16 | $29

Downtown | Macy's | 251 Geary St., 6th fl. (Stockton St.) | 415-296-4272 | www.fleurdelyssf.com

"Lobster on your burger?" – *oui*, the "options are endless" at "star chef" Hubert Keller's Downtown "hamburger joint on steroids" where "grown-ups" "design" their own "out-of-this-world" sliders and Kobe beef variations, sip "spiked milkshakes while watching the game on their booth's personal TV", drink in *Vertigo* views of Union Square" and purchase "thongs with [the restaurant's] name in glitter" post-meal; but Fleur de Lys fans deem the "Saks menu for a Macy's" "tourist" crowd a "complete mismatch", scoffing it's "overpriced hoopla."

Burger Joint *Burgers*
18 | 12 | 15 | $14

AT&T Park | 242 King St. (bet. 3rd & 4th Sts.) | 415-371-1600
Lower Haight | 700 Haight St. (Pierce St.) | 415-864-3833
Mission | 807 Valencia St. (19th St.) | 415-824-3494
www.burgerjointsf.com

Whenever they "want a juicy, tasty" Niman Ranch burger, carnivores "indulge cow cravings" at this "no-frills" Bay Area mini-chain; it may not have "as much variety" as the "gourmet" guys, but the squeaky-"clean" "retro vibe is fun" and "you never hear 'do you want fries with that?'", cuz they're "always included."

BurgerMeister ⊄ *Burgers*
20 | 12 | 16 | $16

Castro | 138 Church St. (Duboce Ave.) | 415-437-2874
Cole Valley | 86 Carl St. (Cole St.) | 415-566-1274
North Beach | 759 Columbus Ave. (Greenwich St.) | 415-296-9907
www.burgermeistersf.com

If a "big, sloppy" "customizable" grilled hamburger ("regular or veggie"), "concocted" in a "delicious manner" and washed down with an "excellent" tap beer or the "lactose-y goodness" of a "great milkshake", is "what you crave", this Bay Area–wide "semi-fast food" chainlet is a "burger must-er"; the quality Niman Ranch beef and all those "add-ons" can make "prices a bit steep", but "servings are huge" and always set mouths "a-watering."

ⓩ Burma Superstar *Burmese*   24 | 15 | 19 | $26

Inner Richmond | 309 Clement St. (4th Ave.) | 415-387-2147 | www.burmasuperstar.com

The "signature tea leaf salad" is "magic in your mouth", simultaneously "savory, sweet, spicy, crunchy and refreshing", aver adventurous eaters who make an "enlightening" "excursion" to these "bargain" Burmese joints; true, the wait to get into the "cramped" Inner Richmond locale can "feel like you're taking the long flight" to Myanmar, but "give the hostess your cell phone number" and "she'll call when your table is ready"; P.S. the Alameda and Oakland outposts are "faster" and more "nicely designed" than the original.

Bursa Kebab *Mediterranean*   21 | 19 | 21 | $30

West Portal | 60 W. Portal Ave. (bet. Ulloa & Vicente Sts.) | 415-564-4006

Kudos go out to this "king of kebabs" "providing much-needed flavor to the West Portal neighborhood", with "delicious" Turkish skewers and other "spiced-just-right" Med dishes; though not quite a "destination", it offers "friendly, efficient" service in a "lovely" atmosphere, as well as "amazing value", especially for lunch.

Bushi-tei *Asian/French*   22 | 21 | 20 | $49

Japantown | 1638 Post St. (bet. Laguna & Webster Sts.) | 415-440-4959 | www.bushi-tei.com

Bushi-tei Bistro *Asian/French*

Japantown | 1581 Webster St. (Post St.) | 415-409-4959 | www.bushiteibistro.com

Hardly "your typical" J-Town option, this fine-dining Asian fusion "gem" showcases "Samurai chef" Waka's combinations "exquisitely prepared" with "French techniques" that "respect" the "subtle flavors" of "Japanese ingredients", all "presented as works of art" in an equally "chic" wood-paneled setting; while omakase dinners "wow your palate", it's "much more affordable for lunch" or brunch, while the bistro satellite is "perfect for a pre-movie bite" – even if it "still needs to find its voice."

Butler & The Chef Bistro, The Ⓜ *French*   21 | 18 | 18 | $23

SoMa | 155A South Park Ave. (bet. 2nd & 3rd Sts.) | 415-896-2075 | www.butlerandthechef.com

With its "giant bowls of café au lait" and "French antiques", this "adorable little cafe (emphasis on the little)" hawking *"authentique"* Gallic goodness – including a croque vegetarian that "dreams are made of" – "brings you back to your Paris days" (only it's green-certified and "friendly"); "it's a nice respite from the rest of SoMa", especially "if you sit outside" overlooking South Park, but expect "long lines on Sunday morning"; P.S. open till 3 PM.

Butterfly Ⓜ *Asian/Californian*   22 | 24 | 21 | $41

Embarcadero | Pier 33 (Bay St.) | 415-864-8999 | www.butterflysf.com

"A delightful stop when strolling the Embarcadero", this "convenient but not-too-commercial" Cal-Asian dishes up "creative" plates that "tickle the taste buds" and a "fabulous view of the Bay" from its "hip", "spacious" dining room; most maintain the staff "goes out of its way" to please, and while some sniff that the fusion fare is "mediocre" and "so three years ago", at least the happy-hour specials are an "awesome deal."

Cafe Bastille ☒ *French*

17 | 16 | 17 | $36

Downtown | 22 Belden Pl. (bet. Bush & Pine Sts.) | 415-986-5673 | www.cafebastille.com

"Sitting outside on a warm San Francisco day" is the highlight of a visit to this "likable" bistro whose sidewalk tables bring "*un peu de* Paris" to Belden Place; though some call the "simple" meals a bit of a "yawn" and say the staff "tries to turn tables too quickly", it's an "oh-so-reasonable" fix when you "miss the ambiance" of the "city of love."

Café Claude *French*

22 | 20 | 21 | $40

Downtown | 7 Claude Ln. (Sutter St.) | 415-392-3515 | www.cafeclaude.com

"Francophiles" find a "secluded" setting for an "intimate rendezvous" at this "adorable" "oasis" "tucked away" in a Downtown "alley", delivering "delicious" bistro fare whose "authenticity is hard to equal"; despite a few service "lapses", the staff's "Bay Area *joie de vivre*" and "great jazz" Thursday-Saturday keep it a "well-priced winner", but consider "calling for directions", since it can be "hard to find."

Café de la Presse *French*

18 | 19 | 18 | $34

Downtown | 352 Grant Ave. (bet. Bush & Sutter Sts.) | 415-249-0900

"Francophiles" and "European visitors" stop for "hearty" bistro dishes and "well-priced wines" at this "handy", "international-feeling" cafe on the "border of Chinatown" and Union Square; though service can be "a bit slow", it's "lovely" to "linger over espresso" at the "tiny tables" while "people-watching" or browsing the "fashion magazines and journals" that "line the walls."

🆕 Café des Amis *French*

- | - | - | M

Cow Hollow | 2000 Union St. (Buchanan St.) | 415-563-7700 | www.cafedesamissf.com

Looking every bit the bustling sidewalk French brasserie that it hopes to emulate, this nouveau-comer in Cow Hollow (from the folks behind Spruce and Village Pub) turns out rustic and refined offerings from crispy frogs' legs and charcuterie to late-night fruits de mer; a coveted mezzanine overlooks the 175-seat dining room outfitted with black wood, red leather banquettes and marble floors, while at the long zinc bar, bartenders pour classic cocktails and apéritifs.

Café Gratitude *Vegan*

16 | 13 | 15 | $26

Mission | 2400 Harrison St. (20th St.) | 415-824-4652 | www.cafegratitude.com

"Interesting or weird, depending on your point of view", this "perky" raw-vegan cafe trio in the Mission, Berkeley and San Rafael delivers "clean", "hearty" and "crunchy (literally and figuratively)" dishes with names like 'I Am Dazzling' and 'I Am Devoted' in a "hippie-dippy" environment; "if you can get past the cheesy affirmations" and "overbearing" service, the "pricey" vittles might "please your palate", but guests with "grated" nerves sneer "I Am Snarky" and wonder why "it takes forever" to get "something that's not even cooked."

Cafe Jacqueline ☒ *French*

25 | 19 | 21 | $51

North Beach | 1454 Grant Ave. (bet. Green & Union Sts.) | 415-981-5565

Serving mainly "exquisite", expensive soufflés (along with "soups and salads"), this "small", "quiet" French "gem" is ideal for an "intimate

	FOOD	DECOR	SERVICE	COST

tête-à-tête" in North Beach; it's "not fast food" by any means, and "edgy" service can be a downside, but guests who use the "long prep time" to "bask in the company of their loved one" – and peek into the kitchen to "say hi" to the "cheery" "Madame Jacqueline", who whips up every sweet and savory cloud "with TLC – feel it's "hard to match."

Café Kati 🗷Ⓜ *Asian* | 22 | 16 | 20 | $47 |

Japantown | 1963 Sutter St. (bet. Fillmore & Webster Sts.) | 415-775-7313 | www.cafekati.com

"Gorgeous 'vertical'" Asian Fusion dishes, followed by "killer desserts" ("try the banana split – suffice to say it's not your grandmother's version") are the hallmarks of this "offbeat" "but serious" veteran "boîte" near Japantown; though "a bit pricey" for a "neighborhood spot", it remains the "go-to choice" for "pre-theater meals" and "romantic dinners", plus the "nifty" "dark but festive" back room is spot-on for "small group celebrations."

Café Tiramisu 🗷 *Italian* | 20 | 18 | 19 | $42 |

Downtown | 28 Belden Pl. (bet. Bush & Pine Sts.) | 415-421-7044 | www.cafetiramisu.com

Celebrating "European"-style "wining and dining", this Belden Place trattoria packs them in "elbow-to-elbow" with "excellent" Northern Italian dishes and "super desserts" set down by an "attentive" staff; while some love the sensation of "eating outside" "on a warm day" or beside the "heat lamps", critics grumble that it's "too crowded" and the "overpriced" fare "takes a backseat to the general ambiance."

Cafe Zoetrope Ⓜ *Italian*   ∇ | 20 | 22 | 20 | $29 |

North Beach | 916 Kearny St. (Columbus Ave.) | 415-291-1700 | www.cafeniebaum-coppola.com

"Come on, you could run into Francis' fawn "people-watching" cineastes who quaff an "excellent espresso" – or a "glass of Mr. Coppola's wine" – at this "convivial" "European-styled" sidewalk cafe "strategically located in bustling North Beach"; perhaps "you pay for the charm" and bric-a-brac celebrating "his film achievements", but the "appealing" pizza and Southern Italian specialties "from the famous director's kitchen" "don't disappoint"; P.S. its new offshoot Mammarella's in Napa Airpark serves weekday breakfast and lunch.

Caffe Delle Stelle *Italian* | 16 | 15 | 16 | $34 |

Hayes Valley | 395 Hayes St. (Gough St.) | 415-252-1110 | www.dellestelle.com

A "reliable alternative to flashier" options before "attending the symphony, opera or ballet", this "down-to-earth" Tuscan trattoria in Hayes Valley is known for "tasty" if not exactly "thrilling" Italian eats, proffered in "perfect" portions at a "price that's right"; "thoughtful" servers "get you to the performance before the curtain rises", and the "complimentary sparkling water" is a "nice touch", but the less starry-eyed note it's "not up to par" with the competition.

Caffè Macaroni 🗷🍴 *Italian*   ∇ | 21 | 14 | 19 | $31 |

North Beach | 59 Columbus Ave. (Jackson St.) | 415-956-9737 | www.caffemacaroni.com

Filling up on "old-style, delicious" Southern Italian fare at this "tiny but welcoming trattoria" on the "edge of North Beach" is "like going home

	FOOD	DECOR	SERVICE	COST

to *mamma mia*" for supper; detractors find the noodles "nothing special" but admit it's a "bargain" nonetheless, and with real dry pasta glued to the ceilings, the "kid-friendly" atmosphere is "a hoot!"

Caffè Museo *Italian/Mediterranean* | 19 | 15 | 13 | $21 |

SoMa | SFMOMA | 151 Third St. (bet. Howard & Mission Sts.) | 415-357-4500 | www.caffemuseo.com

Whether you've just "exercised your brain" in the SFMOMA galleries or need to "escape the Moscone Convention crowd", this "super-arty" "self-serve" cafeteria is the "perfect" "place to refresh"; seating can get "chaotic" ("claim" a spot outdoors), but the "beautifully arranged" Italian-Med fare, appealing to the "most modern and postmodern palates", more than compensates; N.B closed Wednesdays and open late on Thursday evenings.

Cajun Pacific ☒Ⓜ *Cajun* | ▽ 22 | 16 | 22 | $37 |

Outer Sunset | 4542 Irving St. (47th Ave.) | 415-504-6652 | www.cajunpacific.com

"Calling it" "postage stamp–sized" "hardly describes" this "sweet" seafood-centric "Big Easy" outpost in the Outer Sunset "decorated like someone was handed a box of Mardi Gras beads"; it's "terrific watching" "the chef and his partner put on a virtuoso performance, cooking up" some of the "best Cajun cuisine you'll get in California", so it's "always worth the wait", but patrons pining for "pecan pie" "wish they were open more" often than Thursday–Saturday.

Campton Place *Californian/Mediterranean* | 25 | 25 | 24 | $69 |

Downtown | Taj Campton Place Hotel | 340 Stockton St. (bet. Post & Sutter Sts.) | 415-955-5555 | www.camptonplace.com

"Suitable for special occasions", like a "blessedly quiet" "romantic" dinner or a "breakfast meeting with clients you want to impress", this "refined" Cal-Med near Union Square is "always pleasing to the palate, if not the pocketbook"; happy campers say their "cares disappear" thanks to the "formal" yet "gracious" service and whisper about their "best-kept secret", a "tiny" bar that's the "perfect refuge from shopping or sightseeing", even if a few fuss that it's all "a little too stuffy" for comfort; P.S. jacket suggested.

Candybar Ⓜ *Dessert* | ▽ 17 | 18 | 19 | $19 |

Western Addition | 1335 Fulton St. (Divisadero St.) | 415-673-7078 | www.candybarsf.com

"Not really a restaurant", this "cool little" lounge in the Western Addition is instead dedicated to "simply divine", sometimes "out-there" desserts, inviting "chocolate snobs" to "indulge in anything" made with cacao, complemented by a few savory choices and "good" sparkling drinks; there's "not a lot of variety, but what they do, they do well", and the "friendly" servers loan out "old board games to play with", which helps make it a "warm, inviting" "alternative to other bars."

☒ Canteen Ⓜ *Californian* | 27 | 14 | 23 | $47 |

Tenderloin | Commodore Hotel | 817 Sutter St. (Jones St.) | 415-928-8870 | www.sfcanteen.com

How "magician" Dennis Leary continuously conjures such "bad-ass" Californian dinners (and weekend brunch) with "incredibly intricate" flavors at this "tiny" "Tenderloin star" "is a mystery, but one to be ap-

FOOD DECOR SERVICE COST

preciated often" assure "eager fans" who angle to "snag" one of the "swift" nightly seatings; the "glorified" lunch-counter setting is part of the "charm", as it lets "serious foodies" watch the chef "go crazy" crafting "miracles out of a minute kitchen"; P.S. the Tuesday night prix fixe is a "deal."

Capannina *Italian*

25 | 20 | 23 | $42

Cow Hollow | 1809 Union St. (Octavia St.) | 415-409-8001 | www.capanninasf.com

The "charming", "bantering" staff makes you feel like "long-lost family" at this "underhyped" Cow Hollow "sleeper" serving "satisfying pasta dishes" among other "delicious" Italian eats; with its "crowded-together" tables, it's "warm, cozy" and "hopping", and the prix fixe menu, served before 6 PM, is "a steal."

Catch *Seafood*

18 | 17 | 19 | $38

Castro | 2362 Market St. (bet. Castro & 16th Sts.) | 415-431-5000 | www.catchsf.com

"Gay urban professionals" "cast their lines to the schools of pretty men" while enjoying "appetizers and cocktails at the bar" or "sitting by the fire" on the "enclosed patio" of this "casual Castro" seafood house; "some real standouts make it better than good", but with a "hit-or-miss" menu and "friendly" but variable service, it "never ascends to grand."

Cav Wine Bar & Kitchen 🖾 *Wine Bar*

20 | 18 | 20 | $43

Hayes Valley | 1666 Market St. (bet. Franklin & Gough Sts.) | 415-437-1770 | www.cavwinebar.com

A wine-bar "gem" opine oenophiles who "rendezvous" at this "delightfully unpretentious" Hayes Valley "favorite" decorated with "corks on the wall" "before or after" the "opera/symphony", or pop by for a "light bite"; with 40 "divine" options by the glass, vino "exploration" "drives the limited menu" (big on cheese and charcuterie) – the only cav-eat is that "there's hardly" a varietal you "recognize", making it a "must" to rely on the "knowledgeable staff"; P.S. a post-Survey chef and menu change is not reflected in the Food score.

Cha Am Thai *Thai*

19 | 13 | 17 | $24

SoMa | Museum Parc | 701 Folsom St. (3rd St.) | 415-546-9711 | www.chaamthaisf.com

These "reliable", separately owned Southeast Asian stalwarts cook up "zesty" "Thai goodies" for "reasonable" tabs; the SoMa location fills up at lunch as "Moscone conventioneers descend", while the Berkeley "institution" could use some "updating", but with "fast", "efficient" service, both offer a "satisfying" "eat-and-run" option.

Cha Cha Cha *Caribbean*

21 | 18 | 18 | $26

Haight-Ashbury | 1801 Haight St. (Shrader St.) | 415-386-5758
Mission | 2327 Mission St. (bet. 19th & 20th Sts.) | 415-648-0504
www.cha3.com

"Rah-rah-rah" cheer the "trendy" "twentysomethings" who "party down" at this "packed" Haight and Mission duo delivering "wonderful" Caribbean small plates and "killer sangria" amid "quirky voodoo decor"; though the "wait can be long", most insist it's "worth it" for an "affordable", "fab-u-lous" "night out with friends."

	FOOD	DECOR	SERVICE	COST

◪ Chapeau! *French* — 26 | 20 | 25 | $52

Inner Richmond | 126 Clement St. (bet. 2nd & 3rd Aves.) | 415-750-9787 |
www.chapeausf.com

"The magic has moved" to this "less-cramped" Inner Richmond location "swoon" "Francophiles, foodies and other famished folk" who say "hats off" to chef/co-owner Philippe Gardelle's "superlative" country French bistro "treasure", where a meal is an "ooh-la-la" "experience" that begins with a "warm" "welcome" from his "gracious wife", Ellen; better yet, the "upgraded menu" of "five-star cuisine at three-star prices" is still a "screaming deal", especially the early-bird and prix fixe dinners.

Charanga ◫ *Pan-Latin* — 23 | 17 | 20 | $31

Mission | 2351 Mission St. (bet. 19th & 20th Sts.) | 415-282-1813 |
www.charangasf.com

It's like a "warm, loud family who loves you so much they've prepared special dishes for you" chime champions of this "brightly painted" "hidden treasure in the Mission" that channels the "casual feel" of a Havana bodega; graze on "inexpensive" Pan-Latin tapas (with a Cuban/Caribbean emphasis) "as good as the big boys and twice the size", down the "super-cheap sangria" and dig the background charanga music – this is "definitely not your typical taqueria."

Chaya Brasserie *French/Japanese* — 22 | 21 | 21 | $52

Embarcadero | 132 The Embarcadero (bet. Howard & Mission Sts.) |
415-777-8688 | www.thechaya.com

"East meets West" on the Embarcadero with the "innovative" French-Japanese dishes served at this "dependably hip" LA import, flaunting both a "sceney" "vibe" and a "gorgeous" view of the Bay Bridge; though a few critics call the "eclectic" fare "confusing" and "pricey", many are won over by the "happy-hour deals" on "awesome" cocktails and "excellent" sushi at the "buzzing" bar.

Cha-Ya Vegetarian — 23 | 11 | 17 | $21

Japanese Restaurant ⊘ *Japanese/Vegan*

Mission | 762 Valencia St. (bet. 18th & 19th Sts.) | 415-252-7825

Both "Japanese-loving vegetarians" and "devout carnivores" "in need of a detox" flock to this Mission and Berkeley pair offering "satisfying", "beautifully presented" vegan fare in the Buddhist tradition "that tastes like there was actually work put into it"; so ignore the "bare-bones" decor and "awful lines" to focus on the "unusual ingredients" that prompt "culinary conversations"; P.S. the Berkeley branch is closed for lunch on Monday.

Cheesecake Factory *American* — 16 | 17 | 17 | $29

Downtown | Macy's | 251 Geary St., 8th fl. (bet. Powell & Stockton Sts.) |
415-391-4444 | www.thecheesecakefactory.com

"Humongous portions and humongous lines" characterize this American chain where the "textbook"-size menu offers "lots of choices" and a "broad price spectrum" to keep families "stuffed and happy"; the "herd 'em in, herd 'em out" feel isn't for everyone and critics knock "mass-produced" fare and "overdone" decor, but overall it's a "crowd-pleaser", especially when it comes to the "amazing" namesake dessert – even if you need to "take it home for much later."

	FOOD	DECOR	SERVICE	COST

Cheese Steak Shop *Cheesesteaks*

21 | 8 | 16 | $12

Western Addition | 1716 Divisadero St. (bet. Bush & Sutter Sts.) | 415-346-3712 | www.cheesesteakshop.com

"Loosen your belt" advise those "born and raised in Philly", because the "gooey, thick, juicy cheesesteaks" (and "first-rate hoagies") served at these local chain joints are "as good as it gets far from home"; though the "divey" surroundings don't offer "much in the way of decor or service", the "cheap" "heart-clogging decadence" they deliver is "indulgence" enough for most.

Chenery Park Ⓜ *American*

22 | 18 | 23 | $41

Glen Park | 683 Chenery St. (Diamond St.) | 415-337-8537 | www.chenerypark.com

"Striking a perfect balance between elegance and unpretentiousness", this "family-friendly" "belle" of Glen Park is also getting "discovered by people who aren't neighbors"; "inviting service" and "cozy" tri-level digs "perfectly complement" the "varied", "economically" priced American "home cooking" done "with Cajun flair", making it HQ for everything from "dates and group celebrations" to "kids' nights" – but those not toting tots should "otherwise steer clear on Tuesdays."

Chez Maman *French*

23 | 14 | 21 | $28

Potrero Hill | 1453 18th St. (bet. Connecticut & Missouri Sts.) | 415-824-7166 | www.chezmamansf.com

"Most patrons sit on stools" pulled up to the counter at this "tiny little" French bistro in Potrero Hill, so you can expect to "sit almost face-to-face" with the chefs who are grilling up "amazing steak frites" or plating "delicious brunch" dishes; "make no mistake", it's "not fancy", but the modestly priced food is just like you wish "your own *maman* had prepared", and the "expat" staff is "charming" to boot.

Chez Papa Bistrot *French*

23 | 21 | 22 | $46

Potrero Hill | 1401 18th St. (Missouri St.) | 415-824-8210

Chez Papa Resto Ⓢ *French*

SoMa | 4 Mint Plaza (bet. Market & Mission Sts.) | 415-546-4134 www.chezpapasf.com

When they "need their Frenchie fix", followers have their pick of these two bistros (now separately owned) where the "cute", "flirty" waiters serve "solidly crafted" Gallic fare; the newer, "gorgeous" Mint Plaza location (with a Provençal twist) has a "hip SoMa crowd", while the Potrero Hill original is "a bit more affordable" and "cozy" in comparison, but *mon dieu*, both can suffer from "scream-over-the-table volume levels" at peak times.

Chez Spencer *French*

25 | 21 | 22 | $60

Mission | 82 14th St. (bet. Folsom & Harrison Sts.) | 415-864-2191 | www.chezspencer.net

Spencer on the Go! Ⓢ Ⓜ *French*

SoMa | Location varies; see website | www.spenceronthego.com

"What a secret gem" agree the "adventurous" who seek out this "quirky" "indoor/outdoor Frenchie" "speakeasy" "hidden" in a "slightly sketchy" Mission neighborhood for its "spectacular" Gallic fare and vibrant "sense of fête", especially on weekends, "when there's live piano" and "beautiful people abound"; still a few gripe that "given the prices", service can be "uneven"; P.S. its "roving" offshoot, the Spencer on the Go! truck, usually parks at 7th and Folsom Streets Wednesday–Saturday evenings.

🆕 Chile Pies & Ice Cream ⊘ Dessert — — — — I

Western Addition | 601 Baker St. (Fulton St.) | 415-614-9411 | www.greenchilekitchen.com/chilepies

At this homey Western Addition sweet shop (located in the original corner outpost of sibling Green Chile Kitchen), an array of traditional and chile-spiked pies and ice creams can be enjoyed separately or – for the ultimate munchie sensation – whirled together into a 'pie shake'; it also serves a few savory options, including a green chile and apple pie with a cheddar crust and a Southwestern-style Frito pie.

Chloe's Cafe ⊘ American 23 13 19 $21

Noe Valley | 1399 Church St. (26th St.) | 415-648-4116

Granted, it's just "oats, not haute", but this "bright" Noe Valley corner cafe serving "crave"-worthy American "comfort food" like the "fluffi-est pancakes" and "divine croissant French toast" is a "super way to start the day"; the digs "feel like grandma's house", and you can duck "outside on sunny days" – just "go on a weekday" or early, as it's "teeny, tiny" and them "yuppies" are willing to "wait for eggs."

Chouchou French 21 18 22 $41

Forest Hills | 400 Dewey Blvd. (Laguna Honda Blvd.) | 415-242-0960 | www.chouchousf.com

"Every evening is a *bon soir*" at this "intimate, seductive" French bistro (and unsung Sunday brunch "nook") that's about "as close to a Paris bistro" as you'll find in "out-of-the-way" Forest Hills; "sardines have more space", but the "lovely food" served by even "lovelier" "charm-ingly accented" *garçons* who "kiss you on both cheeks" makes the "ex-perience" "memorable", as do "*les grandes* tarts", which are indeed "*les grandes* treats."

☑ Chow American 20 15 19 $26

Castro | 215 Church St. (bet. 15th & Market Sts.) | 415-552-2469

☑ Park Chow American

Inner Sunset | 1240 Ninth Ave. (bet. Irving St. & Lincoln Way) | 415-665-9912
www.chowfoodbar.com

It "feels like home only busier" at this mini-chain of "quirky" New American "neighborhood joints" where the "varied" menu offers "high-quality comfort food" with "flair", capped off by "don't-miss" desserts; some sniff that the grub is "uninspired", but it keeps both "young fam-ilies and hipsters" "happy", and the tabs "won't set you back."

Circa American 16 18 19 $33

Marina | 2001 Chestnut St. (Fillmore St.) | 415-351-0175 | www.circasf.com

"Young Marina-ites" converge on this loungey "party" place for ex-travagant American small plates and a scene that hits a "high note" at happy hour; while critics complain the food is "nothing great" since it changed chefs, that doesn't put a damper on the "post-college soror-ity experience" during weekend brunch, fueled by the "most accom-modating bottomless mimosa service ever."

	FOOD	DECOR	SERVICE	COST

NEW Citizen's Band ⓜ *American* | – | – | – | M

SoMa | 1198 Folsom St. (8th St.) | 415-556-4901 | www.citizensbandsf.com
Named for the iconic CB radio, this SoMa newcomer cranks out gussied-up traditional Americana – think franks and beans, fried chicken, mac 'n' cheese – prepared by fine-dining veteran chefs Chris Beerman (ex Boulevard) and Boris Nemchenok (Uva Enoteca), topped off by home-spun desserts from neighboring Pinkie's Bakery; the 40-seat store-front, decorated with vintage CBs and postcards, offers walk-in-only dinner to start (for upper-end moderate prices), but lunch and brunch are slated for early fall.

Citrus Club *Asian* | 21 | 13 | 16 | $18

Haight-Ashbury | 1790 Haight St. (Shrader St.) | 415-387-6366 |
www.citrusclubsf.com
Partial patrons say the "piping hot bowls of soup" at this "cheap" Upper Haight Pan-Asian "can't be beat", since the "huge portions" of "simply prepared" "slurpy noodles", "delicious broth" and loads of veggies "cure the winter blues anytime"; though the "cramped quarters" can be a "mad house", the "turnover is pretty quick", and "takeout" works too.

Cliff House Bistro *Californian* | 19 | 25 | 19 | $41

Outer Richmond | 1090 Point Lobos Ave. (Balboa St.) | 415-386-3330 |
www.cliffhouse.com
"Forget Rice-a-Roni" – this "memorabilia"-filled Outer Richmond "historic landmark" "overlooking the cliffs" and "crashing" waves is the real "San Francisco treat" for "showing off the city" to "tourists"; the glassed-in dining room gets a "seal of approval" – what a "wow" spot for an "elevated" Cal lunch or "sunset cocktails" – and it's "much more reasonably priced" than Sutro's downstairs ("love" the "bonus popovers" and "Wednesday prix fixe deals"); still, "underwhelmed" locals caution "don't waste your money" after dark.

Coco500 Ⓩ *Californian/Mediterranean* | 23 | 19 | 21 | $47

SoMa | 500 Brannan St. (4th St.) | 415-543-2222 | www.coco500.com
Both the "power-lunch spot of SoMa" and the go-to "before moving out for the opening pitch", Loretta Keller's "convivial", way-"modern" Cal-Med haunt drives droves "kookoo" with its small-plate MVPs like "battered green beans" or beef cheeks ("there'd be a riot if they were taken off the menu"); the "creative" kitchen "doesn't stop there" – even the "ultrafine mixologists" score big with "fabulous drinks" – if only it didn't get so "ear-shatteringly loud in the evening."

Ⓩ Coi Ⓢ ⓜ *Californian/French* | 26 | 24 | 27 | $121

North Beach | 373 Broadway (Montgomery St.) | 415-393-9000 |
www.coirestaurant.com
North Beach may be an "odd location for a food wizard", but Daniel Patterson's Cal-French molecular "magic works just the same" at this "West Coast bow to El Bulli"; the prix fixe "edible works of art", "Zen-like setting" and "superb" service elicit "moans of delight" from "true foodies and wine snobs" who claim it's "for all of your senses", but "mere mortals" "highly recommend" à la carte "dining in the lounge" instead, declaring that the "outlandishly" priced main event lacks a certain "*je ne sais coi*."

Colibrí Mexican Bistro *Mexican*   20 | 17 | 18 | $36

Downtown | 438 Geary St. (bet. Mason & Taylor Sts.) | 415-440-2737 |
www.colibrimexicanbistro.com

"Nothing like old Mexican B-grade movies, fresh guac and a true margarita" affirm amigos of this "quick" (some say "rushed") Union Square "pit stop" purveying "upper-end" dishes with "zippy" flavors in a "lively" atmosphere; less-impressed padres "wouldn't go out of their way" for it, but for "pre-theater" dining, it's "one of the best options" in the neighborhood.

NEW Commonwealth Ⓜ *American*   - | - | - | E

Mission | 2224 Mission St. (18th St.) | 415-355-1500 |
www.commonwealthsf.com

The latest feel-good venture from the former Mission Street Food crew, this casual new dinner house offers cutting-edge New American cuisine by Jason Fox (ex Bar Tartine), both à la carte and as part of a $60 six-course weekly set-dinner ($10 of which is donated to charity), complemented by boutique grower-producer wines; the small storefront (with a skylight) exudes a clean midcentury vibe, featuring lots of wood, white-painted brick and air plants suspended in glass globes.

NEW Comstock Saloon ❶Ⓩ *American*   - | - | - | M

North Beach | 155 Columbus Ave. (Pacific Ave.) | 415-617-0071 |
www.comstocksaloon.com

Everything old is new again at this Barbary Coast–inspired gastropub, an ornately detailed, historic North Beach watering hole revived by two former Absinthe bar impresarios, where 21st-century hipsters seek sustenance and liquid courage via updated American saloon fare (including a beef shank and bone marrow pot pie) complemented by old-timey cocktails; the midpriced menu is served till 1 AM, and there's live jazz Tuesday nights.

Contigo Ⓜ *Spanish*   24 | 21 | 21 | $44

Noe Valley | 1320 Castro St. (24th St.) | 415-285-0250 |
www.contigosf.com

"Barcelona comes to Noe Valley" – and so does everyone else, "as evidenced by the crowds" – at this "modern" "neighborhood" "hot spot" built from "recycled materials"; sit at the communal tables or "cute" back patio and graze on "unique" tapas (ok, "more like samples") and larger platillos that "push the envelope without betraying their Catalan inspiration" – especially "divine" with "perfect pairings" of Iberian cava and sherries suggested by the "sweet-talking" servers.

Corner, The Ⓩ *Californian/Italian*   ▽ 19 | 16 | 16 | $26

Mission | 2199 Mission St. (18th St.) | 415-875-9258 |
www.thecornersf.com

"If Fergus Henderson means anything to you", this little-known "casual" European-style corner cafe ("hence the name") recently overhauled by NYC-trained chef Alex Jackson will "rock" you, opine "offal fans"; the "creative" Cal-Ital fare "pays tribute to the snout-to-tail concept" at "Mission prices", while the "terrific wines don't require an M.S. to appreciate"; still a few feel the "coffee-bar decor" and "distracted" service "fall short" of the "kitchen's ambition"; P.S. now serving lunch.

	FOOD	DECOR	SERVICE	COST

Cosmopolitan, The 🗷 *American*
19 | 20 | 21 | $48

SoMa | Rincon Ctr. | 121 Spear St. (bet. Howard & Mission Sts.) | 415-543-4001 | www.thecosmopolitancafe.com

"New York style meets West Coast cuisine" at this SoMa New American whose "well-prepared" fare and "comfortable" setting make it a "business lunch standard"; while some find the food just "ok", the bar beckons for "drinks after work", while "happy-hour specials" add to the "value."

NEW Cotogna *Italian*
– | – | – | M

Downtown | 490 Pacific St. (Montgomery St.) | 415-775-8500

Quince's adjacent trattoria spin-off (slated at press time to open around Labor Day) aims to lure in Downtown denizens with chef-owner Michael Tusk's moderately priced rustic Boot fare, much of which will be prepared on an imported Italian rotisserie grill; in addition, look for wood-fired pizzas and housemade pastas, served in an open dining room outfitted with brick and timber, and at a counter facing the open kitchen.

NEW Credo 🗷 *Italian*
∇ 17 | 18 | 17 | $40

Downtown | 360 Pine St. (Montgomery St.) | 415-693-0360 | www.credosf.com

This "casual" "up-and-comer" in Downtown's FiDi serving "rustic" Italian is "worth checking out" suggest early adopters, if only for the "fun" decor, including walls covered with "thought-provoking quotes based on the 'I believe'" credo; though not everyone's a believer, suggesting the somewhat expensive food is "not up to par" and the service needs "polish", others feel it "has potential."

Crustacean *Vietnamese*
25 | 19 | 20 | $56

Polk Gulch | 1475 Polk St. (California St.) | 415-776-2722 | www.anfamily.com

Seafood lovers "strap on a bib" and "crack away" at the "delectable", "must-have" crab and garlic noodles cloaked in a "killer" sauce at this Polk Vietnamese with "good service" and a "dress code" contrasting against digs showing a bit of "wear and tear"; true, it's "not for a first date", as you'll end up a "complete drippy, gooey mess", but it's "worth the expense" nonetheless.

Delancey Street 🅼 *Eclectic*
18 | 16 | 21 | $29

Embarcadero | 600 The Embarcadero (Brannan St.) | 415-512-5179 | www.delanceystreetfoundation.org

"You can eat well" and "feel good doing it" at this Embarcadero eatery that "helps individuals get a new start on life" by hiring ex-convicts and recovering addicts, all of whom "work hard to please"; the "big", "comforting" Eclectic meals are an "exceptional value", and if the "bright" dining room "does lack a bit of atmosphere", at least the "patio seating" with "beautiful Bay views" is "priceless on a warm night"; P.S. open Mondays if the Giants are in town.

NEW Delarosa ◑ *Italian*
22 | 16 | 20 | $31

Marina | 2175 Chestnut St. (bet. Pierce & Steiner Sts.) | 415-673-7100 | www.delarosasf.com

"Vivacious" and "packed all the time", this "sleek" new Beretta spin-off provides the Marina set with "crisp", "ingredient-driven" thin-crust pizzas complemented by "far-out and fabulous" seasonal Italian bites;

"fantastic cocktails" brought round by "friendly, cool" servers are another plus, though the room's "backless stools" and "communal seating" are "less than desirable" for some; P.S. to avoid "hour waits", take advantage of the "45-minute call-ahead policy."

DeLessio Market & Bakery *Bakery*   22 | 14 | 16 | $22

Hayes Valley | 1695 Market St. (Gough St.) | 415-552-5559
Western Addition | Falletti's Plaza | 302 Broderick St. (Oak St.) |
415-552-8077
www.delessiomarket.com

While you have to fill your own plate and "pay by the pound" at these "gourmet" "deli buffets", "who would object to helping themselves" to a "salad bar of creative concoctions", "terrific sandwiches" and an "inspired" bakery of "delectable delights"?; the "tiny patio" at the Hayes Valley locale is "nice for a quick lunch", while the "smaller" Western Addition branch is geared toward takeout, but either way, be prepared for "sticker shock at the register."

☑ Delfina *Italian*   26 | 19 | 22 | $47

Mission | 3621 18th St. (bet. Dolores & Guerrero Sts.) | 415-552-4055 |
www.delfinasf.com

Chef/co-owner Craig Stoll "hits every note right" at this Mission "must", preparing "simple, soulful", "swoon-worthy" Northern Italian food, matched by a "well-curated" wine list, that's worth the "hoops required to get a reservation"; the "young" staff is "terrific" and prices are "decent", so while the "New York-y" atmosphere can be a "madhouse", most agree it "never ceases to impress."

Destino *Nuevo Latino*   21 | 17 | 20 | $39

Castro | 1815 Market St. (bet. Guerrero St. & Octavia Blvd.) |
415-552-4451 | www.destinosf.com

"A bit of Peru hidden on Market Street", this "fantastic" Nuevo Latino "date place" by the Castro attracts a "great mixture of people" who appreciate everything from the "unique" tapas ("fabulous ceviche") and caipirinhas to the "melt-in-your-mouth *alfajores* cookies for dessert"; the space is a bit "small and loud", but some of the crowd flows into the "chic" Pisco Latin Lounge next door for pre- or post-meal drinks.

Domo Sushi *Japanese*   ▽ 20 | 15 | 18 | $33

Hayes Valley | 511 Laguna St. (Linden St.) | 415-861-8887 |
www.domosf.com

"All the action is on view in the tiny, open kitchen" at this "solid" if "not particularly adventurous" Hayes Valley Japanese where the "cool chefs" prepare "delicate" crudos, sashimi and rolls (including a novel "baked" variety); "get there early", as "there are no reservations and very few seats" (primarily at the bar or outdoor tables), but thankfully the servers ferry out the fin fare "extremely quickly."

Dosa *Indian*   22 | 22 | 20 | $38

Mission | 995 Valencia St. (21st St.) | 415-642-3672
Upper Fillmore | 1700 Fillmore St. (Post St.) | 415-441-3672
www.dosasf.com

"Delectable" dosas and other "imaginative" plates deliver "complex flavors" at these "upscale" South Indian eateries, packing an "ultraspicy" punch that warrants an "exotic" cocktail to extinguish the "fire"; with a "see-and-be-seen" vibe, the "energetic" Mission original and its "gorgeously decorated" Fillmore spin-off can be "hard to get into", but fans insist that the "delish" dishes are "worth the hipper-than-thou attitude."

Dottie's True Blue Cafe   Diner

25 | 12 | 19 | $20

Tenderloin | 522 Jones St. (bet. Geary & O'Farrell Sts.) | 415-885-2767
"Bring your most entertaining friends" to keep you company, because there's always a "long line" at this "teeny" Tenderloiner that's "in the running for the best breakfast" spot in town; the "cooks are a wonder to watch" as they churn out "heavenly pancakes" and specials "so alluring" that some "never really look" at the menu; since there's "no 'tude", hardly anyone minds the "lackluster diner decor" – somehow "the charm of the place is that there is no charm"; P.S. closes at 3 PM.

Dragon Well   Chinese

22 | 15 | 20 | $27

Marina | 2142 Chestnut St. (bet. Pierce & Steiner Sts.) | 415-474-6888 |
www.dragonwell.com
For "terrific" "Cali-healthy Chinese food", "young families" and Marina regulars rely on the "wholesome" "standards" served at this "neighborhood" place by an "accommodating" staff; while purists protest that its "predictable stir-fries" "cannot compare to the real thing", fans find themselves "going back often" for an "inexpensive" "quick bite."

Ducca   American

17 | 20 | 18 | $49

SoMa | Westin San Francisco | 50 Third St. (Market St.) | 415-977-0271 |
www.duccasf.com
Boasting "beautiful, spacious" digs and "one of the great fire pits in the city", this SoMa hotel "oasis" attracts guests seeking a "quiet lunch" as well as "after-work" drinks; still, many feel the "food doesn't live up to the surroundings" and service is "hit-or-miss"; P.S. the kitchen has shifted post-Survey to a stripped-down, midpriced American menu, with a slight nod to Italy.

Dynamo Donut & Coffee   Ⓜ Coffeehouse

- | - | - | I

Mission | 2760 24th St. (Hampshire St.) | 415-920-1978 |
www.dynamodonut.com
Raising the bar on the doughnuts-and-coffee paradigm, this deceptively simply named Mission bakeshop has achieved cult status among sugar-happy habitués who line up early for the kitchen's changing roster of edgy-flavored, yeast-risen organic doughnuts, such as anise-spiced chocolate and maple-apple-bacon, until they run out; the tiny storefront offers little more than the dynamite sweets, strong Four Barrel coffee and the occasional savory focaccia, but there's limited cafe seating and a new garden patio for your dunking exploits.

E&O Trading Company   Asian

19 | 21 | 19 | $38

Downtown | 314 Sutter St. (bet. Grant Ave. & Stockton St.) |
415-693-0303 | www.eotrading.com
"Indiana Jones and the Pacific Rim Culinary Crusades" soldier on at this "overhauled" (mostly) "for the better" Bay Area chainlet of "lively", "cavernous" Southeast Asian grills that recall the "old Trader Vic's" with "mysterious Orient" decor and "exotic cocktails" that "whisk you away"; "arrive with a group" and "trade" the "boldly flavored" small plates, including the corn fritters – they're "soooo good" devotees "would almost do illegal things" for a "tasty bite."

E'Angelo Ⓜ Italian
21 | 11 | 21 | $29

Marina | 2234 Chestnut St. (bet. Pierce & Scott Sts.) | 415-567-6164
The "welcoming" staff "makes you an offer you can't refuse" at this "old-style" "marinara-sauce Italian" "joint" (opened in 1978) where Marina diners sup on "basic but reliable" "plates of comforting pasta" that are among the "best for the price"; so while it's "usually crowded", *bambino,* it's "worth the wait."

Ebisu Japanese
23 | 17 | 19 | $37

NEW Downtown | 336 Kearny St. (bet. Pine & Bush Sts.) | 415-398-2388 Ⓢ
Inner Sunset | 1283 Ninth Ave. (Irving St.) | 415-566-1770 Ⓜ
www.ebisusushi.com
Sporting "fancier" all-bamboo decor (with a "gorgeous" new raw bar) and an "updated", moderately priced menu boasting "different things to keep you coming back", this redone Inner Sunset Japanese "fixture" (with SFO and Downtown satellites) "still delivers" "sparkling sushi" and "artistic" rolls that go "miles beyond the standards"; it's "great for lunch", and though usually "packed" at dinner, you can bide the wait "sipping a beer on the sidewalk" before giving the "entertaining chefs" "free reign."

Eiji Ⓜ Japanese
25 | 12 | 19 | $35

Castro | 317 Sanchez St. (bet. 16th & 17th Sts.) | 415-558-8149
At this "cozy" "gem" "tucked away" in the Castro, "tofu connoisseurs" "revel in the silkiness" of the "one-man" kitchen's signature "out-of-this-world", "made-to-order oboru" ("not your supermarket" variety) prepared tableside by the "attentive" staff; "sushi purists" and other "adventurers" are also "well rewarded for stepping out of their comfort zones" (forget "dragon rolls and teriyaki"), delighting in "authentic" "country Japanese" "delicacies", "tasty fish" dishes and "unbeatable" mochi.

Elite Cafe American
19 | 19 | 19 | $39

Pacific Heights | 2049 Fillmore St. (bet. California & Pine Sts.) | 415-673-5483 | www.theelitecafe.com
For "upscale down-home cooking", like "amazing" biscuits and "killer" Cajun eats, Pac Heights patrons pick this "old-school" American soul-fooder on Fillmore where the "high-backed booths" offer "lots of privacy" and the staff makes everyone "feel like they're from the neighborhood"; still, doubters dub it only "ok, not great", and opine that even if it's "cheaper than a flight to New Orleans", it's still "overpriced."

Eliza's Chinese
22 | 16 | 17 | $25

Pacific Heights | 2877 California St. (bet. Broderick & Divisadero Sts.) | 415-621-4819
This pioneering Pac Heights "Californian-style" Sino "puts other Chinese restaurants to shame", wokking up "supremely delicious" "Hunan fusion" dishes, all "showcased" in a "soothingly beautiful" setting decorated with "museum"-quality "colored glass"; "be prepared to fight for a table" for the low-cost "luncheon rice plates" or opt for takeout, and be advised that service "gets better the better they get to know you" – otherwise "it's rather scowl-y."

	FOOD	DECOR	SERVICE	COST

Ella's *American*

	21	16	19	$23

Presidio Heights | 500 Presidio Ave. (California St.) | 415-441-5669 | www.ellassanfrancisco.com

Devotees of this "perennial brunch favorite" in Presidio Heights have found their "new religion on Sunday mornings", enduring the purgatory of "long, long lines" for the chance to worship "tender" biscuits, "not-to-be-missed" chicken hash and other "scrumptious" American chow; it has an "unpretentious" atmosphere with a "courteous" staff, but a few guests grumble that it's grown "tired" and "pricey for what you get"; P.S. no dinner.

El Metate *Mexican*

	22	14	14	$11

Mission | 2406 Bryant St. (22nd St.) | 415-641-7209 | elmetate.webs.com

"The menu may look like every other one", but this "super-vibrant" "marvelous Mexican in the Mission" goes well "beyond what other taquerias pawn off"; "gotta love" those "Baja-style fish" and "beautiful" chile verde tacos, "bursting", "football-sized tortas" and "amazing" aguas frescas – they're "worth traveling a few extra blocks" for, plus the "owner makes everyone feel welcome"; P.S. snag an outdoor table on "sunny days."

☑ El Tonayense *Mexican*

	24	7	18	$8

Mission | 3150 24th St. (Shotwell St.) | 415-550-9192
Mission | Location varies; see website
www.eltonayense.com

"Excellent carnitas" and "more exotic" "lip-smacking, authentic" Mexican "cheap eats" done "with panache" entice "on-the-run" diners to "pull over" and "indulge" at these "beautifully designed" lunch and late-night taco trucks in the Mission, voted SF's Best Bang for the Buck; the uninitiated can't understand "why I would stand in line to eat in my car" when it "costs the same" at its less-popular "sit-down restaurant", but converts "can't get enough of them."

El Zocalo ◐ *Salvadoran*

	∇ 20	11	18	$17

Bernal Heights | 3230 Mission St. (Valencia St.) | 415-282-2572

Fans of this "wallet-friendly", "late-night" Salvadoran joint in Bernal Heights praise the "pupusas!" and other "down-home" staples, including "excellent slaw" and "menudo every day of the week"; while you'll need to "be ready to wait and wait", when "Central American is called for", this is the place to "get your belly full."

Emmy's Spaghetti Shack *Italian*

	19	15	17	$25

Bernal Heights | 18 Virginia Ave. (Mission St.) | 415-206-2086 | www.emmysspaghettishack.com

"A shack it is, but come anyway" – this late-night Bernal Heights "punk-rock spaghetti" joint is also a "relaxed" "date spot" with weekend DJs, proffering "huge bowls" of pasta with "flavorful meatballs" (as well as more "chichi" dishes) "served by heavily tattooed women"; it does get "crowded", so "slip" into the "connected dive bar" and sip "40-oz. beers" and "good wines by the glass" while you wait.

Emporio Rulli *Dessert/Italian*

	21	20	16	$24

Downtown | Union Square Pavilion | 225 Stockton St. (bet. Geary & Post Sts.) | 415-433-1122 | www.rulli.com
See review in North of San Francisco Directory.

	FOOD	DECOR	SERVICE	COST

Enrico's Sidewalk Cafe *American/Mediterranean* ▽ | 16 | 17 | 16 | $37
North Beach | 504 Broadway (Kearny St.) | 415-982-6223 |
www.enricossf.com

North Beach's original "bohemian cafe" is still a "people-watching paradise", with live jazz adding to a "nice evening" in the brasserie-style
digs or out on the sidewalk; still, some only recommend it for a "cocktail after dinner", given the "pedestrian" quality of the New American-
Med eats; P.S. closed Sundays January–March.

Eos Restaurant & Wine Bar *Asian/Californian* | 23 | 19 | 20 | $42
Cole Valley | 901 Cole St. (Carl St.) | 415-566-3063 | www.eossf.com
This Cole Valley "neighborhood favorite" "hasn't lost any luster" aver
aficionados who are "transported" by its shiitake mushroom dumplings and other "creative", upscale Cal-Asian small plates matched
with "excellent" wines; the next-door bar is a bit more "intimate" than
the main dining room, but both can get "loud" at dinner, so try going
"on either the early or late side of the evening."

Epic Roasthouse *Steak* | 21 | 25 | 22 | $64
Embarcadero | 369 The Embarcadero (bet. Folsom & Harrison Sts.) |
415-369-9955 | www.epicroasthousesf.com

"Spectacular Bay Bridge views" "set the stage" for "scrumptious" burgers and steak at this "premiere" chophouse "right on the Embarcadero"
where "Jan Birnbaum orchestrates" "epic" plates that "really live up to its
name"; still, "you pay a premium to be on the water", which explains
why those not "billing the company or celebrating a special event" opt
for "surprisingly cheap happy-hour" specials in the "high-energy
Quiver Bar upstairs" or weekend brunch – "a steal" in comparison.

Eric's *Chinese* | 20 | 14 | 16 | $25
Noe Valley | 1500 Church St. (27th St.) | 415-282-0919
"Still going strong", this "family-owned" Noe Valley "neighborhood
Chinese" continues to deliver "on a higher level" – the "ingredients are
always fresh", the Victorian "decor, a cut above most", and "it's a bargain to boot"; purists complain it's "so Americanized" "they should
call it Ersatz's", and the "fire-drill service" may be "legendary", but no
matter – "everyone keeps coming back" to eat in or take out.

Esperpento *Spanish* | 23 | 16 | 18 | $30
Mission | 3295 22nd St. (Valencia St.) | 415-282-8867
When they want "a little bit of everything for next to nothing", "young"
"couples" and "groups" pack this "affordable" Spanish tapas joint in the
"heart of the Mission" to share "authentic" small plates and "tasty"
paella; the "lively", "cute" (some say "cheesy") space is "loud, day or
night" and "service suffers when it's packed", but once the "fantastic"
sangria starts "flowing" you'll feel transported "right back to Spain."

Espetus Churrascaria *Brazilian* | 23 | 19 | 22 | $56
Hayes Valley | 1686 Market St. (Gough St.) | 415-552-8792 |
www.espetus.com

Enthusiastic eaters "unbutton their belts" and "embrace their inner
carnivore" at these "expensive" Brazilian churrascarias in Hayes Valley
and San Mateo, offering "nonstop" skewers of "well-seasoned" meats
(the "variety" just "boggles the mind"), purveyed by waiters with "gi-

FOOD | DECOR | SERVICE | COST

ant carving knives"; "sure, there's a salad bar" "to add some rough-
age" "but why?", when "stuffing yourself" on steak alone is enough to
"get your money's worth."

Eureka Restaurant & Lounge *American* ▽ 22 | 19 | 23 | $39
Castro | 4063 18th St. (bet. Castro & Hartford Sts.) | 415-431-6000 |
www.eurekarestaurant.com
"There's always something comfortable" on the midpriced American-
"with-a-Bayou-twist" menu and "something uncomfortably lust-
producing" in the "lively" lounge upstairs – that's where the "hot crowd"
hangs at this Victorian walk-up, a sib to Chenery Park; all in all, it's a
"classy" "place for gays and others to enjoy a night out", and the "interesting, innovative" fare is "better than at many Castro" competitors.

NEW Fang *Chinese* 20 | 20 | 19 | $32
SoMa | 660 Howard St. (bet. New Montgomery & 3rd Sts.) | 415-777-8568 |
www.fangrestaurant.com
Peter Fang brings "favorites" from his House of Nanking in Chinatown,
plus some new "creations", "to the heart of SoMa" at this more "upscale"
Sino "surprise" where the "busy lunch crowd" and nightcrawlers who
hang at the "beautiful" back-lit bar are "thrilled" to sink their fangs
into whatever the owner "orders for you" (let him be your "culinary
guide"); still, cynics hiss, it suffers from "too-sweet" sauces and "Soup
Nazi" service – like its sibling.

Z Farallon *Seafood* 24 | 27 | 24 | $68
Downtown | 450 Post St. (bet. Mason & Powell Sts.) | 415-956-6969 |
www.farallonrestaurant.com
The "underwater dreamscape" decor (think "light fixtures that look like
jellyfish", or simply "Sea World on acid") makes this "stunning" "seafood emporium" by Mark Franz and Pat Kuleto a "favorite" Downtown
destination of those who want to "wow out-of-towners" or just "feel
like a little kid" again while dining on "ingeniously prepared" fin fare;
"efficient" service buoys the meal too, though wags warn "make sure
you grab a life jacket" before the check comes.

Farina *Italian* 24 | 22 | 20 | $48
Mission | 3560 18th St. (bet. Guerrero & Valencia Sts.) | 415-565-0360 |
www.farina-foods.com
A "chic, modern" choice in the Mission, this "authentic" Italian promises
a "food adventure" to Liguria, complete with highlights like "breathtaking Genovese pesto" (a "bright green" sauce that "dances" on the
"silky" handmade pasta) and "stellar" wines; on the downside, tabs
run a bit "high" and it's "difficult to have a conversation" in the "noisy"
interior, but the sidewalk seating is perfect for "sunny days."

Farmerbrown *Soul Food* 21 | 15 | 17 | $29
Tenderloin | 25 Mason St. (bet. Eddy & Turk Sts.) | 415-409-3276 |
www.farmerbrownsf.com
Farmerbrown's Little Skillet ⊠⊄ *Soul Food*
SoMa | 360 Ritch St. (bet. Brannan & Townsend Sts.) | 415-777-2777 |
www.littleskilletsf.com
"Awesome" "Southern vittles" like "light, crunchy" fried chicken and
"greens that could compete with your grandma's" "feed your soul" at
this "funky little place" in the "gritty" Tenderloin, where the "hipster

crowd" knocks back "innovative cocktails" and "beer in a mason jar" to the tune of "DJs spinning" some nights and "live jazz" at weekend brunch; the "counter-service"-only SoMa spin-off serves similar soul-food staples "fast" to those who don't mind "sitting on the sidewalk" or "in the car."

15 Romolo ❶ *Pub Food*   - | - | - | M

North Beach | 15 Romolo Pl. (B'way) | 415-398-1359 | www.15romolo.com
One of the pioneers in the current renaissance of retro Barbary Coast-inspired watering holes, this North Beach bar at the Basque Hotel lures hipsters to its noir-ish, back-alley lair with a crew of crackerjack bartenders mixing market-driven cocktails from happy hour into the wee hours; to soak up all the spirits, the new kitchen serves American pub food like chile-spiked wings – plus a Humphry Slocombe ice cream sandwich – till 1:30 AM nightly.

Fifth Floor 🅢 *American/French*   25 | 24 | 25 | $75

SoMa | Hotel Palomar | 12 Fourth St., 5th fl. (Market St.) | 415-348-1555 | www.fifthfloorrestaurant.com
"Through all the chef transitions", this "classy-to-a-T" SoMa "oasis" remains HQ for "that special dinner when you need to impress", show-casing a "sublime", revamped New American menu that makes it a tad more "approachable" (but still quite "pricey"); while the largely "appealing" decor is "too velvety" for some, the "outstanding service" and "amazing sommelier" Emily Wines' "witty", "to-die-for" vino list "more than make up for it"; P.S. you can "hobnob in style" over drinks and apps in the "status"-y front lounge.

54 Mint 🅢 *Italian*   22 | 19 | 20 | $44

SoMa | 16 Mint Plaza (Mission St.) | 415-543-5100 | www.54mint.com
A *"Dolce Vita* vibe" rules the day at this "convivial" SoMa ristorante and wine bar presenting "authentic, not cookie-cutter" cucina (including "sigh-inducing" ravioli) amid "sleek" surroundings with a "nifty" patio near the Moscone Center; while the staff's "cinematic Italian warmth" has its charms, service tends to be "slow" and "a bit disorganized", so it's best to go when "you don't need to be anywhere in three hours."

Fior d'Italia ❶ *Italian*   20 | 19 | 20 | $43

North Beach | San Remo Hotel | 2237 Mason St. (bet. Chestnut & Francisco Sts.) | 415-986-1886 | www.fior.com
Guests "take a step back in time to old San Francisco" at this "consistent" North Beach "standby" celebrating its 125th birthday and still delivering "crispy" calamari, "pastas that are worth the calories" and other "classic" Northern Italian cuisine; "decent" tabs and "friendly" service are additional pluses, though some opine that it's "out of touch" and there's "just not the same spirit in the new digs" since it re-located to the San Remo Hotel some years back.

Firefly *Eclectic*   24 | 20 | 23 | $46

Noe Valley | 4288 24th St. (Douglass St.) | 415-821-7652 | www.fireflyrestaurant.com
It's the "heart and soul of Noe Valley" agree admirers who reserve "well in advance" to alight at this "downright charming" "neighbor-hood hangout", indulging in "memorable" takes on Eclectic "home cooking"; "don't let the casual surroundings fool you" – the "serious

	FOOD	DECOR	SERVICE	COST

food" "shines", plus the "professional" staff "takes equally good care" of "carnivores and vegetarians"; P.S. the midweek $35 prix fixe menus are a "big-city steal" – and remember that "everyone becomes a *mammelah*" when the chef prepares "fun Jewish holiday" meals.

Fish & Farm 🗷 *American/Seafood* | 20 | 17 | 19 | $46 |

Downtown | 339 Taylor St. (bet. Ellis & O'Farrell Sts.) | 415-474-3474 | www.fishandfarmsf.com

"Artisanal" New American "comfort food" that "reduces your carbon mouthprint on the world" is the come-on of this "homey" Downtown "oasis" (in a somewhat "iffy" area) where "locavores" "feel good about dining out", whether they "go for the fish or the farm" or simply the "best burger" with a "well-made" drink at the bar; though the service varies and a few find it "costly", many deem it an "ideal" "pre-theater" pick; P.S. a post-Survey chef departure and ownership change is not reflected in the ratings.

5A5 Steak Lounge *Steak* | 22 | 23 | 20 | $68 |

Downtown | 244 Jackson St. (bet. Battery & Front Sts.) | 415-989-2539 | www.5a5stk.com

"Bodacious beef", like the "highest-quality" A5 Japanese Wagyu, is the star at this "gorgeous", "modern" Downtown space that's "very Manhattan while maintaining an SF flavor"; it can get "a little loud" (especially on weekends, when DJs turn up the "clubby vibe") and costs can reach "stratospheric" heights, but pluses like "professional" service and "creative cocktails" lead some to say "save up, my steak-loving friends."

🛛 Fleur de Lys 🗷Ⓜ *Californian/French* | 27 | 26 | 26 | $99 |

Downtown | 777 Sutter St. (bet. Jones & Taylor Sts.) | 415-673-7779 | www.fleurdelyssf.com

"Enchanted" fans of "*Top Chef Masters*" contender Hubert Keller "run out of superlatives to describe" his Downtown "grande dame" where the "astonishing" Cal-French prix fixe dinners are "exquisite in every detail"; the "stunning" (some say "stuffy") interior with a "tent motif" provides "romance *abbondanza*" enhanced by "gracious" service, so "if you need to get a yes from someone on a special occasion", "dress up" and go for the "big splurge."

Florio *French/Italian* | 19 | 20 | 21 | $43 |

Pacific Heights | 1915 Fillmore St. (bet. Bush & Pine Sts.) | 415-775-4300 | www.floriosf.com

There are "no surprises" at this "endearing" "neighborhood bistro" (in the Bix family), which pleases "local" Pac Heights patrons with its "awesome French fries" and other "delicious" Gallic and Italian eats; a bar that invites "bellying up" and "waiters who know how to quietly coddle you" help keep it "comfortable", but its detractors deem it merely "mediocre" and note it "needs a slightly fresher menu to really pop."

Flour + Water ◖ *Italian* | 24 | 18 | 20 | $41 |

Mission | 2401 Harrison St. (20th St.) | 415-826-7000 | www.flourandwater.com

An "exceptional" newcomer, this "Mission phenom" "magically converts" its namesake ingredients into "inventive", "soulful" pastas and "wood-fired" Neapolitan pies that are "definitely a contender in this year's pizza playoffs"; a "middle-of-nowhere" locale and late-night hours "add to the mystique", keeping even the "drop-in" communal tables "super-cramped", though some are turned off by the "attitude" and "difficult" reservations.

Fog City Diner   *American*   19 | 19 | 19 | $36

Embarcadero | 1300 Battery St. (The Embarcadero) | 415-982-2000 | www.fogcitydiner.com

"A quintessential San Francisco experience", this Embarcadero "landmark" is "not your typical diner by any means", offering "upscale" New American fare ("truffle fries" and the like) plus "terrific" cocktails as well; the "cool" "retro" train-car design is "a kick", so supporters are "happy to chaperone" their "out-of-town guests" for some "feelgood dining", but contrarians criticize the "spotty" service and say it's "lost its early panache."

NEW Fondue Cowboy Ⓜ *Fondue*   - | - | - | M

SoMa | 1052 Folsom St. (Russ St.) | 415-431-5100 | www.fonduecowboy.com

Urban cowboys can dunk to their hearts' delight at this Wild West-themed fondue hub in SoMa offering cleverly named, moderately priced pots – think the Raw Hide (Gorgonzola with bacon) and the High Noon (white chocolate with balsamic strawberry glaze) – accompanied by a smattering of salads and draft beer; the decor eschews Swiss Miss trappings for a more macho vibe replete with a giant stencil of Clint Eastwood and old spaghetti Westerns playing overhead.

Forbes Island Ⓜ *American/Seafood*   ▽ 19 | 24 | 23 | $60

Fisherman's Wharf | Piers 39 & 41 (The Embarcadero) | 415-951-4900 | www.forbesisland.com

Maritime mavens "entertain" "visiting friends" at this "submerged" American seafooder in a "floating former residence" that's "reached by boat" from Fisherman's Wharf – sometimes captained by "storytelling" co-owner "Forbes himself"; it's "fun" to "watch fish swim by through portholes" during dinner, so even if the eats are "adequate" but "uninspired", it's worth trying "at least once"; P.S. closed Monday–Tuesday.

Foreign Cinema   *Californian/Mediterranean*   23 | 23 | 21 | $49

Mission | 2534 Mission St. (bet. 21st & 22nd Sts.) | 415-648-7600 | www.foreigncinema.com

"For a night out at the movies'" or "an unbeatable romantic dinner" "under the stars", this "edgy" "Mission winner" projecting "foreign flicks on the garden wall" gets a standing ovation from "cinephiles and foodsters"; it oozes "theatrical ambiance" "(inside and out)" with servers who are "hipster character actors", but it's "come a long way since its dot-com days", now starring the "finely scripted" Cal-Med dishes, "creative cocktails" and "scrumptious" sleeper "champagne brunch", including "housemade Pop Tarts."

4505 Meats 🅂Ⓜ⊐ *Hot Dogs*   ▽ 28 | 12 | 21 | $18

Embarcadero | Ferry Plaza Mkt. | 1 Ferry Bldg. (The Embarcadero) | www.4505meats.com

"Sausage connoisseurs" "would stand in line in the pouring rain" to pig out at this "marvelous" lunch stall at the back corner of the Ferry Building's farmer's market, run by "king of meat" Ryan Farr; it offers neither bargains nor seating, but the "delectable" "breakfast sandwiches", "luscious" burgers, spicy 'Zilla haute dogs and chicharrones ("puffy pork magic") are "nothing short of legendary", so "whatever the distance, go!"; P.S. open Thursdays and Saturdays only, until 2 PM.

☑ NEW Frances Ⓜ Californian

27 | 20 | 25 | $51

Castro | 3870 17th St. (Pond St.) | 415-621-3870 | www.frances-sf.com
The "euphoria" is mounting at this "boiling-hot" Castro newcomer where chef-owner and "master at her craft" Melissa Perello (ex Fifth Floor) is "blowing away" the competition, delighting "elbow-to-elbow" "foodies" with a "limited", changing roster of "locally sourced" Californian fare that's "comforting and brilliant at the same time"; "welcoming" service and "delicious house wine by the ounce" add to the "charm", but "reservations are just about impossible" – fortunately, "squeezing" in at the "walk-in" bar is "as good as gold."

Frascati Californian/Mediterranean

25 | 21 | 24 | $50

Russian Hill | 1901 Hyde St. (Green St.) | 415-928-1406 | www.frascatisf.com
"Walk" through the "beautiful neighborhood" or "take the cable car" that "clangs by" this "picture-perfect bistro", a "special date place" in Russian Hill serving "well-conceived", "delectable" Cal-Med meals that are "not inexpensive, but worth it"; with prized "window tables" and a "quieter" second-floor space tended by servers who are "attentive without being obtrusive", it's "utterly charming" all around (as long as you avoid the "impossible" street parking).

Fresca Peruvian

22 | 17 | 19 | $35

West Portal | 24 W. Portal Ave. (Ulloa St.) | 415-759-8087
Noe Valley | 3945 24th St. (bet. Noe & Sanchez Sts.) | 415-695-0549
Upper Fillmore | 2114 Fillmore St. (California St.) | 415-447-2668
www.frescasf.com
"As the name implies", the "nuevo-Peruvian" "delights" served at this "affordable" trio are "wonderfully fresh", especially the "zesty" ceviches, "delicious" lomo sataldo and a roster of "tasty cocktails"; the settings are "high-energy" and there's "often a line", adding to the "chaotic-enough-to-be-fun" feel, but "spotty service" sometimes results as the staff tries to "manage the mayhem."

Fringale Basque/French

24 | 19 | 23 | $49

SoMa | 570 Fourth St. (bet. Brannan & Freelon Sts.) | 415-543-0573 | www.fringalesf.com
The chef composes a "culinary symphony" of "outstanding" Gallic cuisine "with a Basque twist" at this "darling little" SoMa bistro, a "sure thing" that "seduces" with "simple" yet "elegant" eats and "well-selected" wines; oui, it's a "tad crowded", but amis aver that the "crisp, professional" "real French waiters" "add to the enjoyment", and the "reasonable" prices mean many "neighborhood regulars" return for an "intimate" dinner or "relaxed business lunch" (Tuesday–Friday).

Frjtz Fries Belgian

17 | 13 | 13 | $17

Hayes Valley | 581 Hayes St. (Laguna St.) | 415-864-7654
Mission | 590 Valencia St. (17th St.) | 415-863-8272
www.frjtzfries.com
Frites-fanatics "skip the ketchup" and choose from a list of "creative" dipping sauces that's "longer than the rest of the menu" at this "trendy" Mission and Hayes Valley duo, where "hot, crispy" fries and

"Belgian beers on tap" overshadow the "mixed bag" of salads, crêpes and sandwiches; though its "stark white decor" gets mixed reviews ("like one of those design shows that went horribly wrong"), it offers "great value" for a "simple meal" or "quick snack."

Front Porch, The *Caribbean/Southern* | 19 | 15 | 18 | $31 |

Bernal Heights | 65A 29th St. (bet. Mission St. & San Jose Ave.) | 415-695-7800 | www.thefrontporchsf.com
A bucket of "damn good" fried chicken and a "world-class cheap beer and malt-liquor menu" hook hipsters into this Bernal Heights "dive" dishing out "delicious" Southern "down-home cooking" with Caribbean influences; it's "not for the calorie-conscious" and the line gets "long for walk-ins", but the "young" staff doles out pleasant "hospitality" and "clever" wine cocktails "while you wait on the porch."

Gamine *French* | 23 | 16 | 23 | $35 |

Cow Hollow | 2223 Union St. (bet. Fillmore & Steiner Sts.) | 415-771-7771 | www.gaminesf.com
The owner "makes you feel like a regular, whether you are or not" at this "wonderful neighborhood" French in Cow Hollow; while the decor is "a bit functional", the "authentic" menu of "bistro basics" (including "one of the greatest cheeseburgers" around) provides a "satisfying, casual repast" for a moderate price; P.S. reservations taken for six or more.

☒ Garden Court *Californian* | 18 | 29 | 21 | $58 |

Downtown | Palace Hotel | 2 New Montgomery St. (Market St.) | 415-546-5010 | www.gardencourt-restaurant.com
"You can feel the history" at this "classic SF" restaurant in Downtown's Palace Hotel whose "spectacular" stained-glass ceiling and "Belle Epoque" decor would suit "ladies wearing gloves and hats" for an "elegant lunch" or Saturday afternoon tea; it's "in a class by itself" for "celebrating special holiday occasions" over "groaning buffet" brunches, though the "grandiose surroundings" significantly overshadow the service and "just ok", costly Californian fare.

Garibaldis *Californian/Mediterranean* | 22 | 20 | 21 | $46 |

Presidio Heights | 347 Presidio Ave. (bet. Clay & Sacramento Sts.) | 415-563-8841 | www.garibaldisrestaurant.com
This "always dependable", slightly "swanky" Presidio Heights "staple" (and its Oakland offshoot, which has become "more intimate" after a recent remodel) feels like a "second home" to well-heeled regulars who find it "oh-so-comfortable" for "artfully prepared" Cal-Med fare and "genial" service; the "New York-y" digs can be a bit "noisy", but supporters sigh "oh well", at least "it has a buzz."

☒ Gary Danko *American* | 29 | 27 | 28 | $109 |

Fisherman's Wharf | 800 N. Point St. (Hyde St.) | 415-749-2060 | www.garydanko.com
"Who needs a special occasion?" when simply "going to Gary Danko's" Wharf wonder – once again voted No. 1 for Food and Service as well as Most Popular – "*is* the occasion" swoon diners who "save up" and "dress up" (and if need be, drop in at the bar) for a "feast de resistance" starring "magnificent" New American tasting menus with "choices galore" and an "epic wine list"; the "sexy" interior is almost "superfluous" given the "drop-dead gorgeous" plates, purveyed by "ninja" waiters

(invisible, yet there "when you need them"), and it all culminates with a "showstopping" cheese cart and "pastry parting gifts."

Gaylord India *Indian* | 18 | 19 | 19 | $38 |

Downtown | 1 Embarcadero Ctr. (Sacramento St.) | 415-397-7775 | www.gaylords1.com

For "flavorful", "upscale Indian" in a somewhat "sleepy location", lunchtime buffet buffs and Downtowners grabbing "dinner before a movie" meet up at this "attractive" subcontinental "standard" that's part of an international chain; most maintain it's "reliable" if "pricey", with a few "unique" touches, but detractors deem it "dated" and "definitely not dazzling" compared with the competition.

NEW Georges 𝕊 *Californian* | – | – | – | M |

Downtown | Fugazi Bldg. | 415 Sansome St. (Commercial St.) | 415-956-6900 | www.georgessf.com

This weekday-only FiDi newcomer hopes to reel in Downtown clientele with an all-day raw bar and daily changing slate of affordable, sustainable Californian seafood served in an airy, mod setting with an exposed kitchen and reclaimed-wood tables; meanwhile, the green-topped bar beckons with boutique spirits and Mediterranean wines, not to mention complimentary still and sparkling water dispensed from an in-house filtration system.

Gialina *Pizza* | 25 | 16 | 20 | $28 |

Glen Park | 2842 Diamond St. (Kern St.) | 415-239-8500 | www.gialina.com

A "cult foodie" following hits this "artisanal" pizzeria in "sleepy Glen Park" for its "unusual" "thin-crust" pies topped with "seasonal California ingredients" and other "innovative toppings", along with "fantastic salads" and "ever-so-succulent roasts of the day"; "blown-up family pictures" add to its "rustic charm", and the staff has the "right attitude", though it's tough to avoid the nightly "rush and crush" since the "tiny" room "gets full as soon as it opens"; P.S. a second location, to be named Ragazza, is in the works for the fall.

Giordano Bros. *Sandwiches* | ▽ 21 | 13 | 18 | $15 |

North Beach | 303 Columbus Ave. (B'way) | 415-397-2767 | www.giordanobros.com

"Like the 'burgh in North Beach", this sports bar slaps together "crazy good" "big, sloppy" "Primanti Bros.–style sandwiches" "piled high with fries and slaw", just the way "God intended"; it's a "great place to watch a game or just kick it" to the tune of "free live music", plus the counter guys "hustle to make people happy", so "you don't have to be a Steelers fan to eat here (but it helps)."

Giorgio's Pizzeria *Pizza* | 22 | 12 | 19 | $20 |

Inner Richmond | 151 Clement St. (3rd Ave.) | 415-668-1266 | www.giorgiospizza.com

"In the age of artisan pies", this family-friendly "throwback" remains a "Richmond favorite" for its "no-frills" pizzas with a "just-right crust", served in an "old-school" setting complete with "red-checked tablecloths"; "you may have to wait" for a seat, "especially on weekends" or Wednesdays (4–6 PM), when tykes get to "make their own" pies, but the staff helps "keep things moving", plus the lunch special is a "real bargain."

	FOOD	DECOR	SERVICE	COST

Gitane ● 🗷 Ⓜ *French/Spanish*   21 | 24 | 20 | $51

Downtown | 6 Claude Ln. (bet. Bush & Sutter Sts.) | 415-788-6686 |
www.gitanerestaurant.com

"Sexy" decor makes the "tasty tagines" and other Moroccan-accented
Spanish-French fare seem even "better" at this "high-energy" Downtown
"cousin of Café Claude"; it's "romantic" for "date night", but "sit upstairs for dinner", as the "'in'-crowd" is "out in force" tipping back "excellent cocktails" and "exquisite sherries" at the downstairs bar, and
the "noise escalates accordingly"; P.S. the post-Survey arrival of chef
Bridget Batson (ex Hawthorne Lane) is not reflected in the Food score.

Globe ● *Californian/Italian*   21 | 17 | 18 | $44

Downtown | 290 Pacific Ave. (bet. Battery & Front Sts.) | 415-391-4132 |
www.globerestaurant.com

"Hip and vibrant", "especially late at night" when "chefs from top restaurants" unwind, this Downtowner delivers an "excellent variety" of
Cal-Italian eats, from pizza (the "best price performer") to "higher-
end entrees" like the rib-eye for two, plus a market-fresh "Sunday
farmers' menu"; a few feel "some of the luster has worn off", but with
its "moody lighting" and "wine-bar atmosphere", it's a fine "little place
to take a date."

Goat Hill Pizza *Pizza*   20 | 11 | 17 | $20

Potrero Hill | 300 Connecticut St. (18th St.) | 415-641-1440
SoMa | 171 Stillman St. (bet. 3rd & 4th Sts.) | 415-974-1303
www.goathill.com

Dished up by a "friendly, quick" staff, the "old-fashioned" pies at this
Potrero Hill "institution" are "so San Francisco" with "wonderful sourdough crusts" and "plentiful toppings"; while some find the "basic
pizza nothing special", many are won over by the "all-you-can-eat
Mondays" even though they're a "complete zoo"; P.S. the SoMa outpost is now takeout and delivery only.

Godzila Sushi *Japanese*   18 | 12 | 16 | $31

Pacific Heights | 1800 Divisadero St. (Bush St.) | 415-931-1773

"Neighborhood regulars" "listen to Led Zep" and other classic rock at
this "casual" Pac Heights Japanese where "all the basics" are bolstered
by some "interesting roll combos"; low tabs and decor delivering a
"monster film fix" are pluses, though some reviewers cite "mediocre"
quality and "rushed" service, calling it the "cafeteria" of sushi joints.

🆕 Golden West 🗷 *Bakery/Sandwiches*   - | - | - | I

Downtown | 8 Trinity St. (bet. Montgomery & Sutter Sts.) | 415-392-3246

Another small but mighty venture from chef-entrepreneur Dennis
Leary (Canteen, The Sentinel), this tiny Downtown back-alley bakery
aims to fuel FiDi workers with its housemade breads, pastries and
somewhat retro American dishes – think deviled ham, brisket and
bread-in-can; it's strictly a to-go affair, served weekdays only for
breakfast and lunch.

Gold Mountain *Chinese*   20 | 7 | 12 | $25

Chinatown | 644 Broadway (bet. Columbus Ave. & Stockton St.) |
415-296-7733

"Carts circulate constantly" during lunch at this "huge dim sum palace" in Chinatown delivering "pretty good", low-cost eats to a "local

crowd"; sure, it's a little "like dining in a railway station", and the service is "what you'd expect" in such a scenario, but it makes for a memorable "Sunday experience."

Good Luck Dim Sum 🍜 *Chinese*

20 | 4 | 9 | $10

Inner Richmond | 736 Clement St. (bet. 8th & 9th Aves.) | 415-386-3388 | www.goodluckdimsum.com

"Hungry dim sum aficionados" fill up on "tasty little morsels" "for a song" at this Inner Richmond "hole-in-the-wall" where the "lines are long for a reason"; with decor that's "shoddy at best" and "warm greetings" hard to come by, regulars say it's best to "get in line, have your order ready, pay quickly" – then "take your food to go"; P.S. closes at 6:30 PM.

Goood Frikin' Chicken *Mideastern*

18 | 9 | 15 | $17

Mission | 10 29th St. (Mission St.) | 415-970-2428 | www.gfcsf.com

"The name is funky but accurate" at this Outer Mission "standby" turning out "flavorful" rotisserie and grilled chicken (the "secret is in the rub" of "zingy" spices) as well as "reliable" Middle Eastern sides; since the "cold"-feeling digs have "no atmosphere", many opt to "pick up" the "cheap eats."

Gordon Biersch ● *Pub Food*

15 | 16 | 16 | $29

Embarcadero | 2 Harrison St. (The Embarcadero) | 415-243-8246 | www.gordonbiersch.com

"If you can't find a true local microbrewery", this affordable chain (with Embarcadero, Palo Alto and San Jose locations) is a "fine substitute", serving up "delicious" "craft beers" that "beat" the "decent" American pub grub (though all "hail" the "amazing" garlic fries); an "enjoyable happy-hour kinda place", it's not particularly "exciting", but the "relaxed" atmosphere is well suited to "kicking back with friends."

Gott's Roadside Tray Gourmet *Diner*
(fka Taylor's Automatic Refresher)

21 | 13 | 15 | $18

Embarcadero | 1 Ferry Bldg. (Market St.) | 866-328-3663 | www.gottsroadside.com

See review in North of San Francisco Directory.

NEW Gracias Madre *Mexican/Vegan*

∇ 20 | 20 | 21 | $24

Mission | 2211 Mission St. (18th St.) | 415-683-1346 | www.gracias-madre.com

"Even carnivores" "ignore" that they're chowing down on "surprisingly good" vegan vittles at this art-filled Cafe Gratitude offshoot "smack dab in the center of the Mission", where a "kitchen that pulls no punches with heat or flavor" churns out "creative" Mexican fare (including "smoky, subtle mole"); true, some frown upon the "communal tables", but modest tabs and a "friendly" vibe "seal the deal" for most.

Grand Cafe *French*

20 | 24 | 20 | $47

Downtown | Hotel Monaco | 501 Geary St. (Taylor St.) | 415-292-0101 | www.grandcafe-sf.com

To call the "majestic" setting "grand" would be an "understatement" at this "spectacular" art nouveau bistro, whose "soaring" setting is complemented by "beautifully presented" French fare; it has an "ideal" Downtown location for "pre-theater dining", and "doting"

FOOD | DECOR | SERVICE | COST

servers get folks out "in plenty of time" for the curtain, though a few fuss that it "fails to charm" and sigh "if only the food were as good as the decor"; P.S. some opt for a more casual "quick bite in the bar."

Grandeho's Kamekyo *Japanese* ▽ 21 | 18 | 18 | $36

Fisherman's Wharf | 2721 Hyde St. (bet. Beach & N. Point Sts.) | 415-673-6828

A "real find" in touristy Fisherman's Wharf, this long-standing Japanese – run by the original owners, who recently sold their similarly named outpost in Cole Valley – is a fine spot to "watch the ship traffic in San Francisco harbor" while refueling on some "decent" "sushi with style" or "excellent" Vietnamese eats; though the "storefront" space "could use a makeover", the "down-to earth" service is a plus; P.S. dinner served Saturday–Sunday only.

Grand Pu Bah *Asian* 20 | 19 | 18 | $35

Potrero Hill | 88 Division St. (Rhode Island St.) | 415-255-8188 | www.grandpubahrestaurant.com

"At the base of Potrero Hill", this "enjoyable" Pan-Asian draws an "after-work crowd" for "great drinks" and a midpriced assortment of "colorful, exciting dishes", "especially" the "spicy" Thai "street-food" selections; an "electric", "voluptuous atmosphere" keeps the energy running high, but service can be "spotty" and a few "wish it tasted as good as it looks."

Great Eastern ● *Chinese* 19 | 13 | 15 | $33

Chinatown | 649 Jackson St. (bet. Grant Ave. & Kearny St.) | 415-986-2500

"Floppin'" fish straight from the "tanks in the back" (as well as "fabulous dim sum" during the day) are the bait at this seafooder "in the heart of Chinatown"; there's "nothing fancy" about the surroundings or "lackluster" service, but the "wide selection" of "fairly priced" Sino specialties ensures it's "always busy, especially at lunch."

Green Chile Kitchen & Market *Mexican* 21 | 19 | 17 | $18

Western Addition | 1801 McAllister St. (Baker St.) | 415-440-9411 | www.greenchilekitchen.com

"Not quite Santa Fe but close enough", this "great-value" Western Addition Mexican is "different from your average taqueria", thanks to the "quality" "organic ingredients" that go into the "flavorful food" (e.g. "blue-corn enchiladas, posole and green chile stew"); plus, it's now "even better since its move" to "much roomier digs" nearby, though, alas, the "lines are just as long."

✨ Greens *Vegetarian* 24 | 24 | 22 | $43

Marina | Fort Mason Ctr., Bldg. A | Marina Blvd. (Buchanan St.) | 415-771-6222 | www.greensrestaurant.com

"Fantastic now" as it was Zen, this "vegetarian-with-a-vengeance" pioneer in the Marina "still impresses" both "crunchy types" and "die-hard carnivores" with chef Annie Sommerville's "phenomenal", "no-guilt" meals; yes, it's "expensive considering" there's no meat, and the service "doesn't wow", but "knockout views of the Golden Gate Bridge" and "wonderful" wines elevate an experience that's "great by any standards"; P.S. Saturday night is prix fixe only.

	FOOD	DECOR	SERVICE	COST

Hamano Sushi *Japanese*

FOOD 19 | **DECOR** 12 | **SERVICE** 18 | **COST** $34

Noe Valley | 1332 Castro St. (bet. Jersey & 24th Sts.) | 415-826-0825 | www.hamanosushi.com

Sure, the "ambiance could use some work", but fans of this "kid-friendly" Noe Valley Japanese overlook it in favor of "solid", "inventive" sushi and an "extensive" selection of "sashimi, maki and teriyaki"; "warm" service and "reasonable prices" add to the appeal, as do the "terrific lunch deals."

Hard Knox Cafe *Southern*

19 | 14 | 18 | $22

Dogpatch | 2526 Third St. (bet. 22nd & 23rd Sts.) | 415-648-3770
Outer Richmond | 2448 Clement St. (bet. 25th & 26th Aves.) | 415-752-3770
www.hardknoxcafe.com

"If it's dipped in batter, fried and covered with gravy, you'll find it on the menu" at these "accommodating" "little" "Southern soul food" sisters known for "fantastic" chicken with "all the fixin's" in Dogpatch and the Outer Richmond; though a few purists pout that the cooking "wouldn't cut it in Texas", most maintain that "everyone's happy" once they "pig out" on the "hearty" portions and see the "budget"-friendly bill.

Hard Rock Cafe *American*

12 | 19 | 13 | $29

Fisherman's Wharf | Bldg. Q1 | 1 Pier 39 (The Embarcadero) | 415-956-2013 | www.hardrock.com

"Rock memorabilia" is the claim to fame of this "noisy", "nostalgic", guitar-shaped American chain link on Fisherman's Wharf, and if the food doesn't exactly rock, it's fine for "enjoying a burger and a beer"; but those who deem the concept "so yesterday" ("does anyone still think this is cool?") feel it may be best left to "headbangers", "tourists" and youngsters who "love" those T-shirts.

Harris' *Steak*

25 | 22 | 24 | $66

Polk Gulch | 2100 Van Ness Ave. (Pacific Ave.) | 415-673-1888 | www.harrisrestaurant.com

"Booze and beef – what's not to like?" at this Polk Gulch "steakhouse your grandfather would approve of", from the "dry-aged", "perfectly cooked" cuts of meat and "commendable" sides to the "seamless" staff that "tends to your every need"; it's "expensive but worth every penny" to dine in the "clubby, elegant" library room or at the bar, where the sounds of live jazz add to the "old San Francisco" atmosphere.

Hayes Street Grill *Seafood*

23 | 17 | 23 | $49

Hayes Valley | 320 Hayes St. (bet. Franklin & Gough Sts.) | 415-863-5545 | www.hayesstreetgrill.com

Practicing "culinary minimalism at its best", the chef at this "old-school" Hayes Valley pescatarian paradise "sure knows how to cook fish", preparing "super-fresh" sustainable seafood with "careful simplicity"; if a few sniff it's "a bit stodgy" and "pricey", most maintain the "formula still works", and since the "efficient" staff "manages to accommodate" pre-concert diners with "aplomb", it remains a "big hit" with the "culture crowd."

🆕 Heart *Eclectic*

- | - | - | M

Mission | 1270 Valencia St. (24th St.) | 415-285-1200 | www.heartsf.com

"What a scene!" sum up visitors to this edgy wine bar/art gallery mash-up where Mission hipsters pack the communal tables, sharing

FOOD | DECOR | SERVICE | COST

midpriced Eclectic "small plates for anybody's palate" and weekend brunch (all prepped by the Kitchenette crew); the fare's paired with lesser-known wines that are served in mason jars and available for retail, while special events include monthly tasting menus provided by guest chefs on Tuesday nights (when it's usually closed).

Heaven's Dog *Chinese*
20 | 20 | 20 | $38

SoMa | 1148 Mission St. (bet. 7th & 8th Sts.) | 415-863-6008 | www.heavensdog.com

"Nice doggie" coo connoisseurs of this "inventive" foray into "Chinese street food" from Charles Phan (The Slanted Door), a SoMa Grand "oasis" whose "heavenly cocktails" are "almost as much of a star" as the "sustainable" Sino small plates; it's "more expensive than you think it'll be", but tails still wag over the "accommodating" service, "swank" lounge and adjacent noodle bar for "when you just want to eat and not be seen"; P.S. lunch no longer served.

NEW Heirloom
- | - | - | M

Café ⊠ *Californian/Mediterranean*

Mission | 2500 Folsom St. (21st St.) | 415-821-2500 | www.heirloom-sf.com

Orchestrated by sommelier and chef-owner Matthew Straus, this charming new Cal-Med in the Mission offers simple bistro classics – including cassoulet, mussels and a lunchtime burger stuffed with Époisses cheese – accompanied by 21 wines by the glass and plenty of heirloom bottles on the reserve list; the environs give off a homespun vibe, accented with vintage wallpaper, unfinished wood floors and antique light fixtures, and tabs range from modest to more expensive for a set three-course dinner with pairings.

Helmand Palace *Afghani*
23 | 16 | 20 | $31

Russian Hill | 2424 Van Ness Ave. (bet. Green & Union Sts.) | 415-362-0641 | www.helmandpalace.com

The "intriguing" Afghan menu, full of "beautifully spiced" dishes – including "amazing" lamb, "addicting" pumpkin and "oodles of options for vegetarians" – keeps Russian Hill habitués "full and happy" at this "quiet" (and "often overlooked") choice; with "fair prices" and "helpful" service, many consider it a "wonderful place for a change of pace."

Henry's Hunan *Chinese*
20 | 9 | 17 | $21

Downtown | 674 Sacramento St. (Spring St.) | 415-788-2234 ⊠
Noe Valley | 1708 Church St. (bet. Day & 29th Sts.) | 415-826-9189
SoMa | 1016 Bryant St. (bet. 8th & 9th Sts.) | 415-861-5808 ⊠
SoMa | 110 Natoma St. (bet. New Montgomery & 2nd Sts.) | 415-546-4999 ⊠

Hunan *Chinese*

Chinatown | 924 Sansome St. (bet. B'way & Vallejo St.) | 415-956-7727

www.henryshunanrestaurant.com

For "cheap, spicy Chinese and lots of it", there's "nothing like" this "hole-in-the-wall" chain (with a "slicker" Noe branch) that prompts "mad rushes at lunchtime" for fare that's a "slight step up from the usual"; even critics who fire they've "lost some luster" concede they're "tasty and fast", but "don't go for the service or decor."

	FOOD	DECOR	SERVICE	COST

Herbivore *Vegan* — 15 | 13 | 15 | $22

Mission | 983 Valencia St. (bet. Liberty & 21st Sts.) | 415-826-5657
Western Addition | 531 Divisadero St. (bet. Fell & Hayes Sts.) | 415-885-7133
www.herbivorerestaurant.com

For "basic vegan" at an "affordable" price, "non-meat eaters" and "even a carnivore" or two enjoy "healthy good times" at these "casual" veggie cafes with an "international" bent in the Mission, Western Addition and Berkeley; while fans laud "lots of choices", others complain that the "ho-hum" dishes "all taste the same" and that the service, while "friendly", is often "flakey."

NEW Hog & Rocks ◑ *American* — - | - | - | M

Mission | 3431 19th St. (San Carlos St.) | 415-550-8627 |
www.hogandrocks.com

Stoking the city's obsessions with pork and old-timey libations is this casual, self-billed 'ham and oyster bar' in the Mission (from the talents behind Maverick and Tres Agaves), serving up midpriced American comfort fare and raw bar selections till midnight; a boozy lineup of classic cocktails with retro pricing provides additional reasons to knock back the rocks, either at the walnut bar, communal tables or on the forthcoming patio.

Z Hog Island Oyster Co. & Bar *Seafood* — 25 | 17 | 19 | $36

Embarcadero | Ferry Plaza Mkt. | 1 Ferry Bldg. (The Embarcadero) |
415-391-7117 | www.hogislandoysters.com

Shucks, it's "hard to complain when you're sucking down" the "best damn" bivalves at this "pearl of an oyster bar" with a "gorgeous" Bay view on the Embarcadero or at its less-"mobbed" Napa spawn; the "amazingly fresh" raw fare takes "center stage", but clam chowder that'll "rock your world" and "killer grilled cheese" are "equally satisfying", and while you'll "shell out a lot" here, the "incredible" happy hours (with $1 oyster specials) are "worth the hassle."

Home ◑ *American* — 19 | 15 | 18 | $30

Castro | 2100 Market St. (Church St.) | 415-503-0333 | www.home-sf.com

"Healthy portions" of "true comfort food" (like "can't-be-beat" mac 'n' cheese) are matched by "great cocktails" at this "cozy" Castro "go-to" for "late dinners" and "make-your-own Bloody Marys at brunch"; the "bustling" digs can get "impossibly noisy", but the "unpretentious" attitude helps diners "relax", as does the "way-cheap early-bird" special (5–6 PM daily).

Hong Kong Lounge *Chinese* — ▽ 21 | 11 | 14 | $24

Outer Richmond | 5322 Geary Blvd. (bet. 17th & 18th Aves.) | 415-668-8836

"Everything on everyone else's table looks delicious" at this "superior" Outer Richmond Chinese, which makes it difficult to decide which of the "appetizing" dumplings to choose during "crowded" weekend dim sum feasts; the decor "hasn't changed for years" and service is only "average", but in the evening, the "family-style" meals are "a steal."

Hotei *Japanese* — 20 | 15 | 18 | $24

Inner Sunset | 1290 Ninth Ave. (Lincoln Way) | 415-753-6045 |
www.hoteisf.com

"Perfect" on a "cold, foggy day in the Inner Sunset", this "laid-back" "Japanese noodle house" lures "budget-minded" "big eaters" jonesing for "sushi and ramen (the two most important food groups)"; the "out-of-this-world portions" of "superbly soothing soups" come courtesy of "efficient" servers, as does the "excellent" raw fin fare mirroring that of "sister restaurant Ebisu across the street", only with "less of a wait."

Z House, The Asian

27 | 15 | 21 | $42

North Beach | 1230 Grant Ave. (bet. Columbus Ave. & Vallejo St.) | 415-986-8612 | www.thehse.com

"Stellar" Asian fusion fare, like "exceptional" miso-marinated black cod, makes for a "memorable meal" at this "tiny little nook" in North Beach, a real "find" that offers "top value" for your yen; the "unadorned" space and "atomic-blast noise level" are downsides, but aficionados agree "it's all about the food", which "puts many high-end restaurants to shame"; P.S. "reserve ahead of time", since it's "always full to the brim."

House of Nanking Chinese

21 | 7 | 13 | $22

Chinatown | 919 Kearny St. (bet. Jackson St. & Pacific Ave.) | 415-421-1429

Only "amateurs read the menu" remark regulars who "let the chef take charge" and "keep bringing you plates until you beg for mercy" at this "old standard" in Chinatown; the "jostling", "no-nonsense" service and "dingy", "chaotic" digs are "not for the faint of heart", but the "fresh, fiery" Chinese chow keeps the "line out the door for good reason."

Z House of Prime Rib American

25 | 20 | 23 | $53

Polk Gulch | 1906 Van Ness Ave. (Washington St.) | 415-885-4605 | www.houseofprimerib.net

"The name says it all" at this "charming anachronism" in Polk Gulch where "giant slabs" of "melt-in-your-mouth" prime rib are "served from a silver cart" with all the "traditional trimmings" and martinis poured from "your own personal shaker"; "if you're craving something else", "just turn around and go back home", but to celebrate a "guys' night out" "without breaking the bank", "get into the wayback machine and set the dial to 1952" for this "old San Francisco" haunt.

Hunan Home's Restaurant Chinese

21 | 12 | 18 | $26

Chinatown | 622 Jackson St. (bet. Grant Ave. & Kearny St.) | 415-982-2844

Serving up "flavor and value in equal measure", this "inexpensive" Hunan "hole-in-the-wall smack in the middle of Chinatown" (with off-shoots in Los Altos and Palo Alto) "seems to never change", which suits supporters of its "steady", often "spicy" chow just fine; the "dated" decor is "underwhelming", but Hu cares considering the "generous portions" and "prompt service" from a staff that really "hustles"?

Hyde Street Bistro French

21 | 17 | 20 | $43

Russian Hill | 1521 Hyde St. (bet. Jackson St. & Pacific Ave.) | 415-292-4415 | www.hydestreetbistrosf.com

"French to the core" but "without the attitude", this "lovely", "unpretentious" bistro on Russian Hill delivers "old-fashioned, traditional" dishes (such as coq au vin and cassoulet) complemented by "nice" vins de pays; "parking is difficult" and there's "hardly room to breathe", but locals "don't mind the elbows" or "waits on popular nights", since the vittles are such a "good value."

FOOD | DECOR | SERVICE | COST

Il Cane Rosso *Italian*

22 | 10 | 16 | $24

Embarcadero | Ferry Plaza Mkt. | 1 Ferry Bldg. (The Embarcadero) | 415-391-7599 | www.canerossosf.com

"Savor the Coi experience for less cash" (and a "view of the water") at this "locally sourced" take-out rotisserie and sandwich shop ("porchetta, baby") run by Daniel Patterson and Lauren Kiino in the Ferry Building; it's doggone hard "finding a place to sit", service can be "slow" and it's "not inexpensive for a food-court-type meal", but devotees dub the three-course, $25 "sit-down dinner" a "fantastic deal."

Il Fornaio *Italian*

19 | 20 | 19 | $39

Downtown | Levi's Plaza | 1265 Battery St. (bet. Filbert & Greenwich Sts.) | 415-986-0100 | www.ilfornaio.com

Loyalists "love the bread" and "creative" pastas at this "simple" but "civilized" Italian chain that "tries and often succeeds in serving authentic fare with monthly regional specials"; though some say service is "not consistent" and find the food "unremarkable", the "attractive" environs help support its "almost-gourmet prices."

Iluna Basque *Spanish*

18 | 16 | 17 | $36

North Beach | 701 Union St. (Powell St.) | 415-402-0011 | www.ilunabasque.com

Surveyors are split on this North Beach Basque, brainchild of "cute" chef-owner (and *Top Chef* contestant) Mattin Noblia; some tout the "terrific" tapas as a "nice change of pace" and appreciate the "friendly" atmosphere for sharing sangria, perhaps at the communal table during weekday happy hour (5:30–7 PM); others, however, beef it's a "Basque-et case", bemoaning a "bland chain-restaurant" feel and fare that "isn't remarkable."

Imperial Tea Court *Tearoom*

20 | 19 | 19 | $23

Embarcadero | Ferry Plaza Mkt. | 1 Ferry Bldg. (The Embarcadero) | 415-544-9830 | www.imperialtea.com

A "vast" selection of "excellent" teas are "prepared lovingly", along with Chinese "snacks" and "out-of-this-world" "hand-pulled noodles", at this "unique" teahouse duo; the atmosphere at the Ferry Building branch in San Francisco is "soothing", while the Berkeley Teahouse can feel more like a "factory" unless you "sit outside" in the "lovely" garden.

Incanto *Italian*

24 | 21 | 23 | $54

Noe Valley | 1550 Church St. (Duncan St.) | 415-641-4500 | www.incanto.biz

"Omnivorous adventurers" are "head-over-heels" about the "snout-to-tail cuisine" at this remote Noe Valley "gem" where "passionate" chef Chris Cosentino uses "every part of an animal" ("it's not awful, it's offal!") in his "no-holds-barred" Northern Italian cooking; happily, "even the timid" find "wonderful pastas" and "incredible salumi" to enjoy, while "professional" service and "phenomenal" Boot wines make "expensive" tabs more palatable; P.S. a post-Survey refurb of the already "beautiful" space may not be reflected in the Decor score.

Indian Oven *Indian*

22 | 15 | 18 | $29

Lower Haight | 233 Fillmore St. (bet. Haight & Waller Sts.) | 415-626-1628 | www.indianoven-sf.com

It's "one of the best places" in town for "authentic Indian cuisine" exalt expats who give this white-tablecloth "old standby" in the Lower

Haight their "seal of approval"; true, it's "so small you can practically break bread (or naan) with your neighbors", but the "kind" service and "low-key" vibe curry favor with fans who form the "line out front"; P.S. a post-Survey ownership change is not reflected in the ratings.

Indigo ☑ American — 19 | 18 | 22 | $46

Civic Center | 687 McAllister St. (Gough St.) | 415-673-9353 | www.indigorestaurant.com

This "pleasant" blue-hued haunt at Civic Center is "perfect for before the symphony or opera" opine patrons who appreciate the "gracious" servers who "get you in and out"; the "small but well-chosen" New American menu is a real "value" too – with a "bargain" early-bird and "liberal" "free corkage" policy – though it's "easy to forget" according to critics who say "everything is ok, but nothing is extraordinary."

☑ In-N-Out Burger ◐ Burgers — 22 | 10 | 18 | $9

Fisherman's Wharf | 333 Jefferson St. (bet. Jones & Leavenworth Sts.) | 800-786-1000 | www.in-n-out.com

For the "only fast food worth the calories", devotees of this "cult-classic" chain "imported from SoCal" go "in-hungry, out-happy" courtesy of "righteous burgers, fries and shakes" "made to order with fresh ingredients" and "secret-menu" combos ("ya gotta know the lingo" to go "animal-style"); there's "always a line", but the "hard-working kids" behind the counter turn it out on the "double double."

NEW Ironside ☒ Eclectic — 17 | 19 | 16 | $29

South Beach | Chronicle Books Bldg. | 680 Second St. (bet. Brannan & Townsend Sts.) | 415-896-1127 | www.ironsidesf.com

Just "blocks from AT&T Park", this "hip" South Beach Eclectic run by the District folks "fits right in" with the "surrounding lofts", what with its "industrial look" and "upscale" patrons "ok with spending a bit more" for "Four Barrel coffee" at breakfast and a "quick bite" for lunch (including "veggie Cubano sandwiches"); early accounts suggest "dinner needs work" and some dis the "order-at-the-register" regimen, but connoisseurs contend it "deserves another try."

Isa ☒ French — 25 | 19 | 20 | $46

Marina | 3324 Steiner St. (bet. Chestnut & Lombard Sts.) | 415-567-9588 | www.isarestaurant.com

Despite their best intentions to fairly split "as many dishes as possible", fans of this "celebration"-ready, "small-plate" Marina "gem" still "fight for the last morsel" of "surprising", "succulent" French food; some wish that the staff would not "insist that everyone share" and "let you eat in peace", but most are appeased by the "intimate ambiance of the tented back garden" – the "place to be."

Isobune Japanese — 19 | 14 | 17 | $28

Japantown | Kintetsu Mall | 1737 Post St. (bet. Buchanan & Webster Sts.) | 415-563-1030 | www.isobuneburlingame.com

Fishing "your food from moving boats" that sail past your plate "makes eating sushi festive and fast" at this Japantown joint with a branch in Burlingame; the shipshape system is a "boon for kids", and it's "not terribly expensive" either, but those who aren't on board sniff that "sometimes the fish is fresher than at other times", adding it's occasionally "better to ask the chef to make something, even if it's going around."

	FOOD	DECOR	SERVICE	COST

NEW Izakaya Sozai *Japanese*
- | - | - | M

Inner Sunset | 1500 Irving St. (16th Ave.) | 415-742-5122 |
www.izakayasozai.com

Despite the chef-owner's Blowfish Sushi pedigree, the breakout hit at this cozy, recently rebranded Inner Sunset Japanese is comforting, steamy bowls of tonkotsu ramen (made with broth that simmers for two days); other choices on the midpriced menu include yakitori, sashimi and pork belly, along with plenty of sake, soju and beer, the latter of which flows freely during happy hour on Mondays, Wednesdays and Thursdays.

Izzy's Steaks & Chops *Steak*
20 | 17 | 20 | $43

Marina | 3345 Steiner St. (bet. Chestnut & Lombard Sts.) | 415-563-0487 |
www.izzyssteaks.com

"Meat eaters" "celebrate" at this "retro"-feeling Marina steakhouse (with two suburban sibs) where "tender" cuts are "grilled just right" and "stiff drinks" flow courtesy of an "attentive" staff; while some carnivores complain of "uninspired" eats, many maintain that with "giant portions" and "included" sides, it has the "best bang for the buck" of its kind.

Jackson Fillmore Trattoria Ⓜ *Italian*
21 | 13 | 18 | $39

Upper Fillmore | 2506 Fillmore St. (Jackson St.) | 415-346-5288 |
www.jacksonfillmoresf.com

Flush with Upper Fillmore fans who "sit at the counter" and "schmooze with the owner", this "simple", "longtime neighborhood favorite" dishes out "delectable pasta" and other "well-prepared", moderately priced Italian staples; though a minority mutters the food comes "with a 'tude", most maintain that "starting with the bruschetta", the meal "just keeps getting better"; P.S. it's "best to eat early", since the "small" space does get "crowded."

Jai Yun *Chinese*
▽ 24 | 7 | 14 | $63

Chinatown | 680 Clay St. (Kearny St.) | 415-981-7438

Chef Nei Chia Ji is a "genius" gush groupies who put themselves in his "extremely capable hands" for a "spectacular", "surprising" and "beautifully presented" "multicourse feast" in Chinatown that may "ruin" you for "all other Chinese dining experiences"; most aren't deterred by the "poor service" or "dumpy" decor that leaves "much to be desired", but a few fume that the meal is "overrated" and "way overpriced"; P.S. closed Thursdays.

Jake's Steaks *Cheesesteaks*
▽ 21 | 10 | 14 | $11

Marina | 3301 Buchanan St. (bet. Lombard & Magnolia Sts.) | 415-922-2211 |
www.jakessteaks.net

"Now that I've found Jake's I never have to go home again" rave Philadelphia transplants about this "fast, solid" Marina joint assembling "authentic Philly cheesesteaks" on "Amoroso rolls" and topped with "Whiz"; sporting "beer on draft" too, it's a Sunday "must" for "Eagles" fans, though some cheer the most for their "delivery to my apartment."

☒ Jardinière *Californian/French*
26 | 26 | 25 | $71

Civic Center | 300 Grove St. (Franklin St.) | 415-861-5555 |
www.jardiniere.com

A "stylish" "splurge" near the Civic Center, Traci Des Jardins' "deco beauty has it all" - "fabulous", "sumptuous" (and sustainable) Cal-

French food, "resplendent" decor and "first-class" servers who "bust their butts" to ensure the "ritzy" show-goer crowds make "curtain time"; the "center"-stage cocktail bar "offers modest monetary relief" and last-minute seating "for oysters" and champers, but rather than "rush the pleasure by double-booking", many say skip the theater and "let dining be the event of the evening."

Jay's Cheesesteak *Cheesesteaks*   18 | 10 | 15 | $11

Mission | 3285 21st St. (bet. Lexington & Valencia Sts.) | 415-285-5200 ☞
Western Addition | 553 Divisadero St. (bet. Fell & Hayes Sts.) |
415-771-5104

The "delicious", "gut-busting" cheesesteak may not be "traditional", but it's still a "damn good sandwich" swear supporters of this largely take-out duo in the Mission and the Western Addition; even less conventional are "veggie" versions, which have their own "die-hard fans", though eaters "who have tasted some of Philly's best" are a "bit disappointed", dubbing the offerings merely "average."

Joe DiMaggio's
Italian Chophouse Ⓜ *Italian/Steak*   20 | 23 | 22 | $53

North Beach | 601 Union St. (Stockton St.) | 415-421-5633 |
www.joedimaggiosrestaurant.com

"Baseball fans" ogle the "pics of Joltin' Joe in his heyday" at this "old-time" North Beach Italian chophouse before settling into the "big booths" for "tender" steaks and solid service that support the "big bill"; still, the opposing team finds the grub "uninspired", concluding "if the fare were as great as the photos, this place would be a home run."

Joe's Cable Car *Burgers*   23 | 17 | 18 | $21

Excelsior | 4320 Mission St. (bet. Silver Ave. & Tingley St.) | 415-334-6699 |
www.joescablecar.com

Flipping patties "since We Liked Ike", this "landmark" Excelsior burger "bastion" still "grinds its own beef" and offers "more versions than you can shake a bun at", plus "gut-busting shakes and onion rings"; true, it "charges an arm and a leg" for the goods (despite serving on "paper plates"), but "loyal customers" insist it's "worth the extra dollars for the history, the quality", the "neon"-heavy decor and "even Joe himself."

Juban *Japanese*   18 | 14 | 16 | $38

Japantown | Kinokuniya Bldg. | 1581 Webster St. (Post St.) | 415-776-5822 |
www.jubanrestaurant.com

Those who "enjoy cooking" without any of the "prep or cleanup" congregate at this Japanese "yakiniku-house" trio in Japantown, Burlingame and Menlo Park to "grill their own tidbits" at in-table hibachis; the "tender", "high-quality" meats are "marinated well", and kids "love" the action, though some cite "so-so" service and say it can easily "get expensive."

Just Wonton Ⓜ *Chinese*   ▽ 21 | 3 | 15 | $15

Outer Sunset | 1241 Vicente St. (bet. 23rd & 24th Aves.) | 415-681-2999
Despite the name, insiders insist "it's not just the wonton" that stands out at this "no-frills" Outer Sunset Chinese, but also the "other noodle-based dishes" and "delish rice specials"; the "plastic tablecloths" ("like eating in your aunt's old kitchen") and "bare-bones" service are found wanting, but at least the fare "hardly puts a dent" in your wallet.

	FOOD	DECOR	SERVICE	COST

Kabuto ⓜ *Japanese*

26 | 12 | 19 | $48

Outer Richmond | 5121 Geary Blvd. (bet. 15th & 16th Aves.) |
415-752-5652 | www.kabutosushi.com

Fin fanatics "cannot stop eating" at this Outer Richmond Japanese, a "lively" location that "satisfies your taste buds" with high-end sushi elevated to "pure art", particularly when it comes to the "inventive" specials; just "don't expect much" in the way of decor, and "get there early to put your name on the list", since "seating is tight" and the service, though performed "with care", can also be "slow."

Kamekyo *Japanese*

21 | 13 | 20 | $35

(fka Grandeho's Kamekyo)

Cole Valley | 943 Cole St. (bet. Carl St. & Parnassus Ave.) | 415-759-8428

When Cole Valley families "crave sushi but don't want to travel far", this "tiny storefront" "does the trick", turning out "fresh fish" and "classic Japanese dishes"; it's "good for kids" and rewards "favorite customers", but regulars are split on the results since longtime employees bought out the original owners in 2009: some say "nothing seems to have changed" while others sigh it's "not quite the same."

Kan Zaman *Mideastern*

∇ 19 | 18 | 16 | $23

Haight-Ashbury | 1793 Haight St. (bet. Cole & Shrader Sts.) | 415-751-9656

You may feel "teleported to some Arabic nation" at this "chill" Haight-Ashbury hookah bar filled with low-slung furniture and patrons "socializing with friends" over platters of "consistently good" (and affordable) Middle Eastern meze; service gets mixed marks, but few seem to notice "later in the evening", when patrons can "smoke shisha" at the tables and the "belly dancers come out" (Wednesday–Sunday).

Kasa Indian Eatery *Indian*

19 | 10 | 15 | $15

Castro | 4001 18th St. (Noe St.) | 415-621-6940
Marina | 3115 Fillmore St. (bet. Filbert & Pixley Sts.) | 415-896-4008
www.kasaindian.com

"When you're craving a little spice", these "hip", "self-service" subcontinentals in the Castro and Marina serve up a "limited menu" of "tasty" kati rolls (aka "Indian burritos") and "neat-to-eat" Thali plates that "hit the spot"; the "cafeteria-style" digs are "not fancy" and it's a "little confusing how the ordering works", but calorie-minded consumers applaud "fresh, organic" fare that's "rather healthy" – and the "price is right too."

Katana-Ya ⓓ *Japanese*

22 | 11 | 16 | $20

Downtown | 430 Geary St. (Mason St.) | 415-771-1280

"They know what they're doing" at this "tiny" Downtown "ramen joint", whose "multiple combinations" of "chewy noodles and tasty broth" draw "lines out the door"; there's also "delicious" sushi and other Japanese "cheap eats" on offer for Union Square shoppers, "post-theater" noshers and late-night revelers who stop in for a "tasty" "fix" under the glare of neon (read: the "decor needs some work").

Kate's Kitchen ⌿ *Southern*

∇ 22 | 12 | 18 | $16

Lower Haight | 471 Haight St. (bet. Fillmore & Webster Sts.) | 415-626-3984

Awash in a "friendly hipster vibe" and "bargain" prices, this daytime-only Lower Haight kitchen cranks out "fantastic" Southern breakfasts, including a "French toast orgy that's as good as it sounds" and "plenty of options for vegetarians"; sure, "you have to line up" and the "decor is nothing to write home about", but committed carbo-loaders have "fun reading the signs on the walls" while they wait; P.S. cash only.

Katia's Russian Tea Room ☑ *Russian* ▽ 23 | 17 | 22 | $29

Inner Richmond | 600 Fifth Ave. (Balboa St.) | 415-668-9292 | www.katias.com

"When you feel like a change of pace", this "small, comfortable" corner cafe in the Inner Richmond is "quite good" for a "Russian fix of stroganoff, blintzes" and other "basics"; expect a "lively" time whenever owner Katia Troosh "comes out of the kitchen to chat" and on Saturday nights, when there's "live accordion."

Khan Toke Thai House *Thai* 22 | 23 | 22 | $27

Outer Richmond | 5937 Geary Blvd. (bet. 23rd & 24th Aves.) | 415-668-6654

"Removing your shoes and sitting on the floor" to eat at "kotatsu-style tables" "adds to the mystique" of this "super-cool" Siamese in the Outer Richmond whose "authentic" atmosphere makes it one of the "best places to take out-of-towners, meet friends or celebrate something"; it "may not be the cheapest Thai" around, but "reliably good" food and a "classy staff" mean it's "always a hit."

King of Thai *Thai* 18 | 8 | 14 | $15

Downtown | 184 O'Farrell St. (bet. Powell & Stockton Sts.) | 415-677-9991 ◑
Inner Richmond | 346 Clement St. (bet. 4th & 5th Aves.) | 415-831-9953 ◑⊟
Inner Richmond | 639 Clement St. (bet. 7th & 8th Aves.) | 415-752-5198 ◑⊟
North Beach | 1268 Grant Ave. (bet. Fresno & Vallejo Sts.) | 415-391-8219 | www.kingofthainoodlehouse.com ◑
Outer Sunset | 1507 Sloat Blvd. (bet. Everglade & Springfield Drs.) | 415-566-9921 ⊟
Outer Sunset | 1541 Taraval St. (bet. 25th & 26th Aves.) | 415-682-9958 ◑⊟

"Go for the noodles, not the decor" at this chain of "convenient, late-night" Thais that are "always ready when you are" (every outpost save the one on Sloat is open till 1 AM or later); the "fast, filling" dishes might not be "mind-popping", but they're "hard to beat for the bucks", so frugal sorts suggest stopping in for a "quick fix."

☑ Kiss Seafood ☒Ⓜ *Japanese* 27 | 16 | 24 | $73

Japantown | 1700 Laguna St. (Sutter St.) | 415-474-2866

"Hidden" in Japantown, this "mom-and-pop" "gem" is a "tiny slice of Tokyo", where the chef shows "unparalleled love and pride" in "meticulously" crafting omakase dinners with "delightful combinations" of raw fish and cooked dishes, complemented by "superb" sake; since it has only 12 seats, it feels a bit more like a "small inn in rural Japan" than a luxury destination, but "impressed" guests affirm it's still worth the "fat check."

Kitchenette SF ☒⊟ *Sandwiches* ▽ 22 | 6 | 16 | $11

Dogpatch | American Industrial Ctr. | 958 Illinois St. (bet. 20th & 22nd Sts.) | www.kitchenettesf.com

"Worth a (major) detour", this "inventive", weekday-only lunch stop in Dogpatch offers "wonderful, complex" sandwiches and other American

	FOOD	DECOR	SERVICE	COST

eats from a "fresh menu daily", "served very simply" from a warehouse "loading dock"; there are only a few benches for seating in the parking lot, but that fits the bill for a "cheap", "only-in-SF" takeout meal; P.S. open 11:30 AM–1:30 PM; cash only.

Koh Samui & The Monkey *Thai* | 21 | 19 | 17 | $30 |

SoMa | 415 Brannan St. (bet. Ritch & 3rd Sts.) | 415-369-0007 | www.kohsamuiandthemonkey.com

Another Monkey *Thai*

NEW **Mission** | 280 Valencia St. (14th St.) | 415-241-0288 | www.anothermonkeythai.com

Locals go ape for the "savory" "combination of street favorites and up-scale offerings" complemented by "delicious" cocktails at this "elegant" but "funky" SoMa Thai with a new Mission spin-off; though some cite "spotty" service and call the eats "a bit overpriced", others maintain that it's "surprisingly affordable for the quality" (and a "decent value" for the "filling" lunch specials).

Ⓩ Kokkari Estiatorio *Greek* | 27 | 26 | 25 | $54 |

Downtown | 200 Jackson St. (bet. Battery & Front Sts.) | 415-981-0983 | www.kokkari.com

"Exquisite" Greek "delicacies" delight Downtown devotees of this "cosmopolitan" "Hellenic heaven" that "oozes with ambiance", boasting a "gorgeous", "romantic" main room where "spit-roasted meat" turns above a "blazing" fire; since the "superb" staff ensures a "feel-good" experience, it's "packed every night" with a savvy, "eclectic" crowd – including "politicos" and lovebirds "splurging" on a "special occasion" – so "reservations are a must."

Koo Ⓜ *Asian* | 23 | 18 | 19 | $42 |

Inner Sunset | 408 Irving St. (bet. 5th & 6th Aves.) | 415-731-7077 | www.sushikoo.com

"If you want a Japanese dinner beyond just sushi and the usual", "check out" this "cool", contemporary Inner Sunset izakaya where the "personable chefs" dole out "hard-to-find fish" and sake, along with "inventive" Asian fusion dishes ("Spoonfuls of Happiness" chased by shots "are just that"); the "bustling" space is tended by a "staff that treats you like family" and the prices are "decent" too.

Kuleto's *Italian* | 21 | 19 | 20 | $45 |

Downtown | Villa Florence Hotel | 221 Powell St. (bet. Geary & O'Farrell Sts.) | 415-397-7720 | www.kuletos.com

"A longtime favorite for theatergoers", "tourists" and those taking a "break from shopping in Union Square", this "reliable", "unpretentious" Downtowner delivers "well-made" pastas and other "comforting" Northern Italian eats amid "traditional" digs; some suggest "sit at the bar", have a glass of "tasty wine" and "watch the chefs at work" while you "meet new friends", but a few fret about uneven service and fairly "run-of-the-mill" meals for the price.

Kyo-Ya Ⓩ *Japanese* | 24 | 21 | 21 | $60 |

Downtown | Palace Hotel | 2 New Montgomery St. (Market St.) | 415-546-5090 | www.kyo-ya-restaurant.com

"Pristine" sushi stars at this "outstanding" Downtown option for "top-notch" yet "costly office lunches" as well as "elegantly prepared" kaiseki dinners (which need to be reserved three days in advance), "graciously" served in a "quiet", "dignified setting" "in the back of the Palace Hotel"; its "expensive" trappings keep it "often overlooked", but lunch specials and "great happy hours" help lower the price of admission.

La Boulange *Bakery*   21 | 16 | 16 | $16

Cow Hollow | 1909 Union St. (Laguna St.) | 415-440-4450
Cole Valley | 1000 Cole St. (Parnassus St.) | 415-242-2442
Hayes Valley | 500 Hayes St. (Octavia St.) | 415-863-3376
NEW Noe Valley | 3898 24th St. (bet. Sanchez & Vicksburg Sts.) | 415-821-1050
North Beach | 543 Columbus Ave. (bet. Powell & Stockton Sts.) | 415-399-0714
Pacific Heights | 2043 Fillmore St. (bet. California & Pine Sts.) | 415-928-1300
Russian Hill | 2300 Polk St. (Green St.) | 415-345-1107
SoMa | 685 Market St. (bet. Annie & 3rd Sts.) | 415-512-7610 🗷
www.laboulangebakery.com

There are "few better ways to start the day" than with a "buttery" pastry and a "monster" café au lait at this "cute", "piece-of-Paris" bakery chain; lunchtime lures include "awesome" "open-faced sandwiches" among other "savory and sweet treats", though the "crowds" (with a bounty of "babies and strollers") and sometimes "inefficient" service can detract from the "decadence."

La Ciccia 🅼 *Italian*   26 | 16 | 25 | $45

Noe Valley | 291 30th St. (Church St.) | 415-550-8114 | www.laciccia.com

"Not your average Italian", this "genuine" Sardinian "seafood paradise" is a Noe "neighborhood gem that's known throughout the city" for its "magnificent", "refreshing" regional cuisine and wines you'd otherwise "be damned to find in stores"; the "warm" married owners "make you feel like you've come home for dinner", so while it's rather "small" and "out-of-the-way", it's "well worth the trip."

La Corneta *Mexican*   21 | 9 | 15 | $12

Glen Park | 2834 Diamond St. (bet. Bosworth & Chenery Sts.) | 415-469-8757 ⊅
Mission | 2731 Mission St. (bet. 23rd & 24th Sts.) | 415-643-7001
www.lacorneta.com

"Deliciously fresh, super-stuffed burritos" that "few can finish" (also available in "genius" "baby" versions) are tops at this "inexpensive" taqueria trio in Glen Park, the Mission and Burlingame; the "cafeteria-style service" is usually "fast", despite "daunting rush-hour" lines, but it's not ideal for "hanging out", so many "get it to go."

La Cumbre Taqueria *Mexican*   21 | 9 | 15 | $12

Mission | 515 Valencia St. (bet. 16th & 17th Sts.) | 415-863-8205
This Mission Mexican (with a San Mateo sib) has been an "SF institution" for more than 40 years, and it "never goes out of style", dishing up "fantastic" burritos and other "respectable" south-of-the-border bites (topped with hot sauce "if you dare"); the surroundings are humble, but since it's "super-cheap" and open till 2 AM on the weekends, taco-loving tipplers like to swing by "after a night at the bars."

FOOD	DECOR	SERVICE	COST

NEW Lafitte American

-	-	-	M

Embarcadero | Pier 5 | The Embarcadero (B'way) | 415-839-2134 | www.lafittesf.com

In a swashbuckling feat of derring-do, chef Russell Jackson (LA restaurant vet and former Dissident Chef of Sub Culture Dining) has transformed a historic pier building on the Embarcadero into this intimate modern American whose menus change with the seasons and his own whims; though named after a Louisianan pirate, the sleek industrial space (with an enclosed heated patio) forgoes Captain Hook kitsch, deferring the drama instead to the open kitchen and views of the Bay.

☑ La Folie ☒ French

28	25	26	$95

Russian Hill | 2316 Polk St. (bet. Green & Union Sts.) | 415-776-5577 | www.lafolie.com

"After all these years", chef-owner Roland Passot "still wows" at his "cathedral of French cuisine" on Russian Hill, "personally greeting guests" and crafting "rich", *magnifique* tasting menus, "perfectly coupled" with "brother George's fabulous wine program"; the "fussy presentations, fussier service" and "intimate", "elegantly" remodeled digs are tailor-made for "special evenings" and well worth the "considerable investment"; P.S. "for everyday dining, try the lounge next door."

Lahore Karahi Ⓜ Pakistani

▽ 25	5	10	$15

Tenderloin | 612 O' Farrell St. (Leavenworth St.) | 415-567-8603 | www.lahorekarahisanfrancisco.com

Dubbed "the crown jewel of the Tandooriloin" for its "addictive", "authentic" halal fare that's "exactly like what your dear Pakistani uncle would cook for you in his home", this "hole-in-the-wall" is a haven for "cheap" eats (with BYO drinks); though some are skittish about the surroundings, fortunately the "food balances out" the "nonexistent decor", "limited service" and "the ick factor of getting to it."

La Mar Cebicheria Peruana Peruvian

24	23	21	$52

Embarcadero | Pier 1.5 (Washington St.) | 415-397-8880 | www.lamarcebicheria.com

"Viva Peru!" shout fans of this "gorgeous", "sprawling" Embarcadero outpost from "celeb-chef" Gastón Acurio, whose "exciting" seafood-driven menu (with "incredible ceviches") takes you on a "South American excursion"; it's "especially" alluring on the "bayside" patio or at the "fantastic front bar", where "all the pretty people" dive into "delicious but deadly" Pisco Sours – and easily "forget the price tag", somewhat "superficial" service and "bomb-level noise."

La Méditerranée Mediterranean/Mideastern

19	14	18	$23

Castro | 288 Noe St. (bet. Beaver & Market Sts.) | 415-431-7210
Upper Fillmore | 2210 Fillmore St. (bet. Clay & Sacramento Sts.) | 415-921-2956
www.cafelamed.com

"Savory" "phyllo dough–wrapped treats" and "tempting" meze platters keep this trio in the Castro, Upper Fillmore and Berkeley "perpetually popular" among "regulars" "craving a variety" of Middle Eastern–Med fare "on the fly"; the "informal" settings feel "cramped" to some, but "pleasant" sidewalk seating is sometimes an option, and there's "fast" service and plenty of "bang for the buck" besides.

L'Ardoise 🖂 Ⓜ French

| 23 | 21 | 23 | $47 |

Castro | 151 Noe St. (Henry St.) | 415-437-2600 | www.ardoisesf.com

"Tucked away in Duboce Triangle", this "winning", "absolutely delightful" "boîte" is "reminiscent of bistros in France", down to the "imported Gallic waiters" and chalkboard listing "tasty, unfussy" specials among the "beautifully executed" *grand-mère*-style cuisine; the "Parisian salon ambiance" is "perfect for a date", but given its "studio-apartment" size, reservations are a must.

Lark Creek Steak Steak

| 22 | 21 | 21 | $56 |

Downtown | Westfield San Francisco Ctr. | 845 Market St., 4th fl. (bet. 4th & 5th Sts.) | 415-593-4100 | www.larkcreeksteak.com

"Don't be fooled" by its location in an "upscale mall" – this "tranquil", "clubby" meatery in Downtown's Westfield Centre "impresses" with "properly done" steaks, "freshly ground" burgers and an "above-average" wine list; though peeved patrons find it a bit "pretentious" and "pricey", some are appeased by the dinnertime prix fixe option.

La Scene Café & Bar Ⓜ Californian/Mediterranean

| ▽ 21 | 18 | 21 | $49 |

Downtown | Warwick Regis | 490 Geary St. (bet. Mason & Taylor Sts.) | 415-292-6430 | www.warwicksf.com

For a "civilized" Downtown dinner before the curtain, show-goers head to this "lovely" Cal-Med turning out a "reliable" pre-theater prix fixe; while foodies find it's "ok" but "not inspired", most agree the "competent" servers "do a great job" of getting you out on time.

La Taqueria ⊄ Mexican

| 25 | 9 | 14 | $13 |

Mission | 2889 Mission St. (bet. 24th & 25th Sts.) | 415-285-7117

"Terrific tacos" and "top-of-the-line" burritos loaded with "fresh ingredients" (but "no filler" rice) make this Mission Mexican an "icon" for locals and out-of-towners who "plan layovers in San Francisco" just to get "a fix"; the "decor is nonexistent" and it's "always busy", but the staff keeps the line "moving" and "the quality" makes it one of the "best bargains around" for a "quick bite" or "takeout."

La Terrasse French

| 18 | 19 | 16 | $38 |

Presidio | 215 Lincoln Blvd. (Graham St.) | 415-922-3463 | www.laterrassepresidio.com

"Classic French fare" (including a Continental petit déjeuner for breakfast) comes with a "delightful" setting at this "hidden jewel" in the Presidio where the "heated patio" with a "view of the Golden Gate Bridge" is the "real draw"; while some cite "average", "overpriced" meals and "aloof" service from "charm-school dropouts", vista-seekers say it's "still a pleaser" nonetheless.

La Trappe 🖂 Ⓜ Belgian

| ▽ 18 | 23 | 19 | $33 |

North Beach | 800 Greenwich St. (Mason St.) | 415-440-8727 | www.latrappecafe.com

"Serious beer lovers" know to "head down the winding steps" to the brick-lined cellar at this Belgian gastropub in North Beach, where a "mind-blowing" selection of brews accompanies the "hearty" grub; some of the suds "are a little pricey", but "knowledgeable" bartenders are "helpful in navigating" the list, and aficionados aver the "Trappist ale and ambiance are way too cool to pass up."

	FOOD	DECOR	SERVICE	COST

Le Central Bistro 🗓 *French* — 20 | 17 | 20 | $46

Downtown | 453 Bush St. (bet. Grant Ave. & Kearny St.) | 415-391-2233 |
www.lecentralbistro.com

"Lunch with the town's notables" (including "Willie Brown, who eats
here often") is the legendary lure of this "wonderful little time capsule
of a restaurant" that's still "abuzz" with a "French-fueled atmosphere"
and plenty of Downtown "movers and shakers"; *oui*, the "old-school"
waiters can be "crusty", and some say it's "starting to feel a little
aged", but most maintain it's just "right" for "a glass of *vin rouge*"
paired with "enjoyable" Gallic "bistro fare", like the "classic" cassoulet
that's "been cooking for decades."

Le Charm French Bistro Ⓜ *French* — 22 | 17 | 22 | $41

SoMa | 315 Fifth St. (bet. Folsom & Shipley Sts.) | 415-546-6128 |
www.lecharm.com

This "delightful escape" "hidden" in a "sketchy" part of SoMa is "very
charming" "indeed" cheer fans of its "delicious" French bistro fare and
"bargain" prix fixe menu; though it's often "bustling" and "packed in
tight", the "lovely little" patio feels "miles from the city", and since
"service is tops" too, it's a "family favorite" of many Francophiles;
P.S. a recent chef change may not be fully reflected in the Food score.

Le Colonial *French/Vietnamese* — 23 | 24 | 21 | $53

Downtown | 20 Cosmo Pl. (bet. Jones & Taylor Sts.) | 415-931-3600 |
www.lecolonialsf.com

A visit to this "magical", "tropical" Downtowner in an "out-of-the-way
alley" is "like stepping into a movie" set in "old-time Saigon", "especially in the summer", when a "who's who of the pretty people" dines
on the "beautiful" patio, tended to by an "accommodating" staff; the
"delicately flavored" (and "expensive") dishes take French-Vietnamese
fare "up a notch", and it's "fab for cocktails" too, since the "upstairs
oasis" "explodes" with live music and a "DJ dance scene" after dinner.

Le P'tit Laurent *French* — 23 | 19 | 22 | $39

Glen Park | 699 Chenery St. (Diamond St.) | 415-334-3235

"Ooh-la-la", it's like dining "beneath the Eiffel Tower" at this "luscious"
corner bistro "near the Glen Park BART", where habitués sit "cheek-
by-jowl" and "speak French to the waiters" while downing "real" "old-
fashioned" classics; there's "no haughtiness, just warm service"
"watched over by Laurent himself", but "always reserve", as the prix
fixe (Sunday-Thursday) is "a steal" and "eet iz no longer a secret."

Le Soleil *Vietnamese* — ▽ 20 | 15 | 19 | $30

Inner Richmond | 133 Clement St. (bet. 2nd & 3rd Aves.) | 415-668-4848 |
www.lesoleilusa.com

For "super-fresh" Vietnamese vittles, like "delicious" whole roasted
crab with garlic noodles, Inner Richmonders rely on this "pleasant"
"Clement Street gem"; no, there's "not much" in the way of decor, and
some grumble it's "gone downhill" of late, but it's still "not too pricey"
for a casual "group" meal.

Let's Be Frank *Hot Dogs* — 19 | 11 | 18 | $11

NEW **Downtown** | Justin Herman Plaza | The Embarcadero
(Market St.) 🗓 Ⓜ 🖤

(continued)

FOOD | DECOR | SERVICE | COST

(continued)

Let's Be Frank

Marina | 3318 Steiner St. (bet. Chestnut & Lombard Sts.) | 415-674-6755
Presidio | Warming Hut | Crissy Field (Marine Dr.) 🅜🏳
www.letsbefrankdogs.com

"Who knew you could eat a hot dog without feeling guilty?" wonder fans of these "fabulous" frank stands focusing on "organic" ingredients and "great fixin's"; on "sunny" weekends, lunchers hit the original Crissy Field cart to take their pups for "a walk on the Golden Gate Bridge", or sit at the "outdoor tables" at the new Marina brick-and-mortar, but detractors scold the dogs for being "waaay overpriced"; P.S. the new Downtown cart is open Tuesday–Saturday till 4 PM.

Liberty Cafe, The 🅜 *American*   22 | 18 | 21 | $35

Bernal Heights | 410 Cortland Ave. (bet. Andover & Bennington Sts.) |
415-695-8777 | www.thelibertycafe.com

"Sweet or savory, you can't go wrong" at this "cute" American "comfort-food" cafe and bakery "hidden" "in the sticks" of Bernal Heights, where moderately priced eats including "legendary" chicken pot pies (and "must-order banana creams") warm the soul "on a cold winter night"; a "good brunch" and a wine bar out back with a "sunny patio" lend it further appeal, as does the "neighborly service."

Limón *Peruvian*   23 | 18 | 19 | $35

Mission | 524 Valencia St. (bet. 16th & 17th Sts.) | 415-252-0918 |
www.limon-sf.com

Limón Peruvian Rotisserie *Peruvian*

Mission | 1001 S. Van Ness Ave. (21st St.) | 415-821-2134 |
www.limonrotisserie.com

A "chic" redo and new chef (from Spain's touted Arzak) have taken this "popular Nuevo Peruvian" "to the next level", unleashing "upscale", "flavor-packed plates" ("ceviche is the star") in a larger, loftlike space designed with citrus hues; those who miss its old "charm" choose its tinier rotisserie offshoot for "super roast chicken", the same celebrated seafood and "pitchers of sangria" for a "better value."

Little Chihuahua *Mexican*   ∇ 22 | 14 | 17 | $14

NEW **Noe Valley** | 4123 24th St. (Castro St.) | 415-648-4157
Western Addition | 292 Divisadero St. (bet. Haight & Page Sts.) |
415-255-8225
www.thelittlechihuahua.com

Doling out the "best gringo-fied" south-of-the-border food and "$3 beers" to a "youthful, local crowd", this "small" taqueria in the Western Addition (with a new Noe Valley spin-off) is "a little bit more expensive" than others, but "worth it for the excellent quality of all the ingredients"; "funky breakfast options like Mexican French toast" and "passion fruit mimosas" bring in a weekend brunch following, too.

Little Nepal 🅜 *Nepalese*   ∇ 21 | 15 | 19 | $25

Bernal Heights | 925 Cortland Ave. (bet. Folsom & Gates Sts.) |
415-643-3881 | www.littlenepalsf.com

"Go-go for the momos" and "exotic" curries (and "scoop up every bit with the amazing naan") at this "inviting", low-cost Nepalese bringing a "spicy" "taste of the Himalayas" to Bernal Heights; while the space is quite "small", a "lovely" staff adds to the "warm" atmosphere.

	FOOD	DECOR	SERVICE	COST

Little Star Pizza Ⓜ *Pizza* | 24 | 15 | 17 | $23 |

Mission | 400 Valencia St. (15th St.) | 415-551-7827
Western Addition | 846 Divisadero St. (bet. Fulton & McAllister Sts.) | 415-441-1118
www.littlestarpizza.com

With a "fab" cornmeal crust and "copious toppings", the "perfectly pitched pies" at these "hipster pizza joints" provide a deep-dish "slice of Chicago", and the thin-crust varieties are "incredible" too; while "ridiculous waits" and "deafening noise" lead some to resort to "takeout", others stick around for the "'80s-laden" jukebox and "cool vibe."

Local Kitchen & Wine | 20 | 19 | 18 | $37 |
Merchant *Californian/Italian*

SoMa | 330 First St. (bet. Folsom & Harrison Sts.) | 415-777-4200 | www.sf-local.com

A "wonderful variety" of "boldly flavored" Cal-Italian eats, including "light, crackerlike" pizzas, are washed down with wine from an "interesting yet approachable" list at this lofty SoMa space; service tends toward the "sluggish", especially during Sunday's "all-you-can-eat pizza night", and the "oddly partitioned" layout with communal seating calls to mind an "ad agency art department", but it still has "great energy" abetted by "watching the cooks at work."

NEW Local Mission Eatery Ⓜ *Californian* | - | - | - | E |

Mission | 3111 24th St. (bet. Folsom & Shotwell Sts.) | 415-655-3422 | www.localmissioneatery.com

Eat like a local, or at least a locavore, at this ambitious but casually styled Mission newcomer where a married chef team – with a collective résumé that includes Fifth Floor, Fish & Farm and RN74 – slings locally sourced Cal dishes in a wood-and-tile storefront setting; the slightly expensive meals (with flexible large- and small-plate options) are served by the duo themselves, and there are also weekly cooking 'labs' (check the website for the schedule); P.S. no dinner Tuesday nights.

Loló Ⓢ *Mediterranean/Pan-Latin* | ▽ 24 | 21 | 21 | $38 |

Mission | 3230 22nd St. (bet. Bartlett & Mission Sts.) | 415-643-5656 | www.lolosf.com

"The chef is definitely experimental" at this "decidedly offbeat" Pan-Latin–Med mash-up boasting an "incredibly tasty" "mostly-tapas menu" (served till midnight on weekends) and a "wild" interior whose "kitsched-out" decor made from recycled materials "reminds you that you're definitely in the Mission"; it flies under the radar, but those who are *loco* for it cheer "go with friends and enjoy the ride."

L'Osteria del Forno ⌿ *Italian* | 24 | 14 | 19 | $32 |

North Beach | 519 Columbus Ave. (bet. Green & Union Sts.) | 415-982-1124 | www.losteriadelforno.com

"Buried among the tourist traps" of North Beach, this "fabulous" neighborhood joint eking out a "limited" menu of "amazing baked" Northern Italian eats (including "unbeatable" milk-braised pork and "authentic" thin-crust pizzas) along with "old-school aperitifs" and "reasonably priced" wines is a "Columbus Avenue star"; just "take cash and patience", as the "simple surroundings" are tight, "there are no reservations" and the staff sometimes "takes a while to warm up."

	FOOD	DECOR	SERVICE	COST

Lovejoy's Tea Room 🅜 *Tearoom* — 21 | 22 | 22 | $26

Noe Valley | 1351 Church St. (Clipper St.) | 415-648-5895 | www.lovejoystearoom.com

"Girliness" incarnate, this "funky" Noe Valley tearoom that "looks like grandma's attic" filled with "mismatched china cups" is where "BFFs" go when they "want to be a lady (even in jeans)" for a British "tea for two" served with "delicious, fussy little sandwiches" and "warm scones" "with all the toppings"; it requires advanced reservations (due to all those "bridal and baby showers around you"), but it's "worth it for the occasional treat" – "just don't try to inveigle your man into coming."

Luce *Californian/Italian* — 21 | 20 | 20 | $67

SoMa | InterContinental Hotel | 888 Howard St. (bet. 4th & 5th Sts.) | 415-616-6566 | www.lucewinerestaurant.com

"Despite *Iron Chef* finalist Dominique Crenn in the kitchen" and "greeting customers between courses", this "hip" "yet formal" Cal-Italian "near the convention center" at the InterContinental remains an "underrated" SoMa oasis for "exquisite presentations" of "well-balanced, modern" (some say "overly complicated") fare, complete with a tasting menu and "extensive" wine list; "service is first-rate, but so are the prices", so "going for lunch is a more value-oriented" option.

Luella *Californian/Mediterranean* — 22 | 19 | 23 | $47

Russian Hill | 1896 Hyde St. (Green St.) | 415-674-4343 | www.luellasf.com

"Quiet", "comfortable" and *au courant*, this Russian Hill "Hyde-away" "right on the cable-car line" "deserves to be a destination" declare devotees who "always feel welcome" thanks to "thoughtful" servers who "remember their name"; the "small" Cal-Med menu isn't "especially adventurous", but most agree the "fresh, local" food "never fails" and the wines are "well-priced" as well; P.S. it's extra "kid-friendly" on Sunday nights, when there's a special menu for diners under 10 years old.

Luna Park *American/French* — 19 | 16 | 17 | $33

Mission | 694 Valencia St. (18th St.) | 415-553-8584 | www.lunaparksf.com

For a "lively" night out that won't "break the bank", a "happening" crowd hits this "always-jumping" Mission "favorite" for "huge portions" of "comforting", "homestyle" French-New American grub, "excellent" cocktails and desserts that "rock"; the staff is "personable" and the vibe "hip" and "upbeat", but with "long waits" and a menu that could use an "update", some feel it's more about the "social bar scene" than the food.

Lupa Trattoria *Italian* — ▽ 24 | 20 | 26 | $38

Noe Valley | 4109 24th St. (bet. Castro & Diamond Sts.) | 415-282-5872 | www.lupatrattoria.com

"Warm and inviting" with a "welcoming Italian staff", this Noe Valley trattoria proffers "hearty pastas" and other "unfussy, authentic" Roman dishes, plus wines that "match well with the cuisine"; the "quaint" space is not quite a "destination", but a "well-priced", quality "neighborhood place" for "having dinner with friends."

Menus, photos, voting and more - free at ZAGAT.com

	FOOD	DECOR	SERVICE	COST

Magnolia Gastropub & Brewery ● *American/Southern*

| | 20 | 16 | 18 | $27 |

Haight-Ashbury | 1398 Haight St. (Masonic Ave.) | 415-864-7468 | www.magnoliapub.com

Though "the Dead vibe" has faded, this "time-honored" Haight Street haunt still "rocks", attracting a "hip crowd that's serious about beer" to sample its "first-rate" suds "brewed in the basement", complemented by slightly "fancy" Southern-American gastropub grub that's "getting better and better"; while the "stylie" lair is often "noisy as a metal concert", fans find it a prime place to "have a drink and chow down" until midnight.

Maki Ⓜ *Japanese*

| | ▽ 22 | 14 | 18 | $33 |

Japantown | Japan Ctr. | 1825 Post St., 2nd fl. (bet. Fillmore & Webster Sts.) | 415-921-5215

"Blink and you'll miss" this "unique" "oasis" "hidden" in plain sight in the Japan Center mall, "known for *wappa-meshi*" (baskets of steamed rice topped with veggies and meat), along with sushi, sake and other "pleasingly authentic" fare; the family-run space is quite "small (be prepared to wait)" and sparsely decorated with "plastic food", but "heaven"-sent when you need a place to "take your friends from Tokyo who are craving home cooking"; P.S. lunch served Friday–Sunday.

Mamacita *Mexican*

| | 22 | 18 | 17 | $34 |

Marina | 2317 Chestnut St. (Scott St.) | 415-346-8494 | www.mamacitasf.com

It's a "packed" fiesta for the "young" "Marina-goers" who frequent this "haute Mexican" turning out "trendy spins on traditional dishes", such as "awesome" tacos and "spectacular" churros, matched by "killer drinks"; critics complain that the "ear-splitting" volume is like "10 mariachi bands playing at once", but admirers insist that the "food makes up for it all."

Mama's on Washington Square Ⓜ⊄ *American*

| | 25 | 14 | 18 | $22 |

North Beach | 1701 Stockton St. (Filbert St.) | 415-362-6421 | www.mamas-sf.com

"Scrumptious French toast", "phenomenal" eggs and "fresh-baked goodies" served with "incredible homemade jam" explain why eaters endure a "line trailing out the door" at this daytime American in North Beach; the wait can "seem interminable", but once you finally order at the counter you get "service with a smile" and a seat in the "close" but "cute" dining room to savor a "memorable" morning meal.

Mandalay *Burmese*

| | 23 | 16 | 22 | $26 |

Inner Richmond | 4348 California St. (bet. 5th & 6th Aves.) | 415-386-3895 | www.mandalaysf.com

Those who have been to Myanmar might have a "déjà vu moment" at this "authentic" Inner Richmonder where the "marvelous" ginger and tea leaf salads and other "balanced" Burmese bites seduce with their "subtle" flavor; it's a real "value for the money", especially considering the "wonderful" service and "pleasant" if "quirky" decor, and many Rangoon rooters reckon it "rivals" its "competitors on Clement Street", but "without the crowds."

Manora's Thai Cuisine *Thai*   23 | 15 | 19 | $26

SoMa | 1600 Folsom St. (12th St.) | 415-861-6224 | www.manorathai.com
"So reliable" in SoMa, this "old standby" provides "ample portions" of Thai standards made extra "tasty" with "fresh herbs" and "big flavors"; while the "pleasant" but "dated digs could use some freshening up", "fast" service and "reasonable" tabs make it a lunchtime "hot spot."

🆕 Marengo on Union Ⓜ *American*   - | - | - | M

Cow Hollow | 1980 Union St. (Buchanan St.) | 415-441-2575 | www.marengosf.com
Noncommittal chicks and dudes get to sip, sample and nibble their way through a variety of tastes at this new Cow Hollow wine and whiskey bar, where the midpriced American menu featuring sliders (including lamb, chicken and shrimp varieties) and bar bites (including fried pickles) is well suited to soak up value vino and boozy drinks; while ample flat-screens allow for watching the game, the pièce de résistance is the retractable roof in back that allows for catching some rays.

Mario's Bohemian Cigar Store Cafe *Italian*   19 | 18 | 16 | $19

North Beach | 566 Columbus Ave. (bet. Green & Union Sts.) | 415-362-0536
"Stoke up" on cappuccino, "linger" over a "reasonably priced" glass of wine or chow down on one of the "fantastic" sandwiches served on "locally made focaccia" (a "no-brainer") at this "quintessential North Beach" cafe; the Northern Italian "menu is small" and the service "casual", but "you get a lot of food" and "charm" for the price, plus it's ideal for "people-watching" "right on Washington Square."

MarketBar *Mediterranean*   17 | 18 | 18 | $39

Embarcadero | 1 Ferry Bldg. (Market St.) | 415-434-1100 | www.marketbar.com
"When the sun comes out of hiding", this Embarcadero brasserie is "perfect for an afternoon glass of wine at the bar or on the patio" watching the "rollerbladers" and "farmer's market" posse "go by"; the "tasty but not exceptional" Med meals and service "do the job", so while some patrons protest that it's "overpriced", it's an able "understudy when everything" else in the Ferry Building "is booked."

🆕 Marlowe Ⓢ *American*   - | - | - | M

SoMa | 330 Townsend St. (4th St.) | 415-974-5599 | www.marlowesf.com
This SoMa newcomer (replacing South Food + Wine) dishes up affordable Californian bistro fare like burgers, roast chicken and steak frites (served till 11 PM Thursday–Saturday), accompanied by a nicely priced wine list; it has a rustic-chic look, with whitewashed brick walls, a chalkboard menu and popular food quotes – chosen by the public via Twitter – etched into the front window.

Marnee Thai *Thai*   23 | 14 | 17 | $24

Inner Sunset | 1243 Ninth Ave. (bet. Irving St. & Lincoln Way) | 415-731-9999 | www.MarneeThaiSF.com
Outer Sunset | 2225 Irving St. (bet. 23rd & 24th Aves.) | 415-665-9500
Reviewers rave the "real family Thai" dishes are "expertly" prepared and "deeply flavored" at this "inexpensive" Sunset pair where food is served "like the house is on fire"; "chaos rules when things get crowded", and "Mrs. Marnee" and her staff can "be a bit pushy at times", but if they "make a suggestion" on what to order, "take it."

	FOOD	DECOR	SERVICE	COST

🔢 Masa's 🗹Ⓜ *French*

27 | 24 | 27 | $114

Downtown | Hotel Vintage Ct. | 648 Bush St. (bet. Powell & Stockton Sts.) | 415-989-7154 | www.masasrestaurant.com

"Throughout its varying incarnations", this "sublime" Downtown destination "still wows" with its "marvelous", "superbly executed" New French cuisine by Gregory Short, matched with "superior" wines and served by a "top-notch" staff in a "serene jewel-box" setting; a post-Survey move to jettison its elaborate degustation menus for more recession-friendly four- and seven-course prix fixes makes the "pricey", somewhat "formal" meal a touch more accessible, but you still won't spot anyone here "wearing jeans and a baseball cap"; P.S. a three-course prix fixe is available by request.

Matterhorn Swiss Restaurant Ⓜ *Swiss*

22 | 18 | 20 | $42

Russian Hill | 2323 Van Ness Ave. (bet. Green & Vallejo Sts.) | 415-885-6116

For "ooey-gooey cheesy goodness", meat fondue "or the chocolate version", Alpine enthusiasts head to this "enjoyable" Swiss miss in Russian Hill, whose lodgelike dining room suits a "cold winter evening"; it's somewhat "expensive" and a bit "outdated", but since it keeps both adults and children "entertained", it's "worth a shot when you're in the mood for something different."

Maverick *American*

24 | 19 | 23 | $44

Mission | 3316 17th St. (bet. Mission & Valencia Sts.) | 415-863-3061 | www.sfmaverick.com

"Soulful fried chicken" that "can stand its ground with anyone's in the country" and a "small menu" of other "amazing", "memorable" American eats are sought out by Mission mavericks at this "casual but hip" "foodie gem" where the "hands-on" owners and staff "know their wine" and "make sure you're happy"; just remember that "reservations are a must" to squeeze into the "tiny" room during "prime dinnertime"; P.S. a 40-percent discount makes bottles extra "affordable" on Monday nights.

Max's *Deli*

17 | 14 | 17 | $26

Downtown | Hotel Frank | 398 Geary St. (Mason St.) | 415-646-8600
Downtown | 555 California St., concourse level (Montgomery St.) | 415-788-6297 🅱
Civic Center | Opera Plaza | 601 Van Ness Ave. (Golden Gate Ave.) | 415-771-7301
www.maxsworld.com

Homesick Easterners eager to "satisfy their yen for New York deli fare" order "monster pastrami sandwiches" and other "dependable", "easy-on-the-budget" staples at this Bay Area chain with "something for every mood and taste" on the "large" menu; waiters who perform "operatic ditties between courses" add to the "kid-friendly" vibe at some branches, though unsold surveyors call the food "average at best", adding the "big-portion shtick is getting old."

Maya 🅱 *Mexican*

20 | 19 | 17 | $38

SoMa | 303 Second St. (bet. Folsom & Harrison Sts.) | 415-543-2928 | www.mayasf.com

Putting a "new spin" on south-of-the-border bites, this "upscale" SoMa Mex can deliver either "a drink and a snack" (like "top-notch" guacamole at the "lively bar") or a "creative" meal of "gourmet" "regional" dishes with "flair"; some cite "spotty" service and feel it could use a "spruce-up", but since it's "more elegant than the usual Mission joint", most maintain it's a "pleasure" all around.

NEW Mayes Oyster House ● Seafood | ▽ 19 | 16 | 16 | $34

Polk Gulch | 1233 Polk St. (bet. Bush & Fern Sts.) | 415-885-1233 | www.mayessf.com

This "comfortable" reinvented Barbary Coast–era fish house and saloon in Polk Gulch attracts modern-day prospectors with midpriced seafood classics such as "fine", "fresh" oysters and clams on the rocks, as well as newfangled fare like kamikaze shooters and lobster ceviche; open till 2 AM Thursday–Saturday, the dark-lit, tin-ceilinged setting exudes a bordello vibe, with velvet wallpaper, myriad mirrors and a copper-topped bar where guests can nurse a vintage cocktail by the gas fireplace.

Mayflower Chinese | 19 | 11 | 12 | $29

Outer Richmond | 6255 Geary Blvd. (bet. 26th & 27th Aves.) | 415-387-8338 | www.mayflower-seafood.com

"You can easily imagine yourself in Hong Kong" at this "raucous", "reasonably priced" dim sum destination in the Outer Richmond (with outposts in Millbrae and Milpitas too); the digs are "utilitarian at best", and the variable service might be better if you "go with someone who speaks Cantonese", but for "enjoyable" dumpling lunches and "authentic" Chinese food at dinner (especially "great-value banquets"), it's "always a treat."

Maykadeh Persian | ▽ 23 | 17 | 21 | $37

North Beach | 470 Green St. (Grant Ave.) | 415-362-8286 | www.maykadehrestaurant.com

"Authentic" Persian plates, from "exotic" appetizers to "delicious" lamb, provide a "unique" "alternative to Italian" at this "elegant", moderately priced option in North Beach; with "lovely" service adding to the "warm atmosphere", plus "valet parking" (a "rare" perk in this part of town), many customers "can't wait to go back."

McCormick & Kuleto's Seafood | 20 | 23 | 20 | $46

Fisherman's Wharf | Ghirardelli Sq. | 900 N. Point St. (Larkin St.) | 415-929-1730 | www.mccormickandkuletos.com

"Spectacular vistas" over the Bay and "one of the best views of Alcatraz" around "enhance" the eats at this "busy" Fisherman's Wharf chain link, where fin fans savor "oysters galore" and pick from a "zillion choices" of "well-prepared" "fresh seafood"; it's "reliable" for "family get-togethers" and "taking out-of-town visitors", and the "professional" servers "strive to give you a special experience", but critics carp it's "a bit conventional", as well as "expensive for what it is."

Medjool Mediterranean | 19 | 19 | 15 | $36

Mission | 2522 Mission St. (bet. 21st & 22nd Sts.) | 415-550-9055 | www.medjoolsf.com

This "trendy", multilevel Missionite "rocks the casbah", serving "regional menus" of "good but pricey" Mediterranean tapas in the "party"-friendly interior, which "becomes a club after dinner", and a more "limited" selection on the "awesome" rooftop deck – the "star of the show"; still, some unimpressed guests feel it's "overhyped", grumbling "you have to remind the waitress that you're hungry" in order to be served.

Mel's Drive-In ● *Diner*

14 | 15 | 16 | $18

Civic Center | 1050 Van Ness Ave. (bet. Geary & Myrtle Sts.) | 415-292-6358
Inner Richmond | 3355 Geary Blvd. (bet. Beaumont & Parker Aves.) | 415-387-2255
Marina | 2165 Lombard St. (bet. Fillmore & Steiner Sts.) | 415-921-2867
SoMa | 801 Mission St. (4th St.) | 415-227-0793
www.melsdrive-in.com

Go "retro" at this chain of "'50s-style diners" slinging "old-fashioned" burgers, shakes and "classic American breakfasts" for "families" during the day and revelers in the wee hours who "stumble in" to "soak up the alcohol" with "late-night munchies"; despite the "terrific" jukebox and "*American Graffiti*" vibe, though, many maintain that when it comes to the gut-busting fare, "grease" is the word.

Memphis Minnie's BBQ Joint Ⓜ *BBQ*

21 | 13 | 15 | $20

Lower Haight | 576 Haight St. (bet. Fillmore & Steiner Sts.) | 415-864-7675 | www.memphisminnies.com

"Pig out on pulled pork and brisket" plus "down-home" sides you'll "wake up craving" at this low-cost "one-stop tour of American BBQ" in the Lower Haight, a "must-try" when you want to "get your smoke" on; the "down-and-dirty" self-serve "bluegrassy" digs with "paper towels on the table" resemble the "real deal", but 'cuemeisters "from the South" stress it "doesn't compare" to the "heaven" that waits in "Texas (or Memphis for that matter)."

Mescolanza *Italian*

24 | 18 | 21 | $34

Outer Richmond | 2221 Clement St. (bet. 23rd & 24th Aves.) | 415-668-2221 | www.mescolanza.net

"Superb" pastas, "little pizzas" and other "crave"-able Northern Italian eats earn accolades from Outer Richmonders who "love" this "trusted neighborhood trattoria"; it's "nothing too fancy", but the "welcoming atmosphere" and "reasonable prices" make it a "delightful place to dine"; just remember to "come early" or make a reservation, since it's "always crowded" with "regulars."

Mexico DF *Mexican*

18 | 18 | 18 | $35

Embarcadero | 139 Steuart St. (bet. Howard & Mission Sts.) | 415-808-1048 | www.mex-df.com

"Not your typical" Mex, this Embarcadero eatery has "style and sizzle", serving a "mix of modern and traditional" dishes (including "excellent" carnitas) "topped off" with "amazing" margaritas; the bartenders "know their tequila" and the "nice lounge area" is popular for "happy hour" (until 7 PM), but naysayers knock the food as "not particularly inspiring" and insist they'd rather "go to a taqueria in the Mission three times" for the price.

Midi Ⓢ *American/French*

20 | 17 | 18 | $45

Downtown | Galleria Park Hotel | 185 Sutter St. (Kearny St.) | 415-835-6400 | www.midisanfrancisco.com

At this Downtown perch that's "close enough to Union Square" yet a "tad" "away from the FiDi craziness", chef "Michelle Mah channels her talents" in a "delicious" American-French brasserie "direction"; customers count on it to "break up a day of shopping" or grab a "business lunch" and drinks with "flair" in the casual downstairs area, or hightail it upstairs for a "peaceful" dinner and a more "serene experience."

Mifune *Japanese*   17 | 11 | 13 | $20

Japantown | Japan Ctr. | 1737 Post St. (bet. Laguna & Webster Sts.) | 415-922-0337 | www.mifune.com

Ladling up oodles of "slurp-worthy" handmade noodles that are as "big, fat and fluffy as a cloud" along with other "authentic" "filling" "cheap eats" with "rapid" speed, this Japantown "favorite" can't be "beat before a movie at the Kabuki" and is "always a hit with the kids"; but more sober soba-philes slam the "nonexistent decor" and "somewhat unfriendly service", declaring it "just meh-fune."

Mijita *Mexican*   21 | 14 | 15 | $18

NEW **South Beach** | AT&T Park | 24 Willie Mays Plaza (3rd St.) | 415-644-0240

Embarcadero | Ferry Plaza Mkt. | 1 Ferry Bldg. (The Embarcadero) | 415-399-0814

www.mijitasf.com

"Insane" fish tacos and some of "the city's best carnitas" made with "authentic, sustainable" ingredients chased by a "pitcher of homemade sangria" lure Ferry Building wanderers into this "quick"-service, "upscale" Mexican taqueria by Traci Des Jardins (Jardinière); so nail a "not fancy" "oilcloth-covered table" and "enjoy" it all with a "view of San Francisco Bay"; P.S. at the larger AT&T newcomer, the comida can also be taken into the adjacent Public House.

Millennium *Vegan*   25 | 21 | 22 | $49

Downtown | Hotel California | 580 Geary St. (Jones St.) | 415-345-3900 | www.millenniumrestaurant.com

"Even the most skeptical" omnivores agree that the chef performs "culinary magic" at this "hip", "high-end vegan" "paradise" inside Downtown's Hotel California, conjuring up "intricate" "meatless wonders" and desserts that "sing"; "ok, so it's expensive", but the room is "lovely", the service "superb" and the cocktails "seductive", all adding up to an "unforgettable meal" that's worthy of a "big night out."

Miller's East Coast   19 | 8 | 14 | $19
West Delicatessen *Deli/Jewish*

Polk Gulch | 1725 Polk St. (Clay St.) | 415-563-3542 | www.millersdelisf.com

"When you're in the mood" for "fill-your-belly Jewish deli", this Polk Gulcher serves "huge" sandwiches like "good corned beef and pastrami" and matzo ball soup that can be packed up "to go" (handy "when you're really under the weather" or just want to avoid the "utilitarian" dining room); still, though it has "all the right things on the menu", purists pout it's "substandard" and note it would never "fly in Manhattan (or even Nassau County)."

Mission Beach Café *Californian*   25 | 18 | 21 | $35

Mission | 198 Guerrero St. (14th St.) | 415-861-0198 | www.missionbeachcafesf.com

Even without beach access, "breakfastphiles" are willing to "wait forever" at this "small", landlocked, '50s-inspired Mission storefront with "energetic service" for "otherworldly" midday Californian meals ("meat candy" and "mimosas", mmm) and "amazing in-house pastries"; weekend "brunch is the best", though there's no denying that the "hipster comfort food" and "those pies (especially the rabbit pot pie)" at dinnertime are also "consistently excellent."

NEW Mission Chinese Food Chinese | - | - | - | I |
(fka Misson Street Food)

Mission | Lung Shan Restaurant | 2234 Mission St. (18th St.) | 415-863-2800 | www.missionchinesefood.com

The guys behind Mission Street Food (and Commonwealth) have reworked their weekly pop-up into this everyday concept inside the Mission Chinese restaurant Lung Shan, offering a distinct slate of updated Sino small plates alongside the restaurant's (less exciting) full menu; specialties range from spicy ma po tofu to char siu pork belly, and 75 cents from each item is donated to the SF Food Bank.

Mixt Greens 🖂 Health Food/Sandwiches | 22 | 15 | 19 | $14 |

Downtown | Adam Grant Bldg. | 120 Sansome St. (bet. Bush & Pine Sts.) | 415-433-6498
Downtown | 475 Sansome St. (Commercial St.) | 415-296-9292
Downtown | JP Morgan Chase | 560 Mission St. (bet. 1st & 2nd Sts.) | 415-543-2505
www.mixtgreens.com

A "dizzying" array of "outrageously fresh" ingredients goes into the sustainable "salad of your dreams" at this contemporary Downtown trio where FiDi suits brave "painfully long" lines for a "handy", "healthy lunch"; it's a "simple" concept, but it "works" when you want a "huge" helping of "gourmet" greens that "won't leave you hungry an hour later", even if economizing herbivores balk at the "premium price"; P.S. open weekdays-only until 3 PM.

Mochica Peruvian | 23 | 17 | 20 | $37 |

SoMa | 937 Harrison St. (bet. 5th & 6th Sts.) | 415-278-0480 | www.mochicasf.com

"Impressive", moderately priced Peruvian plates, including "ceviche from the gods", lure Lima lovers to this "small", rustic "sleeper" with a "hip" atmosphere; the "enthusiasm of the staff" adds to the "rewarding" experience of sharing the dishes with a date or among friends, making it "worth the trip" to an "uninviting" stretch of SoMa.

Moishe's Pippic 🖂⊄ Deli/Jewish | 18 | 8 | 18 | $14 |

Hayes Valley | 425A Hayes St. (Gough St.) | 415-431-2440

"Perfectly satisfies a pastrami deficiency" declare devotees who also descend on this Hayes Valley "oasis of old-school" noshes for "Chicago dogs" with "authentic" Windy City "fixin's", "thick" "brisket sandwiches on Fridays" ("don't miss it") and other "Jewish-style" deli-cacies; "it's not Langer's" and critics kvetch their bubbe's "kitchen had more atmosphere", but it's probably "as good as it gets in SF"; P.S. closes at 4 PM.

Moki's Sushi & Pacific Grill Japanese | ▽ 19 | 15 | 15 | $34 |

Bernal Heights | 615 Cortland Ave. (bet. Anderson & Moultrie Sts.) | 415-970-9336

"Surfer dudes" and families alike drop anchor at this "kid-friendly" sushi and grill "favorite" in landlocked Bernal Heights, diving into "abso-

FOOD | DECOR | SERVICE | COST

lutely fresh fish" and other "tasty morsels" that aren't exactly "authentic Japanese, but different" in a South Pacific–inspired way ("macadamia nuts in my roll? yes, please!"); down it all with an "excellent selection of cold sakes" – it's "more satisfying than you think it's going to be."

MoMo's *American*

17 | 19 | 17 | $39

South Beach | 760 Second St. (King St.) | 415-227-8660 | www.sfmomos.com

Fine "for a business lunch" most days, this "friendly" South Beacher "across from the ballpark" "attracts an entirely different crowd" "before and after Giants games", when the "patio is full of testosterone" as fans "meet for a bottle of beer" (or more); some say it scores with "basic" but "well-prepared" New American fare and an owner who makes you "feel part of the team", but others mutter "it's more of a party place" than a destination for "discriminating" diners.

Monk's Kettle ● *Californian*

20 | 17 | 18 | $28

Mission | 3141 16th St. (Albion St.) | 415-865-9523 | www.monkskettle.com

"Where else can you get a tallboy of New Zealand lager made with champagne yeast?" demand brewhounds who seek advice from "knowledgeable" bartenders on the "world-class" suds available at this "hip" Mission gastropub with an "Old English" feel; though the "beer is clearly king", many find the Californian "bar food" "surprisingly inventive" and "designed to pair well", and most suggest "come early" because even on "weeknights" it's "always crowded."

NEW Morph *Thai*

- | - | - | M

Outer Richmond | 5344 Geary Blvd. (bet. 17th & 18th Aves.) | 415-742-5093 | www.morphlife.com

Standard Thai fare and more exciting, seasonally changing Asian fusion plates meet on the midpriced menu at this new boîte in the Outer Richmond; the space is decked out with molded white chairs, LED blue lights and postmodern fixtures, setting a clubby mood.

Morton's The Steakhouse *Steak*

24 | 21 | 23 | $71

Downtown | 400 Post St. (bet. Mason & Powell Sts.) | 415-986-5830 | www.mortons.com

A steakhouse "standard-bearer", this "big-ticket" chain (with Downtown and San Jose locales) offers "excellently prepared" cuts of beef and "grand sides" "served professionally" amid an "ambiance of wealth and class"; some find it a bit "staid" and wish they'd "lose the raw-meat presentation" and "high" wine pricing, but the many who love its "traditional" ways consider it "one of the best."

Moss Room *Californian*

20 | 24 | 19 | $50

Inner Richmond | California Academy of Sciences | 55 Music Concourse Dr. (bet. Fulton St. & Lincoln Way) | 415-876-6121 | www.themossroom.com

An "unexpectedly elegant" (and "expensive") "escape from the jungles upstairs", this "exotic" eatery in the "basement of the Academy" offers an "enchanting" setting to "watch the fish tanks" and "living wall" while breaking over "well-executed", sustainable Cal cuisine and cocktails; green-thumb types note "they'll have to rename it the 'Fern Room', as the moss hasn't survived", and wonder whether the "unpolished" service will also "get better"; P.S. a post-Survey chef and menu change isn't reflected in the Food score.

	FOOD	DECOR	SERVICE	COST

Muracci's Japanese
Curry & Grill ⓢ *Japanese*

▽ 22 | 7 | 13 | $12

Downtown | 307 Kearny St. (Bush St.) | 415-773-1101 |
www.muraccis.com

The "amazingly soothing-to-the-soul", "authentic Japanese curry"
is "cooked over two days" until it attains a "delicious flavor" declare
Downtown diners who pour it over "perfectly fried katsu" at this
tiny, weekday-only "take-out" joint (open till 5 or 6 PM); most everything (including teriyaki and sushi) is "made-to-order", while
extra "touches" like "homemade pickles" and Eastern "bottle
drinks" help keep it "well worth the wait"; P.S. the new Los Altos
branch offers full-service dining.

My Tofu House *Korean*

20 | 8 | 14 | $18

Inner Richmond | 4627 Geary Blvd. (bet. 10th & 11th Aves.) | 415-750-1818
On a "cold, foggy day", Korean connoisseurs like to "cuddle up" with a
"spicy, bubbling bowl of tofu soup", bulgogi that's "beefy perfection"
and Seoul-ful BBQ at this "true cultural experience" in the Inner
Richmond; some of the "fiery" fare is "not for everyone", and neither
are the "spartan surroundings", but most agree the "bang for your
buck" is hard to beat.

Naan 'n Curry *Indian/Pakistani*

17 | 7 | 10 | $15

Downtown | 336 O'Farrell St. (bet. Mason & Taylor Sts.) | 415-346-1443 ●
Inner Sunset | 642 Irving St. (bet. 7th & 8th Aves.) | 415-664-7225
North Beach | 533 Jackson St. (Columbus Ave.) | 415-693-0499
Polk Gulch | 690 Van Ness Ave. (Turk St.) | 415-775-1349
www.naancurry.com

For a "quick, currylicious" meal of "Mumbai street food", fans get their
"fix" at this "bare-bones", "cafeteria-style" Indian-Pakistani chain in
SF and Berkeley; the "aloof" staff and "dubious", "depressing" digs can
be deterrents, though, and some sigh "sure, it's cheap, but not cheap
enough" considering the food is merely "serviceable."

🆕 Naked Lunch ⓢⓂ⌷ *Sandwiches*

▽ 26 | 10 | 20 | $18

North Beach | 504 Broadway (Kearny St.) | 415-577-4951 |
www.nakedlunchsf.com

Fans get their "foie gras fix" between bread at this "sensational" North
Beach lunch-only take-out stand whose name tips its hat to William S.
Burroughs and whose "decadent five-star" sandwiches (plus soups,
artisan ice cream and fresh-fruit libations) are slung by a former Cafe
Majestic chef; crusty types "only wish" its "extremely small", spendy
"creations" came in a "Super-Size-Me option", but at least you can
chow down at Enrico's "patio next door."

Namu *Californian/Korean*

23 | 16 | 20 | $36

Embarcadero | Ferry Plaza Mkt. | 1 Ferry Bldg. (The Embarcadero) |
415-386-8332 Ⓜ⌷
Inner Richmond | 439 Balboa St. (6th Ave.) | 415-386-8332
www.namusf.com

"Young in vibe and energy", this "hip", late-night Inner Richmond
"sleeper" is definitely "not your father's Korean", purveying "refreshing",
"unique" Cal-influenced creations (plus limited-run ramen), accompanied by "cool drinks"; if you can't deal with the "impossible parking", stop by its Ferry Building street-food stand at the farmer's market

on Thursday and Saturday mornings to savor "genius" "seaweed-wrapped" kalbi tacos.

Nettie's Crab Shack *Seafood* | 18 | 17 | 17 | $39 |

Cow Hollow | 2032 Union St. (bet. Buchanan & Webster Sts.) | 415-409-0300 | www.nettiescrabshack.com

"Try the lobster roll", the "good clam chowder" or the "special crab feasts in season" at this "lively" taste of "Maine" in Cow Hollow; Yankees yearning for home are high on its "casual" "East Coast" looks, but others get "crabby" about "disappointing" service and feel the quality "falls short for the high prices."

Nick's Crispy Tacos ⊘ *Mexican* | 21 | 10 | 13 | $14 |

Russian Hill | 1500 Broadway (Polk St.) | 415-409-8226

Operating during off-hours in the "tacky" Rouge nightclub, this incongruous Russian Hill Mex boasting "alarmingly" scarlet "velvet booths" and "garish chandeliers" "fills with yuppies" "craving a Corona" and a "sublime crispy" fish taco done "Nick's-style (is there any other way?)"; it's *muy bueno* before an evening "on the town" or for "eating on the cheap", especially on "insane" $2 Taco Tuesdays.

Nihon 🍴Ⓜ *Japanese* | ▽ 21 | 21 | 16 | $47 |

Mission | 1779 Folsom St. (14th St.) | 415-552-4400 | www.nihon-sf.com

"High-end sushi", an "out-of-this-world" single-malt selection and "wonderfully inventive cocktails" go together "perfectly" at this "cool" two-floor izakaya in the Mission that's "free from the sake-bombing clientele" found elsewhere; the Japanese small plates – "priced like you were in downtown Tokyo" and served till late on the weekends – are "delicious" but "not as stunning" as the booze, so "get a designated driver" and indulge – just "don't expect to be heard" over the "loud music" and "happy-hour" crowds.

Nob Hill Café *Italian* | 21 | 16 | 20 | $34 |

Nob Hill | 1152 Taylor St. (bet. Clay & Pleasant Sts.) | 415-776-6500 | www.nobhillcafe.com

Nob Hill habitués head to this "cute", "comfortable neighborhood place" for "hearty" Northern Italian "classics" that are "light on the pocketbook" and served "without pretense" by an "obliging" staff; though the "tables are small and close together", most diners don't mind the "intimate" environs, and sidewalk seating is an "added bonus" – just "be prepared for a wait at dinner" because "no reservations" are accepted.

🆕 Nombe *Japanese* | ▽ 22 | 12 | 18 | $35 |

Mission | 2491 Mission St. (21st St.) | 415-681-7150 | www.nombesf.com

"The chicken skin is everything people say" crow hipsters who dig into the "brilliant", "low-cost", decidedly "different Japanese street food" presented "tapas-style" and accompanied by a "huge sake selection" at this "up-and-coming" Mission izakaya; the two-room "converted '50s-style diner" features a U-shaped bar serving snacks like yakisoba and a late-night window peddling takeout on weekends, staffed by a "super-nice" but still "inexperienced" crew; P.S. open till 2 AM on the weekends.

	FOOD	DECOR	SERVICE	COST

☑ Nopa ◐ *Californian* — 25 | 21 | 22 | $46

Western Addition | 560 Divisadero St. (Hayes St.) | 415-864-8643 |
www.nopasf.com

Denizens of this "late-night" "darling of the foodies" in "the once-unfashionable" Western Addition "sit upstairs and watch the show" or "downstairs in the thick of it" with the "hipster masses" getting "stoked on" "inventive" spirits at the "hopping bar" and "fantastic" "as-California-as-you-get" "farm-fresh" fare for "down-to-earth prices"; despite the "mind-numbing noise", "forever waits" and the reality that "nopa is short for no parking", everyone, including "the waiters, still manages a smile."

Nopalito *Mexican* — 23 | 17 | 20 | $28

Western Addition | Falletti's Plaza | 306 Broderick St. (Oak St.) |
415-437-0303 | www.nopalitosf.com

Perhaps "the best thing since flour tortillas", "nopa's little offspring" in an "inconspicuous" Western Addition "strip mall" "rethinks what Mexican food is", cranking out "mind-blowing" cocina ("porkgasmic carnitas" and "popsicles just like summers in Mexico") and, of late, "margaritas!"; it's "a little expensive for a taqueria", but "you're paying for the sustainability", "efficient service" and "cute atmosphere" (including a "covered patio"), plus the "phone-in waitlist" and free "parking to boot" are "serious bonuses."

North Beach Pizza *Pizza* — 19 | 11 | 16 | $19

Excelsior | 4787 Mission St. (bet. Persia & Russia Aves.) | 415-586-1400
Haight-Ashbury | 800 Stanyan St. (Haight St.) | 415-751-2300
North Beach | 1462 Grant Ave. (Union St.) | 415-433-2444 ◐
Outer Sunset | 3054 Taraval St. (41st Ave.) | 415-242-9100
www.northbeachpizza.net

Hungry patrons "wolf down" pizzas with a "nice thick crust" piled with "lots of gooey cheese" at this long-running North Beach pie parlor with Bay-wide branches; it's "straightforward", "reliable" and provides "lots of food for low prices", but saucy surveyors sniff it's a "step above the Easy-Bake oven" and is "living on past glory."

North Beach Restaurant ◐ *Italian* — 23 | 20 | 22 | $47

North Beach | 1512 Stockton St. (bet. Green & Union Sts.) | 415-392-1700 |
www.northbeachrestaurant.com

A staple for both "local politicos" and Italophiles with "out-of-town guests", this "proud" North Beach "institution" "hits the spot" with its "wonderful", "old-style" Tuscan cuisine; the "impeccably dressed" staff contributes to the "clubby feel", and if it's "a bit expensive", aficionados agree the "one-of-a-kind" wine list and "white-tablecloth" ambiance help it set the "gold standard" for the neighborhood.

Old Jerusalem *Mediterannean/Mideastern* — ▽ 19 | 9 | 17 | $16

Mission | 2976 Mission St. (bet. 25th & 26th Sts.) | 415-642-5958 |
www.oldjerusalemsf.com

"Big portions" of "real homestyle" Middle Eastern favorites like "Israeli hummus", falafel and "tasty" chicken shawarma are more than a Mission mirage for fans who flock to this "caravan-tent of a place" for "authentic" eats; while the decor "isn't too spectacular", the grub is "cheap" and "kindly" served with the "essential" starters; P.S. no alcohol.

	FOOD	DECOR	SERVICE	COST

One Market ⍓ *American* → 23 | 22 | 22 | $58

Embarcadero | 1 Market St. (bet. Spear & Steuart Sts.) | 415-777-5577 | www.onemarket.com

While this "sophisticated" New American on the Embarcadero "impresses" as a "power lunch spot", "it's so much more" aver admirers who say the "sumptuous" "seasonal menu" uses "lots of fresh produce" in "novel ways"; the "cavernous" dining room is a "pleasure" for enjoying the city "at its hustley-bustley best", and though critics quibble it "can feel a bit corporate", the "beautiful" "view of the Bay Bridge" is a boon, and the "chef's table" offers a more "personal" experience.

Oola Restaurant & Bar ● *Californian* → 21 | 18 | 17 | $48

SoMa | 860 Folsom St. (bet. 4th & 5th Sts.) | 415-995-2061 | www.oola-sf.com

"Tops for late-night" bites, this "small" SoMa "hot spot" serves a "creative" menu of "nouveau" Californian cuisine, including "meaty" dishes like "must-have" babyback ribs; the "bar-style setting" has "just enough flash", but a few fret about the "attitude of the staff" and wonder why "all the fuss."

Oriental Pearl *Chinese* → 21 | 14 | 18 | $30

Chinatown | 778 Clay St. (Walter U. Lum Pl.) | 415-433-1817 | www.orientalpearlsf.com

Attracting both "tourists and locals", this Chinese "pearl is a gem", serving "fish fresh from the tank", "excellent Peking duck" and a "bargain" dim sum lunch; the two-story Chinatown digs are "pleasant" for "sharing among a group", while "attentive" servers help steer avid eaters toward "the most adventurous plates."

Orson Ⓜ *Californian* → 19 | 21 | 18 | $46

SoMa | 508 Fourth St. (Bryant St.) | 415-777-1508 | www.orsonsf.com

"Celebrity chef" Elizabeth Falkner's SoMa "factory space" "showing old films behind the huge, horseshoe-shaped bar" is both "edgy" and "glamorous" – "kinda like" her "platinum, spiky hair" – and a fitting setting for her "inventive take-it-or-leave-it, love-it-or-hate-it" Californian creations ("pop rocks as an ingredient") and less-experimental pizzas and burgers; a few put off by the "foam, floss and fluff" simply "go for the drinks" and "tasty" desserts by cousin Citizen Cake (reopening soon at 2125 Fillmore Street).

Osha Thai *Thai* → 20 | 19 | 17 | $27

Cow Hollow | 2033 Union St. (Webster St.) | 415-567-6742 ●
Downtown | 4 Embarcadero Ctr. (Drumm St.) | 415-788-6742
Glen Park | 2922 Diamond St. (Bosworth St.) | 415-586-6742
Mission | 819 Valencia St. (bet. 19th & 20th Sts.) | 415-826-7738 ●
SoMa | 149 Second St. (bet. Howard & Mission Sts.) | 415-278-9991
NEW SoMa | 311 Third St. (bet. Folsom & Harrison Sts.) | 415-896-6742
Tenderloin | 696 Geary St. (Leavenworth St.) | 415-673-2368 ●
www.oshathai.com

"Tasty Thai with a modern flair" is "consistent across the locations" of this increasingly "ubiquitous" mini-chain whose "high-quality", "moderately priced" staples and more unusual "destination dishes" (like "volcanic beef") are "fresh, spiced to order" and served "fast"; though the volume can be "off the charts", the "attractive" surroundings keep the "cool kids" (and "white-collar workers") "coming back for more."

	FOOD	DECOR	SERVICE	COST

Ottimista Enoteca-Café M *Italian/Mediterranean*
| 17 | 18 | 17 | $31 |

Cow Hollow | 1838 Union St. (Octavia St.) | 415-674-8400 | www.ottimistasf.com

Lasses who "love" "grabbing drinks with their girlfriends" and the "recently graduated frat boys" who follow them "drool over the long list" of "hard-to-find" bottles at this Cow Hollow enoteca; while the Italian-Med small plates ranging from "tasty" to "average" aren't the main attraction, it's still a popular "meeting" place, so come early if you want to "snag a table" on the heated patio, and "expect a crowd" for brunch.

Outerlands M *American*
| ▽ 23 | 19 | 19 | $21 |

Outer Sunset | 4001 Judah St. (45th Ave.) | 415-661-6140 | www.outerlandssf.com

"It may be out of the way" (in the Outer Sunset), but the grilled cheese is "out-of-this-world" at this largely organic New American specializing in "top-notch" soups and "filling" sandwiches on "thick" "housemade bread"; the atmosphere is "relaxed", there are "lots of fun beers" and it's inexpensive to boot, making it just right for a bite "near the beach."

Out the Door *Vietnamese*
| 22 | 16 | 18 | $28 |

Downtown | Westfield San Francisco Ctr. | 845 Market St. (bet. 4th & 5th Sts.) | 415-541-9913
Embarcadero | Ferry Plaza Mkt. | 1 Ferry Bldg. (The Embarcadero) | 415-321-3740
NEW Upper Fillmore | 2232 Bush St. (Fillmore St.) | 415-923-9575
www.outthedoors.com

You go "in the door hungry" and "out the door happy" at these three "sisters to the hugely popular Slanted Door", offering "delicate, flavorful" Vietnamese food with "high-quality ingredients"; the Ferry Building branch does "takeout" only, but you can eat in at Downtown's Westfield Centre ("hidden away from the food-court chaos") and the "stylish", "spare" Upper Fillmore branch; a handful huff about the "hefty bill", but most maintain you "get what you pay for", and "without sweating the reservation gauntlet" at the original.

Oyaji M *Japanese*
| 23 | 17 | 20 | $40 |

Outer Richmond | 3123 Clement St. (bet. 32nd & 33rd Aves.) | 415-379-3604

Savants say "put your trust in the sushi chef" and "tell him to stop when you've had enough" of the "super-fresh" fish, "amazing" grilled goods and "authentic" izakaya plates ("served tapas-style") at this Outer Richmond Japanese; with a "large" sake selection and "sassy, hospitable" service, it suits fin fans who are in a "festive sharing mood" and ready for a "party atmosphere."

Ozumo *Japanese*
| 23 | 24 | 20 | $55 |

Embarcadero | 161 Steuart St. (bet. Howard & Mission Sts.) | 415-882-1333 | www.ozumo.com

The "über-cool decor" "doesn't detract from the innovative fare" at this "Tokyo-chic" twosome along the Embarcadero and in Oakland, presenting "decadent sushi" as well as other "surprising", "intoxicating" cooked items with an "East/West" twist; it's "hip" for "cutting a business deal" or meeting "beautiful people" over sake in the "lively" bar, but the service varies and the "super-snazzy" setting "comes at a premium price", so some prefer to put it on the "company credit card."

Pacific Café *Seafood* | 23 | 16 | 22 | $34 |

Outer Richmond | 7000 Geary Blvd. (34th Ave.) | 415-387-7091
"Exquisitely fresh" seafood, "plainly prepared" and "perfectly cooked", is the calling card of this "comfortable" "neighborhood darling" in the Outer Richmond; "little has changed in over 30 years", from the "funky '70s decor" to the "reasonable" price to servers who "treat you right", and though the "no-reservations" policy often results in "long lines", the "free glass of wine while you wait" is a "nice touch."

Pacific Catch *Seafood* | 19 | 14 | 18 | $25 |

Inner Sunset | 1200 Ninth Ave. (Lincoln Way) | 415-504-6905
Marina | 2027 Chestnut St. (bet. Fillmore & Steiner Sts.) | 415-440-1950
www.pacificcatch.com
"Seafood lovers" get serious "cravings" for the fin fare with Pacific Rim "flair" – from "excellent" fish tacos to "healthy" rice bowls – presented by "aim-to-please" servers at this "casual" mini-chain; but be warned, while the Sunset and Marin branches are roomy, the "tiny" Marina outpost can get "crowded", so "bring a shoe horn" or better yet, "get it to go."

Pagan Ⓜ *Burmese* | 18 | 14 | 16 | $20 |

Inner Richmond | 731 Clement St. (bet. 8th & 9th Aves.) | 415-221-3888
Outer Richmond | 3199 Clement St. (33rd Ave.) | 415-751-2598
www.pagansf.com
Dishing up "flavorful", "filling" Burmese food (as well as a limited Thai menu) this Richmond duo offers a "cheaper, easier-to-get-into" "alternative" to its more established competitors; the settings are "no-frills", and a number of critics find the cooking merely "average", but service is "prompt" and the Inner Richmond branch has a lunch buffet.

Pagolac Ⓜ⇄ *Vietnamese* ∇ | 21 | 10 | 16 | $26 |

Tenderloin | 655 Larkin St. (bet. Ellis & Willow Sts.) | 415-776-3234
"A step up" from the norm in "Little Saigon", this "tiny" "hole-in-the-wall" is "well worth a trip to the Tenderloin", since it's "tough to beat" for the "quality and authenticity" of its slightly "more expensive" Vietnamese vittles; though you can "order à la carte", "the thing to get" is the signature "seven courses of beef", a "group"-friendly, "interactive" affair that includes some dishes you assemble yourself.

Pakwan *Pakistani* | 21 | 7 | 11 | $15 |

Mission | 3180-3182 16th St. (bet. Guerrero & Valencia Sts.) | 415-255-2440 ⇄
Tenderloin | 501 O'Farrell St. (Jones St.) | 415-776-0160
www.pakwanrestaurant.com
The "fragrance of searing spices" whets appetites for the "rich, spicy" curries and "wonderful" biryani dishes, among other "intensely flavored" eats, served at these Pakistani counters; while there's "no atmosphere" (save for some "desi tunes"), money saved on the "bargain" menu means wallet-watchers can "buy a beer" to bring along and dig in.

Palio d'Asti Ⓩ *Italian* | 20 | 19 | 22 | $46 |

Downtown | 640 Sacramento St. (bet. Kearny & Montgomery Sts.) | 415-395-9800 | www.paliodasti.com
A magnet more for "business dining than fine dining", this Downtown modern Italian stallion specializing in "refined" regional dishes stays

in the running thanks to "old-time professional" staffers who work the "crowds" during lunch and "after-work gatherings" ("no wonder Alitalia always entertained clients here"); bargain-hunters race in for the "excellent happy hour" ("full-size pizza" free with two drinks), while foodies luxuriate "during truffle season."

Pancho Villa Taqueria ● *Mexican* — 22 | 9 | 15 | $13

Mission | 3071 16th St. (bet. Mission & Valencia Sts.) | 415-864-8840 | www.panchovillasf.com

"Terrific" tacos and "fat, delicious" burritos are "made to order right in front of you" at these "cheap" Mexican mates in the Mission and San Mateo; the "line can be long", but the "friendly" staff in the "assembly-line operation" "efficiently delivers" a "high volume" of south-of-the-border bites, and if they're not exactly "places to linger", the "buzzy" SF location still has "lots of local color."

Pane e Vino *Italian* — 22 | 18 | 21 | $41

Cow Hollow | 1715 Union St. (Gough St.) | 415-346-2111 | www.paneevinotrattoria.com

"Excellent" Northern Italian eats "impress" guests at this "high performer" in Cow Hollow that complements its "classic" cuisine with "inexpensive house wines"; a "favorite neighborhood destination", it's "wonderful for kids" and "group dining", so while some critics cite "suburban" looks and "predictable" cooking, many are won over by the "lively" atmosphere with "lots of personality."

Papalote Mexican Grill *Mexican* — 22 | 11 | 14 | $13

Mission | 3409 24th St. (Valencia St.) | 415-970-8815
Western Addition | 1777 Fulton St. (Masonic Ave.) | 415-776-0106
www.papalote-sf.com

Forget the "arguments about authenticity" and "just order the damned fish tacos" and "better-than-sex" salsa at these "colorful" Mexican "taquerias with imagination" in the Mission and Western Addition, where "fresh ingredients", "grilled-to-order meats" and "veggie and soyrizo" options provide a boffo "burrito experience"; "be prepared to wait forever" (or "phone" ahead) and pay for "extras", but remember, there's a "reason they beat Bobby Flay in a throwdown."

NEW Parada 22 ⊄ *Puerto Rican* — - | - | - | M

Haight-Ashbury | 1805 Haight St. (Shrader St.) | 415-750-1111

The sights, sounds and smells of San Juan fill the air at this casual Haight-Ashbury newcomer showcasing traditional Puerto Rican cooking upgraded with sustainable meats and produce; order at the counter, grab a real Coke (the sugary kind from Mexico) or a Corona and then nab a seat at one of the picnic tables in the colorful storefront, tricked out with vintage signs and a big photo of bomba dancers.

Park Chalet Garden Restaurant *Californian* — 14 | 19 | 15 | $28

Outer Sunset | 1000 Great Hwy. (bet. Fulton St. & Lincoln Way) | 415-386-8439 | www.beachchalet.com

"The setting's the thing" at this "bright, airy space" in the Outer Sunset, since "big, beautiful windows" look out "onto Golden Gate Park" and, "on sunny days", "the whole 'hood is out on the lawn" with their "dogs and kids"; "all kinds of house-brewed beer" and frequent "live music" add to the "blissful" atmosphere, but gourmets grouse the "over-

"priced" New American–Cal eats are "average" at best, and more than a few suspect "the staff just doesn't care."

Pasta Pomodoro *Italian*   17 | 13 | 18 | $23

Laurel Heights | 3611 California St. (Spruce St.) | 415-831-0900
Noe Valley | 4000 24th St. (Noe St.) | 415-920-9904
www.pastapomodoro.com

"You get a lot of bang for your buck" at these "casual" Italians where "reliable" pastas and "carafes of wine" add up to an "unpretentious but satisfying" meal; no, "it's not Firenze", but they do a "remarkable job for a chain", and if crabby critics are put off by the early evening *"Romper Room"* set, parents praise the "kid-friendly" servers who "always leave you with a smile."

Patxi's Chicago Pizza *Pizza*   22 | 14 | 17 | $22

NEW Cow Hollow | 3318 Fillmore St. (Lombard St.) | 415-345-3995
Hayes Valley | 511 Hayes St. (bet. Laguna & Octavia Sts.) |
415-558-9991
www.patxispizza.com

"No need to go to Chi-town" for a "taste of the Windy City" – just "dig into" this outfit's "seriously delicious" "deep-dish" "Chicago-style pizza" that's "well-endowed" enough to sate "a grown man"; the "crunchy, cornmealed" dough makes "converts" out of "thin-crust lovers" – not a "light snack", especially with "$2 PBRs" and "generous salads"; "call ahead" or opt for "par-baked" or delivery to avoid "long waits"; P.S. a Noe Valley branch is slated to open in fall 2010.

Pauline's Pizza 🗷 Ⓜ *Pizza*   22 | 13 | 16 | $26

Mission | 260 Valencia St. (bet. Duboce Ave. & 14th St.) | 415-552-2050
Pauline's Wines 🗷 Ⓜ *Pizza*
NEW Mission | 260 Valencia St. (bet. Duboce Ave. & 14th St.)
www.paulinespizza.com

The first and "one of the best 'pizza-moderne' places", this "treasure" hawking thin cornmeal-crust pies and "wonderful salads", both "topped with organic produce" "straight from its own farm", is the "type" of joint "you'd only find in San Francisco"; "parking is a hassle" and the "homey" digs draw "long lines" of an "unmistakably Mission clientele", but all is ameliorated with a "bottle of the house red", also available at its new late-night wine bar out back.

Paul K Ⓜ *Mediterranean*   22 | 18 | 21 | $45

Hayes Valley | 199 Gough St. (Oak St.) | 415-552-7132 |
www.paulkrestaurant.com

"Unique, modern Mediterranean food" paired with "excellent wines by the glass" makes this "cozy" Hayes Valley haunt "worth the extra couple of blocks walk" to Davies or the Opera House; "the menu doesn't change much" and "it's a little cramped" and "noisy", but it's an "interesting option for pre-performance" or a "bottomless mimosa brunch", with a staff that "moves you out with plenty of time" but "makes the menu come alive with over-the-top descriptions."

Pazzia 🗷 *Italian*   24 | 14 | 21 | $33

SoMa | 337 Third St. (bet. Folsom & Harrison Sts.) | 415-512-1693
"You'll feel like you're in Firenze" by the Uffizi rather than "near the SFMOMA" at this "casual" trattoria turning out "killer thin-crust

pizza" that "definitely earns the extra z in the name" and other "delicious" Tuscan meals "without all the glitz and glam"; the storefront is "too cramped for comfort, but worth the squeeze" thanks to the "super-accommodating" owner and his "cute" "accented" servers, who "contribute" to the "authentic atmosphere."

☑ Perbacco ☒ *Italian* 25 | 22 | 23 | $54

Downtown | 230 California St. (bet. Battery & Front Sts.) | 415-955-0663 | www.perbaccosf.com

Still the "Downtown favorite" ("second only to new spin-off Barbacco "next door") for "power lunches galore", "after-work drinks" or a "night out", this "energetic", expensive "hot spot" draws torrents of "FiDi foodies" who fall for the "handmade pastas", salumi and other "first-rate" Piedmontese specialties; "chic" decor, "professional" service and a "superlative Italian wine list" seal the deal, "but mamma mia, it's noisy", so gray hairs tend to "head upstairs to escape the din" while "gray suits" party on at the bar.

Pesce *Italian/Seafood* 22 | 16 | 20 | $41

Russian Hill | 2227 Polk St. (bet. Green & Vallejo Sts.) | 415-928-8025 | www.pescesf.com

Habitués are happy to swim with the fishes at this "cozy" Italian seafood "gem" "high up on Russian Hill", where chef Ruggero Gadaldi (Beretta, Antica Trattoria, Delarosa) turns out "top-notch", "innovative Venetian cicchetti" and "pasta small plates" so "delicious" "you'll hardly notice" the "cramped" digs; whether you're out on a "date", doing "dinner with the girls" or enjoying the "lively" bar "scene", "just mangia" and enjoy the "tasty" tidbits.

NEW Pi Bar ◑ *Pizza* ▽ 14 | 14 | 14 | $25

Mission | 1432 Valencia St. (25th St.) | 415-970-9670 | www.pibarsf.com

"Thin-crust pies" and quippy pi references such as $3.14 slices abound at this late-night Mission pizzeria where the "not-cheap" namesake dish attracts a "mix of hipsters, families and just about everyone else", though many dub it "just ok"; suds-drinkers insist the "selection and knowledge of beer" is "where it really shines", which explains why the long wood bar gets overrun (and the "pleasant staff gets overworked") during happy hour.

NEW Pica Pica Maize Kitchen *Venezuelan* ▽ 23 | 11 | 15 | $15

Mission | 401 Valencia St. (15th St.) | 415-400-5453 | www.picapicakitchen.com

"Venezuela comes to Napa" thanks to this Oxbow Market counter (with a ceviche bar) and its new Mission satellite (offering Latin-style beer, sangria and virgin fruit shakes); the "options are many" – "pancake-like arepas" to "satisfy any palate", "maizewiches" and "killer yucca fries" – all "tasty", "inexpensive" wheat- and "gluten-free" "alternatives to fast-food restaurants.

Piccino ☒ *Californian/Italian* ▽ 21 | 13 | 18 | $27

Dogpatch | 801 22nd St. (Tennessee St.) | 415-824-4224 | www.piccinocafe.com

A "bite-sized" space in "up-and-coming" Dogpatch, this "industrial-hip" Cal-Italian cafe turns out "very thin-crust pizzas", "inventive" salads and "divine daily specials", all "based on the freshest local ingredients"; "on a sunny day" the sidewalk tables are "perfect for an alfresco brunch", and while they usually demand a "wait", fortunately "totally addictive" Blue Bottle brew can be found at Piccino's coffee bar a few doors down.

Piperade ⊠ *Spanish*

25 | 21 | 23 | $52

Downtown | 1015 Battery St. (bet. Green & Union Sts.) | 415-391-2555 | www.piperade.com

"Basque in the glory" of Gerald Hirigoyen's rustic, "brick"-walled "hideaway" Downtown, where the "ubiquitous" chef ("a real pip!") "greets" guests "like family" as they "arrive" before laying out an "amazing breadth of choices from every corner of the land and sea" (including the "delicious" "namesake" stew), complemented by "hard-to-find wines of both France and Spain"; "there's harmony in all the nuanced flavors" – the "only problem is limiting choices so you don't waddle home."

Piqueo's *Peruvian*

▽ 24 | 17 | 18 | $38

Bernal Heights | 830 Cortland Ave. (Gates St.) | 415-282-8812 | www.piqueos.com

"Simply delightful", "creative" Peruvian small plates go swimmingly with sangria that "rocks" at this "friendly" "neighborhood gem" in Bernal Heights; some dub the digs "dark and romantic" and "love" watching the open kitchen, but less forgiving guests cite a "crammed" space ("be prepared to sit in your neighbor's lap") with "spotty" service and "wish the prices were a little lower."

Pizza Nostra *Pizza*

▽ 22 | 13 | 20 | $27

Potrero Hill | 300 De Haro St. (16th St.) | 415-558-9493 | www.pizzanostrasf.com

"Savory Neapolitan pizzas" with a "crackly" crust, "delicious" salads and "decadent" desserts are "served up with a minimum of fuss" at this moderately priced, "welcome addition to the Potrero Hill foodie scene"; the "good wine selection" is a plus, and while a few fret it's "a bit sterile" inside, the outdoor seating is "wonderful" on a "sunny day"; P.S. a post-Survey ownership change is not reflected in the ratings.

Pizza Place on Noriega *Pizza*

- | - | - | I

Outer Sunset | 3901 Noriega Ave. (46th Ave.) | 415-759-5752 | www.pizzaplacesf.com

"Order a 'pie' not a 'pizza'" to avoid sounding like "the uninitiated" at this "friendly", under-the-radar, bare-bones "East Coast–style" joint a few blocks from the Pacific Ocean in the Outer Sunset; some forgo the dough entirely, opting instead for the "delicious salads, baked cauliflower" and spaghetti 'n' meatballs, washed down with a brew – and "never" walk away "disappointed."

Pizzeria Delfina *Pizza*

25 | 16 | 19 | $27

Mission | 3611 18th St. (Guerrero St.) | 415-437-6800
Pacific Heights | 2406 California St. (bet. Fillmore & Steiner Sts.) | 415-440-1189
www.pizzeriadelfina.com

The "deftly crafted", "thin-crust" pies are "perfection topped with prosciutto", complemented by "must-try" apps, at this "affably" staffed Mission and Pac Heights pair from "the folks who brought you Delfina";

it's "a little pricey for pizza" and can get "crazy hectic" with hungry "young" "hipsters", but those willing to wait (or those who "skip the line and do takeout") find it "hard not to order everything on the menu."

ⓩ Pizzetta 211 ⊄ *Pizza*

27 | 14 | 16 | $28

Outer Richmond | 211 23rd Ave. (California St.) | 415-379-9880 | www.pizzetta211.com

"Right up there with the best of the best", this Outer Richmond pizzeria purveys "lusty", "artistic" pies with "organic, fresh" toppings (including "over-easy eggs") that lead legions to endure a "long, chilly wait" to "squeeze into" the "peanut-size" parlor; it's all "served up with attitude, gratis", but that's "part of the charm" chirp sunny-side surveyors, who know to "bring cash" and "get there early" to avoid hearing those dreaded words: "we're out of dough."

Plant Cafe Organic, The *Health Food*

20 | 19 | 17 | $27

NEW **Downtown** | 101 California St. (Front St.) | 415-693-9730 ⓢ
Embarcadero | Pier 3 (bet. B'way & Washington St.) | 415-984-1973
Marina | 3352 Steiner St. (bet. Chestnut & Lombard Sts.) | 415-931-2777
www.theplantcafe.com

"Eating healthy never tasted so good" enthuse fans of this "affordable" cafe trio whose "enticing" menu features "tasty" sandwiches and other "organic", "veggie-oriented" bites with "bold flavors"; some report "substandard" service, but with a "nice setting" and "outside" tables in the Marina and a "beautiful" "view of the Bay" at Pier 3, it doesn't "bring down" the experience; P.S. the Downtown branch is open weekdays-only, till 3 PM.

Plouf ⓢ *French*

21 | 17 | 18 | $41

Downtown | 40 Belden Pl. (bet. Bush & Pine Sts.) | 415-986-6491 | www.ploufsf.com

"Making a splash with seafood", like "huge bowls" of "top-notch" mussels prepared "every which way", this somewhat "touristy" "Parisian" bistro with "cute" waiters in nautical "striped shirts" is part of the "scene" on Downtown's pedestrian Belden Place; tables "packed tightly" make for a "high-energy" experience, but it really shines when it's "warm enough" to "sit outdoors" and enjoy the "charming" ambiance.

Pluto's Fresh Food
for a Hungry Universe *American*

19 | 12 | 15 | $14

Inner Sunset | 627 Irving St. (bet. 7th & 8th Aves.) | 415-753-8867
Marina | 3258 Scott St. (bet. Chestnut & Lombard Sts.) | 415-775-8867
www.plutosfreshfood.com

"Ginormous happy salads" "tossed to order" with a "wide choice of ingredients", plus "simple" sandwiches and "homey" sides, have a gravitational pull for customers of these "consistent", "upscale cafeterias" orbiting SF and the South Bay; the "ordering system can be confusing" and it's "hard to get a seat" in the "sterile" spaces, but diehards "don't mind waiting in line" for a "healthy meal" that "doesn't dent the wallet."

Poesia *Italian*

21 | 18 | 23 | $51

Castro | 4072 18th St. (bet. Castro & Hartford Sts.) | 415-252-9325 | www.poesiasf.com

"Excellent" Southern Italian food, including "homemade limoncello" and other Calabresi specialties, makes this "cute", "homey" "walk-up" a "welcome blessing in the Castro"; if a few pose that the "overpriced" cucina is not exactly poetry in motion and complain that you might as well "take a gondola" "considering the parking", for most the meals are "magical", with the added eye-candy benefit of "good-looking", "accented" staffers.

Pomelo Eclectic

20 | 13 | 17 | $26

Inner Sunset | 92 Judah St. (bet. 5th & 6th Aves.) | 415-731-6175
Noe Valley | 1793 Church St. (30th St.) | 415-285-2257
www.pomelosf.com

The "seasonal menu" is "always changing" at this "reasonable" Eclectic duo, highlighting "abundant" international noodles and global grains in "healthy, unusual combinations that work well"; while the Noe Valley outpost has "tight quarters", it's giant compared with the "closet-sized space" in the Inner Sunset, where fans love to "cozy up to the bar" "to watch the chefs" at work in the "tiny but efficient kitchen."

Ponzu Asian

20 | 18 | 19 | $43

Downtown | Serrano Hotel | 401 Taylor St. (bet. Geary & O'Farrell Sts.) | 415-775-7979 | www.ponzurestaurant.com

Serving a "creative menu" of "tasty" Pan-Asian plates, this "find" in Downtown's Serrano Hotel draws from Chinese, Japanese, Thai and Vietnamese cuisines; most agree it's "reliable", if a bit "overpriced", for a "pre-theater dinner", though some stick to the "plush chairs" in the "cool" bar, where drinks are a "steal" during the "highly recommended" happy hour.

Pork Store Café American

19 | 10 | 16 | $16

Haight-Ashbury | 1451 Haight St. (bet. Ashbury St. & Masonic Ave.) | 415-864-6981
Mission | 3122 16th St. (bet. Guerrero & Valencia Sts.) | 415-626-5523 | www.porkstorecafe.com

To recover "from a night of partying", "twentysomethings" devour "huge" portions of "real homestyle" grub at this daytime diner duo (though some fear the Mission branch "isn't as greasy good as Haight Street"); it's "always busy" at brunch and service can be "indifferent", but "oinkers" still wait patiently to "line up at the trough"; P.S. the 16th Street branch is also open Thursday–Friday 7 PM–3 AM, and Saturday all day till 3 AM.

Pot de Pho Vietnamese

∇ 19 | 15 | 18 | $24

Inner Richmond | 3300 Geary Blvd. (Parker Ave.) | 415-668-0826 | www.potdepho.com

Ana Mandara's "cute" sidekick in the Inner Richmond ladles up "delicious" pho, elevated with "fresh ingredients", high-quality meats and "good" handmade noodles, along with other organic Vietnamese vittles; it's a "value" option for combating the "cold" and "fog", though purists tut the "Westernized" soups are "pricey" considering "you can go a few blocks for real" (read: down and dirty) renditions.

Presidio Social Club American

19 | 20 | 20 | $40

Presidio | 563 Ruger St. (Lombard St.) | 415-885-1888 | www.presidiosocialclub.com

"Inventive" cocktails that "evoke" the '40s and '50s "without being dated" wash down the "well-executed" New American "comfort food"

	FOOD	DECOR	SERVICE	COST

that's "better than any mess hall" fare at this "airy" "old" army barracks with "disarmingly simple decor" in the Presidio; while some civilians judge the "homey" eats "decent, but not to-die-for", most recruits are happy to "join the club" for a "lively" experience among the thirtysomething "techno-hip" crowd; P.S. the post-Survey return of founding chef-owner Ray Tang is not reflected in the ratings.

NEW Prime Rib Shabu M *Japanese*

▽ 23 | 16 | 20 | $34

Inner Richmond | 308 Fifth Ave. (Geary Blvd.) | 415-379-4678

"All-you-can-eat" "delicious hand-cut American Kobe" and "fatty ribeye" dinner options for less than $30? – "say no more" enthuse DIY types who get their "hot pot" on at this "laid-back" Inner Richmond "shabu house" run by restaurateur Luke Sung (Domo), proffering individual bubbling cauldrons of sliced meats, seafood and noodles; "everything is first-class", from the "fresh vegetables" and "friendly service" to the rustic setting filled with driftwood lanterns and vintage bric-a-brac.

NEW Prospect *American*

- | - | - | E

SoMa | Infiniti Towers | 300 Spear St. (Folsom St.) | 415-247-7770 | www.prospectsf.com

In SoMa's Infiniti Towers, this breezier younger sister to Boulevard aims to lure in a new breed of diners with a less expensive (but still high-end), more contemporary New American menu that's geared toward casual grazing; the handsome yet understated dining room features floor-to-ceiling windows and plush banquettes, but much of the activity revolves around the square-shaped bar dispensing innovative cocktails.

NEW Public House *Pub Food*

- | - | - | M

South Beach | AT&T Park | 24 Willie Mays Plaza (3rd St.) | 415-644-0240 | www.publichousesf.com

Chef-restaurateur Traci Des Jardins spices up this new upscale sports pub at AT&T Park (replacing Acme Chophouse), featuring 26 giant televisions, a wall built out of kegs and a secret entrance to the stadium; the midpriced menu offers re-envisioned ballpark fare like upscale cheesesteaks, sliders, jalapeño poppers and Humphry Slocombe ice cream; P.S. fans can also slide into the adjoining outpost of Mijita (or outside to its sidewalk tables) for Mexican bites and a shot from the stand-alone tequila bar.

Q Restaurant & Wine Bar *American*

18 | 17 | 19 | $27

Inner Richmond | 225 Clement St. (bet. 3rd & 4th Aves.) | 415-752-2298 | www.qrestaurant.com

At this "funky" Inner Richmond "joint", "families" and "SF radicals" alike chow down on "creative", "complex" "all-American" fare from "homey" BBQ to mac 'n' cheese that "makes you forget Kraft ever existed"; "it gets very busy for weekend brunch", making the "edgy" staff "harried", but "bonuses" like "tables full of action figures and magnetic letters on the wall" that "bring you back to first grade" more than compensate.

Z Quince *French/Italian*

26 | 26 | 26 | $85

Downtown | 470 Pacific Ave. (bet. Montgomery St. & Osgood Pl.) | 415-775-8500 | www.quincerestaurant.com

Michael and Lindsay Tusk have taken their former Pacific Heights "neighborhood charmer" "to even greater heights" at this "sensa-

FOOD DECOR SERVICE COST

tional" new Downtown locale, where the "posh", "spacious" digs reflect the caliber of the nightly changing "knock-your-socks-off" French-Italian fare (particularly the "fabulous pastas") and "beyond impeccable service"; "yes, the portions are small" and there's a "heavy sticker price", but even nostalgists who miss the "quaintness" aver it's "still a special place" to create "restaurant memories"; P.S. its long-awaited adjacent cafe, Cotogna, is set to open soon.

NEW Radius *Californian* | - | - | - | M |

SoMa | 1123 Folsom St. (Langton St.) | 415-525-3676 | www.radiussf.com

SoMa locals are already homing in on this side-by-side cafe-restaurant duo serving French-inspired Californian cuisine sourced from within a 100-mile radius of its kitchen and outfitted with lots of reclaimed wood; it's walk-in only at the casual all-day cafe (featuring a mini-market hawking artisanal larder), but reservations are accepted for the more recently opened sit-down dinner house that showcases more highbrow offerings by veteran chef Kelly Hughett (Ritz-Carlton, NYC's Adour Alain Ducasse).

R & G Lounge *Chinese* | 24 | 12 | 15 | $34 |

Chinatown | 631 Kearny St. (bet. Clay & Sacramento Sts.) | 415-982-7877 | www.rnglounge.com

The name must "stand for real good Chinese seafood", because there's a "packed house every night" digging into "sublime salt-and-pepper crab" and other "first-rate" specialties at this "fabulous-value" choice (even if tabs are slightly "high" for the genre); while the service is "subpar" and the "basement seating can feel cramped" (the "banquet tables upstairs are nicer"), some "Hong Kong transplants" insist it's the "only Cantonese restaurant in Chinatown they go to."

Z Range *American* | 27 | 19 | 24 | $55 |

Mission | 842 Valencia St. (bet. 19th & 20th Sts.) | 415-282-8283 | www.rangesf.com

"Experience the edgy side" of "fine dining" at this "low-key", "relatively affordable" New American "hipster" haunt, a "real feather in the Mission's cap" by couple Cameron and Phil West, whose "spectacular" use of "seasonal ingredients" distinguishes both the "killer" dishes and "quirky" "cocktails of the day"; the "tight seating" in the "minimalist", deco-inflected digs kind of "kills the romance", but the "superlative" staff "always makes you feel at home."

Red's Java House *Burgers* | 15 | 11 | 14 | $12 |

Embarcadero | Pier 30 (Bryant St.) | 415-777-5626

When "all you need" is "your basic burger and a beer", there's "nothing better" than this "scrappy" "cheap-eats institution" on the Embarcadero, a "bayside shack" with a "million-dollar view"; the food is "not necessarily the best" ("you gotta problem with grease?"), but it's a "memorable experience" nonetheless – and "a required stop before or after a Giants game", when it stays open past its usual 5 PM closing.

Regalito Rosticeria *Mexican* | ▽ 19 | 14 | 19 | $28 |

Mission | 3481 18th St. (bet. Lexington & Valencia Sts.) | 415-503-0650 | www.regalitosf.com

"Different than your everyday burrito joint", this "cute" Mexican rotisserie regales Missionites with "tasty" ("if not dazzling") comida like a

	FOOD	DECOR	SERVICE	COST

"mean mole" and other "authentic" options; "friendly service", "even better prices" and weekend brunch complete the picture.

Restaurant LuLu *French/Mediterranean*

| 21 | 20 | 19 | $45 |

SoMa | 816 Folsom St. (bet. 4th & 5th Sts.) | 415-495-5775 | www.restaurantlulu.com

"Anything that comes out of the wood-fired oven is delicious", including "standout" iron-skillet mussels, at this once-"hot", now "tried-and-true" French-Med brasserie in SoMa; an "extensive" wine list and "lovely", "comfy" surroundings" bolster the somewhat expensive "family-style dining", though some squawk that their "ears are ringing" from the "rock-concert" volume.

Richmond Restaurant & Wine Bar ☒ *Californian*

| 25 | 20 | 24 | $45 |

Inner Richmond | 615 Balboa St. (bet. 7th & 8th Aves.) | 415-379-8988 | www.therichmondsf.com

Neighborhood "regulars" return "again and again" to this "sleeper" "in the avenues of the Richmond" for "beautifully presented", "superlative Californian cuisine" and "nice wine selections at a fair price"; "personal service" (the chef-owners often "come out to say hello") lends extra warmth to the "hideaway" locale, but be warned that "street parking is difficult."

Ristobar *Italian*

| - | - | - | M |

Marina | 2300 Chestnut St. (Scott St.) | 415-923-6464 | www.ristobarsf.com

Inspired by Italy's casual neighborhood enotecas, chef Gary Rulli has transformed the former Marina location of Emporio Rulli into this Italian small-plater offering a midpriced menu that runs from agrodolce-style lamb meatballs to crackling-thin artisanal pizzas to showstopping dolci; when you're not craning your neck to view the majestic frescoes on the soaring ceiling, check out the newly installed Enomatic machines behind the marble-topped bar.

Ristorante Ideale *Italian*

| 24 | 15 | 22 | $43 |

North Beach | 1309 Grant Ave. (Vallejo St.) | 415-391-4129 | www.idealerestaurant.com

The "exciting" dishes that "one does not find everywhere", from "thin-style pizza" to the "freshest pasta outside of Italia", are anything but "run-of-the-mill" at this "superb" North Beacher that partisans call the "perfect Roman trattoria"; though the "atmospheric" interior can get "cramped", at least it's "less touristy" than its North Beach neighbors, and the "delightful" servers who "love what they are doing" create a "welcoming environment."

Ristorante Milano *Italian*

| 25 | 17 | 23 | $43 |

Russian Hill | 1448 Pacific Ave. (bet. Hyde & Larkin Sts.) | 415-673-2961 | www.milanosf.com

The "fantastic Italian staff" welcomes "strangers and regulars alike" as if they were "long-lost family" at this "charming" trattoria where the "amazing", slightly expensive Northern Italian food is prepared with "enormous skill" and "served just so"; "tucked away on Russian Hill", it's "hidden" from out-of-towners, but the "intimate" space "bustles" with a loyal "following."

	FOOD	DECOR	SERVICE	COST

Ristorante Umbria 🛇 *Italian* — 20 | 15 | 18 | $36

SoMa | 198 Second St. (Howard St.) | 415-546-6985 |
www.ristoranteumbria.com

Run by "real Italian people" who "treat you like a regular the first time you go", this "consistent", moderately priced trattoria "off the tourist path" in SoMa "satisfies cravings" for "homey" Umbrian fare; a "good lunch place" on weekdays, it's especially enticing "when the weather is nice and the tables and conversation spill out onto the sidewalk."

🗹 Ritz-Carlton Dining Room 🛇Ⓜ *French* — 27 | 27 | 27 | $104

Nob Hill | Ritz-Carlton | 600 Stockton St. (bet. California & Pine Sts.) |
415-773-6198 | www.ritzcarltondiningroom.com

"A throwback to another era", this "calm, romantic" Nob Hill "grande dame" remains "one of the few places where you can dress up and feel like you're going out for a special evening", especially once you sample chef Ron Siegel's "exquisite", often "adventurous" New French prix fixes with "Japanese influences"; you'll "need to pay up", of course, but add in a "decadent dessert cart", "one of the best wine cellars" in town and "pampering" service and you've got a "delight from start to finish."

RN74 *French* — 22 | 24 | 22 | $62

SoMa | Millennium Tower | 301 Mission St. (Beale St.) | 415-543-7474 |
www.rn74.com

Oenophiles are "happy to get on board" Michael Mina's "casually elegant" SoMa newcomer, whose "eye-catching" decor – a "modern interpretation of a Euro train station", complete with an "old-style railroad departure board" announcing "wine specials" – vies for attention with "inventive" (and "pricey") New French large and small plates; "jammed" with "young business types" and "wealthy Millennium Tower tenants" sampling the "incredible" vino selection, it's a real "scene", and if some "don't get the hype", the majority deems it a "worthy" arrival.

NEW Roam Artisan Burgers *Burgers* — - | - | - | I

Cow Hollow | 1785 Union St. (bet. Gough & Octavia Sts.) | 415-440-7626 |
www.roamburgers.com

This eco-conscious burger joint in Cow Hollow poses no dilemmas for omnivores thanks to a slate of customizable pasture-to-plate patties (grass-fed beef, free-range turkey, home-on-the-range bison, plus a veggie version) served alongside the likes of housemade natural sodas and Straus Family Creamery organic ice-cream shakes; the counter-style setup features reclaimed wood, funky recycled-glass light fixtures and the requisite communal table, and you know you're not in Kansas anymore when the bar pours kombucha as well as beer and wine on tap.

RoliRoti 🛇Ⓜ *American* — ▽ 25 | 12 | 19 | $12

Embarcadero | Ferry Plaza Mkt. | 1 Ferry Bldg. (The Embarcadero) |
510-780-0300 | www.roliroti.com

Expect "street food at the highest level" at this truckin' rotisserie "treat" that roosts at the Ferry Building farmer's market on Saturday mornings (as well as other Bay Area locales); a "friendly staff" doles out some of the "best chicken and porchetta you can find", hence the "long lines" of "rush hour" loyalists who can devour the feed from a pier perch.

	FOOD	DECOR	SERVICE	COST

Rosamunde
Sausage Grill ⌀ German

	25	9	16	$11

Lower Haight | 545 Haight St. (bet. Fillmore & Steiner Sts.) | 415-437-6851
NEW Mission | 2832 Mission St. (bet. 24th & 25th Sts.) | 415-970-9015
www.rosamundesausagegrill.com

For some of the "best" wursts in town, link lovers head to this "tiny" Lower Haight "legend" where the "quirky" crew grills up a "huge" selection of haute "dawgs" (like duck and fig) – plus "fantastic" off-the-menu burgers on Tuesdays – enjoyed with a beer at the adjacent Toronado bar; for their part, Missionites trot to its newer, larger sib for the luxury of the same "juicy" goodness and "delicious imported" brews in one place.

Rose Pistola Italian

	21	20	20	$47

North Beach | 532 Columbus Ave. (bet. Green & Union Sts.) | 415-399-0499 | www.rosepistolasf.com

"Buono!" cheer boosters of this "buzzy" North Beach boîte, where you can linger at the "bustling bar" or "sit outside and people-watch" while savoring "unique Ligurian cuisine", including "decadent" appetizers and "garlicky" entrees pulled from the "crackling" "wood-fired oven and grill"; it's "still fresh" and "still fun" say fans, but critics carp it's "somewhat costly" considering the fare is "just ok."

Rose's Cafe Italian

	22	18	20	$32

Cow Hollow | 2298 Union St. (Steiner St.) | 415-775-2200 | www.rosescafesf.com

"Popular during the day" for a "clubby" lunch, this tile-floored cafe is also a "comfortable" "place to relax" after work with a "glass of wine" and "honest", midpriced Northern Italian eats; it really blooms "on the weekends", though, when Cow Hollow cohorts sit at the "sunny" sidewalk seats and scarf up "tasty twists on old favorites", like the breakfast pizzas they "dreamed about" the night before.

Roti Indian Bistro Indian

	22	17	19	$31

West Portal | 53 W. Portal Ave. (bet. Ulloa & Vicente Sts.) | 415-665-7684 | www.rotibistro.com

The "tender tandooris", "fantastic fish dishes" and "flavorful curries" are "remarkable" at these "upscale" Indians in SF's "sleepy West Portal" and Burlingame; they're "a bit pricey for this type of food" fuss the frugal, but "worth it" insist customers "captivated" by the "aroma alone" and heartened by service that "makes you feel at home."

Rotunda American

	21	26	21	$41

Downtown | Neiman Marcus | 150 Stockton St. (bet. Geary & O'Farrell Sts.) | 415-362-4777 | www.neimanmarcus.com

At this "classic slice of old SF", "ladies who lunch" dig into "elegant" American meals (think "lobster clubs and popovers") while "bonding" "after a day of shopping" in Union Square; "say what you will" about the "snooty waiters" and "stratospheric prices", but insiders insist it's "worth every penny" just to "sit under" the "gorgeous stained-glass ceiling" at what may be the "best thing that's happened at Neiman Marcus since it spread out from Texas"; P.S. no dinner served.

	FOOD	DECOR	SERVICE	COST

Roy's *Hawaiian* | 23 | 22 | 22 | $53 |

SoMa | 575 Mission St. (bet. 1st & 2nd Sts.) | 415-777-0277 | www.roysrestaurant.com

"Every meal is a delight" effuse fans of this "high-end" SoMa chain link showcasing celeb chef Roy Yamaguchi's "modern mastery" of Hawaiian fusion cuisine, focusing on "beautifully prepared" fish (and "unique" local specialties) among other "innovative creations" with "bold flavors"; the "upbeat" atmosphere and "excellent" service help support the "steep" price, plus the seasonal prix fixe menu is a real "deal."

Ruth's Chris | 24 | 21 | 23 | $66 |
Steak House *Steak*

Polk Gulch | 1601 Van Ness Ave. (California St.) | 415-673-0557 | www.ruthschris.com

Loyalists "love the sizzling platters" of "oh-so-good buttery steaks" at these "top-quality" chophouse chain links in Polk Gulch and Walnut Creek that come through with "winning" sides too; delivering "old-style service" amid "traditional" trappings, they're "expensive" (and "not for the dieter"), but "utterly reliable", especially when you're "entertaining friends and clients."

Ryoko's ◑ *Japanese* | ▽ 23 | 14 | 18 | $40 |

Downtown | 619 Taylor St. (bet. Post & Sutter Sts.) | 415-775-1028

"The sushi chef is an artist" aver afishionados who appreciate the "fantastic" fin fare (with impressive "combinations of flavors") and "delicious" izakaya menu at this Downtown "basement" Japanese whose "loud music" and "late" kitchen hours (till 1:30 AM nightly) make it resemble a "long-running party with a full bar"; a fastidious few fret it feels more "grubby" than "clubby", though, adding it's best left to the "younger crowd."

Saha Arabic | ▽ 26 | 21 | 22 | $39 |
Fusion 🖾Ⓜ *Mideastern*

Tenderloin | Carlton Hotel | 1075 Sutter St. (bet. Hyde & Larkin Sts.) | 415-345-9547 | www.sahasf.com

"Exciting", "unexpected" Arabic cooking is the main attraction at this Tenderloin treat where "adventurous food lovers" "pile up their table" with "modern" "haute Middle Eastern" morsels for moderate tabs; the "super" servers are "more than willing to explain the dishes" (which include "great vegetarian selections"), so it's worth seeking out this "dark", "romantic" dining room in an "unlikely" location.

Saigon Sandwiches ⊄ *Sandwiches/Vietnamese* | 24 | 2 | 11 | $7 |

Tenderloin | 560 Larkin St. (bet. Eddy & Turk Sts.) | 415-474-5698

"Raising the Vietnamese sandwich to new heights of tastiness", this take-out joint in the Tenderloin "distinguishes itself" with "explosively flavorful" banh mi built with "crusty French bread", "succulent" pork and other "fresh fillings"; while that's "fabulous" enough, "unbelievably cheap prices" "push it to out-of-this-world", and if there's an "inevitable line out the door", at least the "industrious" women behind the counter run everything "efficiently"; P.S. closes at 6 PM.

FOOD	DECOR	SERVICE	COST
▽ 25	18	22	$127

Saison ⊠ Ⓜ *American*

Mission | 2124 Folsom St. (17th St.) | 415-828-7990 |
www.saisonsf.com

"Kudos"-awarding customers no longer need to know the "secret password" to sample chef Joshua Skenes' "refreshing, creative" and very expensive New American prix fixes with "excellent wine pairings" since the Mission pop-up started serving dinner five nights a week, both in the refurbished dining room and at a chef's counter in the kitchen; a newly built outdoor hearth (installed post-Survey) expands its culinary possibilities, while a wine bar is in the works as well.

| 21 | 20 | 19 | $48 |

Salt House *American*

SoMa | 545 Mission St. (bet. 2nd St. & Shaw Alley) | 415-543-8900 |
www.salthousesf.com

"Suits and, well, younger suits" grab a "bite before heading back to the desk" or enjoy "after-work drinks" and a "night out with friends" at Town Hall's "trendy" SoMa sib, which boasts a "snappy little" New American menu in a "casual/upscale" gastropub setting; it can be "quite a trick getting in", "crazy loud" and "relatively expensive", but the "down-to-earth" staffers and "electric" vibe (especially at the "lively bar") help make it a "fine experience" for most.

| 20 | 22 | 18 | $25 |

Samovar Tea Lounge *Tearoom*

Castro | 498 Sanchez St. (18th St.) | 415-626-4700
Hayes Valley | 297 Page St. (Laguna St.) | 415-861-0303
SoMa | 730 Howard St. (bet. 3rd & 4th Sts.) | 415-227-9400
www.samovarlife.com

Oolong enthusiasts "come in stressed and leave super-relaxed" at this "tranquil" trio designed for "luxury lounging", where an "unrivaled" selection of "artisan teas" "from all over the world" are paired with similarly cosmopolitan, "unusual but tasty" bites; "it's not exactly cheap", and the "informative" servers can be "slow", but that's just the right speed for "whiling away a few hours with a friend or a book."

| 21 | 19 | 21 | $43 |

Sam's Grill & Seafood Restaurant ⊠ *Seafood*

Downtown | 374 Bush St. (bet. Kearny & Montgomery Sts.) |
415-421-0594

"Thank heaven" "nothing changes" at this supremely "old-school" seafooder, which continues to serve an "unequaled variety" of "unfancy" but "really fine fish" to the Downtown "business lunch" set; request a "curtained wooden booth" to enhance the "turn-of-the-century experience", but no matter where you sit you'll be served by "wonderful" "tuxedoed waiters" who are as "crusty as the sourdough bread."

| 18 | 9 | 13 | $17 |

Sam Wo's ❶⇱ *Chinese*

Chinatown | 813 Washington St. (Grant Ave.) | 415-982-0596

Intrepid eaters "enter through the kitchen" and climb "rickety stairs" to get to the "run-down dining room" of this Chinatown haunt, applauding the "awesome" "experience" surrounding its "cheap Chinese food"; sure, the waiters are "surly" and the choices fairly "unexciting", but it's open till 3 AM (except Sunday nights) and still mythologized by those who "used to get ripped and come here in the '60s."

	FOOD	DECOR	SERVICE	COST

NEW Sandbox Bakery *Bakery* ▽ 26 | 17 | 21 | $8

Bernal Heights | 833 Cortland Ave. (Gates St.) | 415-642-8580 | www.sandboxbakerysf.com

Bernal-ites find "heaven in a bun" at this "experimental" yet kid-friendly "little neighborhood bakery" that thinks outside the sandbox; "headed by a former Slanted Door pastry chef", it doles out "dee-lish-ous" (and "Asian-influenced") "sweets and savories", including a "Danish with yuzu marmalade", scones and "pricey" sammies du jour; P.S. "go early", as it "sells out too fast" and has only a few seats outside.

Sanraku *Japanese* 21 | 14 | 18 | $36

SoMa | Metreon | 101 Fourth St. (Mission St.) | 415-369-6166
Sanraku Four Seasons *Japanese*
Downtown | 704 Sutter St. (Taylor St.) | 415-771-0803
www.sanraku.com

"In a city rife with sushi variety", these Japanese "mainstays" Downtown and in SoMa's Metreon reel in everyone from "MOMA-goers" and "trade-show" reps to "locals and expats" lured by "well-prepared" raw and grilled eats complemented by a "great sake selection"; the "decor is plain", but seasoned eaters appreciate the reasonable prices, "courteous staff" and ability to "pop in without a reservation."

San Tung *Chinese/Korean* 23 | 8 | 13 | $21

Inner Sunset | 1031 Irving St. (bet. 11th & 12th Aves.) | 415-242-0828 | www.santungrestaurant.com

"Crispy, tangy and a little spicy", the dry fried chicken wings are "crack in poultry form" at this "simple little" Inner Sunset joint where the "killer" dish can be complemented with "hand-pulled noodles" and other "satisfying" Chinese-Korean fare; there's "zero atmosphere" in the "cramped" dining room, and a "long wait" for a table, but wing nuts insist it's "well worth it" and "the price is certainly right."

Sauce ◑ *American* 18 | 14 | 20 | $40

Hayes Valley | 131 Gough St. (Oak St.) | 415-252-1369 | www.saucesf.com
Opera fans and those who want to "sleep soundly at the performance" fill up "pre-show" on "well-priced comfort food" at this "consistent" Hayes Valley American (which stays open till 2 AM for a "post-concert" bite); critics who cite "heavy" "over-sauced" dishes and "dark decor" wish the place would "lighten up", but others find the "cozy" if "shabby" atmosphere "pleasant" and praise the "prompt" service.

Savor *Mediterranean* 17 | 14 | 20 | $23

Noe Valley | 3913 24th St. (bet. Noe & Sanchez Sts.) | 415-282-0344
"Massive portions" ("actually *too* big") of Med-style breakfasts served all day at this Noe Valley "crêpe place" – along with salads and other "simple" items – make it an "absolute favorite" for weekend brunch or a "casual" dinner; some brand it "unimaginative", but more savor it for the "reasonable prices", "family-friendly" service and "lovely" patio that "feels far away from city bustle."

Scala's Bistro *Italian* 23 | 23 | 22 | $47

Downtown | Sir Francis Drake Hotel | 432 Powell St. (bet. Post & Sutter Sts.) | 415-395-8555 | www.scalasbistro.com
"Perfect for pre-theater" dining, a "late" weekend bite or to "escape" the "whirl of Union Square shopping" with a "long, lingering lunch", this "el-

egant" Italian in Downtown's Sir Francis Drake Hotel "hums with homey" appeal; admirers advise "tucking into a comfy booth" for "fabulous" fare delivered by a "personable" staff, but some harrumph about the "high noise level", which can "mar the experience" when it's "at capacity."

Schmidt's ⌀ German   ▽ 21 | 17 | 18 | $28

Mission | 2400 Folsom St. (20th St.) | 415-401-0200 | www.schmidts-sf.com
"To satiate occasional schnitzel cravings", the brat pack heads to this "solid" German deli in the Mission, where the "tasty" "favorites" ("lots of sausage choices") and "nice beer pairings" come with "slightly lower prices and faster service" than its "down-the-street" sister Walzwerk; a "community table" welcomes "solo diners", while imported goodies beckon customers to "shop from its shelves" while they wait; P.S. no longer serving lunch.

✓ Scoma's Seafood   22 | 19 | 20 | $46

Fisherman's Wharf | Pier 47 | 1 Al Scoma Way (Jefferson St.) | 415-771-4383 | www.scomas.com
"You don't have to have out-of-town guests" to dine at this "old-time favorite" at Fisherman's Wharf (or its Sausalito sib with a "patio over the water"), as evidenced by the "steady stream of locals" loving the "delicious", "properly prepared" seafood; they may be "a little worn around the gills", but both boast "gorgeous" Bay views that "add to the ambiance", as well as "professional" servers who "have been there forever"; P.S. there are "no reservations" at the SF original, so "get there early."

Sears Fine Food Diner   20 | 13 | 18 | $22

Downtown | 439 Powell St. (bet. Post & Sutter Sts.) | 415-986-0700 | www.searsfinefood.com
"Breakfast is the thing" at this "nostalgic" Downtown diner where locals "happily join" tourists in the "line stretching up the block" for "those little silver-dollar pancakes" and other "filling" morning fare ferried by "feisty waitresses"; "little-changed over the decades", it's a "landmark" that's a "tight squeeze" inside, but pickier patrons beef that the "budget-friendly" American lunches and dinners are "nothing to write home about."

✓ Seasons Seafood/Steak   26 | 25 | 27 | $68

Downtown | Four Seasons Hotel | 757 Market St., 5th fl. (bet. 3rd & 4th Sts.) | 415-633-3838 | www.fourseasons.com
"At the top of any list for a power lunch or dinner", this "luxury" Downtowner is "as wonderful as you would expect from the Four Seasons", providing "superb" steak and "beautifully prepared" seafood served by an "impeccable" staff; the "elegant", "delightful" setting is conducive to "easy conversation", making it a fine "place to celebrate" – especially if someone else is "footing the bill"; P.S. opening at 6:30 AM for breakfast, it also serves a bar menu until midnight.

✓ Sebo Ⓜ Japanese   27 | 18 | 21 | $67

Hayes Valley | 517 Hayes St. (bet. Laguna & Octavia Sts.) | 415-864-2122 | www.sebosf.com
"Adventurous" "raw-fish enthusiasts rejoice" at this "congenial" Hayes Valley Japanese "temple" of "pricey, pristine sushi", especially if they score "one of the few bar seats" and "let the chefs" feed them;

the seafood is "fresh-caught and flown in" daily and complemented by "pairings from True Sake", but "squeamish diners" take note: "if you like California rolls, go elsewhere"; P.S. it offers izakaya on Sundays, jettisoning its signature dish for cooked cuisine; the post-Survey departure of one of the founding chefs is not reflected in the ratings.

Sens Restaurant ⊠ *Mediterranean/Turkish* | 19 | 22 | 18 | $44

Downtown | 4 Embarcadero Ctr. (Drumm St.) | 415-362-0645 | www.sens-sf.com

The "nice view of the Ferry Building and waterfront" "definitely adds a spark" to this rustic "secret" inside the Embarcadero Center, a "pleasant" "biz-lunch venue" for Downtown diners who embark on an "adventure" with "interesting, well-prepared" (though at times "inconsistent") Med-Turkish fare; "awesome cocktails" appeal to the sens-es during weekday happy hour, when there can be a "raucous crowd at the bar" and hookah-smoking on the patio; P.S. closed weekends.

Sentinel, The ⊠ *Sandwiches* | 24 | 9 | 16 | $12

SoMa | 37 New Montgomery St. (bet. Market & Mission Sts.) | 415-284-9960 | www.thesentinelsf.com

There's "no better lunch counter in the city" beam boosters of this takeout-only SoMa "find" where Dennis Leary (Canteen) "brings gourmet food to the masses" via "reasonably priced" sandwiches crafted from "wonderfully paired" ingredients and fresh-baked breads; everything is "served up quickly" – though clock-watchers should "go early to avoid the lines", call ahead or opt for one of the "amazing breakfast pastries"; P.S. open weekdays-only, till 2:30 PM.

Serpentine *American* | 19 | 19 | 18 | $36

Dogpatch | 2495 Third St. (22nd St.) | 415-252-2000 | www.serpentinesf.com

Dogpatch denizens "love the low-key coolness" of this "spiffy", "modern" "offshoot of Slow Club", delivering a "thoughtful", midpriced New American menu that ranges from "rich", "full-on entrees" to "lighter" lunch fare to an "excellent brunch"; still, a handful shrugs that though it "tries hard", the "uneven" food and service "just don't stand out."

Shabu-Sen *Japanese* | ∇ 19 | 16 | 20 | $28

Japantown | 1726 Buchanan St. (bet. Post & Sutter Sts.) | 415-440-0466

For an interactive eating outing that's "different and kind of fun", this "reasonable" DIY Japanese "conveniently" located in Japantown offers diners a "great variety" of meats, seafood and veggies for "consistently good" shabu-shabu and sukiyaki (plus an all-you-can-eat option Monday–Thursday); "service can vary", but given "you're making your own food", it "doesn't impact the meal too much."

Shalimar ⇪ *Indian/Pakistani* | 24 | 4 | 10 | $16

Polk Gulch | 1409 Polk St. (Pine St.) | 415-776-4642
Tenderloin | 532 Jones St. (Geary St.) | 415-928-0333 ●
www.shalimarsf.com

"Intoxicating aromas" signal the arrival of "delicious", "deeply flavored" Indian-Pakistani plates – "satisfying" stuff that's "so hot but so good" – gush groupies of these "chaotic" joints; they may have all the "elegance of a truck stop", but the "ridiculously cheap" eats are always "great for takeout."

	FOOD	DECOR	SERVICE	COST

Shanghai Dumpling King Chinese
| | 23 | 4 | 13 | $17 |

Outer Richmond | 3319 Balboa St. (34th Ave.) | 415-387-2088

"Long live the king!" salute supporters of this Outer Richmond "hole-in-the-wall" where "masters of *xiao long bao*" crank out "steamers" of "amazing" soup dumplings and "authentic Shanghainese" specialties like hand-pulled noodles, plus "sugar puff desserts" that get "snatched up quickly"; there's "absolutely no decor" and it's "off the beaten path", but "fast service" and "rock-bottom prices" mean one thing: "expect to wait."

Showdogs Hot Dogs
| | 19 | 10 | 15 | $14 |

Downtown | 1020 Market St. (6th St.) | 415-558-9560 | www.showdogssf.com

"Exceptional" franks and "unique", sustainably sourced sausages gussied up with a "surprising variety" of "inventive" toppings are paired with "beer tastings" and "addictive fries" at this "upscale fast-food joint" with a Foreign Cinema pedigree (albeit in a "marginal" Downtown locale); the "dogs are tops", but a few critics bark that steep prices ("I've paid less at Disneyland") and "plain white buns spoil the show."

Silks Californian
| | 25 | 24 | 25 | $69 |

Downtown | Mandarin Oriental Hotel | 222 Sansome St., 2nd fl. (bet. California & Pine Sts.) | 415-986-2020 | www.mandarinoriental.com

A "most inviting" menu of Asian-inspired Californian cuisine sets a "high standard" at this "oasis" in the Downtown Mandarin Oriental, where "exemplary service" contributes to the "enjoyable dining experience"; "well-spaced" tables and a "subdued" atmosphere suit both "serious discussions" and "impressive dates", but don't forget to "make a hefty withdrawal" from your bank account, because the "fabulous" food is also "fabulously expensive."

NEW Skool Seafood
| | - | - | - | E |

Potrero Hill | 1725 Alameda St. (De Haro St.) | 415-255-8844 | www.skoolsf.com

Sustainable seafood with Japanese accents is the hook at this new spawn from a team of Blowfish Sushi and Bushi-tei veterans in Potrero Hill's design district; despite a slightly hidden locale, it's already luring in neighbors for midweek lunch and nightly dinners with a too-cool-for-school interior, decked out with floor-to-ceiling windows and custom-made reclaimed-wood furniture, plus a sunny 45-seat patio.

☑ Slanted Door, The Vietnamese
| | 26 | 22 | 22 | $50 |

Embarcadero | 1 Ferry Bldg. (Market St.) | 415-861-8032 | www.slanteddoor.com

Diners experience an "epiphany" "by the Bay" at Charles Phan's "high-end" Vietnamese where "knockout views" enhance the "stupendous" food ("shaking beef, 'nuff said") and "unfamiliar" wines, while "educated" servers hustle in the "industrial-cool" glassed-in Ferry Building digs; true, it's "l-o-u-d", "jammed" and "impossibly" "hard to get in the door, slanted or not", now that everyone from "presidents and locals" to "tourists" "has it on their 'bucket list'", so some savvy types simply "duck into the bar as soon as it opens."

	FOOD	DECOR	SERVICE	COST

Slow Club *American*

22	16	20	$36

Mission | 2501 Mariposa St. (Hampshire St.) | 415-241-9390 | www.slowclub.com

A chef who "really focuses on in-season, fresh ingredients" turns out "thoughtfully presented" New American dishes "done right" at this "lively" Mission bistro with a "hip" yet "experienced" staff; though it can be "dark and noisy", the "vaguely industrial atmosphere" somehow feels "intimate" when you're chowing down and sipping "complicated cocktails" with the rest of the "alt crowd"; P.S. the "creative" weekend brunch is "awesome."

Sociale ⓈItalian

23	21	23	$48

Presidio Heights | 3665 Sacramento St. (bet. Locust & Spruce Sts.) | 415-921-3200 | www.caffesociale.com

"Hidden away" "down a walkway off Sacramento Street", this "Presidio Heights charmer" is a "sweet spot" for "terrific", upscale Northern Italian cucina ("pasta is a star") and an "eclectic wine list that keeps things interesting"; "TLC" proffered by servers "from the moment you arrive" encourages "relaxing", whether you're seated in the "intimate" interior or more "romantic" heated patio "amid the flowers."

NEW Social
Kitchen & Brewery *American*

-	-	-	M

Inner Sunset | 1326 Ninth Ave. (bet. Irving & Judah Sts.) | 415-681-0330 | www.socialbrewsf.com

Beer's the thing at this Inner Sunset brewpub, a sort of SF-style biergarten minus the garden, whether it's being enjoyed on tap or used as an ingredient for midpriced eclectic New American fare, like Kölsch mussels and an ale-braised short rib pot pie; the bi-level dining room with exposed beams furthers the hopped-up theme, with recycled bottles providing materials for the light fixtures.

NEW Sons & Daughters Ⓜ *American*

-	-	-	E

Nob Hill | 708 Bush St. (bet. Mason & Powell Sts.) | 415-391-8311 | www.sonsanddaughterssf.com

Infusing some young blood into a well-trodden Nob Hill haunt (former home of Cafe Mozart), this ambitious new dinner house run by twentysomethings offers fine dining on a budget, presenting customizable, ingredient-driven four-course American tasting menus (with à la carte options), matched by an eclectic yet affordable wine list; the simple, bistro-esque storefront is lined with flowerboxes outside and decorated with chandeliers and black-and-white photos; P.S. closed Monday–Tuesday.

South Park Cafe ⓈFrench

22	19	21	$37

SoMa | 108 South Park St. (bet. 2nd & 3rd Sts.) | 415-495-7275 | www.southparkcafesf.com

At this "sweet", "petite" bistro, "classic French grub" (think steak frites and "wonderful" desserts) are delivered by an "upbeat" staff in a "European atmosphere" that brings a "bit of Lyon" to South Park; it's just as "crowded" as "when the dot-com bubble was still inflating", though, so expect everyone from SoMa workers who "get there early for lunch" to "romantics" who come 'round for "excellent prix fixe menus" that are "quite 'le bargain.'"

	FOOD	DECOR	SERVICE	COST

⬛NEW Spice Kit ⊠ *Asian* — — — I

SoMa | 405 Howard St. (bet. 1st & Fremont Sts.) | 415-882-4581 | www.spicekit.com

Fine-dining veterans from the French Laundry and the Ritz-Carlton Dining Room channel their talents into affordable Pan-Asian street food at this new quick-service gourmet sandwich shop in SoMa, an indoor-outdoor space offering Vietnamese banh mi, Korean ssäm and salads, which worker bees can customize with a variety of farm-fresh fillings; P.S. lunch-only on Saturday and closed Sunday.

⬛NEW Spire ⊠ *American* — — — M

South Beach | 685 3rd St. (bet. Brannan & Townsend Sts.) | 415-947-0000 | www.spiresf.com

Located just a fly ball away from AT&T Park, this hip South Beach new-comer aspires to score with the nearby lunch-break and after-work set, sporting an eclectic, moderately priced mix of New American classics as interpreted by a former Waterbar sous chef; the kitchen also features a raw bar and happy-hour menus, available at the low-slung lounge tables, at the high community table or in the exposed-brick main dining room.

Spork *American* 20 15 19 $38

Mission | 1058 Valencia St. (bet. 21st & 22nd Sts.) | 415-643-5000 | www.sporksf.com

While the ironic name and "hipster decor" are what "grab your attention" at this "funky" "reincarnation of a KFC" in the Mission, the "creative twists" on New American "comfort food" - served with your "favorite beer" - are the real reason to "get your spork on" here; if you can "get over the highish price for the casual" (some say "sterile") setting and the "welcoming" though "not polished" service", it's a "fun place to dine."

SPQR *Italian* 24 18 21 $45

Pacific Heights | 1911 Fillmore St. (bet. Bush & Pine Sts.) | 415-771-7779 | www.spqrsf.com

"Roman specialties" "shine" at this "happening" Pac Heights osteria that's "every bit the restaurant" as sib A16, with an "imaginative" new chef "taking it to exciting places"; "the waits are enough to make you challenge the person in front of you to a gladiatorial duel", but easy to forget when sitting at the bar counting "tattoos" and racking up "soulful", if slightly "pricey", small plates (including "well-prepared offal") with "fantastic" wines "you'd never drink at home"; P.S. "now they take reservations!"

⬛ Spruce *American* 26 26 24 $70

Presidio Heights | 3640 Sacramento St. (bet. Locust & Spruce Sts.) | 415-931-5100 | www.sprucesf.com

"The Upper East Side comes" to Presidio Heights at this "lively", "alluring" boîte, a "power scene" boasting "posh" looks and "pampering" service to suit "ladies who lunch", "debutantes and the parents who pay"; the kitchen "dazzles" with "exquisite", "farm"-fresh New American fare matched by a "world-class" wine list, but those "not up for the full press" (and tab) join the "spruced-up" walk-ins for a "burger at the bar."

Stable Café *Coffeehouse*

| - | - | - | I |

Mission | 2128 Folsom St. (bet. 17th & 18th Sts.) | 415-552-1199 | www.stablecafe.com

There's "not a horse in sight" at this converted carriage house–turned-coffeehouse in the Mission, but no matter: supporters say the "hip" bi-level digs, "friendly environment", seasonal sandwiches/salads and "awesome" Sunday brunches make it "everything you're looking for in a cafe"; P.S. closes at 4 PM.

Stacks *American*

| 18 | 13 | 17 | $20 |

Hayes Valley | 501 Hayes St. (Octavia St.) | 415-241-9011 | www.stacksrestaurant.com

"It's a good thing they serve breakfast all day because that's usually how long the wait is" for plates of "enormous", "comforting" pancakes and other AM staples (plus lunch) at these "cheery", "casual" American joints in Hayes Valley, Burlingame and Menlo Park; while "pleasant" service and "free coffee" help ease the pain of "long brunch lines", detractors "don't get" the "popularity" of these "upscale IHOPs."

NEW Starbelly *Californian*

| 20 | 18 | 19 | $33 |

Castro | 3583 16th St. (Market St.) | 415-252-7500 | www.starbellysf.com

The Beretta team's "clever" meat-centric Californian spin-off "captures the hearts" and bellies of Castro "hipsters" with the "new paradigm (pizzas, small plates and booze)", served "without the attitude and prices" of other "hyped" spots; yeah, the "cool", "reclaimed-wood" digs (with "communal table" and patio) get "too damn loud", and there are "big waits" and so many "calorie-laden" offerings it ought to be "named 'fatbelly'", but most agree it's a "welcome addition to the neighborhood."

St. Francis Fountain *Diner*

| 19 | 20 | 19 | $20 |

Mission | 2801 24th St. (York St.) | 415-826-4200

Perhaps the "last of its kind", this vintage soda fountain in the Mission that once churned out homemade ice cream, "cherry Cokes and Green Rivers" is now an "awesome" brunch haven proffering Guinness Floats and "toasted-cheese sandwiches" to "unemployed hipsters and SF General Hospital employees alike"; "casual" servers awash in tattoos help make it a "fun" spot to get a "diner fix", score some vintage trading cards and soak up some "old-fashioned charm."

Stinking Rose, The *Italian*

| 18 | 18 | 18 | $37 |

North Beach | 325 Columbus Ave. (bet. Broadway & Vallejo Sts.) | 415-781-7673 | www.thestinkingrose.com

"Garlic lovers" don't mind "emitting an aroma for a few days" after gorging on the Cal-Northern Italian food at this "memorable" North Beach "novelty" joint where "absolutely everything" is "centered around" the pungent namesake; "p.u." say "vampires" and others who shun the "mediocre" plates, "lackluster" service and "touristy" trappings, but fans insist the garlicky "gimmick" needs "to be experienced, at least once."

Straits Restaurant *Singaporean*

| 20 | 19 | 17 | $38 |

Downtown | Westfield San Francisco Ctr. | 845 Market St., 4th fl. (bet. 4th & 5th Sts.) | 415-668-1783 | www.straitsrestaurants.com

An "eclectic" assortment of "flavorful" Pan-Asian plates with a Singaporean slant "helps wash down" a "wonderful selection" of

	FOOD	DECOR	SERVICE	COST

"unique cocktails" at this "hip", moderately priced Downtowner and its siblings to the south; the "energetic" environs in the Westfield Centre are "exotic enough to make a celebration special", and some salivate over the "waitresses in skimpy outfits" (who can be "a little green"), but strait-laced surveyors "wish they'd tamp down the techno", wailing it's "way too noisy" "when the DJ is playing."

Sunflower Restaurant *Vietnamese*

20	8	16	$18

Mission | 3111 16th St. (bet. Albion & Valencia Sts.) | 415-626-5022 | www.sunflower-restaurant.com
Potrero Hill | 288 Connecticut St. (18th St.) | 415-861-2336 | www.sunflowersf.com

"Generous portions" of "amazing pho" and "tasty rolls" "satisfy cravings" at this "authentic" Vietnamese duo in the Mission and Potrero Hill; the digs are "nothing fancy" (though the Connecticut Street outpost is "slightly more upscale"), but "cheery" service and "cheap" tabs, especially for "lunch specials", appeal for sit-down or "grab-and-go" meals.

NEW Super Duper *Burgers*

-	-	-	I

Castro | 2304 Market St. (bet. Noe & 16th Sts.) | 415-558-8123 | www.superdupersf.com

What makes this Castro burger joint from the Starbelly team potentially more super than its patty peers is the provenance of the ingredients - daily ground Niman Ranch beef, fresh garlic for the frites and Straus organic ice cream for the choco-dipped soft-serve; the simple retro-looking storefront, open 11 AM-11 PM daily, features black-and-white tiled floors, a pressed-plywood counter and a communal table.

Suppenküche *German*

22	16	18	$31

Hayes Valley | 601 Hayes St. (Laguana St.) | 415-252-9289 | www.suppenkuche.com

"Beyond-generous portions" of "stick-to-your-gut" German sustenance (including "addicting" schnitzel) are accompanied by "even bigger glasses" of "glorious beer" at this "Teutonically boisterous" hofbräuhaus in Hayes Valley; it's "sparse on the decor" but "always a madhouse", with a "diverse crowd" of "rowdy" *volk* "mingling" around the "communal tables" and an "über-friendly staff" keeping everyone happy.

Supperclub Ⓜ *Eclectic*

14	22	17	$68

SoMa | 657 Harrison St. (bet. 2nd & 3rd Sts.) | 415-348-0900 | www.supperclub.com

"You never know what they have in store for you" at this "cool" SoMa "freakfest" where diners "lounge" on "comfy beds" while "performance artists" - "from fabulous gender illusionists to acrobats" - put on a "wonderful show"; the expensive Eclectic prix fixe fare is "surprisingly good" say some, who "leave granny at home" for a "semi-risque" night out, but many maintain it's only "a destination for the spectacle - not the food."

Suriya Thai *Thai*

∇ 26	19	22	$26

SoMa | 1532 Howard St. (bet. 11th & 12th Sts.) | 415-355-9999
Veteran chef-owner Khun Suriya continues to helm one of the most "underrated Thai restaurants in San Francisco" muse those in on the

"secret", who have followed him from the Mission to his new, "worth-the-trip" SoMa location (boasting "better parking" and a "beautiful" look); "favorites" like the deep-fried "money bags" starter and "outstanding pumpkin curry" are as "consistent as always", as is the service; P.S. credit cards now accepted.

Sushi Groove *Japanese*　　　22 | 17 | 16 | $37

Russian Hill | 1916 Hyde St. (bet. Green & Union Sts.) | 415-440-1905
SoMa | 1516 Folsom St. (bet. 11th & 12th Sts.) | 415-503-1950 🛢

Touting "adventurously styled" sushi and groovy "urban-chic" decor, these Japanese sibs are packed to the gills with a "young, energetic crowd" sampling the "great" sake concoctions; expect "high-quality" food at both, but listen as the "cable car clangs by" at the "cozy" Russian Hill haunt, while the sashimi comes "with a DJ" at the SoMa branch (i.e. it "gets really loud").

☑ Sushi Zone 🛢🚲 *Japanese*　　27 | 11 | 15 | $33

Castro | 1815 Market St. (Pearl St.) | 415-621-1114

Talk about getting into the Zone: the "brutal waits" at this "tiny" sushi "gem" in the Castro "will melt the life out of you" ("even if you arrive before opening"), and once seated, the "chef is slower than an elderly gent behind the wheel of a Buick"; nevertheless, devotees declare "it's worth it" for the "glorious", "California-ized" rolls (i.e. "full of mangos and macadamias"), and it's one of the "best values" in town to boot.

Sutro's at the Cliff House *Californian*　　20 | 25 | 20 | $50

Outer Richmond | 1090 Point Lobos Ave. (Great Hwy.) | 415-386-3330 | www.cliffhouse.com

Yes, "you're paying for the view" – "crashing waves" and "thrilling sunsets" – at this Outer Richmond "landmark" with a "fantastic cliff location at Ocean Beach", but the Californian menu with "tempting seafood" choices is "surprisingly good" as well (ok, some say it "could be better for the price" and location); add in a "buffet-style" Sunday brunch, "well-stocked" bar and "seasoned service", and even picky locals concede it's "not just for tourists."

☑ Swan Oyster Depot 🛢🚲 *Seafood*　　27 | 12 | 22 | $31

Polk Gulch | 1517 Polk St. (bet. California & Sacramento Sts.) | 415-673-1101

The "no-frills, straight-up seafood", "from freshly shucked oysters to bangin' chowda", is "so fresh you can feel the ocean spray" at this "tiny lunch counter" and fish market in Polk Gulch; "amazingly anachronistic", it's staffed by a "band of friendly brothers" who "provide great entertainment as well as great service", which is why fin fans endure a "daunting" line to snag one of the "uncomfortable stools"; P.S. closes at 5:30 PM.

NEW TacoBar *Mexican*　　　- | - | - | I

Pacific Heights | 2401 California St. (Fillmore St.) | 415-674-7745 | www.415tacobar.com

Hoping to raise the bar on Mexican food in Pacific Heights, this inexpensive newcomer (run by Mexico City native and Nick's Crispy Taco alum Jack Schwartz) focuses on sustainably sourced ingredients; the compact, eco-chic space features reclaimed wood and mosaic wall tiling, and booze options include margaritas, sangria and even tequila-spiked ice cream.

FOOD | DECOR | SERVICE | COST

NEW Tacolicious *Mexican*

23 | 17 | 20 | $21

Embarcadero | Ferry Plaza Mkt. | 1 Ferry Bldg. (The Embarcadero)⑤Ⓜ
Marina | 2031 Chestnut St. (Fillmore St.) | 415-346-1966
www.tacolicioussf.com

Hawking the same "tasty tacos" that draw "long lines" at its Thursday-only Ferry Building stand, this "terrific" new Marina entry ups the ante with sit-down service and an additional selection of ceviche, soups and nightly specials; "full of attractive peeps" and lucha libre art, it gets "louder than an Irish bar on St. Patrick's Day", but "delish" tequila cocktails, "fresh ingredients" and "super salsa" compensate.

☑ Tadich Grill ⑤ *Seafood*

23 | 21 | 21 | $45

Downtown | 240 California St. (bet. Battery & Front Sts.) | 415-391-1849

Whether you "score a private booth" or "sit at the counter" and "watch all the action", this Downtown seafooder established in 1849 "transports you back" to the "Barbary Coast" era, with its "crusty" "career waiters" and "classic" "men's club environment"; it "still has the magic touch", serving "simply prepared" "fresh-from-the-sea" specialties, making it a "can't-miss proposition for a business lunch", but "go early to avoid the lines", or pass the time tippling a "perfectly crafted martini."

Takara *Japanese*

▽ 20 | 12 | 19 | $28

Japantown | 22 Peace Plaza (bet. Laguna & Webster Sts.) | 415-921-2000

"High-quality sushi" and other "authentic" Japanese fare, like "excellent" *chawanmushi* (a savory egg custard "that you can't find elsewhere"), is a "breath of fresh air" at this "hidden nook" in Japantown; "pleasant" but "plain" in appearance, it offers "bargain" lunches and more "expensive" dinners that are still "satisfying for the price."

Taqueria Can-Cun ●⇄ *Mexican*

21 | 9 | 15 | $10

Downtown | 1003 Market St. (6th St.) | 415-864-6773
Mission | 2288 Mission St. (19th St.) | 415-252-9560
Mission | 3211 Mission St. (Valencia St.) | 415-550-1414

Despite "dumpy" digs, die-hards declare this trio "one of your best bets" for "awesome" "burritos as large as your arm", "freshly prepared at super speed"; "you'll find everyone from day-laborers to PYTs here" getting their Mex fix, but "drinking buddies" are especially grateful for the "cheap", "greasy" "late-night tacos" at both Mission branches.

☑ Tartine Bakery *Bakery*

27 | 14 | 15 | $16

Mission | 600 Guerrero St. (18th St.) | 415-487-2600 |
www.tartinebakery.com

"Who needs a sign?"- just "let your nose lead you" to this Mission patisserie proffering what may be the "best carbohydrates on the West Coast", including "unparalleled" pastries, "desserts to dream about" and "extraordinary" bread that emerges "fresh from the oven at 5 PM" each day (and is "probably devoured by 5:15"); the "ridiculously long lines" and "attitude-ridden" staffers "get old" fast, but most happily endure both for chow "in a class by itself."

Tataki Sushi & Sake Bar *Japanese*

▽ 22 | 15 | 18 | $43

Pacific Heights | 2815 California St. (Divisadero St.) | 415-931-1182 |
www.tatakisushibar.com

"Grab a seat at the bar and talk to the chefs" at this "casual" Japanese in Pacific Heights that gets "high marks" for using "sustainable fish", resulting in "unique" sushi and sashimi saluted by regulars who "wait in line forever" to "squish into the tiny space"; naturally, it all comes with "expensive" tabs, but "helpful" servers who "interpret the menu and offer suggestions" ease the pain.

Ten-Ichi *Japanese*

| 20 | 15 | 19 | $29 |

Upper Fillmore | 2235 Fillmore St. (bet. Clay & Sacramento Sts.) | 415-346-3477 | www.tenichisf.com

"Consistent throughout the years", this "solid neighborhood sushi joint" in Upper Fillmore serves up "fresh", "creative" versions of "classic rolls and nigiri" along with "hearty", sometimes "unexpected" Japanese dishes; the "quiet", "comfortable" digs are "plain-Jane" (some say "stuck in the '70s"), but the "competent", "no-rush" service and "reasonable prices" keep regulars coming "back for more"; P.S. no lunch on weekends.

Terzo *Mediterranean*

| 23 | 21 | 21 | $47 |

Cow Hollow | 3011 Steiner St. (Union St.) | 415-441-3200 | www.terzosf.com

Maybe it's the "bubbly hostess" or the "roaring fireplace", but Cow Hollow habitués feel perfectly "cozy" at this "lovely neighborhood" Mediterranean that's a "go-to" "date spot"; there's "always something new" on the "creative" but "totally approachable" menu, and while a few pout it's "pricey for small plates", there are some "great wine specials" Sunday–Thursday.

Thai House Express *Thai*

| 23 | 11 | 15 | $22 |

Castro | 599 Castro St. (19th St.) | 415-864-5000
Tenderloin | 901 Larkin St. (Geary St.) | 415-441-2248 ◗
www.thhexpress.com

These "inexpensive" Siamese twins are "not fancy", but they remain "old standbys" for some of the "most authentic Thai food in town"; the "minimalist decor" of the Castro branch is fitting for the area, while the "gritty" late-night Tenderloin sib features "service so quick, your order arrives before you even have time to say 'please'" after placing it.

Thanh Long Ⓜ *Vietnamese*

| 24 | 15 | 18 | $52 |

Outer Sunset | 4101 Judah St. (46th Ave.) | 415-665-1146 | www.anfamily.com

When "addicted" claw-noisseurs "get a craving" for "roasted Dungeness crab and garlic noodles", they put on their "polyester pants with stretch waistbands" and scamper into Crustacean's Outer Sunset Vietnamese sib, where the "pricey" "main attraction" "enchants their senses from headtop to toenail"; the "tired" decor looks "like Saigon in '72" and some gripe the "rest of the menu is pretty mundane", but no matter: most "can't wait to go back."

Thep Phanom Thai Cuisine *Thai*

| 23 | 16 | 19 | $30 |

Lower Haight | 400 Waller St. (Fillmore St.) | 415-431-2526 | www.thepphanom.com

This "favorite" in the Lower Haight is the "king of Thai restaurants" espouse loyal subjects who "crave" "authentic, hot and spicy" flavors; if a few tut "it upgraded the interior but hasn't returned to its former glory", most maintain the "only problem" is "if you come after 6 PM" – when the "tiny" room gets "busy and noisy" and the parking situation gets worse.

	FOOD	DECOR	SERVICE	COST

NEW Thermidor ☒ American
- | - | - | E

SoMa | 8 Mint Plaza (bet. Market & Mission Sts.) | 415-896-6500 | www.thermidorsf.com

The duo behind Spork pays homage to the heyday of 1960s country-club dining at this Mint Plaza newcomer in SoMa offering updated spins on rich American classics, including its namesake lobster dish, accompanied by retro cocktails and a decidedly modern dessert called Coffee, Cigarettes and Doughnuts; the indoor/outdoor setting features midcentury touches, such as white molded-plastic chairs, as well as more sumptuous black leather seating in the lounge.

1300 on Fillmore Soul/Southern
23 | 24 | 22 | $47

Western Addition | 1300 Fillmore St. (Eddy St.) | 415-771-7100 | www.1300fillmore.com

"West meets South" at this "hot spot" in the Western Addition's "jazz district", where an "eclectic" crowd convenes in the "simply cool" lounge sipping "superb cocktails" before moving on to "dressed-up", "insanely rich" soul food "classics" ("mama never cooked this well"); complete with "on-point" service, it's particularly "perfect for dinner before going to Yoshi's" or for the "fabulous gospel brunch" on Sundays.

Three Seasons Vietnamese
21 | 19 | 18 | $39

Marina | 3317 Steiner St. (bet. Chestnut & Lombard Sts.) | 415-567-9989 | www.threeseasonsrestaurant.com

Cooking up "creative combinations" of "tasty" Vietnamese fare, this "lively" duo offers "something for everyone", including an "amazing" "variety of spring rolls", "luscious" fish dishes and "great cocktails"; both get "noisy", but the "memorable" setting in Palo Alto (try a "warm day on the terrace") and "intimate" Marina branch make for a "pleasant" if "pricy" night out.

Ti Couz French
21 | 14 | 16 | $23

Mission | 3108 16th St. (bet. Guerrero & Valencia Sts.) | 415-252-7373

The "impressive" selection of crêpes ("a staple of Brittany gastronomy") comes in "satisfying" savory buckwheat varieties and "tender" sweet styles at this "informal" Mission bistro known for its "hearty" ciders too; outdoor seating attracts *amis* who want to "watch the funky 16th Street world go by", but some aren't so keen on the "sassy" service.

Tipsy Pig American
19 | 16 | 17 | $32

Marina | 2231 Chestnut St. (bet. Pierce & Scott Sts.) | 415-292-2300 | www.thetipsypigsf.com

More "total Marina scene" than "storied English pub", this upscale neighborhood tavern features "rich" American fare (plus a "fantastic brunch") that's a "notch above the usual", along with "generous" libations served in "mason jars"; it's a "nice change" when you want to "pig out", but quiet types should "sit in the library" or on the "relaxing patio" and flee before the "frat/drunk/yuppie rush hour", when service drags and it's "noisier than a rock concert."

Tokyo Go Go Japanese
21 | 16 | 17 | $37

Mission | 3174 16th St. (bet. Guerrero & Valencia Sts.) | 415-864-2288 | www.tokyogogo.com

Seeming "more like a bar than a typical Japanese restaurant", this Mission hangout serves up "fresh fish" in a "loungelike" setting; some "hit up the sushi bar" and banter with the "friendly chefs" over "decent", "pricey" plates, and while it's "not as crowded as it was in flusher times", it still reels in the young set with its "trendy" ambiance and "awesome" happy-hour deals.

Tommaso's ⓜ *Italian*

24	16	20	$29

North Beach | 1042 Kearny St. (bet. B'way & Pacific Ave.) | 415-398-9696 | www.tommasosnorthbeach.com

"You always know what you'll get" at this affordable, "unpretentious" eatery in North Beach, and that's "superb" "thin-crust" pizzas pulled from a "wood-burning oven", as well as other "old-school" Neapolitan fare (think "lots of red sauce"); it's "nothing fancy" and the impatient "hate the wait" (there are "no reservations"), but "once you're seated" it's "loads of fun", since the "subterranean" space "feels like one big Italian dinner table."

Tommy's Mexican Restaurant *Mexican*

18	14	18	$27

Outer Richmond | 5929 Geary Blvd. (bet. 23rd & 24th Aves.) | 415-387-4747 | www.tommystequila.com

The "solid" Mexican menu has "something for everyone" at this "jumping" joint in the Outer Richmond , but the "best thing" about it is the "huge selection of tequila" curated by "knowledgeable" agave guru Julio Bermejo; "spot-on" margaritas ease the discomfort of being "crammed together" in the "loud", "crowded" digs, but teetotalers tut you can find better fare "for the price."

Tommy Toy's Cuisine Chinoise *Chinese*

24	25	24	$62

Downtown | 655 Montgomery St. (bet. Clay & Washington Sts.) | 415-397-4888 | www.tommytoys.com

"Sophisticated" Chinese cuisine "with a French twist" makes for a "memorable meal" at this "swank" Downtowner that's "grand in every way", from the "beautifully presented" plates to "waiters in tuxes" who "pay attention to the details"; whether you go for the "bargain" lunch special or shell out the "big bucks" for the "fantastic" tasting menu at dinner, it's an "elegant" experience all around.

Tonga Room ⓜ *Asian/Pacific Rim*

14	24	17	$45

Nob Hill | Fairmont Hotel | 950 Mason St. (bet. California & Sacramento Sts.) | 415-772-5278 | www.fairmont.com

It's "corny" and packed with "tourists", but tiki-teers insist "you have to go at least once" to this "fabulously campy" "tropical paradise" in Nob Hill "before it's gone"; true, just about everyone pupus the "over-priced theme food" ("make a meal out of" the Pan-Asian–Pacific Rim happy hour instead), but the "complimentary leis", "floating band" and "intermittent" indoor "monsoons" replete with "thunder and lightning" are "still fun after all these years" – particularly after a few "kitcshy" "umbrella drinks."

Ton Kiang *Chinese*

24	12	16	$30

Outer Richmond | 5821 Geary Blvd. (bet. 22nd & 23rd Aves.) | 415-387-8273 | www.tonkiang.net

"Go during the week" to avoid the "crowds" at this Outer Richmond "dim sum shop", a "no-brainer" "away from the tourists and Chinatown" that's revered for its "endless variety" of "high-quality" small plates "served all day, every day" (plus "Hakka specialties" at dinner); "thread-bare" digs and "iffy service" aside, it's "one of the more solid options in the city" – just "pace yourself" or "you could run up some serious debt."

Tony's Pizza Napoletana Ⓜ *Italian*   26 | 15 | 20 | $30

North Beach | 1570 Stockton St. (Union St.) | 415-835-9888 | www.tonyspizzanapoletana.com

"Real-deal pizzaiolo" Tony Gemignani tosses some of the "best dough for not too much dough" at this "fantastic addition to North Beach", a "friendly" "slice of Italy" offering "different styles of pizza" – including American, Neapolitan and Sicilian – courtesy of multiple ovens; however, you'll need to "get there early" to sample the "award-winning margherita" pie ("only make 73 a day"), which can be enjoyed in the "lively" dining room or at "outside tables"; P.S. no reservations, so "grab a beer and wait" in the "great bar"; the adjacent Tony's Coal-Fired Pizza & Slice House is set to open shortly.

Town Hall *American*   23 | 20 | 21 | $50

SoMa | 342 Howard St. (Fremont St.) | 415-908-3900 | www.townhallsf.com

Once "you get past the suits", you're in for a "special" time at this "happening" SoMa New American serving up "so-dependable-it's-scary" "gourmet comfort food" with "Southern flair" (including "some of the best desserts"); it's all set in an "unfussy", exposed-brick space overseen by "attentive" servers, making it "ideal" for "business lunches", a "night out" or "after-work" cocktails – which explains why even the "communal table fills up fast."

Town's End
Restaurant & Bakery Ⓜ *American/Bakery*   20 | 15 | 19 | $29

Embarcadero | South Beach Marina Apts. | 2 Townsend St. (The Embarcadero) | 415-512-0749 | www.townsendrb.com

"Comfort food that makes you smile" is the draw at this "simple" New American cafe where the "good basic" breakfast is "worth it just for a basket of housemade" pastries ("try eating only one mini-muffin") and the Tuesday dinner special is a "deal"; service is generally "helpful", and while the "nice space" is humble, with windows onto the Embarcadero, there's "not a bad view either."

Trademark Grill Ⓢ *American*   ▽ 19 | 17 | 18 | $42

Downtown | 56 Belden Pl. (bet. Bush & Pine Sts.) | 415-397-8800 | www.trademarksf.com

Downtowners applaud the "old Elite crew" for bringing its "killer biscuits", "great oyster selection" and deviled eggs with cumin to this handsome pedestrian-alley spin-off, where outdoor seating beckons for "sipping cocktails" and noshing on affordable New American eats; however, while FiDi folks "love the locale" and 'closing bell' happy-hour specials (2:30-6 PM), the underwhelmed scoff that it needs to "try a lot harder" given "superior competitors."

Trattoria Contadina *Italian*   23 | 15 | 22 | $38

North Beach | 1800 Mason St. (Union St.) | 415-982-5728 | www.trattoriacontadina.com

"On a quiet corner off the main drag" in North Beach, this "sweet little neighborhood Italian joint" "manages to avoid being a tourist trap", instead attracting locals who "keep coming back" for "amazing" yet "affordable" "traditional" fare like "fresh pastas" with "lively sauces" and "lots of great wine choices too"; the interior may be "intimate (read: cramped)" and the crowd "cacophonous", "but that just makes everyone feel like family" enthuse fans, who love the "warm" staff as well.

Tres Agaves *Mexican*   17 | 18 | 16 | $34

South Beach | 130 Townsend St. (bet. 2nd & 3rd Sts.) | 415-227-0500 | www.tresagaves.com

"Knowledgeable bartenders take you on the tequila experience of your life", pouring an "incredible selection" at this "group"-friendly South Beach Mex where the margs are "killer" and the "solid" menu goes beyond "your ordinary burritos"; it "delivers" "before a baseball game" with a "good-time atmosphere", but peeved patrons pout it's "too noisy" and find the "overpriced" "faux taqueria" fare "nothing to rave about."

Tropisueño *Mexican*   19 | 16 | 17 | $28

SoMa | 75 Yerba Buena Ln. (bet. Market & Mission Sts.) | 415-243-0299 | www.tropisueno.com

"Festive decor", "strong margaritas" and "generous", "tasty" Mexican plates – "what more could a girl" (or conventioneer) "ask for?" marvel tequila-lovin' loyalists of this "surprise" "tucked away" in SoMa; operating as a taqueria by day and "upscale" joint at night, it "fills the gap" for lunch or "happy hour" when you "don't want to pay FiDi prices", even if it gets a bit "crowded and noisy."

Troya *Turkish*   23 | 18 | 22 | $29

Inner Richmond | 349 Clement St. (5th Ave.) | 415-379-6000 | www.troyasf.com

For a "Turkish treat", Inner Richmonders descend upon this "gem on Clement" for "delicious" Mediterranean favorites like "aromatic" kebabs and "divine" *manti* (ravioli); still, with "competent" service, an "unpretentious" setting and an enticing happy hour, fans can't help but wonder "why are there always so few people in there?"

Truly Mediterranean *Mediterranean*   26 | 7 | 15 | $13

Mission | 3109 16th St. (Valencia St.) | 415-252-7482 | www.trulymedsf.com

"Crispy meets creamy meets spicy meets tangy" at this "tiny" (and "cheap") Mission Med–Middle Eastern doling out "delicious" shawarma, "super falafel" and enough meat-free offerings to ensure a "big vegetarian party in your mouth"; there are "only a few stools and a counter", so "don't even think about eating in" – just "line up" for takeout and "prepare to be awed."

Tsunami Sushi &
Sake Bar ●🅼 *Japanese*   22 | 22 | 20 | $48

South Beach | 301 King St. (4th St.) | 415-284-0111
Western Addition | 1306 Fulton St. (Divisadero St.) | 415-567-7664
www.nihon-sf.com

"Sushi lovers who think they've had it all" learn otherwise at these "accommodating" Western Addition and South Beach eateries known for their "unique" preparations of "super-fresh" fish; a "great sake list", "loud music" and a "loungey" atmosphere attract a "hip crowd" until "late" (midnight or 1 AM), but beyond the "bargain" happy hour ("the best thing going" here), they're "a bit on the pricey side."

	FOOD	DECOR	SERVICE	COST

Tu Lan ☒⚑ *Vietnamese* · 21 | 3 | 10 | $13

SoMa | 8 Sixth St. (Market St.) | 415-626-0927

The "amazing" Vietnamese chow that "Julia [Child] loved" is "as good as ever" report the "starving students" and brave chowhounds who "don't look at the floors" and simply enjoy the "fast", "cheap" and "copious" meals at this SoMa "Formica palace"; "just watch your step and don't linger at night", as the crowd inside and out is a "mix of the good, the bad, and the very ugly."

2223 Restaurant *Californian* · 21 | 20 | 21 | $39

Castro | 2223 Market St. (bet. Noe & Sanchez Sts.) | 415-431-0692 | www.2223restaurant.com

"Still hanging on as the 'A choice'" in the "gayborhood" (but fine to "take your straight friends"), this "loud", "modern swank" joint is "as Castrofab as it gets", with a "sweet", "engaging" staff, "entertaining" crowd and "delicious" drinks; while the "reliable" Cal-New American "comfort food" is outshined by the "scene", it's a "bargain" on Tuesday nights (with $12 entrees) and "terrific" for Sunday "brunch-a-rama."

Udupi Palace ⚑ *Indian/Vegetarian* · 20 | 8 | 14 | $18

Mission | 1007 Valencia St. (21st St.) | 415-970-8000 | www.udupipalaceca.com

"The curries will clear your sinuses" and the dosas are big "enough to feed a small country but good enough to eat alone" at this "quality" South Indian vegetarian trio where you will "not miss the meat" (or the "wheat", for the "gluten-challenged"); though both the Berkeley and Sunnyvale settings are "less than bland", in the Mission "Bollywood music videos" entertain hipster crowds downing "real-deal" chow at prices that "can't be beat."

Umami Ⓜ *Japanese* · 23 | 22 | 19 | $42

Cow Hollow | 2909 Webster St. (Union St.) | 415-346-3431 | www.umamisf.com

"Tasty" sushi and other "tempting" Japanese bites satisfy after-work appetites at this "trendy" Cow Hollow izakaya whose first floor is "always a scene" at the bar, complete with "half-price" bottles of wine during "happy hour"; those who wish to "enjoy their spicy tuna roll in peace" choose to "sit upstairs", where they can also watch the "incredibly fast" chefs at work.

Underdog Hot Dog & Sausage ⚑ *Hot Dogs* · ▽ 21 | 12 | 20 | $12

Inner Sunset | 1634 Irving St. (bet. 17th & 18th Aves.) | 415-665-8881

The "delicious organic and vegan sausages" at this Inner Sunset "hole-in-the-wall" may be a "long way from the Coney Island original", but green grazers agree the "yummy-with-no-guilt" dogs are a "rare find" – and with "great buns" to boot; they're complemented by "more good stuff" (tater tots, natural soft drinks, etc.), though, frankly, the limited seating suggests takeout is the way to go.

Unicorn Pan Asian Cuisine ☒ *Asian* · 22 | 19 | 19 | $31

Downtown | 191 Pine St. (Battery St.) | 415-982-9828 | www.unicorndining.com

Downtown denizens horn in on this "fashionable" "standby" for a satisfying selection of "delicious" Pan-Asian fare with "interesting" flavors (e.g. "green onion roti") paired with an "extensive" wine list; though it gets "crazy-busy at lunch", "helpful service" moves things along, and "if you have to work late" it's a "good option" for a "quiet" dinner, when the "prix fixe is the way to go."

Universal Cafe ⓜ American

| 23 | 17 | 20 | $38 |

Mission | 2814 19th St. (bet. Bryant & Florida Sts.) | 415-821-4608 | www.universalcafe.net

"Driven by ingredients and imagination", the ever-changing menu at this "outstanding" Missionite features "original, delicious" New American food at "reasonable prices"; true, the "minimalist" space (including "sunny" outdoor tables) can get "chaotic", especially during the "dazzling" brunch, but it's "worth it" to eat at an "institution" that "keeps doing simple things right"; P.S. Tuesday is dinner-only.

Urban Tavern American

| 17 | 18 | 17 | $40 |

Downtown | Hilton | 333 O'Farrell St. (bet. Mason & Taylor Sts.) | 415-771-1400 | www.urbantavernsf.com

"Nice for a hotel restaurant", this Downtown New American gastropub with a "hip design" is a "good value for lunch" and "great before the theater" assert Urban-ites, though critics contend that it's a "little off" somehow, noting there's "not a great beer selection" for a bar and grousing "they need to bring" the "average" eats "up a notch."

Uva Enoteca Italian

| 21 | 19 | 21 | $36 |

Lower Haight | 568 Haight St. (bet. Fillmore & Steiner Sts.) | 415-829-2024 | www.uvaenoteca.com

A "sophisticated" "standout" in the Lower Haight, this "laid-back" enoteca is a "one-stop shop" for Italy's holy trinity, proffering "superb" "cured meats, cheeses and wine" ("what more does one need?") to oenophiles who make a "meal" out of "nibbles" "you won't find anywhere else"; weekend brunch and "reasonable prices" are other lures, though sensitive types counsel the "chic" brick digs gets "loud", especially around "happy hour."

NEW Velvet Room Californian

| - | - | - | M |

Downtown | Clift Hotel | 495 Geary St. (bet. Mission & Taylor Sts.) | 415-929-2300 | www.clifthotel.com

Philippe Starck's striking interior, decked out with red velvet curtains and Murano glass chandeliers, continues to set the stage for Downtown hobnobbing at this newcomer in the Clift Hotel (replacing Asia de Cuba), although now the kitchen is turning out midpriced, locally sourced Californian fare; diners can gaze at themselves via mirror-topped communal tables, while the adjacent Redwood Room affords more traditional people-watching.

Venticello Italian

| 23 | 21 | 22 | $50 |

Nob Hill | 1257 Taylor St. (Washington St.) | 415-922-2545 | www.venticello.com

With "the clang of the cable cars going by" and "charming" servers who are "attentive without being intrusive", this "inviting", upscale trattoria "high up on Nob Hill" oozes "pure romance", making it a popular place for "that special dinner with that special someone"; the "excellent" cooking and "extensive" wine list "transport you to Northern Italy in a nano-second" say admirers, while "awesome views" over the city toward the Bay Bridge are "so San Francisco."

	FOOD	DECOR	SERVICE	COST

Vitrine *American* ▽ 21 | 21 | 21 | $45

SoMa | St. Regis | 125 Third St., 4th fl. (Mission St.) | 415-284-4049 | www.stregis.com/sanfrancisco

"Tucked away" in the St. Regis hotel, this "well-kept secret near the Moscone Center and SoMa museums" is "perfect for that sedate dining experience you want with a client", serving "decadent" breakfasts and "killer" New American lunches; of course it's "not cheap", but enthusiasts "on an expense account" sing about the "beautiful setting", saying the "serene atmosphere" "lowers their blood pressure with every passing moment"; P.S. closes at 2 PM.

Walzwerk *German* 21 | 16 | 18 | $28

Mission | 381 S. Van Ness Ave. (bet. 14th & 15th Sts.) | 415-551-7181 | www.walzwerk.com

Those "nostalgic for old Ostdeutschland" find "Eastern Bloc bliss" at this "kitschy" Missionite that "re-creates the feel" of Berlin "during the wall" with "cold-war-sparse" decor; expect "schnitzel to dream of" and other affordable, "no-fuss" East German "comfort food" washed down with an "outstanding" assortment of native brews, all served by a "charming staff" that's "actually from Germany."

Warming Hut 13 | 15 | 12 | $14
Café & Bookstore *Sandwiches*

Presidio | Crissy Field, Bldg. 983 | Marine Dr. (Long Ave.) | 415-561-3040 | www.crissyfield.org

"What a view!" coo "Crissy Field wanderers" who warm up, get "caffeinated" and refuel at this "adorable" cafe/bookstore in the Presidio overlooking the Golden Gate Bridge; the "organic" fare (soups, sandwiches, cookies) strikes some as an "expensive" "afterthought" and the counter crew "could be a lot faster", but the "unbeatable setting" makes it an "oasis" nonetheless, particularly "after a long walk in the fog."

Waterbar *Seafood* 20 | 26 | 20 | $58

Embarcadero | 399 The Embarcadero (Folsom St.) | 415-284-9922 | www.waterbarsf.com

"Watch the antics of the sea life" in the "floor-to-ceiling" "aquarium columns" (sure to "wow the out-of-towners"), the "beautiful-people" "action at the bar" or just drink in the "spectacular" "Bay Bridge outside" at Pat Kuleto's "water-themed" Embarcadero fish house; finatics find the seafood "rock solid", adding you "can't beat" the "$1 oyster specials" for "happy hour", but sharkier sorts snap "unfortunately" the "pricey" "food does not measure up" to the "killer view."

Waterfront Restaurant *Californian/Seafood* 18 | 22 | 19 | $53

Embarcadero | Pier 7 (B'way) | 415-391-2696 | www.waterfrontsf.com

The "terrific" "bayside setting" translates into "million-dollar views" at this "swanky" Embarcadero "old-schooler" serving "dependable" Californian seafood; many find it's "good for groups" and "out-of-town visitors", but others are in a flap about "hit-or-miss service" and mutter that the "mediocre" menu is "mismatched" with the "lovely" locale and "pricey" tab; P.S. a recent chef change may not be fully reflected in the Food score.

	FOOD	DECOR	SERVICE	COST

NEW Wayfare Tavern American

| - | - | - | E |

Downtown | 558 Sacramento St. (bet. Montgomery & Sansome Sts.) | 415-772-9060 | www.wayfaretavern.com

Celebrity chef Tyler Florence's ode to the Barbary Coast lures power-lunchers and Downtown diners with upscale Traditional American fare, like organic fried chicken and steak and eggs, proffered in a stunning turn-of-the-century building tricked out with Victorian hunting bric-a-brac and dark leather booths; the tri-level setting includes a gentlemen's club-esque billiards room upstairs, plus two bars mixing retro cocktails (courtesy of the Bon Vivants) and pouring Golden State wines.

Weird Fish ⊠ Seafood

| 20 | 18 | 20 | $25 |

Mission | 2193 Mission St. (18th St.) | 415-863-4744 | www.weirdfishsf.com

"Inventive pescatarian" and vegetarian vittles lure a "funky crowd" to this "always packed", "aptly named" "hole-in-the-wall", a "little" (and we "do mean little") nautical nook in the Mission; "weird and wonderful" is the way, from the "suspicious fish dish – always a fun surprise" – to "fried pickles" and "amazing" weekend brunch options like soy chorizo omelets, all served "down and quick"; P.S. its new Schwinn-powered 'Taco Bike' offerings can be tracked via Twitter.

Wexler's ⊠ BBQ

| 22 | 18 | 22 | $39 |

Downtown | 568 Sacramento St. (Montgomery St.) | 415-983-0102 | www.wexlerssf.com

"Ridiculously delicious" Southern-inspired American dishes showcasing "elevated", "unique twists on BBQ" and a "sleek setting" replete with a room-length "wood sculpture" representing black plumes make this "happening" Downtowner a "must-try", especially for "FiDi folks"; whet your whistle with a "speakeasy-type" drink, then take a "tasty" "journey through smoke-cooking" with a detour through "heavenly" Scotch eggs – but "come early" because "even the bar fills up" quickly.

'Wichcraft Sandwiches

| 18 | 13 | 14 | $17 |

Downtown | Westfield San Francisco Ctr. | 868 Mission St., ground fl. (bet. 4th & 5th Sts.) | 866-942-4272 | www.wichcraftsf.com

"Sandwiches like your mama never put in your Lucy lunchbox" "delight" Downtowners who marvel how a "simple meal can be turned into a gourmet experience" at this "modern" "cafeteria-style" mall stop by celeb chef Tom Colicchio; some unmoved eaters aren't feeling the magic, however, citing "overpriced" fare that's just not a "big deal" – even if it's "blessed by a judge from *Top Chef*"; P.S. closes at 6 PM.

Woodhouse Fish Company Seafood

| 20 | 15 | 19 | $31 |

Castro | 2073 Market St. (14th St.) | 415-437-2722
Pacific Heights | 1914 Fillmore St. (bet. Bush & Pine Sts.) | 415-437-2722
www.woodhousefish.com

"New Englanders give the seal of approval" to these Castro and Pac Heights "clam shacks" where you can "roll up your sleeves" and get to "cracking crab shells" or chow down on other "honest" seafood and "wash it all down with a crisp glass of white or a cold beer"; the "engaging" service is a plus, but the no-rez policy often results in "long lines", and some cranky Cape Codders call it "expensive for what you get."

FOOD | DECOR | SERVICE | COST

Woodward's Garden 🗷 Ⓜ *American/Californian* 24 | 18 | 20 | $49

Mission | 1700 Mission St. (Duboce St.) | 415-621-7122 |
www.woodwardsgarden.com

"Don't let the proximity of the freeway put you off", because this Mission
"original" is "serious about food", turning "really top ingredients" into
"consistently creative" Cal–New American dishes in its "tiny open
kitchen"; the "funky" digs attract the "under-30" set, but some more-
seasoned surveyors suggest the "dreary" decor is ripe for a "revamp"
and cite a little "sticker shock" with the bill.

XYZ *American/Californian* 20 | 22 | 20 | $48

SoMa | W Hotel | 181 Third St. (Howard St.) | 415-817-7836 |
www.xyz-sf.com

"Smart and trendy", this "stylish" Cal-American in SoMa's W Hotel
"surprises" many with its "delicious", slightly "expensive" "seasonal
creations" served by a "pleasant" staff; while more-demanding diners
feel it focuses too much on the "action at the bar" ("XYZ needs to follow
the ABCs of running a restaurant"), others are happy to "park here after work" and soak in "the ambiance and energy" of the "scene."

Yabbies Coastal Kitchen *Seafood* 22 | 17 | 19 | $41

Russian Hill | 2237 Polk St. (bet. Green & Vallejo Sts.) | 415-474-4088 |
www.yabbiesrestaurant.com

"Don't forget" about this "fun local joint" recommend Russian Hill
habitués, who like its "fresh and tasty" (if "basic") seafood, including
a "good raw bar and interesting specials", served amid seacoast murals; a crabby few are "not impressed" by either the food or service,
but most approve of the "reasonable" tabs.

Yamo 🗷⊅ *Burmese* ▽ 21 | 6 | 13 | $11

Mission | 3406 18th St. (Mission St.) | 415-553-8911
This "cute" Mission "secret" may be "tiny", but the "authentic"
Burmese flavors in dishes like the "tasty pan-fried noodles" and "great
mango chicken" are "big, bold" and "satisfying" ("cheap too!");
though service can be "brusque" and decor is "nonexistent", the
owner "knows how to run a tight ship", so it doesn't take long to grab
takeout or nab "counter seating."

🗷 Yank Sing *Chinese* 25 | 17 | 19 | $37

SoMa | Rincon Ctr. | 101 Spear St. (Mission St.) | 415-957-9300
SoMa | 49 Stevenson St. (bet. 1st & 2nd Sts.) | 415-541-4949
www.yanksing.com

"Plan to nap after" "eating your fill" at this "Cartier of dim sum" and
"then some", a "gold-standard" Cantonese "banquet-hall" duo in SoMa
packed with "attorneys", "tourists" and Chinatown-averse diners; it's
easy to spend "Benjamins" aplenty on lunch or brunch as the "enticing"
"little carts" loaded with "phenomenal" dumplings "descend like lo-
custs", but the "civilized setting", "helpful staff" (fulfilling "special orders" via "headsets") and "added fresh factor" make the bill "worth it."

Yoshi's San Francisco *Japanese* 21 | 24 | 19 | $50

Western Addition | Fillmore Heritage Ctr. | 1330 Fillmore St. (Eddy St.) |
415-655-5600 | www.yoshis.com

"Original" Japanese fare "taken to the next level", "excellent sake" and
"enchanting" jazz – now that's a "jam for the ages" quip music lovers

who dig dining at this "beautifully designed" Western Addition "cousin" of the famed Oakland supper club; "darn tootin'" the "portions are small and expensive", and service can be "slow", "especially before a show", but "treats" like "priority seating" and "dessert while enjoying" the performance keep the "good" times humming.

Yuet Lee ● *Chinese* | 20 | 5 | 13 | $23

Chinatown | 1300 Stockton St. (B'way) | 415-982-6020

While some are put off by the "ugly-on-ugly color scheme" and "fluorescent-lit" dining room that can probably "be seen from space", and others are "astonished" by the "flopping fish brought to the table for inspection before cooking", many champion the "sensational" seafood and other "cheap" Cantonese eats served at this Chinatown "pit"; since it's open weekends till 3 AM, it's a "quick and dirty" stop for a "late-night grub session."

Yumma's *Mideastern* | ▽ 19 | 8 | 18 | $12

Inner Sunset | 721 Irving St. (bet. 8th & 9th Aves.) | 415-682-0762

Whether you're craving "the best" organic "shawarma this side of the Middle East", "excellent falafel" or "authentic" hummus "like your Lebanese grandmother's" (if you had one), you'll find it at this Inner Sunset "surprise"; "there's not a whole lot going on" decorwise and no alcohol is served either, but never mind: "there's not a dud on the menu"; P.S. soiree planners can also order "party platters."

Zadin Ⓜ *Vietnamese* | ▽ 23 | 20 | 23 | $32

Castro | 4039 18th St. (Hartford St.) | 415-626-2260 | www.zadinsf.com

"An orchestra of flavors" awaits at this "under-the-radar" Vietnamese venue offering a "pleasant reprieve from the Castro" "bar-hopping"/ "power-shopping" "scene"; the "intimate" room, "chill vibe", "attentive staff" and "bold", "flavorful" dishes (including "gluten-free" options) add up to the "perfect" "intermediary night out", with "no cheek-by-jowl tables" as a bonus, so it's definitely a step up from the usual "pho" houses.

Z & Y *Chinese* | - | - | - | M

Chinatown | 655 Jackson St. (bet. Grant & Kearny Sts.) | 415-981-8988 | www.zandyrestaurant.com

Nestled in the heart of Chinatown, this Sino find decorated with the requisite red lanterns and wall hangings may look low-key, but it's run by a top expat chef who now woks up authentic, flaming-hot Sichuan specialties that make diners comfortably numb (along with some tame dishes for uninitiated Midwestern tourists); his accommodating wife paces the meal, ferrying much-needed pitchers of water and bottles of Tsing Tao; P.S. validates two-hour free parking at the nearby Portsmouth Square Garage.

Zante Pizza & Indian Cuisine *Indian/Pizza* | ▽ 18 | 8 | 11 | $20

Bernal Heights | 3489 Mission St. (Cortland St.) | 415-821-3949 | www.zantespizza.com

"Fantabulous Indian pizza" and "vegetarian versions" like naan-other keep city slickers "addicted" to this subcontinental in Bernal Heights; surprisingly, the "flavors don't come on too strong" – who knew that "tandoori chicken" and "some curry" spices could make such an "amazing topping"? – and to seal the deal "it's still hot" when they deliver.

	FOOD	DECOR	SERVICE	COST

Zaré at Fly Trap ⑤ *Californian/Mediterranean* | 23 | 20 | 22 | $47 |

SoMa | 606 Folsom St. (2nd St.) | 415-243-0580 |
www.zareflytrap.com

"Welcoming" chef-owner Hoss Zaré is a "total love biscuit", and his Californian cuisine "infused" with a "Persian twang" reveals his "joyful take on life" exclaim enthusiasts who "feel like family-plus" at his Mediterranean-inspired SoMa casbah, set in the "former Fly Trap"; "everything comes together here", from the "explosive, nuanced", "zingy flavors" and "amazing cocktails" to the "attentive" staff and "sexy" vibe – "I'd go back here in a second on my magic carpet."

Zarzuela ⑤Ⓜ *Spanish* | 24 | 17 | 21 | $39 |

Russian Hill | 2000 Hyde St. (Union St.) | 415-346-0800

"Terrific" "tapas are the thing", along with "traditional Spanish paella" that's a "delight to behold even before" you tuck into it, at this "lively", moderately priced locale in Russian Hill that's a natural for "impressing a date or out-of-town guests"; "courteous" waiters provide a "warm welcome", and though the "lack of reservations" can be "a drawback", optimists advise "ordering a glass of sangria" and "watching the cable cars" while you wait.

Zazie *French* | 22 | 18 | 20 | $29 |

Cole Valley | 941 Cole St. (bet. Carl St. & Parnassus Ave.) |
415-564-5332 | www.zaziesf.com

"Showstopping" gingerbread pancakes and "amazing" riffs on eggs Benedict make this "welcoming" Cole Valley bistro in an 1870s schoolhouse one of "z best" for brunch, so no wonder there's always a "line, rain or shine"; its affordable French fare "satisfies" for other meals too (and "free-corkage Tuesdays" are a "nice perk"), but many brave it simply for the "sunny" patio that's a "real treat"; P.S. in cooler weather, outdoor "heat lamps ward off the chill."

Zeitgeist ⓞⒻ *Burgers* | 16 | 17 | 11 | $14 |

Mission | 199 Valencia St. (Duboce Ave.) | 415-255-7505 |
www.zeitgeistsf.com

"Not fine dining by any means", this "dark dive bar" is packed with "hipsters" sporting "multiple body piercings, tattoos and skinny jeans" who spill out into the backyard to enjoy "great greasy burgers", "beers and big Bloody Marys at bargain prices"; prepare to "be patient" and expect some "abuse" from the staff, but it "rocks on a hot day", when you can "make new biker friends" at one of the picnic tables; P.S. "an added bonus is the Tamale Lady", who makes "her rounds" here regularly.

Ⓝ̲Ⓔ̲Ⓦ̲ Zero Zero *Italian/Pizza* | - | - | - | M |

SoMa | 826 Folsom St. (4th St.) | 415-348-8800 |
www.zerozerosf.com

Bruce Hill (Picco, Pizzeria Picco and Bix) brings his pizzaiolo mojo to this new SoMa Italian specializing in Neapolitan-style wood-fired pies, along with house-cured meats, pastas and his signature softserve ice creams; the name refers to the brand of flour used to achieve the perfect crust, while the design of the bi-level eatery pays homage to the 1900s, with flame-inspired lighting and bars upstairs and down pouring classic cocktails.

| | FOOD | DECOR | SERVICE | COST |

Z Zuni Café M *Mediterranean*   25 21 22 $52

Hayes Valley | 1658 Market St. (bet. Franklin & Gough Sts.) | 415-552-2522 | www.zunicafe.com

"Like an old girlfriend who never seems to age", Judy Rodgers' Hayes Valley "treasure" "filled with light and laughter" still "holds onto the hearts" of "locavores" with its "simple but amazing" Med fare; "noon or night", it's "always buzzing", with everyone from "politicians" to "drag queens" devouring the "perfect" "wood-fired chicken" for two, "legendary Caesar salad" and the "best burgers" (at lunch and after 10 PM) or indulging in "super Bloodys" and oysters at the "cool zinc bar", so most don't mind the occasional "attitude."

Zuppa *Italian*   20 17 19 $39

SoMa | 564 Fourth St. (bet. Brannan & Bryant Sts.) | 415-777-5900 | www.zuppa-sf.com

"Lovely" presentations of pizza, pasta and other "rustic" dishes appeal at this "casual" SoMa Southern Italian where the "high ceilings in a warehouse setting" give it a "cool" "industrial" vibe; "happy-hour bargains" are a plus, but claustrophobes criticize "close-together" tables and say it feels a bit "stark."

Z Zushi Puzzle Ø *Japanese*   27 11 19 $46

Marina | 1910 Lombard St. (Buchanan St.) | 415-931-9319 | www.zushipuzzle.com

"Overlook the tired decor" of this Japanese dive in the Marina and you'll be rewarded with the "widest variety" of "pristine, perfectly prepared" "exotic fish" "this side of Tokyo" (including "live scallops – don't tell PETA"); "dropping in is nearly impossible" since the "secret is out", so reserve first, then "squeeze up to the bar" and "enjoy the ride" as "master" owner Roger Chong "takes care of you" ("you won't get the same service or food at a table"); sure, you might "drop a bundle", but this sushi "rivals" the "best."

EAST OF SAN FRANCISCO

Top Food

__28__ Erna's Elderberry | *Cal./French*
Chez Panisse | *Cal./Med.*

__27__ Chez Panisse Café | *Cal./Med.*
Commis | *American*
Rivoli | *Californian/Med.*
Cheese Board | *Bakery/Pizza*

__26__ Bakesale Betty | *Bakery*
BayWolf | *Californian/Med.*

__25__ Tratt. La Siciliana | *Italian*
Pizzaiolo | *Pizza*

Dopo | *Italian*
Ajanta | *Indian*
Wood Tavern | *Cal.*
Lalime's | *Californian/Med.*
Tamarindo Antojeria | *Mex.*
Wolfdale's | *Californian*
Esin | *American/Med.*

__24__ Wente Vineyards | *Cal./Med.*
Great China | *Chinese*
Oliveto Restaurant | *Italian*

BY CUISINE

AMERICAN
__27__ Commis
__25__ Esin
__24__ Moody's Bistro
__23__ Digs Bistro
Lark Creek

CALIFORNIAN
__28__ Chez Panisse
__27__ Chez Panisse Café
__25__ Wood Tavern
Wolfdale's
__24__ Wente Vineyards

CHINESE
__24__ Great China
__23__ Koi Garden
__20__ Rest. Peony▽
Berkeley Tea
__19__ Shen Hua

FRENCH
__28__ Erna's Elderberry
__24__ À Côté
__23__ Café Fanny
Artisan Bistro
Chevalier

INDIAN
__25__ Ajanta
__24__ Shalimar
__23__ Vik's Chaat Corner
__20__ Udupi Palace
Breads of India

ITALIAN
__25__ Tratt. La Siciliana
Pizzaiolo

Dopo
__24__ Oliveto Restaurant
Prima

JAPANESE
__24__ Kirala
Uzen
__23__ Ozumo
Cha-Ya Vegetarian
O Chamé

MEDITERRANEAN
__28__ Chez Panisse
__27__ Chez Panisse Café
Rivoli
__26__ BayWolf
__25__ Lalime's

MEXICAN/PAN-LATIN
__25__ Tamarindo Antojeria
__23__ Tacubaya
__22__ César
Fonda Solana
__21__ Bocanova

PIZZA
__27__ Cheese Board
__25__ Pizzaiolo
__24__ Little Star Pizza
Zachary's Pizza
Boot & Shoe Service

SOUTHEAST ASIAN
__24__ Xyclo
Soi4
__20__ Pho 84
Le Cheval
__19__ Cha Am Thai

Excludes places with low votes, unless otherwise indicated

Menus, photos, voting and more – free at ZAGAT.com

BY SPECIAL FEATURE

BREAKFAST/BRUNCH

24 Wente Vineyards
23 Café Fanny
   Bette's Oceanview
   Oliveto Cafe
   Lark Creek

CHILD-FRIENDLY

24 Great China
   Zachary's Pizza
23 Lark Creek
21 Pizza Antica
   Picante Cocina

MEET FOR A DRINK

23 Adesso
22 César
   Flora
20 Luka's Tap Room
   Sidebar

OPEN LATE

23 Adesso
22 César
   Fonda Solana
19 Home of Chicken/Waffles
18 Caspers Hot Dogs

OUTDOOR SEATING

24 Wente Vineyards
   Prima
   À Côté
   Va de Vi
22 César

PEOPLE-WATCHING

27 Chez Panisse Café
25 Wood Tavern

24 À Côté
   Va de Vi
   Moody's Bistro

ROMANCE

28 Erna's Elderberry
   Chez Panisse
25 Lalime's
   Wolfdale's
24 Wente Vineyards

SMALL PLATES

24 À Côté
   Va de Vi
23 Mezze
   Adesso
22 César

TRENDY

24 À Côté
   Boot & Shoe Service
23 Adesso
22 Flora
14 Lake Chalet

VIEWS

28 Erna's Elderberry
27 Rivoli
25 Wolfdale's
24 Wente Vineyards
22 Dragonfly

WINNING WINE LISTS

28 Erna's Elderberry
   Chez Panisse
27 Chez Panisse Café
   Rivoli
26 BayWolf

BY LOCATION

BERKELEY

28 Chez Panisse
27 Chez Panisse Café
   Rivoli
   Cheese Board
25 Tratt. La Siciliana

LAKE TAHOE AREA

25 Wolfdale's
   Manzanita∇

24 Moody's Bistro
23 PlumpJack Cafe
22 Dragonfly

OAKLAND

27 Commis
26 Bakesale Betty
   BayWolf
25 Pizzaiolo
   Dopo

Top Decor

29	Ahwahnee Din. Rm.		Picán
27	Erna's Elderberry		Bridges
25	Lake Chalet		Postino
	Wente Vineyards		Gar Woods Grill
24	Bocanova		Chez Panisse Café
	Ozumo		Rivoli
	Sunnyside Resort		Five
	Bing Crosby's	22	Prima
23	Chez Panisse		Flora
	Venezia		Esin

Top Service

27	Erna's Elderberry	23	Wolfdale's
	Commis		Digs Bistro
26	Chez Panisse		Ruth's Chris
25	Chez Panisse Café		Wente Vineyards
	Rivoli		Ajanta
	Lalime's		Lark Creek
	BayWolf		Wood Tavern
24	Esin		Bakesale Betty
	Prima		Mezze
	Peasant & Pear	22	Postino

Best Buys

In order of Bang for the Buck rating.

1. In-N-Out	11. Fentons Creamery
2. Arinell Pizza	12. Bette's Oceanview
3. Caspers Hot Dogs	13. Café Fanny
4. Bakesale Betty	14. Picante Cocina
5. Cheese Board Collective	15. Tacubaya
6. Cheese Steak Shop	16. Barney's
7. Gioia Pizzeria	17. Brown Sugar Kitchen
8. Cactus Taqueria	18. Juan's Place
9. Vik's Chaat Corner	19. Mama's Royal Cafe
10. BurgerMeister	20. Blackberry Bistro

OTHER GOOD VALUES

Ajanta	Emilia's Pizzeria
Barlata	Encuentro
Bo's BBQ	Le Cheval
Boot & Shoe Service	Pho 84
Breads of India	Revival Bar
Chop Bar	SR24
Chow	Trueburger

Menus, photos, voting and more – free at ZAGAT.com

East of San Francisco

À Côté *French/Mediterranean* 24 | 20 | 21 | $41

Oakland | 5478 College Ave. (Taft Ave.) | 510-655-6469 |
www.acoterestaurant.com

Even a "mom with three kids and a minivan" will "feel urbane and sophisticated" in the "plush atmosphere" of this "top Rockridge" choice,
a "fabulous" French-Med small-plate specialist where "every dish is
delish"; "ingenious" cocktails and wines that go "beyond the California
usuals" are also delivered by a "knowledgeable" staff to the "young
and restless" crowd, which spills out from the "tight quarters" into the
back patio – a welcome "escape."

Adagia Restaurant Ⓢ *Californian* 18 | 21 | 18 | $39

Berkeley | Westminster Hse. | 2700 Bancroft Way (College Ave.) |
510-647-2300 | www.adagiarestaurant.com

This "grand old" "Arthurian-looking dining hall" with a "huge fireplace"
provides a "special" setting for dinner "before a Zellerbach performance" on the Berkeley campus, or for pre-game brunches in the
"pleasant" courtyard; while the "reasonable" Cal-Med menu is "tasty"
but a little "boring", and service swings from "super" to "slow", many feel
that whatever's lacking in the meal is "regained in ambiance" alone.

Adesso ●Ⓢ *Italian* 23 | 16 | 19 | $36

Oakland | 4395 Piedmont Ave. (Pleasant Valley Ave.) | 510-601-0305

"Like a sushi bar for salumi", this bite-sized Oakland "hot spot" (spun off
from Dopo) crafts a "limited" but "delectable" aperitivo menu of "amazing" cured meats and cheeses "washed down with creative cocktails"
or "wines by the glass"; just remember to "leave your vegan friends at
home" and bring "sharp elbows" if you go for the twice-nightly happy
hours (offering "free apps" from 5–7 PM and 10:30 PM–midnight),
which get "too crowded by half."

⒵ Ahwahnee Dining Room *American/Californian* 19 | 29 | 21 | $58

Yosemite | Ahwahnee Hotel | 1 Ahwahnee Way (Tecoya Rd.) |
Yosemite National Park | 209-372-1489 | www.yosemitepark.com

"For those who like to rough it" and still enjoy a "dress-up", "fine-dining
experience", "nothing beats" this "stunning", "cathedral-like room", a
"masterpiece" "overlooking the granite peaks of Yosemite"; the "expensive" Cal-American fare and service hardly "live up" to the scen-
ery, but the "famous" Sunday brunch and "special events" (like the
Bracebridge Dinner and Chefs' Holidays) get "higher marks", leaving
"parkitecture" partisans to conclude the "food is acceptable, but the
place itself is delicious."

Ajanta *Indian* 25 | 20 | 23 | $29

Berkeley | 1888 Solano Ave. (bet. The Alameda & Fresno Ave.) |
510-526-4373 | www.ajantarestaurant.com

It's "no curry in a hurry" attest Berkeley admirers of this "wowing"
"white-tablecloth" Indian whose "committed" chef-owner turns out
"top-notch" food with a focus on organic ingredients and "outrageously
flavorful" "monthly regional specialties"; the "sophisticated interior"
and "superb, well-priced" wine list add to the "remarkable" meal.

	FOOD	DECOR	SERVICE	COST

Amanda's *Californian/Health Food*   ▽ 21 | 14 | 18 | $11
Berkeley | 2122 Shattuck Ave. (Center St.) | 510-548-2122 |
www.amandas.com

If you're not lovin' it at typical fast-food joints, this "healthier quick-lunch option" in Berkeley dishes up "excellent, cheap" Cal eats, like "homemade veggie burgers" and "oven-roasted sweet potato fries", with a "Slow Food" sensibility; though some gripe about its "dainty portion sizes" and "stark interior", most feel "we need more like it."

Amber Bistro *Californian*   22 | 20 | 21 | $40
Danville | 500 Hartz Ave. (Church St.) | 925-552-5238 |
www.amberbistro.com

A prix fixe menu option helps deliver "good value for the money" at this "lively local bistro" in Danville serving Californian fusion (including some "nice tapas" at happy hour) that's "always reliable"; with "restful" decor and "friendly" service, it's a "pleasant" option, even if it's too "loud" for some.

Amici's East Coast Pizzeria *Pizza*   19 | 14 | 17 | $21
Danville | Rose Garden Ctr. | 720 Camino Ramon (Sycamore Valley Rd.) |
925-837-9800
Dublin | 4640 Tassajara Rd. (bet. Central Pkwy. & Dublin Blvd.) |
925-875-1600
www.amicis.com
See review in City of San Francisco Directory.

Arinell Pizza ⌀ *Pizza*   21 | 5 | 12 | $8
Berkeley | 2119 Shattuck Ave. (Addison St.) | 510-841-4035
See review in City of San Francisco Directory.

Artisan Bistro Ⓜ *Californian/French*   23 | 17 | 21 | $47
Lafayette | 1005 Brown Ave. (Mt. Diablo Blvd.) | 925-962-0882 |
www.artisanlafayette.com

"Why go to SF" when you can enjoy "ambitious" Cal-French fare "on the 'burbs side of the tunnel"? ask advocates of this Lafayette bistro whose chef-owner is an "artist" crafting "French Laundry cooking at East Bay prices"; though its "noisy" setting in a "small renovated house" feels "out-of-sync" to some, the service "tries hard" and the patio is perfectly "enjoyable."

Asqew Grill *Californian*   16 | 11 | 14 | $17
Emeryville | Bay Street Mall | 5614 Bay St. (Shellmound St.) |
510-595-7471 | www.asqewgrill.com
See review in City of San Francisco Directory.

Bakesale Betty *Bakery*   26 | 11 | 23 | $13
NEW Oakland | 2228 Broadway (W. Grand Ave.) | 510-251-2100 Ⓢ
Oakland | 5098 Telegraph Ave. (51st St.) | 510-985-1213 Ⓜ
www.bakesalebetty.com

Gung-ho guests "gobble" "alfresco" at "makeshift ironing-board tables" at this "cult" bakery and takeout counter where the "heaping", "rocking" desserts and "fantastic" fried chicken sandwiches are "da bomb"; "don't be discouraged" by "lines that snake around the block" and "halfway to Downtown Oakland" (where a second branch recently opened), since the "quick" staff keeps things humming "like a sewing machine", doling out a "cheerful" attitude and often "free cookies."

EAST OF SAN FRANCISCO

	FOOD	DECOR	SERVICE	COST

Barlata *Spanish* — 21 | 17 | 19 | $34

Oakland | 4901 Telegraph Ave. (49th St.) | 510-450-0678 |
www.barlata.com

There's a whole "lotta *lata*" (items served in tin cans), "tasty" small plates and "wonderful" paella going on at this "vibrant" Temescal tapas bar by Catalan native Daniel Olivella (B44); though service can be "slow" at times, it's a "pleasingly raucous" place "to go with friends" for an "affordable" "glass of *tinto*" or to share a "late supper" at the "big, sprawling table"; P.S. lunch Wednesday-Friday only.

**Barney's Gourmet
Hamburgers** *Burgers* — 19 | 12 | 16 | $17

Berkeley | 1591 Solano Ave. (Ordway St.) | 510-526-8185
Berkeley | 1600 Shattuck Ave. (Cedar St.) | 510-849-2827
Oakland | 4162 Piedmont Ave. (Linda Ave.) | 510-655-7180
Oakland | 5819 College Ave. (Chabot Rd.) | 510-601-0444
www.barneyshamburgers.com

See review in City of San Francisco Directory.

**Baxter's
Bistro & Lounge** *Californian* — - | - | - | M

Truckee | Village at Northstar | 8001 Northstar Dr. (N. Shore Rd.) |
530-562-3200 | www.baxtersbistro.com

At this year-round Truckee sib to Moody's, skiers, boarders, bikers and hikers can enjoy seasonally driven midpriced Cal cuisine without having to leave Northstar; in addition to a dapper deco dining room, there's also an outside patio with a fire pit, plus live jazz Friday–Saturday nights.

BayWolf Ⓜ *Californian/Mediterranean* — 26 | 21 | 25 | $50

Oakland | 3853 Piedmont Ave. (Rio Vista Ave.) | 510-655-6004 |
www.baywolf.com

"It's been around" since 1975, but Michael Wild's Oakland "pioneer" "never gets old", "still cranking out" "fresh, innovative and just plain good" monthly changing Cal-Med meals (boasting "can't-miss" duck dishes) that are "graciously" served and complemented by "well-chosen, reasonably priced" wines; so while it's "not at all trendy", it remains "king" for "civilized" "special occasions" in a "warm old" "Craftsman"-style house, or for wolfing down a "casual lunch" on the "front porch."

Bellanico *Italian* — 22 | 18 | 21 | $37

Oakland | 4238 Park Blvd. (Wellington St.) | 510-336-1180 |
www.bellanico.net

"Italy should be so lucky" to have this "wonderful" Glenview "gem" whose "rustic preparations" of "non-mainstream" Boot dishes stand up to those at its "San Francisco counterpart", Aperto; the "small but warm" setting suits a "night out with the family", while the four-course $24 tasting menu (available Sunday-Thursday) and "creative" wine flights are a "terrific bargain."

Berkeley Teahouse *Tearoom* — 20 | 19 | 19 | $23

Berkeley | Epicurious Gdn. | 1511 Shattuck Ave. (bet. Cedar & Vine Sts.) |
510-540-8888 | www.imperialtea.com

See Imperial Tea Court review in City of San Francisco Directory.

	FOOD	DECOR	SERVICE	COST

Bette's Oceanview Diner *Diner* — 23 | 17 | 19 | $19

Berkeley | 1807 Fourth St. (bet. Hearst Ave. & Virginia St.) | 510-644-3230 | www.bettesdiner.com

Despite the name, there's "no ocean to be seen" at this daytime-only Berkeley diner, known for its "delicious", "eclectic" American breakfasts (including soufflé pancakes) as well as "colorful" service and jukebox tunes; since it's "always packed", though, many opt for "top-quality" pastries and other portables at the next-door take-out shop.

Bing Crosby's *American* — 19 | 24 | 19 | $48

Walnut Creek | 1342 Broadway Plaza (S. Main St.) | 925-939-2464 | www.bingcrosbysrestaurant.com

"Upscale baby boomers" and "lounge lizards" convene at this "plush", "retro" Walnut Creek American as they duck into "big booths", nurse "great martinis" and sway to the "fabulous jazz pianist in the bar"; though many find the fare "well done" but "unimaginative", and the atmosphere "a bit staid", the "people-watching" is often "worth the price."

Bistro Liaison *French* — 21 | 19 | 20 | $39

Berkeley | 1849 Shattuck Ave. (bet. Delaware St. & Hearst Ave.) | 510-849-2155 | www.liaisonbistro.com

"Berkeley meets Bordeaux" at this "real find" turning out "simple" French bistro fare and prix fixe "bargains" that are "exceptional for the quality, the service and the surroundings"; it does get "boisterous", particularly for "pre-theater" dinners, but just admire the scene in the "mirrors along the wall", and "you'd swear you were in Paris."

Blackberry Bistro *Southern* — 18 | 14 | 16 | $18

Oakland | 4240 Park Blvd. (Wellington St.) | 510-336-1088

"Amazing" prawns and grits and "rich" French toast stand out among the "bountiful breakfasts" at this Southern cafe in the Oakland hills; though there's "usually a line" on weekends and "service is sloowww", most neighbors don't mind the "leisurely" meal; P.S. no dinner.

Blackhawk Grille *Californian* — 21 | 21 | 20 | $47

Danville | The Shops at Blackhawk | 3540 Blackhawk Plaza Circle (Camino Tassajara) | 925-736-4295 | www.blackhawkgrille.com

With a "lovely setting in Blackhawk Plaza", this Danville Californian has "stood the test of time", serving a "solid" menu that's "perfect for a business lunch or romantic dinner"; many adore "sitting outside on a warm summer day" by the fountains, while others applaud the live music on weekends – though some disappointed diners dub it "pricey" "country-club" fare in a scene that's "too formal for its britches."

Z NEW Blue Bottle Roastery & Coffee Bar *Californian/Coffeehouse* — 23 | 14 | 18 | $9

Oakland | 300 Webster St. (3rd St.) | 510-653-3394 | www.bluebottlecoffee.net

See review in City of San Francisco Directory.

NEW Bocanova *Pan-Latin* — 21 | 24 | 19 | $42

Oakland | Jack London Sq. | 55 Webster St. (The Embarcadero) | 510-444-1233 | www.bocanova.com

This upscale new Pan-Latin "delight" delivers "exciting", "exotic" dishes in a "hip", "beautiful" setting, making it "the best thing that's happened to the Oakland waterfront since Jack London himself landed here"; a "large bar area" separates two sleek indoor dining zones, but "if you sit outside on the deck, be prepared to be ignored by the staff" – though you will have a "wonderful view of the Bay."

NEW Boot & Shoe Service 🅼 *Italian/Pizza* | 24 | 20 | 22 | $31 |

Oakland | 3308 Grand Ave. (Elmwood Ave.) | 510-763-2668 |
www.bootandshoeservice.com

"Despite the name", there's no boot service and the "pizzas do not taste like shoe leather" at this "happening" new Pizzaiolo spin-off in Oakland's Grand Lake area providing "appropriately blistered" pies and a "limited" slate of "affordable" Italian small plates that "shine"; "the no-res policy has 'em lining up at opening time" and loud music "bombards" the exposed-brick room, but "creative cocktails" and "even better food" served "without attitude" are the rewards.

Bo's Barbecue 🅼 *BBQ* | 22 | 11 | 14 | $24 |

Lafayette | 3422 Mt. Diablo Blvd. (Brown Ave.) | 925-283-7133
"Lick-sticking", "high-quality" ribs and brisket are "the star of the show" at Bo McSwine's Southern-style BBQ joint, which "for all the quirks" ("no service, no decor, no reason to have it") lures a "loyal following" out to Lafayette; among other pluses are its "many hard-to-find bottled brews", an outdoor deck and "live jazz overflowing" on weekend nights, making it "well worth a visit."

Breads of India & Gourmet Curries *Indian* | 20 | 14 | 18 | $23 |

Berkeley | 2448 Sacramento St. (Dwight Way) | 510-848-7684
Oakland | 948 Clay St. (bet. 9th & 10th Sts.) | 510-834-7684 🆂
Walnut Creek | 1358 N. Main St. (bet. Cypress & Duncan Sts.) |
925-256-7684 🅼
www.breadsofindia.com

"It isn't called 'Breads of India' for nothing" note carb cravers who claim the "naan is where it's at", bolstering an "always changing" menu of "fresh", "not too spicy" Indian eats at this East Bay mini-chain; though some critics contend the quality is "variable" and "there's just no depth or nuance" to the cooking, most agree it's a strong "value" for a "fast" meal prepared with "humanely sourced" ingredients.

Bridges Restaurant *Asian/Californian* | 22 | 23 | 21 | $52 |

Danville | 44 Church St. (Hartz Ave.) | 925-820-7200 |
www.bridgesdanville.com

Fans of this "reliable fixture" in Downtown Danville feel it's making a "comeback" of late, offering "excellent" Cal-Asian cuisine boosted by "consistently professional service"; "in the summer, outdoor seating and live music" are a plus, while the "convivial" happy hour is a "deal for fine food", though a few long for a menu "overhaul" with more "variety."

Bridgetender Tavern *Pub Food* | ▽ 18 | 16 | 17 | $22 |

Tahoe City | 65 W. Lake Blvd. (Rte. 89) | 530-583-3342
Perfect "after a day of skiing, rafting" or simply "to spend the day drinking and eating", this "popular" pub "next to Fanny Bridge" is a "must-stop" on Tahoe's North Shore; "despite the average food and kitschy decor", "locals love" the burgers, "ultracasual" service and "true Tahoe ambiance" with views of the "meandering river" and mountains, so "arrive willing to wait for a table (cuz you will)."

FOOD | DECOR | SERVICE | COST

Brown Sugar Kitchen M *Soul Food* | 23 | 18 | 19 | $22

Oakland | 2534 Mandela Pkwy. (26th St.) | 510-839-7685 | www.brownsugarkitchen.com

Whether "you're from the South or not", "you'll leave whistling Dixie" after chowing down on "rich" breakfast and lunch dishes like "damn good fried chicken" and "light-as-a-feather" cornmeal waffles at this "gracious" soul food "treasure" in "scruffy" West Oakland; though it's "a bit pricey", "hipsters" are still sweet on it, happily enduring "long weekend waits."

Bucci's Ⓔ *Californian/Italian* | 21 | 19 | 22 | $35

Emeryville | 6121 Hollis St. (bet. 59th & 61st Sts.) | 510-547-4725 | www.buccis.com

"Those who know" this "lively", "welcoming" lunchtime "hangout" for "artists and power brokers" in Emeryville "love it for life", praising the "generous drinks" and "soul-satisfying" Cal-Italian fare that's a "bargain to boot"; adorned with chalkboard witticisms and rotating art and "overseen by Bucci" herself, the "converted brick warehouse" exudes a "supper-party" vibe, making it a "favorite" for "last-minute" dinners too.

BurgerMeister *Burgers* | 20 | 12 | 16 | $16

Alameda | 2319 Central Ave. (bet. Oak & Park Sts.) | 510-865-3032 | www.burgermeistersf.com

See review in City of San Francisco Directory.

Ⓩ Burma Superstar *Burmese* | 24 | 15 | 19 | $26

Alameda | 1345 Park St. (Central Ave.) | 510-522-6200 M
Oakland | 4721 Telegraph Ave. (47th St.) | 510-652-2900
www.burmasuperstar.com

See review in City of San Francisco Directory.

Cactus Taqueria *Mexican* | 20 | 10 | 15 | $13

Berkeley | 1881 Solano Ave. (bet. The Alameda & Fresno Ave.) | 510-528-1881
Oakland | 5642 College Ave. (bet. Keith Ave. & Ocean View Dr.) | 510-658-6180
www.cactustaqueria.com

Get a "tasty" "Mexican fix" at this "stunningly cheap" pair preparing "high-quality" "fast food" like "crispy chicken tacos" and "ginormous burritos" with "fresh salsas to spice things up", plus housemade aguas frescas that "taste like fresh-picked fruits"; just beware, whether it's Berkeley or Rockridge, there are "more kids in this place than tortillas", so "call in your to-go order and minimize your exposure to the chaos."

Café Fanny *French* | 23 | 12 | 16 | $17

Berkeley | 1603 San Pablo Ave. (Cedar St.) | 510-524-5447 | www.cafefanny.com

"Get your fanny over" to Alice Waters' "distinctly Berkeley" zinc-topped food bar command regulars who "dream" about "curated" (if "brusquely" served) breakfast and lunch dishes like "wonderful" egg salad sandwiches and "sublime" "bowls of café au lait" – then "have nightmares about where the hell to sit" in the "elbow-to-elbow" lair; it all "feels so *français*" and a "bit precious", but the food is a "heavenly start to the day" – and "worth the extra moola."

	FOOD	DECOR	SERVICE	COST

Café Fiore *Italian* ▽ 25 | 18 | 21 | $39

South Lake Tahoe | 1169 Ski Run Blvd. (Tamarack Ave.) | 530-541-2908 | www.cafefiore.com

It's "worth skiing all day to feast at night" at this Northern Italian "jewel" in South Lake Tahoe, where the "excellent" dishes and wines (including many half bottles) are served in "attentive" fashion; it's so "tiny" that some groups "have a hard time making reservations", but those who call ahead discover a "cozy" cabin "when it's snowing", and a "cool, comfy" patio "in the summer."

Café Gratitude *Vegan* 16 | 13 | 15 | $26

Berkeley | 1730 Shattuck Ave. (bet. Francisco & Virginia Sts.) | 415-824-4652 | www.cafegratitude.com
See review in City of San Francisco Directory.

Café Rouge *French/Mediterranean* 20 | 19 | 19 | $40

Berkeley | Market Plaza | 1782 Fourth St. (bet. Hearst Ave. & Virginia St.) | 510-525-1440 | www.caferouge.net

When you're "feeling carnivorous", "do as the Berzerklians do" and "bask" in the pleasures of "top-quality" burgers and Bloody Marys at this "eco"-conscious French-Med cafe with an "amazing butcher shop in back"; "it's like the Zuni of the East Bay", with "noisy" ambiance, "great oysters" and a "spacious bar" where you can "comfortably while away the afternoon", plus a terrace to "watch the street scene"; P.S. lunch-only on Mondays.

Camino *Californian/Mediterranean* 23 | 21 | 19 | $48

Oakland | 3917 Grand Ave. (Sunny Slope Ave.) | 510-547-5035 | www.caminorestaurant.com

Be ready to "go with the flow" at "Chez Panisse graduate" Russell Moore's Oakland "hot spot" that "brings out the caveman" in diners with its "ultrashort" menu of "crafty" organic Cal-Med dishes "cooked over open flames" (yup, "even the eggs" at brunch); "three choices are more than enough" when everything is worth "savoring", and enhanced by "inventive" drinks, and while the tables are "mostly communal", they're "still private enough to have a conversation"; P.S. closed Tuesdays.

Casa Orinda *Italian/Steak* 16 | 15 | 18 | $39

Orinda | 20 Bryant Way (Moraga Way) | 925-254-2981 | www.casaorinda.net

A "blast-from-the-past" dating back to 1932, this Orinda Italian steakhouse with "Western decor", showcasing "meat and guns (in a nice way)", along with "famous" "crispy" fried chicken, may be "riding on its history" but it's not galloping into the sunset; a "loyal following" of "seniors and leftover cowboys" still saddles up to the "lively bar" for "old-fashioned brown drinks" and appreciates the "friendly service" and "throwback prices."

Caspers Hot Dogs ⊄ *Hot Dogs* 18 | 7 | 16 | $8

Albany | 545 San Pablo Ave. (bet. Brighton Ave. & Garfield St.) | 510-527-6611
Dublin | 6998 Village Pkwy. (Dublin Blvd.) | 925-828-2224
Hayward | 21670 Foothill Blvd. (Grove Way) | 510-581-9064 ◐
Hayward | 951 C St. (bet. Main St. & Mission Blvd.) | 510-537-7300

(continued)

(continued)

Caspers Hot Dogs

Oakland | 5440 Telegraph Ave. (55th St.) | 510-652-1668
Pleasant Hill | 6 Vivian Dr. (Contra Costa Blvd.) | 925-687-6030 ◐
Richmond | 2530 MacDonald Ave. (Civic Center St.) | 510-235-6492
Walnut Creek | 1280 Newell Hill Pl. (bet. Newell Ave. & San Miguel Dr.) |
925-930-9154
www.caspershotdogs.com

Frank fans affirm the "snappy", "flavorful" dogs "loaded" with toppings will "more than meet your wiener cravings" at this "cheap",
"retro" East Bay chain; the "little old ladies" behind the counter are a
"crack-up" in their "smocks and hairnets", but that's all part of the
"character" that harks back to an "earlier era."

César España ◐ *Spanish*   22 | 20 | 20 | $35

Berkeley | 1515 Shattuck Ave. (bet. Cedar & Vine Sts.) |
510-883-0222

César Latino ◐ *Pan-Latin*

Oakland | 4039 Piedmont Ave. (bet. 40th & 41st Sts.) |
510-883-0222
www.barcesar.com

"Is this Madrid or Berkeley?" ask amigos of this "festive" Spanish
"streetside" cafe whose "fab bar" and "communal tables" are HQ for
a "tapas rendezvous" with "late-evening" libations that "rival" the
food; at the more "spacious", "trendy" Oakland offshoot (also an alfresco lunch and "breakfast favorite"), a recent "switch" to Pan-Latin
antojitos keeps it "interesting", but both tend to get hectic, so you
may have to "flag down the servers."

Cha Am Thai *Thai*   19 | 13 | 17 | $24

Berkeley | 1543 Shattuck Ave. (Cedar St.) | 510-848-9664
See review in City of San Francisco Directory.

Cha-Ya Vegetarian   23 | 11 | 17 | $21
Japanese Restaurant *Japanese/Vegan*

Berkeley | 1686 Shattuck Ave. (bet. Cedar & Virginia Sts.) | 510-981-1213
See review in City of San Francisco Directory.

☑ Cheese Board   27 | 12 | 20 | $14
Collective ⬛Ⓜ⌗ *Bakery/Pizza*

Berkeley | 1512 Shattuck Ave. (bet. Cedar & Vine Sts.) | 510-549-3055 |
www.cheeseboardcollective.coop

"Nothing beats" the "superb", "famous sourdough-crusted" pizza
du jour ("always vegetarian", always "a flavor explosion" – "always
blown away") at this "quintessential Berkeley" "grassroots" pie
co-op where you can "devour it on the median" "local"-style or,
come evening, scramble for a seat inside to "listen to live jazz"; the
"line around the block" "goes quickly", plus there's an "adjacent
bakery and cheese shop" for "partially baked" pizzas, "excellent
breads and morning pastries."

Cheesecake Factory *American*   16 | 17 | 17 | $29

Pleasanton | Stoneridge Shopping Ctr. | 1350 Stoneridge Mall Rd.
(Foothill Rd.) | 925-463-1311 | www.thecheesecakefactory.com
See review in City of San Francisco Directory.

	FOOD	DECOR	SERVICE	COST

Cheese Steak Shop *Cheesesteaks* — 21 | 8 | 16 | $12

Alameda | 2671 Blanding Ave. (Tilden Way) | 510-522-5555
Berkeley | 1054 University Ave. (bet. San Pablo Ave. & 10th St.) |
510-845-8689
Lafayette | 3455 Mount Diablo Blvd. (2nd St.) | 925-283-1234
Oakland | 3308 Lakeshore Ave. (bet. Lake Park Ave. & Mandana Blvd.) |
510-832-6717
Pleasanton | Gateway Square Shopping Ctr. | 4825 Hopyard Rd.
(Stoneridge Dr.) | 925-734-0293
Walnut Creek | 1626 Cypress St. (bet. California Blvd. & Locust St.) |
925-934-7017
www.cheesesteakshop.com
See review in City of San Francisco Directory.

Chevalier Ⓜ *French* — 23 | 18 | 22 | $45

Lafayette | 960 Moraga Rd. (Moraga Blvd.) | 925-385-0793 |
www.chevalierrestaurant.com
"The chef-owner takes great care" at this "charming Gallic", making
you "forget you're in a strip mall in Lafayette" with his "well-executed",
slightly "expensive" French cuisine; service is "breezily correct without stuffiness" and there's "inviting" "garden dining in the summer" –
just be prepared for "difficult" parking at lunch.

Ⓩ Chez Panisse Ⓩ *Californian/Mediterranean* — 28 | 23 | 26 | $83

Berkeley | 1517 Shattuck Ave. (bet. Cedar & Vine Sts.) | 510-548-5525 |
www.chezpanisse.com
"Alice may not live here as much anymore", but her "landmark" kitchen
still "works wonders", crafting the "freshest organic" ingredients into
"simple" yet "outstanding" Cal-Med prix fixes, served by a "courteous" staff to patrons on a "pilgrimage" to this "gastronomic sanctu-
ary"; it's "very Berkeley", down to the Arts and Crafts decor, and while
some find the ambiance "a little too holy", most effuse it's "everything
it's cracked up to be" – "well worth the cost" and the "tough reservation."

Ⓩ Chez Panisse — 27 | 23 | 25 | $52

Café Ⓩ *Californian/Mediterranean*
Berkeley | 1517 Shattuck Ave. (bet. Cedar & Vine Sts.) | 510-548-5049 |
www.chezpanisse.com
"Never has walking up a few steps resulted in reaching foodie heaven at
such a savings" "gloat" Berkeleyites who "skip the religious experience
downstairs" and grab an à la carte lunch or dinner at Alice Waters'
"reliable-as-the-sunrise", "Craftsman-style" cafe; the "shockingly
simple" yet "sublime" Cal-Med dishes (including pizzas with "pristine" toppings) and "exemplary" service are "every bit as good" as the
original, plus you can "go in jeans" and still "tour the joint."

NEW Chop Bar *Californian* — ▽ 22 | 21 | 22 | $27

Oakland | 247 Fourth St. (Alice St.) | 510-834-2467 | www.chopbar510.com
"Local is the theme" at this 'hip' new warehouse cafe near Oakland's
Jack London Square, where everything from the "delicious" Californian
"homestyle cooking that you feel good eating" to the wine and beer is
regionally sourced; early adopters enthuse it's a "fantastic addition to
the neighborhood" that's "run by great people", praising the "relaxed
vibe" and slew of community events like pig roasts and movie nights
on the outdoor patio.

☒ Chow *American*

20 | 15 | 19 | $26

Danville | 445 Railroad Ave. (San Ramon Valley Blvd.) | 925-838-4510
Lafayette | La Fiesta Sq. | 53 Lafayette Circle (Mt. Diablo Blvd.) | 925-962-2469
www.chowfoodbar.com

See review in City of San Francisco Directory.

Christy Hill ◩ *Californian/Mediterranean*

▽ 20 | 27 | 21 | $57

Tahoe City | 115 Grove St. (Rte. 28) | 530-583-8551 | www.christyhill.com

With its "fabulous views" of the Lake, idyllic summer patio and "wonderful" service, this "oh-so-romantic" "special-occasion" destination in Tahoe City has long been considered the "best on the West Shore"; fans hope the quality continues, as it "changed hands" in May 2010 to the folks behind Pianeta and Pacific Crest Grill and now serves a more seasonal Cal-Med menu (with a small-plate focus) and soju cocktails in a remodeled, contemporary dining room; P.S. the ownership change is not reflected in the ratings.

☒ Commis ◩ *American*

27 | 20 | 27 | $78

Oakland | 3859 Piedmont Ave. (W. MacArthur Blvd.) | 510-653-3902 | www.commisrestaurant.com

There's "no sign" and only a "few seats" at this "small but mighty" Oakland "shoebox" where the "somewhat austere" setting keeps the focus "centered on the kitchen"; "rising star" James Syhabout "plays with texture and confounds expectations", conjuring up "groundbreaking" New American prix fixe menus "right in front of your eyes" that leave you "scraping the dish for more", while the staff delivers "meticulous" service that matches the hefty tab; P.S. the menu format is changing from three-course to four-course in September 2010.

Corso Trattoria *Italian*

23 | 18 | 21 | $37

Berkeley | 1788 Shattuck Ave (Delaware St.) | 510-704-8004 | www.trattoriacorso.com

"Lower-priced rustic Italian fare from the Rivoli folks" boasts "cutting-edge" cred at this "refined yet casual" "Florentine bistro" in Berkeley, where guests can "sit at the counter and watch the action" or gaze at "Italian movies over the bar" while sipping wines from a "fine list", proffered by a "pleasant" staff; the "noise" can be a "drawback", but most find, "like a well-balanced Chianti, it hits the spot."

Cottonwood *Eclectic*

▽ 21 | 19 | 22 | $49

Truckee | 10142 Rue Hilltop (Old Brockway Rd.) | 530-587-5711 | www.cottonwoodrestaurant.com

Just "what a mountain restaurant should be", this "hilltop" haunt overlooking Downtown Truckee has deck seating for catching "spectacular sunsets" and dining "under the stars", as well as slightly upscale Eclectic dinners that are "as good as anything in the flatlands", served by an "attentive" crew; with plenty of memorabilia documenting its "historic bones", it's "a bit on the funky side, but in the Sierra, that seems to fit in well."

Digs Bistro *American/Mediterranean*

23 | 20 | 23 | $39

Berkeley | 1453 Dwight Way (bet. Edwards & Sacramento Sts.) | 510-548-2322 | www.digsbistro.com

"East Bay eaters in-the-know" head to this "tiny" Berkeley "pleasure" for "big-flavored" New American-Med dinners and "accessible wines" "served with care"; some "wish" for "more variety on the menu", but most dig that it feels "like dining in someone's house, especially near the fireplace", and savor the twice-monthly Mondays when "kids are entertained in a separate room" while parents enjoy a "real adult meal"; P.S. closed Tuesday-Wednesday.

Doña Tomás 🖼 M *Mexican*   21 | 18 | 19 | $37

Oakland | 5004 Telegraph Ave. (bet. 49th & 51st Sts.) | 510-450-0522 | www.donatomas.com

There's "nothing wrong with taco trucks", but when carnitas-craving Oaklanders "want to sit down to some" "top-quality" Mexican comida with margaritas that'll "knock you on your ass", they "get in line" at this trendy Temescal "haute" cantina; though the "wait at the bar" and in the "sparse dining room" can be "frustrating", it's a treat to "sit on the back patio on a hot summer" night.

Dopo 🖼 *Italian*   25 | 17 | 22 | $36

Oakland | 4293 Piedmont Ave. (Echo Ave.) | 510-652-3676 | www.dopoadesso.com

"Outstanding" "housemade" salumi, "exceptional" pastas and "crisp" pizzas "from people who really know their way around a crust" – plus "great recommendations" from the staff on "bargain" Boot bottles – keep the "hungry hordes lining up" at this "dope" Oakland trattoria; a patio "warmed by the overhead heaters" and "lap blankets" entices, but "go really early or late" to beat the "impossible wait", or better yet for some regulars, "stop coming here, please!"

Dragonfly *Asian/Californian*   22 | 19 | 19 | $40

Truckee | Porter Simon Bldg. | 10118 Donner Pass Rd., 2nd fl. (Spring St.) | 530-587-0557 | www.dragonflycuisine.com

"A nice place to unwind after a day on the slopes", or "outside on the deck in summer", this "second-floor aerie" dishing up "creative" Cal-Asian fare (including "delicate" noodles and "decent" sushi) "brings some excitement" to Downtown Truckee; both the food and service can be a little "uneven", but the "beautiful view of the Sierras" is a bonus.

Duck Club, The *American*   21 | 22 | 22 | $51

Lafayette | Lafayette Park Hotel & Spa | 3287 Mt. Diablo Blvd. (Pleasant Hill Rd.) | 925-283-3700 | www.lafayetteparkhotel.com

See review in South of San Francisco Directory.

NEW Emilia's Pizzeria 🖼 M 🍴 *Pizza*   ▽ 27 | 15 | 23 | $16

Berkeley | 2995 Shattuck Ave. (Ashby Ave.) | 510-704-1794 | emiliaspizzeria.com

A "must-try" for "pizza aficionados", this "popular" Lilliputian Berkeley storefront (look for the orange interior) is a serious contender in the East Bay pizza smackdown; the "extraordinary" gas-fired "thin-crust" offerings topped with a few "fresh ingredients" show a "true dedication to the craft of New York–style" pies, and since there are no slices and only eight seats inside, it's best to "order well in advance."

NEW Encuentro Cafe & Wine Bar *Vegetarian*   – | – | – | M

Oakland | 200 Second St. (Jackson St.) | 510-832-9463 | www.encuentrooakland.com

Headed up by Millennium chef Eric Tucker, this new, under-the-radar vegetarian enoteca in Oakland's up-and-coming Jack London Square

FOOD | DECOR | SERVICE | COST

area wows early samplers with a "limited menu" of "indescribably" "delicious" "creative fare" that's "satisfying" enough for "carnivores"; it's served with "hearty pours of interesting" biodynamic wines in a "cool", "comfortable" setting with a bamboo-topped bar.

☑ Erna's Elderberry House *Californian/French* 28 | 27 | 27 | $88

Oakhurst | Château du Sureau | 48688 Victoria Ln. (Hwy. 41) | 559-683-6800 | www.elderberryhouse.com

Experience "complex" French-Californian cuisine and "European sophistication" at this "fanciful baroque" "foodie paradise" in a "fantastic" B&B that's "worth a special trip" to "unlikely" Oakhurst in the Sierra foothills; what with "mind-blowing" (if "high-priced") prix fixe menus, "not-to-be-missed Sunday brunch" and "visits" from Erna herself, you'll be "treated royally", making it "one of the greatest lodging/dining" "jewels" – especially "if you want to see Yosemite without roughing it."

Esin Restaurant & Bar *American/Mediterranean* 25 | 22 | 24 | $44

Danville | Rose Garden Ctr. | 750 Camino Ramon (Sycamore Valley Rd.) | 925-314-0974 | www.esinrestaurant.com

The "mingling" owners "take pride in their food" at this "upscale" "favorite", providing "extraordinary" New American–Med meals that conclude with "amazing" desserts, particularly the "heavenly" daily changing bread pudding; slightly "swanky" with "beautiful", new-ish "digs in Danville", it has a "hopping" bar and "superb" service to seal the deal.

Evan's American Gourmet Cafe *American* ▽ 25 | 18 | 22 | $66

South Lake Tahoe | 536 Emerald Bay Rd. (15th St.) | 530-542-1990 | www.evanstahoe.com

Evan's to Betsy, "you'd expect mom to come out of the kitchen" at this "charming small cottage" in the Sierras, but instead the "delicious" New American dishes (with Asian influences), extensive selection of single malts and West Coast wines served by an "excellent staff" "match up to the fancier places in SF" – at "more reasonable prices"; "booking is essential" in the high season, as it's "about the only gourmet stop on the south side of Lake Tahoe" and only seats 40.

NEW Eve Ⓢ Ⓜ *American* ▽ 25 | 18 | 22 | $42

Berkeley | 1960 University Ave. (bet. Bonita Ave. & Milvia St.) | 510-868-0735 | www.eve-berkeley.com

"High-art" dinners "impress foodies" at this ambitious Berkeley arrival offering "inventive", "beautiful" New American dishes ("lots of foam") with à la carte and prix fixe options, served in an industrial storefront space; "personalized" attention is another plus, though a few cite "tiny portions" and a pricing system that's "innovative" but "adds up", assessing "it has potential but isn't there yet."

Everett & Jones Barbeque *BBQ* 20 | 11 | 14 | $23

Alameda | 1518 Webster St. (Haight Ave.) | 510-749-7084
Berkeley | 1955 San Pablo Ave. (University Ave.) | 510-548-8261
Hayward | 296 A St. (Filbert St.) | 510-581-3222
Oakland | Jack London Sq. | 126 Broadway (bet. The Embarcadero & 2nd St.) | 510-663-2350
www.eandjbbq.com

'Cue-heads commend the "smoky" "slabs" of "fall-off-the-bone ribs sauced with the most perfect blend of sweet and tart" and served up "with a side of sass" at these East Bay take-out joints; the service and decor are "blah", and a few connoisseurs call the grub "only average", but most simply advise just "take your Lipitor" then "bliss out" with some of the "bestest cheapest BBQ around"; P.S. the Jack London Square branch is a real "sit-down" location with "live music" Saturdays.

FatApple's Diner
17 | **13** | **17** | **$19**

Berkeley | 1346 Martin Luther King Jr. Way (bet. Berryman & Rose Sts.) | 510-526-2260
El Cerrito | 7525 Fairmount Ave. (bet. Carmel & Ramona Aves.) | 510-528-3433

Known for its "juicy, delicious" burgers, this "informal", "kid-friendly" diner duo in Berkeley and El Cerrito turns out "reliable comfort food" that's "well worth sampling", along with baked goods that "will make you crazy if you're on a diet"; it's "nothing amazing" over the food forward, who note it "never changes", but a "loyal following" finds it "fun for breakfast" and a "good value" for dinner.

Fentons Creamery Ice Cream
20 | **15** | **17** | **$17**

Oakland | Terminal 2 | 1 Airport Dr. (Doolittle Dr.)
Oakland | 4226 Piedmont Ave. (bet. Entrada & Glenwood Aves.) | 510-658-7000
www.fentonscreamery.com

"What's not to love" about an "old-fashioned ice creamery"? ask Oakland admirers who have made a "family tradition" of ordering "humongous" "gooey sundaes" at this "always crowded" "classic soda fountain" (which "got a salute in the movie *Up*"); the sweet-toothed say "don't bother with the other food", but some suggest "splitting" the "excellent crab sandwich" "with your tablemate" before "pigging out" on the "wildly indulgent" desserts; P.S. the Oakland airport outpost can be "counted on" for a "quick fix" of "fantastic cones" "before your flight."

Five American/Californian
22 | **23** | **19** | **$44**

Berkeley | Hotel Shattuck Plaza | 2086 Allston Way (Shattuck Ave.) | 510-845-7300 | www.five-berkeley.com

Its name "stands for the five senses", and this "ritzy", "refurbished" "black-and-white" lobby restaurant in Berkeley's Hotel Shattuck Plaza "strives to delight them all"; from the "marvelous ambiance" to the "terrific" Californian "twists" on retro American cooking to the "inventive" drinks at the "spectacular bar" ("have two" – it's near BART), it's a "real treat" for a "reasonable price"; still, if the "deafening" "acoustics" didn't "overpower" conversation and service weren't so "inconsistent", meals could be "properly savored."

Flora 🗓Ⓜ American
22 | **22** | **21** | **$45**

Oakland | 1900 Telegraph Ave. (19th St.) | 510-286-0100 | www.floraoakland.com

Uptown Oakland is "coming of age" (or, rather, "returning to the '30s") thanks to this "hip", "bustling" Doña Tomás offshoot set in a restored art deco floral depot building; while the "modern" New American fare, including a "wonderful Saturday brunch", is "dependably delicious", the "bartenders are really the stars", handcrafting "masterpiece" cocktails that go down easy – and help dull the "ear-piercing noise" and "splurge" prices.

	FOOD	DECOR	SERVICE	COST

Fonda Solana ❶ *Pan-Latin* — 22 | 20 | 21 | $37

Albany | 1501A Solano Ave. (Curtis St.) | 510-559-9006 |
www.fondasolana.com

"If there's such a thing as Albany trendsetters", they're "crowding around a table" at this "happening" brick-red corner cafe, "lingering" past midnight over "vibrant", "addictive Latino small plates" with "a kick" and "fabulous festive drinks"; all of those "duck tacos" and "high-end tequilas" prompt "prices to skyrocket quickly", but the "spirited vibe" and "all-day happy-hour bargains" easily appease.

Forbes Mill Steakhouse *Steak* — 22 | 20 | 21 | $59

Danville | 200 Sycamore Valley Rd. W. (San Ramon Valley Blvd.) |
925-552-0505 | www.forbesmillsteakhouse.com
See review in South of San Francisco Directory.

Garibaldis *Californian/Mediterranean* — 22 | 20 | 21 | $46

Oakland | 5356 College Ave. (bet. Bryant & Manila Aves.) | 510-595-4000 |
www.garibaldisrestaurant.com
See review in City of San Francisco Directory.

Gar Woods Grill & Pier *American/Mediterranean* — 17 | 23 | 18 | $41

Carnelian Bay | 5000 N. Lake Blvd. (Center St.) | 530-546-3366 |
www.garwoods.com

A "wonderful waterside location" ("accessible by boat") paired with an "active bar scene" makes "battling the weekend warrior crowds worthwhile" at this Carnelian Bay boîte; "even blasé gourmets" concede the "pedestrian" New American–Med food "tastes better" after sipping a signature "Wet Woody or two", and besides, when you're "enjoying a gorgeous Tahoe day or evening right above the Lake", "who needs foie gras?"

☒NEW Gather *Californian* — - | - | - | M

Berkeley | David Brower Ctr. | 2200 Oxford St. (Allston Way) |
510-809-0440 | www.gatherrestaurant.com

An ambitious new Berkeley gathering place, this feel-good cafe and wine bar, located near campus and the area's performing arts venues, delivers a diverse menu of affordable farm-to-table Cal dishes (about half of which are vegetarian) complemented by organic wines and spirits; the eco-friendly digs are fashioned from 'gathered' materials like old redwood high-school bleachers repurposed as banquettes and tabletops.

Gioia Pizzeria *Pizza* — 24 | 7 | 17 | $13

Berkeley | 1586 Hopkins St. (bet. McGee & Monterey Aves.) |
510-528-4692 | www.gioiapizzeria.com

Homesick New Yorkers "stand patiently in line" for the "almost pitch-perfect" "thin-crust" pizza piled with "quality ingredients" in "interesting combinations" at this Berkeley "treasure"; since it's "tiny", with only six stools at the "narrow counter", most pick up the "addictive", "inexpensive" slices and pies to "take home" (or eat on a "nearby bench").

Great China *Chinese* — 24 | 10 | 13 | $27

Berkeley | 2115 Kittredge St. (bet. Fulton St. & Shattuck Ave.) |
510-843-7996 | www.greatchinaberkeley.com

"If only they would expand" lament fans of this "cheap", "always mobbed" Berkeley Chinese "favorite" serving "amazingly authentic" dishes like the "must-order" Peking duck; despite its "indifferent" service and "dismal"-looking room, East Bayers feel "lucky" to "wait their turn", knowing "when the food comes you're focused only on what's on the table."

Grégoire *French* | 23 | 9 | 17 | $20

Berkeley | 2109 Cedar St. (bet. Shattuck Ave. & Walnut St.) | 510-883-1893
Oakland | 4001B Piedmont Ave. (40th St.) | 510-547-3444
www.gregoirerestaurant.com

"The foodies' alternative to the microwave", these "fancy" French take-out joints whipping up "amazing sandwiches" and "scrumptious" dinners in "clever hexagonal boxes" "fit the bill" for Berkeley "coeds" and "busy" Oakland "professionals"; everything's "prepared before your eyes" and "changes monthly" except for the "signature potato puffs" (they "rule"), so while there's almost "nowhere to sit", "where else can you get" such a "gourmet" meal for such a "great price"?

Herbivore *Vegan* | 15 | 13 | 15 | $22

Berkeley | 2451 Shattuck Ave. (Haste St.) | 510-665-1675 |
www.herbivorerestaurant.com
See review in City of San Francisco Directory.

NEW Hibiscus *Caribbean* | ▽ 21 | 26 | 21 | $47

Oakland | 1745 San Pablo Ave. (18th St.) | 510-444-2626 |
www.hibiscusoakland.com

"Rockin' good" cooking, "inventive cocktails" and a "gorgeous", West Indies–inspired setting replete with hibiscus paintings and church-pew seating lend a vivacious vibe to this "hipster hangout" next to Uptown's New Parish Music Hall; the full menu of affordable Caribbean-Creole creations from chef Sarah Kirnon (ex Front Porch), including her signature fried chicken and "amazing" grits, is also available in the adjacent bar, decked out with vintage bric-a-brac.

Home of Chicken and Waffles ● *Southern* | ▽ 19 | 11 | 18 | $21

Oakland | 444 Embarcadero W. (B'way) | 510-836-4446
Though it "can't touch" LA's more famous Roscoes, this "friendly", late-night Oaklander is "loved" by "locals" for its "delicious" soul food, ordered off an "adorable mural" menu; while the "high calories/low prices" combination may require you to "have your cardiologist on auto-dial", most leave wondering "what could be better than fried chicken and waffles anyway?"

Il Fornaio *Italian* | 19 | 20 | 19 | $39

Walnut Creek | 1430 Mt. Diablo Blvd. (bet. B'way & Main St.) |
925-296-0100 | www.ilfornaio.com
See review in City of San Francisco Directory.

☒ In-N-Out Burger *Burgers* | 22 | 10 | 18 | $9

Oakland | 8300 Oakport St. (bet. Pendleton & Roland Ways) |
800-786-1000 | www.in-n-out.com
See review in City of San Francisco Directory.

Izzy's Steaks & Chops *Steak* | 20 | 17 | 20 | $43

San Ramon | 200 Montgomery St. (bet. Alcosta Blvd. & Market Pl.) |
925-830-8620 | www.izzyssteaks.com
See review in City of San Francisco Directory.

	FOOD	DECOR	SERVICE	COST

Jake's on the Lake *Californian* | 16 | 21 | 17 | $39 |

Tahoe City | Boatworks Mall | 780 N. Lake Blvd. (Jackpine St.) | 530-583-0188 | www.jakestahoe.com

A prime place to "wow a date" or "bring the whole family", this Sierra docksider "scores points" for its "spectacular setting" overlooking the Tahoe City Marina and the "amazing views" that go with it; despite "so-so" Californian eats and "spotty service", "reservations are suggested" in-season, though it's always "busy with locals" on weekend nights, when the bar features live music.

Jimmy Beans *Diner* | 19 | 10 | 14 | $19 |

Berkeley | 1290 Sixth St. (Gilman St.) | 510-528-3435 | www.jimmybeans.com

With "special omelets" and "crave"-worthy silver-dollar pancakes at "rock-bottom prices", it's a boon to have "breakfast all day" at this Berkeley diner where regulars overlook the "industrial location" and "slapdash" setting and "order at the counter"; despite the crowds, you "can usually get seated" on weekend mornings, or try dinner, when there's table service and a daily three-course "bargain" for $15.

Juan's Place *Mexican* | 16 | 12 | 18 | $18 |

Berkeley | 941 Carleton St. (9th St.) | 510-845-6904

"Fake margaritas", "big bowls of tortilla chips" and "lotsa cheap", "basic" chow make this "old-school" Berkeley Mexican a "frat boy's delight"; it looks as if it's been around since "California belonged to Mexico", but the "atmosphere is always lively", the staff is "friendly" and, besides, it's "fun to wear the sombrero."

Kirala *Japanese* | 24 | 14 | 17 | $33 |

Berkeley | 2100 Ward St. (Shattuck Ave.) | 510-549-3486

Kirala 2 *Japanese*

Berkeley | Epicurious Gdn. | 1511 Shattuck Ave. (bet. Cedar & Vine Sts.) | 510-649-1384

www.kiralaberkeley.com

"Wonderful" robata rivals the "super-fresh sushi" at this perpetually jammed Japanese filled with Berkeleyites who "save up and line up" for the "standout" fare; it's especially enjoyable (and usually quicker) to "sit at the counter and watch the action" or noodle around at the sake bar, but diners who hate to "wait" only to get "rushed" out grab their bento and sashimi spoils to go at Epicurious Garden.

Koi Garden *Chinese* | 23 | 16 | 12 | $33 |

Dublin | Ulferts Ctr. | 4288 Dublin Blvd. (bet. Glynnis Rose Dr. & John Monego Ct.) | 925-833-9090 | www.koipalace.com

See Koi Palace review in South of San Francisco Directory.

Koryo Wooden Charcoal BBQ *Korean* | ∇ 22 | 11 | 15 | $29 |

Oakland | 4390 Telegraph Ave. (bet. 43rd & 44th Sts.) | 510-652-6007 | www.gotsushiandsake.com

"A standout in a sea of delicious Korean restaurants", this affordable hole-in-the-wall in Oakland's Kyoro Plaza is the "go-to place" for ribs and "some of the best bibimbop in town", along with "fantastic pickles and other banchan" that "start the meal in a great way"; it's "unique" for "out-of-towners", and the DIY "wood BBQ" "never gets old, unlike the lines on the weekends" and the "cursory" service.

	FOOD	DECOR	SERVICE	COST

Lake Chalet *Californian*

| | 14 | 25 | 15 | $39 |

Oakland | Lake Merritt Boathse. | 1520 Lakeside Dr. (bet. 14th & 17th Sts.) | 510-208-5253 | www.thelakechalet.com

Even Gertrude Stein couldn't "wish for more in urban Oakland" than this "lovely former boathouse on Lake Merritt", boasting outdoor seating with "stunning views"; typical to "most waterfront dining", the "so-so" seafood and Cal fare and "amateurish" service "don't match up to the price", but "excellent happy hours" at the "endless" bar keep it jumping; P.S. a post-Survey chef change is not reflected in the Food score.

Lalime's *Californian/Mediterranean*

| | 25 | 22 | 25 | $55 |

Berkeley | 1329 Gilman St. (bet. Neilson St. & Peralta Ave.) | 510-527-9838 | www.lalimes.com

"Inspired" Cal-Med menus "highlight the seasons" at this "fine-dining" "destination" (and leader of the K2 restaurant "empire") tended by a "top-notch" staff in a "hidden"-away "Berkeley house"; most diners "like the new, contemporary decor", adding that while it's "a little pricey", it remains a "relative bargain" for "special celebrations"; P.S. a post-Survey chef change is not reflected in the Food score.

La Méditerranée *Mediterranean/Mideastern*

| | 19 | 14 | 18 | $23 |

Berkeley | 2936 College Ave. (bet. Ashby Ave. & Russell St.) | 510-540-7773 | www.cafelamed.com

See review in City of San Francisco Directory.

Lanesplitter Pub & Pizza ● *Pizza*

| | 16 | 10 | 15 | $16 |

Berkeley | 1051 San Pablo Ave. (Monroe St.) | 510-527-8375
Berkeley | 2033 San Pablo Ave. (bet. Addison St. & University Ave.) | 510-845-1652
NEW **Emeryville** | 3645 San Pablo Ave. (Adeline St.) | 510-594-9400 ·
Oakland | 4799 Telegraph Ave. (48th St.) | 510-653-5350
NEW **Oakland** | 536 Lake Park Ave. (Lakeshore Ave.) | 510-893-4001
www.lanesplitterpizza.com

These "old-style" pizza places filled with "motorcycle decor" sling "almost NY" pies (with vegan options), enhanced by "excellent Cali beers" and "ginormous salads"; though the "basic food" and "diffident" service is "not up to the standard of the artisan" vendors nearby, they're "fast, cheap" and "open late too"; P.S. the 1051 San Pablo and new Lake Park Avenue 'pit stops' offer takeout and delivery only.

La Note *French*

| | 22 | 20 | 18 | $26 |

Berkeley | 2377 Shattuck Ave. (bet. Channing Way & Durant Ave.) | 510-843-1535 | www.lanoterestaurant.com

Berkeley locals have a "love affair" with this "cozy" French cafe turning out "wonderful", "rustic" brunches, "zingy" lunches and "honest" country dinners (Thursday–Saturday), serenaded by a "live accordionist" in the evenings; while the "transporting" outdoor garden feels "like the South of France", the service is a bit less blissful, and the "happening" scene gets "swamped" on weekend mornings.

Lark Creek *American*

| | 23 | 21 | 23 | $45 |

Walnut Creek | 1360 Locust St. (bet. Cypress St. & Mt. Diablo Blvd.) | 925-256-1234 | www.larkcreek.com

"Farm-fresh comfort food" is the hallmark of this "tried-and-true" "Walnut Creek institution" whose "light, open" room sets a "relaxed" mood for a leisurely "date" or dinner "before a show"; though some note it's "not particularly adventurous", the "reasonably priced" "standards", "memorable" specials and "excellent" service generally add up to a "rewarding" meal.

Le Cheval *Vietnamese*

20 | 15 | 17 | $27

Oakland | 1007 Clay St. (10th St.) | 510-763-8495
Walnut Creek | 1375 N. Broadway (bet. Cypress & Duncan Sts.) | 925-938-2288 Ⓜ

Le Petit Cheval Ⓢⓟ *Vietnamese*

Berkeley | YWCA | 2600 Bancroft Way (Bowditch St.) | 510-704-8018
www.lecheval.com

"All Downtown Oakland seems to be" at this "noisy barn of a setting" (with a "classier" Walnut Creek offshoot and a "college lunchtime hangout" "near UC Berkeley campus") proffering an "endless" selection of relatively "upscale", "high-quality" "Viet-licious" classics that can be "finished off with a sweet, strong coffee" or "after-work" drinks; the breakneck service is "almost too swift", but the "waiting crowds" offer "testimony to the good food and low prices."

Little Star Pizza Ⓜ *Pizza*

24 | 15 | 17 | $23

NEW Albany | 1175 Solano Ave. (Cornell Ave.) | 510-526-7827 | www.littlestarpizza.com
See review in City of San Francisco Directory.

NEW Locanda da Eva ● *Italian*

- | - | - | M

Berkeley | 2826 Telegraph Ave. (bet. Oregon & Stuart Sts.) | 510-665-9601 | www.locandadaeva.com

Hewing to a tried-and-true winning formula – ingredient-driven rustic Italian cuisine, affordable vino and artisanal cocktails – this bamboo-floored Berkeley newcomer hopes to outfox a cursed location with a slate of wood-fired pizzas, housemade pastas and sustainably sourced fish, fowl and flora, complemented by 20 food-friendly wines by the glass; the innovative drink list, featuring lots of aperitifs and digestifs, is offered along with the bar menu until midnight.

Lo Coco's Restaurant & Pizzeria Ⓜ *Italian*

21 | 14 | 19 | $27

Berkeley | 1400 Shattuck Ave. (Rose St.) | 510-843-3745
Oakland | 4270 Piedmont Ave. (Echo Ave.) | 510-652-6222
www.lococospizzeria.com

The "real Sicilian pizza" and – "oh, mamma mia" – "terrific homemade meatballs" that top "wonderful pasta" "totally satisfy any Italian hankering" at this "family-owned" duo of "tiny", "friendly" trattorias in Berkeley and Oakland; while they're "usually pretty packed", *amici* are willing to wait for the "old-school" experience.

Luka's Taproom & Lounge *Californian/French*

20 | 14 | 18 | $30

Oakland | 2221 Broadway (Grand Ave.) | 510-451-4677 | www.lukasoakland.com

Pleased patrons say "there isn't a single dish to dislike" at this "relaxed" Oakland brasserie offering a "glorious" Belgian beer selection to wash down the "good burgers" and other "simple" Cal-French eats; it's "got the Uptown scene going" with a "hopping" bar and DJs spinning every night, but watch out for a serious "din" that may drown out your "dinner guests"; P.S. "make a reservation" to avoid a "daunting" wait.

	FOOD	DECOR	SERVICE	COST

Mama's Royal Cafe ⌷ *American*

21 | 15 | 17 | $20

Oakland | 4012 Broadway (40th St.) | 510-547-7600 |
www.mamasroyalcafeoakland.com

Catering to a "broad" audience, from the enduring "tie-dyed" set to revelers "after a brutal night of partying", this "popular" daytime diner does "breakfast to-die-for" (think "strong" coffee and "amazing" huevos rancheros) and American lunches too; it's a "real Oakland experience", from the "funky" digs to the "great" waitresses who "have style", but "beware" on the weekends, when there's usually a queue "out the door."

NEW Manzanita

▽ 25 | 25 | 25 | $54

Lake Tahoe *Californian/French*

Truckee | Ritz-Carlton Highlands | 13031 Ritz Carlton Highlands Ct. (Hwy. 267) | 530-562-3050 | www.manzanitalaketahoe.com

This slope-side "winner" at Truckee's luxury Ritz-Carlton Highlands resort is Lake Tahoe's "new place to see and be seen", presenting "Traci-good", "seasonal" Californian-French cooking (courtesy of Jardinière mega chef and partner Des Jardins) matched by "courteous" service and "incredible" sweeping views of Northstar's runs; outfitted with lots of wood, stone and leather, the "dramatic" "lodge"-like setting offers fireside terrace seating with an oversized oval-shaped bar that's perfect for "people-watching"; P.S. no ski boots allowed.

Marica *Seafood*

▽ 23 | 18 | 22 | $37

Oakland | 5301 College Ave. (B'way) | 510-985-8388 |
www.maricafood.wordpress.com

"Fish is the strong suit" at this "steady", "family-run" "neighborhood locale" in Rockridge delivering "fresh", often "brilliant" seafood (i.e. the signature twice-cooked Maine lobster) accompanied by "thoughtful" sides; "warm", "personal service" and "kind-to-the-budget" touches like dollar oysters and daily $5 cocktail specials at the oak bar keep it an "excellent yet affordable" option.

Marzano *Italian/Pizza*

21 | 18 | 20 | $35

Oakland | 4214 Park Blvd. (Glenfield Ave.) | 510-531-4500
NEW Oakland | 5356 College Ave. (bet. Bryant & Manila Aves.) |
510-595-4058
www.marzanorestaurant.com

"Every neighborhood should have one" of these rustic Southern Italians turning out "hot and bubbly", "wood-fired" pizzas with "imaginative" toppings – and now the Glenview original has a twin on College (made by "splitting" sib Garabaldis); sure, they're a "bit of a scene", and "packed so tight you'll know more than you ever cared to" about the next table, but "accommodating" service and "affordable" tabs keep them "simply fab" – just remember, "reservations are a must."

Max's *Deli*

17 | 14 | 17 | $26

Oakland | Oakland City Ctr. | 500 12th St. (bet. B'way & Clay St.) |
510-451-6297 🖩
San Ramon | 2015 Crow Canyon Pl. (Crow Canyon Rd.) | 925-277-9300
www.maxsworld.com
See review in City of San Francisco Directory.

NEW Meritage at The Claremont *Californian*

▽ 25 | 23 | 25 | $68

Berkeley | The Claremont Hotel | 41 Tunnel Rd. (Claremont Ave.) | 510-549-8510 | www.claremontresort.com

Like a finely crafted meritage wine, this tony eno-oriented "hip" redux in the Claremont Hotel (formerly Jordan's) blends together "destination"-worthy Cal cuisine, "excellent service" and "terrific views" of the Bay to create a "wow" experience; the "chef leads with the wine", crafting "small and large" "feast"-worthy plates designed to pair with specific varietals, and also whips up a "fabulous" Sunday brunch buffet; P.S. "be sure to check out the bar menu" and weekend pianists in the lounge.

Metro *Californian/French*

22 | 19 | 22 | $42

Lafayette | 3524 Mt. Diablo Blvd. (bet. 1st St. & Moraga Rd.) | 925-284-4422 | www.metrolafayette.com

The "parking-lot" location of this Cal-French "jewel" in Lafayette might be "inauspicious", but really, it's "city dining in the 'burbs", with "superior" food, "sophisticated", "minimalist" decor and a sweet "summer patio"; boasting "handcrafted cocktails" and "excellent" service as well, it's "like a little black dress: perfect for almost any occasion, casual or festive" – though some caution the nighttime volume can be "hard to bear"; P.S. a $35 three-course prix fixe is available.

Mezze *Californian/Mediterranean*

23 | 21 | 23 | $42

Oakland | 3407 Lakeshore Ave. (bet. Mandana Blvd. & Trestle Glen Rd.) | 510-663-2500 | www.mezze.com

A "neighborhood treasure" with "world-class food", this "wonderful" Oakland bistro concocts "creative" Cal-Med fare suitable for both "special occasions" and everyday dinners (the "three-course prix fixe menus" are "a steal"); with "outstanding cocktails" and "no-corkage" nights (Monday–Wednesday) as well as service that "makes you feel at home", local devotees dub it their "favorite" on Lakeshore.

Miss Pearl's Jam House *Caribbean*

16 | 19 | 17 | $37

Oakland | Waterfront Plaza Hotel | 1 Broadway (Embarcadero W.) | 510-444-7171 | www.misspearlsjamhouse.com

"If you're in Oakland, make a beeline" to this "nouveau Caribbean" for "savory" eats insist loyalists who relish its "reincarnation" "from the late '80s", replete with funky Southern mansion decor; it's "the place" for an "excellent weekend brunch", and on "warm evenings" when you want to "play it cool" you can jam to live music in the bar, though a few lament it's "lost a bit" of its "island spice" and find service a little "jerky."

Moody's Bistro & Lounge *American*

24 | 20 | 22 | $55

Truckee | Truckee Hotel | 10007 Bridge St. (Donner Pass Rd.) | 530-587-8688 | www.moodysbistro.com

"Fantastic", "fresh" New American dishes, augmented by "stiff drinks" and "exceptional service" ("relatively speaking") keep this upscale "hip hangout" in Downtown Truckee "crowded with the après-ski" and "summer-activities" crew; the "make-your-own s'mores please kids and adults alike", while "live jazz" (Thursday–Saturday) and the eternal "hope for a Paul McCartney" repeat visit "brighten" the mood of the "dark" "deco" room.

	FOOD	DECOR	SERVICE	COST

Naan 'n Curry *Indian/Pakistani* — 17 | 7 | 10 | $15

Berkeley | 2366 Telegraph Ave. (bet. Channing Way & Durant Ave.) |
510-841-6226 | www.naancurry.com
See review in City of San Francisco Directory.

Naked Fish, The *Japanese* — ▽ 23 | 16 | 18 | $32

South Lake Tahoe | 3940 Lake Tahoe Blvd. (bet. Hwy. 50 & Pioneer Trail) |
530-541-3474 | www.thenakedfish.com
It's "unbelievable" that you can get "incredible sushi in a mountain
community" rave regulars hooked on this "no-frills" nautical nook "in
the middle of a tourist strip in South Lake Tahoe"; the drill: shed your
gear and "go straight" over, joining the "fun crowd" for "fresh" fish and
weekday happy hours; if you "take a nap after that ski or hike", the
"wait gets longer as the evening" unfolds and "service gets backed up."

Nan Yang Rockridge *Burmese* — ▽ 20 | 13 | 18 | $26

Oakland | 6048 College Ave. (Claremont Ave.) | 510-655-3298 |
www.nanyangrockridge.com
"Wonderful Burmese food" – or is it "Myanmar"? – "whichever, the
food is great" at this "inexpensive" Rockridge eatery whose salads
"sparkle with complex flavors" and noodles make you go "mmm";
while the "subdued" surroundings don't draw raves, the "fresh, well-
prepared" fare leaves reviewers feeling "lucky" it's "not busy."

North Beach Pizza *Pizza* — 19 | 11 | 16 | $19

Berkeley | 1598 University Ave. (California St.) | 510-849-9800 |
www.northbeachpizza.net
See review in City of San Francisco Directory.

O Chamé *Japanese* — 23 | 21 | 21 | $38

Berkeley | 1830 Fourth St. (bet. Hearst Ave. & Virginia St.) | 510-841-8783
"Pure, clean flavors" define the "simple", sometimes "sublime" specialties, like "silky noodles" nestled in a "superb broth", at this "beautifully tranquil" Japanese with a "wonderful Zen ambiance"; it offers a
"calming" escape from the "Berkeley Fourth Street" shopping "craziness", though a few reviewers are ruffled by the "precious serving
sizes" and sigh it's "too expensive" for what you get; P.S. no sushi.

Oliveto Cafe *Italian* — 23 | 19 | 20 | $37

Oakland | 5655 College Ave. (Shafter Ave.) | 510-547-5356 |
www.oliveto.com
When you're craving "amazing" "rustic" Italian cucina but don't want to
pay the "crazy" tabs of its "upstairs" "counterpart", this "European"-
style corner "cafe and espresso bar" next to Oakland's Market Hall
and the BART is the "perfect solution"; "start the day" with a "breakfast
pizza with a fried egg on top", or stop in "early evening" for "superb"
pasta and wine – all "worth the price of admission", especially while
"watching Berkeley-hip types parade by."

Oliveto Restaurant *Italian* — 24 | 21 | 22 | $58

Oakland | 5655 College Ave. (Shafter Ave.) | 510-547-5356 |
www.oliveto.com
"College Avenue meets foodie heaven" at this Oakland Market Hall
"gold standard", a "remarkably unfussy" upstairs perch that's "still
damned good after all these years"; its "dedication to Slow Food pre-

cepts" takes center stage, with "imaginative" "housemade" pastas, salumi and "excellent" "wood-oven" Tuscan "treats for your senses" complemented by equally "special" wines; though a few take issue with "price, portion and attitude", fans aren't fazed, lauding the "not-to-be-missed" "legendary regional and ingredient-themed dinners."

Ozumo Ⓩ *Japanese* | 23 | 24 | 20 | $55 |

Oakland | 2251 Broadway (Grand Ave.) | 510-286-9866 | www.ozumo.com
See review in City of San Francisco Directory.

Pacific Crest Grill at | - | - | - | E |
Bar of America *Mediterranean*

Truckee | 10042 Donner Pass Rd. (Bridge St.) | 530-587-2626 |
www.barofamerica.net

Another fixture on Downtown Truckee's historic main drag, this year-round, white-tablecloth bistro, adjacent to its down-and-dirty Bar of America bro, lures après skiers and summer visitors with all-day seasonal Cal-Med offerings (think cassoulet in the winter, fresh seafood in the summer), much of which has been sourced in the Sierra foothills, including many of the selections on the sustainably leaning wine list; the cozy, 40-seat room is filled with antique books, a vintage back bar and big booths.

Pakwan *Pakistani* | 21 | 7 | 11 | $15 |

Fremont | 41068 Fremont Blvd. (Irvington Ave.) | 510-226-6234 Ⓜ⇄
Hayward | 25168 Mission Blvd. (Central Blvd.) | 510-538-2401
www.pakwanrestaurant.com
See review in City of San Francisco Directory.

Pappo Ⓜ *Californian/Mediterranean*   ∇ | 22 | 21 | 23 | $40 |

Alameda | 2320 Central Ave. (bet. Oak & Park Sts.) | 510-337-9100 |
www.papporestaurant.com

Alamedans who "wish they still lived in SF" inhabit this "intimate, urbanlike" bistro in their own backyard, where the "chef pours his heart" into a Cal-Med menu that uses local ingredients in "new taste combos"; a "great wine selection" and "good service" add to the appeal, whether "you want to impress" or just "grab a bite" before "catching a movie" across the street; P.S. closed Monday–Tuesday, no lunch Wednesday–Thursday.

Pasta Pomodoro *Italian* | 17 | 13 | 18 | $23 |

Emeryville | Bay Street Mall | 5614 Shellmound St. (Bay St.) |
510-923-1173
Oakland | 5500 College Ave. (Lawton Ave.) | 510-923-0900
www.pastapomodoro.com
See review in City of San Francisco Directory.

Peasant & the Pear, The Ⓜ *Mediterranean* | 24 | 21 | 24 | $40 |

Danville | 267 Hartz Ave. (Diablo Blvd.) | 925-820-6611 |
www.thepeasantandthepear.com

"Food made both mindfully and lovingly" is praised by diners at this "absolutely charming" Danville Med known for its "outstanding" lamb shank among other "seasonal" "favorites"; "excellent" service and a "warm atmosphere" with a "lively" (and "loud") bar complete the picture, so many feel it's "perfect for a power lunch, drinks with friends or a date"; P.S. it's "surprisingly kid-friendly" too.

Pho 84 🏿 Vietnamese
20 | 13 | 17 | $21

Oakland | 354 17th St. (bet. Franklin & Webster Sts.) | 510-832-1338 | www.pho84.com

While pho-natics stick to "generous" bowls of the eponymous dish at this "typical Vietnamese noodle stop" in Downtown Oakland, others aim to "try everything" on the "extensive" menu, since the "authentic" dishes are "always fresh and well prepared"; while there are "long lines at lunch", "efficient" servers keep up the pace and deliver a real "value" to boot.

Pianeta Italian
∇ 21 | 18 | 21 | $44

Truckee | 10096 Donner Pass Rd. (Brockway Rd.) | 530-587-4694 | www.pianetarestaurant.com

Whether you make this "welcoming" bi-level Italian-Med a "detour stop on the way to North Shore" after "walking the Downtown" of Truckee or following a "long day on the slopes", you'll be greeted with "fine" "homemade pastas" among other hearty eats; you "can't beat" the old-world ambiance, replete with a stone-walled dining room boasting Da Vinci-style murals, so no wonder it usually gets "crowded with après-skiers on weekend nights", making "reservations are must."

Piatti Italian
19 | 19 | 19 | $39

Danville | 100 Sycamore Valley Rd. W. (San Ramon Valley Blvd.) | 925-838-2082 | www.piatti.com

"Solid" cooking "satisfies" at these "bustling" Bay Area Italians where "all are made to feel welcome" by the "professional" staff; each location has its own charms (like the "delightful" deck "right on the Bay" in Mill Valley, or the "cozy fireplace" in Danville), and while some foodies find the fare "lacks panache", others seek them out for a "dependable", "fairly priced" meal.

Picán Southern
21 | 23 | 21 | $47

Oakland | 2295 Broadway (23rd St.) | 510-834-1000 | www.picanrestaurant.com

"Soul food" goes "upscale" at this "popular" newcomer, a "nice addition" to the "Oaktown" scene, where a "diverse crowd" digs into "über-cool 21st-century 'Hotlanta' cuisine" amid "snazzy" surroundings not far from the Paramount Theatre; there's also an "encyclopedic bourbon collection" and "welcoming Southern hospitality", though a few wags warn that this "butterfat and fried-food fest" can get "expensive."

Picante Cocina Mexicana Mexican
21 | 13 | 15 | $17

Berkeley | 1328 Sixth St. (bet. Camelia & Gilman Sts.) | 510-525-3121 | www.picanteberkeley.com

Though it's "always packed", fans know the line "goes sooo fast" to order "healthy", "Berkeley"-style south-of-the-border staples (with "house-made tortillas") as well as some "unique", "well-crafted" plates at this "high-quality" "Mexican food hall"; "popular among the mommy-and-daddy crowd", it's "noisy with kids", so some "bring the aspirin" while others take refuge in "killer top-shelf margaritas" on the patio.

Pizza Antica Pizza
21 | 15 | 17 | $27

Lafayette | 3600 Mt. Diablo Blvd. (Dewing Ave.) | 925-299-0500 | www.pizzaantica.com

See review in South of San Francisco Directory.

	FOOD	DECOR	SERVICE	COST

Pizzaiolo ⧉ *Pizza*

25 | 18 | 20 | $35

Oakland | 5008 Telegraph Ave. (51st St.) | 510-652-4888 |
www.pizzaiolooakland.com

"Chez Panisse progeny" Charlie Hallowell's "neighborhood-y" "artisanal pizzeria" in Temescal provides "homemade doughnuts for breakfast" and "outstanding" Southern Italian appetizers and "primi pastas" for dinner, yet the "stars of the show" remain the "innovative", "fantastic wood-oven" California pizzas; like its new li'l "sister Boot & Shoe Service", it also has a "young, lively vibe" and "fantastic cocktails", plus a smidge of "attitude", a "drag of a wait" and "way too loud" music – all softened by a "sweet garden in back."

Pizza Rustica *Pizza*

21 | 12 | 18 | $21

Oakland | 5422 College Ave. (bet. Kales & Manila Aves.) |
510-654-1601
Oakland | 6106 La Salle Ave. (Mountain Blvd.) | 510-339-7878
www.caferustica.com

Oaklanders "can always count on good pizza" with "nontraditional" toppings, "creative salads" and "succulent" rotisserie chicken at this East Bay pizzeria pair; while the "tiny" College Avenue location has a "hip" retro atmosphere, there's "no decor at Montclair", leading many to opt for "prompt" takeout or delivery when pining for a pie.

NEW Plum *Californian*

- | - | - | M

Oakland | 2214 Broadway (Grand Ave.) | 510-444-7586

Enterprising chef Daniel Patterson (Coi, Il Cane Rosso) will be spreading his savoir faire from SF to Uptown Oakland with this moderately priced newcomer, slated at press time to open in September 2010; showcasing progressive Northern Californian cuisine, the kitchen will provide plenty of reasons to eat your fruits and vegetables, though meat is on the menu too; an adjacent artisanal cocktail bar is in the works as well.

PlumpJack Cafe *Californian/Mediterranean*

23 | 19 | 21 | $57

Olympic Valley | PlumpJack Squaw Valley Inn | 1920 Squaw Valley Rd. (Hwy. 89) | 530-583-1576 | www.plumpjackcafe.com

Snag a seat "next to the gorgeous fireplace while snow falls gently outside" to truly experience the "more-than-perfect ambiance" of this "slopeside" "oasis" in North Tahoe's Olympic Valley, an "intimate" go-to for the "snow-boots-and-woolly-sweater" set; the "outstanding" Cal-Med fare is matched by a "reasonably priced", "deep wine list", and you might even indulge in some "people-watching" too ("hey, there's the mayor with a Getty").

Postino *Italian*

21 | 23 | 22 | $52

Lafayette | 3565 Mt. Diablo Blvd. (Lafayette Cir.) | 925-299-8700 |
www.postinorestaurant.com

Diners declare this "one-time post office" in Lafayette "delivers" with its "imaginative menu" of "substantial Italian food" that's expensive but "not at all precious", served amid "lovely", fireplace-warmed surroundings by an "attentive" staff; though some critics complain that it's a bit "uneven" in the kitchen (claiming some dishes are "heavier than Dumbo"), most find it "enjoyable" all around.

Prima *Italian*

24 | 22 | 24 | $55

Walnut Creek | 1522 N. Main St. (bet. Bonanza St. & Lincoln Ave.) | 925-935-7780 | www.primawine.com

"Wonderful dinners with winemakers" are a highlight at this Walnut Creek "classic" whose "authentic Italian fare", "superb" vino selection and "top-notch" service, as well as "fab" Tuscan ambiance, all suit a "special occasion"; though it's "been open forever", the "owners take great care" to "stay on top of their game", so the meals are "refined" "without being boring"; P.S. also check out its "wine shop next door."

Red Hut Café *Diner*

▽ 21 | 11 | 18 | $15

South Lake Tahoe | 2749 Lake Tahoe Blvd. (Al Tahoe Blvd.) | 530-541-9024
South Lake Tahoe | Ski Run Ctr. | 3660 Lake Tahoe Blvd. (Hwy. 50) | 530-544-1595
www.redhutcafe.com

"Wholesome" "all-American breakfasts" are "hearty" enough to "take you through to dinner" at these down-home diners in South Lake Tahoe (both closing at 2 PM daily); "frequented by most of the locals", they tend to get "busy", so "expect a wait" and prepare to "sit very close to your friends"; P.S. "if you like the retro vibe here, you'll like" the third hut just across the border "in Stateline too."

Restaurant Peony *Chinese*

▽ 20 | 13 | 10 | $28

Oakland | Pacific Renaissance Plaza | 388 Ninth St. (bet. Franklin & Webster Sts.) | 510-286-8866 | www.restaurantpeony.com

Dumpling devotees gorge on "pristine dim sum" at this "huge" Oakland Chinese where lunchtime is "just like Hong Kong" with "lots of carts, lots of choices", and dinner delivers "elegant" Cantonese food, including "as-good-as-it-gets" Peking duck; despite dowdy digs and service for "masochists", it gets "busy on weekends", so "be prepared to wait."

NEW Revival Bar & Kitchen ⓈⓂ *Californian*

- | - | - | M

Berkeley | 2102 Shattuck Ave. (Addison St.) | 510-549-9950 | www.revivalbarandkitchen.com

The past and the present collide at this newcomer in a revived 1901 Berkeley building, where Venus chef Amy Murray uses every part of the beast on her nightly changing, midpriced Californian menu; fresh cocktails served in vintage glasses from a zinc bar complement the 'mixed piggy platter' and other contemporary farm-to-table fare.

Rick & Ann's *American*

21 | 14 | 18 | $23

Berkeley | 2922 Domingo Ave. (bet. Ashby & Claremont Aves.) | 510-649-8538 | www.rickandanns.com

"All Berkeley wakes up and thinks of breakfast" at this "mecca" for "comfort food supreme", though there's "good American" chow for lunch and dinner too; on the downside, "it ain't comfortable", service can be "surly" and the weekend waits are "crazy-long", but advocates assure you'll leave "satisfied and humming."

River Ranch Lodge & Restaurant *Californian*

▽ 15 | 19 | 14 | $39

Tahoe City | 2285 River Rd. (Alpine Meadows Rd.) | 530-583-4264 | www.riverranchlodge.com

It's "hard to beat beer and a burger on the deck" at this Tahoe City watering hole "after a leisurely rafting trip down the Truckee River" or

FOOD | DECOR | SERVICE | COST

simply kicking back and watching others "disembark" below; you'll need to "get here early and stake your claim" outside in the summer, but during ski season the rustic interior with a stone fireplace offers "great ambiance" for refueling on the "usual" Californian "mountain fare", even if it's "mediocre" for the price.

Z Rivoli *Californian/Mediterranean*   27 | 23 | 25 | $50

Berkeley | 1539 Solano Ave. (bet. Neilson St. & Peralta Ave.) | 510-526-2542 | www.rivolirestaurant.com

Delivering "genius"-level "city food at East Bay prices", this Berkeley "star" continues to shine for a "special night out", delighting "foodies" with its "rustic" yet "beautifully prepared" seasonal Cal-Med meals, "perfectly orchestrated" by a "caring" crew; a "full bar is a welcome addition" to the "recently renovated", "Zen"-like room, where guests enjoy the "theater" of bartenders in action and "peaceful views" of the "wildlife from the glassed-off garden in the back."

Ruth's Chris Steak House *Steak*   24 | 21 | 23 | $66

Walnut Creek | 1553 Olympic Blvd. (bet. Locust & Main Sts.) | 925-977-3477 | www.ruthschris.com

See review in City of San Francisco Directory.

Saul's Restaurant & Delicatessen *Deli*   17 | 14 | 17 | $21

Berkeley | 1475 Shattuck Ave. (bet. Rose & Vine Sts.) | 510-848-3354 | www.saulsdeli.com

You'll "keep waiting for George Costanza to walk in" at this "good approximation" of a "real NY deli", whose "kitschy charm", "credible pastrami on rye" and requisite brunch "nosh" make it "about the only place for transplanted New Yorkers to get the flavors of home"; true, a few loyalists lament it's "not what it used to be", but more "appreciate it for what it is" – even if it's "more Berkeley" than Brooklyn (with sustainable ingredients and "no gruffness").

Scott's Seafood *Seafood*   19 | 19 | 20 | $43

Oakland | 2 Broadway (The Embarcadero) | 510-444-3456 | www.scottseastbay.com

Walnut Creek | 1333 N. California Blvd. (bet. Bonanza St. & Mt. Diablo Blvd.) | 925-934-1300 | www.scottswc.com

"Steady-eddy seafood" keeps customers "coming for years" and "taking the family" to this "competent" American mini-chain where additional lures include "beautiful marina views" in Oakland or "live music" at some outposts; while the rooms are "classy" and the service "welcoming", critics find them a "yawn" and assert the "quality does not match the price"; P.S. the Palo Alto and San Jose pair is separately owned.

Sea Salt *Seafood*   21 | 17 | 20 | $40

Berkeley | 2512 San Pablo Ave. (Dwight Way) | 510-883-1720 | www.seasaltrestaurant.com

"Both rustic and more refined approaches" to "sustainable" seafood please patrons at this spawn of Lalime's, housed in a "funky old Berkeley storefront" filled with "marine blue" hues, where it's tough to "decide what to order" (though the fish 'n' chips are "hard to pass up"); while some carp about "kinda small" portions and "uneven" quality, it "mostly hits the mark", plus the "congenial service" and $1 happy-hour oysters set an "inviting" tone.

	FOOD	DECOR	SERVICE	COST

Shalimar ⊄ *Indian/Pakistani* | 24 | 4 | 10 | $16 |

Fremont | 3325 Walnut Ave. (bet. Liberty St. & Paseo Padre Pkwy.) |
510-494-1919 | www.shalimarsf.com
See review in City of San Francisco Directory.

Shen Hua *Chinese* | 19 | 16 | 17 | $26 |

Berkeley | 2914 College Ave. (bet. Ashby Ave. & Russell St.) | 510-883-1777
Fans find the food is as "tasty" "as the room is loud" at this sizable
Berkeley Sichuan serving a "mile-long menu" of "flavorful", easy-on-
the-wallet Chinese; still, some disappointed diners point to "greasy"
dishes and "spotty" service, declaring it's "gone downhill" of late.

Sidebar 🖾 *Californian* | 20 | 19 | 21 | $36 |

Oakland | 542 Grand Ave. (bet. Euclid Ave. & MacArthur Blvd.) |
510-452-9500 | www.sidebar-oakland.com
"Juicy hamburgers" and other "satisfying", "modestly priced" Cal-Med
eats, plus "amazing 'locavore' drinks" (made with locally produced li-
quors), have Oaklanders sidling up to this "trendy neighborhood" gastropub; despite the "tiny, tiny menu", "what they do, they do well", and
service is "excellent", adding up to a "class act."

Soi4 *Thai* | 24 | 19 | 21 | $33 |

Oakland | 5421 College Ave. (bet. Kales & Manila Aves.) | 510-655-0889 |
www.soifour.com
Eaters encounter a "taste-bud extravaganza" at this "fabulous"
"Rockridge jewel" whose "artful" Thai cooking offers a "fresh take" on
the cuisine; boasting a "hip", "trendy" setting (and luckily "no wait"),
it has an "upscale" ambiance with moderate tabs "to match";
P.S. "don't be pretentious" – say "soy", not "swa."

Soule Domain *American* | ▽ 25 | 27 | 26 | $52 |

Kings Beach | 9983 Cove Ave. (Stateline Rd.) | 530-546-7529 |
www.souledomain.com
A "cozy, romantic" log cabin sets the stage for "some of the best food" in
Kings Beach at this Tahoe "treat" that's "tucked away up the street from
the Stateline casinos"; expect a one-two punch of "attentive" service
and "inventive" New American dinners showcasing "unexpected combinations", prompting partisans to proclaim "don't miss this one."

🆕 SR24 🖾 *American* | - | - | - | M |

Oakland | 5179 Telegraph Ave. (51st St.) | 510-655-9300 |
www.sr24food.com
Named after nearby State Route 24, this American newcomer in
Oakland's Temescal neighborhood offers affordable, sustainably
sourced lunch and dinner – along with a selection of microbrews – in a
quaint, red-walled setting; happy hour from 3-6:30 PM fills the void in
between, featuring discount libations and bargain bar bites (check its
Facebook page for the daily password that earns you a free drink).

Sunnyside Resort *Seafood/Steak* | 17 | 24 | 17 | $37 |

Tahoe City | 1850 W. Lake Blvd. (bet. Pineland Dr. & Sequoia Ave.) |
530-583-7200 | www.sunnysideresort.com
This "idyllic" Tahoe City spot "right on the lake" is the "place to be on
the West Shore", whether you dine by the fireplace in winter or "come
by boat" in the summer to enjoy a "cocktail on the patio"; the "expen-

sive" surf 'n' turf is "ok, not great" and service is "fine", but with that "terrific view", "who pays attention to the food?" – just "pick a sunny day and you won't be disappointed."

Tacubaya *Mexican*   23 | 13 | 14 | $18

Berkeley | 1788 Fourth St. (bet. Hearst Ave. & Virginia St.) | 510-525-5160 | www.tacubaya.net

Serving "seasonal" Mexican "fast food" as "artfully good" as that of "big sister" Doña Tomas (but "without the wait"), this Berkeley taqueria provides a "wonderfully authentic" pit stop for Fourth Street shoppers to "grab a bite" and chill on the patio; decor and service are "virtually nonexistent", it gets "crowded" and some find "prices a bit high", but perks like "freshly made churros" and aguas frescas keep connoisseurs "going back."

Tamarindo Antojeria Mexicana ⊠ *Mexican*   25 | 18 | 19 | $36

Oakland | 468 Eighth St. (bet. B'way & Washington St.) | 510-444-1944 | www.tamarindoantojeria.com

There's "terrific talent in the kitchen" at this "true find" in "Old Oakland" turning out tapas-style plates of "creative, authentic regional Mexican cooking – without the ubiquitous burrito"; as the "sharp"-looking surroundings are rather "tiny and cramped", some "wish they would give in and take a reservation", but "efficient service" and cocktails like the "tamarind margarita" keep the crowds coming.

Thai Buddhist Temple   ∇ 19 | 12 | 14 | $15
Mongkolratanaram Ⓜ⇄ *Thai*

Berkeley | 1911 Russell St. (bet. Martin Luther King Jr. Way & Otis St.) | 510-849-3419

Brunch "doesn't get more Berkeley" than this "unique", "only-on-Sundays" Thai pit stop at a Buddhist monastery where "hipsters, college professors and yuppies" "buy tokens" for "solid curries and noodle dishes", then "sit outside" at "long communal tables"; so maybe "you don't go for the magnificent cuisine", but the "carnival atmosphere" is easy to "enjoy", plus it's "cheap, cheap, cheap"; P.S. open 10 AM-1 PM.

Townhouse Bar & Grill ⊠ *Californian*   20 | 18 | 21 | $39

Emeryville | 5862 Doyle St. (bet. 59th & Powell Sts.) | 510-652-6151 | www.townhousebarandgrill.com

"As comfortable as an old glove", this "far-off-the-beaten-path" Emeryville "fixture" is "worth seeking out" say townies who "never get bored" of its "terrific" Californian fare; true, the former speakeasy resembles a "biker bar" from outside, but the valet-parked "BMWs, Audis and Mercedeses" tip off that within lies a "lively" dining spot, enhanced by "lovely" service, "fantastic mojitos" and "character in all the right places."

Trader Vic's *Polynesian*   17 | 20 | 19 | $47

Emeryville | 9 Anchor Dr. (Powell St.) | 510-653-3400 | www.tradervics.com

The "kitschy" South Seas setting is a "blast from the past" at this "over-the-top" pair in the Polynesian chain that "pioneered the pupu platter" in the States; many "go for a mai tai or two" among a "dizzying array" of "out-of-this world" tiki drinks, but modernists maintain it's "way past its pull-date" and ding the "dated", "high-priced" cuisine;

P.S. the Emeryville locale boasts a "marina view", while the Palo Alto spin-off sports a "great collection of South Pacific and Asian art."

Trattoria La Siciliana ⊅ *Italian*   25 | 15 | 18 | $35

Berkeley | 2993 College Ave. (bet. Ashby Ave. & Webster St.) | 510-704-1474 | www.trattorialasiciliana.com

"If you like garlic, you're home" at this "bit of Sicily in Berkeley", where "mama's in the kitchen" turning out "toothsome", "family-style" Italian for an excellent "value"; the decor's a little "kitschy", they don't take "plastic" and there's "always a line", but the "dreamy" pastas make "having to sit on your neighbor's lap totally worth it."

T Rex Barbecue *BBQ*   17 | 17 | 17 | $32

Berkeley | 1300 10th St. (Gilman St.) | 510-527-0099 | www.t-rex-bbq.com

"I am carnivore, hear me roar!" 'cue-nasours cry, contemplating "delicious" brisket, ribs and "wonderful sides" at this Berkeley joint in the Lalime's family; brunch is a "plus" with "maple sugar beignets", and happy hour in the "sports-bar atmosphere" is "smokin' fun", so while some dub the goods "yuppie versions of BBQ", all visitors might still "have to be rolled back out to the parking lot."

NEW Trueburger ⑤ *Burgers*   - | - | - | I

Oakland | 146 Grand Ave. (bet. Harrison & Valdez Sts.) | 510-208-5678 | www.trueburgeroakland.com

At this new modern-day soda fountain near Lake Merritt, a duo of veteran fine-dining chefs prepares the platonic ideal of fast food – houseground Angus beef burgers and hand-spun milkshakes – without the transfat or guilt; the simply adorned storefront (with a black-and-white mural of Oakland landmarks) serves lunch every day but Sunday, with dinner service Thursday–Saturday.

Udupi Palace ⊅ *Indian/Vegetarian*   20 | 8 | 14 | $18

Berkeley | 1901-1903 University Ave. (Martin Luther King Jr. Way) | 510-843-6600
Newark | 5988 Newpark Mall Rd. (bet. Cedar Blvd. & Mowry Ave.) | 510-794-8400
www.udupipalaceca.com

See review in City of San Francisco Directory.

Uzen ⑤ *Japanese*   24 | 16 | 19 | $35

Oakland | 5415 College Ave. (bet. Kales & Manila Aves.) | 510-654-7753

"Creative" sushi "so fresh that they write the day's selection out for you" is the draw at this Oakland "hole-in-the-wall", though there are also "some well-prepared hot Japanese dishes" for a "reasonable price"; some say the staff is "a bit austere, as is the decor", but "put your trust in the sushi chef–owner" and "you can't go wrong."

Va de Vi *Eclectic*   24 | 21 | 21 | $48

Walnut Creek | 1511 Mt. Diablo Blvd. (Main St.) | 925-979-0100 | www.vadevibistro.com

At this "rare standout" in Walnut Creek, there's "lots of people watching" to go with a "terrific selection" of "imaginative" Eclectic small plates to "share (or hoard)", plus "first-rate" wine flights, all served by a "bustling staff"; just be warned, the narrow space is "tight" and "noisy" (though the patio is more "idyllic") – and "everything is so good, it's easy to get carried away" and "boost" your bill.

Vanessa's Bistro *French/Vietnamese*

23 | 17 | 21 | $35

Berkeley | 1715 Solano Ave. (Ensenada Ave.) | 510-525-8300 |
www.vanessasbistro.com

Fans adore this "fabulous neighborhood" French-Vietnamese bistro in
Northern Berkeley that "dazzles with innovation and panache", thanks
to chef-owner Vanessa Dang and daughter Vi, a "family that really
cares about food"; with a "sophisticated" touch and service that's "always personal and attentive", it's a midpriced "find" that garners lots
of "love"; P.S. closed Tuesday.

Venezia *Italian*

21 | 23 | 21 | $33

Berkeley | 1799 University Ave. (Grant St.) | 510-849-4681 |
www.caffevenezia.com

Look up for the "best underwear display in the Bay Area" among the
"laundry hanging" in the "*trompe l'oeil* piazza interior" of this "whimsical" Berkeley "neighborhood place" serving "standard" but "delicious"
Italian eats; "popular for family parties", it's also "enjoyable" for a
date and offers "delightful opera nights" – but "parking can be a pain."

Venus *Californian*

21 | 16 | 19 | $33

Berkeley | 2327 Shattuck Ave. (bet. Bancroft Way & Durant Ave.) |
510-540-5950 | www.venusrestaurant.net

Baby, "she's got it!" bust out groupies of this "affordable" Downtown
Berkeley "treasure", where each Californian dish, made from "organic,
often local" ingredients, has a "unique personality and depth of character"; while it gets "crowded" and service can be mixed, the "charming new decor" adds appeal, and even skeptics advise "overlook the
insufferable blah-blah about sustainability and enjoy the food."

Vic Stewart's Ⓜ *Steak*

21 | 20 | 19 | $58

Walnut Creek | 850 S. Broadway (bet. Mt. Diablo Blvd. & Newell Ave.) |
925-943-5666 | www.vicstewarts.com

Travel "back to a bygone era" at this Walnut Creek train depot from
the late 1800s, converted into an "intimate", "classy" steakhouse,
complete with an attached Pullman dining car; the wine list is "thick as
a phone book", the service is "decent" and the beef is "tender", though
a few feel that it's not quite "on par" with the price.

Vik's Chaat Corner Ⓜ *Indian*

23 | 8 | 12 | $14

Berkeley | 2390 4th St. (Channing Way) | 510-644-4432 |
www.vikschaatcorner.com

The "brand-new location" of this Berkeley "Indian street-food" "crown
jewel" feels "less like a converted auto repair shop and more like a converted warehouse", but "you'll be too busy chowing down" on the
"low-cost" eats "to whine about the ambiance"; there's a "dazzling array
of flavors" in the "savory" dishes, so just overlook the "cafeteria-style
service" and "Styrofoam dish-trays" and "enjoy"; P.S. closes at 6 PM
Tuesday–Friday, 8 PM Saturday–Sunday.

Wente Vineyards,
The Restaurant at *Californian/Mediterranean*

24 | 25 | 23 | $56

Livermore | 5050 Arroyo Rd. (Wetmore Rd.) | 925-456-2450 |
www.wentevineyards.com

The view is "glorious" at this "worthy destination" "nestled into" a
"lovely vineyard setting" in Livermore, making it "perfect for special

occasions" or simply a "romantic" meal on the patio; though expensive, it's an "excellent value", with "impeccable" Cal-Med cuisine (including an "outstanding" pork chop), a "first-class wine list" and service that's "right on the money", as well as "wonderful music" during the summer concert series.

Wild Goose ⓂAmerican — | — | — | E

Tahoe Vista | 7320 N. Lake Blvd. (Pino Grande Ave.) | 530-546-3640 | www.wildgoosetahoe.com

Now anyone can enjoy lakeshore happy hour and dinner on the fire-warmed patio at this once-private New American in aptly named Tahoe Vista; the two-tiered dining room, built to resemble a 1920s wooden cruiser, serves moderately priced to expensive fare, from the familiar (meatloaf) to the fanciful (Kobe shabu shabu with lobster butter); open Wednesday–Sunday from mid-May to mid-October.

Wolfdale's Californian 25 | 22 | 23 | $55

Tahoe City | 640 N. Lake Blvd. (Grove St.) | 530-583-5700 | www.wolfdales.com

It's impossible to "go wrong" with "stunning views of the Lake" agree "families and couples" who have a "howl" at this "go-to" Tahoe City spot, one of the North Shore's "most sophisticated" and "certainly the best for fish" and other "eclectic", "Asian-influenced" Californian fare; touches like "sunset dinners" on the deck, custom-made dinnerware and "bocce ball after drinks" add to the "memorable experience."

Wood Tavern Californian 25 | 20 | 23 | $44

Oakland | 6317 College Ave. (bet. Alcatraz Ave. & 63rd St.) | 510-654-6607 | www.woodtavern.net

"Woodies" "don't want to tell you how good" this "hip", "perpetually packed" Rockridge "star" staffed by a "pro" crew really is, but both the "limited" Cal menu (fit for "pork fiends") and cocktails are "killer"; while it's often "difficult to get in", all in all it's "hog heaven", with the "unholy noise level" balanced out by the "reasonable" bill; P.S. late "lunch service" is calmer, and the "best hot pastrami sandwich" is available then, to boot.

Xyclo Vietnamese 24 | 17 | 19 | $30

Oakland | 4218 Piedmont Ave. (bet. Entrada & Ridgeway Aves.) | 510-654-2681 | www.xyclorestaurant.com

"Pho-riffic", with "amazingly fresh ingredients" and "creative presentations", this "small but pleasant" Vietnamese "manages to stick out nicely even on crowded Piedmont Avenue"; though some connoisseurs contend it's "not authentic", the "decently priced", "interesting takes" on the standards win over most.

Yankee Pier New England/Seafood 18 | 16 | 18 | $35

Lafayette | Lafayette Mercantile Bldg. | 3593 Mt. Diablo Blvd. (bet. Dewing Ave. & Lafayette Circle) | 925-283-4100 | www.yankeepier.com

See review in North of San Francisco Directory.

Yoshi's at Jack London Square Japanese 20 | 20 | 19 | $46

Oakland | Jack London Sq. | 510 Embarcadero W. (bet. Clay & Washington Sts.) | 510-238-9200 | www.yoshis.com

For a "Jack London kind of night with the fog horns blaring beyond the Bay" and "congas banging" next door, hepcats strut to this "lovely", "ultramodern" Japanese supper club at Oakland's "legendary jazz" venue, where the "inspired sushi" "adds to the chorus"; "it's not the Yoshi's your father used to eat at" report come-latelies who sing the praises of the "significantly upgraded" cuisine and "interesting cocktails", noting that a pre-show meal is the way to "reserve good seats."

Z Zachary's Chicago Pizza *Pizza* | 24 | 12 | 17 | $21 |

Berkeley | 1853 Solano Ave. (The Alameda) | 510-525-5950
Oakland | 5801 College Ave. (bet. Claremont Ave. & Grove Shafter Fwy.) | 510-655-6385
San Ramon | 3110 Crow Canyon Pl. (Crow Canyon Rd.) | 925-244-1222
www.zacharys.com

"Sorry, Chicago", pie-eyed pizzaholics proclaim this "beloved" East Bay trio turns out "the best deep-dish pizza in the country", with an "outer crust" that's "nice and crispy, while the middle is oozing with cheese and filling" (in fact, "a slice could be mistaken for a portion of lasagna"); yes, the environs are often "a zoo" with "giant lines", but indefatigable fans insist it's "worth waiting years for" (or just "call ahead and get takeout").

Zatar Ⓢ Ⓜ ⌿ *Mediterranean*   ∇ | 25 | 19 | 23 | $42 |

Berkeley | 1981 Shattuck Ave. (University Ave.) | 510-841-1981 | www.zatarrestaurant.com

"You want to savor every bite" says the "fanatically loyal clientele" of this "favorite find" in Berkeley serving "healthy" eclectic Med food using "home-grown vegetables" from its own organic garden; a "warm" ambiance and "personal" service enhance its appeal, so while it's "sardine-can" small and a bit "expensive", most agree there's "nothing like it"; P.S. open for dinner Wednesday–Saturday, lunch on Friday; no reservations for groups smaller than six.

NORTH OF SAN FRANCISCO

Top Food Ratings

29 French Laundry | *Amer./French*
28 Cyrus | *French*
   Hana Japanese | *Japanese*
27 La Toque | *French*
   Sushi Ran | *Japanese*
   Redd | *Californian*
   Farmhouse Inn | *Cal.*
   Ad Hoc | *American*
26 Auberge du Soleil | *Cal./French*
   Cafe La Haye | *American/Cal.*

   Terra | *American*
   Rosso Pizzeria | *Italian/Pizza*
   Ubuntu | *Californian/Vegan*
   Madrona Manor | *Amer./Fr.*
   Meadowood Rest. | *Cal.*
   Martini House | *American*
   Bouchon | *French*
   Bottega | *Italian*
25 Pizzeria Picco | *Pizza*
   Bistro des Copains | *French*

BY CUISINE

AMERICAN
29 French Laundry
27 Ad Hoc
26 Cafe La Haye
   Terra
   Madrona Manor

CALIFORNIAN
27 Redd
   Farmhouse Inn
26 Auberge du Soleil
   Ubuntu
   Meadowood Rest.

ECLECTIC
25 Willi's Wine Bar
24 Willow Wood Mkt.
   Wine Spectator
23 Go Fish
   Celadon

FRENCH
28 Cyrus
27 La Toque
26 Bouchon
25 Bistro des Copains
   Bistro Jeanty

ITALIAN
26 Rosso Pizzeria
   Bottega

25 Pizzeria Picco
   Picco
   Osteria Stellina

JAPANESE/SUSHI
28 Hana Japanese
27 Sushi Ran
24 Osake▽
23 Go Fish
19 Robata Grill

MEDITERRANEAN
25 Central Market
24 Ledford House
   Underwood Bar*
   Willow Wood Mkt.
23 El Dorado Kitchen

PIZZA
26 Rosso Pizzeria
25 Pizzeria Picco
24 Diavola
21 Azzurro Pizzeria
   Pizza Antica

SEAFOOD/STEAK
25 Fish
   Hog Island Oyster
24 Press
   Cole's Chop House
   Willi's Seafood

Excludes places with low votes, unless otherwise indicated

Menus, photos, voting and more – free at ZAGAT.com

BY SPECIAL FEATURE

BREAKFAST/BRUNCH
- 24 Willow Wood Mkt.
- Downtown Bakery
- 22 Alexis Baking Co
- 19 Tavern at Lark Creek
- Dipsea Cafe

CHILD-FRIENDLY
- 26 Rosso Pizzeria
- 25 Fish
- 21 Gott's Roadside Tray
- Pizza Antica
- Pizzeria Tra Vigne

OUTDOOR SEATING
- 26 Auberge du Soleil
- Martini House
- 24 Tra Vigne
- Murray Circle
- Étoile

PEOPLE-WATCHING
- 26 Martini House
- Bouchon
- Bottega
- 25 Mustards Grill
- 24 Bistro Don Giovanni

ROMANCE
- 28 Cyrus
- 27 Farmhouse Inn
- 26 Auberge du Soleil
- Terra
- Madrona Manor

SMALL PLATES
- 25 Picco
- Willi's Wine Bar
- 24 Underwood Bar
- Willi's Seafood
- 22 Oxbow Wine

TASTING MENUS
- 29 French Laundry
- 28 Cyrus
- 27 La Toque
- Redd
- 26 Meadowood Rest.

VIEWS
- 26 Auberge du Soleil
- 24 Ledford House
- Murray Circle
- 21 Caprice
- 18 Napa Wine Train

WINE BARS
- 26 Martini House
- 25 Willi's Wine Bar
- Fig Cafe & Winebar
- 24 Étoile
- 19 Bounty Hunter

WINNING WINE LISTS
- 29 French Laundry
- 28 Cyrus
- 27 La Toque
- 26 Terra
- Meadowood Rest.

BY LOCATION

MARIN COUNTY
- 27 Sushi Ran
- 25 Pizzeria Picco
- Picco
- Fish
- 24 Marché aux Fleurs

MENDOCINO COUNTY
- 24 Cafe Beaujolais
- Ledford House
- Mendo Bistro
- Moosse Café
- Albion River Inn

NAPA COUNTY
- 29 French Laundry
- 27 La Toque
- Redd
- Ad Hoc
- 26 Terra

SONOMA COUNTY
- 28 Cyrus
- 27 Farmhouse Inn
- 26 Cafe La Haye
- Rosso Pizzeria
- Madrona Manor

Top Decor

28	Auberge du Soleil		Martini House
	Cyrus		Bottega
27	French Laundry		Murray Circle
	Farm		Farmhouse Inn
	Meadowood Rest.	24	Dry Creek Kitchen
26	Étoile		St. Orres
	Press		Wine Spectator
	Madrona Manor		Tra Vigne
	John Ash & Co.		Terra
25	La Toque		Caprice

Top Service

28	French Laundry		Ad Hoc
	Cyrus		Redd
27	La Toque	24	Martini House
	Meadowood Rest.		Terra
26	Auberge du Soleil		Cafe Beaujolais
	Farmhouse Inn		Marché aux Fleurs
	Étoile		Solbar
	Madrona Manor		Cafe La Haye
25	Albion River Inn		Ledford House*
	Bistro des Copains		Mirepoix

Best Buys

In order of Bang for the Buck rating.

1. In-N-Out	11. Barney's
2. Cheese Steak Shop	12. Betty's Fish & Chips
3. Downtown Bakery	13. Alexis Baking Co.
4. La Boulange	14. Emporio Rulli
5. Sol Food	15. Asqew Grill
6. Model Bakery	16. Amici's Pizzeria
7. Avatar's	17. Pizzeria Picco
8. Joe's Taco	18. Lotus/Anokha
9. Jimtown Store	19. Bovolo
10. Gott's Roadside Tray	20. Della Fattoria

OTHER GOOD VALUES

Brick & Bottle	Pica Pica Maize
Cafe Citti	Restaurant P/30
C Casa	Royal Thai
Neela's	Spoonbar
Norman Rose Tavern	Table Café
Oenotri	Terrapin Creek

* Indicates a tie with restaurant above

North of San Francisco

☑ Ad Hoc *American*

27 | 21 | 25 | $58

Yountville | 6476 Washington St. (bet. Mission St. & Oak Circle) | 707-944-2487 | www.adhocrestaurant.com

Grandma's cookin' "amped up" with "French Laundry–quality ingredients" and "technique" is "what's for dinner" at Thomas Keller's "foodie" "boarding house" in Yountville where "omnivores" "roll the dice" and always win with "positively brilliant" "family-style" set-menu suppers (and Sunday brunch) served by "jean-clad" waiters; those few who cluck about "expensive" tabs for "homey" meals (including the "incredible" fried chicken served "every other Monday") have the option of dining "à la carte at the bar"; P.S. closed Tuesday–Wednesday.

AKA Bistro *American*

15 | 16 | 16 | $44

St. Helena | 1320 Main St. (Hunt Ave.) | 707-967-8111 | www.akabistro.com

"Locals know" that this breezy St. Helena bistro by LA's Robert Simon (Bistro 45) offers a "great ambiance" to "drop in for a burger" at the "fire-warmed" lounge or a multicourse American meal in the main room; still, the "Napa-centric" 'Wall of Wine' "seems to be the focus rather than the food" or service, which are "nothing remarkable", though a few suggest a late-Survey chef change "has improved" matters.

Albion River Inn *Californian*

24 | 24 | 25 | $52

Albion | 3790 N. Hwy. 1 (Spring Grove Rd.) | 707-937-1919 | www.albionriverinn.com

"Amazing on all counts", this "cliffside" Californian on the "rugged Mendocino coast" offers "gorgeous" "vistas galore" ("especially at sunset") as well as "fantastic food and "charming", "professional" service "fit for a special dinner"; the "lovely" piano music and "large bar" stocked with a "remarkable" selection of wines and single malts "add another level of delight" – not to mention an excuse to "stay over" in Albion.

Alexis Baking Company *Bakery*

22 | 13 | 16 | $19

(aka ABC)

Napa | 1517 Third St. (bet. Church & School Sts.) | 707-258-1827 | www.alexisbakingcompany.com

"For a real Napa" experience, "arrive early and beat the midmorning crowd" at this "insider's" bakery and coffee shop cranking out "the best huevos rancheros in existence", "unbelievable desserts" and "reasonably" priced sandwiches without the "fancy-schmancy hype"; looking like a cross between a "drive-thru oil changer" and a "bustling" "Haight-Ashbury" cafe, it offers plenty of "camaraderie", though the service "can be spacey"; P.S. breakfast and lunch only.

All Seasons Bistro Ⓜ *Californian*

▽ 23 | 20 | 24 | $41

Calistoga | 1400 Lincoln Ave. (Washington St.) | 707-942-9111 | www.allseasonsnapavalley.net

When they're "tired of overpriced ego palaces", Calistogans choose this "unpretentious" bistro on the town's main drag, where the "varied" menu of "seasonal" Californian cooking is matched by a "wonderful collection of hard-to-find wines" (oenophiles can even "browse in the

FOOD DECOR SERVICE COST

back-room wine shop and pay retail" plus the modest $15 corkage); the "simple" dining room with a red ceiling may not be as "glamorous" as its neighbors, but the "stellar" service is "always a hit."

Amici's East Coast Pizzeria *Pizza* 19 | 14 | 17 | $21

San Rafael | 1242 Fourth St. (bet. B & C Sts.) | 415-455-9777 | www.amicis.com
See review in City of San Francisco Directory.

Angèle *French* 23 | 22 | 22 | $47

Napa | 540 Main St. (3rd St.) | 707-252-8115 | www.angelerestaurant.com

"Like a Paris bistro on the Napa River", this "relaxed" enclave sports a dog-friendly patio that "begs you to dine alfresco" when it's "warm", and a "cozy" boathouse bar where "everyone seems to know everyone else"; it "may not make it onto all the hot lists", but enjoys "staying power" thanks to its "honest" (though somewhat expensive) "country French fare", "attractive" wine list and "gracious" service.

Annalien ⊠ⓂVietnamese 22 | 16 | 19 | $38

Napa | 1142 Main St. (bet. 1st & Pearl Sts.) | 707-224-8319
This "upscale Vietnamese" "find" proffering "terrific", "carefully prepared" Saigon staples "brings a welcome bit of diversity" to the Napa dining scene; though a few purists pout it's "a little pricey" and "not much better than your average pho joint", most concede that "super proprietress" Annalien's "animated" service and her "quaint" Indochine surroundings "certainly are."

Applewood
Inn & Restaurant ⊠Ⓜ *Californian* 24 | 20 | 22 | $52

Guerneville | 13555 Hwy. 116 (River Rd.) | 707-869-9093 | www.applewoodinn.com

Surrounded by "soaring redwoods", old apple trees and "beautiful gardens", this Russian River retreat has a "romantic" "cabin-in-the-woods feel", making for a "magical evening" of "fine dining that's not stuffy"; despite a change in ownership last year, the same chef continues to showcase "tantalizing", "locally sourced" Californian dishes ("try the tasting menu") along with regional wines "chosen with care" and proffered by a "pampering" staff.

Asqew Grill *Californian* 16 | 11 | 14 | $17

Mill Valley | Strawberry Vill. | 800 Redwood Hwy. (Belvedere Dr.) | 415-383-9011 | www.asqewgrill.com
See review in City of San Francisco Directory.

⊿ Auberge du Soleil *Californian/French* 26 | 28 | 26 | $84

Rutherford | Auberge du Soleil | 180 Rutherford Hill Rd. (Silverado Trail) | 707-967-3111 | www.aubergedusoleil.com

"Breathtaking views of Napa Valley" are matched by "magnificent" Cal-French cuisine, "awesome" wines and "superb" service by a staff that "makes you feel like the only guests in the room" at this Rutherford "paradise"; the "blow-the-budget" prix fixe menus are a "luxury", but even "taking the cheap way out" with "summer lunch on the deck" or "sunset cocktails" is enough to make you feel "astronomically lucky."

	FOOD	DECOR	SERVICE	COST

Avatar's 🖄 *Indian*

23 | 10 | 21 | $18

Sausalito | 2656 Bridgeway (Coloma St.) | 415-332-8083

Avatar's Punjabi Burrito *Indian*

Mill Valley | 15 Madrona St. (bet. Lovell & Throckmorton Aves.) |
415-381-8293 🖄🕏

NEW **Petaluma** | 131 Kentucky St. (bet. Washington St. & Western Ave.) |
707-765-9775
www.enjoyavatars.com

"Exciting" Indian burritos filled with "zippy" curries deliver "two favorite foods rolled into one" at this "inventive", "affordable" and "charismatic" quick-service Sausalito "hole-in-the-wall" and its spin-offs in Petaluma and Mill Valley (where "there's virtually no seating"); since there's "a rush every lunch and dinner", "fanatical followers" often "get it to go."

Azzurro Pizzeria & Enoteca *Pizza*

21 | 18 | 19 | $29

Napa | 1260 Main St. (Clinton St.) | 707-255-5552 | www.azzurropizzeria.com

"Crispy" "designer pizzas", "tasty salads" and "expertly selected wines" served by a "helpful" staff lure lots of "locals" to this Downtown Napa pie place with a "family atmosphere"; while the "closeness of the tables" contributes to the high volume, many "forgive" the din and stay for "soft-serve" ice cream for dessert.

Balboa Cafe *American*

19 | 18 | 19 | $36

Mill Valley | 38 Miller Ave. (Presidio Ave.) | 415-381-7321 |
www.plumpjack.com
See review in City of San Francisco Directory.

BarBersQ *BBQ*

22 | 16 | 19 | $33

Napa | Bel Aire Plaza | 3900 Bel Aire Plaza (Redwood Rd.) |
707-224-6600 | www.barbersq.com

Forget the "froufrou fare Up Valley" – this "upscale BBQ" joint is a prime "pig-out spot in Napa" where "locals" "wash down" those "unbeatable" ribs "with a great NV cab" and "holla praise" for the "fried chicken dinners"; considering the "fresh", sustainable ingredients, "pleasant" service and "amazing" music, most don't mind the "higher-end" prices and "parking-lot" locale.

Bardessono *American*

21 | 24 | 22 | $64

Yountville | Bardessono Hotel & Spa | 6526 Yount St. (bet. Finnell Rd. &
Washington St.) | 707-204-6030 | www.bardessono.com

"Exquisite", "contemporary" surroundings set the stage for the "ultimate green experience" at this "sustainable" resort New American in Yountville; some feel the dishes are "fresh" and "beautifully composed" yet "lack oomph", especially considering the "high" cost, but most find the staff "pleasant" and love "sitting outside in the tranquil setting"; P.S. the unique restrooms are a "must-see."

Barndiva 🖄 *American*

20 | 23 | 18 | $46

Healdsburg | 231 Center St. (Matheson St.) | 707-431-0100 |
www.barndiva.com

"The 'in' spot in Healdsburg", this "beautiful" boîte housed in a "spacious", updated old barn exudes just "the right balance of urban and small-town chic", offering "locals" and "wine visitors" a "delightful" place to "mingle"; the lounge is "SoHo-like" and the patio a "treat",

FOOD   DECOR   SERVICE   COST

though some insist the "super drinks" trump the "in-season" but "variable" American eats, not to mention the often "indifferent" service ("diva, indeed").

Barney's Gourmet Hamburgers *Burgers* | 19 | 12 | 16 | $17 |

San Rafael | 1020 Court St. (4th St.) | 415-454-4594 |
www.barneyshamburgers.com
See review in City of San Francisco Directory.

Betty's Fish & Chips *Seafood* | 23 | 12 | 19 | $19 |

Santa Rosa | 4046 Sonoma Hwy. (bet. Bush Creek Rd. & Mission Blvd.) |
707-539-0899

Anglophiles get "weekly cravings" for "generous portions" of "simply delicious" fish 'n' chips and "fabulous" fruit pies at this "affordable", "family run" "Santa Rosa classic" "right off Highway 12"; though it resembles a "home kitchen done with a seaside motif", "when the food is this good, who cares?"

Bistro des Copains *French* | 25 | 20 | 25 | $45 |

Occidental | 3782 Bohemian Hwy. (bet. Coleman Valley & Graton Rds.) |
707-874-2436 | www.bistrodescopains.com

Hidden amid the "glaring neon" of Occidental's "Italian-heavy offerings" lies this "locally popular" "bistro in the woods" whose "remarkable" "Southern France-meets-Sonoma" meals coaxed "from a wood-burning oven" make it "worth the harrowing ride out" to "the boonies"; add in "excellent" service, "fairly priced" à la carte and prix fixe options, and "no corkage Tuesdays" on Sonoma wines, and no wonder it's "no longer a secret."

Bistro Don Giovanni *Italian* | 24 | 22 | 22 | $48 |

Napa | 4110 Howard Ln. (bet. Oak Knoll & Salvador Aves.) | 707-224-3300 |
www.bistrodongiovanni.com

"Local vintners" and "visitors alike" commend this "convivial" "wine-country standard" in Napa, where the "spot-on", "soul-satisfying" Italian cucina (with a French influence) is accompanied by "fairly priced" vino; the "beautiful" setting, "with gardens and vineyards to admire", "will make you feel as if you're on vacation in Tuscany", as will host Giovanni Scala, who "knows how to take care of his customers."

☑ Bistro Jeanty *French* | 25 | 21 | 23 | $52 |

Yountville | 6510 Washington St. (Mulberry St.) | 707-944-0103 |
www.bistrojeanty.com

"Check your pretensions" and "go native" at Philippe Jeanty's "jolly" "Yountville classic" proffering "hearty", "pure country French" bistro fare and "plenty of wine" "without the snobbery"; the "ma-and-pa" decor could stand a refresh, but whether you get your "gastro fix" "by the fire", at the "community table" or "alfresco", it's a "wonderful" "stop for nonbillionaires" and a "welcome alternative" to all that "over-the-top-cuisine."

Bistro Ralph ☒ *Californian/French* | 23 | 18 | 23 | $48 |

Healdsburg | 109 Plaza St. (Healdsburg Ave.) | 707-433-1380 |
www.bistroralph.com

"It may not be the 'latest'", but "if you don't want to spend an arm and a leg" this veteran Healdsburg bistro is a "hometown favorite" for a "casual lunch" or dinner of "delicious", "straightforward" Cal-French fare, served in "laid-back" style; the "comfy" bar has a "cool vibe", enhanced by "interesting Sonoma wines" and "huge" martinis, plus there are a couple of outdoor tables for "watching the action" on the square.

Boca *Argentinean/Steak*

22 | 21 | 22 | $44

Novato | 340 Ignacio Blvd. (Rte. 101) | 415-883-0901 | www.bocasteak.com
"An oasis in Novato" "when you're hankerin' for a well-aged steak", "fries cooked in duck fat" and South American specialties like empanadas, this stylish Argentinean meatery (with token salads and a "kids' menu" to appease "Marin diners"), "carries the day" (midweek) and "night"; a few beef it "could be better" for the price, but most "come back for the bar scene" that's HQ for a "fabulous happy-hour menu" and "half-priced wines on Tuesdays."

Boon Fly Café *Californian*

22 | 19 | 20 | $31

Napa | Carneros Inn | 4048 Sonoma Hwy. (Los Carneros Ave.) | 707-299-4900 | www.thecarnerosinn.com
"You may have to wait", but "your patience will be rewarded" with "creative" Californian "comfort food made with fresh local ingredients" at this "casual" Napa Californian where breakfast brings "delicious" "warm doughnut holes" among other "treats", and dinners are "dynamite as well"; a few feel it's grown a bit "complacent", but the "personable" staff and "stylish" if somewhat "spartan" dining room on the grounds of the "posh" Carneros Inn are pluses.

☑ Bottega *Italian*

26 | 25 | 23 | $60

Yountville | V Mktpl. | 6525 Washington St. (Yount St.) | 707-945-1050 | www.botteganapavalley.com
Michael Chiarello's "Yountville hot spot" showcasing "big, bold" and "brilliant" Italian cuisine feels like a "Napa reality show", with the "*Top Chef* master" himself "holding court" and "glad-handing" guests who fill the "colorful", "glamorous" "villa" setting, complete with a fireplace-warmed patio; despite the "hype", though, the "tremendous value" and a "wonderfully informal" vibe keep it a "worthy" contender, with cooking to "impress even hardened foodies."

☑ Bouchon *French*

26 | 23 | 23 | $56

Yountville | 6534 Washington St. (Yount St.) | 707-944-8037 | www.bouchonbistro.com
Thomas Keller "can do no wrong" swear supporters of his "quintessential French bistro" in Yountville, "your next best bet" (and a "wallet-friendly" alternative) when "you can't secure a reservation at the French Laundry"; "casual perfection is the watchword here", from the "inspired", "superb" dishes to the "crisp" service to the "upbeat" "Paris-in-Napa" setting, so no wonder "there's always a crowd" filling the "close" tables that force you to "get to know your neighbor."

Bounty Hunter Wine Bar & Smokin' BBQ *BBQ*

19 | 17 | 19 | $33

Napa | 975 First St. (Main St.) | 707-226-3976 | www.bountyhunterwine.com
"Wine steals the show" and is "lovingly displayed" at this "kitschy" Western-style "hangout" by the Napa River, where grape "geeks" and "local jokels" saddle up to the stools for 40 options by the glass and "decent plates of barbecue" to go with them; the "beer-can chicken rules" for a "quick meal" "after work" or vineyard-hopping, but mostly

"it's the place to be" for the "fun crowd", "pleasant service" and "clubby" weekend scene.

Bovolo *Italian*
22 | 12 | 17 | $23

Healdsburg | Copperfield's Bookstore | 106 Matheson St. (Healdsburg Ave.) | 707-431-2962 | www.bovolorestaurant.com

"Bring on the bacon" bellow boosters of this "everything-pork" whistle stop "inside a bookstore on the Healdsburg square", known for "perfect pizzas", Italian-inspired sandwiches and breakfasts boasting "artisan-cured meats", all worthy of its Zazu pedigree; "it's basically take-out" and the waits are strictly "Slow Food", but it's enjoyable for a "quick bite or longer lunch on the patio" when "weather permits"; P.S. closes at 4 PM most weekdays, later on weekends.

Brannan's Grill *American/French*
22 | 22 | 21 | $42

Calistoga | 1374 Lincoln Ave. (Washington St.) | 707-942-2233 | www.brannansgrill.com

For a "pleasant" repast "after a spa" day, guests go for the "straight-ahead", slightly "upscale" American-French fare at this "warm" "Calistoga standard"; though the menu strikes some as merely "average", most "keep coming back" to "people-watch at the window tables" overlooking the street, and it "can be quite lively on weekends" for a "nightcap" during live jazz sets.

NEW Brick & Bottle *Californian*
- | - | - | M

Corte Madera | 55 Tamal Vista Blvd. (Sandpiper Circle) | 415-924-3366 | www.brickandbottle.com

Peripatetic chef Scott Howard returns to the Marin dining scene at this decidedly casual Corte Madera newcomer boasting something for everyone – affordable yet sophisticated Californian comfort food for foodies, a build-your-own pizza counter for the kiddies and plenty of artisanal drinks at the long copper bar (touted as the county's largest) for cocktailers; if that weren't enough, there's a happy hour, a late-night menu and an outdoor patio with views of Mount Tamalpais.

Brix *Californian/Mediterranean*
23 | 23 | 22 | $51

Napa | 7377 St. Helena Hwy. (Yount Mill Rd.) | 707-944-2749 | www.brix.com

Pleased patrons say "there's no prettier place to sit in the Valley than the patio that looks out to the vineyards" at this quintessential "wine-country dining" stop-over in Napa where chef Anne Gingrass-Paik prepares "excellent" Cal-Med meals using "ingredients from the garden"; free of the "pretentious trappings" found elsewhere (and often easier on the "budget"), it's a "favorite for happy hour" or during lunch or Sunday brunch, when it's "neat" to walk the grounds, "then eat the largess", matched by a "small-vineyard wine."

Z Buckeye Roadhouse *American/BBQ*
23 | 23 | 22 | $46

Mill Valley | 15 Shoreline Hwy. (Hwy. 101) | 415-331-2600 | www.buckeyeroadhouse.com

"As consistent as the sun rising in the east", this "jovial" Mill Valley roadhouse with a "hunting-lodge" atmosphere is always "jam-packed" with everyone from Marin Headlands hikers making a "pit stop" to "local singles" who linger in the "lively bar" to buckaroos "celebrating" a "special occasion" next to the "roaring fireplace"; fortunately the staff handles the "hustle and bustle" "with aplomb", and the "down-home"

New American food "soothes the soul", especially for 'cue connoisseurs who commend the "savory ribs" from the "smokehouse out back."

Bungalow 44 *American* | 22 | 21 | 21 | $44 |

Mill Valley | 44 E. Blithedale Ave. (Sunnyside Ave.) | 415-381-2500 | www.bungalow44.com

The "40-plus Mill Valley set" soaks up a "sexy scene" at this "vibrant" sister to the Buckeye, while tucking into "upscale" New American "comfort food" that "sings with flavor and imagination"; "neighborly service" keeps it "popular", but since the "loud" bar threatens to "overwhelm" the main Arts and Crafts dining room, some suggest sitting "in front of the fireplace" on the covered patio.

Cafe Beaujolais *Californian/French* | 24 | 22 | 24 | $54 |

Mendocino | 961 Ukiah St. (School St.) | 707-937-5614 | www.cafebeaujolais.com

"Through all of its ownership changes" and expansions, this "Mendocino hideaway" set in a Victorian farmhouse with a "quaint coastal atmosphere" "remains a must-go"; "dress up" for "that getaway dinner" of "inventive" Cal-French fare and "local Anderson Valley wines in the "lovely" dining room, "decompress" with an "affordable lunch" (Wednesday–Sunday) on the garden patio – or just follow the "tantalizing" aroma of "freshly baked bread emerging" from the attached bakery.

Cafe Citti *Italian* | 23 | 13 | 19 | $25 |

Kenwood | 9049 Sonoma Hwy./Hwy. 12 (Shaw Ave.) | 707-833-2690 | www.cafecitti.com

The "modest appearance from Highway 12" conceals the "fine" Tuscan food on offer – including a "delicious garlicky Caesar salad" that's "not for the faint of heart" – at this "kid-friendly" "Kenwood klassic" where you "tell 'em what you want at the counter", then sit on the "charming patio" or get "wine-country picnic" provisions to go; another "revelation": the "roadside location" and "no corkage fee" help "keep the prices down."

Café Gratitude *Vegan* | 16 | 13 | 15 | $26 |

San Rafael | 2200 Fourth St. (bet. Alexander Ave. & Santa Margarita Dr.) | 415-824-4652 | www.cafegratitude.com

See review in City of San Francisco Directory.

Cafe La Haye ⚠Ⓜ *American/Californian* | 26 | 20 | 24 | $51 |

Sonoma | 140 E. Napa St. (bet. E. 1st & 2nd Sts.) | 707-935-5994 | www.cafelahaye.com

The "chef has changed but the quality rolls on" at this "intimate" bitty "boîte" just "off the square" in Sonoma, where the "fresh, flavorful" New American–Cal cuisine is as "creative" as the "wonderful changing" roster of "cool art"; watch the "on-game" "cooks in action" – and be sure to "book early", as "it's no longer a secret" that they "do a bang-up job" in such "close quarters."

NEW Cantinetta Piero *Italian* | ▽ 21 | 23 | 21 | $53 |

Yountville | Hotel Luca | 6774 Washington St. (Madison St.) | 707-299-5015 | www.hotellucanapa.com

"House-cured meats rule" at this "spirited" new Yountville sidekick to Carmel's Cantinetta Luca that's big on "sampler plates" of salumi, wood-fired pizzas and housemade pastas; the "spiffy" setting in the "quaint" Hotel Lucca feels like a "real Tuscan farmhouse", plus there's an exhibition curing room and an outdoor courtyard that's "lovely in the warm weather", so even those who quibble it's "still settling in" vow to "try again."

Caprice, The 🅜 American — 21 | 24 | 22 | $56

Tiburon | 2000 Paradise Dr. (Mar W. St.) | 415-435-3400 | www.thecaprice.com

"Recently revamped and more downscale than its previous incarnation" (though still expensive), this "quiet" Tiburon grand dame boasts a view so "marvelous" it "seems like you can reach out and touch Angel Island and the Golden Gate Bridge" while dining on "delicious" New American fare; many recommend "going at sunset", especially on a "very special something kinda day", though a few feel the vista is the "only thing memorable."

Carneros Bistro & Wine Bar California — ▽ 22 | 20 | 20 | $44

Sonoma | The Lodge at Sonoma | 1325 Broadway (bet. Clay St. & Leveroni Rd.) | 707-931-2042 | www.thelodgeatsonoma.com

"Well worth a visit" whether or not "you're staying at the Lodge", this under-the-radar Californian kitchen serves up "pretty amazing" meals "for a hotel restaurant"; admirers applaud the "inventive" chef and sommelier, who create "dynamic" pairings of "Sonoma wines and ingredients" ("often picked from the garden just outside"), and also laud the bartenders for their "unusual, tasty" drinks.

NEW C Casa Mexican — - | - | - | I

Napa | Oxbow Public Mkt. | 644 First St. (bet. Silverado Trail & Socol Ave.) | 707-226-7700 | www.myccasa.com

This new quick-service Mex in Downtown Napa's Oxbow Public Market specializes in made-to-order tortillas filled with chile-rubbed rotisserie meats, fish and unconventional local larder such as microgreens and goat cheese, prepared by brothers Erasto and Pablo Jacinto (protégés of Cindy Pawlcyn); Mexican Coca-Cola, housemade aguas frescas, beer and wine top off the menu, all of which can be enjoyed inside or overlooking the river.

Celadon American/Eclectic — 23 | 20 | 24 | $51

Napa | The Historic Napa Mill | 500 Main St. (5th St.) | 707-254-9690 | www.celadonnapa.com

Like the patina on a "piece of Chinese porcelain", the "well-executed" American-Eclectic comfort food attains a "marvelously creative" polish at Greg Cole's upscale but "unpretentious" ol' "reliable" "tucked into" Downtown's Napa Mill "close to the river"; "pull your chair up to the bar and meet some locals" or hit the "covered patio" – "perfect" for a midweek lunch or "on a warm evening."

Central Market Californian/Mediterranean — 25 | 20 | 22 | $43

Petaluma | 42 Petaluma Blvd. N. (Western Ave.) | 707-778-9900 | www.centralmarketpetaluma.com

"Join the festivities" at this "justly popular" Downtown Petaluma "destination" and "you'll never walk away hungry" assure admirers who enjoy "splendid" Cal-Med Slow Food with friends in the "open-air" environs of an old restored brick building; when he's not manning the "accomplished kitchen", "gracious" "chef's chef" Tony Najiola "works the room", making diners "feel welcome" and spreading a "touch of New Orleans" bonhomie.

Chapter & Moon Ⓜ American
▽ 23 | 17 | 20 | $31

Fort Bragg | 32150 N. Harbor Dr. (S. Main St.) | 707-962-1643
It's "not high cuisine", but this "definite jewel" "perched at the far edge of Noyo Harbor" in Fort Bragg is far "more than a 'chapter'" thanks to a "happy-to-please" chef who prepares appealing breakfasts, "house-made breads" and "wonderful" seafood-centric American eats; the "homey" digs are merely a footnote, but the "fantastic views" speak "volumes" – especially when you "watch the sun set as fishing boats sail back with the day's catch."

Charcuterie French
21 | 16 | 20 | $38

Healdsburg | Healdsburg Plaza | 335 Healdsburg Ave. (Plaza St.) | 707-431-7213 | www.charcuteriehealdsburg.com
"Don't let the name fool you" – there's more than "excellent charcuterie" at this "unpretentious" "value-find" with the feel of a "small French village bistro" ("if you like pigs, you'll like the decor") "right off the Healdsburg square"; "close" quarters mean you might "knock elbows" with "neighbors", but "what the heck" – the "daily chalkboard menu" of "delicious" pastas and salads is worth oinking out on before or "after wine tasting."

Cheesecake Factory American
16 | 17 | 17 | $29

Corte Madera | The Village at Corte Madera | 1736 Redwood Hwy. (Hwy. 101) | 415-945-0777 | www.thecheesecakefactory.com
See review in City of San Francisco Directory.

Cheese Steak Shop Cheesesteaks
21 | 8 | 16 | $12

Santa Rosa | 750 Stony Point Rd. (Sebastopol Rd.) | 707-527-9877 | www.cheesesteakshop.com
See review in City of San Francisco Directory.

Cindy's Backstreet Kitchen California
24 | 20 | 23 | $45

St. Helena | 1327 Railroad Ave. (bet. Adams St. & Hunt Ave.) | 707-963-1200 | www.cindysbackstreetkitchen.com
There's "no froufrou" at this "laid-back" "discovery" ("dubbed Mustards North") on a "true backstreet of St. Helena" – just "imaginative", "upscale" Californian "comfort food with a few ethnic twists" (including "divine duck burgers") that's "vintage Cindy"; the "cheery" decor and "oh-so-friendly" staff make it a "magnet" for locals and tourists who "mingle" "elbow-to-elbow" at the "lively bar", while the "sweet terrace" is "perfect" for a "between-wine-stops lunch."

Cole's Chop House Steak
24 | 21 | 22 | $62

Napa | 1122 Main St. (bet. 1st & Pearl Sts.) | 707-224-6328 | www.coleschophouse.com
"If you have a hankerin' for cow", rustle up your "meat fix" at this "carnivore's dream" in Downtown Napa, where "hospitable" chef-owner Greg Cole (Celadon) presents "off-the-charts" "dry-aged" cuts "cooked to perfection" plus "terrific" sides and the Valley's "great big red wines" "to go with them"; the historic "stone building and bar" and creekside patio are also "hangout"-"central" for "movers and shakers" who don't flinch over the "fabulous" "expense-account"-priced martinis.

	FOOD	DECOR	SERVICE	COST

Cook St. Helena *Italian*   25 | 16 | 21 | $40

St. Helena | 1310 Main St. (Hunt Ave.) | 707-963-7088 |
www.cooksthelena.com

"Growers, winemakers and shopkeepers" "rub elbows" at this "true locals'" "favorite" in St. Helena, a "skinny little space" that "fills quickly" and "delivers much more than its storefront façade suggests"; the "excellent", "made-from-scratch" Italian cooking ("especially pastas") makes it a "must-stop" to "sop up" all that "wine after too many tastings", and it all costs "about a quarter of the price" of the "glitzy" places.

Cucina Paradiso ⊠ *Italian*   24 | 20 | 21 | $40

Petaluma | 114 Petaluma Blvd. N. (Western Ave.) | 707-782-1130 |
www.cucinaparadisopetaluma.com

The "homemade pasta is a must" for Petaluma regulars who stay on "repeat mode", frequenting this trattoria for its "beautiful presentation" of "sophisticated" Southern Italian cooking, served by a "helpful" staff for "reasonable" tabs; just be sure to make reservations, because even with its "fancier", "more spacious" new surroundings, it still "gets crowded early."

Cucina Restaurant & Wine Bar Ⓜ *Italian*   ▽ 23 | 16 | 21 | $43

San Anselmo | 510 San Anselmo Ave. (Tunstead Ave.) | 415-454-2942 |
www.cucinarestaurantandwinebar.com

Loyalists "love, love, love" the "honest Italian cooking" complemented by "reasonably priced" wines at this San Anselmo trattoria; though the "limited menu" could stand to "change" more often, the "friendly" staff and "relaxing" setting make it a "neighborhood favorite" for "family" dinners and other "casual" get-togethers.

Cuvée *American*   ▽ 20 | 21 | 19 | $47

Napa | 1650 Soscol Ave. (Vallejo St.) | 707-224-2330 |
www.cuveenapa.com

Easy to "drive by" on "busy Soscol" Avenue, this "comfortable" American turns out "all the usual suspects, done very well", and it's "tough to beat the price" on Wednesdays, when the bargain three-course dinner and "no-corkage policy" help "pack the house with locals"; "half-priced cocktails" during happy hour and a "nice outdoor patio" are further draws, but some suggest it's merely "ok" for Napa; P.S. a recent chef change may not be fully reflected in the Food score.

Ⓩ Cyrus *French*   28 | 28 | 28 | $130

Healdsburg | 29 North St. (Foss St.) | 707-433-3311 |
www.cyrusrestaurant.com

"Traveling foodies" know they're in for a night of "sheer indulgence" when the servers begin by "measuring the caviar against a gold coin" at this "beautiful", "incomparable" "temple of high cuisine" in Healdsburg that "puts the fine in dining"; sure, you can eat "à la carte at the bar", but most "go for broke" (literally) over chef-owner Douglas Keane's "mind-blowing" New French tasting menus embellished by "abounding carts", and while it's a bit "overwrought" for "sleepy Sonoma", the "outstanding" service makes for "memorable" "dinner theater"; P.S. dinner Thursday–Monday, plus Saturday lunch.

	FOOD	DECOR	SERVICE	COST

Della Fattoria
Downtown Café ☒ *Bakery/Eclectic*   25 | 16 | 18 | $26

Petaluma | 141 Petaluma Blvd. N. (bet. Washington St. & Western Ave.) | 707-763-0161 | www.dellafattoria.com

Devotees of its "magnificent bread" "love" this "quaint" bakery in Downtown Petaluma, where the "pricey" Eclectic "gastronomic delights" include "sandwiches made on fresh-baked" loaves, "fresh-from-the-farm" salads and "lattes in soup-sized mugs", plus the "staff is 'hey girlfriend!' friendly"; it's ground zero for "decadent" brunches and lunches as well as Friday night dinners" served at the "communal table", though the display cases "make it hard to not eat dessert first."

Della Santina's *Italian*   22 | 19 | 21 | $39

Sonoma | 133 E. Napa St. (1st St.) | 707-935-0576 | www.dellasantinas.com

Set in a "cute" locale off the Sonoma square, this "reasonably priced" trattoria offers "tourists" and locals a "relaxing" "place to linger, have another glass of wine" and savor Tuscan-style "grilled meats" and "gnocchi better than my nonna's"; some paesani wish the kitchen would "take more risks", but dining "alfresco" "on the lovely patio during spring and summer" is thoroughly "enjoyable", particularly if you let the "accommodating owner" "choose your meal."

Diavola Pizzeria & Salumeria *Italian*   24 | 19 | 22 | $36

Geyserville | 21021 Geyserville Ave. (Hwy. 128) | 707-814-0111 | www.diavolapizzeria.com

"Not your everyday pizza joint", this "porktastic" Geyserville "oasis" cranks out "top-of-the-line" pies, "innovative" salads and enough "sophisticated" Italian lunch and dinner options to appeal to "foodies and common folks" alike; despite a devil of a no-res policy, souls are soothed by the "country-store-looking" digs, "reasonable wine pricing" and "excellent" house-cured meats to go.

Dipsea Cafe, The *American*   19 | 15 | 16 | $22

Mill Valley | 200 Shoreline Hwy./Hwy. 1 (Tennessee Valley Rd.) | 415-381-0298 | www.dipseacafe.com

Morning is prime time at this Mill Valley "breakfast institution" where "crowds" of "families and carbo-loading hikers" are willing "to wait" for "huge portions" of "comfort food" like "homemade biscuits" and special "scrambles"; the country decor is a bit "kitschy", but most love the "fireplace and creek view", which help distract when the "busy" scene makes it hard to have a "quality conversation."

Downtown Bakery &
Creamery ⊄ *Bakery*   24 | 9 | 15 | $15

Healdsburg | 308A Center St. (bet. Matheson & Plaza Sts.) | 707-431-2719 | www.downtownbakery.net

"Start your day" at this "artisan bakery" that's "the spot in H'burg" (with a "stall at the Ferry Building" in SF) to pick up "don't-miss" sticky buns among other "fabulous pastries" and "killer breads" from the "dangerous counter"; "portable" lunches are another attraction, as well as a weekend breakfast that's "worth the long wait and cramped picnic-table seating" in the "throwback" "candy-striped" space; P.S. no dinner.

Drake's Beach Café 🅜 *Californian*

▽ 20 | 19 | 18 | $31

Inverness | Point Reyes Nat'l Seashore | 1 Drake's Beach Rd. (Sir Francis Drake Blvd.) | 415-669-1297

Surprisingly, the "youngsters who run this little" wind-blown Californian shack next to the Point Reyes Visitor Center in Inverness (with "Drakes Bay right out of the window") "really know how to cook"; it's primarily a daytime cafe, with rezzies required for the "wonderful" Saturday prix fixe dinners, when "free corkage" and "not knowing what you'll be served are part of the fun"; P.S. hours vary by season, so call ahead.

Dream Farm *American*

▽ 21 | 18 | 22 | $39

San Anselmo | 198 Sir Francis Drake Blvd. (bet. Bank St. & Tunstead Ave.) | 415-453-9898 | www.dreamfarmmarin.com

"It's hardly a farm, but the dream aspect comes true" at this two-room San Anselmo storefront (a "creative economical rebirth" of its predecessor Fork) where the "tasty", "down-home" New American fare could be "called 'comfort food' but it's too good"; though some say "there's no wow factor", others are satisfied by the "modest but interesting", small-producer wine list, "knowledgeable" service and "pleasant" atmosphere, complementing a meal that "doesn't bust the bank."

Dry Creek Kitchen *Californian*

24 | 24 | 24 | $67

Healdsburg | Hotel Healdsburg | 317 Healdsburg Ave. (Matheson St.) | 707-431-0330 | www.charliepalmer.com

The "first-rate", "artfully prepared" Californian "tasting menus", "free Sonoma wine corkage" and "amazing setting on the square" make this "Charlie Palmer outpost" in Healdsburg a "favorite" for "chef groupies" and local "winemakers" alike; expect "New York prices", but the staff is "always on-point", and "when 'the man' is running the show" it's "one of the best anywhere"; P.S. lunch served Friday–Sunday.

Duck Club, The *American*

21 | 22 | 22 | $51

Bodega Bay | Bodega Bay Lodge & Spa | 103 S. Hwy. 1 (Doran Park Rd.) | 707-875-3525 | www.bodegabaylodge.com

See review in South of San Francisco Directory.

E&O Trading Company *Asian*

19 | 21 | 19 | $38

Larkspur | 2231 Larkspur Landing Circle (Sir Francis Drake Blvd.) | 415-925-0303 | www.eotrading.com

See review in City of San Francisco Directory.

El Dorado Kitchen *Californian/Mediterranean*

23 | 22 | 22 | $49

Sonoma | El Dorado Hotel | 405 First St. W. (Spain St.) | 707-996-3030 | www.eldoradosonoma.com

"Beautiful people" hanging out under the "huge fig tree" on the "gorgeous patio" savor the "stylish" ambiance and "uncomplicated" Cal-Med dishes "bursting with flavor" at this "high-energy" "Sonoma haunt" in the El Dorado Hotel; "killer cocktails" and "friendly" service contribute to the "happening" bar scene, though the tabs can get "expensive."

Emporio Rulli *Dessert/Italian*

21 | 20 | 16 | $24

Larkspur | 464 Magnolia Ave. (bet. Cane & Ward Sts.) | 415-924-7478 | www.rulli.com

"Kill a morning" with "pricey" "pastries worthy of a photo-op" and a "terrific" latte while "watching" the "Lycra set" "stroll by", or just "grab a gelato" or "fantastic" panini at Larkspur's primo "authentic Italian bakery"-cafe; a pared-down alfresco offshoot at SF's Union Square attracts "colorful tourists" refueling "during shopping excursions", but counter service is "scant" at both and lacks the "warm-and-fuzzies."

Estate *Californian/Italian*

23 | 24 | 23 | $48

Sonoma | 400 W. Spain St. (W. 4th St.) | 707-933-3663 | www.estate-sonoma.com

Sondra Bernstein's "wonderfully homey", slightly upscale "new kid" (sib to The Girl & the Fig) set in an "enchanting" "restored Victorian" feels like a "true gem" amid Sonoma's "tourist wonderland", where you can "eat a little or go crazy" sharing "awesome" Cal-Ital "housemade pasta", salumi and "atypical vegetable preparations" accompanied by "excellent wines"; the interior is "full of character", but outside by the fireplace is the "place to be" on "dreamy" "summer evenings" or brunchtime on Sundays.

☑ Étoile *Californian*

24 | 26 | 26 | $81

Yountville | Domaine Chandon Winery | 1 California Dr. (St. Helena Hwy./Rte. 29) | 707-944-2892 | www.chandon.com

"The perfect setting for a romantic" "alfresco lunch" or "long, leisurely" dinner "in the heart of Napa", this Yountville "aristocrat" overlooking the Domaine Chandon Winery's landscaped gardens seduces admirers with "incredible service" and "simply stellar" Californian à la carte and tasting menus designed to "match with the excellent sparklers" and bottles "from other vineyards"; whether you "journey through" the grounds beforehand or just wine and dine, it provides a "visual and taste treat you won't forget"; P.S. closed Tuesday-Wednesday and the month of January.

☑ Farm *American*

23 | 27 | 24 | $66

Napa | Carneros Inn | 4048 Sonoma Hwy. (Los Carneros Ave.) | 707-299-4882 | www.thecarnerosinn.com

"Sexy yet comfortable", with an "agri-tourist setting", this "high-style, high-priced" New American "Napa outpost" "draws foodies galore"; have "a drink outdoors by the amazing" fire pits (it feels like a "lovely" "open-air living room"), indulge in "terrific preparations of locally sourced everything", or better yet, "stay at the Carneros Inn" – that way you can "go after the wine list with abandon" then "walk to your room."

☑ Farmhouse
Inn & Restaurant *Californian*

27 | 25 | 26 | $75

Forestville | Farmhouse Inn | 7871 River Rd. (bet. Trenton & Wohler Rds.) | 707-887-3300 | www.farmhouseinn.com

Set in a "restored" Forestville "farmhouse", this "romantic Russian River foodie destination" feels like a "true country escape", yet delivers "city-quality" Californian dishes, an "upscale feel" and "excellent service" without "the airs"; the "elegant" menu offerings "change seasonally", but you can always count on 'thumper three ways'", a "killer cheese cart" and sommelier-selected standouts; if a few find the "waiters in tuxes a little much", urban cowboys counter it's "well worth the price" for a "special occasion."

NEW Farmstead *Californian*

| - | - | - | E |

St. Helena | Long Meadow Ranch | 738 Main St. (Charter Oak St.) | 707-963-9181 | www.farmsteadnapa.com

Truly walking the farm-to-table path, this ambitious newcomer situated in St. Helena's Long Meadow Ranch showcases Cal-American cuisine made with olive oil, vegetables and grass-fed beef produced on-site, hitting modest to higher-end price points; decorated with vintage pitchforks, the former nursery barn now encompasses a central open kitchen, booth and communal seating, and alfresco dining under apple trees.

Fig Cafe & Winebar *French*

| 25 | 20 | 22 | $40 |

Glen Ellen | 13690 Arnold Dr. (bet. Carmel Ave. & Odonnell Ln.) | 707-938-2130 | www.thefigcafe.com

Let "the tourists go to The Girl & the Fig" jokes the "local, vocal crowd" that squeezes into the "tight quarters" of this "crazy-busy" "off-the-beaten-path" figlet in Glen Ellen, chowing down on "amazing", lower priced country French food and "creative" brunches; they "love the free corkage" too, plus service is "friendly and efficient"; P.S. no reservations.

Fish ⊅ *Seafood*

| 25 | 15 | 16 | $35 |

Sausalito | 350 Harbor Dr. (Clipper Yacht Harbor) | 415-331-3474 | www.331fish.com

Pescatarians fall "hook, line and sinker" for this "no-frills" "cash-only" fish "shack" "overlooking the Sausalito yacht harbor", tucking into "ridiculously good", "sustainable" "boat-to-table" fin fare washed down with drinks in "mason jars" (a "snazzy touch"); if carpers quibble that the "linen-napkin prices" have "officially jumped the shark" considering you have to "stand in line" and share "rustic" picnic tables, most counter it's "seafood alfresco at its best" – with a "free seagull serenade" to boot.

NEW Fish Story *Seafood*

| - | - | - | E |

Napa | Napa Riverfront | 790 Main St. (3rd St.) | 707-251-5600 | www.fishstorynapa.com

Not just another fish story, this forthcoming sustainable seafooder set at press time to wash ashore mid-September, hopes to reel in visitors and locals to downtown Napa's new Riverfront with fresh catches prepared daily for lunch and dinner by chef Stephen Barber (ex BarBersQ), as well as artisan meats and seasonal veggies, for moderate-to-expensive tabs; along with a 12-ft. raw bar and tanks for live crab and lobster, there will be a wall displaying guest-submitted fishing tales, plus lots of outdoor riverside seating.

Flavor *Californian/Eclectic*

| 19 | 17 | 18 | $31 |

Santa Rosa | 96 Old Courthouse Sq. (bet. 3rd & 4th Sts.) | 707-573-9600 | www.flavorbistro.com

"A nice break from high-end Sonoma", this "easy-on-the-pocketbook" "no-rez" Santa Rosa bistro boasts a "vast" Cal-Eclectic menu with "something for everyone", including "salads so fresh they deserve a slap" and "pasta that's not like your mama makes"; half-glass wine options and "incomparable" local Moonlight beer are pluses for the "noisy", "energetic crowd", but critics contend the food "lacks any special flavors" and find service "distracted."

	FOOD	DECOR	SERVICE	COST

NEW Fort Bragg Bakery ⓂBakery/Eclectic ▽ | 27 | 17 | 19 | $19 |

Fort Bragg | 360 N. Franklin St. (Laurel St.) | 707-964-9647 |
www.fortbraggbakery.com

There's plenty to brag about at this "wonderful new" artisanal bakery
and cafe "hangout" in Fort Bragg, where "locals" "love watching"
Christopher Kump (ex Cafe Beaujolais) coax "rich, chewy" breads,
"European"-style pastries and "excellent" individual pizzas from a
massive, lovingly restored wood-fired oven; there are only 20 seats,
but many agree it's "the only place" Downtown for "perfect" Eclectic
breakfasts and lunches; P.S. open Wednesday–Sunday till 4 PM.

Frantoio Italian — 22 | 20 | 21 | $44 |

Mill Valley | 152 Shoreline Hwy. (Hwy. 101) | 415-289-5777 |
www.frantoio.com

Paesani "can never get beyond the heavenly gnochetti" at this "cavernous" Mill Valley ristorante whose "authentic" preparations and
Boot bottlings satisfy that taste for "Tuscany in Marin", as does its
picturesque olive oil mill" that presses "amazing housemade" EVOO
in season" (October–December); though some critics contend the
kitchen is "coasting" and the ambiance is a bit "cold", others are partial to the "fair prices" and "service with flair."

Fremont Diner Diner ▽ | 22 | 19 | 15 | $24 |

Sonoma | 2698 Fremont Dr. (S. Central Ave.) | 707-938-7370

Doling out "comfort food at its best", this vintage-looking roadside
diner tucked among vineyards and farms on the outskirts of Sonoma
is winning favors with locals who brake for a "fabulous" blackboard
menu of Southern breakfasts, pulled-pork sandwiches and burgers,
washed down with sweet tea, floats and malts; "if you have not been
here, it's a must" insist early samplers, who eat inside amid bric-a-
brac for sale, or alfresco at picnic tables; P.S. no dinners.

⬛ French Laundry, The American/French | 29 | 27 | 28 | $275 |

Yountville | 6640 Washington St. (Creek St.) | 707-944-2380 |
www.frenchlaundry.com

This one goes to 11!" exclaim reviewers who run out of "superlatives"
to describe Thomas Keller's "glorious" stone lair in Yountville, where
they "melt away" the afternoon (Friday–Sunday) or evening with an
unforgettable" New American–French tasting "extravaganza" that's
so far out of the box, you can't compare it to any other restaurant";
the "exceptional" staff "puffs out its chest a bit", but the wine pairings
take the meal from fabulous to magical", and "what's another few
$100" for an experience this tough to "afford" (or "snag") more than
once in a lifetime"?

Fumé Bistro & Bar American | 19 | 15 | 21 | $39 |

Napa | 4050 Byway E. (Avalon Ct.) | 707-257-1999 |
www.fumebistro.com

The "warm, welcoming" service at this Napa "neighborhood bar and
grill" helps everyone feel "like locals" as they dine on a "diverse",
honest" menu of New American dishes that while "not crazy gourmet" are "tasty to be sure"; the "lovely patio" and "convivial" bar make
up for the location "right off busy highway 29", while "moderate prices"
and "thrifty" deals keep the crowds coming to "hang."

Gary Chu's 🅜 *Chinese*   21 | 19 | 18 | $31

Santa Rosa | 611 Fifth St. (bet. D St. & Mendocino Ave.) | 707-526-5840 |
www.garychus.com

Chef Chu's sturdy Santa Rosa "winner" presenting "modern Chinese
in an equally modern setting" remains among the "prettiest and
tastiest" of its type in the North Bay, delivering "carefully prepared" Mandarin and Sichuan plates, "pleasant" service and
"lunch-special" steals; choosy sorts chirp it's "getting a little tired"
but concede that much like its "sister Osake", it offers a "nice alternative to wine-country cuisine."

Girl & the Fig, The   *French*   24 | 21 | 22 | $44

Sonoma | Sonoma Hotel | 110 W. Spain St. (1st St. W) | 707-938-3634 |
www.thegirlandthefig.com

"Freshly picked" ingredients, "killer" fromage and "fantastic" regional
Cal-Rhônes "reign" at this "well-appointed", "country French" cafe in
an "old hotel" "right on the square"; "delightful lunches in the garden"
and "downright tasty dinners" (including "some outstanding figgy
preparations") enhanced by the staff's "Sonoma hospitality" have
made it an "insanely popular" stop "on the wine trail", but it maintains
a "real local feel" nonetheless.

Go Fish   *Eclectic/Seafood*   23 | 21 | 21 | $51

St. Helena | 641 Main St. (bet. Charter Oak Ave. & Mills Ln.) |
707-963-0700 | www.gofishrestaurant.net

"Careful, you can get hooked" on this "cheery" whale of a restaurant
in St. Helena, a "bravura attempt" by Cindy Pawlcyn (Mustards Grill,
Cindy's Backstreet Kitchen) to provide Valley-ites with "fresh-as-the-
moment" Eclectic seafood, including "stunning, seductive sushi"; a
"well-priced" wine selection (including a list of 27 for $27) takes some
of the sting out of otherwise "expensive" tabs, as do the "attentive"
servers and "divine" patio.

Gott's Roadside Tray Gourmet   *Diner*   21 | 13 | 15 | $18
(fka Taylor's Automatic Refresher)

Napa | Oxbow Public Mkt. | 644 First St. (bet. Silverado Trail & Soscol Ave.) |
707-224-6900
St. Helena | 933 Main St. (Pope St.) | 707-963-3486
www.gottsroadside.com

"If you're looking for the dollar menu, you're in the wrong place", but
for "fresh, upscale fast food", including the "ultimate" burger, "take
the kids" to this "nostalgic" trio of "recently renamed" "roadside
stands"; there's indoor seating at the Napa and SF spin-offs, and "it's
a kick" to eat and sip "high-end wine" in the "fenced-in picnic area" in
St. Helena, though a tour bus "beached out front" can add to the
"ridiculously long lines."

Guaymas   *Mexican*   17 | 20 | 17 | $36

Tiburon | 5 Main St. (Tiburon Blvd.) | 415-435-6300 |
www.guaymasrestaurant.com

The "stunning" view "overlooking San Francisco Bay" is reason enough
to "take the ferry to Tiburon with friends" aver amigos of this Mexican
seafooder, who "shake off the week" tippling "top-shelf tequila" on the
"gorgeous" deck; true, "no one goes here solely for the food" (which

ranges from "decent" to "so-so"), and service can be "spotty", but it's an "amazing" setting for "spending a lazy Saturday" sipping "excellent margaritas"; P.S. make a reservation, since it "fills up quickly."

🔲 Hana Japanese Restaurant *Japanese* 28 | 17 | 22 | $45

Rohnert Park | 101 Golf Course Dr. (Roberts Lake Rd.) | 707-586-0270 | www.hanajapanese.com

Offering an "exceptional selection of raw fish", "traditional" dishes and "exquisitely crafted" Sonoma-inspired specials, chef-owner Ken Tominaga strives for "perfection" at this "must-stop" "sushi spot" that's definitely "one of the best Japanese restaurants in the area"; a "sake sommelier" only enhances the "great dining experience", making it even harder to "believe it's in a Rohnert Park" strip mall.

Harmony Restaurant *Chinese* 20 | 19 | 20 | $33

Mill Valley | Strawberry Vill. | 800 Redwood Hwy. (Belvedere Dr.) | 415-381-5300 | www.harmonyrestaurantgroup.com

"Organic", "creative" Chinese chow, including "tasty" dim sum (available "in the evening" as well as at lunch), is prepared in a "healthy" style "without the MSG" at this "pretty" Mill Valley locale; the "to-go counter" is convenient for dumpling devotees who can "never drive by without wanting to go in", but foes find the "food can be bland" and contend the "itty-bitty portions" are "overpriced."

Harvest Moon Café *Californian/Mediterranean* ▽ 25 | 18 | 22 | $45

Sonoma | 487 First St. W. (W. Napa St.) | 707-933-8160 | www.harvestmooncafesonoma.com

From the "excellently prepared", "constantly changing" and ingredient-driven Cal-Med menu to the "warm, personal service", insiders insist "you can't go wrong" at this "charming" Sonoma haunt that's "one of the absolute best" in town; run by a couple that "knows how to make you feel at home", it's set in a "slightly funky" "little space" that can seem "tight", so "sit in the garden" in "warm weather" and enjoy Sunday brunch or "drink the night away"; P.S. closed Tuesdays.

Healdsburg Bar & Grill *American* 19 | 16 | 18 | $31

Healdsburg | 245 Healdsburg Ave. (bet. Matheson & Mill Sts.) | 707-433-3333 | www.healdsburgbarandgrill.com

The "Cyrus boys do burgers (and do them well)" at this "lively" pub offering a "welcome break" from the area's "trendy see-and-be-seen places", along with "reasonably priced" American grub, "local beers on tap" and a no-corkage policy to "remind you you're in wine country"; a "large patio" provides refuge from the often "crowded" interior, and though some snipe about "hit-and-miss" food and service, most maintain it's "just what Healdsburg needed."

🔲 Hog Island Oyster Co. & Bar *Seafood* 25 | 17 | 19 | $36

Napa | Oxbow Public Mkt. | 610 First St. (bet. Silverado Trail & Soscol Ave.) | 707-251-8113 | www.hogislandoysters.com

See review in City of San Francisco Directory.

Hopmonk Tavern *Eclectic* 18 | 18 | 17 | $28

Sebastopol | 230 Petaluma Ave. (bet. Abbott Ave. & Burnett St.) | 707-829-7300 | www.hopmonk.com

Dean Biersch (of Gordon Biersch fame) has "done an excellent job" creating an "authentic" tavern vibe at this all-day Sebastopol "hang-

FOOD | DECOR | SERVICE | COST

out" where the "better-than-average" Eclectic pub food is nonetheless "eclipsed" by a "fabulous" "selection of brews"; it gets "rather loud" and some tap it as "relatively expensive", but pluses include a "nifty beer garden out back" and "live entertainment" that draws "West County youngsters" who "drink and boogie" the night away.

Hurley's Restaurant & Bar *Californian/Mediterranean*

22 | 20 | 21 | $48

Yountville | 6518 Washington St. (Yount St.) | 707-944-2345 | www.hurleysrestaurant.com

Both "locals" and wayfarers "traveling up to wine country" "always feel welcome" in the "gorgeous bar" or out on the patio at this Yountville Cal-Med that "holds its own" with "comforting" fare and wows with "wild game preparations" in season; still, detractors maintain that even with "lower prices than most", it "suffers in comparison" to the big names.

Il Davide ⓜ *Italian*

20 | 17 | 21 | $34

San Rafael | 901 A St. (bet. 3rd & 4th Sts.) | 415-454-8080 | www.ildavide.net

The "cozy" interior and "fun" outdoor tables create an "appealing" atmosphere for "solid" Tuscan eats and "delectable" wines at this San Rafael "sleeper"; it's a "good value" (especially for the "bargain" lunch specials) and the "accommodating" staff is a plus, so no wonder returning guests "see the same faces time after time."

Il Fornaio *Italian*

19 | 20 | 19 | $39

Corte Madera | Town Center Corte Madera | 223 Corte Madera Town Ctr. (Madera Blvd.) | 415-927-4400 | www.ilfornaio.com
See review in City of San Francisco Directory.

🇿 In-N-Out Burger ❷ *Burgers*

22 | 10 | 18 | $9

Mill Valley | 798 Redwood Hwy. (Belvedere Dr.)
Napa | 820 Imola Ave./Hwy. 121 (Napa Vallejo Hwy.)
800-786-1000 | www.in-n-out.com
See review in City of San Francisco Directory.

Insalata's *Mediterranean*

23 | 22 | 22 | $44

San Anselmo | 120 Sir Francis Drake Blvd. (Barber Ave.) | 415-457-7700 | www.insalatas.com

"Creative", locally sourced Med fare complemented by a "wine list equal to the food" (including "fine vegetarian dishes") makes this long-running San Anselmo "treat" a "standby for date night" and "celebrations"; "warm, attentive" servers oversee the "comfortable", high-ceilinged space, which is also home to a "lunch menu as inviting as dinner" and an "outstanding take-out counter."

Jimtown Store *Deli*

21 | 18 | 17 | $20

Healdsburg | 6706 Hwy. 128 (Alexander Valley Rd.) | 707-433-1212 | www.jimtown.com

"Take a break from quaffing vino" en route to Healdsburg and "do all your Christmas shopping" at the same time at this "old-fashioned" Alexander Valley "general store" and deli crammed with "vintage candy" and "retro gifts"; "prices are a bit high" for the "inventive" breakfasts and lunches with a "country twang", but many find it a "must stop" anyway, particularly when you can "sit on the patio."

	FOOD	DECOR	SERVICE	COST

Joe's Taco Lounge & Salsaria *Mexican*
| 19 | 17 | 17 | $18 |

Mill Valley | 382 Miller Ave. (bet. Evergreen & Montford Aves.) | 415-383-8164

A "gazillion varieties of hot sauce line the walls" at this "colorful" Mill Valley taqueria, a "teeny" "dive" slinging some of the "best fish tacos outside of Mexico" and other *delicioso* "cheap" chow; all in all, it's a "family-friendly" "post-surfing or -mountain-biking" hang, but all of Marin knows it, so expect a "crowded nightmare every weekend."

John Ash & Co. *Californian*
| 22 | 26 | 23 | $59 |

Santa Rosa | 4330 Barnes Rd. (River Rd.) | 707-527-7687 | www.vintnersinn.com

"Finish a day of tasting on an up note" at this veteran Santa Rosa "stand-out", which proffers "farm-fresh Sonoma ingredients" and a regional "wine list to drool over" in a "gorgeous setting" overlooking a vineyard; whether you perch "near the fireplace, on the terrace" or in the "cozy" bar, the "atmosphere is outstanding" and the staff "well trained", though a few fret the "expensive" Cal cuisine is "less inspired" these days.

Jole *American*
| ∇ 25 | 21 | 23 | $50 |

Calistoga | Mount View Hotel | 1457 Lincoln Ave. (bet. Fair Way & Washington St.) | 707-942-5938 | www.jolerestaurant.com

The "talented" couple behind this Calistoga "farm-to-table" New American provides "innovative", "exceptional" small plates that "reflect the season", complemented by "amazing desserts" and a "novel" wine list; while the staff is "down-to-earth" and the "trendy LA-feeling" interior "intimate", take care as you "construct your own tasting menu" because the "tab can run up."

K&L Bistro ☒ *French*
| 24 | 17 | 22 | $46 |

Sebastopol | 119 S. Main St. (bet. Bodega Ave. & Burnett St.) | 707-823-6614

"Cranking out some of the better food in the North Bay", this "often-times buzzing bistro" in "small-town" Sebastopol delivers "stylish" "big-town" French fare "prepared with an emphasis on local products"; it's relatively "easy on the wallet" and the married chef-owners serve up "lots of TLC", so though some find the "storefront" setting "cramped", others consider it "comfortable."

Kenwood Ⓜ *American/French*
| 21 | 20 | 21 | $51 |

Kenwood | 9900 Sonoma Hwy./Hwy. 12 (Libby Ave.) | 707-833-6326 | www.kenwoodrestaurant.com

Along with a "beautiful patio" for enjoying lunch and a convivial bar for "evenings after a day of tasting", this "pleasant" Kenwood roadhouse features "solid" New American-French meals, a "wine list heavy on Sonoma County" labels and "welcoming" staffers who "make customers feel right at home"; true, a few consider the menu "too expensive" and a bit "tired", but "who cares when you can gaze over a vineyard?"

La Boulange *Bakery*
| 21 | 16 | 16 | $16 |

Mill Valley | Strawberry Vill. | 800 Redwood Hwy. (Belvedere Dr.) | 415-381-1260

Novato | Hamilton Mktpl. | 5800 Nave Dr. (bet. N. Hamilton Pkwy. & Roblar Dr.) | 415-382-8594
www.laboulangebakery.com
See review in City of San Francisco Directory.

FOOD | DECOR | SERVICE | COST

La Gare ⓜ *French* ▽ 21 | 18 | 21 | $40

Santa Rosa | 208 Wilson St. (3rd St.) | 707-528-4355 |
www.lagarerestaurant.com
This "old-fashioned" French in Santa Rosa's "burgeoning Railroad
Square" maintains an "immutable" menu, delivering "classic" cuisine
in "grand style"; the "contagious" congeniality of the staff means most
forgive that it's "not the trendiest place" ("the decor is a bit
'grandma's kitchen' from 1984"), though the less impressed tut that
it's "tired"; P.S. open Wednesday–Sunday for dinner only.

La Ginestra ⓜ *Italian* 21 | 11 | 20 | $33

Mill Valley | 127 Throckmorton Ave. (bet. Madrona St. & Miller Ave.) |
415-388-0224
"If we don't answer the door at home, check here" josh "frequent diners" of this longtime Mill Valley "favorite", providing "old-fashioned"
Southern Italian fare like "homemade ravioli" and pizzas in "welcoming" style; though a few sniff that both the food and "no-nonsense"
digs are "dated", most find it a perfectly "charming" "family place"
that's "priced just right"; P.S. no reservations.

La Petite Rive *French* ▽ 26 | 21 | 24 | $52

Little River | 7750 North Hwy. 1 (north of Little River Airport Rd., next to
Van Damme Beach State Park) | 707-937-4945 | www.lapetiterive.com
With only "two seatings nightly", this "tiny", "romantic" Little River respite "overlooking the ocean" is "hard to get into" but "worth the effort"
(and the expense) for its "dreamily delicious" French prix fixes (guests
choose the entree and "then the chef fills in the rest"); indeed, it feels
a little "like you're eating on the Seine", so while the pace is "slow", it's
become a "go-to restaurant on the coast"; P.S. closed Tuesdays.

LaSalette *Portuguese* 24 | 19 | 24 | $47

Sonoma | Mercado Ctr. | 452 First St. E. (bet. Napa & Spain Sts.) |
707-938-1927 | www.lasalette-restaurant.com
"Portugal's Azores meets Sonoma wine country" at this "charming"
"mom-and-pop" "hidden off the Sonoma square" that "draws in locals
and tourists alike" with its "flavorful", "transporting" dishes (highlighting seafood) from the "wood-fired" oven; "reasonably priced"
wines, "gracious" service and "unpretentious" "European-style" surroundings, including a "delightful patio", help "seal the deal."

Las Camelias *Mexican* ▽ 18 | 13 | 19 | $27

San Rafael | 912 Lincoln Ave. (bet. 3rd & 4th Sts.) | 415-453-5850 |
www.lascameliasrestaurant.com
"Nicer" than your "run-of-the-mill" Mex, this San Rafael "go-to" puts
a "twist" on the "standards", providing "satisfying plates" inspired by
the "chef's hometown of Cuautla" and served in a simple but "charming" setting that feels like a "friend's house"; while there are no "real
margaritas", housemade sangria complements the affordable,
"better-than-average" grub.

ⓩ La Toque *French* 27 | 25 | 27 | $103

Napa | Westin Verasa | 1314 McKinstry St. (Soscol Ave.) | 707-257-5157 |
www.latoque.com
"Hats off" to chef Ken Frank whose "move down to Napa only improved" what's "frankly one of the best restaurants" in the Valley,

proffering "pricey" but "extraordinary" New French tasting menus (including "awesome annual truffle" dinners) with "exceptional" wine pairings; the "beautiful" albeit hotel-like digs and "wonderful" service make you feel "pampered" for a "special" evening, while his adjacent Bank Café allows for more "casual" dining.

Ledford House Ⓜ *Californian/Mediterranean* 24 | 23 | 24 | $48

Albion | 3000 N. Hwy. 1 (Spring Grove Rd.) | 707-937-0282 | www.ledfordhouse.com

"Year in and year out", this upscale Albion bistro situated "not too far from the bustle of Mendocino" "rocks" the house with its "beautiful view over the ocean", "splendidly prepared" Cal-Med "comfort food" "by chef Lisa" and "caring service" "from host" and husband Tony; "as a bonus, there's always remarkably good jazz that still allows for conversation" while you "watch the sunset over the Pacific"; P.S. closed Monday–Tuesday.

Left Bank *French* 19 | 20 | 18 | $42

Larkspur | Blue Rock Inn | 507 Magnolia Ave. (Ward St.) | 415-927-3331 | www.leftbank.com

When they "crave steak frites and a glass of wine", or maybe just a "dose of French ambiance", many bank on this "tried-and-true" trio of "boisterous" brasseries in Larkspur, Menlo Park and San Jose, each of which boasts "lovely" outdoor seating that "adds to the pleasure" of the meal; they're "reasonably priced" to boot, and if a few fret that the fare is "by-the-numbers" and the service "mixed", most maintain they've found "a formula that works."

Little River Inn *Californian/Seafood* 21 | 21 | 22 | $50

Little River | Little River Inn | 7901 N. Hwy. 1 (Little River Airport Rd.) | 707-937-5942 | www.littleriverinn.com

With its "lovely" views, "wonderful" "old-fashioned" dining room and "excellent service", this Little River "retreat" is a "favorite near Mendocino" for "killer breakfasts", including "hotcakes like no other"; while weekend brunch is the "highlight", some feel the "predictable" Californian seafood dinners are "improving", but "locals" prefer to "eat at the bar" for the "best value", along with "spectacular" ocean vistas and the "area's best characters".

Lotus Cuisine of India *Indian* 23 | 16 | 21 | $26

San Rafael | 704 Fourth St. (Tamalpais Ave.) | 415-456-5808 | www.lotusrestaurant.com

Anokha Cuisine of India *Indian*

Novato | 811 Grant Ave. (Reichert Ave.) | 415-892-3440 | www.anokharestaurant.com

Café Lotus *Indian*

Fairfax | 1912 Sir Francis Drake Blvd. (Claus Dr.) | 415-457-7836 | www.cafelotusfairfax.com

Diners adore this "suburban San Rafael" subcontinental (with "sister" acts in Novato and Fairfax), where the "fast, accommodating" staff ferries out "fresh, flavorful" "health-conscious" Northern Indian specialties; while the "terrific" lunch buffet is a "bargain", dinner is more upscale in the "attractive", ornament-filled setting, which is especially inviting on "warm evenings", when the "roof skylight" is opened.

MacCallum House *Californian*　　23 | 23 | 22 | $51

Mendocino | MacCallum House Inn | 45020 Albion St. (bet. Hesser & Kasten Sts.) | 707-937-5763 | www.maccallumhouse.com

Prime for a "romantic weekend" in Mendocino, this "antique Victorian" B&B with a "wonderful view of the Pacific in the distance" and a "roaring fireplace to snuggle up with your honey" offers "exciting", regionally sourced Californian dinners and wines "without the crunchy-granola aesthetic"; while it's "expensive" to sup in the main dining room, the "less formal bar area" is a better "value" option, and breakfast on the porch is "always a treat."

Madrona Manor Ⓜ *American/French*　　26 | 26 | 26 | $90

Healdsburg | Madrona Manor | 1001 Westside Rd. (W. Dry Creek Rd.) | 707-433-4231 | www.madronamanor.com

A "great romantic getaway", this "elegant" "old mansion" "decorated in all sorts of Victoriana" and graced by "gardenside" dining on the "beautiful grounds" proffers "superlative" French–New American à la carte and tasting menus accompanied by "wonderful local wines"; as the "above-and-beyond" staff delivers "white-glove service without the glove", it's hardly cheap, but gives hotter Healdsburg destinations a "run for their money."

🆕 **Mammarella's** Ⓩ *Coffeehouse/Italian*　▽ 20 | 22 | 20 | $29

Napa | Napa Airport | 630 Airpark Rd. (Airport Blvd.) | 707-256-3441 | www.cafecoppola.com

See Cafe Zoetrope review in City of San Francisco Directory.

Marché aux Fleurs ⓈⓂ *French*　　24 | 22 | 24 | $52

Ross | 23 Ross Common (Lagunitas Rd.) | 415-925-9200 | www.marcheauxfleursrestaurant.com

A "worthy getaway from the city", this "charmer" in Ross provides "first-rate" New French fare focusing on "local, organic" ingredients, matched by an "inspired" wine list that's "filled with bottles from small and often unknown" producers; "warm", "wonderful" service enhances the "comfortable" setting, and the "patio is practically perfect for a romantic" "summer supper"; P.S. Thursday's "burger night" offers a "lower-cost" way to go.

Marinitas ⚫ *Pan-Latin*　　18 | 20 | 18 | $34

San Anselmo | 218 Sir Francis Drake Blvd. (Bank St.) | 415-454-8900 | www.marinitas.net

They've "done it again" marvel amigos of this "festive", "high-end" cantina "run by the Insalata folks" that's "quickly become a hot spot" in "sleepy" San Anselmo, proffering "tasty" Mexican and Pan-Latin eats with "fab margaritas" till midnight; despite complaints that it can be "hit-or-miss" and "a little expensive for rice", the "wacky decor" and "happening scene" ("sometimes five-deep at the bar") make it a "blast."

Market *American*　　22 | 20 | 22 | $40

St. Helena | 1347 Main St. (bet. Adams St. & Hunt Ave.) | 707-963-3799 | www.marketsthelena.com

Perfect for "when the rest of Napa is booked" or for tourists "tired of all the pretension", this "beautiful stone-walled" stop in St. Helena dishes up "reasonably priced" American "home cooking with a bam"

	FOOD	DECOR	SERVICE	COST

(like "grown-up mac 'n' cheese") and "superb Valley" vino with "tiny mark-ups"; "hospitable" all around, it keeps the "who's who of the wine business" and other "locals" "coming back regularly."

Martini House *American*

| | 26 | 25 | 24 | $66 |

St. Helena | 1245 Spring St. (bet. Main St. & Oak Ave.) | 707-963-2233 | www.martinihouse.com

"Right up there with the Napa big boys", this "lovely" restored "Arts and Crafts cottage" in St. Helena is perennially filled with foodies "sitting next to Valley royalty" in the "beautiful garden" or the "rustic" Pat Kuleto–designed dining room, where fungus-"freak" chef Todd Humphries puts on a culinary "show", presenting "spectacular", high-end New American meals and "full-blown" "mushroom-madness" tasting menus; "for a more casual vibe", customers grab a "Kobe burger" or early-bird "family meal" in the "downstairs bar", which also supplies "terrific" wines and "first-class" cocktails.

Max's *Deli*

| | 17 | 14 | 17 | $26 |

Corte Madera | 60 Madera Blvd. (Hwy. 101) | 415-924-6297 | www.maxsworld.com

See review in City of San Francisco Directory.

Meadowood, The Grill *Californian*
(aka The Grill at Meadowood)

| | 22 | 21 | 24 | $57 |

St. Helena | Meadowood Napa Valley | 900 Meadowood Ln. (Silverado Trail) | 707-963-3646 | www.meadowood.com

After an "exhausting afternoon" spent at the pool, wine tasting or playing croquet, this "little hideaway nestled into" the "excellent" St. Helena resort feels like a "welcome alternative" to the more formal restaurant; guests graze on "good, solid" country-"club"-style fare while taking in the "beautiful" fairways and "peacefulness that is Meadowood", or relax over dinner and enjoy the "old-fashioned" service; even if some find it "very modest" given the surroundings, it's still "just fine."

☑ Meadowood, The
Restaurant ☑ *Californian*
(aka The Restaurant at Meadowood)

| | 26 | 27 | 27 | $107 |

St. Helena | Meadowood Napa Valley | 900 Meadowood Ln. (Silverado Trail) | 707-967-1205 | www.meadowood.com

"Set deep" in St. Helena's "woodsy" Meadowood resort, this "splendiferous" "special-occasion destination" steeped in "pure romance" "rivals" "wine country's tops", providing "delightful" haute Californian tasting menus by chef Christopher Kostow with pairings that "amaze and surprise"; yes, "you'll pay dearly for the experience", but you "can't beat the combination of the view", "synchronized" service and food that's as "inventive" as it is "pretty" – indeed, the "memories will linger for a long, long time."

Melting Pot *Fondue*

| | 17 | 19 | 19 | $46 |

Larkspur | 125 E. Sir Francis Drake Blvd. (Larkspur Landing Circle) | 415-461-6358 | www.meltingpot.com

"It's all about sharing" and "cooking your own food" at this Larkspur chain link serving "every kind of fondue", including "delicious" chocolate pots; while it's a "romantic" "treat" for "younger couples" and "fun to do with a group", critics contend it's "overpriced" and "preten-

"tious", and would prefer a "more casual" setup; P.S. go with a large party if you want "two burners."

Mendo Bistro   *American*   24 | 18 | 22 | $37

Fort Bragg | The Company Store | 301 N. Main St., 2nd fl. (Redwood Ave.) | 707-964-4974 | www.mendobistro.com

"Chef Nicholas Petti brings city-level "flair" to Fort Bragg at this "funky" "gem" on the second floor of an "old" Arts and Crafts–style "logging store", "nourishing body and soul" with "playful", regionally sourced New American eats and a "comprehensive local wine list"; the "inspired (and affordable) choices" appeal to everyone from "foodies to kids to dyed-in-the-wool vegans", while the "wonderful views" of Downtown add to the "feel-good" Mendo experience.

Mendocino Café   *Eclectic*   20 | 15 | 20 | $34

Mendocino | 10451 Lansing St. (Albion St.) | 707-937-6141 | www.mendocinocafe.com

"A funky and very Mendocino cafe", this Eclectic stalwart with a "beautiful garden" and ocean view is the "perfect mixture" of "location and feel" for both lunch and "fine family dining"; "yes, other places have higher-end food and Napa Valley drama", but it's "one of the few" that's "reasonably priced", so "if you're staying in town" it "totally fits" the bill.

Mendocino Hotel   *Californian*   19 | 22 | 20 | $46

Mendocino | Mendocino Hotel | 45080 Main St. (bet. Kasten & Lansing Sts.) | 707-937-0511 | www.mendocinohotel.com

"Step back" into the late "19th century, when Mendocino was a lumber town", at this "beautifully restored Victorian" hotel, a "must-visit for tourists" replete with an "evocative ambiance" and fine "view of the fog"; "save a few bucks" and eat at the "cozy" antique carved-wood bar of the Lobby Lounge bistro, or "splurge" on "wonderful" Californian fare and "a huge selection of regional wines" in the "romantic" dining room – either way, you'll be "super comfortable, especially on a cold night."

Meritage Martini   ▽ 21 | 18 | 22 | $42
Oyster Bar & Grille   *Italian*

Sonoma | 165 W. Napa St. (bet. 1st & 2nd Sts.) | 707-938-9430 | www.sonomameritage.com

Both "locals" and "tourists" love stopping in for a "super lunch of just oysters and salad", "relaxing" over "wonderfully creative" Northern Italian food, or simply sipping the "wild" martinis at this "little hideaway" near Sonoma Plaza; the room's "old-fashioned California" feel strikes some as "a little tired", but "prompt, friendly" service ups its appeal as a "wine country destination"; P.S. closed Tuesday.

Mirepoix 🅂 Ⓜ *French*   24 | 18 | 24 | $59

Windsor | 275 Windsor River Rd. (bet. Honsa Ave. & Windsor Rd.) | 707-838-0162 | www.restaurantmirepoix.com

Though it recently "moved a little further upscale" by shifting to "tasting menus" only, this "romantic" "gem" "off-the-beaten-path" in "tiny Windsor" is still "outstanding", complementing "imaginative", "often exquisite" French food with a "reasonably priced" wine list that "shows the same care"; the "very small" space means "reservations are a must", but once you're seated the "personable" owners ensure "excellent" service; P.S. open Wednesday–Saturday.

	FOOD	DECOR	SERVICE	COST

Model Bakery *Bakery*

21 | 11 | 16 | $16

Napa | Oxbow Public Mkt. | 644 First St. (bet. Silverado Trail & Soscol Ave.) | 707-963-8192
St. Helena | 1357 Main St. (bet. Adams St. & Hunt Ave.) | 707-963-8192
www.themodelbakery.com

It's the "real deal" cry carbo-loaders who "stroll by" this mom-and-daughter duo's "funky" "daytime only" St. Helena bakery and coffee-house and its "take-and-go" Napa Oxbow branch for a cup of joe and "killer morning buns" or "freshly baked" brick-oven pizzas, "sammies" and other "wine country"–bound "picnic supplies"; those "moist cakes" and "exceptional" goodies sure "tempt from the cases" – no wonder "snagging a seat" is "tough."

Monti's Rotisserie & Bar *American/Mediterranean*

21 | 18 | 20 | $37

Santa Rosa | Montgomery Village Shopping Ctr. | 714 Village Ct. (Farmers Ln.) | 707-568-4404 | www.montisroti.net

The "wood-fired stove" adds an "extra-cozy" touch to this "casual" Santa Rosa roost purveying "solid" New American–Med eats, including "hard-to-beat" daily rotisserie specials; since the "longtime staff makes you feel absolutely at home", it's "deservedly popular" among locals, who disregard the "odd placement in a shopping mall" and "go back often" to dine and sip "generous cocktails" at the "lively bar."

Moosse Café *Californian*

24 | 20 | 22 | $45

Mendocino | The Blue Heron Inn | 390 Kasten St. (Albion St.) | 707-937-4323 | www.themoosse.com

"Sitting near the garden is a total treat" attest fans who flock to this "cute" "homey" Californian "favorite" with a New England feel in The Blue Heron Inn after "browsing the shops" in town or for a "relaxing evening out"; if a few find the digs too "plain"-Jane and the tabs too "high", for most the "consistently creative", "well-prepared" "comfort food" and "dedicated owners and staff" truly "surpass" other "Mendocino eateries."

NEW Morimoto Napa *Japanese*

- | - | - | VE

Napa | 610 Main St. (5th St.) | 707-252-1600 | www.morimotonapa.com

The first West Coast branch of Masaharu Morimoto's empire arrives on Downtown Napa's revitalized Riverfront, where the dramatic, traditional-meets-modern digs include a dining room, sushi bar and waterfront patio, and the pricey menu pairs fish flown in from Tokyo with Californian ingredients; the offerings are rounded out by soups, noodles and rice dishes and complemented by NorCal wines, imported sakes, artisanal cocktails and a selection of beers, including the chef's own line of Rogue Brewery suds.

Mosaic Restaurant & Wine Lounge *Californian*

25 | 20 | 22 | $53

Forestville | 6675 Front St. (Mirabel Rd.) | 707-887-7503 | www.mosaiceats.com

"You'd never expect such" "reliably excellent" Californian fare "when you drive up" to this "out-of-the-way place" in Forestville marvel "pleasantly surprised" diners, but "wow" the chef-owner "can cook", whether whipping up a "sublime" brunch or a "stellar" "special occasion" "summer dinner" (best enjoyed "outside on the lovely patio"); as a plus, the "local" Russian River Valley wine list is totally "delightful."

Murray Circle *Californian* | 24 | 25 | 23 | $70 |

Sausalito | Cavallo Point Resort in Fort Baker | 602 Murray Circle (Sausalito Lateral Rd.) | 415-339-4750 | www.murraycircle.com
Elevating fine dining to "a whole new level for Marin", this "remodeled army post" "at the foot of the Golden Gate Bridge" in Sausalito seduces with "postcard views of the Bay" and "sensational" Californian fare; lunch can "make any ordinary Joe feel like a CEO", while sipping "cocktails on the porch" or by the fireplace bar as the city "lights come on" heightens its "special occasion" status; if you can "stand the dent in your wallet", "splurge" on the "grand tasting menu" and "top-notch" wine pairings.

Z Mustards Grill *American/Californian* | 25 | 20 | 22 | $49 |

Yountville | 7399 St. Helena Hwy./Hwy. 29 (bet. Oakville Grade Rd. & Washington St.) | 707-944-2424 | www.mustardsgrill.com
Chef Cindy Pawlcyn is on the "pulse of what people like", as evidenced by all the "happy" diners "fueling up" on her "marvelous" Cal-New American "gourmet comfort food" at this "well-appointed roadhouse" with "helpful" service in Yountville; it's "always packed" and "a little frenetic", so "it's best to make reservations" or try "eating at the bar", where you can "mix with locals" while sipping some vino from the "fantastic", "well-priced" list.

Napa General Store *Californian/Eclectic* | 19 | 15 | 16 | $26 |

Napa | 540 Main St. (5th St.) | 707-259-0762 | www.napageneralstore.com
"Love" the "cozy, old-time" "general store feel" and "nice location" overlooking the revitalized Napa riverfront agree admirers who gather at this "casual" Cal-Eclectic cafe for an "enjoyable breakfast" or "light" alfresco lunch; picnickers also pronounce it "pretty special" for "picking up some deliciousness" and local vino – all the "wine country fixings" you need to "work your way through" the Valley; P.S. closes at 5 PM.

Napa Valley Wine Train *Californian* | 18 | 24 | 21 | $75 |

Napa | 1275 McKinstry St. (bet. 1st St. & Soscol Ave.) | 707-253-2111 | www.winetrain.com
"There's a certain romance" to this "civilized dining experience", during which passengers watch "the Napa Valley as it passes by" while supping on "pretty good" Californian cuisine in a "splendid" "old train car"; it's "a kick" that's best "during the day" "so you can actually see" the "amazing" views, but those who aren't on board opine it's "overpriced" and fume that the food is "just fair."

Neela's Ⓜ *Indian* | – | – | – | M |

Napa | 975 Clinton St. (Main St.) | 707-226-9988 | www.neelasnapa.com
Wine country natives say namaste and "beat tracks" to this "mecca of exquisite Indian food in Napa (yes, Napa)" where Neela Paniz (ex LA's Bombay Cafe) turns out "beautifully seasoned" pan-regional cuisine; the contemporary, colorful storefront features Bollywood videos playing in the bar, creating a lively backdrop for "bargain Thali" lunches and weekly dinner specials, matched by a food-friendly wine list.

	FOOD	DECOR	SERVICE	COST

Nick's Cove *Californian*
19 | 22 | 19 | $48

Marshall | Nick's Cove & Cottages | 23240 Hwy. 1 (4 mi. north of Marshall-Petaluma Rd.) | 415-723-1071 | www.nickscove.com

A "wonderful destination" "on your way up or down the coast", Pat Kuleto's gussied-up "restored roadhouse" in "sleepy" Marshall offers an "idyllic setting" "right on Tomales Bay" for savoring Californian seafood, including "pristine oysters (in all of their forms)"; if clam-counters counter that prices are "high" and note service "could use a little polishing", even they admit that a "drink out on the jetty" while "watching the sun set" and "birds swoop into the water" is "escapism at its best."

955 Ukiah Ⓜ *American/French*
23 | 20 | 21 | $46

Mendocino | 955 Ukiah St. (School St.) | 707-937-1955 | www.955restaurant.com

"You'll find a lot of locals eating" at this "bucolic", "hidden spot in the village of Mendocino", where the "imaginative" New American-French dinners, based on locally grown ingredients, are matched by a "diverse wine list" sourced from nearby vineyards; the "family-run" space, resembling an "artist's studio", is "cozy" for a "date" and the tabs are "decent" too, making it a worthwhile "rival to the better-known restaurant next door"; P.S. closed Monday-Wednesday.

NEW Norman Rose Tavern *American*
∇ 20 | 22 | 19 | $31

Napa | 1401 First St. (Franklin St.) | 707-258-1516 | www.normanrosenapa.com

"After a hard day of exploring the wines of Napa", join "packs" of "lo-cals" at the Azzurro folks' "inviting" new "neighborhood tavern" set in "an old bank building" Downtown for "uncomplicated", "well-prepared" sustainably sourced American "pub grub", including one of the "best burgers"; belly up to the bar for "beers on tap", watch sports on the "ring of flat-screens" and "enjoy the lively atmosphere" while waiting, as no reservations are taken.

North Coast Brewing Company *American*
17 | 15 | 17 | $26

Fort Bragg | 455 N. Main St. (Pine St.) | 707-964-3400 | www.northcoastbrewing.com

The "locally crafted" brews are "worth the trip" up the Mendocino coast to this "Northern Californian beer mecca" and taproom set in a historic Fort Bragg building across the street from the microbrewery; but while some find the American "pub food" "surprisingly good" and events like Pint Night and Taco Tuesdays "fun", underwhelmed mugs foam that the fare "doesn't measure up" to the "delicious" suds.

Oco Time Ⓢ *Japanese*
- | - | - | M

Ukiah | 111 W. Church St. (School St.) | 707-462-2422 | www.ocotime.com

This "small" hippie-dippy Japanese cafe in Ukiah may fly under the ra-dar, but "make a reservation or you won't get in" warn residents who know that any time is a great time to enjoy the "best sushi and sashimi on the North Coast" (also available at its take-out annex, It's Time); the signature okonomiyaki - a savory pancake layered with noodles, meat and vegetables and considered the soul food of Hiroshima - rounds out the menu, along with sake, beer and wine.

	FOOD	DECOR	SERVICE	COST

NEW Oenotri *Italian* | – | – | – | E

Napa | Napa Sq. | 1425 First St. (bet. Franklin & School Sts.) |
707-252-1022 | www.oenotri.com

Breaking away from the conventional Cal-Ital wine country offerings,
this new trattoria in Downtown's Napa Square (run by a duo of Oliveto
veterans) showcases the authentic, rustic flavors of Southern Italy –
most notably an ever-changing array of pastas, house-cured salumi
and Neapolitan-style pizzas baked in the open kitchen's wood-fired
oven; in keeping with its name (an ancient term meaning 'vine cultiva-
tors'), the wine list favors food-friendly regional vini; P.S. open till
midnight Thursday–Saturday.

Olema Inn *Californian* | 19 | 22 | 19 | $49

Olema | Olema Inn | 10000 Sir Francis Drake Blvd. (Hwy. 101) |
415-663-9559 | www.theolemainn.com

Weekenders "driving up the coast" love to "stumble upon" this old
country inn, an "elegant but not fancy" "oasis" in Olema serving "homey"
Californian fare and "wonderful" "boutique wines"; despite a "succes-
sion of owners and chefs", its "timeless" setting with a "beautiful garden" makes it HQ for "romantic" occasions, though a few report their
interest has "gone down" since the "prices went way up."

Osake ☒ *Californian/Japanese* | ▽ 24 | 18 | 22 | $33

Santa Rosa | 2446 Patio Ct. (Farmers Ln.) | 707-542-8282 |
www.garychus.com

Chef-owner "Gary Chu is a familiar face" at his Santa Rosa sushi place,
often "holding court" behind the bar and "schmoozing" with regulars
while he "slices and dices" "fresh", "tasty" fish, complemented by
other moderately priced, "well-prepared" Cal-Japanese eats as well as
"good sake"; despite an "odd location" in a "strip mall", fans note it's
"nice" once you're inside.

Osteria Stellina *Italian* | 25 | 17 | 22 | $40

Point Reyes Station | 11285 Hwy. 1 (bet. 2nd & 3rd Sts.) |
415-663-9988 | www.osteriastellina.com

"Get in your car or bike" and hightail it to this shining "star in a distant
constellation" in "funky little Point Reyes Station" that "fashions"
Italian-inspired locavore dishes, "pulling off oyster pizza", braised goat
and other "wonderful surprises" with a "real sense of place and vivid,
rich flavors"; the "simple" storefront gets "crowded and noisy", but everyone "quits complaining" once the meals – "worthy of SF's best" –
and "regional wine" "gems" arrive; P.S. now serving weekend brunch.

Oxbow Wine | 22 | 20 | 21 | $28
Merchant *Californian/Mediterranean*

Napa | Oxbow Public Mkt. | 610 First St. (bet. Silverado Trail & Soscol
Ave.) | 707-257-5200 | www.oxbowwinemerchant.com

"Go for the cheese" at this Cal-Med "hipster-doodle" Oxbow Market
"hangout" boasting the "best foreign and domestic" fromage selection, "stay to watch the sunset" from the deck "overlooking" the
"lovely" river; some serious sippers sidle up to the "nifty wine bar" to
sample "before buying new Cabs" while "munching" charcuterie dispensed by the knowledgeable crew – either way it's a "wonderful"
"scene"; P.S. a move into the main market hall is planned for Fall 2010.

	FOOD	DECOR	SERVICE	COST

Pacific Catch *Seafood* — 19 | 14 | 18 | $25

Corte Madera | Town Center Corte Madera | 133 Corte Madera Town Ctr. (off Hwy. 101) | 415-927-3474 | www.pacificcatch.com
See review in City of San Francisco Directory.

Pasta Pomodoro *Italian* — 17 | 13 | 18 | $23

Mill Valley | Strawberry Vill. | 800 Redwood Hwy. (Belvedere Dr.) | 415-388-1692
San Rafael | Montecito Plaza | 421 3rd St. (bet. Grand Ave. & Mary St.) | 415-256-2401
www.pastapomodoro.com
See review in City of San Francisco Directory.

Patrona Restaurant & Lounge 🗷Ⓜ *Californian* — - | - | - | E

Ukiah | 130 W. Standley St. (School St.) | 707-462-9181 | www.patronarestaurant.com
"A real find in Ukiah", this locavore Californian near the County Courthouse Square pays homage to Mendocino's bounty, turning out "innovative", hyper-regional lunches and dinners, paired with "excellent" North Coast wines; the eco-chic setting in a former grocery with natural wood tables, old exposed-brick walls and a cocktail lounge (stocked with the area's largest selection of absinthe) is fast becoming "the most happening place Downtown."

Pearl 🗷Ⓜ *Californian* — ▽ 21 | 15 | 20 | $35

Napa | 1339 Pearl St. (bet. Franklin & Polk Sts.) | 707-224-9161 | www.therestaurantpearl.com
Napa foodies who "care more about flavor than decor" head Downtown to this aptly named, long-running mom-and-pop bistro for what else but "awesome oysters", along with seasonal eclectic Californian eats and some of the region's best and least-known wines; the "attention paid to the food served is obvious" – "everything on the menu is fabulous" and cheaper than most Up Valley haunts.

Peter Lowell's *Italian* — ▽ 21 | 17 | 19 | $31

Sebastopol | 7385 Healdsburg Ave. (Florence Ave.) | 707-829-1077 | www.peterlowells.com
Veggie-loving visitors "can't stop going back" to this "very West County" "organic neighborhood cafe" on Sebastopol's "main drag", a "reliable stop" that's "part of the local scene", but "outsider-friendly" too; the "well-prepared" food, including Italianate breakfasts, "great wood-fired pizzas" and "a minimum of meat" and fish is a locavore affair, befitting the "super-cozy" LEED-certified storefront, replete with a recycled paper-stone biodynamic-focused wine bar; P.S. eat alfresco on a "nice day."

Piaci Pub & Pizzeria *Pizza* — ▽ 27 | 14 | 19 | $23

Fort Bragg | 120 W. Redwood Ave. (Hwy. 1) | 707-961-1133 | www.piacipizza.com
A "good time is literally had by all" at this Fort Bragg pub with "its own personality and flair" set in an "off-Main Street location", where the "crowded, rushed" atmosphere is "part of the fun" and a "wait for a table" de rigueur; what a "cool spot to hang out" "with the old Mendocino hippies" and indulge in "excellent" "adult"-style "thin-crust pizza",

and in addition, one of the "best selections in town of artisan beers and wines by the glass."

Piatti *Italian*   19 | 19 | 19 | $39

Mill Valley | 625 Redwood Hwy. (Hwy. 101) | 415-380-2525 | www.piatti.com

See review in East of San Francisco Directory.

Piazza D'Angelo *Italian*   21 | 20 | 20 | $40

Mill Valley | 22 Miller Ave. (bet. Sunnyside & Throckmorton Aves.) | 415-388-2000 | www.piazzadangelo.com

"Delicious" pastas and other "simple" Italian "comfort food" inspire some to visit this "bustling" Mill Valley venue "almost daily"; "the food is always good", and the staff "make you feel like family", but social surveyors are partial to "people-watching" and "mixing with the crowd", a "who's who" of locals (including many "middle-age divorcées") who like to "see and be seen" in the "big, busy" bar.

Pica Pica Maize Kitchen *Venezuelan*   ▽ 23 | 11 | 15 | $15

Napa | Oxbow Public Mkt. | 610 First St. (bet. Silverado Trail & Soscol Ave.) | 707-251-3757 | www.picapicakitchen.com

See review in City of San Francisco Directory.

Picco *Italian*   25 | 21 | 23 | $49

Larkspur | 320 Magnolia Ave. (King St.) | 415-924-0300 | www.restaurantpicco.com

Many a "Marin dweller's favorite" Cal-Ital haunt, this "cozy brick" "standout" owned by "talented" chef Bruce Hill (Bix and neighboring Pizzeria Picco) "always" delivers "something seasonal and marvelous to eat"; the "flavors" of the "dead-perfect", "inspired" ("albeit pricey") but not-so-"small plates" "are as bright as the lighting is muted", and while the "vivacious" vibe can be "noisy" and "a little too cougarish" for a few, believers brag it doesn't get "any better than this."

Piccolo Teatro *Italian*   ▽ 22 | 21 | 18 | $41

Sausalito | 739 Bridgeway Blvd. (Anchor St.) | 415-332-0739 | www.piccoloteatrodisausalito.com

Ready for the big stage since the recent installment of veteran chef Amey Shaw, this "attractive" Sausalito cafe serving "interesting", "Venetian-inspired" plates is the "perfect" "place to pause" for an "unhurried lunch" "during nice weather", when "one end opens up into sidewalk seating"; it's equally simpatico for a "casual" dinner by the "cozy fireplace" (enhanced by live jazz on Wednesdays) or under "lap blankets" and "heaters on the patio."

Pine Cone Diner ⊟ *Diner*   ▽ 22 | 15 | 17 | $26

Point Reyes Station | 60 Fourth St. (B St.) | 415-663-1536 | www.pineconediner.com

Day-trippers passing through "lovely" Point Reyes Station (as well as lots of "locals") "always make a point to stop" at this "quirky" diner where breakfasts (the "best corned beef hash on the West Coast") and New American lunches satisfy a "healthy appetite"; the "kitschy" "retro" setting has "lots of atmosphere", with "pleasant" outdoor tables too, and if some say "service can be surly", most maintain the "sassy waitresses" are "friendly" at heart; P.S. closes at 3 PM daily.

	FOOD	DECOR	SERVICE	COST

Pizza Antica *Pizza* — 21 | 15 | 17 | $27

Mill Valley | Strawberry Vill. | 800 Redwood Hwy. (Belvedere Dr.) |
415-383-0600 | www.pizzaantica.com

See review in South of San Francisco Directory.

Pizzavino 707 Ⓜ *Pizza* — - | - | - | M

Sebastopol | 6948 Sebastopol Ave. (bet. Main St. & Petaluma Ave.) |
707-829-9500 | www.pizzavino707.com

Still relatively unknown outside the 707 area, this Cal-Ital redux on the
Sebastopol plaza turns out "truly delicious pizza" and a "nice wine selection", along with salumi and wood-fired small plates from an open
kitchen; the front bar hosts happy hours, while a second center bar
doubles as a tasting room and retail shop for the Sonoma County Wine
Collective (Friday–Sunday); rounding out the ambitious offerings: an
upstairs pool lounge and a "lovely outdoor setting" for alfresco lunches.

Pizzeria Picco *Pizza* — 25 | 17 | 20 | $27

Larkspur | 316 Magnolia Ave. (King St.) | 415-945-8900 |
www.pizzeriapicco.com

Picco's "jammed but quaint" "biker-themed" Southern Italian offshoot
and wine shop sets taste buds salivating with "amazing" "wood-oven
pizzas", "fresh salads" that "rotate seasonally" and "killer organic
soft-serve" ("olive oil" optional) for dessert; if "you're lucky enough"
to "score" a seat "at the cozy bar" or outside "on a warm evening"
amid the "hilarious" "sidewalk scene" "you feel as though you've
gone to heaven."

Pizzeria Tra Vigne *Pizza* — 21 | 16 | 16 | $28

St. Helena | Inn at Southbridge | 1016 Main St. (bet. Charter Oak Ave. &
Pope St.) | 707-967-9999 | www.pizzeriatravigne.com

For a "welcome break from all the tastings", vino-vacationers hit this
St. Helena Italian (spun off from Tra Vigne) for "can't-go-wrong" salads
and "delicious", "chewy-crust" pizzas paired with "wines and beers"
from the menu or from Napa vineyard hopping ("no corkage fee");
while some are underwhelmed by "weak" service and long "waits for
a table", "it's not a bad value for the area", especially if you score a
courtyard table "under the stars."

Poggio *Italian* — 23 | 24 | 22 | $47

Sausalito | Casa Madrona | 777 Bridgeway (Bay St.) | 415-332-7771 |
www.poggiotrattoria.com

With plenty of "*buon giornos*", "*bellas* and *bellos* to go around", this
"soulful", "rustic" Tuscan trattoria transcends "touristy Sausalito",
showcasing "fantastic pastas" "made fresh each day", "perfect" "grilled
meats" and garden-grown veggies "matched by terrific service" and
vini; relish it all in the "gorgeous" terracotta-tiled room with "lighting
that takes years off your dining companions", or, on a "leisurely day",
"on the sidewalk overlooking the Bay."

Press Ⓢ Ⓜ *American/Steak* — 24 | 26 | 24 | $70

St. Helena | 587 St. Helena Hwy. (White Ln.) | 707-967-0550 |
www.presssthelena.com

"Hunks" of "charred red meat and big red wines" at "big prices" are the
siren call of this St. Helena American with a "neat" farmhouse feel;
prepare to "save up" for the locally sourced steaks "prepared with un-

rivaled attention" "over an open fire" and accompanied by "excellent sides", though thankfully "Sunday Suppers" and Wednesday blue-plate specials at the "beautiful bar" (which stocks its "own 209 gin") are "a steal."

Ravenous Cafe ⓜ Californian/Eclectic — 21 | 17 | 18 | $42

Healdsburg | 420 Center St. (bet. North & Piper Sts.) | 707-431-1302

"Sit outside if you can" on the "awesome" patio at this "lovely little cafe" set in a 1930s "Craftsman house", which is just "off the beaten path" in Healdsburg but nonetheless "gets crazy busy" with fans of its "consistently good" Cal-Eclectic chow and "huge wine-by-the-glass list"; it's "definitely a scene", but a "ravenous" few warn a "tiny kitchen" and occasional "spotty service" can make it a "longggg night."

Ravens' Restaurant Vegan — ▽ 22 | 23 | 22 | $42

Mendocino | Stanford Inn & Spa | 44850 Comptche Ukiah Rd. (Hwy. 1) | 707-937-5615 | www.stanfordinn.com

"You don't have to be a vegetarian" or vegan to appreciate the "creativity and flair evident in every dish" at this "romantic" Mendocino inn-sider where the "hearty" breakfast and dinner fare, primarily sourced from the eco-resort's gardens, is matched by a strong wine list (a "treat"); boosters insist you won't question "where's the beef?", though a few counter it's "expensive, elitist" and not everyone's cup of chamomile tea.

☒ Redd Restaurant Californian — 27 | 22 | 25 | $70

Yountville | 6480 Washington St. (bet. Mission St. & Oak Circle) | 707-944-2222 | www.reddnapavalley.com

Thanks to its "tantalizing" Cal dishes "showcasing local ingredients" and "divine" desserts that "shouldn't be missed", foodies "won't sing the blues" at chef-owner Richard Reddington's "delightful" destination, deemed "one of Yountville's best – and that's saying something"; surveyors are torn over the "über-modern" decor ("welcome departure" vs. "uptight New Yorker") and wallet-watchers blast an "expensive" wine list, but service that's so "attentive it's almost embarrassing" and otherwise "fair prices" more than compensate.

Rendezvous Inn & Restaurant ⓜ French — ▽ 27 | 20 | 24 | $52

Fort Bragg | 647 N. Main St. (bet. Bush & Fir Sts.) | 707-964-8142 | www.rendezvousinn.com

Kim Badenhop "puts out some of the finest food on the Mendocino Coast" at this "romantic" spot in a "lovely" Fort Bragg Craftsman B&B, where he "delights" diners with "fantastic" fireside French feasts topped by "ethereal soufflés"; it's all paired with "great" California wines at "real prices" and "excellent service", enhanced by a "chef who does not miss visiting every table"; P.S. closed Monday–Tuesday.

Restaurant, The American/Eclectic — ▽ 25 | 17 | 25 | $37

Fort Bragg | 418 N. Main St. (Laurel St.) | 707-964-9800 | www.therestaurantfortbragg.com

It's "one of the longest-lasting restaurants on the often finicky Mendocino Coast", so it's "doing something right" declare devotees of this Fort Bragg "favorite" where the "excellent" if "expensive" New American–Eclectic eats come with "comfortable service"; filled with oil paintings by Olaf Palm, the "oldish but quaint" setting remains a defacto choice for "elegant" occasions, though a few suggest the menu could use some "updating"; P.S. closed Tuesday–Wednesday.

Restaurant at Stevenswood, The *American* ▽ 24 | 21 | 21 | $62

Little River | Stevenswood Lodge | 8211 Shoreline Hwy./N. Hwy. 1 (1 mi. south of Mendocino) | 707-937-2810 | www.stevenswood.com

For a "fine night out in the ocean wilds", Little River diners descend upon this "delightful" New American nook "nestled in a forestlike setting", where a "creative", "ever-changing" menu is offered Friday-Saturday in the "cozy", fireplace-lit dining room; during the rest of the week, only breakfast and an "abbreviated" casual grill menu are available, though "warm" service is a constant.

NEW Restaurant P/30 Ⓜ *American* – | – | – | M

Sebastopol | 9890 Bodega Hwy. (bet. Ferguson & Montgomery Rds.) | 707-861-9030 | www.restaurantp30.com

An off-the-beaten-path newcomer, this Sebastopol roadhouse is already packed to the rafters nightly with West County denizens lapping up the affordable yet chic New American comfort fare (e.g. locally sourced chicken and waffles) amid oversized Pop Art canvases; it's currently open Wednesday-Sunday, and only accepts rezzies for large groups.

Risibisi *Italian* ▽ 22 | 20 | 23 | $39

Petaluma | 154 Petaluma Blvd. N. (Washington St.) | 707-766-7600 | www.risibisirestaurant.com

"Charming and intimate", this "unpretentious" Venetian venue "holds its own" in Downtown Petaluma, dishing up "substantial portions" of "carefully prepared", "intriguing" Italian eats with "good wine"; since the owner "Marco is a terrific host", habitués like to "linger" despite the "tight" seating; P.S. there's a "lovely prix fixe menu for lunch."

Robata Grill & Sushi *Japanese* 19 | 14 | 19 | $33

Mill Valley | 591 Redwood Hwy. (Seminary Dr.) | 415-381-8400 | www.robatagrill.com

For "delicious" sushi and robata-style grill items ("without the wait and cost" of competitors), this "large, comfortable, though sometimes crowded" Mill Valley Japanese "right off 101" lures "local families and young professionals"; while critics claim it's "not quite top-quality", most find it pleasant and "fairly priced" nonetheless.

Rocker Oysterfellers Ⓜ *American* ▽ 21 | 15 | 22 | $35

Valley Ford | Valley Ford Hotel | 14415 Hwy. 1 (School St.) | 707-876-1983 | www.rockeroysterfellers.com

This American "roadside" pit stop in the "cow town" of Valley Ford serving "comforting" "Southern-style" dinners and "even better" Sunday brunch is a fine "place to stop on your way home from the coast"; so kick back and "sit on a rocking chair on the front porch letting time slip by", or "feel part of the local scene" at the bar featuring live music and "briny, sweet" dollar oysters at Thursday's happy hour; P.S. closed Monday-Tuesday.

Rosso Pizzeria & Wine Bar *Italian/Pizza* 26 | 17 | 24 | $30

Santa Rosa | Creekside Ctr. | 53 Montgomery Dr. (3rd St.) | 707-544-3221 | www.rossopizzeria.com

"Fantastic" "artisanal pies", salad-topped flatbreads (heaped with "high-quality, unusual ingredients") and "interesting daily specials like suckling pig" keep this Slow Food–inspired trattoria "packed" despite a "down economy" and "dorky Santa Rosa shopping-center" locale; all in all, it's a "pizza slice of Umbria", where the "service couldn't be friendlier" and the "well-priced" wine is available in "multiple sizes – from small tastes to carafes to bottles."

Royal Thai *Thai*   22 | 18 | 18 | $26
San Rafael | 610 Third St. (Irwin St.) | 415-485-1074 | www.royalthaisanrafael.com
Keeping it regal since 1983, this "traditional Thai" in San Rafael still "beats out" the competition with its "delightful" menu ranging from "sweet and savory" appetizers to "fantastic" fish to "smooth, spicy" curries with "super-fresh" vegetables; it may not be "glamorous", but "attentive" service enhances the affordable meal.

NEW Rustic, Francis's Favorites *Italian*   - | - | - | E
Geyserville | Frances Coppola Winery | 300 Via Archimedes (Fredson Rd.) | 707-857-1400 | www.franciscoppolawinery.com
Making wine country visitors an offer they can't refuse, this new Italian at Francis Ford Coppola's extravagantly renovated Geyserville winery (with a swimming pool and bocce court on the grounds) offers an atmospheric indoor and outdoor setting overlooking vineyards for enjoying the director's favorite foods, from Neapolitan pizzas and Mrs. Scorsese's lemon chicken to meats cooked on an Argentinean-style *parrilla* in the center of the dining room, complemented by bottles from both his collection and others.

Rutherford Grill *American*   23 | 20 | 21 | $40
Rutherford | 1180 Rutherford Rd. (Hwy. 29) | 707-963-1792 | www.hillstone.com
"Consistently excellent" American fare, including "super ribs", "satisfies all appetites" at this Rutherford link in the Hillstone chain, a "popular" "place to refuel" "after a day of wine tasting"; the "wonderful" "no-corkage policy brings in the locals in droves", so expect "long lines" without a reservation (accepted after 5 PM only), but at least the "patio bar is a pleasant spot" to "wait for your table."

Santé *Californian/French*   ▽ 23 | 20 | 22 | $73
Sonoma | Fairmont Sonoma Mission Inn & Spa | 100 Boyes Blvd. (Sonoma Hwy.) | 707-939-2415 | www.fairmont.com
Guests at the Fairmont Sonoma Mission Inn appreciate that they "don't need to leave the hotel" for a "most pleasing" dining experience, specifically "beautifully presented" Cal-French "tasting menus with wine pairings" that are "deceptively simple yet ultimately satisfying"; a "warm, gracious" staff and "hard-to-beat setting" add to the allure, though a picky few counter it's "not worth the price."

Santi *Italian*   24 | - | 23 | $48
Santa Rosa | Fountaingrove Vill. | 2097 Stagecoach Rd. (Fountaingrove Pkwy.) | 707-528-1549 | www.santirestaurant.com
Reopened post-Survey in the "big city of Santa Rosa", this former "Geyserville boonies" Northern Italian continues to showcase longtime chef Liza Hinman's "authentic", "earthy" "housemade everything" in her new open kitchen, outfitted with a wood-burning oven; it'll "cost you some serious" lire, but the total package, including a patio, is a pleaser.

	FOOD	DECOR	SERVICE	COST

Ⓩ Scoma's *Seafood* — 22 | 19 | 20 | $46

Sausalito | 588 Bridgeway (Princess St.) | 415-332-9551 |
www.scomassausalito.com
See review in City of San Francisco Directory.

Scopa Ⓜ *Italian* — 25 | 17 | 22 | $43

Healdsburg | 109A Plaza St. (bet. Center St. & Healdsburg Ave.) |
707-433-5282 | www.scopahealdsburg.com
Perhaps the "best deal in Sonoma", this "heavenly" Healdsburg "hole-in-the-wall" "packs a big punch" with "gutsy Italian food", "enthusias-tic" service and a "wonderfully informal" vibe; "if you can squeeze in" or nab a spot outside, "you'll likely be seated between winemakers" (who work the floor Wednesday nights), another reason it remains a "hot spot" despite the "funky" setting and "loud" decibel level.

Solbar *Californian* — 25 | 23 | 24 | $49

Calistoga | Solage Resort | 755 Silverado Trail (bet. Brannan St. & Pickett Rd.) | 707-226-0850 | www.solbarnv.com
The "best of LA and Napa in one heavenly location", this Solage Resort Californian delivers a "little bit of hip city life in laid-back" Calistoga, courtesy of a "modern" space – complete with a "wonderful bar and fireplaces" – that sets the scene for French Laundry vet Brandon Sharp's "innovative" fare; it's predictably "pricey", but since it's all coupled with "incredible wines" and an "A+ staff", few seem to care.

Sol Food *Puerto Rican* — 22 | 15 | 16 | $17

San Rafael | 732 Fourth St. (Lincoln Ave.) | 415-451-4765
San Rafael | 901 Lincoln Ave. (3rd St.) | 415-451-4765
www.solfoodrestaurant.com
These "lively" San Rafael "favorites" (both the "sit-down" original and the take-out "shack" on Fourth Street) crank out "inexpensive", "ridic-ulously good" Puerto Rican "treats" that are "slightly healthier" than "what *abuelita* used to make"; it all comes with "killer hot sauce" and "refreshing" limeades, and while fans sol-ute the venues' "tropical ambiance" and late hours ("by Marin standards"), beware they're even "more popular" since being "featured on *Diners, Drive-Ins and Dives*."

NEW Spoonbar *Mediterranean* — - | - | - | M

Healdsburg | H2hotel | 219 Healdsburg Ave. (bet. W. Matheson & Mill Sts.) |
707-433-7222 | www.spoonbar.com
Not your father's wine country restaurant, this hip newcomer in Downtown Healdsburg's eco-chic H2hotel spoon-feeds overnight guests and late-night grazers alike with a slightly upscale, cosmopoli-tan Med menu by chef Rudy Mihal, complemented by Sonoma wines on tap (to lower your carbon mouthprint) and farm-to-glass cocktails mixed by ex-Cyrus startender Scott Beattie; the entire room, outfitted with a reclaimed-wood communal table and colorful Eames chairs, opens onto the street through cantina doors.

**Starlight Wine
Bar & Restaurant** Ⓜ *American* — ▽ 22 | 23 | 21 | $35

Sebastopol | 6167 Sebastopol Ave. (bet. Morris St. & Petaluma Ave.) |
707-823-1943 | www.starlightwinebar.com
This "cute" Sebastopol wine bar set in a shiny art-deco "railroad car" is a nifty "place to visit if you have nostalgia for old trains" declare din-

ers on board with its "quintessential" New American–Creole "comfort food" and small-producer bottlings; a few find the experience "up and down", but the "delightful" husband-and-wife owners generally keep everything on track.

Station House Cafe *Californian* 18 | 15 | 16 | $33
Point Reyes Station | 11180 State Rte. 1 (2nd St.) | 415-663-1515 | www.stationhousecafe.com

A "dependable" "stop after a long day of hiking", this "moderately priced" place in Point Reyes Station serves "homestyle" Cal cooking based on "local" ingredients; the "nice garden area" is a boon "when the weather is warm enough", and occasional live music notches up the "neighborly feeling", but critics carp the "service can be slow" and the kitchen is "resting on its laurels"; P.S. closed Wednesdays.

St. Orres *Californian* 22 | 24 | 23 | $62
Gualala | St. Orres Hotel | 36601 S. Hwy. 1 (Seaside School Rd.) | 707-884-3303 | www.saintorres.com

"Overlooking" the "dramatic North Coast shoreline" in the "middle of nowhere" (read: Gualala), this "rustic lodge" is where Mendocino-bound travelers brake to enjoy "locally sourced" Californian repasts and regional wines in a "beautiful setting"; it's "expensive" and some suggest the menu is "stuck in the past", but those smitten by the "Russian onion dome", "lovely solarium next to the bar" and "pleasant service" insist it's "worth the trip."

☑ Sushi Ran *Japanese* 27 | 20 | 23 | $56
Sausalito | 107 Caledonia St. (bet. Pine & Turney Sts.) | 415-332-3620 | www.sushiran.com

"If God opened a sushi bar", it might resemble this "posh" Sausalito spot that's "worth the trip over the bridge", since it proffers "top-notch" fish "flown in from Japan" and "wonderful cooked dishes" in "tranquil" digs; "Marin attitude and crowds can be a drag" and it's "no bargain", but savvy surveyors who sample it during the "busy lunch hour" snag delicious "deals", while sake-seekers who "enhance the experience" with the "insane" selection at the next-door "wine bar" "almost never wait."

Syrah ⓈⓂ *Californian/French* 25 | 18 | 24 | $52
Santa Rosa | 205 Fifth St. (Davis St.) | 707-568-4002 | www.syrahbistro.com

"Beautiful presentations" of "perfectly prepared seasonal produce" and "mouthwatering desserts" are "the star" at this "dependable" Cal-French bistro in Santa Rosa, but the "deep wine list" ("far more than just syrah") is also "superb"; the "personable" chef/co-owner helps make the atmosphere "homey and warm", suitable for a "splurge" or "any special occasion", but most maintain the "exposed" atrium is less appealing than the "intimate" interior.

Table Café ⓈⓂ *Californian* ▽ 23 | 14 | 19 | $20
Larkspur | 1167 Magnolia Ave. (Estelle Ave.) | 415-461-6787 | www.table-cafe.com

A tempting daytime eatery tucked away in a Larkspur strip mall, this "little" Californian specializes in "creative" dosas, salads and chalkboard specials brimming with "top-quality", market-fresh and sustainable ingredients; there's only a handful of tables (inside and out), but dinners and housemade desserts are available for takeout.

Table 28 *Californian*
(fka Boonville Hotel)

| 23 | 20 | 22 | $48 |

Boonville | Boonville Hotel | 14050 Hwy. 128 (Lambert Ln.) | 707-895-2210 | www.boonvillehotel.com

It's "easy to miss" this recently reenvisioned "roadside cafe" set in an "old-school country inn" in Boonville, but it's a "relaxing" "place to grab dinner on the way up to Mendocino", particularly on the deck "when weather permits"; the "limited" Californian set dinners served family-style are "surprisingly fine" (though not for "picky eaters") and the Shaker dining room with "fireplace ablaze" books up with hotel guests, so be sure to call ahead; P.S. closed Tuesday–Wednesday, and hours change seasonally.

Tavern at Lark Creek *American*

| 19 | 23 | 20 | $39 |

Larkspur | 234 Magnolia Ave. (Madrone Ave.) | 415-924-7766 | www.tavernatlarkcreek.com

Thanks to a "simplified", "lower-priced" menu" that's "right for the times", this Marin "landmark" dishing up "delicious" New American fare in a "light, airy" Larkspur home (complete with a "blissful" creek-side patio) "continues to be a destination" for everyone from families to "city people" "escaping to the country"; if some nostalgists say it's "lost its character", more revel in the fact they can now drop in on a lark "instead of just for special occasions."

Tea Room Café ♥ *American*

▽ | 21 | 14 | 12 | $19 |

Petaluma | 316 Western Ave. (bet. Howard & Liberty Sts.) | 707-765-0199 | www.tearoomcafe.com

"What an eye-opener!" declare Petalumans who rise and shine at this "comfortable" daytime cafe steeped in "excellent coffees and teas", as well as "yummy breakfasts", "creative desserts" and "wonderful" lunch fare ("love the grilled shrimp sandwich"); the "annoying ordering system" and ensuing "fight for a table" can be a buzzkill, but sitting "outside in the sun" offers a "nice respite" nonetheless.

Terra *American*

| 26 | 24 | 24 | $72 |

St. Helena | 1345 Railroad Ave. (bet. Adams St. & Hunt Ave.) | 707-963-8931 | www.terrarestaurant.com

"After all these years", this St. Helena "celebratory destination" from chef-owners Hiro Sone and Lissa Doumani (SF's Ame) continues to "wow", from the "mind-blowing" "Asian spins" on New American cuisine and "knock-your-socks-off" desserts to the "sublime" wines, "outstanding service" and "romantic" setting in an "old stone house"; if some "foodies" fawn it's on par with the "great ones", there are differences: "you can actually get a reservation" here, and "prices are within reach of mere mortals."

Terrapin Creek Ⓜ *Californian*

▽ | 28 | 19 | 24 | $41 |

Bodega Bay | 1580 Eastshore Rd. (Hwy. 1) | 707-875-2700 | www.terrapincreekcafe.com

"Walk the beach, then hunker down and warm up" at this "cozy", under-the-radar Californian bistro "tucked off the main road", where the "adorable" chef-owners "vividly" blend "Asian influences" with "seasonal Sonoma County ingredients"; add in "friendly" service and a small patio with water views, and no wonder acolytes aver it's a "jewel" in the "overcrowded Bodega Bay corridor"; P.S. only open Thursday–Sunday.

NEW Tjukiji Sushi Ⓜ _Japanese_   - | - | - | M

Mill Valley | 24 Sunnyside Ave. (Parkwood St.) | 415-383-1382 | www.tsukijisushimv.com

In a converted Mill Valley bungalow (previously home to Ora), this casual Japanese is warmed up with two black brick fireplaces and twin sunrooms lined with picture windows, as well as outdoor patio seating; the menu delivers numerous small plates and a handful of entrees, plus standout sushi (much flown in from Tokyo's Tsukiji market) with a staggering number of rolls from longtime Sushi Ran chef Haruo Komatsu, who uses only top-tier Koshihikari rice.

Toast _American_   18 | 14 | 17 | $23

Mill Valley | 31 Sunnyside Ave. (bet. Blithedale & Miller Aves.) | 415-388-2500 | www.toastmillvalley.com
Novato | Hamilton Mktpl. | 5800 Nave Dr. (bet. N. Hamilton Pkwy. & Roblar Dr.) | 415-382-1144 | www.toastnovato.com

Though "breakfast is what they do best", the "food is more interesting than you'd expect" at these "jammed" Marin Americans offering "something for everyone", from "pancakes all day" for the kids to "reliable" lunch and dinner specials for mom and dad; choose between the "diner-like" Mill Valley original or its more modern "industrial" Novato outpost, which share "reasonable prices" and sometimes "spotty" service.

Tra Vigne _Italian_   24 | 24 | 23 | $58

St. Helena | 1050 Charter Oak Ave. (Main St.) | 707-963-4444 | www.travignerestaurant.com

St. Helena's "oldie but goodie" tucked "among the vines" off Highway 29 continues to deliver "crazy good" Northern Italian fare as "richly satisfying" as the "people-watching" in the "Tuscan dream"-like setting; "even with all the tourists", the "efficient" service and "festive atmosphere" in the bar or on the "romantic" courtyard "never get tiresome", while the "unmatched wine list" and "no-corkage-fee" policy (which helps with "expensive" tabs) make it the "perfect" spot to "pop a cork."

NEW Tyler Florence
Rotisserie & Wine _French_   - | - | - | M

Napa | Napa Riverfront | Main St. (3rd St.)

Another heavy-hitter slated to open mid-September in Downtown Napa's Riverfront, this forthcoming 120-seat, quick-service pit stop from celebrity chef Tyler Florence (also Wayfare Tavern) will offer wine country visitors a casual indoor/outdoor perch to sip local vintages and refuel on a daily selection of midpriced rotisserie meats and other local, seasonal American lunch and dinner fare; between meals, diners can pop into Florence's adjacent new kitchen store.

Ubuntu _Californian/Vegan_   26 | 22 | 23 | $54

Napa | 1140 Main St. (Pearl St.) | 707-251-5656 | www.ubuntunapa.com

The beet goes on at this Downtown Napa "treasure" where the "newly promoted chef" continues to create "complex" "seed-to-stalk" cuisine out of what "others send to the compost heap", complemented by "in-

credible biodynamic wines", "beautiful" stone surroundings and "enthusiastic" service; true, a "vegetarian restaurant with a yoga studio"
"upstairs" sounds "sooo California", but even "avid carnivores" who
go with an "open mind" and a big wallet can't help but "slow down and
just enjoy" the "good karma"; P.S. a recent chef change may not be
fully reflected in the Food score.

Ukiah Brewing Company & Restaurant Pub Food

▽ 16 | 14 | 17 | $26

Ukiah | 102 S. State St. (Perkins St.) | 707-468-5898 |
www.ukiahbrewingco.com

"Who ever heard of an organic pub?" ponder suds-seekers who hop-
pen upon this eco-conscious brewery sidekick that's "better than you
might expect for an old hippie hangout in Ukiah"; since the service and
"typical" bar chow are merely "ok", most stop in for the "good brews"
(a proprietary collection of ales and lagers) and to enjoy the historic
digs' "kick-ass atmosphere" and nightly live music.

Underwood Bar & Bistro Ⓜ Mediterranean

24 | 22 | 23 | $42

Graton | 9113 Graton Rd. (Edison St.) | 707-823-7023 |
www.underwoodgraton.com

Few outsiders "have discovered" this "upscale" bistro in "middle-of-
nowhere" Graton, but "open the door" and you "can't swing a dead cat
without hitting a winery insider" and other "West County residents"
who "spend hours sitting at the bar" or in the dark-wood dining room
downing "exceptional drinks" and "imaginative" Southern Med small
plates; it "over-delivers in every way" (from the "personable service"
to the patio and "bocce court"), and there's a bonus: the "noise comes
at no extra charge."

Uva Trattoria & Bar Italian

▽ 20 | 16 | 20 | $35

Napa | 1040 Clinton St. (bet. Brown & Main Sts.) | 707-255-6646 |
www.uvatrattoria.com

For "old-fashioned family and date-night Italian", this "quirky, popular"
Napa spot is a "bargain" – especially with "live jazz" Wednesday-
Sunday; while new owners leave some fretting that "the menu is similar
but not as good", loyal "locals" savor the wine selection, generous
BYO policy (no corkage on the first bottle) and "friendly" atmosphere.

Vin Antico Ⓜ Italian

▽ 19 | 21 | 21 | $38

San Rafael | 881 Fourth St. (bet. Cijos St. & Lootens Pl.) | 415-454-4492 |
www.vinantico.com

"Hipper than most venues in Marin", this "urban trattoria" brings a bit
of "chic to San Rafael", with its "warm" ambiance and bar where you
can "belly up" to "watch the chefs" in action; "efficient" servers ferry
the "limited" menu of "tasty" Italian eats (marred by "occasional
misses"), but the "tight quarters" mean you might learn more about
your neighbors "than you ever cared to"; P.S. a recent chef change may
not be fully reflected in the Food score.

Volpi's Ristorante & Bar Ⓜ Italian

▽ 18 | 15 | 20 | $29

Petaluma | 124 Washington St. (bet. Keokuk St. & Petaluma Blvd.) |
707-762-2371

A Petaluma "secret", this affordable family-run Italian has "been
around forever", with its "old-school checkered tablecloths, Chianti-

bottle candles and warped wooden floor"; the *piatti* are "classic, straight-ahead" and "extra-large", the staff "can handle everything from screaming children to folks who need 25 minutes to choose an entree" – and if you're lucky grandpa will be playing the accordion.

Water Street Bistro ⵚ *French*

▽ 24 | 16 | 17 | $28

Petaluma | 100 Petaluma Blvd. N. (Western Ave.) | 707-763-9563

If you can, "stop in on a sunny day" to enjoy the "great views" (from the "little tables" aside the Petaluma River) and "anything chocolate" at this "cozy", somewhat "funky" bistro; the "friendly" chef-owner turns out "amazing", "gourmet French" daytime fare at "coffee-shop prices", and if "awkward seating" vexes some, cognoscenti return regularly for the "exquisitely themed" monthly dinners.

Willi's Seafood & Raw Bar *Seafood*

24 | 20 | 22 | $45

Healdsburg | 403 Healdsburg Ave. (North St.) | 707-433-9191 | www.williseafood.net

The "beautifully presented" raw bar bites and tapas with a "seafood emphasis" are "beyond scrumptious" at this "hip, happening" haunt near Healdsburg Plaza, where you can "sit at the bar" and "slurp oysters" (along with "creative" cocktails and a "wide variety of wines by the glass") or "catch a table outside" to watch the "beautiful people" pass by; either way, the service is "pleasant", but the "little plates add up to a big bill if you're hungry."

Willi's Wine Bar *Eclectic*

25 | 19 | 23 | $47

Santa Rosa | Orchard Inn | 4404 Old Redwood Hwy. (Ursuline Rd.) | 707-526-3096 | www.williswinebar.net

"Come with several people" because you may be "tempted to sample" "more than you can eat" at this "wonderfully unexpected" Eclectic stop in an "out-of-the-way" stretch of Santa Rosa, serving up "inventive" tapas and a "fabulous" "changing wine list" featuring "lovely flights"; "helpful" service is a plus, though given how easy it is to "rack up" a high tab, it's "not the place to go if you're on a budget."

Willow Wood
Market Cafe *Eclectic/Mediterranean*

24 | 18 | 19 | $30

Graton | 9020 Graton Rd. (Edison St.) | 707-823-0233 | www.willowwoodgraton.com

West County "locals" "drink at Underwood", but for "scrumptious" Eclectic-Med meals, including the "best brunch" around, they hit its "properly funky" "casual little sister" cafe "across the street"; yup, you have to be looking for the "neat little town" of "Graton to find it", but it's "always packed" with "locals and tourists", all "mad" for the "sunny garden" and "adorable" general store upfront stocking vintage "childhood toys" and other gifts.

Wine Spectator Greystone *Californian*

24 | 24 | 22 | $59

St. Helena | Culinary Institute of America | 2555 Main St. (Deer Park Rd.) | 707-967-1010 | www.ciachef.edu

"Watch the professionals" and toques "in-training" preparing the day's "inventive", "well-executed" Cal-Eclectic dishes at this "spectacular" medieval-looking "old winery", a "show-off spot for out-of-towners" on the St. Helena campus of the CIA; "service is technically not run by students", though it sometimes "feels it", but "sharing bites

	FOOD	DECOR	SERVICE	COST

and sips of everything, including flights of wine", while sitting "on the terrace" overlooking the "lovely" valley more than compensates.

Yankee Pier   *New England/Seafood* | 18 | 16 | 18 | $35 |

Larkspur | 286 Magnolia Ave. (bet. King St. & William Ave.) | 415-924-7676 | www.yankeepier.com

"You can count on the American seafood classics" say contented cap'ns of this "kid-friendly" New England–style mini-chain where "tasteful nautical" decor (and "tables close enough to make you think you are in a ship's cabin") set the scene for "winning" lobster rolls and other "respectable" midpriced fare; still some miffed mateys maintain "Bradley Ogden missed the boat with this one", citing "inconsistent" service and "ordinary" grub.

Zazu   Ⓜ *American/Italian* | 25 | 18 | 23 | $51 |

Santa Rosa | 3535 Guerneville Rd. (Willowside Rd.) | 707-523-4814 | www.zazurestaurant.com

"Now you're talking" declare devotees of this "quirky" "roadhouse" "out in the sticks" of Santa Rosa, where a "super" couple keeps their New American–Northern Italian dishes "fresh" with produce picked from the "backyard garden"; "anything made with black pig" (a house specialty) "will not disappoint", but then again, all of the "imaginative", "ever-changing" offerings are "winners"; P.S. Pizza & Pinot nights featuring "local", "hard-to-get" wines provide a "welcome change of pace" from the "pricier" provender.

Zin   *American* | 23 | 18 | 22 | $40 |

Healdsburg | 344 Center St. (North St.) | 707-473-0946 | www.zinrestaurant.com

Wine country dining bares its "Southern side" at this Healdsburg New American where many of the "rustic, flavorful" dishes (like "addictive" "beer-battered green beans") come "fresh from the chef-owner's garden" and are enhanced by "excellent local" vintages – including "lots of Zins (big surprise)"; the "pleasant staff" and "relaxed" atmosphere make it a "perfect" place to "sit next to winemakers" and "take a break", and it's a "good deal" to boot.

Zinsvalley   *American* | 18 | 18 | 19 | $39 |

Napa | 1106 First St. (Main St.) | 707-224-0695 | www.zinsvalley.com

This local haunt has moved to "fancy new digs in Downtown Napa", but the "priced-right" New American "comfort food" has "moved uptown", with an "expanded menu" and bar bites served till midnight; a "helpful" staff adds to the "inviting" atmosphere, but a few "disappointed" diners dub the chow "nondescript" and say "the charm is now gone"; P.S. no corkage fee on the first two BYO bottles.

ZuZu   *Spanish* | 24 | 18 | 22 | $39 |

Napa | 829 Main St. (bet. 2nd & 3rd Sts.) | 707-224-8555 | www.zuzunapa.com

Even "Spain" might be "envious" of this Downtown Napa "local hangout" that "always pleases" with "fantastic tapas", a "well-paired wine selection" ("including sherries") that "won't set you back an arm and a leg" and a "staff that helps explain" it all; go "with a group" in order to "try everything", but hit it "early", as the candlelit room gets "jumping" (and "sardine-crowded") as the night wears on.

SOUTH OF SAN FRANCISCO

Top Food

28 Sierra Mar | *Cal./Eclectic*

27 Kaygetsu | *Japanese*
Marinus | *French*
Manresa | *American*
Cafe Gibraltar | *Med.*
Evvia | *Greek*

26 La Forêt | *Continental/French*
Le Papillon | *French*
Alexander's | *Japanese/Steak*
Village Pub | *American*

Nick's on Main | *American*

25 Dio Deka | *Greek*
Chantilly | *French/Italian*
Tamarine | *Vietnamese*
Aubergine | *Californian*
Pacific's Edge | *Amer./French*
Passionfish | *Cal./Seafood*
Sent Sovi | *Californian*
Anton & Michel | *Continenta*
Plumed Horse | *Californian*

BY CUISINE

AMERICAN

27 Manresa
26 Village Pub
Nick's on Main
25 Pacific's Edge
24 Navio

ASIAN

25 Tamarine
24 Flying Fish (Carmel)
21 Three Seasons
Xanh
20 Krung Thai

CALIFORNIAN

28 Sierra Mar
25 Sent Sovi
Plumed Horse
Flea St Café
24 John Bentley's

CHINESE

24 Tai Pan
23 Koi Palace
22 O'mei
21 Hunan Home/Garden
Chef Chu's

CONTINENTAL

26 La Forêt
25 Anton & Michel
24 Ecco▽
22 Bella Vista

FRENCH

27 Marinus
26 Le Papillon
25 Chantilly

Aubergine
24 Marché

INDIAN

24 Amber India
Shalimar
23 Sakoon
22 Mantra
Junnoon

ITALIAN

24 Donato Enoteca
23 Cantinetta Luca
Casanova
22 Pasta Moon
Mezza Luna/Caffè

JAPANESE

27 Kaygetsu
26 Alexander's Steak
24 Gochi
Jin Sho
23 Naomi Sushi

MED./GREEK

27 Cafe Gibraltar
Evvia
25 Dio Deka
22 Fandango
20 Cetrella

SEAFOOD

25 Passionfish
24 Flying Fish (Carmel)
23 Koi Palace
Flying Fish (Half Moon Bay)
21 Old Port Lobster

Excludes places with low votes, unless otherwise indicated

Menus, photos, voting and more – free at ZAGAT.com

BY SPECIAL FEATURE

BREAKFAST/BRUNCH

26 La Forêt
24 Navio
   Gayle's Bakery
23 Madera
   Koi Palace

OUTDOOR SEATING

28 Sierra Mar
25 Anton & Michel
   Roy's
19 Sam's Chowder Hse.
17 Nepenthe

PEOPLE-WATCHING

27 Evvia
26 Village Pub
25 Dio Deka
   Tamarine
20 Joya

ROMANCE

28 Sierra Mar
27 Marinus
26 La Forêt
25 Pacific's Edge
23 Casanova

SINGLES SCENES

24 Cin-Cin Wine Bar
22 Junnoon
21 Xanh
19 Sino
18 Red Lantern

SMALL PLATES

25 Tamarine
22 Junnoon
21 Three Seasons
20 Straits
19 Lavanda

TASTING MENUS

27 Kaygetsu
   Marinus
   Manresa
25 Aubergine
22 Chez TJ

WINNING WINE LISTS

28 Sierra Mar
27 Marinus
26 Village Pub
25 Passionfish
   Plumed Horse

BY LOCATION

CARMEL/MONTEREY

27 Marinus
25 Aubergine
   Pacific's Edge
   Anton & Michel
24 Flying Fish Grill

HALF MOON BAY/ COAST

27 Cafe Gibraltar
24 Navio
23 Flying Fish Grill
22 Pasta Moon
   Mezza Luna

PALO ALTO/MENLO PK

27 Kaygetsu
   Evvia
25 Tamarine
   Bistro Elan
   Flea St. Café

PENINSULA

26 Village Pub
25 Chantilly
24 John Bentley's
   Martins West
   Donato Enoteca

SANTA CRUZ/ CAPITOLA

24 Gayle's Bakery
22 O'mei
21 Gabriella Café
18 Shadowbrook
   Hula's

SILICON VALLEY

27 Manresa
26 La Forêt
   Le Papillon
   Alexander's Steak
   Nick's on Main

Top Decor

29 Sierra Mar	Aubergine
28 Pacific's Edge	Manresa
27 Navio	24 Alexander's Steak
Marinus	Chantilly
26 Roy's	Dio Deka
Nepenthe	Village Pub
25 Madera	Casanova
Anton & Michel	La Forêt
Shadowbrook*	Tai Pan
Plumed Horse	23 Sakoon

Top Service

27 Marinus	24 Navio
Sierra Mar	Bella Vista
Manresa	Sent Sovi
26 Kaygetsu	Passionfish
Le Papillon	Dio Deka
25 Aubergine	Plumed Horse*
La Forêt	Flea St. Café
Alexander's Steak	John Bentley's
Village Pub	Nick's on Main
Chantilly	Marché

Best Buys

In order of Bang for the Buck rating.

1. In-N-Out
2. Cheese Steak Shop
3. La Cumbre Taqueria
4. Pancho Villa
5. La Corneta
6. Burger Joint
7. Pluto's Fresh Food
8. BurgerMeister
9. Gayle's Bakery
10. Cool Café
11. Stacks
12. Udupi Palace
13. North Beach Pizza
14. Patxi's Pizza
15. Amici's Pizzeria
16. Flying Fish (Half Moon Bay)
17. Shalimar
18. Barbara's Fish Trap
19. Krung Thai
20. Pasta Pomodoro

OTHER GOOD VALUES

Amber India
Basque Cultural Ctr.
Big Sur Bakery
Café Brioche
Cannery Row Brewing
Cellar Door Café
Cool Café

Dishdash
Duarte's Tavern
Hotaru
Mundaka
Rist. Avanti
SliderBarCafe
Soif Wine Bar

* Indicates a tie with restaurant above

South of San Francisco

AcquaPazza Ristorante *Italian*   ▽ 21 | 17 | 22 | $41

San Mateo | 201 E. Third Ave. (bet. B St. & San Mateo Dr.) |
650-375-0903 | www.acqua-pazza.com

Perhaps it's "not haute Italian", but there are "some fine dishes" served
in a "lively" ambiance at this "reasonably priced", "excellent addition to
the San Mateo scene"; Positano ceramics enhance the simple space, and
the owners "could not make you feel more welcome", but call ahead for
the entertainment schedule if "loud dinner music" is not your thing.

Alexander's Steakhouse *Japanese/Steak*   26 | 24 | 25 | $83

Cupertino | Cupertino Sq. | 10330 N. Wolfe Rd. (bet. Rte. 280 &
Stevens Creek Blvd.) | 408-446-2222 | www.alexanderssteakhouse.com

This "swanky" "carnivore's castle" in Cupertino (with an SF branch in
the works) purveys "outstanding" "dry-aged" "steakhouse staples" as
well as "to-die-for Wagyu" among other "modern" Japanese fare; a
"mind-blowing" "wall of meat in the lobby" leads to a "stunning"
interior, and the "precisely choreographed" service "makes you feel
special, no matter what the occasion", so it lends itself to a "break-
the-bank" "splurge"; P.S. "homemade flavored cotton candy" delivered with the bill is a "sweet way to end the night."

☑ Amber India *Indian*   24 | 20 | 20 | $38

Mountain View | Olive Tree Shopping Ctr. | 2290 W. El Camino Real
(bet. Ortega & S. Rengstorff Aves.) | 650-968-7511
San Jose | 377 Santana Row (Olin Ave.) | 408-248-5400

☑ Amber Café *Indian*

Mountain View | 600 W. El Camino Real (View St.) | 650-968-1751
www.amber-india.com

"Everyone melts" for the "heavenly butter chicken" and other "alluring" Indian eats at this "refined" curry quartet, including the Mountain
View "original" in a "plain-Jane strip mall" and SoMa's "glam" branch
that's "beautiful enough for a business client"; "tops for taste and
value", the "bounteous" lunch buffet (not available at the cafe) is the
"best bet" for those who want to "try a little bit of everything."

Amici's East Coast Pizzeria *Pizza*   19 | 14 | 17 | $21

Cupertino | 10310 S. De Anza Blvd. (Rodrigues Ave.) |
408-252-3333
Mountain View | 790 Castro St. (Yosemite Ave.) | 650-961-6666
Redwood Shores | 226 Redwood Shores Pkwy. (Twin Dolphin Dr.) |
650-654-3333
San Jose | 225 W. Santa Clara St. (bet. N. Almaden Ave. & Notre Dame St.) |
408-289-9000
San Mateo | 69 Third Ave. (San Mateo Dr.) | 650-342-9392
www.amicis.com
See review in City of San Francisco Directory.

Anton & Michel Restaurant *Continental*   25 | 25 | 23 | $58

Carmel | Mission St. (bet. Ocean & 7th Aves.) | 831-624-2406 |
www.antonandmichel.com

"Sumptuous" Continental cuisine and "old-world" service (see the
"rack of lamb carved tableside") are signatures of this "high-priced"
"classic" in Carmel; its fireplaces and "beautiful courtyard with foun-

tains" ensure a "restful", "lovely-to-look-at" setting, so while those who dub it "stuffy" say it "needs a new look" and some "young blood", devoted diners declare "it doesn't get any better than this."

Aquarius *American*   ▽ 23 | 22 | 20 | $44

Santa Cruz | Santa Cruz Dream Inn | 175 W. Cliff Dr. (Bay St.) | 831-460-5012 | www.aquariussantacruz.com

The "setting alone", with a "terrific view of the pier" and the Pacific, makes this "beautiful" new beachside restaurant in Santa Cruz's renovated Dream Inn "worth visiting", but the "bright" New American menu also gets "points" for its "fresh", "sustainable" seafood matched by "interesting" regional wines; though the service impresses less, "what's not to like" about hanging ten in a "hip", "retro-modern" room replete with a "shimmering surfboard light arrangement"?

Arcadia *American*   21 | 20 | 19 | $61

San Jose | San Jose Marriott | 100 W. San Carlos St. (Market St.) | 408-278-4555 | www.michaelmina.net

"Über-rich comfort food for the über-rich" is "well worth the occasional splurge", even for less-flush fans who are sold on "special treats" like "lobster pot pie", as well as the "delicious" steaks, at Michael Mina's American outpost in the San Jose Marriott; still, what strikes some as "lovely mod decor" is "boring" to others, and the sometimes "aloof" service can be off-putting at a place "of this caliber."

NEW Attic ⌧Ⓜ *Asian*   - | - | - | M

San Mateo | 234 S. B St. (2nd Ave.) | 650-342-450 | www.atticrestaurant.com

At this funky-looking two-story newcomer in Downtown San Mateo, chef Tim Luymn (ex the shuttered Poleng Lounge) prepares his signature Pan-Asian street food and Filipino favorites, gussied-up with modern presentations and complemented by fanciful tropical cocktails; the upstairs dining room is tricked out with wooden lanterns, low-slung gong-topped tables and windows overlooking the street, while a small downstairs bar (dubbed Under the Attic) serves more Americanized drinks and happy-hour bites such as oysters and fish tacos.

Aubergine *Californian*   25 | 25 | 25 | $94

Carmel | L'Auberge Carmel | Monte Verde St. (7th Ave.) | 831-624-8578 | www.laubergecarmel.com

"Wonderful for a romantic dinner", this "tiny jewel box" at L'Auberge Carmel presents "exceptional", "memorable" Cal-French prix fixe meals paired with "incredible" wines; while some claim the "portions are startlingly small for the price" and detect a "pretentious" air, most are content to have a "small staff attending to your needs", adding to the "whole experience"; P.S. jacket suggested.

Barbara's Fish Trap ⇄ *Seafood*   20 | 13 | 17 | $24

Princeton by the Sea | 281 Capistrano Rd. (Hwy. 1) | 650-728-7049

Known for its "sea air" and "serious" fried seafood, plus "full-of-flavor" clam chowder, this "no-frills" nautical "shack" on the edge of Princeton's harbor has a "genuine" "New England" feel; it's "a bit pricey for what it is", but "exactly the spot you want" when "daytripping" on the coast, particularly if you "hit the speedy take-out window" and "relax on a bench" with a brew.

	FOOD	DECOR	SERVICE	COST

Basin, The *American* · 21 | 19 | 21 | $48

Saratoga | 14572 Big Basin Way (5th St.) | 408-867-1906 |
www.thebasin.com

A "local" "favorite", this Saratoga supper club is "perfect" for "date night" or "even just to sit at the bar" (or under the old oak trees in summer) to enjoy martinis and apps; the "upscale", "seasonally changing" New American dinners (with Spanish and Italian influences) are "by no means exceptional", but thanks to a "quaint" atmosphere and an owner who "treats all his guests like family", it adds up to a "nice evening."

Basque Cultural Center ⓜ *French* · 21 | 13 | 20 | $31

South San Francisco | Basque Cultural Ctr. | 599 Railroad Ave. (bet. Orange & Spruce Aves.) | 650-583-8091 | www.basqueculturalcenter.com

"Culinary adventurers" and "friendly folks who have been here for decades" hit this "community" "banquet hall" in South City for "plentiful", "flavorful" French Basque food and wine at "shockingly low prices"; the setting and service are definitely "kicking it old-school", but where else can you "watch *pilota*" or have a group of "gray-haired" "guys at the next table singing songs" "invite you for an after-dinner drink"?

NEW Baumé ⓜ *French* · ▽ 28 | 28 | 28 | $129

Palo Alto | 201 S. California Ave. (Park Ave.) | 650-328-8899 |
www.baumerestaurant.com

"Palo Alto now has its destination restaurant" declare diners who have sampled this molecular-gastronomy-geared newcomer (named after an 18th-century chemist), providing "phenomenal" French prix fixes prepared by chef Bruno Chemel (ex Chez TJ), along with "amazing" service in a pared-down setting brightened by citrus-orange walls; it's an "intellectual food experience" that's not to be missed "if you can afford it", though a few find themselves "laughing" about "vanishingly small" portions – that is, until "the bill comes."

Bella Vista 🅂ⓜ *Continental* · 22 | 23 | 24 | $57

Woodside | 13451 Skyline Blvd. (5 mi. south of Rte. 92) | 650-851-1229 |
www.bvrestaurant.com

"Stunning views" are the "star" at this "romantic" Woodside "hideaway" that "takes you back to another age in dining", bolstered by "elegant" Continental dishes – such as steak Diane flambéed "tableside" by tuxedoed "pros" – that "win supporting-cast awards"; true, it's a helluva "drive up the mountain" and some feel the cooking "doesn't match the cost", but "grab a window table on a clear night and you'll be in heaven."

Benihana *Japanese* · 17 | 16 | 19 | $40

Burlingame | 1496 Old Bayshore Hwy. (Mahler Rd.) | 650-342-5202
Cupertino | Cupertino Sq. | 2074 Vallco Fashion Park (Vallco Pkwy.) |
408-253-1221
www.benihana.com

See review in City of San Francisco Directory.

Big Sur Bakery & Restaurant *American/Bakery* · 21 | 16 | 18 | $35

Big Sur | Hwy. 1 (½ mi. south of Pfeiffer State Pk.) | 831-667-0520 |
www.bigsurbakery.com

Fulfilling "high expectations", this "out-in-nature" roadside bakery by "SoCal transplants" is a "delightful stopping place" in Big Sur for "exceptional" baked goods and "steaming cups of coffee", as well as "fabulous" wood-fired pizzas and other "lovingly prepared", affordable American dishes for lunch, dinner and brunch; sit-down customers can savor the grub inside the funky "old wooden" ranch house or out on the "sunny deck"; P.S. only the bakery is open Mondays.

Bistro Elan 🗷Ⓜ *Californian/French*   25 | 18 | 22 | $50

Palo Alto | 448 S. California Ave. (bet. Birch St. & El Camino Real) | 650-327-0284 | www.bistroelan.com

This "perennial favorite" for "special occasions" and "business lunches" in Palo Alto "carefully crafts" "produce fresh from the farmer's market" into Cal-French bistro fare "extraordinaire", served in an "urbane" atmosphere; though the "sophisticated" staff strikes some as "snobby", and others pout the "petite" dining room feels "cramped", pleased patrons find a piece of "Provence" on the "sun-dappled patio."

Bistro Moulin 🗷 *French*   ▽ 29 | 21 | 25 | $48

Monterey | 867 Wave St. (bet. David & Irving Aves.) | 831-333-1200 | www.bistromoulin.com

Though it's "stumbling distance from Cannery Row" and the Monterey Bay Aquarium, you'll find "all locals dining" at this "fab" French bistro considered the "best bet in the area" to "meet friends" and break bread over "authentic" dishes and "excellent" wines; the "tiny", "romantic" setting is run by a "caring" couple, who also oversee the attached gourmet shop; P.S. lunch served Wednesday-Saturday.

Bistro Vida *French*   19 | 19 | 19 | $36

Menlo Park | 641 Santa Cruz Ave. (bet. Curtis St. & El Camino Real) | 650-462-1686 | www.bistrovidamp.com

A "few high spots" of "tasty bistro fare" stand out at this "cute", "French-ish" Menlo Park "sleeper", which has been known to induce a "happy food coma" "without breaking the bank"; still, the "inconsistent kitchen screams 'stick to the basics'", and "uneven" service also merits a *comme ci, comme ça*, as some praise the "personal" attention, while others find the "Parisian"-style staff "a bit rude."

Blowfish Sushi To Die For *Japanese*   21 | 20 | 18 | $44

San Jose | 335 Santana Row (bet. Moorpark Ave. & Stevens Creek Blvd.) | 408-345-3848 | www.blowfishsushi.com

See review in City of San Francisco Directory.

Buca di Beppo *Italian*   15 | 16 | 17 | $28

Campbell | Pruneyard Shopping Ctr. | 1875 S. Bascom Ave. (Campbell Ave.) | 408-377-7722
Palo Alto | 643 Emerson St. (bet. Forest & Hamilton Aves.) | 650-329-0665
San Jose | Oakridge Mall | 925 Blossom Hill Rd. (bet. Santa Teresa & Winfield Blvds.) | 408-226-1444
www.bucadibeppo.com

See review in City of San Francisco Directory.

Burger Joint *Burgers*   18 | 12 | 15 | $14

Burlingame | 1401 Burlingame Ave. (Primrose Rd.) | 650-558-9232
South San Francisco | San Francisco Int'l Airport | Int'l Terminal, Boarding Area A (Hwy. 101) | 650-821-0582
www.burgerjointsf.com

See review in City of San Francisco Directory.

	FOOD	DECOR	SERVICE	COST

BurgerMeister *Burgers*

| 20 | 12 | 16 | $16 |

Daly City | 507 Westlake Ctr. (John Daly Blvd.) | 650-755-1941 |
www.burgermeistersf.com

See review in City of San Francisco Directory.

Café Brioche *Californian/French*

| 21 | 17 | 18 | $34 |

Palo Alto | 445 S. California Ave. (bet. Ash St. & El Camino Real) |
650-326-8640 | www.cafebriochepaloalto.com

It's "nothing too fancy", but this "charming" Cal-Provençal bistro in
Palo Alto is a "relative bargain" for "savory" "French classics" delivered
with "cheerful service"; just "get there early" – especially for the "wonderful" weekend brunch – because it's "very small" and "often crowded"
with "lots of regulars"; P.S. "reservations recommended" for dinner.

☑ Cafe Gibraltar Ⓜ *Mediterranean*

| 27 | 21 | 23 | $43 |

El Granada | 425 Avenue Alhambra (Palma St.) | 650-560-9039 |
www.cafegibraltar.com

At this "oasis on the coast" in "unlikely" El Granada you can sit "cross-
legged" at "popular tent tables" and sample the "extraordinary assortment" of wood-fired meze, "locally grown" veggies and "fragrant
vegan soups" that reveals the "entire sweep" of the Mediterranean;
service isn't always "up to par" with the "memorable" meals, but Moor
important, the "good-value wines" and prix fixes "won't force you into
a second mortgage."

Café Rustica Ⓜ *Californian*

| 23 | 21 | 19 | $38 |

Carmel Valley | 10 Del Fino Pl. (Carmel Valley Rd.) | 831-659-4444 |
www.caferusticacarmelvalley.com

"Tucked away in Carmel Valley", this "welcoming", "casual" "favorite"
draws in "repeat" guests with "lovely" surroundings that offer a view
of "the hills" and "fresh", "well-prepared" Californian cuisine, including "paper-thin"-crust pizzas and "generous salads" at a "reasonable
price"; since it tends to get "busy", just "make reservations" and ask
for a table on the "charming garden patio."

Calafia *Californian*

| 19 | 17 | 19 | $29 |

Palo Alto | Town & Country Vill. | 855 El Camino Real (Embarcadero Rd.) |
650-322-9200 | www.calafiapaloalto.com

To call the Cal cuisine of "ex-Google chef" Charlie Ayers "eclectic" would
be "an understatement", but the "quirky" dishes that "tease the flavor
out of each element" appeal to adventurous Palo Altans seeking "organic", "healthy" choices for a "relatively decent price"; it's "popular" for
breakfast and lunch, but some prefer picking up "pre-made meals" and
skipping the "loud", "bunker"-like dining room.

**ⓃⒺⓌ Cannery Row
Brewing Company** *American*

| - | - | - | M |

Monterey | 95 Prescott Ave. (Wave St.) | 831-643-2722 |
www.canneryrowbrewingcompany.com

On the historic Downtown Monterey strip that inspired John Steinbeck's
novel, this sprawling, casual all-day hang, with fire pits warming up
the patio, serves an approachable selection of midpriced American
eats by chef Mark Ayers (ex Pacific's Edge); open late on the weekends, the bar pours over 70 beers on tap, though despite its moniker,
none are crafted on-site.

	FOOD	DECOR	SERVICE	COST

Cantinetta Luca *Italian* — 23 | 22 | 21 | $49

Carmel | Dolores St. (bet. Ocean & 7th Aves.) | 831-625-6500 |
www.cantinettaluca.com

"*The* place to go" deep "in the heart of Carmel", this "swell" looker
"captures the essence" of a true "Italian cantinetta" concur regulars who
wedge into the "always crowded" rustic room or belly up to the bar for
"great wines by the glass"; the "spendy" but "smokin'" salumi, cheese
platters, pizza, "you name it" are all worth "swooning over" – so just
"take a megaphone" if you want conversation.

Casanova *French/Italian* — 23 | 24 | 22 | $55

Carmel | Fifth Ave. (bet. Mission & San Carlos Sts.) | 831-625-0501 |
www.casanovarestaurant.com

"Take your wife, and make her into your girlfriend" at this "romantic"
"little cottage" serving "Old World" Northern Italian–French "comfort
food" in "copper pans" that perfectly "captures the Carmel charm";
underscoring its "transporting" allure: a "dog-friendly" "covered outdoor" patio with a "tree growing in the middle" and an "unbelievable
wine cellar with bottles stashed in every cubbyhole"; P.S. "lunch is a
better value, and easier to get seated for", than the "pricey" dinner.

Cascal *Pan-Latin* — 19 | 20 | 18 | $39

Mountain View | 400 Castro St. (California St.) | 650-940-9500 |
www.cascalrestaurant.com

"Your tongue gets a holiday" to "exotic ports of call" at this "hopping"
place for Pan-Latin fare, where Mountain View groups "graze" on "tapas
galore" and "fantastic drinks" to the tune of "live music on the weekends"; the "wonderful outdoor patio" is "always in high demand" on
"balmy summer evenings", and the staff "keeps up the festive feeling",
but the "deafening" noise indoors defeats those who didn't "bring Dixie
cups on a string", and the frugal fuss it "sure does get expensive quickly."

Cellar Door Café Ⓜ *Californian* — ▽ 22 | 22 | 20 | $41

Santa Cruz | Bonny Doon Winery | 329 Ingalls St. (bet. Fair Ave. &
Swift St.) | 831-425-6771 | www.bonnydoonvineyard.com

Revealing "winemaker Randall Grahm's wacky whimsy" this "welcome
addition to Santa Cruz", "connected to the Bonny Doon" Vineyard
tasting room, is kinda "quirky", "just like the man", with a wood-
planked, "lofty" look and communal tables; executive chef "Charlie
Parker of Manresa fame" "has it going on", serving "clean, green and
sourced-to-a-T" Californian dishes (with "affordable" nightly prix fixe
options), all best paired with a "bottle or two" of those "eclectic but
terrific" biodynamic wines; P.S. open for dinner Wednesday–Sunday,
with lunch on the weekends.

Cetrella Ⓜ *Mediterranean* — 20 | 21 | 19 | $49

Half Moon Bay | 845 Main St. (Monte Vista Ln.) | 650-726-4090 |
www.cetrella.com

A "romantic destination after a sunset beach walk", this "oasis in the
middle of Half Moon Bay" brings a "French sensibility" to its "flavorful"
Mediterranean dinners and whips up a "marvelous" Sunday brunch to
boot; the "cozy stone fireplace" and "terrific jazz" (Thursday–Saturday)
add to the ambiance, though some feel both the food and service are
too "uneven" for the price.

	FOOD	DECOR	SERVICE	COST

Chantilly 🖼 *French/Italian*
25 | 24 | 25 | $63

Redwood City | 3001 El Camino Real (Selby Ln.) | 650-321-4080 | www.chantillyrestaurant.com

"Old-style dining elegance" is "defined" at this French–Northern Italian "classic" in Redwood City, providing "outstanding" if "traditional" dishes and a "great wine list", with "impeccable" service by a seasoned staff; the "quiet, formal" dining room and "very expensive" menu may deter some, but it's still a prime place to "bring your parents or grandparents" for a "special occasion."

Cheesecake Factory *American*
16 | 17 | 17 | $29

Palo Alto | 375 University Ave. (bet. Florence & Waverly St.) | 650-473-9622
San Jose | 925 Blossom Hill Rd. (bet. Santa Teresa & Winfield Blvds.) | 408-225-6948
Santa Clara | Westfield Shoppingtown Valley Fair | 3041 Stevens Creek Blvd. (N. Winchester Blvd.) | 408-246-0092
www.thecheesecakefactory.com
See review in City of San Francisco Directory.

Cheese Steak Shop *Cheesesteaks*
21 | 8 | 16 | $12

San Jose | Monterey Plaza | 5524 Monterey Rd. (Blossom Hill Rd.) | 408-972-0271
Sunnyvale | 832 W. El Camino Real (Hollenbeck Ave.) | 408-530-8159
www.cheesesteakshop.com
See review in City of San Francisco Directory.

Chef Chu's *Chinese*
21 | 16 | 19 | $28

Los Altos | 1067 N. San Antonio Rd. (El Camino Real) | 650-948-2696 | www.chefchu.com

An "institution" since 1970, this Sino standby in Los Altos is "still going strong" under famed "founder-owner" Larry Chu and son, who "warmly welcome" guests to the "always-crowded" dining room; the sociable suggest "taking a group" and "spinning the lazy Susans" for a sampling of "excellent" Mandarin dishes prepared with "high-quality" ingredients, but a minority maintains it's largely "unremarkable", "Americanized" chow – like the kind "you grew up with in the Midwest."

Chez Shea *Eclectic*
∇ 23 | 13 | 15 | $25

Half Moon Bay | 408 Main St. (Mill St.) | 650-560-9234 | www.chez-shea.com

"Satisfy the palate" at Cafe Gibraltar's "far more casual" semi-self-serve "little sister" cafe in Downtown Half Moon Bay suggest "locals" who rave about the "amazing prices" and "phenomenal" "tastes they get out of one kitchen" – Eclectic comfort food and tapas from the "Mediterranean, Mexico" (and beyond) "with more umami than you would believe"; the "back patio is great on a sunny day" – though "the wait after you order is another story."

Chez TJ 🖼 Ⓜ *French*
22 | 18 | 20 | $112

Mountain View | 938 Villa St. (bet. Castro St. & Shoreline Blvd.) | 650-964-7466 | www.cheztj.com

Now at the helm of this Mountain View "treat for grown-ups" that's "been around forever", French Laundry alum Scott Nishiyama "does his alma mater proud", presenting "whimsical platings" of "killer" prix fixe New French fare coupled with "inventive wine pairings"; still, some complain the dishes are "too edgy" , too "tiny" or just "not spectacular", also decrying the "wildly out-of-date" Victorian digs and a staff that's "not as polished" as the "heavy price tag" deserves.

Cin-Cin Wine Bar & Restaurant 🅂 *Eclectic*   24 | 21 | 22 | $43

Los Gatos | 368 Village Ln. (Saratoga Los Gatos Rd.) | 408-354-8006 | www.cincinwinebar.com

Attracting South Bay "thirtysomethings", this "high-energy" Cascal sib in Los Gatos offers a global array of "scrumptious small plates" and an "extensive but not overwhelming" selection of wines (by the glass, bottle and flight), served by a "knowledgeable" staff; though a few pout it's "pricey", the happy-hour menu is an affordable way to sample "remarkable" vintages or kick off a meal before the "loud" dinner rush; P.S. the "backless chairs" at some tables aren't for everyone.

Club XIX 🅂 🅜 *Californian/French*   ▽ 22 | 26 | 26 | $73

Pebble Beach | The Lodge at Pebble Beach | 1700 17 Mile Dr. (Cypress Dr.) | 831-625-8519 | www.pebblebeach.com

Link lovers time tee-off to end their round with "drinks on the patio" and "watch the sun go down" over the "world-famous golf course" at this clubby Pebble Beach hideaway where "money, money, money" buys you a "lovely" Cal-French dinner, a "marvelous view" and "outstanding service"; if a few quibble that it's "deadly quiet", for most it's a "special-occasion" score – the exhaustive wine list alone is worth the "17 Mile Drive fee"; P.S. jacket suggested.

Cool Café *Californian*   20 | 16 | 13 | $18

Menlo Park | 1525 O'Brien Dr. (University Ave.) | 650-325-3665 🅂
Palo Alto | Stanford Univ. Cantor Arts Ctr. | 128 Lomita Dr. (Museum Way) | 650-725-4758 🅜
www.cooleatz.com

"What's better" on a "sunny day" – or Thursday night – than perusing the "gorgeous" "Rodin sculpture garden" while enjoying the "always locally sourced", "satisfying" organic Californian sandwiches and salads by chef-owner Jesse Cool (Flea St. Cafe) at this Cantor Arts Center eatery with an "upscale Stanford vibe"; though it's "not a destination" ("lunchtime lines" feel like a "dorm cafeteria"), the "bucolic" campus makes for a "lovely experience"; P.S. the Menlo Park branch serves weekday lunch only.

Crouching Tiger *Chinese*   ▽ 21 | 18 | 18 | $22

Redwood City | 2644 Broadway St. (El Camino Real) | 650-298-8881 | www.crouchingtigerrestaurant.com

No hidden dragons here, just a "vast range" of "Chinese regional cuisine" at this "creative" Redwood City "oasis", bolstered by "fresh, contemporary" decor and "warm" service; some say "stick to the Sichuan dishes" and avoid the more "Americanized" options, but otherwise the "only dilemma" is whether to "take out or eat in."

Dasaprakash *Indian*   ▽ 21 | 19 | 20 | $20

Santa Clara | 2636 Homestead Rd. (bet. Kiely Blvd. & San Tomas Expwy.) | 408-246-8292 | www.dasaprakash.com

"When you taste this stuff" – "authentic" South Indian eats with "loads of spices" – you'll see "why Columbus was sailing to India" declare "masala dosa" devotees; even though it's "in an old strip-mall" in Santa Clara, it's a "surprising delight" with a "comfortable" "open"

FOOD | DECOR | SERVICE | COST

dining room whose "cool" ambiance and "friendly" service make it "perfect for a date."

Davenport Roadhouse Restaurant & Inn ⓜ *Californian/Coffeehouse*

▽ 19 | 19 | 18 | $32

Davenport | 1 Davenport Ave. (Hwy. 1) | 831-426-8801 | www.davenportroadhouse.com

This "charming" roadhouse "right on Highway 1" in "tiny seaside Davenport" ("with whale-watching just feet away") is a prime "place to stop between San Francisco and Santa Cruz" for "better-than-it-should-be" Californian fare (including "solid b'fast"), followed by a "stroll on the beach"; a "magnificent stone fireplace" and "live music" on Tuesdays and Saturdays beckon on "foggy coastal" evenings.

Deetjen's Big Sur Restaurant *Californian*

23 | 23 | 22 | $43

Big Sur | Deetjen's Big Sur Inn | 48865 Hwy. 1 (30 mi. south of Carmel) | 831-667-2378 | www.deetjens.com

"Big Sur to a T", this "one-of-a-kind" "bohemian" boîte on PCH is a "funky favorite" for "breakfast in the redwoods in sight of the ocean" or "terrific" Californian dinners paired with fine wines; the "hippie romantic ambiance" of the "driftwood palace" surroundings will "take you back to the days of Miller and Kerouac", and though it's "not for fussy status seekers", it displays an "attention to quality missing at comparably priced places in the area"; P.S. no lunch.

Dio Deka *Greek*

25 | 24 | 24 | $60

Los Gatos | Hotel Los Gatos | 210 E. Main St. (High School Ct.) | 408-354-7700 | www.diodeka.com

Bring your big fat wallet to this transporting "high-end" estiatorio that feels more "like a swanky restaurant on Santorini" than a Los Gatos hotel hang; the "exceptional nouveau Hellenic"-Med cuisine, enhanced by a "dynamic" vibe and owners who treat you "like family", works for "small plates" in the "beautiful-people lounge", "business dinners or a night on the town", though the whole package is a touch too "flashy" for some.

Dishdash ⓩ *Mideastern*

22 | 15 | 18 | $27

Sunnyvale | 190 S. Murphy Ave. (Washington Ave.) | 408-774-1889 | www.dishdash.net

With a menu that "extends well beyond falafel and hummus", this affordable Sunnyvaler serves "generous" plates of "amazing" Middle Eastern food, including the "can't-be-beat" *mansaf* (stewed lamb with yogurt) as well as "interesting" veggie options; service can be "harried", especially during "weekday lunches", when it's "packed" with Silicon Valley "engineers", so "go early or late to beat the rush."

Donato Enoteca *Italian*

24 | 21 | 21 | $43

Redwood City | 1041 Middlefield Rd. (bet. Jefferson Ave. & Main St.) | 650-701-1000 | www.donatoenoteca.com

"Donato can cook" cry fans of the "bold" chef's new "true trattoria" ("without the stereotypical boring" choices) in Downtown Redwood City that's an "oasis" for Northern Italian food on the Peninsula; whether "sitting at the bar" or chef's counter, luxuriating in the "white-tablecloth ambiance" of the back dining room, or relaxing "outside on a warm night", diners are rewarded by the "same super", "fairly priced" cuisine, "attentive" service and "unique" vino selection, available "by the glass, carafe or bottle."

Don Pico's Original Mexican Bistro ⌧Ⓜ Mexican

| 21 | 13 | 18 | $26 |

San Bruno | 461 El Camino Real (Jenevein Ave.) | 650-589-1163 | www.donpicosbistro.com

"Big platters" with "lots of seafood", plus "excellent margaritas", add up to a "pleasant surprise" at this San Bruno "neighborhood joint" whose grub is "not the cheapest Mex around, but certainly among the best"; while the surroundings fall a bit short, frequent "live music", "interesting artwork" and a "schmoozing" staff all add to the "lively environment."

Duarte's Tavern American

| 21 | 13 | 18 | $30 |

Pescadero | 202 Stage Rd. (Pescadero Creek Rd.) | 650-879-0464 | www.duartestavern.com

"Daytrippers" are delighted to "find a golden nugget" like this "funky" "over-100-year-old" roadhouse in the "one-streetlight town" of Pescadero, joining "Santa Cruz surfers" and a "cast of characters" in the "Western bar" for a "pint", as well as "legendary" artichoke soup, cioppino and "simple, time-tested" American eats; "trendy" it ain't, but the olallieberry pie is "out of this world", and both the "history" and "the 'hon' from the longtime waitresses" bring back a "bygone era."

Duck Club, The American

| 21 | 22 | 22 | $51 |

Menlo Park | Stanford Park Hotel | 100 El Camino Real (Sand Hill Rd.) | 650-330-2790 | www.stanfordparkhotel.com

Duck Club Grill American

Monterey | Monterey Plaza Hotel & Spa | 400 Cannery Row (Wave St.) | 831-646-1700 | www.woodsidehotels.com

Diners who duck into these "upscale" hotel restaurants discover "elegant" settings for "reliable" New American cuisine, including, of course, "well-prepared" versions of the namesake bird; "quiet" rooms tended by servers who are "efficient without being overbearing" are conducive to "important" conversations, but they're "nothing to rave about" quack some critics, who find the surroundings "stuffy" and the food "acceptable but not exciting"; P.S. the Monterey and Bodega Bay locations benefit from "dreamy" waterfront views.

E&O Trading Company Asian

| 19 | 21 | 19 | $38 |

San Jose | 96 S. First St. (San Fernando St.) | 408-938-4100 | www.eotrading.com

See review in City of San Francisco Directory.

Ebisu Japanese

| 23 | 17 | 19 | $37 |

South San Francisco | San Francisco Int'l Airport | Int'l Terminal, Main Hall, N. Food Court (Hwy. 101) | 650-588-2549 | www.ebisusushi.com

See review in City of San Francisco Directory.

Ecco Restaurant ⌧ Californian/Continental

▽ 24 | 22 | 26 | $49 |

Burlingame | 322 Lorton Ave. (bet. Burlingame & Donnelly Aves.) | 650-342-7355 | www.eccorestaurant.com

"If you haven't tried it yet, you don't know what you're missing" argue advocates of this Burlingame "gem" boasting "top-flight" (and somewhat "pricey") Continental-Californian cuisine with "fantastic daily specials"; "excellent" servers provide apt "suggestions for wine pairings", and since the setting is quite "pleasant", most maintain they "will definitely return."

Espetus Churrascaria *Brazilian*

23 | 19 | 22 | $56

San Mateo | 710 S. B St. (bet. 7th & 8th Aves.) | 650-342-8700 | www.espetus.com
See review in City of San Francisco Directory.

☑ Evvia *Greek*

27 | 23 | 23 | $52

Palo Alto | 420 Emerson St. (bet. Lytton & University Aves.) | 650-326-0983 | www.evvia.net
"Absolutely first-rate Greek food", like grilled fish that's "pure bliss" and lamb chops that claim a "cult following", is served amid a "beautiful", "rustic" interior that transports you to a "warm summer evening on the Mediterranean coast" at this Palo Alto sister of SF's Kokkari; though the owners are "not shy about prices", it remains "packed", since their "professional, personable" staff ensures a "welcoming" atmosphere.

Fandango *Mediterranean*

22 | 21 | 21 | $46

Pacific Grove | 223 17th St. (bet. Laurel & Lighthouse Aves.) | 831-372-3456 | www.fandangorestaurant.com
"Treat time!" chorus acolytes who dance over to this Pacific Grove "favorite" for a "special European-flavored experience" replete with "mouthwatering", "Old World" Med standards like osso buco and paella, an "atmospheric" French country "homelike setting" and "charming" service; if a handful shrug "the menu is tired", "longtime guests" counter with the koan "sometimes the best surprise is no surprise."

Fishwife at Asilomar Beach *Californian/Seafood*

21 | 15 | 19 | $30

Pacific Grove | 1996½ Sunset Dr. (Asilomar Ave.) | 831-375-7107 | www.fishwife.com
"It doesn't look like much on the outside", but this "friendly fish house" "a stone's throw" from "beautiful Asilomar Beach" is an "untouristy favorite of locals", prized for its "sensibly priced", "simple, substantial and super-fresh seafood" with a Caribbean "bent"; while "it's more like home cooking than gourmet cuisine" and the decor's "colorful", not "high class", "you can be better fed here" than at Pacific Grove's "more pricey places."

Flea St. Café ☑ *American*

25 | 20 | 24 | $54

Menlo Park | 3607 Alameda de las Pulgas (Avy Ave.) | 650-854-1226 | www.cooleatz.com
Jesse Ziff Cool is "Menlo Park's Alice Waters", and her "original", "elegant" yet "cozy" "enviro-friendly" "gem" with a "small but inviting" bar "remains a Peninsula powerhouse" where she and staffers "lovingly" deliver "deftly prepared" "organic Cal-American cuisine at its best"; "food is the star here" – indeed, her "devotion" to the "locavore movement" "goes to extremes", down to the "great collection" of sustainable wines and beer – and "you'll pay plenty for" it, but what a "fantastic foodie experience."

Flying Fish Grill *Californian/Seafood*

24 | 19 | 22 | $46

Carmel | Carmel Plaza | Mission St. (bet. Ocean & 7th Aves.) | 831-625-1962
"Delicate, savory" seafood (and "excellent" beef shabu-shabu) draws diners "down the stairs" to this little "subterranean" "jewel" with a

"Japanese country inn" feel in Carmel Plaza; the "heavenly" Cal-Asian fusion "combinations" just might trump the nearby "aquarium as the reason to see the area", and it's a "nice break from all the European" and "touristy" places, plus the "warm feeling from the genial hosts" is "just as it should be."

Flying Fish Grill *Californian/Seafood*   23 | 12 | 18 | $22

Half Moon Bay | 99 San Mateo Rd. (bet. Cabrillo Hwy. & Main St.) | 650-712-1125 | www.flyingfishgrill.net

"Bet you can't eat just one" "legendary", "fresh-from-the-boat fish taco" bait believers who also get their fill of "crabby cheesy bread" and other Californian seafood specialties at this "funky" "roadside dive" in Half Moon Bay that feels "like some beach shack in the tropics"; it's "worth a stop if you're going up (or down) Highway 1" and will leave you with "enough" dough to "buy gas to get home."

Forbes Mill Steakhouse *Steak*   22 | 20 | 21 | $59

Los Gatos | 206 N. Santa Cruz Ave. (Royce St.) | 408-395-6434 | www.forbesmillsteakhouse.com

These "classic" steakhouses in Danville and Los Gatos are prime places "for a celebration" or "dad's night out" according to acolytes who praise the "delicious" cuts and "smooth martinis"; with a "lively" setting and solid service, they offer a welcome "alternative" to better-known temples to beef, though less-impressed eaters rate them "run-of-the-mill" and "not good enough to justify the price."

Fuki Sushi *Japanese*   22 | 19 | 20 | $46

Palo Alto | 4119 El Camino Real (bet. Arastradero & Page Mill Rds.) | 650-494-9383 | www.fukisushi.com

"Carefully created", "artfully presented" sushi and "thick cuts of sashimi" are the stars at this "traditional", "exceedingly dependable" Palo Alto mainstay where the "high-quality" fish is "expensive but worth it"; the "authentic" Japanese setting, complete with "tatami rooms" tended by servers clad in "beautiful" kimonos, strikes a few as "nearly kitschy", but most find it "relaxing" and "elegant."

Gabriella Café *Californian/Italian*   21 | 18 | 19 | $43

Santa Cruz | 910 Cedar St. (bet. Church & Locust Sts.) | 831-457-1677

Offering "excellent quality for the price", this long-running locavore in Santa Cruz still "dazzles" with "adventurous" Cal-Italian dishes that "vary with the season", accompanied by "interesting wines by the glass"; "attentive" service and "sweet" decor set the stage for a "quiet" "romantic" dinner (or "fabulous" brunch), though some say the "beyond-intimate" setting "occasionally verges on cramped."

Gayle's Bakery & Rosticceria *Bakery*   24 | 13 | 17 | $19

Capitola | Upper Capitola Shopping Ctr. | 504 Bay Ave. (Capitola Ave.) | 831-462-1200 | www.gaylesbakery.com

"Leave your diet at the door" of this "no-nonsense" Capitola bakery known for its "awesome" "pastries, cakes and confections" that's a "must-stop" "between SF and Monterey", be it for "breakfast croissants, delicious sandwiches on homemade bread" or "terrific" blue-plate dinners; the "crowds and the price are deep", but the "new enclosed patio is a plus" and the "inspired" "picnic fixin's" suit a "day at the beach."

SOUTH OF SAN FRANCISCO

	FOOD	DECOR	SERVICE	COST

Gochi Japanese Fusion Tapas ⓈJapanese `24` `17` `17` `$43`
Cupertino | 19980 Homestead Rd. (bet. Blarney & Heron Aves.) |
408-725-0542 | www.gochifusiontapas.com

"A menu full of surprises and international influences" makes it easy
to "over-order" at this "cool" "little izakaya" in Cupertino purveying
"marvelous, unusual" Tokyo-style tapas designed to go down easily
with beer or soju cocktails; the service "varies", but menus in two lan-
guages and the option of "taking your shoes off" add to the "authentic" feel, and lunchtime offers some delicious "deals."

Gordon Biersch *Pub Food* `15` `16` `16` `$29`
Palo Alto | 640 Emerson St. (bet. Forest & Hamilton Aves.) | 650-323-7723
San Jose | 33 E. San Fernando St. (bet. S. 1st & 2nd Sts.) | 408-294-6785
www.gordonbiersch.com
See review in City of San Francisco Directory.

Grasing's Coastal Cuisine *Californian* `22` `20` `21` `$51`
Carmel | Jordan Ctr. | Sixth Ave. (Mission St.) | 831-624-6562 |
www.grasings.com

Chef/co-owner Kurt Grasing (Kurt's Carmel Chop House) is "always
front and center" at this "small" Carmel "favorite" known for its "appealing" California coastal cuisine and Golden State wines, plus a
"pleasant", pooch-friendly patio for bottomless-mimosa brunches;
service gets mixed marks ("unobtrusive" vs. "inattentive") and a few
fret that the cooking isn't "up to the latest trends", but at least a "prix
fixe menu" helps with "pricey" tabs.

Hachi Ju Hachi Ⓜ *Japanese* `–` `–` `–` `E`
Saratoga | 14480 Big Basin Way (3rd St.) | 408-647-2258 |
www.hachijuhachi88.com

A fine "new addition to the neighborhood", this "subdued" Saratogan
is a labor of love from chef Suzuki-san, who brings "true Osaka-style
dishes to the Bay Area" (down to the handmade tofu); with "excellent
sushi" too (though not the "rainbow-roll" sort), it's popular with in-
the-know eaters who grab a ringside seat at the blond-wood bar.

Half Moon Bay Brewing Company *Pub Food/Seafood* `15` `15` `15` `$33`
Half Moon Bay | 390 Capistrano Rd. (bet. Cabrillo Hwy. & Prospect
Way) | 650-728-2739 | www.hmbbrewingco.com

There's "nothin' better" than "sitting out on the patio around the fire
pit" with "Fido" enjoying the "water views", "house brews" and live
music (Friday–Sunday) moon fans of this long-running "casual"
Californian in Half Moon Bay; while not a highlight, the "dependable"
seafood-focused pub grub is "reasonably priced" and the staff
"doesn't rush you along", "making it easy to return time after time."

Happy Cafe Restaurant ⏁ *Chinese* ▽ `21` `4` `14` `$16`
San Mateo | 250 S. B St. (bet. 2nd & 3rd Aves.) | 650-340-7138

"Shanghai dumplings", "handmade" noodles and savory steamed
buns make for happy campers at this no-frills, cash-only "hole-in-the-
wall" in San Mateo; the brunch bunch sighs the "weekend dim sum"
still gets "too busy", so impatient sorts may want to consider the "affordable" "Chinese plate lunches and homestyle" dinners served
midweek; P.S. closed Tuesdays.

Hotaru *Japanese* · 20 | 10 | 15 | $22

San Mateo | 33 E. Third Ave. (bet. El Camino Real & San Mateo Dr.) | 650-343-1152 | www.hotarurestaurant.com

"Fresh" sushi, "perfectly cooked" tempura and "comforting" noodles make this "reliable" Japanese joint a "favorite" of San Mateans; the "lines are frequently long" (though they "move quickly"), and the "small", "no-frills" dining room can feel "cramped", but "you can't beat the prices" for the "homey" fare, especially the "bang-for-the-buck" bento boxes and "generous" combination meals.

Hula's *Asian/Eclectic* · 18 | 17 | 17 | $27

Monterey | 622 Lighthouse Ave. (Hoffman Ave.) | 831-655-4852
Santa Cruz | 221 Cathcart St. (bet. Cedar St. & Pacific Ave.) | 831-426-4852
www.hulastiki.com

There's "no need to go to Waikiki" for a "party atmosphere" and "killer mai tais" explain the "young crowds" who sashay into these "funky" "tiki huts" in Downtown Monterey and Santa Cruz, serving up "tasty" if "basic" Hawaiian chow with Asian influences; the "aloha" vibe extends to the "leisurely" yet "caring" service and "community-minded" owners, who donate part of 'Mahalo Monday' sales to charity.

Hunan Home's Restaurant *Chinese* · 21 | 12 | 18 | $26

Los Altos | 4880 El Camino Real (Jordan Ave.) | 650-965-8888 | www.hunanhomes.com

Hunan Garden *Chinese*

Palo Alto | 3345 El Camino Real (bet. Fernando & Lambert Aves.) | 650-565-8868

See review in City of San Francisco Directory.

Iberia *Spanish* · 22 | 21 | 16 | $46

Menlo Park | 1026 Alma St. (Ravenswood Ave.) | 650-325-8981 | www.iberiarestaurant.com

"Excellent" plates and "potent" sangria "that will have you speaking fluent Spanish by the second glass" "rule" at this Menlo Park hangout where enthusiasts urge "stick with" the bar (the only place tapas are served at dinnertime) and warm up to the "crackling fire"; "pricey" paella is the thing in the somewhat "stuffy" main dining room and on the "wonderful" patio, though the "steep" automatic tip vexes surveyors who say the "slow" service "doesn't measure up."

Il Fornaio *Italian* · 19 | 20 | 19 | $39

Burlingame | 327 Lorton Ave. (Donnelly Ave.) | 650-375-8000
Carmel | The Pine Inn | Ocean Ave. (Monte Verde St.) | 831-622-5100
Palo Alto | Garden Court Hotel | 520 Cowper St. (bet. Hamilton & University Aves.) | 650-853-3888
San Jose | Sainte Claire Hotel | 302 S. Market St. (San Carlos St.) | 408-271-3366
www.ilfornaio.com

See review in City of San Francisco Directory.

Il Postale *Italian* · 22 | 16 | 21 | $38

Sunnyvale | 127 W. Washington Ave. (bet. Frances St. & Murphy Ave.) | 408-733-9600 | www.ilpostale.com

For an "Italian night out" or a "lunch meeting" over "delicious" dishes and "interesting selections" from an "impressive wine list", the

	FOOD	DECOR	SERVICE	COST

"Silicon Valley crowd" heads to this "oh-so-friendly", "good-value" Sunnyvale bistro; the "old post office decor" creates a "pleasant" ambiance, and while it can get "noisy", it's still "great fun when it's crowded"; P.S. reservations accepted for five or more.

☑ In-N-Out Burger ● Burgers `22 | 10 | 18 | $9`
Millbrae | 11 Rollins Rd. (bet. Adrian Rd. & E. Millbrae Ave.)
Mountain View | 1159 N. Rengstorff Ave. (Amphitheatre Pkwy.)
Mountain View | 53 W. El Camino Real (bet. Bay St. & Grant Rd.)
NEW **San Jose** | 550 Newhall St. (Chestnut St.)
San Jose | 5611 Santa Teresa Blvd. (Blossom Hill Rd.)
Daly City | 260 Washington St. (Sullivan Ave.)
800-786-1000 | www.in-n-out.com
See review in City of San Francisco Directory.

Isobune Japanese `19 | 14 | 17 | $28`
Burlingame | 1451 Burlingame Ave. (bet. El Camino Real & Primrose Rd.) | 650-344-8433 | www.isobuneburlingame.com
See review in City of San Francisco Directory.

Izzy's Steaks & Chops Steak `20 | 17 | 20 | $43`
San Carlos | 525 Skyway Rd. (Hwy. 101) | 650-654-2822 | www.izzyssteaks.com
See review in City of San Francisco Directory.

Jin Sho ☒ Japanese `24 | 17 | 18 | $54`
Palo Alto | 454 S. California Ave. (bet. Ash St. & El Camino Real) | 650-321-3454 | www.jinshorestaurant.com

"The Nobu influence is unmistakable" at this "modern" Japanese in Palo Alto, opened by alums of that NYC restaurant, delivering "excellent" sushi and other "slam-dunk" dishes with "delightful", "unusual" touches; on the downside, service is a bit "patchy" and tabs are "expensive", particularly if you splurge on the omakase.

John Bentley's ☒ Californian `24 | 21 | 24 | $59`
Redwood City | 2915 El Camino Real (Selby Ln.) | 650-365-7777 | www.johnbentleys.com

Peninsula diners are "reluctant to spread the word" about their "favorite place", as this "standout" Redwood City bistro delivering "dependable" Cal "classics" and an appealing (if "pricey") wine list is already "wildly popular"; the "chic" digs are "not as intimate" as the now-shuttered Woodside location, but concerns are alleviated by a staff that's "beyond compare", overseen by an "owner who cares."

Joya Restaurant Nuevo Latino `20 | 23 | 18 | $45`
Palo Alto | 339 University Ave. (Florence St.) | 650-853-9800 | www.joyarestaurant.com

A "vibrant bar scene", "good-looking staff" and "live musical beats" add up to "one of the hipper places on the Peninsula" at this "happening" Palo Altan, where "beautiful people in a beautiful setting" nosh on "refreshing", "unusual" Nuevo Latino tapas and sip sangria that "rocks"; "alfresco" seating offers "people-watching along the sidewalk", but the frugal fuss it's "not cheap" and the small plates "lack sparkle."

Juban Japanese `18 | 14 | 16 | $38`
Burlingame | 1204 Broadway (Laguna Ave.) | 650-347-2300

(continued)

(continued)

Juban

Menlo Park | 712 Santa Cruz Ave. (bet. Chestnut & Curtis Sts.) | 650-473-6458
www.jubanrestaurant.com
See review in City of San Francisco Directory.

Junnoon *Indian*

| 22 | 21 | 19 | $44 |

Palo Alto | 150 University Ave. (High St.) | 650-329-9644 | www.junnoon.com
"Not your typical" tandoori place, this "upscale" Indian in Palo Alto "transcends" the competition by adding "contemporary pizzazz" to "traditional" fare, with its "artfully presented" large and small plates accompanied by "party-pleasing" cocktails; since the "lovely", loungey ambiance is as "hot as a Mumbai night", most keep "coming back" to "enjoy the sleekness of it all", but dissenters declare it "misses too frequently to warrant" the "high price."

Kabul Afghan Cuisine *Afghan*

| 23 | 16 | 19 | $30 |

Burlingame | 1101 Burlingame Ave. (California Dr.) | 650-343-2075
San Carlos | San Carlos Plaza | 135 El Camino Real (bet. Hull Dr. & Oak St.) | 650-594-2840
www.kabulcuisine.com
"Wonderful" Afghan eats – from "succulent" kebabs to "crave"-able pumpkin dishes – take customers down the "Khyber Pass" at this "exotic" Burlingame eatery and the "less crowded" "original" in a San Carlos strip mall; "portions large enough to share" contribute to the "good quality-price ratio", and despite "unimaginative" decor, the "gracious" staff ensures a "welcoming" atmosphere.

Kanpai ⊠ *Japanese*

| ▽ 24 | 18 | 21 | $40 |

Palo Alto | 330 Lytton Ave. (bet. Bryant & Florence Sts.) | 650-325-2696
"Omakase is the way to go" pronounce Peninsulans smitten by the "wonderful fresh fish" at this Downtown Palo Alto Japanese "owned by the fine folks of Naomi", a "hip" spot for "sake flights and the chef's delights" (plus "super sushi" and more standard fare); add in an "accommodating" staff, and most agree "you won't be disappointed."

☑ Kaygetsu Ⓜ *Japanese*

| 27 | 20 | 26 | $84 |

Menlo Park | Sharon Heights Shopping Ctr. | 325 Sharon Park Dr. (Sand Hill Rd.) | 650-234-1084 | www.kaygetsu.com
"Close your eyes and you could be in Tokyo" at this "labor of love" tucked into a Menlo Park "shopping plaza", where the "exquisite" kaiseki dinners – matched with "rare" sakes – have "no peer outside of Japan"; it costs a "fortune" (though à la carte options and the prix fixe lunch are "cheaper") and the atmosphere is "more traditional" than a "Nobu-type" joint, but a "server-to-diner ratio that seems to be 1:1" and the parade of "textures and tastes" "almost too lovely to eat" add up to an "unforgettable culinary experience."

Kitchen, The ❶ *Chinese*

| ▽ 19 | 9 | 12 | $27 |

Millbrae | 279 El Camino Real (Le Cruz Ave.) | 650-692-9688
Someone's definitely in the kitchen at this Cantonese hole-in-the-wall where the "authentic" country-style Chinese specialties and "excellent dim sum" (lunch only) stand out among all the "competition" in Millbrae; on the downside, "you need to have sharp elbows to get a ta-

FOOD | DECOR | SERVICE | COST

ble" and the staff tends to be "grumpy", but it's conveniently located near SFO and stays open late.

Koi Palace Chinese
23 | 16 | 12 | $33

Daly City | Serramonte Plaza | 365 Gellert Blvd. (bet. Hickey & Serramonte Blvds.) | 650-992-9000 | www.koipalace.com

Always "filled to the rafters" with "Chinese families" chowing down on delicacies from the wheeled-around carts, this "massive" Daly City dim sum house (with a "modern" Dublin sib) delivers some of the most "heavenly" dumplings "outside of Asia"; brunch-goers have to endure "teeth-gnashing waits" and "typical brusque service", but "VIP guests" gamely circle back for "decadent", "pricey" "banquet dinners" showcasing "Hong Kong-style" seafood fresh from the tank.

Krung Thai Thai
20 | 14 | 15 | $23

Mountain View | San Antonio Shopping Ctr. | 590 Showers Dr. (bet. California & Latham Sts.) | 650-559-0366

San Jose | 642 S. Winchester Blvd. (bet. Moorpark Ave. & Riddle Rd.) | 408-260-8224 | www.newkrungthai.com

An "explosion" of "authentic" flavors wows fans at these "popular" Peninsula Thais in Mountain View and San Jose delivering inexpensive noodles and curries; with a no-frills atmosphere and servers who "clear your table" the second "you stop to take a breath", it's "not the place for a special meal", but "dependable" "for a tasty one."

La Corneta Mexican
21 | 9 | 15 | $12

Burlingame | 1123 Burlingame Ave. (bet. Hatch Ln. & Lorton Ave.) | 650-340-1300 | www.lacorneta.com

See review in City of San Francisco Directory.

NEW La Costanera ●Ⓜ Peruvian
▽ 24 | 28 | 18 | $56

Montara | 8150 Cabrillo Hwy. (bet. 1st & 2nd Sts.) | 650-728-1600 | www.lacostanerarestaurant.com

Perched over the Pacific in Montara Beach, this contemporary new Peruvian from Carlos Altamirano (SF's Piqueo's and Mochica) is a "beautiful remodel of the old Chart House" whose "to-die-for" "ocean views" and "quality" regional cuisine (including "great ceviches) makes it a "treat for the eyes and the tummy"; service "doesn't match" up, but "happy-hour" habitués and late-night revelers admit it's easy to "settle in" for Pisco Sours at the "comfortable" bar or on the patio.

La Cumbre Taqueria Mexican
21 | 9 | 15 | $12

San Mateo | 28 N. B St. (bet. Baldwin & Tilton Aves.) | 650-344-8989

See review in City of San Francisco Directory.

La Forêt Ⓜ Continental/French
26 | 24 | 25 | $79

San Jose | 21747 Bertram Rd. (Almaden Rd.) | 408-997-3458 | www.laforetrestaurant.com

Those who brave the trip to "the boonies" (i.e. the outskirts of San Jose) to find this "quiet" Continental-French "tucked away" in a "house by a creek" are rewarded with a "leisurely evening" of "wonderfully prepared" food, particularly if they opt for the "incredible wild game" or "exquisite" tasting menu; it's quite "pricey", but most agree the "romantic country" ambiance and "attentive" service complete the package for a "special occasion."

	FOOD	DECOR	SERVICE	COST

La Posta ☑ *Italian* — ▽ 21 | 16 | 21 | $36

Santa Cruz | 538 Seabright Ave. (Watson St.) | 831-457-2782 | www.lapostarestaurant.com

"Showing a real commitment to quality and freshness" that "rivals SF", this Santa Cruz trattoria set in a former post office has customers "swooning" over the "outstanding" cucina that highlights "different regions in Italy", complemented by housemade bread and "excellent" bottles, all for a "great price"; it gets "a bit noisy when busy", and on Tuesday nights, when there's live music, but otherwise suits a "relaxed" night out.

La Strada *Italian* — 20 | 17 | 18 | $34

Palo Alto | 335 University Ave. (bet. Bryant & Florence Sts.) | 650-324-8300 | www.lastradapaloalto.com

"Fresh", "slightly unusual" Italian cuisine, including appetizers that "amuse the palate", makes this trattoria a "favorite" in Downtown Palo Alto; picky patrons fuss the "food is only fair", but devotees declare that grabbing an outdoor table and "people-watching" adds up to a "*perfetto*" way to dine.

Lavanda *Mediterranean* — 19 | 19 | 20 | $48

Palo Alto | 185 University Ave. (Emerson St.) | 650-321-3514 | www.lavandarestaurant.com

Palo Altans are partial to this "warm", "trendy" locale providing "rustic but refined" Mediterranean cooking matched by a "fabulous" wine list "showcasing interesting varietals"; the Sunday prix fixe meals are a "superb value", and while a few sigh that the "small plates are hit-or-miss" (and the service too), sold surveyors recommend it to "score with a business colleague, a date or even your own spouse."

LB Steak *Steak* — 22 | 23 | 22 | $51

San Jose | Santana Row | 334 Santana Row (Stevens Creek Blvd.) | 408-244-1180 | www.lbsteak.com

An "excellent update of the traditional steakhouse", this "upscale off-shoot of Left Bank" shows some "French flair", providing "properly cooked" cuts followed up by Gallic "treats from the dessert cart"; the "beautiful dark-wood decor" sets a "swanky yet comfortable" tone, and the "outdoor seating is great on a sunny day", leaving most carnivores to conclude it's a "terrific find" on San Jose's Santana Row.

Left Bank *French* — 19 | 20 | 18 | $42

Menlo Park | 635 Santa Cruz Ave. (Doyle St.) | 650-473-6543
San Jose | Santana Row | 377 Santana Row (Olsen Dr.) | 408-984-3500
www.leftbank.com

See review in North of San Francisco Directory.

☑ Le Papillon *French* — 26 | 23 | 26 | $84

San Jose | 410 Saratoga Ave. (Kiely Blvd.) | 408-296-3730 | www.lepapillon.com

Chef Scott Cooper "spoils" diners with his "incredible culinary gifts" at this high-end San Jose "treasure" where the "beautifully presented" New French fare is "absolutely delectable"; since "impeccable" service complements the "romantic" room – which is pleasantly "subdued" despite being "next to a strip mall" – you "can't go wrong" when you're willing to "break the bank."

	FOOD	DECOR	SERVICE	COST

Lion & Compass ⓈＺ American
▽ 20 | 19 | 22 | $43

Sunnyvale | 1023 N. Fair Oaks Ave. (Weddell Dr.) | 408-745-1260 |
www.lionandcompass.com

"Still a place to be for the Silicon Valley crowd" ("does Nolan Bushnell still hang at the bar?") this Sunnyvale stalwart provides "good" New American food and "exemplary" service amid "airy" colonial Caribbean decor; while many have "never actually paid to eat" here – "it's somewhere the company takes you for meetings" or power lunches – it's generally "packed, so the economy must be improving."

MacArthur Park American
17 | 19 | 18 | $42

Palo Alto | 27 University Ave. (El Camino Real) | 650-321-9990 |
www.macarthurparkpaloalto.com

The "expansive, airy" dining room in a "Julia Morgan–designed landmark building" creates a "glowing" setting for Traditional American meals at this Palo Alto "standby" for "business meetings" and the Stanford set; the "finger-lickin' ribs" are "favorites", but reviewers who remark they've "been there, done that" suggest upgrading the "slow" service and "doing something new" with the "marginal", "overpriced" menu.

Madera American
23 | 25 | 22 | $64

Menlo Park | Rosewood Sand Hill | 2825 Sand Hill Rd. (Hwy. 280) |
650-561-1540 | www.maderasandhill.com

Ducky for "drinks and dinner on the Peninsula", this "hot spot" inside Menlo Park's "upscale Rosewood" resort serves "innovative", "nicely prepared" New American food accompanied by "fantastic views" of the mountains "from the patio" and a "vibrant" "cougar bar and lounge at night"; it's "expensive for the area", but a "haven for the high-tech set", especially "when the VCs from across Sand Hill Road are paying."

Ma Maison Ⓜ French
▽ 20 | 16 | 20 | $52

Aptos | 9051 Soquel Dr. (Rio Del Mar Blvd.) | 831-688-5566 |
www.mamaisonrestaurant.com

This little-known mom-and-pop bistro serving Gallic classics in a "quiet, romantic" converted 1928 house feels more "like a little country cottage in France" than something you'd "stumble on" in Aptos, "especially when French-born chef Lionel comes and talks to you at your table"; opinions of the food range from "first-class" to "average" "for the price", but the patio lunches and fireside dinners have an "inviting" touch.

Mandaloun Californian/Mediterranean
▽ 20 | 18 | 20 | $36

Redwood City | 2021 Broadway St. (bet. Jefferson Ave. & Main St.) |
650-367-7974 | www.mandaloun.biz

It's a "keeper" agree supporters of this Redwood City hangout who suggest "settling in near the big fire" on a cold day (there's a patio for summer dining too) and chowing down on "flavorful", "well-prepared" Cal-Med dishes served by a "knowledgeable" staff; it's "definitely a good value" and the "bar area is nice as well", but some doubters dub the food merely "decent" and "not at all memorable."

Ｚ Manresa Ⓜ American
27 | 25 | 27 | $128

Los Gatos | 320 Village Ln. (bet. N. Santa Cruz & University Aves.) |
408-354-4330 | www.manresarestaurant.com

"Mad scientist" chef-owner David Kinch creates "visionary", "knockout" prix fixe meals in his "movie-set kitchen" at this New American "food paradise" in Los Gatos, using his own biodynamic produce and tying everything together with "fantastic" wines; "the expense is deep, but the experience" – from the "slightly bent presentations" to the "incredible" service – is "like going to the opera", delivering a command "performance" "you'll remember for a lifetime"; P.S. plans to add a front lounge with a small-bites menu are slated to begin in fall 2010.

Mantra *Californian/Indian* | 22 | 21 | 20 | $45 |

Palo Alto | 632 Emerson St. (bet. Forest & Hamilton Aves.) | 650-322-3500 | www.mantrapaloalto.com

"California meets Mumbai" at this "high-end" Palo Alto "hybrid" where the "sumptuous" Cal-Indian food is matched by "hip" surroundings, drawing "venture capital financiers" and folks from "Facebook" to enjoy an "upmarket early-bird special" during the "dynamite" happy hour; still, a minority deems the dishes only "decent" and declares it "doesn't seem as innovative" as it once was.

Marché ⊠ *French* | 24 | 23 | 24 | $67 |

Menlo Park | 898 Santa Cruz Ave. (University Dr.) | 650-324-9092 | www.restaurantmarche.com

"Genius" New French cuisine "shines" at this "true star" in Menlo Park, where "local produce" is transformed into "unique presentations" that "make dinner a culinary delight"; service is "excellent" in the "intimate", artful dining room, though diners who find the tabs "awfully expensive" tend to save it for a "special occasion" or go for the "superb" prix fixe.

ⓩ Marinus *French* | 27 | 27 | 27 | $96 |

Carmel Valley | Bernardus Lodge | 415 Carmel Valley Rd. (Laureles Grade Rd.) | 831-658-3500 | www.bernardus.com

For some of the finest dining "in Monterey County by a mile", foodies make the "wonderful" (albeit "far") drive through Carmel Valley and "splurge" at this "beautifully landscaped resort" where Cal Stamenov prepares "stellar" Cal-French tasting menus and the sommelier provides "inspired suggestions"; whether you sit at the chef's table or by the grand fireplace that "could melt even the coldest critic", it's the "meal of a lifetime" – even "nicer" if you "stay at the lodge."

Martins West ⊠ *Scottish* | 24 | 23 | 23 | $39 |

Redwood City | 831 Main St. (bet. B'way & Stambaugh St.) | 650-366-4366 | www.martinswestgp.com

Gastropub-goers agree the "innovative, hearty" grub at this "chic" Redwood City arrival has enough "inspiring", "sustainable" touches to defy "what you think of as Scottish fare" – from an "incredible" burger to "rocking" desserts, and even the "haggis on a stick is delicious (no kidding!)"; the "super-friendly" service and "interesting" cocktails also impress, so most maintain it's a "must-try."

Max's *Deli* | 17 | 14 | 17 | $26 |

Burlingame | 1250 Old Bayshore Hwy. (B'way) | 650-342-6297
Palo Alto | Stanford Shopping Ctr. | 711 Stanford Shopping Ctr. (Sand Hill Rd.) | 650-323-6297
Redwood City | Sequoia Station | 1001 El Camino Real (James Ave.) | 650-365-6297
www.maxsworld.com
See review in City of San Francisco Directory.

	FOOD	DECOR	SERVICE	COST

Mayfield Bakery & Café *Bakery/Californian*
| 19 | 19 | 17 | $37 |

Palo Alto | Town & Country Vill. | 855 El Camino Real (Embarcadero Rd.) | 650-853-9200 | www.mayfieldbakery.com

The "hip"-enough "19th-century farmhouse" decor almost makes you "forget you're in a shopping mall" muse mavens who congregate on the "lovely patio" or inside this "always packed" "cousin to the Village Pub" in Palo Alto; carb-lovers praise the "artfully re-imagined breakfasts" and other "homey" Cal meals at prices that don't "crack the credit card", but a few fume "service is shambolic", fueling up instead on "terrific homemade breads" and desserts in the next-door bakery.

Mayflower *Chinese*
| 19 | 11 | 12 | $29 |

Milpitas | 428 Barber Ln. (Bellew Dr.) | 408-922-2700

Hong Kong Flower Lounge *Chinese*
Millbrae | 51 Millbrae Ave. (bet. Broadway & El Camino Real) | 650-692-6666 www.mayflower-seafood.com

See review in City of San Francisco Directory.

McCormick & Schmick's *Seafood*
| 21 | 19 | 20 | $48 |

San Jose | The Fairmont | 170 S. Market St. (San Carlos St.) | 408-283-7200 | www.mccormickandschmicks.com

An "enjoyable" choice for "business and pleasure", this "upscale" seafood chain link in San Jose offers a "daily changing" menu of "freshly caught" fare in an "upbeat" atmosphere; though it feels too "stamped-out-of-a-mold" for some, its "professional" service is a plus and the "happy-hour bar menu" wins over the after-work crowd.

Mezza Luna *Italian*
| 22 | 19 | 22 | $37 |

Princeton by the Sea | 459 Prospect Way (Capistrano Rd.) | 650-728-8108

Caffè Mezza Luna *Italian*
Half Moon Bay | 240 Capistrano Rd. (Hwy. 1) | 650-560-0137 www.mezzalunabythesea.com

"They know fish and they know sauce" at this "peaceful" "coastside" Southern Italian in Princeton by the Sea, where the "excellent", moderately priced cuisine and "personable" service bring "warmth to even the foggiest of days"; its sister cafe in Half Moon Bay is worth a stop for simpler sandwiches and focaccia-style pizza, as well as "great espresso" and "authentic" pastries.

Mistral ⒵ *French/Italian*
| 19 | 19 | 19 | $39 |

Redwood Shores | 370-6 Bridge Pkwy. (Marine Pkwy.) | 650-802-9222 | www.mistraldining.com

"Always packed" with "business types" from "Oracle" and the like, this "pleasant" Redwood Shores bistro "on the lagoon" is "the place to do lunch" or "meet after work" for "solid", "seasonal" French-Italian food and "well-selected" wines; the "beautiful" "heated patio" is a "delight" on "balmy summer evenings", though adventurous eaters opine the "slightly overpriced", "average" eats can "get a little boring."

Montrio Bistro *Californian*
| 22 | 22 | 21 | $42 |

Monterey | 414 Calle Principal (Franklin St.) | 831-648-8880 | www.montrio.com

"One of the best places" to "eat well" for "less" in Downtown Monterey for "nearly 15 years", this "cute", "cozy" converted 1910 firehouse "just far enough away from the aquarium" "keeps it fresh" with "sustainable" ingredients and an "eclectic" slate of "delicious" Californian eats (with Southwestern and Italian touches), plus "nice" wines by the glass; the "friendly service" and "super" options make it a "lovely" choice for "groups with different tastes", who declare we'll "definitely go back!"

Morton's The Steakhouse *Steak*

| 24 | 21 | 23 | $71 |

San Jose | 177 Park Ave. (bet. Almaden Blvd. & Market St.) | 408-947-7000 | www.mortons.com
See review in City of San Francisco Directory.

Mundaka *Spanish*

| - | - | - | E |

Carmel | San Carlos St. (bet. Ocean & 7th Aves.) | 831-624-7400 | www.mundakacarmel.com

Infusing a bit of olé into Downtown Carmel is this Spaniard aglow with atmospheric lighting and built entirely from reclaimed materials; patrons share upscale tapas and paella, crafted by chef Brandon Miller (ex Stokes), while downing vino from a *porrón* and grooving to live DJs on select nights, making for a festive atmosphere.

NEW Muracci's Japanese Curry & Grill ☒ *Japanese*

| ▽ 22 | 7 | 13 | $12 |

Los Altos | 244 State St. (bet. 2nd & 3rd Sts.) | 650-917-1101 | www.muraccis.com
See review in City of San Francisco Directory.

Naomi Sushi ☒ *Japanese*

| 23 | 13 | 20 | $37 |

Menlo Park | 1328 El Camino Real (bet. Glenwood & Oak Grove Aves.) | 650-321-6902 | www.naomisushi.com

"The interior is pretty standard", but the "fresh, delicious, unusual" sushi "sure isn't" at this "friendly neighborhood" Japanese in Menlo Park, whose regulars recommend "sitting at the bar", "admiring the masters at work and letting them decide what to serve you"; with an "awesome" sake list and "affordable" tabs to boot, it's an "all-time favorite" in the area.

☒ Navio *American*

| 24 | 27 | 24 | $79 |

Half Moon Bay | Ritz-Carlton Half Moon Bay | 1 Miramontes Point Rd. (Hwy. 1) | 650-712-7000 | www.ritzcarlton.com

"For an ocean setting", complete with "killer views" of the "crashing Pacific" *and* the "18th green", this "swanky" cliffside New American at the Ritz-Carlton Half Moon Bay is "hard to surpass"; along with "uniformly outstanding" food and wine pairings, there's an open kitchen for "watching all the action" and what may be the "single greatest buffet brunch in the universe", all of which costs a "bundle"; P.S. the Conservatory lounge offerings are "cheaper."

Nepenthe *American*

| 17 | 26 | 17 | $37 |

Big Sur | 48510 Hwy. 1 (¼ mi. south of Ventana Inn & Spa) | 831-667-2345 | www.nepenthebigsur.com

"Sit outside" and find "nirvana" at this "iconic Big Sur" "aerie" (a former "love nest of Orson Welles") with the "wilderness at your back, crashing Pacific Ocean below" and "vistas that stretch" "as long as the lines to get in"; the "pedestrian" "burgers and Bloodys" are "secondary", while the "slow service" emerging from the "far-out, hippie-inspired" space is actually "a plus" while "lazing away" until sunset.

	FOOD	DECOR	SERVICE	COST

Nick's on Main 🅂 Ⓜ *American*
26 | 20 | 24 | $53

Los Gatos | 35 E. Main St. (College Ave.) | 408-399-6457 |
www.nicksonmainst.com

Chef-owner Nick Difu not only "welcomes each diner personally" to his "darling", "bedroom-small" bistro in the "quaint village" of Los Gatos, he also whips up "soul-satisfying" New American "comfort food" that "elevates you beyond" the "noise" and the surroundings; even those sitting "tightly bunched" at the "long, middle table" have a "delightful time" forming "friendships" with "strangers", so little wonder it's "tough to get a reservation" ("walk-ins" are "just not happening"), but "worth the effort."

North Beach Pizza *Pizza*
19 | 11 | 16 | $19

San Mateo | 240 E. Third Ave. (B St.) | 650-344-5000 |
www.northbeachpizza.net

See review in City of San Francisco Directory.

Old Port Lobster Shack *Seafood*
21 | 12 | 15 | $29

Redwood City | 851 Veteran's Blvd. (bet. Jefferson Ave. & Middlefield Rd.) |
650-366-2400 | www.oplobster.com

"Homesick" New Englanders who "can't get theah from heah" "line up" at this ersatz "down-east" "port stand" in an "oddly located" Redwood "strip mall" for a "real" "Atlantic" "lobstah roll" – "naked or dressed" – and "chowda", "with Maine beer to wash it back"; the "kitschy" "seaside ambiance" is "definitely family-friendly", though a few pout about "eyebrow-raising prices", considering the "counter" service, "wooden picnic table" seating and "paper-towel napkins."

O'mei Ⓜ *Chinese*
22 | 11 | 14 | $33

Santa Cruz | 2316 Mission St. (Fair Ave.) | 831-425-8458 |
www.omeichow.com

The "legendary" gan pung chicken and other "varied", "exotic offerings" show off "Chinese food in a new light" say Sinophiles of this Santa Cruz stalwart whose "sensational" fare trumps its "strip-center location"; still, others opine "O'mei? O'nay!", noting "inconsistent" cooking, "bad service" and *chi* that "feng shui specialists were born to fix", and take issue with the mandatory tip "added to every meal."

Original Joe's ⓿ *American/Italian*
18 | 15 | 18 | $32

(aka Joe's, OJ's)

San Jose | 301 S. First St. (San Carlos St.) | 408-292-7030 |
www.originaljoes.com

When they want to "time travel to the 1950s", nostalgists "sit at the counter and watch the chefs cook" "surprisingly good steaks" and other Italian-American "classics" at this "entertaining" vintage eatery in San Jose; servers who "have been there since the invention of tomato sauce" "are a trip", and "tremendous" portions mean "you'll have enough for lunch the next day", though contemporary critics kvetch the "bland" fare "doesn't cut it today" (it's "'old' maybe, but certainly not 'original'").

Osteria 🅂 *Italian*
22 | 15 | 19 | $36

Palo Alto | 247 Hamilton Ave. (Ramona St.) | 650-328-5700
"Expertly prepared" pastas that are "full of flavor" set the "gold standard" for Palo Alto patrons who keep this "homey Italian trattoria"

FOOD | DECOR | SERVICE | COST

"tightly packed"; some cite "uninventive" food and "surly" servers and find it "uncomfortable" "sitting a hair's breadth away from you neighbor", but for most it's an "affordable" option that's "worth th squeeze" – just "don't show up without a reservation."

Oswald Restaurant Ⓜ American ▽ 25 | 17 | 21 | $51

Santa Cruz | 121 Soquel Ave. (Front St.) | 831-423-7427 | www.oswaldrestaurant.com

Back on the scene "after a few years' hiatus", with a "bigger" Downtown setting, this "innovative" "standout in the restaurant dead zone o Santa Cruz" reclaims its "jewel" status with "stylish", "locally" sourced New American offerings, "decadent" desserts, "signature cocktails" and "excellent service"; the "concrete industrial" corner digs get "noisy", but everyone "always seem to be having a good time", includ-ing "da man" – chef Damani Thomas – who's "visible cooking from in-side" the "very open kitchen."

⚡ Pacific's Edge American/French 25 | 28 | 23 | $75

Carmel | Hyatt Highlands Inn | 120 Highlands Dr. (Hwy. 1) | 831-620-1234 | www.pacificsedge.com

"Not to be missed when in Carmel", this "glass-enclosed" "fine dining" aerie "overlooking the crashing waves" of the Pacific "romances from the minute you walk in" to the final course of the "sensational" New American–French tasting menu, gilded by "spot-on" wine pairings; if a few fret about "doll's portions at king's prices", even they concede that the "spectacular view" "before the sun sets" compensates, and some advise "you can have as much fun" – and the same vista – at the bar; P.S. a post-Survey chef change is not reflected in the Food score.

Pampas Brazilian 21 | 20 | 21 | $57

Palo Alto | 529 Alma St. (bet. Hamilton & University Aves.) | 650-327-1323 | www.pampaspaloalto.com

"Hardcore carnivores" "feast" away at this "huge" "all-you-can-eat" Brazilian churrascaria in Palo Alto, indulging in an "unbeatable selec-tion" of skewers that "just keep coming", complemented by a "sump-tuous" salad bar; with "wonderful" live jazz on weekends beefing up the "modern" ambiance, it's well-suited to "celebrations", but "be pre-pared to pay handsomely for the privilege" of eating "unlimited meat"; P.S. à la carte options are also available.

Pancho Villa Taqueria Mexican 22 | 9 | 15 | $13

San Mateo | 365 S. B St. (bet. 3rd & 4th Aves.) | 650-343-4123 | www.panchovillasm.ypguides.net

See review in City of San Francisco Directory.

Parcel 104 Californian 23 | 21 | 22 | $63

Santa Clara | Santa Clara Marriott | 2700 Mission College Blvd. (bet. Freedom Cir. & Great America Pkwy.) | 408-970-6104 | www.parcel104.com

"Fresh" "local" ingredients, many of them "organic", get the "modern treatment" at this "consistent" "high-end" Californian "in an expected location" (the Santa Clara Marriott); delivering "beautifully presented" plates and "attentive service", it's "popular" for "quiet" "business lunches and dinners", but it's "a bit expensive" cry critics, who save it for dining on the "corporate account."

	FOOD	DECOR	SERVICE	COST

Passage to India *Indian* ▽ 17 | 13 | 17 | $26

Mountain View | 1991 W. El Camino Real (Clark Ave.) | 650-969-9990 |
www.passagetoindia.net

Aficionados affirm it's "all about the buffet" – an "affordable" lunch
spread (also served Friday–Saturday dinner) that "satisfies" with a
"nice variety" of Indian and Desi Chinese dishes – at this simply decorated Mountain View venue; the à la carte menu offers some "excellent"
choices as well, and the staff is "helpful", making it a local "favorite."

Passionfish *Californian/Seafood* 25 | 20 | 24 | $47

Pacific Grove | 701 Lighthouse Ave. (Congress Ave.) | 831-655-3311 |
www.passionfish.net

"In a town awash with seafood restaurants", this "off-the-tourist-path",
"environmentally conscious" Californian in Pacific Grove "bobs above
the waves", "stunning" diners with "sustainable" "local catches" that
seem to "swim from the ocean straight to your plate" (along with "turf
for carnivores"); the staff has a "passion" for "flawlessly handling" the
customers despite "close tables", but the real hook for "rejoicing wine
lovers" is the "amazing" vino selection with "ridiculously low prices."

Pasta Moon *Italian* 22 | 19 | 21 | $42

Half Moon Bay | 315 Main St. (Kelly St.) | 650-726-5125 |
www.pastamoon.com

Ingredients "fresh from the local farmers down the road" are "treated
with respect" as they're fashioned into "delicious" Italian eats "with an
eclectic touch" at this "cute", "homey" hangout in Half Moon Bay;
though some doubters describe the food as "decent but not outstanding"
and a little "expensive", the "charming" owner and staff "make you
feel special", "creating a warmth" here "on even the foggiest of days."

Pasta Pomodoro *Italian* 17 | 13 | 18 | $23

Redwood City | 490 El Camino Real (Whipple Ave.) | 650-474-2400
San Bruno | Bayhill Center | 811A Cherry Ave. (San Bruno Ave.) |
650-583-6622
San Jose | Evergreen Mkt. | 4898 San Felipe Rd. (Yerba Buena Blvd.) |
408-532-0271
San Mateo | Bay Meadows | 1060 Park Pl. (Saratoga Dr.) | 650-574-2600
www.pastapomodoro.com
See review in City of San Francisco Directory.

Patxi's Chicago Pizza *Pizza* 22 | 14 | 17 | $22

Palo Alto | 441 Emerson St. (bet. Lytton & University Aves.) |
650-473-9999 | www.patxispizza.com
See review in City of San Francisco Directory.

Piatti *Italian* 19 | 19 | 19 | $39

Carmel | Sixth Ave. (Junipero Ave.) | 831-625-1766
Santa Clara | 3905 Rivermark Plaza (Montague Expwy.) | 408-330-9212
www.piatti.com
See review in East of San Francisco Directory.

Pizza Antica *Pizza* 21 | 15 | 17 | $27

San Jose | Santana Row | 334 Santana Row (Stevens Creek Blvd.) |
408-557-8373 | www.pizzaantica.com

"For a chain", this "grown-up" "trattoria-type" suburban outfit ferrying
out "freaking delicious" Italian-style "flatbread pizzas" enhanced by

FOOD | DECOR | SERVICE | COST

"inventive" "Northern California" toppings (and "seasonal salads") is "far better than the ordinary shopping-mall" pie stop; the servers are sorta "puppy dog–like" and "children run wild at family hours", but a "full bar" with "carafes of good wine" and a patio for "soaking up the sun" "help make the noise" and "no-reservations policy" "more tolerable."

Plumed Horse ☒ *Californian* | 25 | 25 | 24 | $98
Saratoga | 14555 Big Basin Way (4th St.) | 408-867-4711 |
www.plumedhorse.com
"Bringing urban sophistication to sleepy Saratoga", this "beautifully remodeled" haute "foodie must" is the place "to impress", starting with a "champagne cart" and culminating with "creative" Californian "degustation menus" that "rival anything in SF"; the "modern" setting, featuring a "dazzling, two-story glass wine cellar", is fitting for a "special-occasion dinner", but "gold-diggers" and scene-seekers "stick with" the "hip" lounge, "enjoying" "sensational" appetizers and weekend piano music without the "outrageous" outlay.

Pluto's Fresh Food for a Hungry Universe *American* | 19 | 12 | 15 | $14
Palo Alto | 482 University Ave. (Cowper St.) | 650-853-1556
San Jose | 3055 Olin Ave. (Winchester Blvd.) | 408-247-9120
www.plutosfreshfood.com
See review in City of San Francisco Directory.

Quattro Restaurant & Bar *Italian* | 21 | 23 | 22 | $60
East Palo Alto | Four Seasons Hotel | 2050 University Ave. (Woodland Ave.) |
650-470-2889 | www.fourseasons.com
Filled with "VCs and CEOs", this "luxurious" lair in East Palo Alto's equally "upscale Four Seasons" provides "excellent" cuisine, thanks to a chef who "really knows his Italian food"; "professional" servers maintain a "proper pace" to suit plenty of "dealmaking", but the frugal fuss the "pricey" plates are "not worth a special trip" unless "you're on an expense account."

Red Lantern *Asian* | 18 | 20 | 16 | $36
Redwood City | 808 Winslow St. (B'way) | 650-369-5483 |
www.redlanternrwc.com
Exuding "great energy" and a touch of exotica in "the 'burbs", this "beautiful", "suitably atmospheric" Pan-Asian in Redwood City projecting images of Southeast Asia on the walls is a "perfect place to sit at the bar" and share "tasty" small plates and cocktails; however, red-flag wavers warn that "inconsistent" food and service don't measure up to the "cool setting", which "turns into a dance club" on Friday nights.

NEW Restaurant at Ventana, The *Californian* | ▽ 22 | 25 | 23 | $60
Big Sur | Ventana Inn & Spa | 48123 Hwy. 1 (Coast Ridge Rd.) |
831-667-2331 | www.ventanainn.com
Romantics feel as if they're "just this side of heaven" at this resort Californian, thanks to the "amazing" patio views of the "Big Sur coast" and an interior, featuring "exposed wood rafters", that's been "beautifully restored" since wildfires ravaged the area; the "expensive", locally sourced cuisine is "better than it needs to be", but to "get the true value", "come for lunch" or cocktails "before the sun goes down."

	FOOD	DECOR	SERVICE	COST

Rio Grill *Californian*   22 | 19 | 20 | $41

Carmel | Crossroads Shopping Ctr. | 101 Crossroads Blvd. (Rio Rd.) |
831-625-5436 | www.riogrill.com

"Carmel locals" "return time and again" (and sometimes "take the
kids") to this "see-and-be-seen spot" serving "generous" portions of
"always enjoyable" Californian cuisine with "Southwestern touches";
diners undeterred by the "strip-mall" setting report "attentive" service and decor that's "as comfortable as an old shoe", and since prices
are "reasonable" for the region, most maintain it pleases both the
"palate and the purse."

Ristorante Avanti *Californian*   ▽ 23 | 18 | 24 | $34

Santa Cruz | Palm Shopping Ctr. | 1711 Mission St. (Bay St.) |
831-427-0135 | www.ristoranteavanti.com

"Highlighting" the "local, sustainable" "bounty of the Monterey Bay to
full effect", this Santa Cruz strip-mall "find" delivers "superior" Cal-
Italian fare amid "bustling", "true trattoria" surroundings "adorned
with pottery"; adding to its appeal are a "reasonably priced" wine list
(including "older" vintages from Europe) and "excellent" service – "a
rare thing in this laid-back beach town."

Ristorante Capellini *Italian*   ▽ 18 | 18 | 18 | $39

San Mateo | 310 Baldwin Ave. (B St.) | 650-348-2296 | www.capellinis.com
It's "everything you want" in an Italian ristorante declare devotees of this
"reliable", midpriced San Matean, where the "pleasant" digs designed
by Pat Kuleto are "perfect for a romantic date or business dinner"; the
"pastas are always well prepared" and "service is appropriately attentive", but novelty-seekers sigh the "standard" fare is "nothing special"
and say it "seems like it hasn't changed" in years.

Roti Indian Bistro *Indian*   22 | 17 | 19 | $31

Burlingame | 209 Park Rd. (bet. Burlingame & Howard Aves.) |
650-340-7684 | www.rotibistro.com
See review in City of San Francisco Directory.

☑ Roy's at Pebble Beach *Hawaiian*   25 | 26 | 24 | $59

Pebble Beach | The Inn at Spanish Bay | 2700 17 Mile Dr. (Congress Rd.) |
831-647-7423 | www.pebblebeach.com
Roy Yamaguchi's "delightful" Pebble Beach golf-course outpost "feels
like Hawaii" decree duffers who savor his signature slate of "outstanding" "South Pacific" fusion fare while soaking up the "dreamy ocean
views"; it's "rather pricey", but the staff "keeps grinding out the aloha",
so at the very least it's "worth the trip" for "drinks around the outside
fireplace" to hear the "bagpiper bring in the last foursome at dusk."

Sakae Sushi Noboru *Japanese*   ▽ 26 | 19 | 19 | $65

Burlingame | 243 California Dr. (bet. Burlingame & Howard Aves.) |
650-348-4064 | www.sakaesushi.com
Doling out "high-quality", "unique" "fresh fish from Japan" along with
"scrumptious" tempura, this expensive eatery (formerly called Noboru
in its San Mateo days) has relocated to "more spacious, pleasant"
Burlingame digs, but still has followers who consider it "the best sushi
place on the Peninsula"; while a few find it "pretentious" and feel the
food "needs repricing", dozens of sakes on offer and weekend karaoke
in the back lounge help solidify its standing among expats.

Sakoon   Indian

23 | 23 | 22 | $37

Mountain View | 357 Castro St. (bet. California & Dana Sts.) | 650-965-2000 | www.sakoonrestaurant.com

For "modern Indian done right", Silicon Valley sorts swamp this "innovative" Mountain View subcontinental where chef Sachin Chopra puts a "tasty twist on traditional dishes" using "authentic spicing"; add in "superb lunch buffets", "gracious service" and "eye-popping" decor (e.g. "fiber-optic lights", bright hues), and most gladly pay tabs that run a "bit pricier" than usual.

Sam's Chowder House   Seafood

19 | 19 | 17 | $35

Half Moon Bay | 4210 N. Cabrillo Hwy. (Capistrano Rd.) | 650-712-0245 | www.samschowderhouse.com

For "fresh seafood at the beach", "locals and day-trippers" trek to this "slightly touristy" fish shack in an "unsurpassed" Half Moon Bay setting to "watch the sunset" and savor a "killer" "cup of New England chowda" or a lobster roll that's "da bomb" ("it better be for $20"); true, a few decry "so-so" fin fare and "underwhelming" service, but it's "always packed" nonetheless – "even on the foggiest days."

Sardine Factory   American/Seafood

20 | 21 | 21 | $59

Monterey | 701 Wave St. (Prescott Ave.) | 831-373-3775 | www.sardinefactory.com

"Tourists in shorts and flip-flops" descend upon this "pricey" Cannery Row "stalwart", where "traditional waiters" whisk "good, not fabulous" sustainable American seafood to tables in an "old-fashioned" dining space; loyalists insist it's "worth stopping in" to check out the "spectacular conservatory", "fantastic bartenders" or "working wine cellar", while the less-impressed deem it all "a bit tired" ("you'll love it if you're from Nebraska").

Scott's of Palo Alto   Seafood

19 | 19 | 20 | $43

Palo Alto | Town & Country Vill. | 855 El Camino Real (Embarcadero Rd.) | 650-323-1555 | www.scottsseafoodpa.com

Scott's of San Jose   Seafood

San Jose | 185 Park Ave. (bet. S. Almaden Blvd. & S. Market St.) | 408-971-1700 | www.scottsseafoodsj.com

See review in East of San Francisco Directory.

Sent Sovi   Ⓜ   Californian

25 | 20 | 24 | $77

Saratoga | 14583 Big Basin Way (5th St.) | 408-867-3110 | www.sentsovi.com

"You can see the passion" of the young couple running this "special-occasion" restaurant in Saratoga, which regales its "Silicon Valley clientele" with "personal service" and "surprisingly inventive" Californian cuisine in a "charming" space the "size of my mother's shoe closet"; "fantastic" weekly specials and "theme dinners" make it "possible to get out of here" for less, but to "get the full experience", regulars recommend you "save for the splurge."

71 Saint Peter   🅱 Californian/Mediterranean

20 | 19 | 21 | $43

San Jose | San Pedro Sq. | 71 N. San Pedro St. (bet. W. Santa Clara & W. St. John Sts.) | 408-971-8523 | www.71saintpeter.com

A "family-run" "refuge" on San Jose's San Pedro Square, this "cozy" bistro provides "delicious" "seasonal" Cal-Med cooking and "friendly" service for a "good value"; though a few critics carp it's "nothing to write home about", many seek it out "in the summertime", when it's a coup to score" an outdoor table.

Shadowbrook *American/Californian*
| 18 | 25 | 19 | $49 |

Capitola | 1750 Wharf Rd. (Capitola Rd.) | 831-475-1511 |
www.shadowbrook-capitola.com

The "adorable little" tram (or "hillivator") that takes you "through the lush gardens" to this "lovely" Capitola "hideaway" sets the tone for a "unique experience", while the "spectacular setting" makes it "irresistible" for "special celebrations"; many are pleased too with "well-executed" Cal-New American fare and "responsive" servers, but demanding diners deem the menu "uninspired" and advise "just come for cocktails" or a bite "in the bar."

Shalimar ⇔ *Indian/Pakistani*
| 24 | 4 | 10 | $16 |

Sunnyvale | 1146 W. El Camino Real (bet. Bernardo & Grape Aves.) |
408-530-0300 | www.shalimarsv.com

See review in City of San Francisco Directory.

Shokolaat ⌧Ⓜ *Californian*
| 21 | 20 | 18 | $47 |

Palo Alto | 516 University Ave. (Cowper St.) | 650-289-0719 |
www.shokolaat.com

An "ambitious" eatery that's equal parts patisserie and Californian bistro, this "undiscovered gem" in Palo Alto offers "unique presentations" of French-inflected fare, complemented by "well-chosen wines" and "heavenly" "handcrafted desserts" that "tickle the tongue"; most surveyors are sweet on the "attractive dining room", but sourpusses pout that the "uneven" eats and service aren't up to what the "prices lead you to expect."

☒ Sierra Mar *Californian/Eclectic*
| 28 | 29 | 27 | $89 |

Big Sur | Post Ranch Inn | Hwy. 1 (30 mi. south of Carmel) | 831-667-2800 |
www.postranchinn.com

"Relax" "on a bluff above the Pacific" and "feel at one with nature" as you take in the "unsurpassed" "view extraordinaire" from this "stunning" glass-enclosed aerie at the Post Ranch Inn, voted No. 1 for Decor in the Bay Area; "irrespective of location", the "unique, flavorful" Cal-Eclectic fare, "encyclopedia-sized wine list" and servers who "spoil you" will "please any gourmand", but since the "tab is as close to the clouds as you are", consider going for "lunch out on the deck."

Sino *Chinese*
| 19 | 20 | 16 | $37 |

San Jose | Santana Row | 377 Santana Row (Olsen Dr.) | 408-247-8880 |
www.sinorestaurant.com

"Delicious" dim sum and other appealing eats at the "upper end of Chinese" draw Sinophiles to Chris Yeo's trendy, richly decorated restaurant and lounge on San Jose's Santana Row; during the day it's "great to eat outdoors", and later on the "young professional happyhour crowd" convenes, but the "thumping music" and "clubby" "attitude" at night are too much for some.

ⓃⒺⓌ SliderBarCafe ◑ *Burgers*
| - | - | - | I |

Palo Alto | 324 University Ave. (bet. Bryant & Waverly Sts.) |
650-322-7300 | www.sliderbarcafe.com

Sliders of every stripe – from beef to veggie to a dessert rendition (chocolate chip cookies filled with frozen yogurt) – made with sustainable ingredients are the draw at this quick-service American that recently slid into Palo Alto; the sunny storefront, with floor to-ceiling windows that fold open onto the street, also serves breakfast all day and stays open till midnight, pouring an array of microbrews and wines.

Soif Wine Bar *Californian* ▽ 24 | 20 | 22 | $40

Santa Cruz | 105 Walnut Ave. (Pacific Ave.) | 831-423-2020 | www.soifwine.com

Boasting "phenomenal" vintages available by the "glass, taste or bottle" courtesy of its "adjacent store", this largely "undiscovered" Californian eatery/enoteca is a "trendy" spot to "meet a fellow wine lover" (along with "some Santa Cruz characters") for a "couple of flights" and "creative" "small and large plates"; jazz on Tuesdays and "various classes are a real treat", as are the "attentive" servers, who "know their stuff."

Stacks *American* 18 | 13 | 17 | $20

Burlingame | 361 California Dr. (Lorton Ave.) | 650-579-1384
Menlo Park | 600 Santa Cruz Ave. (El Camino Real) | 650-838-0066
www.stacksrestaurant.com
See review in City of San Francisco Directory.

St. Michael's Alley Ⓢ Ⓜ *Californian* 22 | 21 | 22 | $44

Palo Alto | 140 Homer Ave. (High St.) | 650-326-2530 | www.stmikes.com

The "eclectic" Cal cuisine – "fresh, festive dishes that rotate with the seasons" – is "popular with the Silicon Valley set" and "ladies who lunch" at this "unpretentious" "neighborhood gem" in Palo Alto; when it relocated to "spiffed-up digs" in 2009, it may have "lost some of its coziness", but gained "extra space", "lots of light" and outdoor tables that "make alfresco dining a pleasure", all while maintaining "welcoming" service; P.S. weekend brunch is still served at the "homey" original location at 806 Emerson Street.

Straits Restaurant *Singaporean* 20 | 19 | 17 | $38

Burlingame | 1100 Burlingame Ave. (California Dr.) | 650-373-7883
San Jose | 333 Santana Row (bet. Alyssum & Tatum Lns.) | 408-246-6320
www.straitsrestaurants.com

Straits Cafe *Singaporean*

Palo Alto | 3295 El Camino Real (Lambert Ave.) | 650-494-7168 | www.straitscafepaloalto.com
See review in City of San Francisco Directory.

Sumika Ⓜ *Japanese* ▽ 24 | 15 | 17 | $44

Los Altos | 236 Central Plaza (bet. 2nd & 3rd Sts.) | 650-917-1822 | www.sumikagrill.com

Orenci Ramen's yakitori-bar offshoot hidden in a Los Altos alleyway lures "Japanese businessmen on expense accounts" and kushi-yaki mavens who insist the special "binchotan" charcoal that "brings superior flavor" to the "delicious" array of "authentic" grilled goodies (including chicken hearts and pork cheeks) is worth the extra yen; service can be "slow" and the modern digs are unremarkable, but the "excellent donburi" lunches and $3 draft Sapporos at happy hour (Tuesday–Thursday) provide further incentive.

	FOOD	DECOR	SERVICE	COST

Tai Pan *Chinese*
24 | 24 | 23 | $38

Palo Alto | 560 Waverley St. (bet. Hamilton & University Aves.) | 650-329-9168 | www.taipanpaloalto.com

"Delectable" dim sum and "perfectly prepared" Cantonese entrees made with "top-notch ingredients" delight "locals and visiting Stanford parents" at this "upscale Chinese" in Palo Alto; offering "serene", "elegant" surroundings and "gracious" service as well, it's on the "expensive" side for the genre, but admirers agree it's a real "value" for "special occasions."

Tamarine *Vietnamese*
25 | 23 | 21 | $53

Palo Alto | 546 University Ave. (bet. Cowper & Webster Sts.) | 650-325-8500 | www.tamarinerestaurant.com

"A cool, hip vibe" infuses this "upscale Vietnamese" "winner" ("the Slanted Door for the Peninsula") where an "attractive Palo Alto crowd" sips "seasonal drinks" at the "long bar" or shares "sensational", "expertly prepared" and "beautifully served" small plates in the "modern" yet "warm" dining room; true, it all comes "with a price tag", but it's "worth the splurge" for a meal "you'll dream about."

Taqueria Tlaquepaque *Mexican*
∇ 24 | 9 | 10 | $18

San Jose | 2222 Lincoln Ave. (bet. Curtner & Franquette Aves.) | 408-978-3665

San Jose | 699 Curtner Ave. (Canoas Garden Ave.) | 408-448-1230 🖪

San Jose | 721 Willow St. (Delmas Ave.) | 408-287-9777

This trinity of San Jose "burrito and taco joints" follows in the "tradition of all great hole-in-the-wall Mexican restaurants", whereby the "homestyle" comida is "sublime" but the "spotty service" and "barely functioning" decor "leave something to be desired"; happily, most overlook any deficiencies thanks to the "wonderful chile verde" and tortilla chips "you can't stop eating", complemented by "sangria ordered by the pitcher" and "frosty mugs" of the tequila-spiked "Super Chavela."

Tarpy's Roadhouse *American*
21 | 21 | 19 | $41

Monterey | 2999 Monterey-Salinas Hwy. (Canyon Del Rey Blvd.) | 831-647-1444 | www.tarpys.com

A longtime "destination (and it has to be, given its location)" for explorers venturing "home from Monterey or Carmel", this "consistently good" American set in a "rustic-chic" 1917 stone building dishes up "reasonably priced" "comfort food" and Sunday brunch; service can be "spotty", but the "classic roadhouse ambiance" and "pleasant outdoor seating" ensure it's "always packed."

Thea Mediterranean
Cuisine *Greek/Mediterranean*
19 | 21 | 17 | $35

San Jose | Santana Row | 3090 Olsen Dr. (S. Winchester Blvd.) | 408-260-1444 | www.thearestaurant.com

The "light, airy atmosphere" inspires "instant relaxation" at this mid-priced Hellenic haunt serving a "colorful", "consistently good" Mediterranean menu; add in an "extensive" drink selection and it's a "favorite" for a "romantic" meal on San Jose's Santana Row; P.S. belly dancers do their thing Friday–Saturday nights.

	FOOD	DECOR	SERVICE	COST

Three Seasons *Vietnamese* 　　　　21 | 19 | 18 | $39
Palo Alto | 518 Bryant St. (University Ave.) | 650-838-0353 |
www.threeseasonsrestaurant.com
See review in City of San Francisco Directory.

Trader Vic's *Polynesian* 　　　　17 | 20 | 19 | $47
Palo Alto | Dina's Garden Hotel | 4269 El Camino Real (bet. Charleston &
San Antonio Rds.) | 650-849-9800 | www.tradervicspaloalto.com
See review in East of San Francisco Directory.

Twist Bistro 🚫Ⓜ *American/French* 　　20 | 15 | 17 | $38
Campbell | 245 E. Campbell Ave. (bet. 1st & 2nd Sts.) | 408-370-2467 |
www.twist-bistro.com

Twist Café Ⓜ *American/French*
Campbell | 247 E. Campbell Ave. (bet. 1st & 2nd Sts.) | 408-374-8982 |
www.twist-cafe.com
"What a twist" – Campbell suburbanites can get their "French fix" at
these side-by-side "foodie places", a sidewalk cafe serving breakfast
and lunch and its "fine urban-bistro" kin, where the "friendly" chef-
owner prepares New American dinners with a Gallic spin; if a few critics charge the fare "needs more punch", the "soothing", "Paris-like"
atmosphere is a plus.

231 Ellsworth 🚫 *American* 　　　　23 | 21 | 23 | $60
San Mateo | 231 S. Ellsworth Ave. (bet. 2nd & 3rd Aves.) |
650-347-7231 | www.231ellsworth.com
Wheelers and dealers "on expense accounts" and couples enjoying
"date night in Downtown San Mateo" both appreciate this "mainstay
on the mid-Peninsula", whose "sophisticated" New American fare is
served at "comfortably spaced tables" – a "rare luxury these days";
"professional" service enhances the "subdued" surroundings, but critics contend it "seems like your father's business restaurant" and
"needs an update."

Udupi Palace *Indian/Vegetarian* 　　20 | 8 | 14 | $18
Sunnyvale | 976 E. El Camino Real (Poplar Ave.) | 408-830-9600 |
www.udupipalaceca.com
See review in City of San Francisco Directory.

Ⓩ Village Pub, The *American* 　　26 | 24 | 25 | $67
Woodside | 2967 Woodside Rd. (Whiskey Hill Rd.) | 650-851-9888 |
www.thevillagepub.net
You can "feel the venture capital money in the air" in this "swanky", "off-
the-beaten-path" haunt's "richly textured room", where Woodside's
"horsey set" "impresses" clients and spouses, sipping "velvety drinks"
and dining fireside on "creative", "luxe" New American fare; the "splendid" staff welcomes you "whether you're in stilettos or sneakers",
making it all "feel like home" – just get ready to drop "some serious
money", or hit the casual bar for the "justifiably famous burger."

Viognier *Californian/French* 　　23 | 21 | 22 | $72
San Mateo | Draeger's Mktpl. | 222 E. Fourth Ave. (bet. B St. &
Ellswoth Ave.) | 650-685-3727 | www.viognierrestaurant.com
Don't let the "strange location" ("on the second floor of Draeger's
Marketplace") "put you off", because the "vibrant", "creative" Cal-

FOOD | DECOR | SERVICE | COST

French dinners and "wonderful" wine list make this a "first-rate" choice for a "special evening" in San Mateo; the "quiet" room with "widely spaced tables" (some "in front of a fireplace") "inspires conversation", and the "knowledgeable" staff is "welcoming" as well, but detractors are disappointed by the "switch to a fixed-price" menu and save it for when they're "feeling flush."

Wicket's Bistro *Californian*

∇ 24 | 21 | 22 | $44

Carmel Valley | Bernardus Lodge | 415 Carmel Valley Rd. (Laureles Grade Rd.) | 831-658-3400 | www.bernardus.com

"It's all about the setting" and the home-grown ingredients at this "delightful" Californian bistro at the Bernardus Lodge resort in Carmel Valley, where alfresco diners can watch "lawn bowling and croquet" "between courses" or cozy up to the outdoor fireplace in cooler weather; the Euro-accented menu may be "limited" compared with its wicked-expensive on-site sibling Marinus, but for a "casual night out" it's "never a disappointment."

Will's Fargo Dining House & Saloon *Seafood/Steak*

∇ 23 | 19 | 21 | $49

Carmel Valley | Carmel Valley Vill. | 16 W. Carmel Valley Rd. (El Caminito Way) | 831-659-2774 | www.bernardus.com

Feeding the troops "delicious" surf 'n' turf since 1959, this "charming" vintage roadhouse with a "saloon" feel "remains one of the best steakhouses" in Carmel Valley, and a "bargain" to boot; check out the meat "display as you walk in the door", settle in for a stiff cocktail or "local" vino from the owner's own Bernardus Winery or just break bread and enjoy the novelty of "carrying on a conversation" – "perfection" incarnate; P.S. closed Tuesday–Wednesday.

Xanh *Vietnamese*

21 | 21 | 18 | $38

Mountain View | 110 Castro St. (Evelyn Ave.) | 650-964-1888 | www.xanhrestaurant.com

"For a dash of nightclub with your dinner", this "stylish" Mountain View venue delivers "upscale" "nouveau Vietnamese" that "wows" in a "glitzy" atmosphere with "dim lighting and decor in shades of blue"; service is generally "solid", and though a few "wish they'd turn down the volume a bit", there's little chance of that when the DJs spin and "it really starts hopping" on the weekends; P.S. there's a new weekday lunch buffet too.

Yankee Pier *New England/Seafood*

18 | 16 | 18 | $35

San Jose | 378 Santana Row (Stevens Creek Blvd.) | 408-244-1244
South San Francisco | San Francisco Int'l Airport | United Domestic Departure Terminal 3 (Hwy. 101) | 650-821-8938 | www.yankeepier.com

See review in North of San Francisco Directory.

Zibibbo ⊠ *Mediterranean*

19 | 20 | 18 | $45

Palo Alto | 430 Kipling St. (bet. Lytton & University Aves.) | 650-328-6722 | www.zibibborestaurant.com

There's "always an upbeat crowd" at this "happening", "upscale" Palo Altan (sib to SF's Restaurant Lulu) savoring "simple yet delicious" Mediterranean small plates and "family-style" "specialties from the wood-fired oven"; it's "inviting" for "catching up with friends" over "wine flights" at the bar, though a minority mutters that the "reception"-sized space, "variable" service and somewhat "tired" menu are already for a "refresh."

Zitune *Moroccan*

| 23 | 20 | 22 | $45 |

Los Altos | 325 Main St. (2nd St.) | 650-947-0247 | www.zitune.com
"Casablanca meets California in the sleepy suburb of Los Altos" at this "tranquil" place where the Moroccan menu, "modernized with fresh local ingredients" and "novel" preparations, offers many "intriguing" choices (the starters especially "shine"); "service is a lot friendlier than at the medina in Marrakesh", and though the price "can climb quickly" at dinner, the prix fixe lunch is a "real bargain."

Zucca Ristorante *Mediterranean*

| ∇ 18 | 19 | 18 | $39 |

Mountain View | 186 Castro St. (bet. Evelyn Ave. & Villa St.) | 650-864-9940 | www.zuccaristorante.com
A "seasonal menu" of "simple" Med plates (both large and small) paired with a "decent wine list" keep this "quaint little" place "reliable for a "reasonably priced" lunch or "a date in Mountain View"; it's "especially nice when you can sit outside", where a guitarist plays Thursday–Saturday, but a fussier few say that while it "tries hard", it's "not quite there."

INDEXES

LOCATION MAPS

All places are in San Francisco unless otherwise noted (East of San Francisco=E; North of San Francisco=N; South of San Francisco=S).

Cuisines

Includes names, locations and Food ratings.

AFGHAN

Helmand Palace | **Russian Hill** — 23
Kabul Afghan | **multi.** — 23

AMERICAN

🅩 Ad Hoc | **Yountville/N** — 27
🅩 Ahwahnee | **Yosemite/E** — 19
AKA Bistro | **St. Helena/N** — 15
Ame | **SoMa** — 26
NEW Amer. Cupcake | **Cow Hollow** — ⊥
NEW Amer. Grilled Cheese | **SoMa** — ⊥
Aquarius | **Santa Cruz/S** — 23
Arcadia | **San Jose/S** — 21
NEW Baker/Banker | **Upper Fillmore** — 25
Balboa Cafe | **multi.** — 19
Bardessono | **Yountville/N** — 21
Bar Jules | **Hayes Valley** — 25
Barndiva | **Healdsburg/N** — 20
Basin | **Saratoga/S** — 21
Beach Chalet | **Outer Sunset** — 14
NEW Benu | **SoMa** — ⊥
🅩 Big 4 | **Nob Hill** — 23
Big Sur | **Big Sur/S** — 21
Bing Crosby's | **Walnut Creek/E** — 19
🅩 Bix | **Downtown** — 24
Blue Plate | **Mission** — 23
Boulette Larder | **Embarcadero** — 25
🅩 Boulevard | **Embarcadero** — 27
Brannan's Grill | **Calistoga/N** — 22
Brazen Head | **Cow Hollow** — 21
🅩 Buckeye | **Mill Valley/N** — 23
Bungalow 44 | **Mill Valley/N** — 22
Cafe La Haye | **Sonoma/N** — 26
NEW Cannery Row Brew | **Monterey/S** — ⊥
Caprice | **Tiburon/N** — 21
Celadon | **Napa/N** — 23
Chapter & Moon | **Ft Bragg/N** — 23
Cheesecake Fac. | **multi.** — 16
Chenery Park | **Glen Pk** — 22
Chloe's Cafe | **Noe Valley** — 23
🅩 Chow/Park Chow | **multi.** — 20
Circa | **Marina** — 16
NEW Citizen's Band | **SoMa** — ⊥
🅩 Commis | **Oakland/E** — 27
NEW Commonwealth | **Mission** — ⊥
NEW Comstock | **N Beach** — ⊥
Cosmopolitan | **SoMa** — 19

Cuvée | **Napa/N** — 20
Digs Bistro | **Berkeley/E** — 23
Dipsea Cafe | **Mill Valley/N** — 19
Dream Farm | **San Anselmo/N** — 21
Duarte's | **Pescadero/S** — 21
Duck Club | **multi.** — 21
Elite Cafe | **Pacific Hts** — 19
Ella's | **Presidio Hts** — 21
Enrico's | **N Beach** — 16
Esin | **Danville/E** — 25
Eureka | **Castro** — 22
Evan's | **S Lake Tahoe/E** — 25
NEW Eve | **Berkeley/E** — 25
🅩 Farm | **Napa/N** — 23
NEW Farmstead | **St. Helena/N** — ⊥
15 Romolo | **N Beach** — ⊥
Fifth Floor | **SoMa** — 25
Fish & Farm | **Downtown** — 20
Five | **Berkeley/E** — 22
Flea St. Café | **Menlo Pk/S** — 25
Flora | **Oakland/E** — 22
Fog City Diner | **Embarcadero** — 19
Forbes Island | **Fish. Wharf** — 19
🅩 French Laundry | **Yountville/N** — 29
Fumé Bistro | **Napa/N** — 19
Gar Woods | **Carnelian Bay/E** — 17
🅩 Gary Danko | **Fish. Wharf** — 29
Gordon Biersch | **multi.** — 15
Gott's Roadside | **multi.** — 21
Hard Rock | **Fish. Wharf** — 12
Healdsburg B&G | **Healdsburg/N** — 19
NEW Hog & Rocks | **Mission** — ⊥
Home | **Castro** — 19
🅩 House of Prime | **Polk Gulch** — 25
Indigo | **Civic Ctr** — 19
🅩 In-N-Out | **multi.** — 22
Jole | **Calistoga/N** — 25
Kenwood | **Kenwood/N** — 21
Kitchenette SF | **Dogpatch** — 22
NEW Lafitte | **Embarcadero** — ⊥
Lark Creek | **Walnut Creek/E** — 23
Liberty Cafe | **Bernal Hts** — 22
Lion/Compass | **Sunnyvale/S** — 20
Luna Park | **Mission** — 19
MacArthur Pk. | **Palo Alto/S** — 17
Madera | **Menlo Pk/S** — 23
Madrona | **Healdsburg/N** — 26
Magnolia | **Haight-Ashbury** — 20
Mama's on Wash. | **N Beach** — 25
Mama's Royal | **Oakland/E** — 21

CUISINES

BAKERIES

Alexis Baking	Napa/N	22
NEW Amer. Cupcake	Cow Hollow	-
Bakesale Betty	Oakland/E	26
Big Sur	Big Sur/S	21
☑ Cheese Board	Berkeley/E	27
DeLessio	multi.	22
Della Fattoria	Petaluma/N	25
Downtown Bakery	Healdsburg/N	24
Dynamo Donut	Mission	-
Emporio Rulli	multi.	21
NEW Fort Bragg Bakery	Ft Bragg/N	27
Gayle's Bakery	Capitola/S	24
NEW Golden West	Downtown	-
La Boulange	multi.	21
Liberty Cafe	Bernal Hts	22
Mama's on Wash.	N Beach	25
Mayfield	Palo Alto/S	19
Model Bakery	multi.	21
NEW Sandbox	Bernal Hts	26
☑ Tartine	Mission	27
Town's End	Embarcadero	20

BARBECUE

Baby Blues BBQ	Mission	20
BarBersQ	Napa/N	22
Bo's BBQ	Lafayette/E	22
Bounty Hunter	Napa/N	19
☑ Buckeye	Mill Valley/N	23
Everett/Jones	multi.	20
Memphis Minnie	Lower Haight	21
Q Rest.	Inner Rich	18
T Rex BBQ	Berkeley/E	17
Wexler's	Downtown	22

BELGIAN

Frjtz Fries	multi.	17
La Trappe	N Beach	18

BRAZILIAN

Espetus	multi.	23
Pampas	Palo Alto/S	21

BRITISH

Betty's Fish	Santa Rosa/N	23
Lovejoy's Tea	Noe Valley	21

BURGERS

NEW Acme Burger	W Addition	18
Balboa Cafe	Cow Hollow	19
Barney's	multi.	19
NEW Burger Bar	Downtown	19
Burger Joint	multi.	18
BurgerMeister	multi.	20
NEW Cannery Row Brew	Monterey/S	-
FatApple's	multi.	17
Gott's Roadside	multi.	21
Healdsburg B&G	Healdsburg/N	19
☑ In-N-Out	multi.	22
Joe's Cable Car	Excelsior	23
Mel's Drive-In	multi.	14
Red's Java	Embarcadero	15
NEW Roam	Cow Hollow	-
NEW SliderBar	Palo Alto/S	-
NEW Super Duper	Castro	-
NEW Trueburger	Oakland/E	-
Zeitgeist	Mission	16

BURMESE

☑ Burma Superstar	multi.	24
Mandalay	Inner Rich	23
Nan Yang	Oakland/E	20
Pagan	multi.	18
Yamo	Mission	21

CAJUN

Cajun Pacific	Outer Sunset	22
Chenery Park	Glen Pk	22
Elite Cafe	Pacific Hts	19

CALIFORNIAN

Adagia	Berkeley/E	18
☑ Ahwahnee	Yosemite/E	19
Albion River Inn	Albion/N	24
All Seasons	Calistoga/N	23
Amanda's	Berkeley/E	21
Amber Bistro	Danville/E	22
Americano	Embarcadero	18
Applewood Inn	Guerneville/N	24
Artisan Bistro	Lafayette/E	23
AsiaSF	SoMa	17
Asqew Grill	multi.	16
☑ Auberge/Soleil	Rutherford/N	26
Aubergine	Carmel/S	25
NEW Bar Agricole	SoMa	-
Baxter's Bistro	Truckee/E	-
BayWolf	Oakland/E	26
Bistro Aix	Marina	-
Bistro Boudin	Fish. Wharf	20
Bistro Elan	Palo Alto/S	25
Bistro Ralph	Healdsburg/N	23
Blackhawk Grille	Danville/E	21
Blue Barn	Marina	21
☑ Blue Bottle	multi.	23
Boon Fly	Napa/N	22

NEW Brick/Bottle | Corte Madera/N	–
Bridges | **Danville/E**	22
Brix | **Napa/N**	23
Bucci's | **Emeryville/E**	21
Butterfly | **Embarcadero**	22
Cafe Beaujolais | **Mendocino/N**	24
Café Brioche | **Palo Alto/S**	21
Cafe La Haye | **Sonoma/N**	26
Café Rustica | **Carmel Valley/S**	23
Calafia | **Palo Alto/S**	19
Camino | **Oakland/E**	23
Campton Place | **Downtown**	25
⊿ Canteen | **Tenderloin**	27
Carneros Bistro | **Sonoma/N**	22
Cellar Door Café | **Santa Cruz/S**	22
Central Market | **Petaluma/N**	25
⊿ Chez Panisse | **Berkeley/E**	28
⊿ Chez Panisse Café | **Berkeley/E**	27
NEW Chop Bar | **Oakland/E**	22
Christy Hill | **Tahoe City/E**	20
Cindy's | **St. Helena/N**	24
Cliff House | **Outer Rich**	19
Club XIX | **Pebble Bch/S**	22
Coco500 | **SoMa**	23
⊿ Coi | **N Beach**	26
Cool Café | **multi.**	20
Corner | **Mission**	19
Davenport Rdhse. | **Davenport/S**	19
Deetjen's | **Big Sur/S**	23
Dragonfly | **Truckee/E**	22
Drake's | **Inverness/N**	20
Dry Creek | **Healdsburg/N**	24
Ecco | **Burlingame/S**	24
El Dorado | **Sonoma/N**	23
Eos | **Cole Valley**	23
⊿ Erna's Elderberry | **Oakhurst/E**	28
Estate | **Sonoma/N**	23
⊿ Étoile | **Yountville/N**	24
⊿ Farmhouse Inn | **Forestville/N**	27
NEW Farmstead | **St. Helena/N**	–
Fishwife | **Pacific Grove/S**	21
Five | **Berkeley/E**	22
Flavor | **Santa Rosa/N**	19
Flea St. Café | **Menlo Pk/S**	25
⊿ Fleur de Lys | **Downtown**	27
Flying Fish | **Carmel/S**	24
Flying Fish | **Half Moon Bay/S**	23
Foreign Cinema | **Mission**	23
⊿ **NEW** Frances | **Castro**	27
Frascati | **Russian Hill**	25
Gabriella Café | **Santa Cruz/S**	21
⊿ Garden Court | **Downtown**	18
Garibaldis | **multi.**	22

NEW Gather | **Berkeley/E**	–
NEW Georges | **Downtown**	–
Globe | **Downtown**	21
Grasing's Coastal | **Carmel/S**	22
Half Moon Brew | **Half Moon Bay/S**	15
Harvest Moon | **Sonoma/N**	25
NEW Heirloom | **Mission**	–
Hurley's | **Yountville/N**	22
Jake's/Lake | **Tahoe City/E**	16
⊿ Jardinière | **Civic Ctr**	26
John Ash | **Santa Rosa/N**	22
John Bentley | **Redwood City/S**	24
Lake Chalet | **Oakland/E**	14
Lalime's | **Berkeley/E**	25
La Scene | **Downtown**	21
Ledford Hse. | **Albion/N**	24
Little River Inn | **Little River/N**	21
Local Kitchen | **SoMa**	20
NEW Local Mission | **Mission**	–
Luce | **SoMa**	21
Luella | **Russian Hill**	22
Luka's Taproom | **Oakland/E**	20
MacCallum | **Mendocino/N**	23
Mandaloun | **Redwood City/S**	20
Mantra | **Palo Alto/S**	22
NEW Manzanita | **Truckee/E**	25
⊿ Marinus | **Carmel Valley/S**	27
NEW Marlowe | **SoMa**	–
Mayfield | **Palo Alto/S**	19
Meadowood Grill | **St. Helena/N**	22
⊿ Meadowood Rest. | **St. Helena/N**	26
Mendo Hotel | **Mendocino/N**	19
NEW Meritage/Claremont | **Berkeley/E**	25
Metro | **Lafayette/E**	22
Mezze | **Oakland/E**	23
Mission Bch. Café | **Mission**	25
Monk's Kettle | **Mission**	20
Montrio Bistro | **Monterey/S**	22
Moosse Café | **Mendocino/N**	24
Mosaic | **Forestville/N**	25
Moss Room | **Inner Rich**	20
Murray Circle | **Sausalito/N**	24
⊿ Mustards | **Yountville/N**	25
Namu | **Inner Rich**	23
Napa General | **Napa/N**	19
Napa Wine Train | **Napa/N**	18
Nick's Cove | **Marshall/N**	19
⊿ Nopa | **W Addition**	25
Olema Inn | **Olema/N**	19
Oola | **SoMa**	21
Orson | **SoMa**	19
Osake | **Santa Rosa/N**	24

Oxbow Wine | Napa/N	22
Pacific Crest | Truckee/E	-
Pappo | Alameda/E	22
Parcel 104 | Santa Clara/S	23
Park Chalet | Outer Sunset	14
Passionfish | Pacific Grove/S	25
Patrona | Ukiah/N	-
Pearl | Napa/N	21
Piccino | Dogpatch	21
Picco | Larkspur/N	25
Pizzavino | Sebastopol/N	-
NEW Plum | Oakland/E	-
Plumed Horse | Saratoga/S	25
PlumpJack | Olympic Valley/E	23
NEW Radius | SoMa	-
Ravenous | Healdsburg/N	21
Z Redd | Yountville/N	27
NEW Rest. at Ventana | Big Sur/S	22
NEW Revival Bar | Berkeley/E	-
Richmond Rest. | Inner Rich	25
Rio Grill | Carmel/S	22
Rist. Avanti | Santa Cruz/S	23
River Ranch | Tahoe City/E	15
Z Rivoli | Berkeley/E	27
Santé | Sonoma/N	23
Sent Sovi | Saratoga/S	25
71 St. Peter | San Jose/S	20
Shadowbrook | Capitola/S	18
Shokolaat | Palo Alto/S	21
Sidebar | Oakland/E	20
Z Sierra Mar | Big Sur/S	28
Silks | Downtown	25
Soif Wine Bar | Santa Cruz/S	24
Solbar | Calistoga/N	25
NEW Starbelly | Castro	20
Station House | Pt Reyes/N	18
Stinking Rose | N Beach	18
St. Michael's | Palo Alto/S	22
St. Orres | Gualala/N	22
Sutro's | Outer Rich	20
Syrah | Santa Rosa/N	25
Table 28 | Boonville/N	23
Table Café | Larkspur/N	23
Terrapin Creek | Bodega Bay/N	28
Townhouse B&G | Emeryville/E	20
2223 | Castro	21
Ubuntu | Napa/N	26
NEW Velvet Room | Downtown	-
Venus | Berkeley/E	21
Viognier | San Mateo/S	23
Waterfront | Embarcadero	18
Wente Vineyards | Livermore/E	24
Wicket Bistro | Carmel Valley/S	24
Wine Spectator | St. Helena/N	24

Wolfdale's | Tahoe City/E	25
Wood Tavern | Oakland/E	25
Woodward's Gdn. | Mission	24
XYZ | SoMa	20
Zaré/Fly Trap | SoMa	23

CAMBODIAN

Angkor Borei | Bernal Hts	23

CARIBBEAN

Cha Cha Cha | multi.	21
Fishwife | Pacific Grove/S	21
Front Porch | Bernal Hts	19
NEW Hibiscus | Oakland/E	21
Miss Pearl's | Oakland/E	16

CHEESESTEAKS

Cheese Steak Shop | multi.	21
Jake's Steaks | Marina	21
Jay's | multi.	18

CHICKEN

Goood Frikin' Chicken | Mission	18
Green Chile | W Addition	21
Home of Chicken | Oakland/E	19
Il Cane Rosso | Embarcadero	22
RoliRoti | Embarcadero	25

CHINESE

(* dim sum specialist)

Alice's | Noe Valley	20
Imperial/Berkeley* | multi.	20
Brandy Ho's | multi.	19
Chef Chu's | Los Altos/S	21
Crouching Tiger | Redwood City/S	21
Dragon Well | Marina	22
Eliza's | Pacific Hts	22
Eric's | Noe Valley	20
NEW Fang | SoMa	20
Gary Chu's | Santa Rosa/N	21
Gold Mountain* | Chinatown	20
Good Luck* | Inner Rich	20
Great China | Berkeley/E	24
Great Eastern* | Chinatown	19
Happy Cafe* | San Mateo/S	21
Harmony* | Mill Valley/N	20
Heaven's Dog* | SoMa	20
Henry's Hunan | multi.	20
Mayflower/HK Flower* | multi.	19
Hong Kong Lounge | Outer Rich	21
House of Nanking | Chinatown	21
Hunan | multi.	21
Jai Yun | Chinatown	24
Just Wonton | Outer Sunset	21
Kitchen* | Millbrae/S	19

Koi*	**multi.**	23
NEW Mission Chinese	**Mission**	–
O'mei	**Santa Cruz/S**	22
Oriental Pearl	**Chinatown**	21
R&G Lounge	**Chinatown**	24
Rest. Peony*	**Oakland/E**	20
Sam Wo's	**Chinatown**	18
San Tung	**Inner Sunset**	23
Shanghai Dumpling	**Outer Rich**	23
Shen Hua	**Berkeley/E**	19
Sino*	**San Jose/S**	19
Tai Pan*	**Palo Alto/S**	24
Tommy Toy	**Downtown**	24
Ton Kiang*	**Outer Rich**	24
☑ Yank Sing*	**SoMa**	25
Yuet Lee	**Chinatown**	20
Z & Y	**Chinatown**	–

COFFEEHOUSES

☑ Blue Bottle	**multi.**	23
Dynamo Donut	**Mission**	–
Stable Café	**Mission**	–
Warming Hut	**Presidio**	13

COFFEE SHOPS/ DINERS

Alexis Baking	**Napa/N**	22
Bette's Oceanview	**Berkeley/E**	23
Dottie's	**Tenderloin**	25
FatApple's	**multi.**	17
Fog City Diner	**Embarcadero**	19
Fremont Diner	**Sonoma/N**	22
Gott's Roadside	**multi.**	21
Jimmy Beans	**Berkeley/E**	19
Joe's Cable Car	**Excelsior**	23
Mel's Drive-In	**multi.**	14
Pine Cone Diner	**Pt Reyes/N**	22
Red Hut	**S Lake Tahoe/E**	21
Sears Fine Food	**Downtown**	20
St. Francis	**Mission**	19

CONTINENTAL

Anton/Michel	**Carmel/S**	25
Bella Vista	**Woodside/S**	22
Ecco	**Burlingame/S**	24
La Forêt	**San Jose/S**	26

CREOLE

Brenda's	**Civic Ctr**	24
NEW Hibiscus	**Oakland/E**	21
Starlight	**Sebastopol/N**	22

DELIS

Boccalone	**Embarcadero**	24
Jimtown Store	**Healdsburg/N**	21
Max's	**multi.**	17
Miller's Deli	**Polk Gulch**	19
Moishe's Pippic	**Hayes Valley**	18
Saul's Rest./Deli	**Berkeley/E**	17
Schmidt's	**Mission**	21

DESSERT

Cafe Jacqueline	**N Beach**	25
Candybar	**W Addition**	17
Cheesecake Fac.	**multi.**	16
NEW Chile Pies	**W Addition**	–
DeLessio	**multi.**	22
Downtown Bakery	**Healdsburg/N**	24
Emporio Rulli	**multi.**	21
☑ Farallon	**Downtown**	24
Gayle's Bakery	**Capitola/S**	24
La Boulange	**multi.**	21
Mayfield	**Palo Alto/S**	19
Model Bakery	**Napa/N**	21
Orson	**SoMa**	19
Shokolaat	**Palo Alto/S**	21
☑ Tartine	**Mission**	27
Town Hall	**SoMa**	23

ECLECTIC

Academy Cafe	**Inner Rich**	19
Alembic	**Haight-Ashbury**	22
Andalu	**Mission**	20
Celadon	**Napa/N**	23
Chez Shea	**Half Moon Bay/S**	23
Cottonwood	**Truckee/E**	21
Delancey St.	**Embarcadero**	18
Della Fattoria	**Petaluma/N**	25
Firefly	**Noe Valley**	24
Flavor	**Santa Rosa/N**	19
NEW Fort Bragg Bakery	**Ft Bragg/N**	27
Go Fish	**St. Helena/N**	23
NEW Heart	**Mission**	–
Hopmonk	**Sebastopol/N**	18
NEW Ironside	**S Beach**	17
Mendo Café	**Mendocino/N**	20
Napa General	**Napa/N**	19
Pomelo	**multi.**	20
Ravenous	**Healdsburg/N**	21
Restaurant	**Ft Bragg/N**	25
☑ Sierra Mar	**Big Sur/S**	28
Supperclub	**SoMa**	14
Va de Vi	**Walnut Creek/E**	24
Willi's Wine	**Santa Rosa/N**	25
Willow Wood	**Graton/N**	24
Wine Spectator	**St. Helena/N**	24

ETHIOPIAN

Axum Cafe | **Lower Haight** 21

FILIPINO

NEW Attic | **San Mateo/S** −

FONDUE

NEW Fondue Cowboy | **SoMa** −
Matterhorn Swiss | **Russian Hill** 22
Melting Pot | **Larkspur/N** 17

FRENCH

À Côté | **Oakland/E** 24
Ana Mandara | **Fish. Wharf** 22
Angèle | **Napa/N** 23
☒ Auberge/Soleil | 26
  Rutherford/N
Aubergine | **Carmel/S** 25
Basque Cultural | 21
  S San Francisco/S
NEW Baumé | **Palo Alto/S** 28
Bistro Aix | **Marina** −
Bistro/Copains | **Occidental/N** 25
Bistro Moulin | **Monterey/S** 29
☒ Bix | **Downtown** 24
Brannan's Grill | **Calistoga/N** 22
Bushi-tei | **Japantown** 22
Cafe Beaujolais | **Mendocino/N** 24
Café Fanny | **Berkeley/E** 23
Cafe Jacqueline | **N Beach** 25
Casanova | **Carmel/S** 23
Chantilly | **Redwood City/S** 25
Chaya | **Embarcadero** 22
Chevalier | **Lafayette/E** 23
Chez Spencer | **Mission** 25
Chez TJ | **Mtn View/S** 22
Club XIX | **Pebble Bch/S** 22
☒ Coi | **N Beach** 26
☒ Cyrus | **Healdsburg/N** 28
☒ Erna's Elderberry | **Oakhurst/E** 28
Fifth Floor | **SoMa** 25
Fig Cafe/Wine | **Glen Ellen/N** 25
☒ Fleur de Lys | **Downtown** 27
☒ French Laundry | **Yountville/N** 29
Gitane | **Downtown** 21
Grégoire | **multi.** 23
Isa | **Marina** 25
☒ Jardinière | **Civic Ctr** 26
Kenwood | **Kenwood/N** 21
La Boulange | **multi.** 21
☒ La Folie | **Russian Hill** 28
La Forêt | **San Jose/S** 26
La Gare | **Santa Rosa/N** 21
La Petite Rive | **Little River/N** 26
☒ La Toque | **Napa/N** 27

Le Colonial | **Downtown** 23
☒ Le Papillon | **San Jose/S** 26
Luna Park | **Mission** 19
Madrona | **Healdsburg/N** 26
Ma Maison | **Aptos/S** 20
NEW Manzanita | **Truckee/E** 25
Marché | **Menlo Pk/S** 24
Marché/Fleurs | **Ross/N** 24
☒ Marinus | **Carmel Valley/S** 27
☒ Masa's | **Downtown** 27
Metro | **Lafayette/E** 22
Mirepoix | **Windsor/N** 24
Mistral | **Redwood Shores/S** 19
955 Ukiah | **Mendocino/N** 23
☒ Pacific's Edge | **Carmel/S** 25
☒ Quince | **Downtown** 26
Rendezvous Inn | **Ft Bragg/N** 27
Rest. LuLu/Petite | **SoMa** 21
☒ Ritz-Carlton | **Nob Hill** 27
RN74 | **SoMa** 22
Santé | **Sonoma/N** 23
Twist | **Campbell/S** 20
NEW Tyler Florence | **Napa/N** −
Vanessa's Bistro | **Berkeley/E** 23
Viognier | **San Mateo/S** 23

FRENCH (BISTRO)

Alamo Sq. | **W Addition** 20
Artisan Bistro | **Lafayette/E** 23
Baker St. Bistro | **Marina** 22
NEW Bistro Central Parc | −
  W Addition
Bistro Elan | **Palo Alto/S** 25
☒ Bistro Jeanty | **Yountville/N** 25
Bistro Liaison | **Berkeley/E** 21
Bistro Ralph | **Healdsburg/N** 23
Bistro St. Germain | 20
  Lower Haight
Bistro Vida | **Menlo Pk/S** 19
Bodega Bistro | **Tenderloin** 24
☒ Bouchon | **Yountville/N** 26
Butler & Chef | **SoMa** 21
Cafe Bastille | **Downtown** 17
Café Brioche | **Palo Alto/S** 21
Café Claude | **Downtown** 22
Café de la Presse | **Downtown** 18
Café Rouge | **Berkeley/E** 20
☒ Chapeau! | **Inner Rich** 26
Charcuterie | **Healdsburg/N** 21
Chez Maman | **Potrero Hill** 23
Chez Papa | **multi.** 23
Chez Spencer | **SoMa** 25
Chouchou | **Forest Hills** 21
Florio | **Pacific Hts** 19
Fringale | **SoMa** 24

Menus, photos, voting and more – free at ZAGAT.com

Gamine | **Cow Hollow**	23
Girl & Fig | **Sonoma/N**	24
Grand Cafe | **Downtown**	20
Hyde St. Bistro | **Russian Hill**	21
K&L Bistro | **Sebastopol/N**	24
La Note | **Berkeley/E**	22
L'Ardoise | **Castro**	23
La Terrasse | **Presidio**	18
Le Central Bistro | **Downtown**	20
Le Charm Bistro | **SoMa**	22
Le P'tit Laurent | **Glen Pk**	23
Plouf | **Downtown**	21
South Park | **SoMa**	22
Syrah | **Santa Rosa/N**	25
Ti Couz | **Mission**	21
Water St. Bistro | **Petaluma/N**	24
Zazie | **Cole Valley**	22

FRENCH (BRASSERIE)

🛂 Absinthe | **Hayes Valley**	22
NEW Café des Amis | **Cow Hollow**	–
Left Bank | **multi.**	19
Luka's Taproom | **Oakland/E**	20
Midi | **Downtown**	20

GASTROPUB

Alembic | Eclectic | **Haight-Ashbury**	22
NEW Bar Agricole | Cal. | **SoMa**	–
NEW Comstock | Amer. | **N Beach**	–
15 Romolo | Amer. | **N Beach**	–
Hopmonk | Eclectic | **Sebastopol/N**	18
La Trappe | Belgian | **N Beach**	18
Magnolia | Amer. | **Haight-Ashbury**	20
Martins West | Scottish | **Redwood City/S**	24
Monk's Kettle | Cal. | **Mission**	20
NEW Norman Rose | Amer. | **Napa/N**	20
Salt House | Amer. | **SoMa**	21
Sidebar | Cal. | **Oakland/E**	20
NEW Social Kitchen | Amer. | **Inner Sunset**	–
Tipsy Pig | Amer. | **Marina**	19
Urban Tavern | Amer. | **Downtown**	17

GERMAN

Rosamunde | **multi.**	25
Schmidt's | **Mission**	21
Suppenküche | **Hayes Valley**	22
Walzwerk | **Mission**	21

GREEK

Dio Deka | **Los Gatos/S**	25
🛂 Evvia | **Palo Alto/S**	27
🛂 Kokkari | **Downtown**	27
Thea Med. | **San Jose/S**	19

HAWAIIAN

Hula's | **multi.**	18
Roy's | **SoMa**	23
🛂 Roy's | **Pebble Bch/S**	25

HEALTH FOOD

(See also Vegetarian)

Amanda's | **Berkeley/E**	21
Beautifull | **multi.**	17
Mixt Greens | **Downtown**	22
Plant Cafe | **multi.**	20

HOT DOGS

Caspers Hot Dogs | **multi.**	18
4505 Meats | **Embarcadero**	28
Let's Be Frank | **multi.**	19
Showdogs | **Downtown**	19
Underdog | **Inner Sunset**	21

ICE CREAM PARLORS

Fentons | **Oakland/E**	20

INDIAN

Ajanta | **Berkeley/E**	25
🛂 Amber India | **multi.**	24
Avatar's | **multi.**	23
Breads of India | **multi.**	20
Dasaprakash | **Santa Clara/S**	21
Dosa | **multi.**	22
Gaylord India | **Downtown**	18
Indian Oven | **Lower Haight**	22
Junnoon | **Palo Alto/S**	22
Kasa Indian | **multi.**	19
Lotus/Anokha | **multi.**	23
Mantra | **Palo Alto/S**	22
Naan/Curry | **multi.**	17
Neela's | **Napa/N**	–
Passage to India | **Mtn View/S**	17
Roti Indian | **multi.**	22
Sakoon | **Mtn View/S**	23
Shalimar | **multi.**	24
Udupi Palace | **multi.**	20
Vik's Chaat | **Berkeley/E**	23
Zante | **Bernal Hts**	18

ITALIAN

(N=Northern; S=Southern)

AcquaPazza | S | **San Mateo/S**	21
🛂 Acquerello | **Polk Gulch**	28

Adesso | **Oakland/E**	23
Albona Rist. | N | **N Beach**	23
Alioto's | S | **Fish. Wharf**	18
Antica Trattoria | **Russian Hill**	23
Aperto | **Potrero Hill**	24
☑ A16 | S | **Marina**	25
Azzurro Pizzeria | **Napa/N**	21
Bacco | **Noe Valley**	22
NEW Barbacco | **Downtown**	25
Bar Bambino | **Mission**	23
Bellanico | **Oakland/E**	22
Bella Trattoria | S | **Inner Rich**	22
Beretta | **Mission**	23
Bistro Don Giovanni | **Napa/N**	24
NEW Boot/Shoe | **Oakland/E**	24
☑ Bottega | **Yountville/N**	26
Bovolo | **Healdsburg/N**	22
Buca di Beppo | **multi.**	15
Bucci's | **Emeryville/E**	21
Cafe Citti | N | **Kenwood/N**	23
Café Fiore | N | **S Lake Tahoe/E**	25
Café Tiramisu | N | **Downtown**	20
Cafe Zoetrope/Mammarella's | S | **multi.**	20
Caffe Delle Stelle | N | **Hayes Valley**	16
Caffè Macaroni | S | **N Beach**	21
Caffè Museo | **SoMa**	19
Cantinetta Luca | **Carmel/S**	23
NEW Cantinetta Piero | **Yountville/N**	21
Capannina | **Cow Hollow**	25
Casanova | N | **Carmel/S**	23
Casa Orinda | **Orinda/E**	16
Chantilly | N | **Redwood City/S**	25
Cook St. Helena | N | **St. Helena/N**	25
Corner | **Mission**	19
Corso | N | **Berkeley/E**	23
NEW Cotogna | **Downtown**	–
NEW Credo | **Downtown**	17
Cucina Paradiso | S | **Petaluma/N**	24
Cucina Rest. | **San Anselmo/N**	23
NEW Delarosa | **Marina**	22
☑ Delfina | N | **Mission**	26
Della Santina | N | **Sonoma/N**	22
Diavola | **Geyserville/N**	24
Donato | N | **Redwood City/S**	24
Dopo | **Oakland/E**	25
E'Angelo | **Marina**	21
Emmy's Spaghetti | **Bernal Hts**	19
Emporio Rulli | **multi.**	21
Estate | **Sonoma/N**	23
Farina | **Mission**	24
54 Mint | **SoMa**	22
Fior d'Italia | N | **N Beach**	20

Florio | **Pacific Hts**	19
Flour + Water | **Mission**	24
Frantoio | N | **Mill Valley/N**	22
Gabriella Café | **Santa Cruz/S**	21
Gialina | **Glen Pk**	25
Globe | **Downtown**	21
Il Cane Rosso | **Embarcadero**	22
Il Davide | N | **San Rafael/N**	20
Il Fornaio | **multi.**	19
Il Postale | **Sunnyvale/S**	22
Incanto | N | **Noe Valley**	24
Jackson Fillmore | **Upper Fillmore**	21
Joe DiMaggio | **N Beach**	20
Kuleto's | N | **Downtown**	21
La Ciccia | **Noe Valley**	26
La Ginestra | S | **Mill Valley/N**	21
La Posta | **Santa Cruz/S**	21
La Strada | **Palo Alto/S**	20
Local Kitchen | **SoMa**	20
NEW Locanda da Eva | **Berkeley/E**	–
Lo Coco | S | **multi.**	21
L'Osteria | N | **N Beach**	24
Luce | **SoMa**	21
Lupa Trattoria | S | **Noe Valley**	24
Mario's Bohemian | N | **N Beach**	19
Marzano | S | **Oakland/E**	21
Meritage Martini | N | **Sonoma/N**	21
Mescolanza | N | **Outer Rich**	24
Mezza Luna/Caffè | S | **multi.**	22
Mistral | **Redwood Shores/S**	19
Nob Hill Café | N | **Nob Hill**	21
North Bch. Rest. | N | **N Beach**	23
NEW Oenotri | S | **Napa/N**	–
Oliveto Cafe | **Oakland/E**	23
Oliveto Rest. | **Oakland/E**	24
Original Joe's | **San Jose/S**	18
Osteria | **Palo Alto/S**	22
Osteria Stellina | **Pt Reyes/N**	25
Ottimista | **Cow Hollow**	17
Palio d'Asti | **Downtown**	20
Pane e Vino | N | **Cow Hollow**	22
Pasta Moon | **Half Moon Bay/S**	22
Pasta Pomodoro | **multi.**	17
Pazzia | **SoMa**	24
☑ Perbacco | **Downtown**	25
Pesce | N | **Russian Hill**	22
Peter Lowell | **Sebastopol/N**	21
Piaci | **Ft Bragg/N**	27
Pianeta | N | **Truckee/E**	21
Piatti | **multi.**	19
Piazza D'Angelo | **Mill Valley/N**	21
Piccino | **Dogpatch**	21
Picco | **Larkspur/N**	25
Piccolo Teatro | **Sausalito/N**	22

Pizza Antica | **multi.**	21
Pizzaiolo | S | **Oakland/E**	25
Pizzavino | **Sebastopol/N**	-
Pizzeria Delfina | **Pacific Hts**	25
Pizzeria Picco | S | **Larkspur/N**	25
Pizzeria Tra Vigne | **St. Helena/N**	21
Poesia | S | **Castro**	21
Poggio | N | **Sausalito/N**	23
Postino | **Lafayette/E**	21
Prima | N | **Walnut Creek/E**	24
Quattro | **E Palo Alto/S**	21
☑ Quince | **Downtown**	26
Risibisi | N | **Petaluma/N**	22
Ristobar | **Marina**	-
Rist. Avanti | **Santa Cruz/S**	23
Rist. Capellini | **San Mateo/S**	18
Rist. Ideale | S | **N Beach**	24
Rist. Milano | N | **Russian Hill**	25
Rist. Umbria | N | **SoMa**	20
Rose Pistola | N | **N Beach**	21
Rose's Cafe | N | **Cow Hollow**	22
Rosso Pizzeria | **Santa Rosa/N**	26
NEW Rustic | **Geyserville/N**	-
Santi | N | **Santa Rosa/N**	24
Scala's Bistro | **Downtown**	23
Scopa | **Healdsburg/N**	25
Sociale | N | **Presidio Hts**	23
SPQR | S | **Pacific Hts**	24
Stinking Rose | N | **N Beach**	18
Tommaso's | S | **N Beach**	24
Tony's Pizza | **N Beach**	26
Tratt. Contadina | **N Beach**	23
Tratt. La Sicil. | S | **Berkeley/E**	25
Tra Vigne | N | **St. Helena/N**	24
Uva Enoteca | **Lower Haight**	21
Uva Trattoria | **Napa/N**	20
Venezia | **Berkeley/E**	21
Venticello | N | **Nob Hill**	23
Vin Antico | **San Rafael/N**	19
Volpi's Rist. | **Petaluma/N**	18
Zazu | N | **Santa Rosa/N**	25
NEW Zero Zero | **SoMa**	-
Zuppa | S | **SoMa**	20

JAPANESE

(* sushi specialist)

Ace Wasabi's* | **Marina**	20
Alexander's | **Cupertino/S**	26
Anzu* | **Downtown**	22
Ariake* | **Outer Rich**	23
Benihana | **multi.**	17
Blowfish Sushi* | **multi.**	21
Bushi-tei | **Japantown**	22
Chaya | **Embarcadero**	22
Cha-Ya Veg.* | **multi.**	23

Domo Sushi* | **Hayes Valley**	20
Ebisu* | **multi.**	23
Eiji* | **Castro**	25
Fuki Sushi* | **Palo Alto/S**	22
Gochi | **Cupertino/S**	24
Godzila Sushi* | **Pacific Hts**	18
Grandeho Kamekyo* | **Fish. Wharf**	21
Hachi Ju Hachi* | **Saratoga/S**	-
Hamano Sushi* | **Noe Valley**	19
☑ Hana* | **Rohnert Pk/N**	28
Hotaru* | **San Mateo/S**	20
Hotei* | **Inner Sunset**	20
Isobune* | **multi.**	19
NEW Izakaya Sozai | **Inner Sunset**	-
Jin Sho* | **Palo Alto/S**	24
Juban | **multi.**	18
Kabuto* | **Outer Rich**	26
Kamekyo* | **Cole Valley**	21
Kanpai* | **Palo Alto/S**	24
Katana-Ya | **Downtown**	22
☑ Kaygetsu* | **Menlo Pk/S**	27
Kirala* | **Berkeley/E**	24
☑ Kiss Seafood* | **Japantown**	27
Koo* | **Inner Sunset**	23
Kyo-Ya* | **Downtown**	24
Maki* | **Japantown**	22
Mifune | **Japantown**	17
Moki's Sushi* | **Bernal Hts**	19
NEW Morimoto* | **Napa/N**	-
Muracci's* | **multi.**	22
Naked Fish* | **S Lake Tahoe/E**	23
Naomi Sushi* | **Menlo Pk/S**	23
Nihon | **Mission**	21
NEW Nombe | **Mission**	22
O Chamé | **Berkeley/E**	23
Oco Time* | **Ukiah/N**	-
Osake* | **Santa Rosa/N**	24
Oyaji* | **Outer Rich**	23
Ozumo* | **multi.**	23
NEW Prime Rib Shabu | **Inner Rich**	23
Robata Grill* | **Mill Valley/N**	19
Ryoko's* | **Downtown**	23
Sakae Sushi* | **Burlingame/S**	26
Sanraku* | **multi.**	21
☑ Sebo* | **Hayes Valley**	27
Shabu-Sen | **Japantown**	19
Sumika | **Los Altos/S**	24
Sushi Groove* | **multi.**	22
☑ Sushi Ran* | **Sausalito/N**	27
☑ Sushi Zone* | **Castro**	27
Takara* | **Japantown**	20
Tataki Sushi* | **Pacific Hts**	22
Ten-Ichi* | **Upper Fillmore**	20
NEW Tjukiji Sushi* | **Mill Valley/N**	-

CUISINES

Tokyo Go Go*	**Mission**	21
Tsunami*	**multi.**	22
Umami*	**Cow Hollow**	23
Uzen*	**Oakland/E**	24
Yoshi's*	**Oakland/E**	20
Yoshi's SF	**W Addition**	21
Z Zushi Puzzle*	**Marina**	27

JEWISH

Miller's Deli	**Polk Gulch**	19
Moishe's Pippic	**Hayes Valley**	18
Saul's Rest./Deli	**Berkeley/E**	17

KOREAN

(* barbecue specialist)

Brother's Korean*	**Inner Rich**	22
Koryo BBQ*	**Oakland/E**	22
My Tofu*	**Inner Rich**	20
Namu	**multi.**	23
San Tung	**Inner Sunset**	23

MEDITERRANEAN

Z Absinthe	**Hayes Valley**	22
À Côté	**Oakland/E**	24
Adagia	**Berkeley/E**	18
Arlequin	**Hayes Valley**	18
Bar Tartine	**Mission**	23
BayWolf	**Oakland/E**	26
Brix	**Napa/N**	23
Bursa Kebab	**W Portal**	21
Z Cafe Gibraltar	**El Granada/S**	27
Café Rouge	**Berkeley/E**	20
Caffè Museo	**SoMa**	19
Camino	**Oakland/E**	23
Campton Place	**Downtown**	25
Central Market	**Petaluma/N**	25
Cetrella	**Half Moon Bay/S**	20
Z Chez Panisse	**Berkeley/E**	28
Z Chez Panisse Café	**Berkeley/E**	27
Christy Hill	**Tahoe City/E**	20
Coco500	**SoMa**	23
Digs Bistro	**Berkeley/E**	23
Dio Deka	**Los Gatos/S**	25
El Dorado	**Sonoma/N**	23
Enrico's	**N Beach**	16
Esin	**Danville/E**	25
Fandango	**Pacific Grove/S**	22
Foreign Cinema	**Mission**	23
Frascati	**Russian Hill**	25
Garibaldis	**multi.**	22
Gar Woods	**Carnelian Bay/E**	17
Harvest Moon	**Sonoma/N**	25
NEW Heirloom	**Mission**	-
Hurley's	**Yountville/N**	22

Insalata's	**San Anselmo/N**	23
Lalime's	**Berkeley/E**	25
La Méditerranée	**multi.**	19
La Scene	**Downtown**	21
Lavanda	**Palo Alto/S**	19
Ledford Hse.	**Albion/N**	24
Loló	**Mission**	24
Luella	**Russian Hill**	22
Mandaloun	**Redwood City/S**	20
MarketBar	**Embarcadero**	17
Medjool	**Mission**	19
Mezze	**Oakland/E**	23
Monti's	**Santa Rosa/N**	21
Ottimista	**Cow Hollow**	17
Oxbow Wine	**Napa/N**	22
Pacific Crest	**Truckee/E**	-
Pappo	**Alameda/E**	22
Paul K	**Hayes Valley**	22
Peasant/Pear	**Danville/E**	24
Pianeta	**Truckee/E**	21
PlumpJack	**Olympic Valley/E**	23
Rest. LuLu/Petite	**SoMa**	21
Z Rivoli	**Berkeley/E**	27
Savor	**Noe Valley**	17
Sens	**Downtown**	19
71 St. Peter	**San Jose/S**	20
Sidebar	**Oakland/E**	20
NEW Spoonbar	**Healdsburg/N**	-
Terzo	**Cow Hollow**	23
Thea Med.	**San Jose/S**	19
Truly Med.	**Mission**	26
Underwood Bar	**Graton/N**	24
Wente Vineyards	**Livermore/E**	24
Willow Wood	**Graton/N**	24
Zaré/Fly Trap	**SoMa**	23
Zatar	**Berkeley/E**	25
Zibibbo	**Palo Alto/S**	19
Zucca	**Mtn View/S**	18
Z Zuni Café	**Hayes Valley**	25

MEXICAN

Cactus Taqueria	**multi.**	20
NEW C Casa	**Napa/N**	-
Colibrí	**Downtown**	20
Doña Tomás	**Oakland/E**	21
Don Pico	**San Bruno/S**	21
El Metate	**Mission**	22
Z El Tonayense	**multi.**	24
NEW Gracias	**Mission**	20
Green Chile	**W Addition**	21
Guaymas	**Tiburon/N**	17
Joe's Taco	**Mill Valley/N**	19
Juan's	**Berkeley/E**	16
La Corneta	**multi.**	21
La Cumbre	**multi.**	21

Restaurant	Location	Score
Las Camelias	**San Rafael/N**	18
La Taqueria	**Mission**	25
Little Chihuahua	**multi.**	22
Mamacita	**Marina**	22
Marinitas	**San Anselmo/N**	18
Maya	**SoMa**	20
Mexico DF	**Embarcadero**	18
Mijita	**multi.**	21
Nick's Crispy	**Russian Hill**	21
Nopalito	**W Addition**	23
Pancho Villa	**multi.**	22
Papalote	**multi.**	22
Picante Cocina	**Berkeley/E**	21
Regalito Rosticeria	**Mission**	19
NEW TacoBar	**Pacific Hts**	-
NEW Tacolicious	**multi.**	23
Tacubaya	**Berkeley/E**	23
Tamarindo	**Oakland/E**	25
Taqueria Can-Cun	**multi.**	21
Taqueria Tlaquepaque	**San Jose/S**	24
Tommy's Mex.	**Outer Rich**	18
Tres Agaves	**S Beach**	17
Tropisueño	**SoMa**	19

MIDDLE EASTERN

Restaurant	Location	Score
Dishdash	**Sunnyvale/S**	22
Goood Frikin' Chicken	**Mission**	18
Kan Zaman	**Haight-Ashbury**	19
La Méditerranée	**multi.**	19
Old Jerusalem	**Mission**	19
Saha	**Tenderloin**	26
Truly Med.	**Mission**	26
Yumma's	**Inner Sunset**	19

MOROCCAN

Restaurant	Location	Score
Z Aziza	**Outer Rich**	26
Zitune	**Los Altos/S**	23

NEPALESE

Restaurant	Location	Score
Little Nepal	**Bernal Hts**	21

NEW ENGLAND

Restaurant	Location	Score
Old Port Lobster	**Redwood City/S**	21
Yankee Pier	**multi.**	18

NOODLE SHOPS

Restaurant	Location	Score
Citrus Club	**Haight-Ashbury**	21
Hotaru	**San Mateo/S**	20
Hotei	**Inner Sunset**	20
Katana-Ya	**Downtown**	22
King of Thai	**multi.**	18
Mifune	**Japantown**	17
O Chamé	**Berkeley/E**	23

Restaurant	Location	Score
Osha Thai	**multi.**	20
San Tung	**Inner Sunset**	23

NUEVO LATINO

Restaurant	Location	Score
Destino	**Castro**	21
Joya	**Palo Alto/S**	20
Limón	**Mission**	23

PACIFIC RIM

Restaurant	Location	Score
Pacific Catch	**multi.**	19
Tonga	**Nob Hill**	14

PAKISTANI

Restaurant	Location	Score
Lahore Karahi	**Tenderloin**	25
Naan/Curry	**multi.**	17
Pakwan	**multi.**	21
Shalimar	**multi.**	24

PAN-LATIN

Restaurant	Location	Score
NEW Bocanova	**Oakland/E**	21
Cascal	**Mtn View/S**	19
César	**Oakland/E**	22
Charanga	**Mission**	23
Fonda Solana	**Albany/E**	22
Loló	**Mission**	24
Marinitas	**San Anselmo/N**	18

PERSIAN

Restaurant	Location	Score
Maykadeh	**N Beach**	23

PERUVIAN

Restaurant	Location	Score
Fresca	**multi.**	22
NEW La Costanera	**Montara/S**	24
La Mar	**Embarcadero**	24
Limón	**Mission**	23
Mochica	**SoMa**	23
Piqueo's	**Bernal Hts**	24

PIZZA

Restaurant	Location	Score
Amici's	**multi.**	19
Arinell Pizza	**multi.**	21
Azzurro Pizzeria	**Napa/N**	21
Beretta	**Mission**	23
NEW Boot/Shoe	**Oakland/E**	24
Cafe Zoetrope/Mammarella's	**N Beach**	20
Z Cheese Board	**Berkeley/E**	27
NEW Delarosa	**Marina**	22
Diavola	**Geyserville/N**	24
NEW Emilia's	**Berkeley/E**	27
Flour + Water	**Mission**	24
Gialina	**Glen Pk**	25
Gioia Pizzeria	**Berkeley/E**	24
Giorgio's	**Inner Rich**	22
Goat Hill Pizza	**multi.**	20

La Ginestra | **Mill Valley/N**	21
Lanesplitter | **multi.**	16
Little Star | **multi.**	24
Local Kitchen | **SoMa**	20
Lo Coco | **multi.**	21
Marzano | **Oakland/E**	21
North Bch. Pizza | **multi.**	19
Palio d'Asti | **Downtown**	20
Patxi's Pizza | **multi.**	22
Pauline's | **Mission**	22
Piaci | **Ft Bragg/N**	27
NEW Pi Bar | **Mission**	14
Pizza Antica | **multi.**	21
Pizzaiolo | **Oakland/E**	25
Pizza Nostra | **Potrero Hill**	22
Pizza Pl./Noriega | **Outer Sunset**	-
Pizza Rustica | **Oakland/E**	21
Pizzavino | **Sebastopol/N**	-
Pizzeria Delfina | **multi.**	25
Pizzeria Picco | **Larkspur/N**	25
Pizzeria Tra Vigne | **St. Helena/N**	21
Z Pizzetta 211 | **Outer Rich**	27
Rosso Pizzeria | **Santa Rosa/N**	26
NEW Rustic | **Geyserville/N**	-
NEW Starbelly | **Castro**	20
Tommaso's | **N Beach**	24
Tony's Pizza | **N Beach**	26
Z Zachary's Pizza | **multi.**	24
Zante | **Bernal Hts**	18
NEW Zero Zero | **SoMa**	-

POLYNESIAN

Trader Vic's | **multi.**	17

PORTUGUESE

LaSalette | **Sonoma/N**	24

PUB FOOD

Bridgetender | **Tahoe City/E**	18
Gordon Biersch | **multi.**	15
Half Moon Brew | **Half Moon Bay/S**	15
NEW Public House | **S Beach**	-
Ukiah Brew | **Ukiah/N**	16

PUERTO RICAN

NEW Parada 22 | **Haight-Ashbury**	-
Sol Food | **San Rafael/N**	22

RUSSIAN

Katia's Tea | **Inner Rich**	23

SALVADORAN

El Zocalo | **Bernal Hts**	20

SANDWICHES

NEW Amer. Grilled Cheese | **SoMa**	-
Bakesale Betty | **Oakland/E**	26
Bocadillos | **N Beach**	23
Boccalone | **Embarcadero**	24
Cheese Steak Shop | **multi.**	21
Downtown Bakery | **Healdsburg/N**	24
NEW Fort Bragg Bakery | **Ft Bragg/N**	27
Gayle's Bakery | **Capitola/S**	24
Giordano | **N Beach**	21
NEW Golden West | **Downtown**	-
Il Cane Rosso | **Embarcadero**	22
Jimtown Store | **Healdsburg/N**	21
Kitchenette SF | **Dogpatch**	22
NEW Local Mission | **Mission**	-
Mario's Bohemian | **N Beach**	19
Max's | **multi.**	17
Mixt Greens | **Downtown**	22
Model Bakery | **multi.**	21
NEW Naked Lunch | **N Beach**	26
Plant Cafe | **multi.**	20
Pluto's | **multi.**	19
Saigon Sandwich | **Tenderloin**	24
Sentinel | **SoMa**	24
NEW Spice Kit | **SoMa**	-
Warming Hut | **Presidio**	13
'Wichcraft | **Downtown**	18

SCOTTISH

Martins West | **Redwood City/S**	24

SEAFOOD

Alamo Sq. | **W Addition**	20
Alioto's | **Fish. Wharf**	18
Anchor & Hope | **SoMa**	21
Anchor Oyster | **Castro**	23
Aquarius | **Santa Cruz/S**	23
Barbara's | **Princeton Sea/S**	20
Bar Crudo | **W Addition**	25
Betty's Fish | **Santa Rosa/N**	23
Cajun Pacific | **Outer Sunset**	22
Catch | **Castro**	18
Chapter & Moon | **Ft Bragg/N**	23
Z Farallon | **Downtown**	24
Fish | **Sausalito/N**	25
Fish & Farm | **Downtown**	20
NEW Fish Story | **Napa/N**	-
Fishwife | **Pacific Grove/S**	21
Flying Fish | **Carmel/S**	24
Flying Fish | **Half Moon Bay/S**	23

orbes Island | **Fish. Wharf**	19
NEW Georges | **Downtown**	-
Go Fish | **St. Helena/N**	23
Great Eastern | **Chinatown**	19
Guaymas | **Tiburon/N**	17
Half Moon Brew | **Half Moon Bay/S**	15
Hayes St. Grill | **Hayes Valley**	23
NEW Hog & Rocks | **Mission**	-
Z Hog Island Oyster | **multi.**	25
Koi | **Daly City/S**	23
Lake Chalet | **Oakland/E**	14
La Mar | **Embarcadero**	24
Little River Inn | **Little River/N**	21
Marica | **Oakland/E**	23
NEW Mayes | **Polk Gulch**	19
Mayflower/HK Flower | **Outer Rich**	19
McCormick/Kuleto | **Fish. Wharf**	20
McCormick/Schmick | **San Jose/S**	21
Meritage Martini | **Sonoma/N**	21
Nettie's Crab | **Cow Hollow**	18
Old Port Lobster | **Redwood City/S**	21
Pacific Café | **Outer Rich**	23
Pacific Catch | **multi.**	19
Passionfish | **Pacific Grove/S**	25
Pesce | **Russian Hill**	22
Plouf | **Downtown**	21
R&G Lounge | **Chinatown**	24
Sam's Chowder | **Half Moon Bay/S**	19
Sam's Grill | **Downtown**	21
Sardine Factory | **Monterey/S**	20
Z Scoma's | **multi.**	22
Scott's | **multi.**	19
Sea Salt | **Berkeley/E**	21
Z Seasons | **Downtown**	26
NEW Skool | **Potrero Hill**	-
Sunnyside | **Tahoe City/E**	17
Z Swan Oyster | **Polk Gulch**	27
Z Tadich Grill | **Downtown**	23
Waterbar | **Embarcadero**	20
Waterfront | **Embarcadero**	18
Weird Fish | **Mission**	20
Willi's Seafood | **Healdsburg/N**	24
Will's Fargo | **Carmel Valley/S**	23
Wolfdale's | **Tahoe City/E**	25
Woodhse. | **multi.**	20
Yabbies Coastal | **Russian Hill**	22
Yankee Pier | **multi.**	18

SINGAPOREAN

Straits | **multi.**	20

SMALL PLATES

(See also Spanish tapas specialist)

Z Absinthe | French/Med. | **Hayes Valley**	22
À Côté | French/Med. | **Oakland/E**	24
Adesso | Italian | **Oakland/E**	23
NEW Amer. Cupcake | Amer. | **Cow Hollow**	-
Andalu | Eclectic | **Mission**	20
AsiaSF | Asian/Cal. | **SoMa**	17
NEW Barbacco | Italian | **Downtown**	25
Basil | Thai | **SoMa**	23
NEW Boot/Shoe | Italian | **Oakland/E**	24
Cascal | Pan-Latin | **Mtn View/S**	19
César | Pan-Latin | **Oakland/E**	22
Cha Cha Cha | Carib. | **multi.**	21
Charanga | Pan-Latin | **Mission**	23
Chez Shea | Eclectic | **Half Moon Bay/S**	23
Circa | Amer. | **Marina**	16
E&O Trading | Asian | **multi.**	19
Eos | Asian/Cal. | **Cole Valley**	23
Grand Pu Bah | Thai | **Potrero Hill**	20
NEW Heart | Eclectic | **Mission**	-
Isa | French | **Marina**	25
Jole | Amer. | **Calistoga/N**	25
Joya | Nuevo Latino | **Palo Alto/S**	20
Junnoon | Indian | **Palo Alto/S**	22
Lavanda | Med. | **Palo Alto/S**	19
Medjool | Med. | **Mission**	19
Mezze | Cal./Med. | **Oakland/E**	23
Monti's | Med. | **Santa Rosa/N**	21
Nihon | Japanese | **Mission**	21
Orson | Cal. | **SoMa**	19
Ottimista | Italian/Med. | **Cow Hollow**	17
Oxbow Wine | Cal. | **Napa/N**	22
Park Chalet | Amer. | **Outer Sunset**	14
Pesce | Italian/Seafood | **Russian Hill**	22
Picco | Italian | **Larkspur/N**	25
Piqueo's | Peruvian | **Bernal Hts**	24
Ponzu | Asian | **Downtown**	20
Ristobar | Italian | **Marina**	-
RN74 | French | **SoMa**	22
NEW Starbelly | Cal. | **Castro**	20
Straits | Singapor. | **multi.**	20
Tamarine | Viet. | **Palo Alto/S**	25
Terzo | Med. | **Cow Hollow**	23
Three Seasons | Viet. | **multi.**	21
NEW Tjukiji Sushi | Japanese | **Mill Valley/N**	-

Underwood Bar | Med. | **Graton/N** 24

Va de Vi | Eclectic | **Walnut Creek/E** 24

Willi's Seafood | Seafood | **Healdsburg/N** 24

Willi's Wine | Eclectic | **Santa Rosa/N** 25

Zibibbo | Med. | **Palo Alto/S** 19

Zucca | Med. | **Mtn View/S** 18

SOUL FOOD

Broken Record | **Excelsior** 22
Brown Sugar | **Oakland/E** 23
Elite Cafe | **Pacific Hts** 19
Farmerbrown | **multi.** 21
Hard Knox | **multi.** 19
Home of Chicken | **Oakland/E** 19
Picán | **Oakland/E** 21
Starlight | **Sebastopol/N** 22
1300/Fillmore | **W Addition** 23

SOUTHERN

Baby Blues BBQ | **Mission** 20
Blackberry Bistro | **Oakland/E** 18
Brenda's | **Civic Ctr** 24
Everett/Jones | **multi.** 20
Front Porch | **Bernal Hts** 19
Hard Knox | **multi.** 19
Home of Chicken | **Oakland/E** 19
Kate's Kitchen | **Lower Haight** 22
Magnolia | **Haight-Ashbury** 20
Picán | **Oakland/E** 21
1300/Fillmore | **W Addition** 23

SOUTHWESTERN

Boogaloos | **Mission** 18

SPANISH

(* tapas specialist)
Alegrias* | **Marina** 20
Barlata* | **Oakland/E** 21
B44* | **Downtown** 21
Bocadillos* | **N Beach** 23
César* | **Berkeley/E** 22
Contigo* | **Noe Valley** 24
Esperpento* | **Mission** 23
Fonda Solana* | **Albany/E** 22
Gitane | **Downtown** 21
Iberia* | **Menlo Pk/S** 22
Iluna Basque* | **N Beach** 18
Mundaka* | **Carmel/S** -
Piperade | **Downtown** 25
Zarzuela* | **Russian Hill** 24
ZuZu* | **Napa/N** 24

STEAKHOUSES

Alexander's | **Cupertino/S** 26
Alfred's Steak | **Downtown** 22
Arcadia | **San Jose/S** 21
Boca | **Novato/N** 22
Casa Orinda | **Orinda/E** 16
Cole's Chop | **Napa/N** 24
Epic Roasthse. | **Embarcadero** 21
Espetus | **multi.** 23
5A5 Steak | **Downtown** 22
Forbes Mill | **multi.** 22
Harris' | **Polk Gulch** 25
🆉 House of Prime | **Polk Gulch** 25
Izzy's Steak | **multi.** 20
Joe DiMaggio | **N Beach** 20
Lark Creek Steak | **Downtown** 22
Morton's | **multi.** 24
Press | **St. Helena/N** 24
Ruth's Chris | **multi.** 24
🆉 Seasons | **Downtown** 26
Sunnyside | **Tahoe City/E** 17
Vic Stewart | **Walnut Creek/E** 21
Will's Fargo | **Carmel Valley/S** 23

SWISS

Matterhorn Swiss | **Russian Hill** 22

TEAROOMS

Imperial/Berkeley | **multi.** 20
Lovejoy's Tea | **Noe Valley** 21
Samovar Tea | **multi.** 20

THAI

Basil | **SoMa** 23
Cha Am Thai | **multi.** 19
Grand Pu Bah | **Potrero Hill** 20
Khan Toke | **Outer Rich** 22
King of Thai | **multi.** 18
Koh Samui/Another | **multi.** 21
Krung Thai | **multi.** 20
Manora's Thai | **SoMa** 23
Marnee Thai | **multi.** 23
NEW Morph | **Outer Rich** -
Osha Thai | **multi.** 20
Royal Thai | **San Rafael/N** 22
Soi4 | **Oakland/E** 24
Suriya Thai | **SoMa** 26
Thai Buddhist | **Berkeley/E** 19
Thai House | **multi.** 23
Thep Phanom | **Lower Haight** 23

TURKISH

A La Turca | **Tenderloin** 23
Bursa Kebab | **W Portal** 21
Sens | **Downtown** 19
Troya | **Inner Rich** 23

VEGETARIAN

(* vegan)

Café Gratitude* | **multi.**	16
Cha-Ya Veg.* | **multi.**	23
NEW Encuentro | **Oakland/E**	–
NEW Gracias* | **Mission**	20
Z Greens | **Marina**	24
Herbivore* | **multi.**	15
Millennium* | **Downtown**	25
Ravens'* | **Mendocino/N**	22
Ubuntu* | **Napa/N**	26
Udupi Palace | **multi.**	20

VENEZUELAN

Pica Pica Maize | **multi.**	23

VIETNAMESE

Ana Mandara | **Fish. Wharf**	22
Annalien | **Napa/N**	22
Bodega Bistro | **Tenderloin**	24
Crustacean | **Polk Gulch**	25
Le Cheval | **multi.**	20
Le Colonial | **Downtown**	23
Le Soleil | **Inner Rich**	20
Out the Door | **multi.**	22
Pagolac | **Tenderloin**	21
Pho 84 | **Oakland/E**	20
Pot de Pho | **Inner Rich**	19
Saigon Sandwich | **Tenderloin**	24
Z Slanted Door | **Embarcadero**	26
Sunflower | **multi.**	20
Tamarine | **Palo Alto/S**	25
Thanh Long | **Outer Sunset**	24
Three Seasons | **multi.**	21
Tu Lan | **SoMa**	21
Vanessa's Bistro | **Berkeley/E**	23
Xanh | **Mtn View/S**	21
Xyclo | **Oakland/E**	24
Zadin | **Castro**	23

WEST AFRICAN

Bissap Baobob | **Mission**	22

Locations

Includes names, cuisines, Food ratings and, for locations that are mapped, top list with map coordinates.

City of San Francisco

AT&T PARK/ SOUTH BEACH
(See map on page 291)

TOP FOOD

Tsunami	*Japanese*	**G5**	22
Mijita	*Mex.*	**H5**	21
Amici's	*Pizza*	**G5**	19

LISTING

Amici's	*Pizza*	19
Burger Joint	*Burgers*	18
NEW Ironside	*Eclectic*	17
Mijita	*Mex.*	21
MoMo's	*Amer.*	17
NEW Public House	*Pub*	-
NEW Spire	*Amer.*	-
Tres Agaves	*Mex.*	17
Tsunami	*Japanese*	22

BERNAL HEIGHTS

Angkor Borei	*Cambodian*	23
El Zocalo	*Salvadoran*	20
Emmy's Spaghetti	*Italian*	19
Front Porch	*Carib./Southern*	19
Liberty Cafe	*Amer.*	22
Little Nepal	*Nepalese*	21
Moki's Sushi	*Japanese*	19
Piqueo's	*Peruvian*	24
NEW Sandbox	*Bakery*	26
Zante	*Indian/Pizza*	18

CASTRO
(See map on page 292)

TOP FOOD

Sushi Zone	*Japanese*	**A6**	27
Frances	*Cal.*	**D4**	27
Eiji	*Japanese*	**C4**	25
Thai House	*Thai*	**E3**	23
Anchor Oyster	*Seafood*	**E3**	23

LISTING

Anchor Oyster	*Seafood*	23
Brandy Ho's	*Chinese*	19
BurgerMeister	*Burgers*	20
Catch	*Seafood*	18
Z Chow/Park Chow	*Amer.*	20
Destino	*Nuevo Latino*	21
Eiji	*Japanese*	25

Eureka	*Amer.*	22
Z NEW Frances	*Cal.*	27
Home	*Amer.*	19
Kasa Indian	*Indian*	19
La Méditerranée	*Med./Mideast.*	19
L'Ardoise	*French*	23
Poesia	*Italian*	21
Samovar Tea	*Tea*	20
NEW Starbelly	*Cal.*	20
NEW Super Duper	*Burgers*	-
Z Sushi Zone	*Japanese*	27
Thai House	*Thai*	23
2223	*Cal.*	21
Woodhse.	*Seafood*	20
Zadin	*Viet.*	23

CHINA BASIN/ DOGPATCH

Hard Knox	*Southern*	19
Kitchenette SF	*Sandwiches*	22
Piccino	*Cal./Italian*	21
Serpentine	*Amer.*	19

CHINATOWN
(See map on page 288)

TOP FOOD

R&G Lounge	*Chinese*	**G7**	24
House of Nanking	*Chinese*	**F7**	21
Hunan	*Chinese*	**F6**	21

LISTING

Brandy Ho's	*Chinese*	19
Gold Mountain	*Chinese*	20
Great Eastern	*Chinese*	19
House of Nanking	*Chinese*	21
Henry's Hunan	*Chinese*	20
Hunan	*Chinese*	21
Jai Yun	*Chinese*	24
Oriental Pearl	*Chinese*	21
R&G Lounge	*Chinese*	24
Sam Wo's	*Chinese*	18
Yuet Lee	*Chinese*	20
Z & Y	*Chinese*	-

COW HOLLOW
(See map on page 290)

TOP FOOD

Capannina	*Italian*	**H5**	25
Gamine	*French*	**F5**	23
Betelnut Pejiu	*Asian*	**G5**	23

Menus, photos, voting and more – free at ZAGAT.com

Umami | *Japanese* | **G5** — 23
Terzo | *Med.* | **F5** — 23

LISTING

NEW Amer. Cupcake | *Amer./Bakery* — -
Balboa Cafe | *Amer.* — 19
Betelnut Pejiu | *Asian* — 23
Brazen Head | *Amer.* — 21
NEW Café des Amis | *French* — -
Capannina | *Italian* — 25
Gamine | *French* — 23
La Boulange | *Bakery* — 21
NEW Marengo | *Amer.* — -
Nettie's Crab | *Seafood* — 18
Osha Thai | *Thai* — 20
Ottimista | *Italian/Med.* — 17
Pane e Vino | *Italian* — 22
Patxi's Pizza | *Pizza* — 22
NEW Roam | *Burgers* — -
Rose's Cafe | *Italian* — 22
Terzo | *Med.* — 23
Umami | *Japanese* — 23

DOWNTOWN

(See map on page 288)

TOP FOOD

Masa's | *French* | **H5** — 27
Fleur de Lys | *Cal./French* | **I4** — 27
Kokkari | *Greek* | **F8** — 27
Seasons | *Seafood/Steak* | **J6** — 26
Quince | *French/Italian* | **F7** — 26

LISTING

Alfred's Steak | *Steak* — 22
Anzu | *Japanese* — 22
NEW Barbacco | *Italian* — 25
B44 | *Spanish* — 21
Z Bix | *Amer./French* — 24
NEW Burger Bar | *Burgers* — 19
Cafe Bastille | *French* — 17
Café Claude | *French* — 22
Café de la Presse | *French* — 18
Café Tiramisu | *Italian* — 20
Campton Place | *Cal./Med.* — 25
Cheesecake Fac. | *Amer.* — 16
Colibrí | *Mex.* — 20
NEW Cotogna | *Italian* — -
NEW Credo | *Italian* — 17
E&O Trading | *Asian* — 19
Ebisu | *Japanese* — 23
Emporio Rulli | *Dessert/Italian* — 21
Z Farallon | *Seafood* — 24
Fish & Farm | *Amer./Seafood* — 20
5A5 Steak | *Steak* — 22

Z Fleur de Lys | *Cal./French* — 27
Z Garden Court | *Cal.* — 18
Gaylord India | *Indian* — 18
NEW Georges | *Cal.* — -
Gitane | *French/Spanish* — 21
Globe | *Cal./Italian* — 21
NEW Golden West | *Bakery/Sandwiches* — -
Grand Cafe | *French* — 20
Henry's Hunan | *Chinese* — 20
Il Fornaio | *Italian* — 19
Katana-Ya | *Japanese* — 22
King of Thai | *Thai* — 18
Z Kokkari | *Greek* — 27
Kuleto's | *Italian* — 21
Kyo-Ya | *Japanese* — 24
Lark Creek Steak | *Steak* — 22
La Scene | *Cal./Med.* — 21
Le Central Bistro | *French* — 20
Le Colonial | *French/Viet.* — 23
Let's Be Frank | *Hot Dogs* — 19
Z Masa's | *French* — 27
Max's | *Deli* — 17
Midi | *Amer./French* — 20
Millennium | *Vegan* — 25
Mixt Greens | *Health/Sandwiches* — 22
Morton's | *Steak* — 24
Muracci's | *Japanese* — 22
Naan/Curry | *Indian/Pakistani* — 17
Osha Thai | *Thai* — 20
Out the Door | *Viet.* — 22
Palio d'Asti | *Italian* — 20
Z Perbacco | *Italian* — 25
Piperade | *Spanish* — 25
Plant Cafe | *Health* — 20
Plouf | *French* — 21
Ponzu | *Asian* — 20
Z Quince | *French/Italian* — 26
Rotunda | *Amer.* — 21
Ryoko's | *Japanese* — 23
Sam's Grill | *Seafood* — 21
Sanraku | *Japanese* — 21
Scala's Bistro | *Italian* — 23
Sears Fine Food | *Diner* — 20
Z Seasons | *Seafood/Steak* — 26
Sens | *Med./Turkish* — 19
Showdogs | *Hot Dogs* — 19
Silks | *Cal.* — 25
Straits | *Singapor.* — 20
Z Tadich Grill | *Seafood* — 23
Taqueria Can-Cun | *Mex.* — 21
Tommy Toy | *Chinese* — 24
Trademark Grill | *Amer.* — 19
Unicorn | *Asian* — 22
Urban Tavern | *Amer.* — 17

LOCATIONS

NEW Velvet Room	*Cal.*	-
NEW Wayfare Tav.	*Amer.*	-
Wexler's	*BBQ*	22
'Wichcraft	*Sandwiches*	18

EMBARCADERO

Americano	*Cal.*	18
🅩 Blue Bottle	*Cal./Coffee*	23
Boccalone	*Sandwiches*	24
Boulette Larder	*Amer.*	25
🅩 Boulevard	*Amer.*	27
Butterfly	*Asian/Cal.*	22
Chaya	*French/Japanese*	22
Delancey St.	*Eclectic*	18
Epic Roasthse.	*Steak*	21
Fog City Diner	*Amer.*	19
4505 Meats	*Hot Dogs*	28
Gordon Biersch	*Pub*	15
Gott's Roadside	*Diner*	21
🅩 Hog Island Oyster	*Seafood*	25
Il Cane Rosso	*Italian*	22
Imperial/Berkeley	*Tea*	20
NEW Lafitte	*Amer.*	-
La Mar	*Peruvian*	24
MarketBar	*Med.*	17
Mexico DF	*Mex.*	18
Mijita	*Mex.*	21
Namu	*Cal./Korean*	23
One Market	*Amer.*	23
Out the Door	*Viet.*	22
Ozumo	*Japanese*	23
Plant Cafe	*Health*	20
Red's Java	*Burgers*	15
RoliRoti	*Amer.*	25
🅩 Slanted Door	*Viet.*	26
NEW Tacolicious	*Mex.*	23
Town's End	*Amer./Bakery*	20
Waterbar	*Seafood*	20
Waterfront	*Cal./Seafood*	18

EXCELSIOR

Broken Record	*Soul*	22
Joe's Cable Car	*Burgers*	23
North Bch. Pizza	*Pizza*	19

FISHERMAN'S WHARF

(See map on page 288)

TOP FOOD

Gary Danko	*Amer.*	**B2**	29
Scoma's	*Seafood*	**A4**	22
Ana Mandara	*Viet.*	**B2**	22

LISTING

Alioto's	*Italian*	18
Ana Mandara	*Viet.*	22

Bistro Boudin	*Cal.*	20
Forbes Island	*Amer./Seafood*	19
🅩 Gary Danko	*Amer.*	29
Grandeho Kamekyo	*Japanese*	21
Hard Rock	*Amer.*	12
🅩 In-N-Out	*Burgers*	22
McCormick/Kuleto	*Seafood*	20
🅩 Scoma's	*Seafood*	22

FOREST HILLS/ WEST PORTAL

Bursa Kebab	*Med.*	21
Chouchou	*French*	21
Fresca	*Peruvian*	22
Roti Indian	*Indian*	22

GLEN PARK

Chenery Park	*Amer.*	22
Gialina	*Pizza*	25
La Corneta	*Mex.*	21
Le P'tit Laurent	*French*	23
Osha Thai	*Thai*	20

HAIGHT-ASHBURY/ COLE VALLEY

Alembic	*Eclectic*	22
Asqew Grill	*Cal.*	16
BurgerMeister	*Burgers*	20
Cha Cha Cha	*Carib.*	21
Citrus Club	*Asian*	21
Eos	*Asian/Cal.*	23
Kamekyo	*Japanese*	21
Kan Zaman	*Mideast.*	19
La Boulange	*Bakery*	21
Magnolia	*Amer./Southern*	20
North Bch. Pizza	*Pizza*	19
NEW Parada 22	*Puerto Rican*	-
Pork Store	*Amer.*	19
Zazie	*French*	22

HAYES VALLEY/ CIVIC CENTER

🅩 Absinthe	*French/Med.*	22
Arlequin	*Med.*	18
Bar Jules	*Amer.*	25
🅩 Blue Bottle	*Cal./Coffee*	23
Brenda's	*Creole/Southern*	24
Caffe Delle Stelle	*Italian*	16
Cav Wine Bar	*Wine*	20
DeLessio	*Bakery*	22
Domo Sushi	*Japanese*	20
Espetus	*Brazilian*	23
Frjtz Fries	*Belgian*	17
Hayes St. Grill	*Seafood*	23
Indigo	*Amer.*	19

ⓩ Jardinière	*Cal./French*	26
La Boulange	*Bakery*	21
Max's	*Deli*	17
Mel's Drive-In	*Diner*	14
Moishe's Pippic	*Deli/Jewish*	18
Patxi's Pizza	*Pizza*	22
Paul K	*Med.*	22
Samovar Tea	*Tea*	20
Sauce	*Amer.*	18
ⓩ Sebo	*Japanese*	27
Stacks	*Amer.*	18
Suppenküche	*German*	22
ⓩ Zuni Café	*Med.*	25

INNER RICHMOND

Academy Cafe	*Eclectic*	19
Bella Trattoria	*Italian*	22
Brother's Korean	*Korean*	22
B Star Bar	*Asian*	22
ⓩ Burma Superstar	*Burmese*	24
ⓩ Chapeau!	*French*	26
Giorgio's	*Pizza*	22
Good Luck	*Chinese*	20
Katia's Tea	*Russian*	23
King of Thai	*Thai*	18
Le Soleil	*Viet.*	20
Mandalay	*Burmese*	23
Mel's Drive-In	*Diner*	14
Moss Room	*Cal.*	20
My Tofu	*Korean*	20
Namu	*Cal./Korean*	23
Pagan	*Burmese*	18
Pot de Pho	*Viet.*	19
NEW Prime Rib Shabu	*Japanese*	23
Q Rest.	*Amer.*	18
Richmond Rest.	*Cal.*	25
Troya	*Turkish*	23

INNER SUNSET

Beautifull	*Health*	17
ⓩ Chow/Park Chow	*Amer.*	20
Ebisu	*Japanese*	23
Hotei	*Japanese*	20
NEW Izakaya Sozai	*Japanese*	-
Koo	*Asian*	23
Marnee Thai	*Thai*	23
Naan/Curry	*Indian/Pakistani*	17
Pacific Catch	*Seafood*	19
Pluto's	*Amer.*	19
Pomelo	*Eclectic*	20
San Tung	*Chinese/Korean*	23
NEW Social Kitchen	*Amer.*	-
Underdog	*Hot Dogs*	21
Yumma's	*Mideast.*	19

JAPANTOWN

Benihana	*Japanese*	17
Bushi-tei	*Asian/French*	22
Café Kati	*Asian*	22
Isobune	*Japanese*	19
Juban	*Japanese*	18
ⓩ Kiss Seafood	*Japanese*	27
Maki	*Japanese*	22
Mifune	*Japanese*	17
Shabu-Sen	*Japanese*	19
Takara	*Japanese*	20

LAUREL HEIGHTS/ PRESIDIO HEIGHTS

Asqew Grill	*Cal.*	16
Beautifull	*Health*	17
Ella's	*Amer.*	21
Garibaldis	*Cal./Med.*	22
Pasta Pomodoro	*Italian*	17
Sociale	*Italian*	23
ⓩ Spruce	*Amer.*	26

LOWER HAIGHT

Axum Cafe	*Ethiopian*	21
Bistro St. Germain	*French*	20
Burger Joint	*Burgers*	18
Indian Oven	*Indian*	22
Kate's Kitchen	*Southern*	22
Memphis Minnie	*BBQ*	21
Rosamunde	*German*	25
Thep Phanom	*Thai*	23
Uva Enoteca	*Italian*	21

MARINA

(See map on page 290)

TOP FOOD

Zushi Puzzle	*Japanese*	**G4**	27
Isa	*French*	**F4**	25
A16	*Italian*	**E3**	25
Greens	*Veg.*	**G2**	24
Tacolicious	*Mex.*	**F3**	23

LISTING

Ace Wasabi's	*Japanese*	20
Alegrias	*Spanish*	20
Amici's	*Pizza*	19
ⓩ A16	*Italian*	25
Asqew Grill	*Cal.*	16
Baker St. Bistro	*French*	22
Barney's	*Burgers*	19
Bistro Aix	*Cal./French*	-
Blue Barn	*Cal.*	21
Circa	*Amer.*	16
NEW Delarosa	*Italian*	22
Dragon Well	*Chinese*	22

E'Angelo	*Italian*	21
Z Greens	*Veg.*	24
Isa	*French*	25
Izzy's Steak	*Steak*	20
Jake's Steaks	*Cheesestks.*	21
Kasa Indian	*Indian*	19
Let's Be Frank	*Hot Dogs*	19
Mamacita	*Mex.*	22
Mel's Drive-In	*Diner*	14
Pacific Catch	*Seafood*	19
Plant Cafe	*Health*	20
Pluto's	*Amer.*	19
Ristobar	*Italian*	-
NEW Tacolicious	*Mex.*	23
Three Seasons	*Viet.*	21
Tipsy Pig	*Amer.*	19
Z Zushi Puzzle	*Japanese*	27

MISSION

(See map on page 292)

TOP FOOD

Range	*Amer.*	**E6**	27
Tartine	*Bakery*	**D6**	27
Delfina	*Italian*	**D6**	26
Truly Med.	*Med.*	**C6**	26
Chez Spencer	*French*	**B8**	25

LISTING

Andalu	*Eclectic*	20
Arinell Pizza	*Pizza*	21
Baby Blues BBQ	*BBQ/Southern*	20
Bar Bambino	*Italian*	23
Bar Tartine	*Med.*	23
Beretta	*Italian*	23
Bissap Baobab	*Senegalese*	22
Blowfish Sushi	*Japanese*	21
Blue Plate	*Amer.*	23
Boogaloos	*SW*	18
Burger Joint	*Burgers*	18
Café Gratitude	*Vegan*	16
Cha Cha Cha	*Carib.*	21
Charanga	*Pan-Latin*	23
Cha-Ya Veg.	*Japanese/Vegan*	23
Chez Spencer	*French*	25
NEW Commonwealth	*Amer.*	-
Corner	*Cal./Italian*	19
Z Delfina	*Italian*	26
Dosa	*Indian*	22
Dynamo Donut	*Coffee*	-
El Metate	*Mex.*	22
Z El Tonayense	*Mex.*	24
Esperpento	*Spanish*	23
Farina	*Italian*	24
Flour + Water	*Italian*	24
Foreign Cinema	*Cal./Med.*	23

Frjtz Fries	*Belgian*	17
Goood Frikin' Chicken	*Mideast.*	18
NEW Gracias	*Mex./Vegan*	20
NEW Heart	*Eclectic*	-
NEW Heirloom	*Cal./Med.*	-
Herbivore	*Vegan*	15
NEW Hog & Rocks	*Amer.*	-
Jay's	*Cheesestks.*	18
Koh Samui/Another	*Thai*	21
La Corneta	*Mex.*	21
La Cumbre	*Mex.*	21
La Taqueria	*Mex.*	25
Limón	*Peruvian*	23
Little Star	*Pizza*	24
NEW Local Mission	*Cal.*	-
Loló	*Med./Pan-Latin*	24
Luna Park	*Amer./French*	19
Maverick	*Amer.*	24
Medjool	*Med.*	19
Mission Bch. Café	*Cal.*	25
NEW Mission Chinese	*Chinese*	-
Monk's Kettle	*Cal.*	20
Nihon	*Japanese*	21
NEW Nombe	*Japanese*	22
Old Jerusalem	*Med./Mideast.*	19
Osha Thai	*Thai*	20
Pakwan	*Pakistani*	21
Pancho Villa	*Mex.*	22
Papalote	*Mex.*	22
Pauline's	*Pizza*	22
NEW Pi Bar	*Pizza*	14
Pica Pica Maize	*Venezuelan*	23
Pizzeria Delfina	*Pizza*	25
Pork Store	*Amer.*	19
Z Range	*Amer.*	27
Regalito Rosticeria	*Mex.*	19
Rosamunde	*German*	25
Saison	*Amer.*	25
Schmidt's	*German*	21
Slow Club	*Amer.*	22
Spork	*Amer.*	20
Stable Café	*Coffee*	-
St. Francis	*Diner*	19
Sunflower	*Viet.*	20
Taqueria Can-Cun	*Mex.*	21
Z Tartine	*Bakery*	27
Ti Couz	*French*	21
Tokyo Go Go	*Japanese*	21
Truly Med.	*Med.*	26
Udupi Palace	*Indian/Veg.*	20
Universal Cafe	*Amer.*	23
Walzwerk	*German*	21
Weird Fish	*Seafood*	20
Woodward's Gdn.	*Amer./Cal.*	24

Menus, photos, voting and more – free at ZAGAT.com

Yamo	*Burmese*	21
Zeitgeist	*Burgers*	16

NOB HILL

(See map on page 288)

TOP FOOD

Ritz-Carlton	*French*	**H6**	27
Big 4	*Amer.*	**H4**	23
Venticello	*Italian*	**G4**	23

LISTING

☑ Big 4	*Amer.*	23
Nob Hill Café	*Italian*	21
☑ Ritz-Carlton	*French*	27
NEW Sons/Daughters	*Amer.*	-
Tonga	*Asian/Pac. Rim*	14
Venticello	*Italian*	23

NOE VALLEY

(See map on page 292)

TOP FOOD

La Ciccia	*Italian*	**K5**	26
Firefly	*Eclectic*	**H2**	24
Contigo	*Spanish*	**H3**	24
Incanto	*Italian*	**I5**	24
Chloe's Cafe	*Amer.*	**H5**	23

LISTING

Alice's	*Chinese*	20
Bacco	*Italian*	22
Barney's	*Burgers*	19
Chloe's Cafe	*Amer.*	23
Contigo	*Spanish*	24
Eric's	*Chinese*	20
Firefly	*Eclectic*	24
Fresca	*Peruvian*	22
Hamano Sushi	*Japanese*	19
Henry's Hunan	*Chinese*	20
Incanto	*Italian*	24
La Boulange	*Bakery*	21
La Ciccia	*Italian*	26
Little Chihuahua	*Mex.*	22
Lovejoy's Tea	*Tea*	21
Lupa Trattoria	*Italian*	24
Pasta Pomodoro	*Italian*	17
Pomelo	*Eclectic*	20
Savor	*Med.*	17

NORTH BEACH

(See map on page 288)

TOP FOOD

House	*Asian*	**E6**	27
Coi	*Cal./French*	**F7**	26
Tony's Pizza	*Italian*	**E6**	26
Mama's on Wash.	*Amer.*	**D6**	25
Cafe Jacqueline	*French*	**E6**	25

LISTING

Albona Rist.	*Italian*	23
Bocadillos	*Spanish*	23
BurgerMeister	*Burgers*	20
Cafe Jacqueline	*French*	25
Cafe Zoetrope/Mammarella's	*Italian*	20
Caffè Macaroni	*Italian*	21
☑ Coi	*Cal./French*	26
NEW Comstock	*Amer.*	-
Enrico's	*Amer./Med.*	16
15 Romolo	*Pub*	-
Fior d'Italia	*Italian*	20
Giordano	*Sandwiches*	21
☑ House	*Asian*	27
Iluna Basque	*Spanish*	18
Joe DiMaggio	*Italian/Steak*	20
King of Thai	*Thai*	18
La Boulange	*Bakery*	21
La Trappe	*Belgian*	18
L'Osteria	*Italian*	24
Mama's on Wash.	*Amer.*	25
Mario's Bohemian	*Italian*	19
Maykadeh	*Persian*	23
Naan/Curry	*Indian/Pakistani*	17
NEW Naked Lunch	*Sandwiches*	26
North Bch. Pizza	*Pizza*	19
North Bch. Rest.	*Italian*	23
Rist. Ideale	*Italian*	24
Rose Pistola	*Italian*	21
Stinking Rose	*Italian*	18
Tommaso's	*Italian*	24
Tony's Pizza	*Italian*	26
Tratt. Contadina	*Italian*	23

OUTER RICHMOND

Ariake	*Japanese*	23
☑ Aziza	*Moroccan*	26
Cliff House	*Cal.*	19
Hard Knox	*Southern*	19
Hong Kong Lounge	*Chinese*	21
Kabuto	*Japanese*	26
Khan Toke	*Thai*	22
Mayflower/HK Flower	*Chinese*	19
Mescolanza	*Italian*	24
NEW Morph	*Thai*	-
Oyaji	*Japanese*	23
Pacific Café	*Seafood*	23
Pagan	*Burmese*	18
☑ Pizzetta 211	*Pizza*	27
Shanghai Dumpling	*Chinese*	23
Sutro's	*Cal.*	20
Tommy's Mex.	*Mex.*	18
Ton Kiang	*Chinese*	24

LISTING

LOCATIONS

OUTER SUNSET

Beach Chalet	*Amer.*	14
Cajun Pacific	*Cajun*	22
Just Wonton	*Chinese*	21
King of Thai	*Thai*	18
Marnee Thai	*Thai*	23
North Bch. Pizza	*Pizza*	19
Outerlands	*Amer.*	23
Park Chalet	*Cal.*	14
Pizza Pl./Noriega	*Pizza*	-
Thanh Long	*Viet.*	24

PACIFIC HEIGHTS

Elite Cafe	*Amer.*	19
Eliza's	*Chinese*	22
Florio	*French/Italian*	19
Godzila Sushi	*Japanese*	18
La Boulange	*Bakery*	21
Pizzeria Delfina	*Pizza*	25
SPQR	*Italian*	24
NEW TacoBar	*Mex.*	-
Tataki Sushi	*Japanese*	22
Woodhse.	*Seafood*	20

POLK GULCH
(See map on page 288)

TOP FOOD

Acquerello	*Italian*	**G1**	28
Swan Oyster	*Seafood*	**H1**	27
Harris'	*Steak*	**F1**	25

LISTING

Z Acquerello	*Italian*	28
Crustacean	*Viet.*	25
Harris'	*Steak*	25
Z House of Prime	*Amer.*	25
NEW Mayes	*Seafood*	19
Miller's Deli	*Deli/Jewish*	19
Naan/Curry	*Indian/Pakistani*	17
Ruth's Chris	*Steak*	24
Shalimar	*Indian/Pakistani*	24
Z Swan Oyster	*Seafood*	27

POTRERO HILL

Aperto	*Italian*	24
Chez Maman	*French*	23
Chez Papa	*French*	23
Goat Hill Pizza	*Pizza*	20
Grand Pu Bah	*Thai*	20
Pizza Nostra	*Pizza*	22
NEW Skool	*Seafood*	-
Sunflower	*Viet.*	20

PRESIDIO

La Terrasse	*French*	18
Let's Be Frank	*Hot Dogs*	19

Presidio Social	*Amer.*	19
Warming Hut	*Sandwiches*	13

RUSSIAN HILL
(See map on page 288)

TOP FOOD

La Folie	*French*	**E1**	28
Frascati	*Cal./Med.*	**E3**	25
Rist. Milano	*Italian*	**F2**	25

LISTING

Antica Trattoria	*Italian*	23
Frascati	*Cal./Med.*	25
Helmand Palace	*Afghani*	23
Hyde St. Bistro	*French*	21
La Boulange	*Bakery*	21
Z La Folie	*French*	28
Luella	*Cal./Med.*	22
Matterhorn Swiss	*Swiss*	22
Nick's Crispy	*Mex.*	21
Pesce	*Italian/Seafood*	22
Rist. Milano	*Italian*	25
Sushi Groove	*Japanese*	22
Yabbies Coastal	*Seafood*	22
Zarzuela	*Spanish*	24

SOMA
(See map on page 291)

TOP FOOD

Ame	*Amer.*	**H2**	26
Yank Sing	*Chinese*	**I1** **J2**	25
Fifth Floor	*Amer./French*	**F1**	25
Sentinel	*Sandwiches*	**H1**	24
Fringale	*Basque/French*	**G4**	24

LISTING

Z Amber India	*Indian*	24
Ame	*Amer.*	26
NEW Amer. Grilled Cheese	*Amer./Sandwiches*	-
Anchor & Hope	*Seafood*	21
AsiaSF	*Asian/Cal.*	17
NEW Bar Agricole	*Cal.*	-
Basil	*Thai*	23
NEW Benu	*Amer.*	-
Z Blue Bottle	*Cal./Coffee*	23
Buca di Beppo	*Italian*	15
Butler & Chef	*French*	21
Caffè Museo	*Italian/Med.*	19
Cha Am Thai	*Thai*	19
Chez Papa	*French*	23
Chez Spencer	*French*	25
NEW Citizen's Band	*Amer.*	-
Coco500	*Cal./Med.*	23
Cosmopolitan	*Amer.*	19
Ducca	*Amer.*	17

Menus, photos, voting and more – free at ZAGAT.com

NEW Fang	*Chinese*	20
Farmerbrown	*Soul*	21
Fifth Floor	*Amer./French*	25
54 Mint	*Italian*	22
NEW Fondue Cowboy	*Fondue*	-
Fringale	*Basque/French*	24
Goat Hill Pizza	*Pizza*	20
Heaven's Dog	*Chinese*	20
Henry's Hunan	*Chinese*	20
Koh Samui/Another	*Thai*	21
La Boulange	*Bakery*	21
Le Charm Bistro	*French*	22
Local Kitchen	*Cal./Italian*	20
Luce	*Cal./Italian*	21
Manora's Thai	*Thai*	23
NEW Marlowe	*Amer.*	-
Maya	*Mex.*	20
Mel's Drive-In	*Diner*	14
Mochica	*Peruvian*	23
Oola	*Cal.*	21
Orson	*Cal.*	19
Osha Thai	*Thai*	20
Pazzia	*Italian*	24
NEW Prospect	*Amer.*	-
NEW Radius	*Cal.*	-
Rest. LuLu/Petite	*French/Med.*	21
Rist. Umbria	*Italian*	20
RN74	*French*	22
Roy's	*Hawaiian*	23
Salt House	*Amer.*	21
Samovar Tea	*Tea*	20
Sanraku	*Japanese*	21
Sentinel	*Sandwiches*	24
South Park	*French*	22
NEW Spice Kit	*Asian*	-
Supperclub	*Eclectic*	14
Suriya Thai	*Thai*	26
Sushi Groove	*Japanese*	22
NEW Thermidor	*Amer.*	-
Town Hall	*Amer.*	23
Tropisueño	*Mex.*	19
Tu Lan	*Viet.*	21
Vitrine	*Amer.*	21
XYZ	*Amer./Cal.*	20
☑ Yank Sing	*Chinese*	25
Zaré/Fly Trap	*Cal./Med.*	23
NEW Zero Zero	*Italian/Pizza*	-
Zuppa	*Italian*	20

TENDERLOIN

(See map on page 288)

TOP FOOD

Canteen	*Cal.*	**I4**	27
Dottie's	*Diner*	**J4**	25
Bodega Bistro	*Viet.*	**K2**	24

LISTING

A La Turca	*Turkish*	23
Bodega Bistro	*Viet.*	24
☑ Canteen	*Cal.*	27
Dottie's	*Diner*	25
Farmerbrown	*Soul*	21
Lahore Karahi	*Pakistani*	25
Osha Thai	*Thai*	20
Pagolac	*Viet.*	21
Pakwan	*Pakistani*	21
Saha	*Mideast.*	26
Saigon Sandwich	*Sandwiches/Viet.*	24
Shalimar	*Indian/Pakistani*	24
Thai House	*Thai*	23

UPPER FILLMORE

NEW Baker/Banker	*Amer.*	25
Dosa	*Indian*	22
Fresca	*Peruvian*	22
Jackson Fillmore	*Italian*	21
La Méditerranée	*Med./Mideast.*	19
Out the Door	*Viet.*	22
Ten-Ichi	*Japanese*	20

WESTERN ADDITION

NEW Acme Burger	*Burgers*	18
Alamo Sq.	*French/Seafood*	20
Bar Crudo	*Seafood*	25
NEW Bistro Central Parc	*French*	-
Candybar	*Dessert*	17
Cheese Steak Shop	*Cheesestks.*	21
NEW Chile Pies	*Dessert*	-
DeLessio	*Bakery*	22
Green Chile	*Mex.*	21
Herbivore	*Vegan*	15
Jay's	*Cheesestks.*	18
Little Chihuahua	*Mex.*	22
Little Star	*Pizza*	24
☑ Nopa	*Cal.*	25
Nopalito	*Mex.*	23
Papalote	*Mex.*	22
1300/Fillmore	*Soul/Southern*	23
Tsunami	*Japanese*	22
Yoshi's SF	*Japanese*	21

East of San Francisco

ALAMEDA

BurgerMeister	*Burgers*	20
☑ Burma Superstar	*Burmese*	24
Cheese Steak Shop	*Cheesestks.*	21
Everett/Jones	*BBQ*	20
Pappo	*Cal./Med.*	22

ALBANY

Caspers Hot Dogs	*Hot Dogs*	18
Fonda Solana	*Pan-Latin*	22
Little Star	*Pizza*	24

BERKELEY

Adagia	*Cal.*	18
Ajanta	*Indian*	25
Amanda's	*Cal./Health*	21
Arinell Pizza	*Pizza*	21
Barney's	*Burgers*	19
Imperial/Berkeley	*Tea*	20
Bette's Oceanview	*Diner*	23
Bistro Liaison	*French*	21
Breads of India	*Indian*	20
Cactus Taqueria	*Mex.*	20
Café Fanny	*French*	23
Café Gratitude	*Vegan*	16
Café Rouge	*French/Med.*	20
César	*Spanish*	22
Cha Am Thai	*Thai*	19
Cha-Ya Veg.	*Japanese/Vegan*	23
Z Cheese Board	*Bakery/Pizza*	27
Cheese Steak Shop	*Cheesestks.*	21
Z Chez Panisse	*Cal./Med.*	28
Z Chez Panisse Café	*Cal./Med.*	27
Corso	*Italian*	23
Digs Bistro	*Amer./Med.*	23
NEW Emilia's	*Pizza*	27
NEW Eve	*Amer.*	25
Everett/Jones	*BBQ*	20
FatApple's	*Diner*	17
Five	*Amer./Cal.*	22
NEW Gather	*Cal.*	-
Gioia Pizzeria	*Pizza*	24
Great China	*Chinese*	24
Grégoire	*French*	23
Herbivore	*Vegan*	15
Jimmy Beans	*Diner*	19
Juan's	*Mex.*	16
Kirala	*Japanese*	24
Lalime's	*Cal./Med.*	25
La Méditerranée	*Med./Mideast.*	19
Lanesplitter	*Pizza*	16
La Note	*French*	22
Le Cheval	*Viet.*	20
NEW Locanda da Eva	*Italian*	-
Lo Coco	*Italian*	21
NEW Meritage/Claremont	*Cal.*	25
Naan/Curry	*Indian/Pakistani*	17
North Bch. Pizza	*Pizza*	19
O Chamé	*Japanese*	23
Picante Cocina	*Mex.*	21

NEW Revival Bar	*Cal.*	-
Rick & Ann	*Amer.*	21
Z Rivoli	*Cal./Med.*	27
Saul's Rest./Deli	*Deli*	17
Sea Salt	*Seafood*	21
Shen Hua	*Chinese*	19
Tacubaya	*Mex.*	23
Thai Buddhist	*Thai*	19
Tratt. La Sicil.	*Italian*	25
T Rex BBQ	*BBQ*	17
Udupi Palace	*Indian/Veg.*	20
Vanessa's Bistro	*French/Viet.*	23
Venezia	*Italian*	21
Venus	*Cal.*	21
Vik's Chaat	*Indian*	23
Z Zachary's Pizza	*Pizza*	24
Zatar	*Med.*	25

DANVILLE

Amber Bistro	*Cal.*	22
Amici's	*Pizza*	19
Blackhawk Grille	*Cal.*	21
Bridges	*Asian/Cal.*	22
Z Chow/Park Chow	*Amer.*	20
Esin	*Amer./Med.*	25
Forbes Mill	*Steak*	22
Peasant/Pear	*Med.*	24
Piatti	*Italian*	19

DUBLIN

Amici's	*Pizza*	19
Caspers Hot Dogs	*Hot Dogs*	18
Koi	*Chinese*	23

EL CERRITO

FatApple's	*Diner*	17

EMERYVILLE

Asqew Grill	*Cal.*	16
Bucci's	*Cal./Italian*	21
Lanesplitter	*Pizza*	16
Pasta Pomodoro	*Italian*	17
Townhouse B&G	*Cal.*	20
Trader Vic's	*Polynesian*	17

FREMONT/NEWARK

Pakwan	*Pakistani*	21
Shalimar	*Indian/Pakistani*	24
Udupi Palace	*Indian/Veg.*	20

HAYWARD

Caspers Hot Dogs	*Hot Dogs*	18
Everett/Jones	*BBQ*	20
Pakwan	*Pakistani*	21

LAFAYETTE

Restaurant	Cuisine	Rating
Artisan Bistro	Cal./French	23
Bo's BBQ	BBQ	22
Cheese Steak Shop	Cheesestks.	21
Chevalier	French	23
🛚 Chow/Park Chow	Amer.	20
Duck Club	Amer.	21
Metro	Cal./French	22
Pizza Antica	Pizza	21
Postino	Italian	21
Yankee Pier	New Eng./Seafood	18

LAKE TAHOE

Restaurant	Cuisine	Rating
Baxter's Bistro	Cal.	-
Bridgetender	Pub	18
Café Fiore	Italian	25
Christy Hill	Cal./Med.	20
Cottonwood	Eclectic	21
Dragonfly	Asian/Cal.	22
Evan's	Amer.	25
Gar Woods	Amer./Med.	17
Jake's/Lake	Cal.	16
NEW Manzanita	Cal./French	25
Moody's Bistro	Amer.	24
Naked Fish	Japanese	23
Pacific Crest	Med.	-
Pianeta	Italian	21
PlumpJack	Cal./Med.	23
Red Hut	Diner	21
River Ranch	Cal.	15
Soule Domain	Amer.	25
Sunnyside	Seafood/Steak	17
Wild Goose	Amer.	-
Wolfdale's	Cal.	25

LIVERMORE

Restaurant	Cuisine	Rating
Wente Vineyards	Cal./Med.	24

OAKLAND

Restaurant	Cuisine	Rating
À Côté	French/Med.	24
Adesso	Italian	23
Bakesale Betty	Bakery	26
Barlata	Spanish	21
Barney's	Burgers	19
BayWolf	Cal./Med.	26
Bellanico	Italian	22
Blackberry Bistro	Southern	18
🛚 Blue Bottle	Cal./Coffee	23
NEW Bocanova	Pan-Latin	21
NEW Boot/Shoe	Italian/Pizza	24
Breads of India	Indian	20
Brown Sugar	Soul	23
🛚 Burma Superstar	Burmese	24
Cactus Taqueria	Mex.	20
Camino	Cal./Med.	23
Caspers Hot Dogs	Hot Dogs	18

Restaurant	Cuisine	Rating
César	Pan-Latin	22
Cheese Steak Shop	Cheesestks.	21
NEW Chop Bar	Cal.	22
🛚 Commis	Amer.	27
Doña Tomás	Mex.	21
Dopo	Italian	25
NEW Encuentro	Veg.	-
Everett/Jones	BBQ	20
Fentons	Ice Cream	20
Flora	Amer.	22
Garibaldis	Cal./Med.	22
Grégoire	French	23
NEW Hibiscus	Carib.	21
Home of Chicken	Southern	19
🛚 In-N-Out	Burgers	22
Koryo BBQ	Korean	22
Lake Chalet	Cal.	14
Lanesplitter	Pizza	16
Le Cheval	Viet.	20
Lo Coco	Italian	21
Luka's Taproom	Cal./French	20
Mama's Royal	Amer.	21
Marica	Seafood	23
Marzano	Italian/Pizza	21
Max's	Deli	17
Mezze	Cal./Med.	23
Miss Pearl's	Carib.	16
Nan Yang	Burmese	20
Oliveto Cafe	Italian	23
Oliveto Rest.	Italian	24
Ozumo	Japanese	23
Pasta Pomodoro	Italian	17
Pho 84	Viet.	20
Picán	Southern	21
Pizzaiolo	Pizza	25
Pizza Rustica	Pizza	21
NEW Plum	Cal.	-
Rest. Peony	Chinese	20
Scott's	Seafood	19
Sidebar	Cal.	20
Soi4	Thai	24
NEW SR24	Amer.	-
Tamarindo	Mex.	25
NEW Trueburger	Burgers	-
Uzen	Japanese	24
Wood Tavern	Cal.	25
Xyclo	Viet.	24
Yoshi's	Japanese	20
🛚 Zachary's Pizza	Pizza	24

ORINDA

Restaurant	Cuisine	Rating
Casa Orinda	Italian/Steak	16

PLEASANT HILL

Restaurant	Cuisine	Rating
Caspers Hot Dogs	Hot Dogs	18

LOCATIONS

PLEASANTON

Cheesecake Fac. | *Amer.* — 16
Cheese Steak Shop | *Cheesestks.* — 21

RICHMOND

Caspers Hot Dogs | *Hot Dogs* — 18

SAN RAMON

Izzy's Steak | *Steak* — 20
Max's | *Deli* — 17
Z Zachary's Pizza | *Pizza* — 24

WALNUT CREEK

Bing Crosby's | *Amer.* — 19
Breads of India | *Indian* — 20
Caspers Hot Dogs | *Hot Dogs* — 18
Cheese Steak Shop | *Cheesestks.* — 21
Il Fornaio | *Italian* — 19
Lark Creek | *Amer.* — 23
Le Cheval | *Viet.* — 20
Prima | *Italian* — 24
Ruth's Chris | *Steak* — 24
Scott's | *Seafood* — 19
Va de Vi | *Eclectic* — 24
Vic Stewart | *Steak* — 21

YOSEMITE/OAKHURST

Z Ahwahnee | *Amer./Cal.* — 19
Z Erna's Elderberry | *Cal./French* — 28

North of San Francisco

BODEGA BAY

Duck Club | *Amer.* — 21
Terrapin Creek | *Cal.* — 28

CALISTOGA

All Seasons | *Cal.* — 23
Brannan's Grill | *Amer./French* — 22
Jole | *Amer.* — 25
Solbar | *Cal.* — 25

CORTE MADERA

NEW Brick/Bottle | *Cal.* — -
Cheesecake Fac. | *Amer.* — 16
Il Fornaio | *Italian* — 19
Max's | *Deli* — 17
Pacific Catch | *Seafood* — 19

FAIRFAX

Lotus/Anokha | *Indian* — 23

FORESTVILLE

Z Farmhouse Inn | *Cal.* — 27
Mosaic | *Cal.* — 25

GEYSERVILLE

Diavola | *Italian* — 24
NEW Rustic | *Italian* — -

GLEN ELLEN/ KENWOOD

Cafe Citti | *Italian* — 23
Fig Cafe/Wine | *French* — 25
Kenwood | *Amer./French* — 21

GUERNEVILLE

Applewood Inn | *Cal.* — 24

HEALDSBURG/ WINDSOR

Barndiva | *Amer.* — 20
Bistro Ralph | *Cal./French* — 23
Bovolo | *Italian* — 22
Charcuterie | *French* — 21
Z Cyrus | *French* — 28
Downtown Bakery | *Bakery* — 24
Dry Creek | *Cal.* — 24
Healdsburg B&G | *Amer.* — 19
Jimtown Store | *Deli* — 21
Madrona | *Amer./French* — 26
Mirepoix | *French* — 24
Ravenous | *Cal./Eclectic* — 21
Scopa | *Italian* — 25
NEW Spoonbar | *Med.* — -
Willi's Seafood | *Seafood* — 24
Zin | *Amer.* — 23

LARKSPUR

E&O Trading | *Asian* — 19
Emporio Rulli | *Dessert/Italian* — 21
Left Bank | *French* — 19
Melting Pot | *Fondue* — 17
Picco | *Italian* — 25
Pizzeria Picco | *Pizza* — 25
Table Café | *Cal.* — 23
Tav./Lark Creek | *Amer.* — 19
Yankee Pier | *New Eng./Seafood* — 18

MENDOCINO COUNTY

Albion River Inn | *Cal.* — 24
Cafe Beaujolais | *Cal./French* — 24
Chapter & Moon | *Amer.* — 23
NEW Fort Bragg Bakery | *Bakery/Eclectic* — 27
La Petite Rive | *French* — 26
Ledford Hse. | *Cal./Med.* — 24
Little River Inn | *Cal./Seafood* — 21
MacCallum | *Cal.* — 23
Mendo Bistro | *Amer.* — 24
Mendo Café | *Eclectic* — 20

Mendo Hotel	*Cal.*	19
Moosse Café	*Cal.*	24
55 Ukiah	*Amer./French*	23
North Coast Brew	*Amer.*	17
Oco Time	*Japanese*	-
Patrona	*Cal.*	-
Piaci	*Pizza*	27
Ravens'	*Vegan*	22
Rendezvous Inn	*French*	27
Restaurant	*Amer./Eclectic*	25
Rest. at Stevenswood	*Amer.*	24
St. Orres	*Cal.*	22
Table 28	*Cal.*	23
Ukiah Brew	*Pub*	16

MILL VALLEY

Asqew Grill	*Cal.*	16
Avatar's	*Indian*	23
Balboa Cafe	*Amer.*	19
☑ Buckeye	*Amer./BBQ*	23
Bungalow 44	*Amer.*	22
Dipsea Cafe	*Amer.*	19
Frantoio	*Italian*	22
Harmony	*Chinese*	20
☑ In-N-Out	*Burgers*	22
Joe's Taco	*Mex.*	19
La Boulange	*Bakery*	21
La Ginestra	*Italian*	21
Pasta Pomodoro	*Italian*	17
Piatti	*Italian*	19
Piazza D'Angelo	*Italian*	21
Pizza Antica	*Pizza*	21
Robata Grill	*Japanese*	19
NEW Tjukiji Sushi	*Japanese*	-
Toast	*Amer.*	18

NAPA

Alexis Baking	*Bakery*	22
Angèle	*French*	23
Annalien	*Viet.*	22
Azzurro Pizzeria	*Pizza*	21
BarBersQ	*BBQ*	22
Bistro Don Giovanni	*Italian*	24
Boon Fly	*Cal.*	22
Bounty Hunter	*BBQ*	19
Brix	*Cal./Med.*	23
Cafe Zoetrope/Mammarella's	*Coffee*	20
NEW C Casa	*Mex.*	-
Celadon	*Amer./Eclectic*	23
Cole's Chop	*Steak*	24
Cuvée	*Amer.*	20
Farm	*Amer.*	23
NEW Fish Story	*Seafood*	-
Fumé Bistro	*Amer.*	19

Gott's Roadside	*Diner*	21
☑ Hog Island Oyster	*Seafood*	25
☑ In-N-Out	*Burgers*	22
☑ La Toque	*French*	27
Model Bakery	*Bakery*	21
NEW Morimoto	*Japanese*	-
Napa General	*Cal./Eclectic*	19
Napa Wine Train	*Cal.*	18
Neela's	*Indian*	-
NEW Norman Rose	*Amer.*	20
NEW Oenotri	*Italian*	-
Oxbow Wine	*Cal./Med.*	22
Pearl	*Cal.*	21
Pica Pica Maize	*Venezuelan*	23
NEW Tyler Florence	*French*	-
Ubuntu	*Cal./Vegan*	26
Uva Trattoria	*Italian*	20
Zinsvalley	*Amer.*	18
ZuZu	*Spanish*	24

NOVATO

Boca	*Argent./Steak*	22
La Boulange	*Bakery*	21
Lotus/Anokha	*Indian*	23
Toast	*Amer.*	18

OCCIDENTAL

Bistro/Copains	*French*	25

PETALUMA

Avatar's	*Indian*	23
Central Market	*Cal./Med.*	25
Cucina Paradiso	*Italian*	24
Della Fattoria	*Bakery/Eclectic*	25
Risibisi	*Italian*	22
Tea Room Café	*Amer.*	21
Volpi's Rist.	*Italian*	18
Water St. Bistro	*French*	24

ROSS

Marché/Fleurs	*French*	24

RUTHERFORD

☑ Auberge/Soleil	*Cal./French*	26
Rutherford Grill	*Amer.*	23

SAN ANSELMO

Cucina Rest.	*Italian*	23
Dream Farm	*Amer.*	21
Insalata's	*Med.*	23
Marinitas	*Pan-Latin*	18

SAN RAFAEL

Amici's	*Pizza*	19
Barney's	*Burgers*	19

Café Gratitude	*Vegan*	16	LaSalette	*Portug.*	24
Il Davide	*Italian*	20	Meritage Martini	*Italian*	21
Las Camelias	*Mex.*	18	Santé	*Cal./French*	23

ST. HELENA

Lotus/Anokha	*Indian*	23
Pasta Pomodoro	*Italian*	17

AKA Bistro	*Amer.*	15
Cindy's	*Amer./Cal.*	24
Cook St. Helena	*Italian*	25
NEW Farmstead	*Cal.*	-
Go Fish	*Eclectic/Seafood*	23
Gott's Roadside	*Diner*	21
Market	*Amer.*	22
Martini Hse.	*Amer.*	26
Meadowood Grill	*Cal.*	22
Z Meadowood Rest.	*Cal.*	26
Model Bakery	*Bakery*	21
Pizzeria Tra Vigne	*Pizza*	21
Press	*Amer./Steak*	24
Terra	*Amer.*	26
Tra Vigne	*Italian*	24
Wine Spectator	*Cal.*	24

Royal Thai | *Thai* | 22
Sol Food | *Puerto Rican* | 22
Vin Antico | *Italian* | 19

SANTA ROSA/ ROHNERT PARK

Betty's Fish	*Seafood*	23
Cheese Steak Shop	*Cheesestks.*	21
Flavor	*Cal./Eclectic*	19
Gary Chu's	*Chinese*	21
Z Hana	*Japanese*	28
John Ash	*Cal.*	22
La Gare	*Fench*	21
Monti's	*Amer./Med.*	21
Osake	*Cal./Japanese*	24
Rosso Pizzeria	*Italian/Pizza*	26
Santi	*Italian*	24
Syrah	*Cal./French*	25
Willi's Wine	*Eclectic*	25
Zazu	*Amer./Italian*	25

TIBURON

Caprice	*Amer.*	21
Guaymas	*Mex.*	17

VALLEY FORD

Rocker Oyster	*Amer.*	21

WEST MARIN/OLEMA

Drake's	*Cal.*	20
Nick's Cove	*Cal.*	19
Olema Inn	*Cal.*	19
Osteria Stellina	*Italian*	25
Pine Cone Diner	*Diner*	22
Station House	*Cal.*	18

SAUSALITO

Avatar's	*Indian*	23
Fish	*Seafood*	25
Murray Circle	*Cal.*	24
Piccolo Teatro	*Italian*	22
Poggio	*Italian*	23
Z Scoma's	*Seafood*	22
Z Sushi Ran	*Japanese*	27

SEBASTOPOL/ GRATON

YOUNTVILLE

Z Ad Hoc	*Amer.*	27
Bardessono	*Amer.*	21
Z Bistro Jeanty	*French*	25
Z Bottega	*Italian*	26
Z Bouchon	*French*	26
NEW Cantinetta Piero	*Italian*	21
Z Étoile	*Cal.*	24
Z French Laundry	*Amer./French*	29
Hurley's	*Cal./Med.*	22
Z Mustards	*Amer./Cal.*	25
Z Redd	*Cal.*	27

Hopmonk	*Eclectic*	18
K&L Bistro	*French*	24
Peter Lowell	*Italian*	21
Pizzavino	*Pizza*	-
NEW Rest. P/30	*Amer.*	-
Starlight	*Amer.*	22
Underwood Bar	*Med.*	24
Willow Wood	*Eclectic/Med.*	24

South of San Francisco

SONOMA

Cafe La Haye	*Amer./Cal.*	26
Carneros Bistro	*Cal.*	22
Della Santina	*Italian*	22
El Dorado	*Cal./Med.*	23
Estate	*Cal./Italian*	23
Fremont Diner	*Diner*	22
Girl & Fig	*French*	24
Harvest Moon	*Cal./Med.*	25

BIG SUR

Big Sur	*Amer./Bakery*	21
Deetjen's	*Cal.*	23

Menus, photos, voting and more – free at ZAGAT.com

Nepenthe	*Amer.*	17
NEW Rest. at Ventana	*Cal.*	22
Z Sierra Mar	*Cal./Eclectic*	28

BURLINGAME

Benihana	*Japanese*	17
Burger Joint	*Burgers*	18
Ecco	*Cal./Continental*	24
Il Fornaio	*Italian*	19
Isobune	*Japanese*	19
Juban	*Japanese*	18
Kabul Afghan	*Afghan*	23
La Corneta	*Mex.*	21
Max's	*Deli*	17
Roti Indian	*Indian*	22
Sakae Sushi	*Japanese*	26
Stacks	*Amer.*	18
Straits	*Singapor.*	20

CAMPBELL

Buca di Beppo	*Italian*	15
Twist	*Amer./French*	20

CARMEL/ MONTEREY PEN

Anton/Michel	*Continental*	25
Aubergine	*Cal.*	25
Bistro Moulin	*French*	29
NEW Cannery Row Brew	*Amer.*	-
Cantinetta Luca	*Italian*	23
Casanova	*French/Italian*	23
Club XIX	*Cal./French*	22
Duck Club	*Amer.*	21
Fandango	*Med.*	22
Fishwife	*Cal./Seafood*	21
Flying Fish	*Cal./Seafood*	24
Grasing's Coastal	*Cal.*	22
Hula's	*Hawaiian*	18
Il Fornaio	*Italian*	19
Montrio Bistro	*Cal.*	22
Mundaka	*Spanish*	-
Z Pacific's Edge	*Amer./French*	25
Passionfish	*Cal./Seafood*	25
Piatti	*Italian*	19
Rio Grill	*Cal.*	22
Z Roy's	*Hawaiian*	25
Sardine Factory	*Amer./Seafood*	20
Tarpy's	*Amer.*	21

CARMEL VALLEY

Café Rustica	*Cal.*	23
Z Marinus	*French*	27
Wicket Bistro	*Cal.*	24
Will's Fargo	*Seafood/Steak*	23

CUPERTINO

Alexander's	*Japanese/Steak*	26
Amici's	*Pizza*	19
Benihana	*Japanese*	17
Gochi	*Japanese*	24

HALF MOON BAY/ COAST

Barbara's	*Seafood*	20
Z Cafe Gibraltar	*Med.*	27
Cetrella	*Med.*	20
Chez Shea	*Eclectic*	23
Davenport Rdhse.	*Cal./Coffee*	19
Duarte's	*Amer.*	21
Flying Fish	*Cal./Seafood*	23
Half Moon Brew	*Pub/Seafood*	15
NEW La Costanera	*Peruvian*	24
Mezza Luna/Caffè	*Italian*	22
Z Navio	*Amer.*	24
Pasta Moon	*Italian*	22
Sam's Chowder	*Seafood*	19

LOS ALTOS

Chef Chu's	*Chinese*	21
Hunan	*Chinese*	21
Muracci's	*Japanese*	22
Sumika	*Japanese*	24
Zitune	*Moroccan*	23

LOS GATOS

Cin-Cin Wine	*Eclectic*	24
Dio Deka	*Greek*	25
Forbes Mill	*Steak*	22
Z Manresa	*Amer.*	27
Nick's on Main	*Amer.*	26

MENLO PARK

Bistro Vida	*French*	19
Cool Café	*Cal.*	20
Duck Club	*Amer.*	21
Flea St. Café	*Amer.*	25
Iberia	*Spanish*	22
Juban	*Japanese*	18
Z Kaygetsu	*Japanese*	27
Left Bank	*French*	19
Madera	*Amer.*	23
Marché	*French*	24
Naomi Sushi	*Japanese*	23
Stacks	*Amer.*	18

MILLBRAE

Mayflower/HK Flower	*Chinese*	19
Z In-N-Out	*Burgers*	22
Kitchen	*Chinese*	19

LOCATIONS

MILPITAS

Mayflower/HK Flower | *Chinese*   19

MOUNTAIN VIEW

Ⓩ Amber India | *Indian*   24
Amici's | *Pizza*   19
Cascal | *Pan-Latin*   19
Chez TJ | *French*   22
Ⓩ In-N-Out | *Burgers*   22
Krung Thai | *Thai*   20
Passage to India | *Indian*   17
Sakoon | *Indian*   23
Xanh | *Viet.*   21
Zucca | *Med.*   18

PALO ALTO/ EAST PALO ALTO

NEW Baumé | *French*   28
Bistro Elan | *Cal./French*   25
Buca di Beppo | *Italian*   15
Café Brioche | *Cal./French*   21
Calafia | *Cal.*   19
Cheesecake Fac. | *Amer.*   16
Cool Café | *Cal.*   20
Ⓩ Evvia | *Greek*   27
Fuki Sushi | *Japanese*   22
Gordon Biersch | *Pub*   15
Hunan | *Chinese*   21
Il Fornaio | *Italian*   19
Jin Sho | *Japanese*   24
Joya | *Nuevo Latino*   20
Junnoon | *Indian*   22
Kanpai | *Japanese*   24
La Strada | *Italian*   20
Lavanda | *Med.*   19
MacArthur Pk. | *Amer.*   17
Mantra | *Cal./Indian*   22
Max's | *Deli*   17
Mayfield | *Bakery/Cal.*   19
Osteria | *Italian*   22
Pampas | *Brazilian*   21
Patxi's Pizza | *Pizza*   22
Pluto's | *Amer.*   19
Quattro | *Italian*   21
Scott's | *Seafood*   19
Shokolaat | *Cal.*   21
NEW SliderBar | *Burgers*   -
St. Michael's | *Cal.*   22
Straits | *Singapor.*   20
Tai Pan | *Chinese*   24
Tamarine | *Viet.*   25
Three Seasons | *Viet.*   21
Trader Vic's | *Polynesian*   17
Zibibbo | *Med.*   19

REDWOOD CITY

Chantilly | *French/Italian*   25
Crouching Tiger | *Chinese*   21
Donato | *Italian*   24
John Bentley | *Cal.*   24
Mandaloun | *Cal./Med.*   20
Martins West | *Scottish*   24
Max's | *Deli*   17
Old Port Lobster | *Seafood*   21
Pasta Pomodoro | *Italian*   17
Red Lantern | *Asian*   18

REDWOOD SHORES

Amici's | *Pizza*   19
Mistral | *French/Italian*   19

SAN BRUNO

Don Pico | *Mex.*   21
Pasta Pomodoro | *Italian*   17

SAN CARLOS

Izzy's Steak | *Steak*   20
Kabul Afghan | *Afghan*   23

SAN JOSE

Ⓩ Amber India | *Indian*   24
Amici's | *Pizza*   19
Arcadia | *Amer.*   21
Blowfish Sushi | *Japanese*   21
Buca di Beppo | *Italian*   15
Cheesecake Fac. | *Amer.*   16
Cheese Steak Shop | *Cheesestks.*   21
E&O Trading | *Asian*   19
Gordon Biersch | *Pub*   15
Il Fornaio | *Italian*   19
Ⓩ In-N-Out | *Burgers*   22
Krung Thai | *Thai*   20
La Forêt | *Continental/French*   26
LB Steak | *Steak*   22
Left Bank | *French*   19
Ⓩ Le Papillon | *French*   26
McCormick/Schmick | *Seafood*   21
Morton's | *Steak*   24
Original Joe's | *Amer./Italian*   18
Pasta Pomodoro | *Italian*   17
Pizza Antica | *Pizza*   21
Pluto's | *Amer.*   19
Scott's | *Seafood*   19
71 St. Peter | *Cal./Med.*   20
Sino | *Chinese*   19
Straits | *Singapor.*   20
Taqueria Tlaquepaque | *Mex.*   24
Thea Med. | *Greek/Med.*   19
Yankee Pier | *New Eng./Seafood*   18

SAN MATEO

AcquaPazza | *Italian* — 21
Amici's | *Pizza* — 19
NEW Attic | *Asian* — -
Espetus | *Brazilian* — 23
Happy Cafe | *Chinese* — 21
Hotaru | *Japanese* — 20
La Cumbre | *Mex.* — 21
North Bch. Pizza | *Pizza* — 19
Pancho Villa | *Mex.* — 22
Pasta Pomodoro | *Italian* — 17
Rist. Capellini | *Italian* — 18
231 Ellsworth | *Amer.* — 23
Viognier | *Cal./French* — 23

SANTA CLARA

Cheesecake Fac. | *Amer.* — 16
Dasaprakash | *Indian* — 21
Parcel 104 | *Cal.* — 23
Piatti | *Italian* — 19

SANTA CRUZ/ APTOS/CAPITOLA/ SOQUEL

Aquarius | *Amer.* — 23
Cellar Door Café | *Cal.* — 22
Gabriella Café | *Cal./Italian* — 21
Gayle's Bakery | *Bakery* — 24
Hula's | *Hawaiian* — 18
La Posta | *Italian* — 21
Ma Maison | *French* — 20
O'mei | *Chinese* — 22

Oswald | *Amer.* — 25
Rist. Avanti | *Cal.* — 23
Shadowbrook | *Amer./Cal.* — 18
Soif Wine Bar | *Cal.* — 24

SARATOGA

Basin | *Amer.* — 21
Hachi Ju Hachi | *Japanese* — -
Plumed Horse | *Cal.* — 25
Sent Sovi | *Cal.* — 25

SOUTH SF/ DALY CITY

Basque Cultural | *French* — 21
Burger Joint | *Burgers* — 18
BurgerMeister | *Burgers* — 20
Ebisu | *Japanese* — 23
Z In-N-Out | *Burgers* — 22
Koi | *Chinese* — 23
Yankee Pier | *New Eng./Seafood* — 18

SUNNYVALE

Cheese Steak Shop | *Cheesestks.* — 21
Dishdash | *Mideast.* — 22
Il Postale | *Italian* — 22
Lion/Compass | *Amer.* — 20
Shalimar | *Indian/Pakistani* — 24
Udupi Palace | *Indian/Veg.* — 20

WOODSIDE

Bella Vista | *Continental* — 22
Z Village Pub | *Amer.* — 26

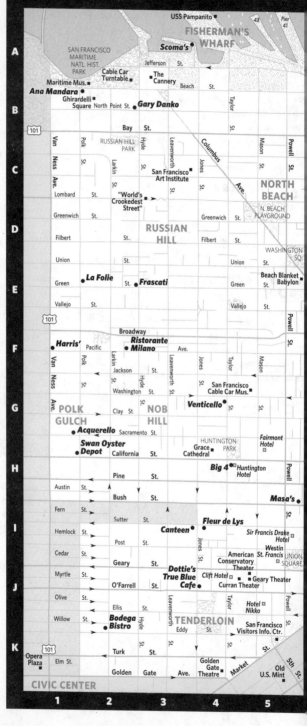

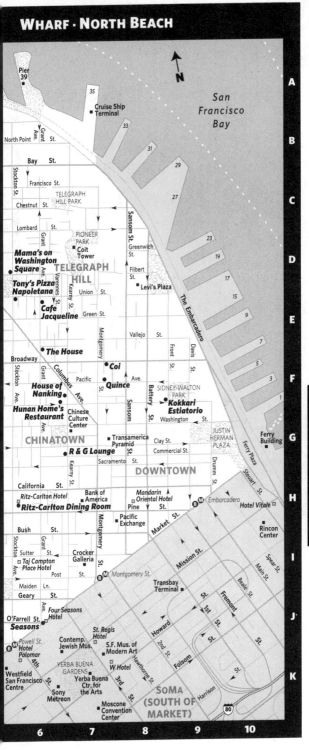

San Francisco Bay

Pier 39

35

Cruise Ship Terminal

33

North Point Ave.

Grant

31

Bay St.

29

Stockton St.

Francisco St.

27

TELEGRAPH HILL PARK

Chestnut

Lombard

Grant

PIONEER PARK

Sansom St.

Greenwich St.

23

Mama's on Washington Square

Coit Tower

19

TELEGRAPH HILL

Varennes St.

Filbert St.

17

Tony's Pizza Napoletana

Kearny St.

Union St.

Levi's Plaza

15

Cafe Jacqueline

St.

Green St.

9

Montgomery

Vallejo St.

Front St.

Davis St.

The Embarcadero

7

The House

5

Broadway

Columbus Ave.

Coi

Pacific Ave.

3

Stockton Ave.

Grant

House of Nanking

Quince

Sansom

Battery St.

SIDNEY-WALTON PARK

1

Hunan Home's Restaurant

Chinese Culture Center

Kokkari Estiatorio

Washington St.

CHINATOWN

Transamerica Pyramid

Clay St.

JUSTIN HERMAN PLAZA

Ferry Building

R & G Lounge

Kearny St.

Sacramento

Commercial St.

Drumm St.

Ferry Plaza

DOWNTOWN

California St.

Bank of America

Mandarin Oriental Hotel

Steuart St.

Embarcadero

Hotel Vitale

Ritz-Carlton Hotel

Ritz-Carlton Dining Room

Pine St.

Pacific Exchange

Rincon Center

Bush St.

Montgomery St.

Market St.

Spear St.

Stockton Ave.

Grant

Sutter St.

Crocker Galleria

Mission St.

Main St.

Taj Campton Place Hotel

St.

Post St.

Montgomery St.

Beale St.

Maiden Ln.

Transbay Terminal

Fremont St.

Geary St.

1st St.

Four Seasons Hotel

O'Farrell St.

Howard St.

Seasons

St. Regis Hotel

2nd St.

Powell St.

Contemp. Jewish Mus.

Hotel Palomar

S.F. Mus. of Modern Art

Folsom St.

4th

YERBA BUENA GARDENS

W Hotel

Hawthorne St.

Westfield San Francisco Centre

Yerba Buena Ctr. for the Arts

SOMA (SOUTH OF MARKET)

Sony Metreon

St.

Harrison

3rd

Moscone Convention Center

80

6   7   8   9   10

A B C D E F G H I J K

MAPS

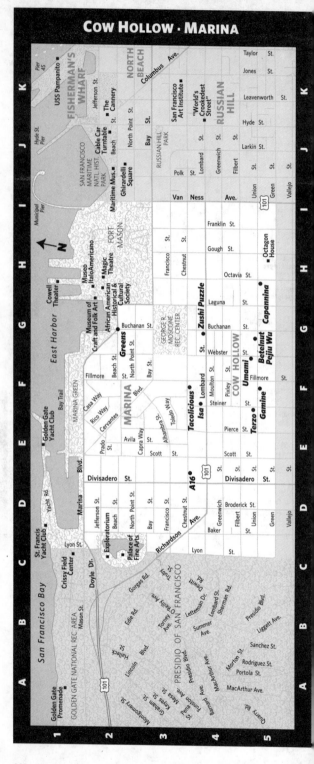

COW HOLLOW · MARINA

Menus, photos, voting and more – free at ZAGAT.com

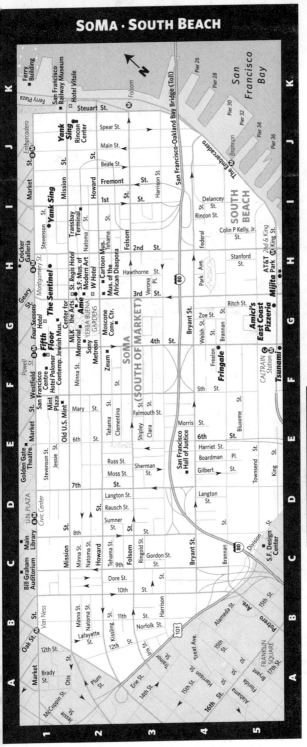

SoMa · SOUTH BEACH

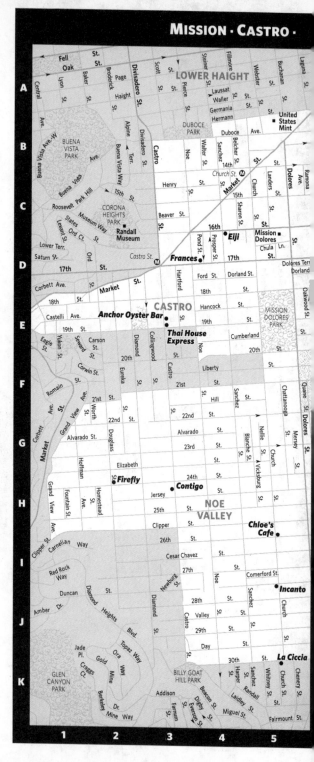

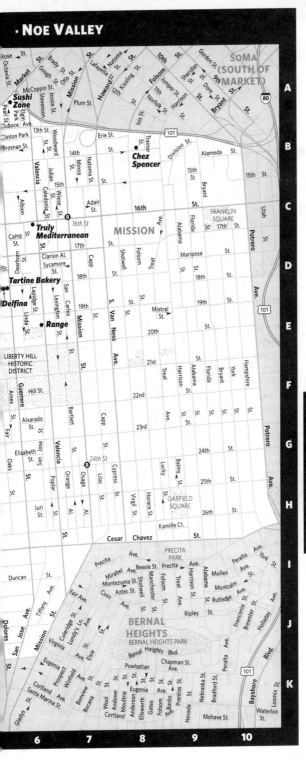

SOMA
(SOUTH OF
MARKET)

Rose St.
Octavia St.
Market St.
Brady St.
Gough St.
Otis St.
Lafayette St.
Natoma St.
10th St.
Gordon St.
Sheridan St.
9th St.
80

McCoppin St.
Jessie St.
Stevenson St.
Mission St.
Howard St.
12th St.
Kissling St.
Folsom St.
Juniper St.
11th St.
Dore St.
Bryant St.

Sushi
Zone
Plum St.
Norfolk St.
Harrison St.
St.

Elgin Park
Pearl St.
Duboce Ave.
13th St.

Clinton Park
Woodward St.
14th St.
Erie St.
101
Trainor St.
Division St.
Alameda St.

Brosnan St.
Valencia St.
Julian St.
Caledonia St.
15th St.
Minna St.
Natoma St.
St.
Chez
Spencer
15th St.
Bryant St.
15th St.
Utah St.

Albion St.
Wiese St.
Adair St.
16th St.
St.
St.
FRANKLIN
SQUARE
17th St.
Potrero Ave.

Camp St.
Truly
Mediterranean
8
16th St
17th St.
MISSION
Florida St.
Alabama St.
Ave.

Dearborn St.
Clarion Al.
Sycamore St.
18th St.
Capp St.
Shotwell St.
Folsom St.
Treat Ave.
Mariposa St.
18th St.
St.

Tartine Bakery
Ladidge St.
Lexington St.
San Carlos St.
19th St.
St.
St.
Mistral St.
19th St.

Delfina
Linda St.
Range
Mission St.
S. Van Ness Ave.
20th
Harrison St.
Alabama St.
Florida St.
Bryant St.
York St.
Hampshire St.

LIBERTY HILL
HISTORIC
DISTRICT
21st
Treat

Ames St.
Guerrero St.
Hill St.
Bartlett St.
22nd
Treat Ave.
Harrison St.
St.
St.
Bryant St.
St.

Fair St.
Alvarado St.
San Jose St.
Capp St.
23rd

Oaks St.
Elizabeth St.
Valencia St.
St.
24th
24th St.

Poplar St.
Orange St.
Osage St.
8
24th St
Cypress St.
Lilac St.
Lucky St.
Balmy St.
25th St.
Potrero Ave.

Juri St.
Al.
Al.
Virgil St.
Horace St.
GARFIELD
SQUARE
26th St.

Kamille Ct.

Cesar Chavez St.

Duncan St.
Precita Ave.
PRECITA
PARK
Precita Ave.
Peralta Ave.
York St.

Mirabel Ave.
Bessie St.
Alabama St.
Mullen Ave.

Tiffany Ave.
Fair Ave.
Montezuma St.
Shotwell St.
Manchester St.
Harrison St.
Treat Ave.
Montcalm St.
Rutledge St.
Franconia St.
Brewster St.
Holladay Ave.

San Jose Ave.
Coso Ave.
Aztec St.
Ripley St.

Dolores St.
Mission St.
Virginia Ave.
Coleridge St.
Lundys Ln.
Elsie St.
BERNAL
HEIGHTS
BERNAL HEIGHTS PARK
Bernal Heights Blvd.

Eugenia Ave.
Prospect Ave.
Winfield St.
Bonview St.
Bocana St.
Wool St.
Andover St.
Moultrie St.
Anderson St.
Powhattan Ave.
Ellsworth St.
Gates St.
Eugenia Ave.
Folsom St.
Banks St.
Prentiss St.
Chapman St.
Ave.
Nevada St.
Nebraska St.
Bradford St.
Peralta Ave.
101
Bayshore Blvd.

Gladys St.
Cortland Ave.
Santa Marina St.
Cortland Ave.
Mohave St.
Waterloo St.
Loomis St.

MAPS

6   7   8   9   10

Special Features

Listings cover the best in each category and include names, locations and Food ratings. Multi-location restaurants' features may vary by branch.

BREAKFAST

(See also Hotel Dining)

Alexis Baking | **Napa/N**	22
Bette's Oceanview | **Berkeley/E**	23
Big Sur | **Big Sur/S**	21
Blackberry Bistro | **Oakland/E**	18
Boulette Larder | **Embarcadero**	25
Butler & Chef | **SoMa**	21
Café Fanny | **Berkeley/E**	23
Chloe's Cafe | **Noe Valley**	23
Dipsea Cafe | **Mill Valley/N**	19
Dottie's | **Tenderloin**	25
Downtown Bakery | **Healdsburg/N**	24
Ella's | **Presidio Hts**	21
Emporio Rulli | **Downtown**	21
FatApple's | **multi.**	17
Gayle's Bakery | **Capitola/S**	24
Il Fornaio | **multi.**	19
Jimmy Beans | **Berkeley/E**	19
Jimtown Store | **Healdsburg/N**	21
Kate's Kitchen | **Lower Haight**	22
Koi | **Daly City/S**	23
La Boulange | **multi.**	21
La Note | **Berkeley/E**	22
Mama's on Wash. | **N Beach**	25
Mama's Royal | **Oakland/E**	21
Mel's Drive-In | **multi.**	14
Model Bakery | **St. Helena/N**	21
Napa General | **Napa/N**	19
Oliveto Cafe | **Oakland/E**	23
Pork Store | **multi.**	19
Red's Java | **Embarcadero**	15
Rick & Ann | **Berkeley/E**	21
Rose's Cafe | **Cow Hollow**	22
Savor | **Noe Valley**	17
Sears Fine Food | **Downtown**	20
☑ Tartine | **Mission**	27
Town's End | **Embarcadero**	20
Venus | **Berkeley/E**	21
Water St. Bistro | **Petaluma/N**	24
Willow Wood | **Graton/N**	24
Zazie | **Cole Valley**	22

BRUNCH

☑ Absinthe | **Hayes Valley**	22
☑ Ahwahnee | **Yosemite/E**	19
Alexis Baking | **Napa/N**	22
Americano | **Embarcadero**	18

Anzu | **Downtown**	22
Baker St. Bistro | **Marina**	22
Balboa Cafe | **Cow Hollow**	19
Beach Chalet | **Outer Sunset**	14
Bistro Liaison | **Berkeley/E**	21
Bistro Vida | **Menlo Pk/S**	19
Blackhawk Grille | **Danville/E**	21
Brenda's | **Civic Ctr**	24
☑ Buckeye | **Mill Valley/N**	23
Campton Place | **Downtown**	25
☑ Canteen | **Tenderloin**	27
Catch | **Castro**	18
Chez Maman | **Potrero Hill**	23
Chloe's Cafe | **Noe Valley**	23
☑ Chow/Park Chow | **multi.**	20
Delancey St. | **Embarcadero**	18
Dottie's | **Tenderloin**	25
Duck Club | **Lafayette/E**	21
Elite Cafe | **Pacific Hts**	19
Ella's | **Presidio Hts**	21
☑ Erna's Elderberry | **Oakhurst/E**	28
Estate | **Sonoma/N**	23
Fandango | **Pacific Grove/S**	22
Five | **Berkeley/E**	22
Foreign Cinema | **Mission**	23
Gabriella Café | **Santa Cruz/S**	21
☑ Garden Court | **Downtown**	18
Garibaldis | **Oakland/E**	22
Gayle's Bakery | **Capitola/S**	24
Girl & Fig | **Sonoma/N**	24
Grand Cafe | **Downtown**	20
☑ Greens | **Marina**	24
Home | **Castro**	19
Insalata's | **San Anselmo/N**	23
Kate's Kitchen | **Lower Haight**	22
La Forêt | **San Jose/S**	26
La Note | **Berkeley/E**	22
Lark Creek | **Walnut Creek/E**	23
Liberty Cafe | **Bernal Hts**	22
Luna Park | **Mission**	19
Madera | **Menlo Pk/S**	23
Marinitas | **San Anselmo/N**	18
Mayfield | **Palo Alto/S**	19
Mission Bch. Café | **Mission**	25
MoMo's | **S Beach**	17
☑ Navio | **Half Moon Bay/S**	24
Nob Hill Café | **Nob Hill**	21
Park Chalet | **Outer Sunset**	14

Menus, photos, voting and more – free at ZAGAT.com

azza D'Angelo | **Mill Valley/N**	21
icante Cocina | **Berkeley/E**	21
Rest. | **Inner Rich**	18
est. LuLu/Petite | **SoMa**	21
ick & Ann | **Berkeley/E**	21
io Grill | **Carmel/S**	22
ose's Cafe | **Cow Hollow**	22
avor | **Noe Valley**	17
cott's | **multi.**	19
Seasons | **Downtown**	26
ow Club | **Mission**	22
t. Michael's | **Palo Alto/S**	22
arpy's | **Monterey/S**	21
av./Lark Creek | **Larkspur/N**	19
300/Fillmore | **W Addition**	23
ipsy Pig | **Marina**	19
own's End | **Embarcadero**	20
rader Vic's | **Emeryville/E**	17
ra Vigne | **St. Helena/N**	24
223 | **Castro**	21
niversal Cafe | **Mission**	23
enus | **Berkeley/E**	21
ente Vineyards | **Livermore/E**	24
illow Wood | **Graton/N**	24
Yank Sing | **SoMa**	25
azie | **Cole Valley**	22
Zuni Café | **Hayes Valley**	25

BUSINESS DINING

Alexander's | **Cupertino/S**	26
Alfred's Steak | **Downtown**	22
Amber India | **multi.**	24
Ame | **SoMa**	26
Americano | **Embarcadero**	18
Anchor & Hope | **SoMa**	21
Anzu | **Downtown**	22
NEW Barbacco | **Downtown**	25
Basin | **Saratoga/S**	21
Big 4 | **Nob Hill**	23
Bing Crosby's | **Walnut Creek/E**	19
Boca | **Novato/N**	22
Bottega | **Yountville/N**	26
Boulevard | **Embarcadero**	27
Bushi-tei | **Japantown**	22
Campton Place | **Downtown**	25
Cha Am Thai | **SoMa**	19
Chantilly | **Redwood City/S**	25
Chaya | **Embarcadero**	22
Chef Chu's | **Los Altos/S**	21
Chez Papa | **SoMa**	23
Cole's Chop | **Napa/N**	24
Cool Café | **Palo Alto/S**	20
Cosmopolitan | **SoMa**	19
NEW Credo | **Downtown**	17

Dio Deka | **Los Gatos/S**	25
Donato | **Redwood City/S**	24
Ducca | **SoMa**	17
Duck Club | **Menlo Pk/S**	21
E&O Trading | **San Jose/S**	19
Evvia | **Palo Alto/S**	27
Farallon | **Downtown**	24
Five | **Berkeley/E**	22
5A5 Steak | **Downtown**	22
Flea St. Café | **Menlo Pk/S**	25
Fuki Sushi | **Palo Alto/S**	22
Gaylord India | **Downtown**	18
NEW Georges | **Downtown**	-
Gitane | **Downtown**	21
Grand Cafe | **Downtown**	20
Harris' | **Polk Gulch**	25
Heaven's Dog | **SoMa**	20
House of Prime | **Polk Gulch**	25
Iberia | **Menlo Pk/S**	22
Il Fornaio | **multi.**	19
Izzy's Steak | **multi.**	20
Jin Sho | **Palo Alto/S**	24
Joe DiMaggio | **N Beach**	20
Joya | **Palo Alto/S**	20
Junnoon | **Palo Alto/S**	22
Kanpai | **Palo Alto/S**	24
Kaygetsu | **Menlo Pk/S**	27
Kokkari | **Downtown**	27
Kuleto's | **Downtown**	21
Kyo-Ya | **Downtown**	24
La Forêt | **San Jose/S**	26
Lark Creek Steak | **Downtown**	22
Lavanda | **Palo Alto/S**	19
LB Steak | **San Jose/S**	22
Le Central Bistro | **Downtown**	20
Le Papillon | **San Jose/S**	26
Lion/Compass | **Sunnyvale/S**	20
Luce | **SoMa**	21
MacArthur Pk. | **Palo Alto/S**	17
Madera | **Menlo Pk/S**	23
NEW Manzanita | **Truckee/E**	25
Marinus | **Carmel Valley/S**	27
MarketBar | **Embarcadero**	17
Martins West | **Redwood City/S**	24
Masa's | **Downtown**	27
Meadowood Grill | **St. Helena/N**	22
NEW Meritage/Claremont | **Berkeley/E**	25
Mexico DF | **Embarcadero**	18
Midi | **Downtown**	20
Mistral | **Redwood Shores/S**	19
Mixt Greens | **Downtown**	22
MoMo's | **S Beach**	17
Morton's | **multi.**	24

SPECIAL FEATURES

Restaurant	Location	
Moss Room	Inner Rich	20
Muracci's	Downtown	22
Murray Circle	Sausalito/N	24
One Market	Embarcadero	23
Osha Thai	multi.	20
Osteria	Palo Alto/S	22
Ozumo	multi.	23
Palio d'Asti	Downtown	20
Pampas	Palo Alto/S	21
Pazzia	SoMa	24
Peasant/Pear	Danville/E	24
☑ Perbacco	Downtown	25
Picco	Larkspur/N	25
Piperade	Downtown	25
Plumed Horse	Saratoga/S	25
Poggio	Sausalito/N	23
Ponzu	Downtown	20
Presidio Social	Presidio	19
Press	St. Helena/N	24
NEW Prospect	SoMa	-
Quattro	E Palo Alto/S	21
Red Lantern	Redwood City/S	18
Rest. LuLu/Petite	SoMa	21
Rist. Umbria	SoMa	20
☑ Ritz-Carlton	Nob Hill	27
RN74	SoMa	22
Roy's	SoMa	23
Ruth's Chris	Polk Gulch	24
Salt House	SoMa	21
Sam's Grill	Downtown	21
Sanraku	multi.	21
☑ Seasons	Downtown	26
Sens	Downtown	19
71 St. Peter	San Jose/S	20
Silks	Downtown	25
Sino	San Jose/S	19
Solbar	Calistoga/N	25
South Park	SoMa	22
St. Michael's	Palo Alto/S	22
☑ Tadich Grill	Downtown	23
Tommy Toy	Downtown	24
Townhouse B&G	Emeryville/E	20
231 Ellsworth	San Mateo/S	23
Urban Tavern	Downtown	17
Viognier	San Mateo/S	23
Waterfront	Embarcadero	18
☑ Yank Sing	SoMa	25
Zaré/Fly Trap	SoMa	23
Zibibbo	Palo Alto/S	19
☑ Zuni Café	Hayes Valley	25
Zuppa	SoMa	20

CATERING

Restaurant	Location	
☑ Acquerello	Polk Gulch	28
Adagia	Berkeley/E	18
Alexis Baking	Napa/N	20
All Seasons	Calistoga/N	2.
Americano	Embarcadero	1(
Asqew Grill	multi.	1(
Barndiva	Healdsburg/N	20
Betelnut Pejiu	Cow Hollow	23
Bistro Liaison	Berkeley/E	21
☑ Bix	Downtown	24
Blowfish Sushi	multi.	21
Bocadillos	N Beach	23
☑ Buckeye	Mill Valley/N	23
Café Kati	Japantown	22
César	Berkeley/E	22
Cha Cha Cha	multi.	21
Charanga	Mission	23
Chef Chu's	Los Altos/S	21
Chenery Park	Glen Pk	22
Chez Papa	Potrero Hill	23
Chez Spencer	Mission	25
Coco500	SoMa	23
Cool Café	Palo Alto/S	20
Cucina Paradiso	Petaluma/N	24
Destino	Castro	21
Ebisu	Inner Sunset	23
Emporio Rulli	Larkspur/N	21
Eos	Cole Valley	23
Fig Cafe/Wine	Glen Ellen/N	25
Fresca	multi.	22
Gayle's Bakery	Capitola/S	24
Grasing's Coastal	Carmel/S	22
☑ Greens	Marina	24
☑ Hana	Rohnert Pk/N	28
Iberia	Menlo Pk/S	22
Il Davide	San Rafael/N	20
Il Fornaio	San Jose/S	19
Insalata's	San Anselmo/N	23
Jimtown Store	Healdsburg/N	21
☑ Kokkari	Downtown	27
La Méditerranée	multi.	19
La Strada	Palo Alto/S	20
Lavanda	Palo Alto/S	19
Left Bank	multi.	19
Marché	Menlo Pk/S	24
☑ Marinus	Carmel Valley/S	27
Max's	Downtown	17
Memphis Minnie	Lower Haight	21
Mochica	SoMa	23
Moki's Sushi	Bernal Hts	19
Monti's	Santa Rosa/N	21
Napa General	Napa/N	19
Nick's Crispy	Russian Hill	21
Ozumo	Embarcadero	23
Piatti	multi.	19

CELEBRITY CHEFS

SPECIAL FEATURES

Thomas Keller
- Z Ad Hoc | **Yountville/N** 27
- Z Bouchon | **Yountville/N** 26
- Z French Laundry | **Yountville/N** 29

Christopher Kump
- NEW Fort Bragg Bakery | **Ft Bragg/N** 27

Mourad Lahlou
- Z Aziza | **Outer Rich** 26

Dennis Leary
- Z Canteen | **Tenderloin** 27
- NEW Golden West | **Downtown** -
- Sentinel | **SoMa** 24

Corey Lee
- NEW Benu | **SoMa** -

Michael Mina
- Arcadia | **San Jose/S** 21
- RN74 | **SoMa** 22

Masaharu Morimoto
- NEW Morimoto | **Napa/N** -

Nancy Oakes
- Z Boulevard | **Embarcadero** 27
- NEW Prospect | **SoMa** -

Daniel Olivella
- Barlata | **Oakland/E** 21
- B44 | **Downtown** 21

Charlie Palmer
- Dry Creek | **Healdsburg/N** 24

Roland Passot
- Z La Folie | **Russian Hill** 28
- LB Steak | **San Jose/S** 22

Daniel Patterson
- Z Coi | **N Beach** 26
- Il Cane Rosso | **Embarcadero** 22
- NEW Plum | **Oakland/E** -

Cindy Pawlcyn
- Cindy's | **St. Helena/N** 24
- Go Fish | **St. Helena/N** 23
- Z Mustards | **Yountville/N** 25

Charles Phan
- Academy Cafe | **Inner Rich** 19
- Heaven's Dog | **SoMa** 20
- Out the Door | **multi.** 22
- Z Slanted Door | **Embarcadero** 26

Richard Reddington
- Z Redd | **Yountville/N** 27

Judy Rodgers
- Z Zuni Café | **Hayes Valley** 25

Mitchell and Steven Rosenthal
- Anchor & Hope | **SoMa** 21
- Salt House | **SoMa** 21
- Town Hall | **SoMa** 23

Gregory Short
- Z Masa's | **Downtown** 27

Ron Siegel
- Z Ritz-Carlton | **Nob Hill** 27

Hiro Sone
- Ame | **SoMa** 26
- Terra | **St. Helena/N** 26

Cal Stamenov
- Z Marinus | **Carmel Valley/S** 27
- Wicket Bistro | **Carmel Valley/S** 24
- Will's Fargo | **Carmel Valley/S** 23

Craig Stoll
- Z Delfina | **Mission** 26
- Pizzeria Delfina | **multi.** 25

Luke Sung
- NEW Prime Rib Shabu | **Inner Rich** 23

Seiji 'Waka' Wakabayashi
- Bushi-tei | **Japantown** 22

Alice Waters
- Café Fanny | **Berkeley/E** 23
- Z Chez Panisse | **Berkeley/E** 28
- Z Chez Panisse Café | **Berkeley/E** 27

Roy Yamaguchi
- Roy's | **SoMa** 23
- Z Roy's | **Pebble Bch/S** 25

Chris Yeo
- Sino | **San Jose/S** 19
- Straits | **multi.** 20

CHILD-FRIENDLY

(Alternatives to the usual fast-food places; * children's menu available)
- Z Ahwahnee* | **Yosemite/E** 19
- Alexis Baking | **Napa/N** 22
- Alice's | **Noe Valley** 20
- Alioto's* | **Fish. Wharf** 18
- Amici's* | **multi.** 19
- Aperto* | **Potrero Hill** 24
- Arcadia* | **San Jose/S** 21
- Asqew Grill* | **multi.** 16
- Azzurro Pizzeria | **Napa/N** 21
- Barbara's* | **Princeton Sea/S** 20
- Barney's* | **multi.** 19
- Basque Cultural* | **S San Francisco/S** 21
- Beach Chalet* | **Outer Sunset** 14
- Bellanico | **Oakland/E** 22
- Bette's Oceanview | **Berkeley/E** 23
- Bistro Boudin* | **Fish. Wharf** 20
- Brandy Ho's | **multi.** 19
- Buca di Beppo* | **multi.** 15
- Z Buckeye* | **Mill Valley/N** 23

Bungalow 44* | Mill Valley/N	22
Burger Joint | multi.	18
☑ Burma Superstar | Inner Rich	24
Cactus Taqueria* | multi.	20
Cafe Citti | Kenwood/N	23
Caffe Delle Stelle | Hayes Valley	16
Caffè Macaroni | N Beach	21
Caffè Museo | SoMa	19
Caspers Hot Dogs | multi.	18
Cetrella* | Half Moon Bay/S	20
Cheesecake Fac.* | multi.	16
Chenery Park | Glen Pk	22
☑ Chow/Park Chow* | multi.	20
Cindy's | St. Helena/N	24
Citrus Club | Haight-Ashbury	21
Cook St. Helena | St. Helena/N	25
Cool Café | Palo Alto/S	20
Delancey St. | Embarcadero	18
Dipsea Cafe* | Mill Valley/N	19
Dottie's | Tenderloin	25
Duarte's* | Pescadero/S	21
Eliza's | Pacific Hts	22
Ella's | Presidio Hts	21
Emmy's Spaghetti* | Bernal Hts	19
Eric's | Noe Valley	20
FatApple's* | multi.	17
Fentons* | Oakland/E	20
Fish | Sausalito/N	25
Flavor* | Santa Rosa/N	19
Fog City Diner* | Embarcadero	19
Forbes Mill* | Danville/E	22
Foreign Cinema* | Mission	23
Front Porch* | Bernal Hts	19
Garibaldis | Oakland/E	22
Gar Woods* | Carnelian Bay/E	17
Giordano | N Beach	21
Giorgio's | Inner Rich	22
Goat Hill Pizza | Potrero Hill	20
Gott's Roadside | multi.	21
Great China | Berkeley/E	24
Great Eastern | Chinatown	19
Guaymas* | Tiburon/N	17
Hard Rock* | Fish. Wharf	12
Healdsburg B&G* | Healdsburg/N	19
Henry's Hunan | multi.	20
Hurley's | Yountville/N	22
Il Fornaio* | multi.	19
Insalata's* | San Anselmo/N	23
Jay's* | multi.	18
Jimmy Beans* | Berkeley/E	19
Joe's Cable Car | Excelsior	23
Joe's Taco* | Mill Valley/N	19
Juan's | Berkeley/E	16
Juban | multi.	18

Koi | Daly City/S	23
Koryo BBQ | Oakland/E	22
Kuleto's | Downtown	21
La Boulange | multi.	21
La Cumbre | Mission	21
La Méditerranée* | multi.	19
Lark Creek* | Walnut Creek/E	23
Lark Creek Steak* | Downtown	22
La Taqueria | Mission	25
Left Bank* | multi.	19
Lo Coco | Berkeley/E	21
Lovejoy's Tea* | Noe Valley	21
Luella* | Russian Hill	22
Mama's on Wash. | N Beach	25
Market | St. Helena/N	22
Max's* | multi.	17
Mel's Drive-In* | multi.	14
Model Bakery | St. Helena/N	21
Napa General* | Napa/N	19
Nepenthe* | Big Sur/S	17
North Bch. Pizza | multi.	19
O'mei | Santa Cruz/S	22
Original Joe's* | San Jose/S	18
Pacific Catch* | multi.	19
Pancho Villa | multi.	22
Parcel 104* | Santa Clara/S	23
Park Chalet* | Outer Sunset	14
Pasta Pomodoro* | multi.	17
Piatti* | multi.	19
Picante Cocina* | Berkeley/E	21
Pizza Antica* | multi.	21
Pizza Rustica | Oakland/E	21
Pizzeria Tra Vigne* | St. Helena/N	21
Q Rest. | Inner Rich	18
Quattro* | E Palo Alto/S	21
R&G Lounge | Chinatown	24
Rest. Peony | Oakland/E	20
Rick & Ann* | Berkeley/E	21
Robata Grill | Mill Valley/N	19
Rosso Pizzeria* | Santa Rosa/N	26
☑ Roy's* | Pebble Bch/S	25
Sam's Chowder* | Half Moon Bay/S	19
Saul's Rest./Deli* | Berkeley/E	17
Savor* | Noe Valley	17
☑ Scoma's* | multi.	22
Sears Fine Food | Downtown	20
Shen Hua | Berkeley/E	19
Taqueria Can-Cun | multi.	21
Tarpy's* | Monterey/S	21
Tommaso's | N Beach	24
Ton Kiang | Outer Rich	24
Tony's Pizza* | N Beach	26
Venezia* | Berkeley/E	21

SPECIAL FEATURES

Willow Wood | **Graton/N** 24
Yankee Pier* | **multi.** 18
Z Yank Sing | **SoMa** 25
Z Zachary's Pizza | **Oakland/E** 24

COCKTAIL SPECIALISTS

Z Absinthe | **Hayes Valley** 22
À Côté | **Oakland/E** 24
Adesso | **Oakland/E** 23
Alembic | **Haight-Ashbury** 22
Z Aziza | **Outer Rich** 26
NEW Bar Agricole | **SoMa** -
Beretta | **Mission** 23
Betelnut Pejiu | **Cow Hollow** 23
Z Bix | **Downtown** 24
NEW Brick/Bottle | **Corte Madera/N** -
NEW Café des Amis | **Cow Hollow** -
Coco500 | **SoMa** 23
NEW Comstock | **N Beach** -
NEW Delarosa | **Marina** 22
Dosa | **multi.** 22
15 Romolo | **N Beach** -
Flora | **Oakland/E** 22
Heaven's Dog | **SoMa** 20
NEW Hog & Rocks | **Mission** -
Z Jardinière | **Civic Ctr** 26
Le Colonial | **Downtown** 23
NEW Locanda da Eva | **Berkeley/E** -
Nihon | **Mission** 21
NEW Nombe | **Mission** 22
Orson | **SoMa** 19
NEW Prospect | **SoMa** -
Z Range | **Mission** 27
NEW Revival Bar | **Berkeley/E** -
NEW Spoonbar | **Healdsburg/N** -
NEW Starbelly | **Castro** 20
NEW Thermidor | **SoMa** -
Tres Agaves | **S Beach** 17
NEW Wayfare Tav. | **Downtown** -
Wood Tavern | **Oakland/E** 25
Zaré/Fly Trap | **SoMa** 23
NEW Zero Zero | **SoMa** -

DANCING

AsiaSF | **SoMa** 17
Enrico's | **N Beach** 16
Kan Zaman | **Haight-Ashbury** 19
Le Colonial | **Downtown** 23
Luka's Taproom | **Oakland/E** 20
NEW Mayes | **Polk Gulch** 19
Medjool | **Mission** 19
Tonga | **Nob Hill** 14

DELIVERY

Alexis Baking | **Napa/N** 22
Amici's | **multi.** 19
Angkor Borei | **Bernal Hts** 23
Basil | **SoMa** 23
Brandy Ho's | **Chinatown** 19
Gary Chu's | **Santa Rosa/N** 21
Goat Hill Pizza | **SoMa** 20
Henry's Hunan | **SoMa** 20
Max's | **multi.** 17
NEW Mission Chinese | **Mission** -
North Bch. Pizza | **multi.** 19
Pakwan | **Hayward/E** 21
Pizza Rustica | **Oakland/E** 21
Z Swan Oyster | **Polk Gulch** 27
Ton Kiang | **Outer Rich** 24
Zante | **Bernal Hts** 18

DINING ALONE

(Other than hotels and places with counter service)
Z Absinthe | **Hayes Valley** 22
Anchor & Hope | **SoMa** 21
Ariake | **Outer Rich** 23
NEW Barbacco | **Downtown** 25
Bar Crudo | **W Addition** 25
Barlata | **Oakland/E** 21
Bar Tartine | **Mission** 23
Beretta | **Mission** 23
Bette's Oceanview | **Berkeley/E** 23
NEW Bistro Central Parc | **W Addition** -
Z Bistro Jeanty | **Yountville/N** 25
Bistro Ralph | **Healdsburg/N** 23
Blowfish Sushi | **multi.** 21
Blue Barn | **Marina** 21
Bocadillos | **N Beach** 23
Z Bouchon | **Yountville/N** 26
Z Boulevard | **Embarcadero** 27
Bovolo | **Healdsburg/N** 22
Z Buckeye | **Mill Valley/N** 23
Bungalow 44 | **Mill Valley/N** 22
Café Claude | **Downtown** 22
Café de la Presse | **Downtown** 18
Café Gratitude | **multi.** 16
Café Rouge | **Berkeley/E** 20
Z Canteen | **Tenderloin** 27
Cascal | **Mtn View/S** 19
Cellar Door Café | **Santa Cruz/S** 22
César | **Berkeley/E** 22
Cetrella | **Half Moon Bay/S** 20
Chez Maman | **Potrero Hill** 23
Chez Papa | **Potrero Hill** 23
NEW Chile Pies | **W Addition** -
NEW Chop Bar | **Oakland/E** 22

Menus, photos, voting and more - free at ZAGAT.com

Coco500 | **SoMa**	23
Contigo | **Noe Valley**	24
Cook St. Helena | **St. Helena/N**	25
Corso | **Berkeley/E**	23
Cuvée | **Napa/N**	20
NEW Delarosa | **Marina**	22
DeLessio | **multi.**	22
Della Fattoria | **Petaluma/N**	25
Domo Sushi | **Hayes Valley**	20
Dosa | **Mission**	22
Duarte's | **Pescadero/S**	21
E&O Trading | **San Jose/S**	19
Ebisu | **multi.**	23
Emporio Rulli | **Larkspur/N**	21
NEW Encuentro | **Oakland/E**	-
Enrico's | **N Beach**	16
Eos | **Cole Valley**	23
NEW Eve | **Berkeley/E**	25
Z Evvia | **Palo Alto/S**	27
Farmerbrown | **Tenderloin**	21
NEW Farmstead | **St. Helena/N**	-
Firefly | **Noe Valley**	24
Flora | **Oakland/E**	22
Fog City Diner | **Embarcadero**	19
NEW Fort Bragg Bakery | **Ft Bragg/N**	27
4505 Meats | **Embarcadero**	28
Fremont Diner | **Sonoma/N**	22
Fringale | **SoMa**	24
Frjtz Fries | **multi.**	17
Gamine | **Cow Hollow**	23
NEW Georges | **Downtown**	-
Godzila Sushi | **Pacific Hts**	18
Gott's Roadside | **Napa/N**	21
NEW Gracias | **Mission**	20
Grandeho Kamekyo | **Fish. Wharf**	21
Grand Pu Bah | **Potrero Hill**	20
Green Chile | **W Addition**	21
Grégoire | **Oakland/E**	23
Hachi Ju Hachi | **Saratoga/S**	-
Hamano Sushi | **Noe Valley**	19
Z Hana | **Rohnert Pk/N**	28
NEW Heart | **Mission**	-
NEW Hibiscus | **Oakland/E**	21
Z Hog Island Oyster | **Embarcadero**	25
Home of Chicken | **Oakland/E**	19
Hopmonk | **Sebastopol/N**	18
Hula's | **Monterey/S**	18
Hurley's | **Yountville/N**	22
NEW Izakaya Sozai | **Inner Sunset**	-
Kabuto | **Outer Rich**	26
Kamekyo | **Cole Valley**	21
Kanpai | **Palo Alto/S**	24
Kasa Indian | **Marina**	19

Z Kaygetsu | **Menlo Pk/S**	27
King of Thai | **multi.**	18
Kirala | **Berkeley/E**	24
Z Kiss Seafood | **Japantown**	27
Kitchenette SF | **Dogpatch**	22
Koo | **Inner Sunset**	23
Krung Thai | **San Jose/S**	20
La Boulange | **multi.**	21
NEW La Costanera | **Montara/S**	24
NEW Lafitte | **Embarcadero**	-
La Note | **Berkeley/E**	22
La Trappe | **N Beach**	18
Left Bank | **Menlo Pk/S**	19
Little Chihuahua | **W Addition**	22
NEW Local Mission | **Mission**	-
Mario's Bohemian | **N Beach**	19
MarketBar | **Embarcadero**	17
NEW Marlowe | **SoMa**	-
Marzano | **Oakland/E**	21
Maverick | **Mission**	24
Mayfield | **Palo Alto/S**	19
Meritage Martini | **Sonoma/N**	21
Mission Bch. Café | **Mission**	25
Model Bakery | **Napa/N**	21
Monk's Kettle | **Mission**	20
Z Mustards | **Yountville/N**	25
Naan/Curry | **Downtown**	17
NEW Naked Lunch | **N Beach**	26
Namu | **Embarcadero**	23
Naomi Sushi | **Menlo Pk/S**	23
NEW Nombe | **Mission**	22
Nopalito | **W Addition**	23
Oliveto Cafe | **Oakland/E**	23
Orson | **SoMa**	19
Ottimista | **Cow Hollow**	17
Outerlands | **Outer Sunset**	23
Out the Door | **multi.**	22
Oxbow Wine | **Napa/N**	22
Oyaji | **Outer Rich**	23
Pacific Catch | **multi.**	19
NEW Parada 22 | **Haight-Ashbury**	-
Pasta Pomodoro | **multi.**	17
Patrona | **Ukiah/N**	-
Peter Lowell | **Sebastopol/N**	21
NEW Pi Bar | **Mission**	14
Pica Pica Maize | **Napa/N**	23
Piccino | **Dogpatch**	21
Piccolo Teatro | **Sausalito/N**	22
Pine Cone Diner | **Pt Reyes/N**	22
Piperade | **Downtown**	25
Pizzeria Delfina | **Pacific Hts**	25
Plant Cafe | **multi.**	20
Pot de Pho | **Inner Rich**	19
NEW Radius | **SoMa**	-

☑ Redd | **Yountville/N**	27
Robata Grill | **Mill Valley/N**	19
Samovar Tea | **multi.**	20
☑ Sebo | **Hayes Valley**	27
Serpentine | **Dogpatch**	19
Shabu-Sen | **Japantown**	19
Sino | **San Jose/S**	19
NEW SliderBar | **Palo Alto/S**	-
Spork | **Mission**	20
SPQR | **Pacific Hts**	24
Stable Café | **Mission**	-
NEW Starbelly | **Castro**	20
NEW Super Duper | **Castro**	-
Suppenküche | **Hayes Valley**	22
☑ Sushi Ran | **Sausalito/N**	27
☑ Sushi Zone | **Castro**	27
☑ Swan Oyster | **Polk Gulch**	27
Table Café | **Larkspur/N**	23
NEW Tacolicious | **Marina**	23
Tataki Sushi | **Pacific Hts**	22
Tea Room Café | **Petaluma/N**	21
Terzo | **Cow Hollow**	23
Ti Couz | **Mission**	21
Town Hall | **SoMa**	23
Tra Vigne | **St. Helena/N**	24
NEW Trueburger | **Oakland/E**	-
Tsunami | **W Addition**	22
Uva Enoteca | **Lower Haight**	21
Vanessa's Bistro | **Berkeley/E**	23
Viognier | **San Mateo/S**	23
Wild Goose | **Tahoe Vista/E**	-
Willi's Seafood | **Healdsburg/N**	24
Will's Fargo | **Carmel Valley/S**	23
Woodhse. | **Castro**	20
Xanh | **Mtn View/S**	21
Yoshi's | **Oakland/E**	20
Yoshi's SF | **W Addition**	21
Zazie | **Cole Valley**	22
Zibibbo | **Palo Alto/S**	19
☑ Zuni Café | **Hayes Valley**	25
☑ Zushi Puzzle | **Marina**	27

ENTERTAINMENT

(Call for days and times
of performances)

☑ Ahwahnee | piano | **Yosemite/E**	19
Albion River Inn | piano | **Albion/N**	24
Ana Mandara | jazz | **Fish. Wharf**	22
AsiaSF | gender illusionists | **SoMa**	17
Beach Chalet | live music | **Outer Sunset**	14
☑ Big 4 | piano | **Nob Hill**	23
Bing Crosby's | piano | **Walnut Creek/E**	19
☑ Bix | live music | **Downtown**	24
Blowfish Sushi | DJ | **San Jose/S**	21
Butterfly | jazz | **Embarcadero**	22
Cafe Bastille | jazz | **Downtown**	17
Café Claude | jazz | **Downtown**	22
Cascal | Spanish music | **Mtn View/S**	19
Cetrella | jazz | **Half Moon Bay/S**	20
☑ Cheese Board | jazz/pop | **Berkeley/E**	27
Enrico's | jazz | **N Beach**	16
Everett/Jones | varies | **Oakland/E**	20
Foreign Cinema | films | **Mission**	23
☑ Garden Court | live music | **Downtown**	18
Giordano | bands | **N Beach**	21
Harris' | live music | **Polk Gulch**	25
Kan Zaman | varies | **Haight-Ashbury**	19
Katia's Tea | accordion | **Inner Rich**	23
La Note | accordion | **Berkeley/E**	22
Ledford Hse. | jazz | **Albion/N**	24
☑ Marinus | jazz | **Carmel Valley/S**	27
Max's | varies | **multi.**	17
☑ Navio | jazz | **Half Moon Bay/S**	24
Olema Inn | jazz | **Olema/N**	19
Plumed Horse | piano | **Saratoga/S**	25
Rose Pistola | jazz | **N Beach**	21
Santé | piano | **Sonoma/N**	23
Sardine Factory | piano | **Monterey/S**	20
Scott's | varies | **multi.**	19
Straits | varies | **multi.**	20
Sushi Groove | DJ | **SoMa**	22
Tonga | live music | **Nob Hill**	14
Townhouse B&G | live music | **Emeryville/E**	20
Uva Trattoria | jazz | **Napa/N**	20
Vic Stewart | piano | **Walnut Creek/E**	21
XYZ | DJ | **SoMa**	20
Yoshi's | jazz | **Oakland/E**	20
Yoshi's SF | live music | **W Addition**	21
☑ Zuni Café | piano | **Hayes Valley**	25

FIREPLACES

Adagia | **Berkeley/E**	18
☑ Ahwahnee | **Yosemite/E**	19
AKA Bistro | **St. Helena/N**	15
Albion River Inn | **Albion/N**	24
Alexander's | **Cupertino/S**	26

Restaurant	Rating
Ame | **SoMa**	26
Anton/Michel | **Carmel/S**	25
Applewood Inn | **Guerneville/N**	24
☑ Auberge/Soleil | **Rutherford/N**	26
Bardessono | **Yountville/N**	21
Barney's | **Berkeley/E**	19
Bella Vista | **Woodside/S**	22
Betelnut Pejiu | **Cow Hollow**	23
☑ Big 4 | **Nob Hill**	23
Bing Crosby's | **Walnut Creek/E**	19
Bistro Don Giovanni | **Napa/N**	24
☑ Bistro Jeanty | **Yountville/N**	25
Boca | **Novato/N**	22
Brannan's Grill | **Calistoga/N**	22
Brix | **Napa/N**	23
☑ Buckeye | **Mill Valley/N**	23
Cafe Citti | **Kenwood/N**	23
NEW Café des Amis | **Cow Hollow**	–
Café Gratitude | **Berkeley/E**	16
NEW Cantinetta Piero | **Yountville/N**	21
Caprice | **Tiburon/N**	21
Casanova | **Carmel/S**	23
Casa Orinda | **Orinda/E**	16
Cetrella | **Half Moon Bay/S**	20
Chantilly | **Redwood City/S**	25
Chapter & Moon | **Ft Bragg/N**	25
Chez Spencer | **Mission**	22
Chez TJ | **Mtn View/S**	20
☑ Chow/Park Chow | **multi.**	–
NEW Comstock | **N Beach**	–
Cottonwood | **Truckee/E**	21
Cuvée | **Napa/N**	20
Davenport Rdhse. | **Davenport/S**	19
Deetjen's | **Big Sur/S**	23
Della Santina | **Sonoma/N**	22
Digs Bistro | **Berkeley/E**	23
Dio Deka | **Los Gatos/S**	25
Dipsea Cafe | **Mill Valley/N**	19
Duck Club | **Bodega Bay/N**	21
E&O Trading | **Larkspur/N**	19
El Dorado | **Sonoma/N**	23
☑ Erna's Elderberry | **Oakhurst/E**	28
☑ Étoile | **Yountville/N**	24
☑ Evvia | **Palo Alto/S**	27
Fandango | **Pacific Grove/S**	22
☑ Farm | **Napa/N**	23
☑ Farmhouse Inn | **Forestville/N**	27
5A5 Steak | **Downtown**	22
Flavor | **Santa Rosa/N**	19
☑ Fleur de Lys | **Downtown**	27
Flying Fish | **Carmel/S**	24
Forbes Island | **Fish. Wharf**	19
Forbes Mill | **Los Gatos/S**	22
Foreign Cinema | **Mission**	23
☑ French Laundry | **Yountville/N**	29
Gar Woods | **Carnelian Bay/E**	17
Gayle's Bakery | **Capitola/S**	24
Guaymas | **Tiburon/N**	17
Half Moon Brew | **Half Moon Bay/S**	15
Harris' | **Polk Gulch**	25
Home | **Castro**	19
☑ House of Prime | **Polk Gulch**	25
Iberia | **Menlo Pk/S**	22
Il Fornaio | **multi.**	19
Izzy's Steak | **Marina**	20
Jake's/Lake | **Tahoe City/E**	16
John Ash | **Santa Rosa/N**	22
Kenwood | **Kenwood/N**	21
Koh Samui/Another | **Mission**	21
☑ Kokkari | **Downtown**	27
Kuleto's | **Downtown**	21
Lake Chalet | **Oakland/E**	14
La Terrasse | **Presidio**	18
☑ La Toque | **Napa/N**	27
LB Steak | **San Jose/S**	22
Ledford Hse. | **Albion/N**	24
Left Bank | **Larkspur/N**	19
Le Soleil | **Inner Rich**	20
Lupa Trattoria | **Noe Valley**	24
MacArthur Pk. | **Palo Alto/S**	17
MacCallum | **Mendocino/N**	23
Madera | **Menlo Pk/S**	23
Madrona | **Healdsburg/N**	26
Ma Maison | **Aptos/S**	20
Mandaloun | **Redwood City/S**	20
☑ Manresa | **Los Gatos/S**	27
☑ Marinus | **Carmel Valley/S**	27
Martini Hse. | **St. Helena/N**	26
NEW Mayes | **Polk Gulch**	19
☑ Meadowood Rest. | **St. Helena/N**	26
Mendo Hotel | **Mendocino/N**	19
Metro | **Lafayette/E**	22
Mezza Luna/Caffè | **Princeton Sea/S**	22
Monti's | **Santa Rosa/N**	21
Moosse Café | **Mendocino/N**	24
Mosaic | **Forestville/N**	25
Murray Circle | **Sausalito/N**	24
Napa General | **Napa/N**	19
☑ Navio | **Half Moon Bay/S**	24
Nepenthe | **Big Sur/S**	17
Nick's Cove | **Marshall/N**	19
Osha Thai | **multi.**	20
☑ Pacific's Edge | **Carmel/S**	25
Parcel 104 | **Santa Clara/S**	23

Park Chalet | **Outer Sunset**	14
Piatti | **multi.**	19
Piazza D'Angelo | **Mill Valley/N**	21
Plouf | **Downtown**	21
Plumed Horse | **Saratoga/S**	25
PlumpJack | **Olympic Valley/E**	23
Postino | **Lafayette/E**	21
Press | **St. Helena/N**	24
Prima | **Walnut Creek/E**	24
Quattro | **E Palo Alto/S**	21
Ravenous | **Healdsburg/N**	21
Ravens' | **Mendocino/N**	22
Rendezvous Inn | **Ft Bragg/N**	27
Rest. at Stevenswood | **Little River/N**	24
Rest. LuLu/Petite | **SoMa**	21
Rio Grill | **Carmel/S**	22
River Ranch | **Tahoe City/E**	15
Samovar Tea | **Hayes Valley**	20
Sam's Chowder | **Half Moon Bay/S**	19
Santé | **Sonoma/N**	23
Sardine Factory | **Monterey/S**	20
Savor | **Noe Valley**	17
Scott's | **Palo Alto/S**	19
Shadowbrook | **Capitola/S**	18
☑ Sierra Mar | **Big Sur/S**	28
Soule Domain | **Kings Bch/E**	25
☑ Spruce | **Presidio Hts**	26
St. Orres | **Gualala/N**	22
Sunnyside | **Tahoe City/E**	17
Table 28 | **Boonville/N**	23
Tarpy's | **Monterey/S**	21
Terzo | **Cow Hollow**	23
NEW Tjukiji Sushi | **Mill Valley/N**	-
Toast | **Novato/N**	18
Townhouse B&G | **Emeryville/E**	20
Troya | **Inner Rich**	23
Venticello | **Nob Hill**	23
Vic Stewart | **Walnut Creek/E**	21
☑ Village Pub | **Woodside/S**	26
Viognier | **San Mateo/S**	23
Wild Goose | **Tahoe Vista/E**	-
Will's Fargo | **Carmel Valley/S**	23
Wine Spectator | **St. Helena/N**	24
Zibibbo | **Palo Alto/S**	19
Zinsvalley | **Napa/N**	18

FOOD STANDS/ TRUCKS

Boccalone | **Embarcadero**	24
Chez/Spencer on the Go! | **SoMa**	25
☑ El Tonayense | **multi.**	24
4505 Meats | **Embarcadero**	28
Kitchenette SF | **Dogpatch**	22

Let's Be Frank | **multi.**	19
Namu | **Embarcadero**	23
RoliRoti | **Embarcadero**	25
NEW Tacolicious | **Embarcadero**	23

GREEN/LOCAL/ ORGANIC

(Places specializing in organic, local ingredients)

Academy Cafe | **Inner Rich**	19
Adagia | **Berkeley/E**	18
☑ Ad Hoc | **Yountville/N**	27
Ajanta | **Berkeley/E**	25
AKA Bistro | **St. Helena/N**	15
Amanda's | **Berkeley/E**	21
Aquarius | **Santa Cruz/S**	23
Artisan Bistro | **Lafayette/E**	23
Aubergine | **Carmel/S**	25
NEW Bar Agricole | **SoMa**	-
Bardessono | **Yountville/N**	21
Bar Jules | **Hayes Valley**	25
Barndiva | **Healdsburg/N**	20
Bellanico | **Oakland/E**	22
Bistro/Copains | **Occidental/N**	25
Bistro Don Giovanni | **Napa/N**	24
Blue Barn | **Marina**	21
Blue Plate | **Mission**	23
☑ Bottega | **Yountville/N**	26
Boulette Larder | **Embarcadero**	25
Bovolo | **Healdsburg/N**	22
Breads of India | **multi.**	20
Brix | **Napa/N**	23
Butler & Chef | **SoMa**	21
Cafe Beaujolais | **Mendocino/N**	24
☑ Cafe Gibraltar | **El Granada/S**	27
Café Gratitude | **multi.**	16
Calafia | **Palo Alto/S**	19
Camino | **Oakland/E**	23
☑ Cheese Board | **Berkeley/E**	27
☑ Chez Panisse | **Berkeley/E**	28
☑ Chez Panisse Café | **Berkeley/E**	27
Chez Shea | **Half Moon Bay/S**	23
☑ Chow/Park Chow | **Inner Sunset**	20
☑ Coi | **N Beach**	26
☑ Commis | **Oakland/E**	27
Contigo | **Noe Valley**	24
Cool Café | **Palo Alto/S**	20
Deetjen's | **Big Sur/S**	23
☑ Delfina | **Mission**	26
Della Fattoria | **Petaluma/N**	25
Della Santina | **Sonoma/N**	22
Digs Bistro | **Berkeley/E**	23
Donato | **Redwood City/S**	24
Doña Tomás | **Oakland/E**	21

Menus, photos, voting and more - free at ZAGAT.com

Dopo	Oakland/E	25
Dosa	multi.	22
Dragonfly	Truckee/E	22
Drake's	Inverness/N	20
Dry Creek	Healdsburg/N	24
NEW Encuentro	Oakland/E	-
Eos	Cole Valley	23
Epic Roasthse.	Embarcadero	21
Z Erna's Elderberry	Oakhurst/E	28
Z Étoile	Yountville/N	24
Eureka	Castro	22
Z Farallon	Downtown	24
Z Farm	Napa/N	23
Farmerbrown	multi.	21
Z Farmhouse Inn	Forestville/N	27
NEW Farmstead	St. Helena/N	-
Fifth Floor	SoMa	25
Fig Cafe/Wine	Glen Ellen/N	25
Firefly	Noe Valley	24
Fish	Sausalito/N	25
Fish & Farm	Downtown	20
Flea St. Café	Menlo Pk/S	25
Z Fleur de Lys	Downtown	27
Flour + Water	Mission	24
Foreign Cinema	Mission	23
Z French Laundry	Yountville/N	29
Gabriella Café	Santa Cruz/S	21
Garibaldis	multi.	22
Z Gary Danko	Fish. Wharf	29
Gialina	Glen Pk	25
Gioia Pizzeria	Berkeley/E	24
Globe	Downtown	21
Grasing's Coastal	Carmel/S	22
Green Chile	W Addition	21
Z Greens	Marina	24
Harmony	Mill Valley/N	20
Harvest Moon	Sonoma/N	25
Hayes St. Grill	Hayes Valley	23
Heaven's Dog	SoMa	20
Herbivore	multi.	15
Imperial/Berkeley	Embarcadero	20
Incanto	Noe Valley	24
Insalata's	San Anselmo/N	23
Z Jardinière	Civic Ctr	26
Jimtown Store	Healdsburg/N	21
John Ash	Santa Rosa/N	22
Junnoon	Palo Alto/S	22
La Ciccia	Noe Valley	26
Z La Folie	Russian Hill	28
Lalime's	Berkeley/E	25
Lark Creek	Walnut Creek/E	23
Las Camelias	San Rafael/N	18
Z La Toque	Napa/N	27
Ledford Hse.	Albion/N	24

Local Kitchen	SoMa	20
NEW Local Mission	Mission	-
Lotus/Anokha	San Rafael/N	23
Luella	Russian Hill	22
MacCallum	Mendocino/N	23
Madera	Menlo Pk/S	23
Madrona	Healdsburg/N	26
Magnolia	Haight-Ashbury	20
Z Manresa	Los Gatos/S	27
Marché	Menlo Pk/S	24
Marché/Fleurs	Ross/N	24
Marinitas	San Anselmo/N	18
Z Marinus	Carmel Valley/S	27
MarketBar	Embarcadero	17
Martini Hse.	St. Helena/N	26
Martins West	Redwood City/S	24
Marzano	Oakland/E	21
Z Masa's	Downtown	27
Maverick	Mission	24
Meadowood Grill	St. Helena/N	22
Z Meadowood Rest.	St. Helena/N	26
Mendo Bistro	Ft Bragg/N	24
Midi	Downtown	20
Millennium	Downtown	25
Mixt Greens	Downtown	22
Montrio Bistro	Monterey/S	22
Mosaic	Forestville/N	25
Moss Room	Inner Rich	20
Z Navio	Half Moon Bay/S	24
Nick's Cove	Marshall/N	19
Nick's Crispy	Russian Hill	21
Z Nopa	W Addition	25
Nopalito	W Addition	23
O Chamé	Berkeley/E	23
Olema Inn	Olema/N	19
Oliveto Cafe	Oakland/E	23
Oliveto Rest.	Oakland/E	24
One Market	Embarcadero	23
Oola	SoMa	21
Osteria Stellina	Pt Reyes/N	25
Pacific Catch	Marina	19
Z Pacific's Edge	Carmel/S	25
Parcel 104	Santa Clara/S	23
Passionfish	Pacific Grove/S	25
Pauline's	Mission	22
Pearl	Napa/N	21
Peter Lowell	Sebastopol/N	21
Piccino	Dogpatch	21
Picco	Larkspur/N	25
Pine Cone Diner	Pt Reyes/N	22
Pizza Antica	Lafayette/E	21
Pizzaiolo	Oakland/E	25
Pizzavino	Sebastopol/N	-
Pizzeria Picco	Larkspur/N	25

Pizzeria Tra Vigne | St. Helena/N	21
🔁 Pizzetta 211 | Outer Rich	27
Plant Cafe | Marina	20
Press | St. Helena/N	24
🔁 Quince | Downtown	26
NEW Radius | SoMa	-
🔁 Range | Mission	27
Ravenous | Healdsburg/N	21
Ravens' | Mendocino/N	22
Regalito Rosticeria | Mission	19
Rendezvous Inn | Ft Bragg/N	27
Rest. at Stevenswood | Little River/N	24
NEW Revival Bar | Berkeley/E	-
Richmond Rest. | Inner Rich	25
Rist. Avanti | Santa Cruz/S	23
🔁 Ritz-Carlton | Nob Hill	27
🔁 Rivoli | Berkeley/E	27
Rocker Oyster | Valley Ford/N	21
Santi | Santa Rosa/N	24
🔁 Sebo | Hayes Valley	27
Serpentine | Dogpatch	19
🔁 Sierra Mar | Big Sur/S	28
🔁 Slanted Door | Embarcadero	26
Slow Club | Mission	22
Sol Food | San Rafael/N	22
NEW Spoonbar | Healdsburg/N	-
SPQR | Pacific Hts	24
🔁 Spruce | Presidio Hts	26
NEW SR24 | Oakland/E	-
St. Orres | Gualala/N	22
Sutro's | Outer Rich	20
Syrah | Santa Rosa/N	25
Table Cafe | Larkspur/N	23
Tacubaya | Berkeley/E	23
Tamarine | Palo Alto/S	25
🔁 Tartine | Mission	27
Tav./Lark Creek | Larkspur/N	19
Terzo | Cow Hollow	23
Tipsy Pig | Marina	19
Town Hall | SoMa	23
Trademark Grill | Downtown	19
Tra Vigne | St. Helena/N	24
T Rex BBQ | Berkeley/E	17
Twist | Campbell/S	20
2223 | Castro	21
Ubuntu | Napa/N	26
Underdog | Inner Sunset	21
Underwood Bar | Graton/N	24
🔁 Village Pub | Woodside/S	26
Viognier | San Mateo/S	23
Warming Hut | Presidio	13
Water St. Bistro | Petaluma/N	24
Weird Fish | Mission	20

Wente Vineyards | Livermore/E	24
Wexler's | Downtown	22
Willi's Seafood | Healdsburg/N	24
Willi's Wine | Santa Rosa/N	25
Wine Spectator | St. Helena/N	24
Wolfdale's | Tahoe City/E	25
Woodward's Gdn. | Mission	24
Yankee Pier | San Jose/S	18
Zaré/Fly Trap | SoMa	23
Zatar | Berkeley/E	25
Zazu | Santa Rosa/N	25
Zin | Healdsburg/N	23
🔁 Zuni Café | Hayes Valley	25

HISTORIC PLACES

(Year opened; * building)

1800 | Market* | St. Helena/N	22
1800 | Stable Café* | Mission	-
1829 | Cindy's* | St. Helena/N	24
1844 | Celadon* | Napa/N	23
1847 | Farmhouse Inn* | Forestville/N	27
1848 | La Forêt* | San Jose/S	26
1849 | Tadich Grill | Downtown	23
1856 | Garden Court* | Downtown	18
1857 | Little River Inn* | Little River/N	21
1860 | Pizza Antica* | Lafayette/E	21
1863 | Cliff House | Outer Rich	19
1863 | Sutro's* | Outer Rich	20
1864 | Estate* | Sonoma/N	23
1864 | Rocker Oyster* | Valley Ford/N	21
1864 | Table 28* | Boonville/N	23
1865 | Mayes* | Polk Gulch	19
1867 | Sam's Grill | Downtown	21
1870 | Bottega* | Yountville/N	26
1870 | Murray Circle* | Sausalito/N	24
1875 | La Note* | Berkeley/E	22
1876 | Olema Inn* | Olema/N	19
1878 | Mendo Hotel* | Mendocino/N	19
1880 | Pianeta* | Truckee/E	21
1881 | Il Fornaio* | Carmel/S	19
1881 | Madrona* | Healdsburg/N	26
1882 | MacCallum* | Mendocino/N	23
1884 | Napa General* | Napa/N	19
1884 | Terra* | St. Helena/N	26
1886 | Cole's Chop* | Napa/N	24
1886 | Fior d'Italia | N Beach	20
1886 | Mendo Bistro* | Ft Bragg/N	24
1886 | Willi's Wine* | Santa Rosa/N	25

Menus, photos, voting and more - free at ZAGAT.com

1888	Bounty Hunter*	**Napa/N**	19
1888	Tav./Lark Creek*	**Larkspur/N**	19
1889	Boulevard*	**Embarcadero**	27
1889	Pacific Café*	**Outer Rich**	23
1890	Chez TJ*	**Mtn View/S**	22
1890	Eureka*	**Castro**	22
1890	Scoma's*	**Sausalito/N**	22
1890	Yankee Pier*	**Larkspur/N**	18
1893	Cafe Beaujolais*	**Mendocino/N**	24
1893	Jimtown Store*	**Healdsburg/N**	21
1894	Duarte's*	**Pescadero/S**	21
1894	Fentons	**Oakland/E**	20
1895	La Posta*	**Santa Cruz/S**	21
1895	Restaurant*	**Ft Bragg/N**	25
1897	Rendezvous Inn*	**Ft Bragg/N**	27
1900	Axum Cafe*	**Lower Haight**	21
1900	Bar Agricole*	**SoMa**	–
1900	Bar Tartine*	**Mission**	23
1900	Central Market*	**Petaluma/N**	25
1900	Cha Cha Cha*	**Mission**	21
1900	French Laundry*	**Yountville/N**	29
1900	Girl & Fig*	**Sonoma/N**	24
1900	La Ginestra*	**Mill Valley/N**	21
1900	Pauline's*	**Mission**	22
1904	Moosse Café*	**Mendocino/N**	24
1904	Paul K*	**Hayes Valley**	22
1905	Hopmonk*	**Sebastopol/N**	18
1906	Coco500*	**SoMa**	23
1906	Davenport Rdhse.*	**Davenport/S**	19
1906	Imperial/Berkeley*	**Embarcadero**	20
1906	Pork Store*	**Haight-Ashbury**	19
1907	Town Hall*	**SoMa**	23
1908	Zaré/Fly Trap*	**SoMa**	23
1909	Campton Place*	**Downtown**	25
1909	Ironside*	**S Beach**	17
1910	Catch*	**Castro**	18
1910	Harris'*	**Polk Gulch**	25
1910	Rest. LuLu/Petite*	**SoMa**	21
1912	Swan Oyster	**Polk Gulch**	27
1913	Balboa Cafe	**Cow Hollow**	19
1913	Zuni Café*	**Hayes Valley**	25
1914	Healdsburg B&G*	**Healdsburg/N**	19
1914	Red's Java*	**Embarcadero**	15
1915	Napa Wine Train*	**Napa/N**	18
1916	Amer. Grilled Cheese*	**SoMa**	–
1917	Pacific's Edge*	**Carmel/S**	25
1917	Tarpy's*	**Monterey/S**	21
1918	MacArthur Pk.*	**Palo Alto/S**	17
1918	St. Francis	**Mission**	19
1919	Albion River Inn*	**Albion/N**	24
1919	Ana Mandara*	**Fish. Wharf**	22
1919	Sauce*	**Hayes Valley**	18
1920	Acquerello*	**Polk Gulch**	28
1920	Albona Rist.*	**N Beach**	23
1920	Bistro Vida*	**Menlo Pk/S**	19
1920	Boogaloos*	**Mission**	18
1920	Florio*	**Pacific Hts**	19
1921	Digs Bistro*	**Berkeley/E**	23
1923	Martini Hse.*	**St. Helena/N**	26
1925	Adagia*	**Berkeley/E**	18
1925	Alioto's	**Fish. Wharf**	18
1925	Farallon*	**Downtown**	24
1925	John Bentley*	**Redwood City/S**	24
1925	Rist. Capellini*	**San Mateo/S**	18
1927	Ahwahnee*	**Yosemite/E**	19
1927	Bella Vista*	**Woodside/S**	22
1927	Townhouse B&G*	**Emeryville/E**	20
1928	Alfred's Steak	**Downtown**	22
1928	Elite Cafe*	**Pacific Hts**	19
1928	Ma Maison*	**Aptos/S**	20
1929	Aubergine*	**Carmel/S**	25
1930	Big 4*	**Nob Hill**	23
1930	Caprice*	**Tiburon/N**	21
1930	Foreign Cinema*	**Mission**	23
1930	Lalime's*	**Berkeley/E**	25
1930	Lo Coco*	**Oakland/E**	21
1930	Ravenous*	**Healdsburg/N**	21
1930	Tea Room Café*	**Petaluma/N**	21
1932	Casa Orinda*	**Orinda/E**	16
1933	Luka's Taproom*	**Oakland/E**	20
1934	Caspers Hot Dogs	**Oakland/E**	18
1935	Tommaso's	**N Beach**	24
1936	Gabriella Café*	**Santa Cruz/S**	21
1937	Buckeye	**Mill Valley/N**	23
1937	Deetjen's*	**Big Sur/S**	23
1937	Postino*	**Lafayette/E**	21
1937	231 Ellsworth*	**San Mateo/S**	23

SPECIAL FEATURES

1938	Sears Fine Food	**Downtown**	20
1945	Tonga	**Nob Hill**	14
1947	Shadowbrook	**Capitola/S**	18
1948	Evan's*	**S Lake Tahoe/E**	25
1949	Gott's Roadside	**St. Helena/N**	21
1949	House of Prime	**Polk Gulch**	25
1949	Nepenthe	**Big Sur/S**	17
1950	Alexis Baking*	**Napa/N**	22
1952	Plumed Horse	**Saratoga/S**	25
1953	Mel's Drive-In*	**Inner Rich**	14
1955	Breads of India*	**Berkeley/E**	20
1956	Original Joe's	**San Jose/S**	18
1958	Enrico's	**N Beach**	16
1958	Yank Sing	**SoMa**	25
1959	Red Hut	**S Lake Tahoe/E**	21
1959	St. Michael's	**Palo Alto/S**	22
1959	Will's Fargo	**Carmel Valley/S**	23
1960	Benihana	**Japantown**	17

HOTEL DINING

Ahwahnee Hotel
🔣 Ahwahnee | **Yosemite/E** — 19

Auberge du Soleil
🔣 Auberge/Soleil | **Rutherford/N** — 26

Bardessono Hotel & Spa
Bardessono | **Yountville/N** — 21

Bernardus Lodge
🔣 Marinus | **Carmel Valley/S** — 27
Wicket Bistro | **Carmel Valley/S** — 24

Blue Heron Inn
Moosse Café | **Mendocino/N** — 24

Blue Rock Inn
Left Bank | **Larkspur/N** — 19

Boonville Hotel
Table 28 | **Boonville/N** — 23

California, Hotel
Millennium | **Downtown** — 25

Carlton Hotel
Saha | **Tenderloin** — 26

Carneros Inn
Boon Fly | **Napa/N** — 22
🔣 Farm | **Napa/N** — 23

Casa Madrona
Poggio | **Sausalito/N** — 23

Cavallo Point Resort in Fort Baker
Murray Circle | **Sausalito/N** — 24

Château du Sureau
🔣 Erna's Elderberry | **Oakhurst/E** — 28

Claremont Hotel
NEW Meritage/Claremont | **Berkeley/E** — 25

Clift Hotel
NEW Velvet Room | **Downtown** — -

Dina's Garden Hotel
Trader Vic's | **Palo Alto/S** — 17

El Dorado Hotel
El Dorado | **Sonoma/N** — 23

Fairmont
McCormick/Schmick | **San Jose/S** — 21

Fairmont Hotel
Tonga | **Nob Hill** — 14

Fairmont Sonoma Mission Inn & Spa
Santé | **Sonoma/N** — 23

Farmhouse Inn
🔣 Farmhouse Inn | **Forestville/N** — 27

Four Seasons Hotel
Quattro | **E Palo Alto/S** — 21
🔣 Seasons | **Downtown** — 26

Frank, Hotel
Max's | **Downtown** — 17

Galleria Park Hotel
Midi | **Downtown** — 20

Garden Court Hotel
Il Fornaio | **Palo Alto/S** — 19

H2hotel
NEW Spoonbar | **Healdsburg/N** — -

Healdsburg, Hotel
Dry Creek | **Healdsburg/N** — 24

Hilton
Urban Tavern | **Downtown** — 17

Huntington Hotel
🔣 Big 4 | **Nob Hill** — 23

Hyatt Highlands Inn
🔣 Pacific's Edge | **Carmel/S** — 25

Inn at Southbridge
Pizzeria Tra Vigne | **St. Helena/N** — 21

Inn at Spanish Bay
🔣 Roy's | **Pebble Bch/S** — 25

InterContinental Hotel
Luce | **SoMa** — 21

Lafayette Park Hotel & Spa
Duck Club | **Lafayette/E** — 21

L'Auberge Carmel
Aubergine | **Carmel/S** — 25

Westin San Francisco
 Ducca | SoMa   17

Westin Verasa
 🇿 La Toque | Napa/N   27

W Hotel
 XYZ | SoMa   20

LATE DINING

(Weekday closing hour)

🇿 Absinthe | 12 AM | 22
 Hayes Valley

NEW Acme Burger | varies | 18
 W Addition

Adesso | varies | Oakland/E   23

Alembic | 12 AM | 22
 Haight-Ashbury

NEW Bar Agricole | 1 AM | -
 SoMa

Beretta | 12 AM | Mission   23

Brazen Head | 1 AM | Cow Hollow   21

Broken Record | 12 AM | 22
 Excelsior

Brother's Korean | varies | 22
 Inner Rich

Caspers Hot Dogs | 11:30 PM | 18
 multi.

NEW Comstock | 1 AM | N Beach   -

NEW Delarosa | 1 AM | Marina   22

El Zocalo | 3:45 AM | Bernal Hts   20

15 Romolo | 1:30 AM | N Beach   -

Fior d'Italia | 12 AM | N Beach   20

Flour + Water | 12 AM | Mission   24

Fonda Solana | 12:30 AM | 22
 Albany/E

Gitane | 12 AM | Downtown   21

Globe | 1 AM | Downtown   21

Gordon Biersch | 12 AM | 15
 Embarcadero

Great Eastern | 12 AM | 19
 Chinatown

NEW Hog & Rocks | 12 AM | -
 Mission

Home | 12 AM | Castro   19

Home of Chicken | varies | 19
 Oakland/E

🇿 In-N-Out | varies | multi.   22

King of Thai | varies | multi.   18

Kitchen | 1 AM | Millbrae/S   19

NEW La Costanera | 12 AM | 24
 Montara/S

Lanesplitter | 12 AM | multi.   16

NEW Locanda da Eva | 12 AM | -
 Berkeley/E

Magnolia | 12 AM | 20
 Haight-Ashbury

Marinitas | 12 AM | 18
 San Anselmo/N

Mel's Drive-In | varies | multi.   14

Monk's Kettle | 1 AM | Mission   20

Naan/Curry | varies | Downtown   17

🇿 Nopa | 1 AM | W Addition   25

North Bch. Pizza | varies | 19
 N Beach

Oola | 1 AM | SoMa   21

Original Joe's | varies | San Jose/S   18

Osha Thai | varies | multi.   20

Pancho Villa | varies | Mission   22

NEW Pi Bar | 12 AM | Mission   14

Ryoko's | 2 AM | Downtown   23

Sam Wo's | 3 AM | Chinatown   18

Sauce | 12 AM | Hayes Valley   18

Shalimar | 11:30 PM | Tenderloin   24

NEW SliderBar | 12 AM | -
 Palo Alto/S

Taqueria Can-Cun | varies | 21
 Mission

Thai House | varies | Tenderloin   23

Tsunami | 12 AM | multi.   22

Zeitgeist | 2 AM | Mission   16

MEET FOR A DRINK

🇿 Absinthe | Hayes Valley   22

Adesso | Oakland/E   23

AKA Bistro | St. Helena/N   15

Alembic | Haight-Ashbury   22

Amber Bistro | Danville/E   22

🇿 Amber India | SoMa   24

Americano | Embarcadero   18

Ana Mandara | Fish. Wharf   22

Anchor & Hope | SoMa   21

Andalu | Mission   20

AsiaSF | SoMa   17

Balboa Cafe | Cow Hollow   19

NEW Bar Agricole | SoMa   -

NEW Barbacco | Downtown   25

Bar Bambino | Mission   23

Bardessono | Yountville/N   21

Barlata | Oakland/E   21

Barndiva | Healdsburg/N   20

Baxter's Bistro | Truckee/E   -

Beach Chalet | Outer Sunset   14

Bellanico | Oakland/E   22

Beretta | Mission   23

Betelnut Pejiu | Cow Hollow   23

🇿 Big 4 | Nob Hill   23

Bing Crosby's | Walnut Creek/E   19

Bistro/Copains | Occidental/N   25

Bistro Don Giovanni | Napa/N   24

🇿 Bix | Downtown   24

🇿 Bottega | Yountville/N   26

🇿 Bouchon | Yountville/N   26

🇿 Boulevard | Embarcadero   27

Brazen Head | Cow Hollow   21

NEW Brick/Bottle | Corte Madera/N	-]
Bridgetender | Tahoe City/E	18]
Broken Record | Excelsior	22]
Z Buckeye | Mill Valley/N	23]
Bungalow 44 | Mill Valley/N	22]
Butterfly | Embarcadero	22]
NEW Café des Amis | Cow Hollow	-]
Café Rouge | Berkeley/E	20]
NEW Cannery Row Brew | Monterey/S	-]
Cascal | Mtn View/S	19]
Cav Wine Bar | Hayes Valley	20]
Cellar Door Café | Santa Cruz/S	22]
César | Berkeley/E	22]
NEW Chop Bar | Oakland/E	22]
Cin-Cin Wine | Los Gatos/S	24]
Circa | Marina	16]
Colibrí | Downtown	20]
NEW Comstock | N Beach	-]
Cosmopolitan | SoMa	19]
Davenport Rdhse. | Davenport/S	19]
NEW Delarosa | Marina	22]
Dio Deka | Los Gatos/S	25]
Donato | Redwood City/S	24]
Doña Tomás | Oakland/E	21]
Ducca | SoMa	17]
E&O Trading | multi.	19]
Elite Cafe | Pacific Hts	19]
NEW Encuentro | Oakland/E	-]
Enrico's | N Beach	16]
Eos | Cole Valley	23]
Epic Roasthse. | Embarcadero	21]
Eureka | Castro	22]
Z Farallon | Downtown	24]
Z Farm | Napa/N	23]
15 Romolo | N Beach	-]
54 Mint | SoMa	22]
Fig Cafe/Wine | Glen Ellen/N	25]
Five | Berkeley/E	22]
5A5 Steak | Downtown	22]
Flora | Oakland/E	22]
Florio | Pacific Hts	19]
Fonda Solana | Albany/E	22]
Foreign Cinema | Mission	23]
Garibaldis | multi.	22]
Gar Woods | Carnelian Bay/E	17]
Gitane | Downtown	21]
Go Fish | St. Helena/N	23]
Gordon Biersch | multi.	15]
Guaymas | Tiburon/N	17]
Half Moon Brew | Half Moon Bay/S	15]
NEW Heart | Mission	-]
Heaven's Dog | SoMa	20]

NEW Heirloom | Mission	-]
NEW Hog & Rocks | Mission	-]
Home | Castro	19]
Hopmonk | Sebastopol/N	18]
Hula's | Santa Cruz/S	18]
Iberia | Menlo Pk/S	22]
NEW Izakaya Sozai | Inner Sunset	-]
Jake's/Lake | Tahoe City/E	16]
Z Jardinière | Civic Ctr	26]
Joya | Palo Alto/S	20]
Junnoon | Palo Alto/S	22]
Kan Zaman | Haight-Ashbury	19]
Z Kokkari | Downtown	27]
NEW La Costanera | Montara/S	24]
La Mar | Embarcadero	24]
Lanesplitter | Oakland/E	16]
La Trappe | N Beach	18]
Lavanda | Palo Alto/S	19]
Le Colonial | Downtown	23]
Left Bank | multi.	19]
Luce | SoMa	21]
Luka's Taproom | Oakland/E	20]
Luna Park | Mission	19]
Magnolia | Haight-Ashbury	20]
Mamacita | Marina	22]
Mantra | Palo Alto/S	22]
NEW Manzanita | Truckee/E	25]
NEW Marengo | Cow Hollow	-]
Marinitas | San Anselmo/N	18]
MarketBar | Embarcadero	17]
Martini Hse. | St. Helena/N	26]
Martins West | Redwood City/S	24]
NEW Mayes | Polk Gulch	19]
Medjool | Mission	19]
Mendo Hotel | Mendocino/N	19]
NEW Meritage/Claremont | Berkeley/E	25]
Meritage Martini | Sonoma/N	21]
Midi | Downtown	20]
Mijita | S Beach	21]
Miss Pearl's | Oakland/E	16]
MoMo's | S Beach	17]
Monk's Kettle | Mission	20]
Moody's Bistro | Truckee/E	24]
Mundaka | Carmel/S	-]
Murray Circle | Sausalito/N	24]
Z Mustards | Yountville/N	25]
Nettie's Crab | Cow Hollow	18]
Nihon | Mission	21]
NEW Nombe | Mission	22]
Z Nopa | W Addition	25]
NEW Norman Rose | Napa/N	20]
North Coast Brew | Ft Bragg/N	17]
Oliveto Cafe | Oakland/E	23]
One Market | Embarcadero	23]

Orson	**SoMa**	19
Oswald	**Santa Cruz/S**	25
Ottimista	**Cow Hollow**	17
Oxbow Wine	**Napa/N**	22
Oyaji	**Outer Rich**	23
Ozumo	**multi.**	23
Pacific Crest	**Truckee/E**	-
Palio d'Asti	**Downtown**	20
Park Chalet	**Outer Sunset**	14
Patrona	**Ukiah/N**	-
NEW Perbacco	**Downtown**	25
NEW Pi Bar	**Mission**	14
Picán	**Oakland/E**	21
Picco	**Larkspur/S**	25
Piccolo Teatro	**Sausalito/N**	22
Plumed Horse	**Saratoga/S**	25
Ponzu	**Downtown**	20
Presidio Social	**Presidio**	19
Prima	**Walnut Creek/E**	24
NEW Prospect	**SoMa**	-
NEW Public House	**S Beach**	-
NEW Radius	**SoMa**	-
Z Range	**Mission**	27
Z Redd	**Yountville/N**	27
Red Lantern	**Redwood City/S**	18
NEW Rest. at Ventana	**Big Sur/S**	22
Rest. LuLu/Petite	**SoMa**	21
NEW Rest. P/30	**Sebastopol/N**	-
NEW Revival Bar	**Berkeley/E**	-
Rist. Avanti	**Santa Cruz/S**	23
River Ranch	**Tahoe City/E**	15
RN74	**SoMa**	22
Rose Pistola	**N Beach**	21
Rose's Cafe	**Cow Hollow**	22
Rosso Pizzeria	**Santa Rosa/N**	26
NEW Rustic	**Geyserville/N**	-
Sardine Factory	**Monterey/S**	20
Sea Salt	**Berkeley/E**	21
Sens	**Downtown**	19
Serpentine	**Dogpatch**	19
Sino	**San Jose/S**	19
NEW SliderBar	**Palo Alto/S**	-
Slow Club	**Mission**	22
NEW Social Kitchen	**Inner Sunset**	-
Soif Wine Bar	**Santa Cruz/S**	24
Solbar	**Calistoga/N**	25
NEW Spoonbar	**Healdsburg/N**	-
NEW Starbelly	**Castro**	20
Starlight	**Sebastopol/N**	22
Sunnyside	**Tahoe City/E**	17
Sushi Groove	**Russian Hill**	22
Tamarine	**Palo Alto/S**	25
Tav./Lark Creek	**Larkspur/N**	19
Terzo	**Cow Hollow**	23

NEW Thermidor	**SoMa**	-
1300/Fillmore	**W Addition**	23
Tipsy Pig	**Marina**	19
Tokyo Go Go	**Mission**	21
Tommy's Mex.	**Outer Rich**	18
Tonga	**Nob Hill**	14
Town Hall	**SoMa**	23
Townhouse B&G	**Emeryville/E**	20
Trader Vic's	**Emeryville/E**	17
Tra Vigne	**St. Helena/N**	24
Tres Agaves	**S Beach**	17
2223	**Castro**	21
Ukiah Brew	**Ukiah/N**	16
Umami	**Cow Hollow**	23
Underwood Bar	**Graton/N**	24
Uva Enoteca	**Lower Haight**	21
Va de Vi	**Walnut Creek/E**	24
Vin Antico	**San Rafael/N**	19
Waterbar	**Embarcadero**	20
NEW Wayfare Tav.	**Downtown**	-
Wexler's	**Downtown**	22
Wicket Bistro	**Carmel Valley/S**	24
Wild Goose	**Tahoe Vista/E**	-
Willi's Seafood	**Healdsburg/N**	24
Will's Fargo	**Carmel Valley/S**	23
Wine Spectator	**St. Helena/N**	24
Wood Tavern	**Oakland/E**	25
Xanh	**Mtn View/S**	21
Yoshi's SF	**W Addition**	21
Zaré/Fly Trap	**SoMa**	23
Zibibbo	**Palo Alto/S**	19
Zin	**Healdsburg/N**	23
Z Zuni Café	**Hayes Valley**	25
ZuZu	**Napa/N**	24

NEWCOMERS

Acme Burger	**W Addition**	18
Amer. Cupcake	**Cow Hollow**	-
Amer. Grilled Cheese	**SoMa**	-
Attic	**San Mateo/S**	-
Baker/Banker	**Upper Fillmore**	25
Bar Agricole	**SoMa**	-
Barbacco	**Downtown**	25
Baumé	**Palo Alto/S**	28
Benu	**SoMa**	-
Bistro Central Parc	**W Addition**	-
Bocanova	**Oakland/E**	21
Boot/Shoe	**Oakland/E**	24
Brick/Bottle	**Corte Madera/N**	-
Burger Bar	**Downtown**	19
Café des Amis	**Cow Hollow**	-
Cannery Row Brew	**Monterey/S**	-
Cantinetta Piero	**Yountville/N**	21
C Casa	**Napa/N**	-
Chile Pies	**W Addition**	-

Chop Bar | **Oakland/E**	22
Citizen's Band | **SoMa**	-
Commonwealth | **Mission**	-
Comstock | **N Beach**	-
Cotogna | **Downtown**	-
Credo | **Downtown**	17
Delarosa | **Marina**	22
Emilia's | **Berkeley/E**	27
Encuentro | **Oakland/E**	-
Eve | **Berkeley/E**	25
Fang | **SoMa**	20
Farmstead | **St. Helena/N**	-
Fish Story | **Napa/N**	-
Fondue Cowboy | **SoMa**	-
Fort Bragg Bakery | **Ft Bragg/N**	27
Frances | **Castro**	27
Gather | **Berkeley/E**	-
Georges | **Downtown**	-
Golden West | **Downtown**	-
Gracias | **Mission**	20
Heart | **Mission**	-
Heirloom | **Mission**	-
Hibiscus | **Oakland/E**	21
Hog & Rocks | **Mission**	-
Ironside | **S Beach**	17
Izakaya Sozai | **Inner Sunset**	-
La Costanera | **Montara/S**	24
Lafitte | **Embarcadero**	-
Local Mission | **Mission**	-
Locanda da Eva | **Berkeley/E**	-
Manzanita | **Truckee/E**	25
Marengo | **Cow Hollow**	-
Marlowe | **SoMa**	-
Mayes | **Polk Gulch**	19
Meritage/Claremont | **Berkeley/E**	25
Mission Chinese | **Mission**	-
Morimoto | **Napa/N**	-
Morph | **Outer Rich**	-
Naked Lunch | **N Beach**	26
Nombe | **Mission**	22
Norman Rose | **Napa/N**	20
Oenotri | **Napa/N**	-
Parada 22 | **Haight-Ashbury**	-
Pi Bar | **Mission**	14
Plum | **Oakland/E**	-
Prime Rib Shabu | **Inner Rich**	23
Prospect | **SoMa**	-
Public House | **S Beach**	-
Radius | **SoMa**	-
Rest. at Ventana | **Big Sur/S**	22
Rest. P/30 | **Sebastopol/N**	-
Revival Bar | **Berkeley/E**	-
Roam | **Cow Hollow**	-
Rustic | **Geyserville/N**	-

Sandbox | **Bernal Hts**	26
Skool | **Potrero Hill**	-
SliderBar | **Palo Alto/S**	-
Social Kitchen | **Inner Sunset**	-
Sons/Daughters | **Nob Hill**	-
Spice Kit | **SoMa**	-
Spire | **S Beach**	-
Spoonbar | **Healdsburg/N**	-
SR24 | **Oakland/E**	-
Starbelly | **Castro**	20
Super Duper | **Castro**	-
TacoBar | **Pacific Hts**	-
Tacolicious | **multi.**	23
Thermidor | **SoMa**	-
Tjukiji Sushi | **Mill Valley/N**	-
Trueburger | **Oakland/E**	-
Tyler Florence | **Napa/N**	-
Velvet Room | **Downtown**	-
Wayfare Tav. | **Downtown**	-
Zero Zero | **SoMa**	-

OFFBEAT

Ace Wasabi's | **Marina**	20
Albona Rist. | **N Beach**	23
AsiaSF | **SoMa**	17
Avatar's | **Sausalito/N**	23
Basque Cultural | **S San Francisco/S**	21
Benihana | **Japantown**	17
Blowfish Sushi | **Mission**	21
Boogaloos | **Mission**	18
Broken Record | **Excelsior**	22
Buca di Beppo | **multi.**	15
Café Gratitude | **multi.**	16
Candybar | **W Addition**	17
Cellar Door Café | **Santa Cruz/S**	22
Cha Cha Cha | **multi.**	21
Cha-Ya Veg. | **multi.**	23
Don Pico | **San Bruno/S**	21
Duarte's | **Pescadero/S**	21
E&O Trading | **Larkspur/N**	19
Fish | **Sausalito/N**	25
Forbes Island | **Fish. Wharf**	19
Home of Chicken | **Oakland/E**	19
Jimtown Store | **Healdsburg/N**	21
Joe's Cable Car | **Excelsior**	23
Kan Zaman | **Haight-Ashbury**	19
Kitchenette SF | **Dogpatch**	22
Loló | **Mission**	24
Lovejoy's Tea | **Noe Valley**	21
Maykadeh | **N Beach**	23
Millennium | **Downtown**	25
Nick's Crispy | **Russian Hill**	21
Orson | **SoMa**	19
Oyaji | **Outer Rich**	23

Ravens' | **Mendocino/N**	22
Red's Java | **Embarcadero**	15
Sol Food | **San Rafael/N**	22
St. Orres | **Gualala/N**	22
Supperclub | **SoMa**	14
Thai Buddhist | **Berkeley/E**	19
Tonga | **Nob Hill**	14
Trader Vic's | **Emeryville/E**	17
Venezia | **Berkeley/E**	21

OUTDOOR DINING

(G=garden; P=patio; S=sidewalk;
T=terrace; W=waterside)

❷ Absinthe | S | **Hayes Valley**	22
À Côté | P | **Oakland/E**	24
Adagia | P | **Berkeley/E**	18
Alexis Baking | S | **Napa/N**	22
Angèle | P, W | **Napa/N**	23
Anton/Michel | G, P | **Carmel/S**	25
Aperto | S | **Potrero Hill**	24
Applewood Inn | G, T | **Guerneville/N**	24
❷ Auberge/Soleil | T | **Rutherford/N**	26
Baker St. Bistro | S | **Marina**	22
NEW Bar Agricole | P | **SoMa**	–
Barbara's | P, S, W | **Princeton Sea/S**	20
Barndiva | G, P | **Healdsburg/N**	20
Barney's | P | **multi.**	19
Basin | P | **Saratoga/S**	21
Beach Chalet | W | **Outer Sunset**	14
Betelnut Pejiu | S | **Cow Hollow**	23
B44 | S | **Downtown**	21
Bistro Boudin | P, W | **Fish. Wharf**	20
Bistro Don Giovanni | P, T | **Napa/N**	24
Bistro Elan | P | **Palo Alto/S**	25
❷ Bistro Jeanty | P | **Yountville/N**	25
Bistro Liaison | P | **Berkeley/E**	21
Bistro Vida | S | **Menlo Pk/S**	19
Blackhawk Grille | P, T, W | **Danville/E**	21
❷ Blue Bottle | S | **SoMa**	23
Blue Plate | G, P | **Mission**	23
Boca | P | **Novato/N**	22
Bo's BBQ | T | **Lafayette/E**	22
❷ Bouchon | P | **Yountville/N**	26
Bridges | P | **Danville/E**	22
Bucci's | P | **Emeryville/E**	21
❷ Buckeye | P | **Mill Valley/N**	23
Bungalow 44 | P | **Mill Valley/N**	22
Cactus Taqueria | S | **Oakland/E**	20
Cafe Bastille | S, T | **Downtown**	17
Cafe Citti | P | **Kenwood/N**	23
Café Claude | S | **Downtown**	22

Café Fanny | P | **Berkeley/E**	23
Café Rouge | P | **Berkeley/E**	20
Café Tiramisu | S | **Downtown**	20
Caffè Museo | S | **SoMa**	19
Casanova | P | **Carmel/S**	23
Cascal | P | **Mtn View/S**	19
Catch | P | **Castro**	18
Celadon | P | **Napa/N**	23
César | P | **Oakland/E**	22
Charanga | P | **Mission**	23
Chaya | P | **Embarcadero**	22
Cheesecake Fac. | P, T | **Downtown**	16
Chez Maman | S | **Potrero Hill**	23
Chez Papa | S | **Potrero Hill**	23
Chez Spencer | G, P | **Mission**	25
Chez TJ | P | **Mtn View/S**	22
Chloe's Cafe | S | **Noe Valley**	23
❷ Chow/Park Chow | P, S, T | **multi.**	20
Cindy's | P | **St. Helena/N**	24
Club XIX | P, W | **Pebble Bch/S**	22
Cole's Chop | T, W | **Napa/N**	24
Cool Café | P | **Palo Alto/S**	20
Delancey St. | P, S | **Embarcadero**	18
Della Santina | P | **Sonoma/N**	22
Doña Tomás | P | **Oakland/E**	21
Dopo | S | **Oakland/E**	25
Dry Creek | S | **Healdsburg/N**	24
Ducca | P | **SoMa**	17
Duck Club | P | **Menlo Pk/S**	21
El Dorado | P, W | **Sonoma/N**	23
Emporio Rulli | P, S | **multi.**	21
Enrico's | P | **N Beach**	16
Epic Roasthse. | P | **Embarcadero**	21
❷ Étoile | P, T | **Yountville/N**	24
Everett/Jones | S | **multi.**	20
Fentons | P | **Oakland/E**	20
Fish | T, W | **Sausalito/N**	25
Flavor | P | **Santa Rosa/N**	19
Flea St. Café | P | **Menlo Pk/S**	25
Fog City Diner | S | **Embarcadero**	19
Fonda Solana | S | **Albany/E**	22
Foreign Cinema | P | **Mission**	23
Frantoio | G, P | **Mill Valley/N**	22
Fumé Bistro | P | **Napa/N**	19
Gabriella Café | G, P | **Santa Cruz/S**	21
Girl & Fig | G, P | **Sonoma/N**	24
Gott's Roadside | G, P | **multi.**	21
Grasing's Coastal | P | **Carmel/S**	22
Grégoire | S | **Berkeley/E**	23
Guaymas | P, T, W | **Tiburon/N**	17
❷ Hog Island Oyster | P, W | **Embarcadero**	25
Home | P | **Castro**	19
Hurley's | P | **Yountville/N**	22

beria | P | **Menlo Pk/S**	22
l Davide | P | **San Rafael/N**	20
l Fornaio | P | **multi.**	19
sa | P | **Marina**	25
Jimmy Beans | S | **Berkeley/E**	19
Jimtown Store | P | **Healdsburg/N**	21
John Ash | P | **Santa Rosa/N**	22
Kenwood | G | **Kenwood/N**	21
La Boulange | S | **multi.**	21
Lake Chalet | T, W | **Oakland/E**	14
La Mar | P, W | **Embarcadero**	24
La Note | P | **Berkeley/E**	22
Lark Creek | P | **Walnut Creek/E**	23
LaSalette | P | **Sonoma/N**	24
La Strada | T | **Palo Alto/S**	20
Le Charm Bistro | P | **SoMa**	22
Le Colonial | P | **Downtown**	23
Left Bank | P, S | **multi.**	19
Lion/Compass | P | **Sunnyvale/S**	20
MacCallum | T | **Mendocino/N**	23
Madrona | T | **Healdsburg/N**	26
Marché/Fleurs | P | **Ross/N**	24
MarketBar | P | **Embarcadero**	17
Martini Hse. | P | **St. Helena/N**	26
Meadowood Grill | T | **St. Helena/N**	22
☑ Meadowood Rest. | T | **St. Helena/N**	26
Medjool | P | **Mission**	19
Meritage Martini | G, P | **Sonoma/N**	21
Mezze | S | **Oakland/E**	23
Mistral | P, W | **Redwood Shores/S**	19
MoMo's | T | **S Beach**	17
Monti's | P | **Santa Rosa/N**	21
Moosse Café | T, W | **Mendocino/N**	24
Murray Circle | P | **Sausalito/N**	24
Napa General | T, W | **Napa/N**	19
Nepenthe | P, W | **Big Sur/S**	17
O Chamé | P | **Berkeley/E**	23
Olema Inn | P | **Olema/N**	19
Oliveto Cafe | S | **Oakland/E**	23
Parcel 104 | P | **Santa Clara/S**	23
Park Chalet | G, P, W | **Outer Sunset**	14
Pasta Moon | P | **Half Moon Bay/S**	22
Pazzia | P | **SoMa**	24
Piatti | P, W | **multi.**	19
Piazza D'Angelo | P | **Mill Valley/N**	21
Picante Cocina | P | **Berkeley/E**	21
Piperade | P | **Downtown**	25
Pizza Antica | P | **multi.**	21
Pizzeria Tra Vigne | P | **St. Helena/N**	21

☑ Pizzetta 211 | S | **Outer Rich**	27
Plouf | T | **Downtown**	21
PlumpJack | P | **Olympic Valley/E**	23
Poggio | S | **Sausalito/N**	23
Postino | P | **Lafayette/E**	21
Press | P | **St. Helena/N**	24
Prima | P | **Walnut Creek/E**	24
Ravenous | P | **Healdsburg/N**	21
Red's Java | P, W | **Embarcadero**	15
Rick & Ann | P | **Berkeley/E**	21
Rose Pistola | S | **N Beach**	21
Rose's Cafe | S | **Cow Hollow**	22
☑ Roy's | P, W | **Pebble Bch/S**	25
NEW Rustic | P | **Geyserville/N**	–
Rutherford Grill | P | **Rutherford/N**	23
Sam's Chowder | P, W | **Half Moon Bay/S**	19
Santi | P | **Santa Rosa/N**	24
Savor | P | **Noe Valley**	17
☑ Scoma's | P, W | **Sausalito/N**	22
Sea Salt | P | **Berkeley/E**	21
71 St. Peter | P | **San Jose/S**	20
☑ Sierra Mar | T, W | **Big Sur/S**	28
NEW Skool | P | **Potrero Hill**	–
Slow Club | S | **Mission**	22
Sociale | G, P | **Presidio Hts**	23
South Park | S | **SoMa**	22
Straits | P | **multi.**	20
☑ Sushi Ran | P | **Sausalito/N**	27
Tarpy's | P | **Monterey/S**	21
☑ Tartine | S | **Mission**	27
Ti Couz | S | **Mission**	21
Townhouse B&G | P | **Emeryville/E**	20
Town's End | P | **Embarcadero**	20
Trader Vic's | T | **Palo Alto/S**	17
Tra Vigne | G, T | **St. Helena/N**	24
Underwood Bar | P | **Graton/N**	24
Universal Cafe | P | **Mission**	23
Va de Vi | S, T | **Walnut Creek/E**	24
Waterbar | P, W | **Embarcadero**	20
Waterfront | P, W | **Embarcadero**	18
Water St. Bistro | P, W | **Petaluma/N**	24
Wente Vineyards | P | **Livermore/E**	24
Willi's Seafood | P | **Healdsburg/N**	24
Willi's Wine | P | **Santa Rosa/N**	25
Wine Spectator | T | **St. Helena/N**	24
Yankee Pier | P, T | **multi.**	18
Yumma's | G | **Inner Sunset**	18
Zazie | G | **Cole Valley**	22
Zibibbo | G, P | **Palo Alto/S**	19
Zinsvalley | P | **Napa/N**	18

SPECIAL FEATURES

Zucca | P | Mtn View/S — 18

Z Zuni Café | S | Hayes Valley — 25

PEOPLE-WATCHING

Z Absinthe | Hayes Valley — 22
Ace Wasabi's | Marina — 20
À Côté | Oakland/E — 24
Ana Mandara | Fish. Wharf — 22
Anchor & Hope | SoMa — 21
AsiaSF | SoMa — 17
Balboa Cafe | multi. — 19
NEW Barbacco | Downtown — 25
Barlata | Oakland/E — 21
Barndiva | Healdsburg/N — 20
Bar Tartine | Mission — 23
Baxter's Bistro | Truckee/E — -
Beretta | Mission — 23
Betelnut Pejiu | Cow Hollow — 23
Bing Crosby's | Walnut Creek/E — 19
Bistro Don Giovanni | Napa/N — 24
Z Bistro Jeanty | Yountville/N — 25
Bistro St. Germain | Lower Haight — 20
Z Bix | Downtown — 24
Blowfish Sushi | Mission — 21
Z Blue Bottle | multi. — 23
NEW Bocanova | Oakland/E — 21
Boogaloos | Mission — 18
Z Bottega | Yountville/N — 26
Z Bouchon | Yountville/N — 26
Z Boulevard | Embarcadero — 27
Bridgetender | Tahoe City/E — 18
Brix | Napa/N — 23
Bungalow 44 | Mill Valley/N — 22
NEW Burger Bar | Downtown — 19
Cafe Bastille | Downtown — 17
Café Claude | Downtown — 22
Café de la Presse | Downtown — 18
Candybar | W Addition — 17
NEW Cannery Row Brew | Monterey/S — -
Cascal | Mtn View/S — 19
Catch | Castro — 18
Cav Wine Bar | Hayes Valley — 20
Central Market | Petaluma/N — 25
César | Berkeley/E — 22
Cha Cha Cha | multi. — 21
Chaya | Embarcadero — 22
Z Chez Panisse Café | Berkeley/E — 27
Chez Papa | SoMa — 23
Cin-Cin Wine | Los Gatos/S — 24
Circa | Marina — 16
NEW Comstock | N Beach — -
Cottonwood | Truckee/E — 21
NEW Delarosa | Marina — 22
Dio Deka | Los Gatos/S — 25

Donato | Redwood City/S — 24
Dosa | multi. — 22
Downtown Bakery | Healdsburg/N — 24
Dragonfly | Truckee/E — 22
Ducca | SoMa — 17
E&O Trading | Larkspur/N — 19
Enrico's | N Beach — 16
Epic Roasthse. | Embarcadero — 21
Z Evvia | Palo Alto/S — 27
Farina | Mission — 24
NEW Farmstead | St. Helena/N — -
54 Mint | SoMa — 22
Fish & Farm | Downtown — 20
Five | Berkeley/E — 22
5A5 Steak | Downtown — 22
Flea St. Café | Menlo Pk/S — 25
Flora | Oakland/E — 22
Flour + Water | Mission — 24
Foreign Cinema | Mission — 23
Frjtz Fries | multi. — 17
Front Porch | Bernal Hts — 19
Gar Woods | Carnelian Bay/E — 17
Gitane | Downtown — 21
Gott's Roadside | Napa/N — 21
Grand Pu Bah | Potrero Hill — 20
Heaven's Dog | SoMa — 20
Z Hog Island Oyster | Napa/N — 25
Hopmonk | Sebastopol/N — 18
NEW Ironside | S Beach — 17
Jake's/Lake | Tahoe City/E — 16
Z Jardinière | Civic Ctr — 26
Joya | Palo Alto/S — 20
Junnoon | Palo Alto/S — 22
La Boulange | Noe Valley — 21
La Mar | Embarcadero — 24
LB Steak | San Jose/S — 22
Left Bank | Larkspur/N — 19
Local Kitchen | SoMa — 20
Luce | SoMa — 21
Magnolia | Haight-Ashbury — 20
Mamacita | Marina — 22
NEW Manzanita | Truckee/E — 25
Marinitas | San Anselmo/N — 18
Mario's Bohemian | N Beach — 19
MarketBar | Embarcadero — 17
Martini Hse. | St. Helena/N — 26
Martins West | Redwood City/S — 24
Marzano | Oakland/E — 21
Maverick | Mission — 24
NEW Mayes | Polk Gulch — 19
Mayfield | Palo Alto/S — 19
Medjool | Mission — 19
Mexico DF | Embarcadero — 18
Midi | Downtown — 20

Menus, photos, voting and more – free at ZAGAT.com

POWER SCENES

SPECIAL FEATURES

Restaurant	Location	Score
NEW Prospect	SoMa	-
Quattro	E Palo Alto/S	21
Z Redd	Yountville/N	27
Z Ritz-Carlton	Nob Hill	27
RN74	SoMa	22
Sam's Grill	Downtown	21
Z Seasons	Downtown	26
Sens	Downtown	19
Silks	Downtown	25
Z Spruce	Presidio Hts	26
Z Tadich Grill	Downtown	23
Tommy Toy	Downtown	24
Town Hall	SoMa	23
Urban Tavern	Downtown	17
Z Village Pub	Woodside/S	26
Viognier	San Mateo/S	23
Waterbar	Embarcadero	20
NEW Wayfare Tav.	Downtown	-
Z Zuni Café	Hayes Valley	25

PRE-THEATER

Restaurant	Location	Score
Z Absinthe	Hayes Valley	22
Anzu	Downtown	22
Arlequin	Hayes Valley	18
Bistro Liaison	Berkeley/E	21
Café Kati	Japantown	22
Colibrí	Downtown	20
Fish & Farm	Downtown	20
Grand Cafe	Downtown	20
Hayes St. Grill	Hayes Valley	23
Z Jardinière	Civic Ctr	26
La Scene	Downtown	21
Paul K	Hayes Valley	22
Ponzu	Downtown	20
Sauce	Hayes Valley	18
Scala's Bistro	Downtown	23
Venus	Berkeley/E	21

PRIVATE ROOMS

(Restaurants charge less at off times; call for capacity)

Restaurant	Location	Score
Z Absinthe	Hayes Valley	22
À Côté	Oakland/E	24
Z Acquerello	Polk Gulch	28
Adagia	Berkeley/E	18
Alegrias	Marina	20
Alexander's	Cupertino/S	26
Alfred's Steak	Downtown	22
Ana Mandara	Fish. Wharf	22
Andalu	Mission	20
Angèle	Napa/N	23
Anton/Michel	Carmel/S	25
Arcadia	San Jose/S	21
Z Auberge/Soleil	Rutherford/N	26

Restaurant	Location	Score
Aubergine	Carmel/S	2
Z Aziza	Outer Rich	26
Barndiva	Healdsburg/N	20
Basin	Saratoga/S	2
BayWolf	Oakland/E	24
Bella Vista	Woodside/S	2
Betelnut Pejiu	Cow Hollow	23
Z Big 4	Nob Hill	2
Bing Crosby's	Walnut Creek/E	1
Bistro Liaison	Berkeley/E	2
Blackhawk Grille	Danville/E	2
Blue Plate	Mission	23
Boca	Novato/N	2
Boulette Larder	Embarcadero	2
Z Boulevard	Embarcadero	2
Buca di Beppo	multi.	1
Z Buckeye	Mill Valley/N	2
Café Kati	Japantown	2
Café Rouge	Berkeley/E	20
Campton Place	Downtown	2
Caprice	Tiburon/N	2
Carneros Bistro	Sonoma/N	2
Casanova	Carmel/S	2
Cetrella	Half Moon Bay/S	20
Cha Cha Cha	Mission	2
Chantilly	Redwood City/S	2
Chez TJ	Mtn View/S	2
Cindy's	St. Helena/N	2
Club XIX	Pebble Bch/S	2
Cosmopolitan	SoMa	1
Z Cyrus	Healdsburg/N	2
Dry Creek	Healdsburg/N	2
Eos	Cole Valley	23
Z Erna's Elderberry	Oakhurst/E	28
Fandango	Pacific Grove/S	2
Z Farallon	Downtown	2
Fifth Floor	SoMa	2
Flea St. Café	Menlo Pk/S	2
Z Fleur de Lys	Downtown	2
Florio	Pacific Hts	1
Foreign Cinema	Mission	2
Frantoio	Mill Valley/N	2
Garibaldis	Oakland/E	2
Gary Chu's	Santa Rosa/N	2
Z Gary Danko	Fish. Wharf	2
Grand Cafe	Downtown	20
Grasing's Coastal	Carmel/S	2
Harris'	Polk Gulch	2
Hurley's	Yountville/N	2
Iberia	Menlo Pk/S	2
Il Fornaio	multi.	1
Incanto	Noe Valley	2
Indigo	Civic Ctr	1
Insalata's	San Anselmo/N	2

a Jardinière | **Civic Ctr**	26
ohn Bentley | **Redwood City/S**	24
.enwood | **Kenwood/N**	21
han Toke | **Outer Rich**	22
Kokkari | **Downtown**	27
a La Folie | **Russian Hill**	28
a Forêt | **San Jose/S**	26
a Strada | **Palo Alto/S**	20
avanda | **Palo Alto/S**	19
e Colonial | **Downtown**	23
eft Bank | **multi.**	19
a Le Papillon | **San Jose/S**	26
ion/Compass | **Sunnyvale/S**	20
ittle River Inn | **Little River/N**	21
MacCallum | **Mendocino/N**	23
Madrona | **Healdsburg/N**	26
a Manresa | **Los Gatos/S**	27
Marché | **Menlo Pk/S**	24
a Marinus | **Carmel Valley/S**	27
Martini Hse. | **St. Helena/N**	26
a Masa's | **Downtown**	27
Maya | **SoMa**	20
Millennium | **Downtown**	25
Montrio Bistro | **Monterey/S**	22
Morton's | **Downtown**	24
Moss Room | **Inner Rich**	20
a Navio | **Half Moon Bay/S**	24
North Bch. Rest. | **N Beach**	23
Olema Inn | **Olema/N**	19
One Market | **Embarcadero**	23
Orson | **SoMa**	19
Ozumo | **Embarcadero**	23
a Pacific's Edge | **Carmel/S**	25
alio d'Asti | **Downtown**	20
arcel 104 | **Santa Clara/S**	23
assionfish | **Pacific Grove/S**	25
auline's | **Mission**	22
a Perbacco | **Downtown**	25
esce | **Russian Hill**	22
iatti | **multi.**	19
iazza D'Angelo | **Mill Valley/N**	21
lumed Horse | **Saratoga/S**	25
lumpJack | **Olympic Valley/E**	23
oggio | **Sausalito/N**	23
onzu | **Downtown**	20
ostino | **Lafayette/E**	21
ress | **St. Helena/N**	24
rima | **Walnut Creek/E**	24
NEW Prospect | **SoMa**	-
R&G Lounge | **Chinatown**	24
est. LuLu/Petite | **SoMa**	21
io Grill | **Carmel/S**	22
a Ritz-Carlton | **Nob Hill**	27
ose Pistola | **N Beach**	21

Roy's | **SoMa**	23
Ruth's Chris | **Polk Gulch**	24
Sardine Factory | **Monterey/S**	20
Sauce | **Hayes Valley**	18
Scala's Bistro | **Downtown**	23
Scott's | **multi.**	19
☑ Seasons | **Downtown**	26
71 St. Peter | **San Jose/S**	20
Shadowbrook | **Capitola/S**	18
Silks | **Downtown**	25
☑ Slanted Door | **Embarcadero**	26
Soi4 | **Oakland/E**	24
NEW Sons/Daughters | **Nob Hill**	-
☑ Spruce | **Presidio Hts**	26
St. Orres | **Gualala/N**	22
Straits | **San Jose/S**	20
Table 28 | **Boonville/N**	23
Tamarine | **Palo Alto/S**	25
Tarpy's | **Monterey/S**	21
Terra | **St. Helena/N**	26
Ti Couz | **Mission**	21
Tommy Toy | **Downtown**	24
Town Hall | **SoMa**	23
Trader Vic's | **multi.**	17
Tra Vigne | **St. Helena/N**	24
231 Ellsworth | **San Mateo/S**	23
2223 | **Castro**	21
Vic Stewart | **Walnut Creek/E**	21
☑ Village Pub | **Woodside/S**	26
Viognier | **San Mateo/S**	23
Waterbar | **Embarcadero**	20
Wente Vineyards | **Livermore/E**	24
☑ Yank Sing | **SoMa**	25
Zarzuela | **Russian Hill**	24
Zibibbo | **Palo Alto/S**	19
Zuppa | **SoMa**	20

PRIX FIXE MENUS

(Call for prices and times)

☑ Absinthe | **Hayes Valley**	22
☑ Acquerello | **Polk Gulch**	28
☑ Ad Hoc | **Yountville/N**	27
Ajanta | **Berkeley/E**	25
Alamo Sq. | **W Addition**	20
Amber Bistro | **Danville/E**	22
Ana Mandara | **Fish. Wharf**	22
AsiaSF | **SoMa**	17
☑ Auberge/Soleil | **Rutherford/N**	26
Aubergine | **Carmel/S**	25
Axum Cafe | **Lower Haight**	21
☑ Aziza | **Outer Rich**	26
Baker St. Bistro | **Marina**	22
Basque Cultural | **S San Francisco/S**	21
NEW Baumé | **Palo Alto/S**	28

Bistro Aix | **Marina**	–
NEW Bistro Central Parc | **W Addition**	–
Bistro/Copains | **Occidental/N**	25
Bistro Liaison | **Berkeley/E**	21
Bistro St. Germain | **Lower Haight**	20
☑ Bix | **Downtown**	24
Bridges | **Danville/E**	22
Cafe Bastille | **Downtown**	17
☑ Cafe Gibraltar | **El Granada/S**	27
Caffe Delle Stelle | **Hayes Valley**	16
☑ Canteen | **Tenderloin**	27
Capannina | **Cow Hollow**	25
Caprice | **Tiburon/N**	21
Cellar Door Café | **Santa Cruz/S**	22
Chantilly | **Redwood City/S**	25
☑ Chapeau! | **Inner Rich**	26
Charcuterie | **Healdsburg/N**	21
☑ Chez Panisse | **Berkeley/E**	28
☑ Chez Panisse Café | **Berkeley/E**	27
Chez Papa | **multi.**	23
Chez Spencer | **Mission**	25
Chez TJ | **Mtn View/S**	22
Cliff House | **Outer Rich**	19
☑ Coi | **N Beach**	26
☑ Commis | **Oakland/E**	27
Cuvée | **Napa/N**	20
☑ Cyrus | **Healdsburg/N**	28
Digs Bistro | **Berkeley/E**	23
Drake's | **Inverness/N**	20
Dry Creek | **Healdsburg/N**	24
Duck Club | **Lafayette/E**	21
Ecco | **Burlingame/S**	24
☑ Erna's Elderberry | **Oakhurst/E**	28
Esin | **Danville/E**	25
Espetus | **Hayes Valley**	23
☑ Étoile | **Yountville/N**	24
NEW Eve | **Berkeley/E**	25
☑ Farallon | **Downtown**	24
Firefly | **Noe Valley**	24
☑ Fleur de Lys | **Downtown**	27
☑ French Laundry | **Yountville/N**	29
Garibaldis | **multi.**	22
☑ Gary Danko | **Fish. Wharf**	29
Girl & Fig | **Sonoma/N**	24
Grand Cafe | **Downtown**	20
Grand Pu Bah | **Potrero Hill**	20
Grasing's Coastal | **Carmel/S**	22
Great China | **Berkeley/E**	24
☑ Greens | **Marina**	24
☑ Hana | **Rohnert Pk/N**	28
Hurley's | **Yountville/N**	22
Hyde St. Bistro | **Russian Hill**	21
Il Davide | **San Rafael/N**	20

Indigo | **Civic Ctr**	19
Isa | **Marina**	25
Isobune | **Burlingame/S**	19
☑ Jardinière | **Civic Ctr**	26
Jimmy Beans | **Berkeley/E**	19
Jin Sho | **Palo Alto/S**	24
Junnoon | **Palo Alto/S**	22
Kyo-Ya | **Downtown**	24
La Forêt | **San Jose/S**	26
La Petite Rive | **Little River/N**	26
Lark Creek Steak | **Downtown**	22
La Scene | **Downtown**	21
La Terrasse | **Presidio**	18
☑ La Toque | **Napa/N**	27
Lavanda | **Palo Alto/S**	19
Le Charm Bistro | **SoMa**	22
Ledford Hse. | **Albion/N**	24
☑ Le Papillon | **San Jose/S**	26
Le P'tit Laurent | **Glen Pk**	23
MacCallum | **Mendocino/N**	23
Madrona | **Healdsburg/N**	26
☑ Manresa | **Los Gatos/S**	27
Mantra | **Palo Alto/S**	22
MarketBar | **Embarcadero**	17
Martini Hse. | **St. Helena/N**	26
☑ Masa's | **Downtown**	27
☑ Meadowood Rest. | **St. Helena/N**	26
Metro | **Lafayette/E**	22
Mezze | **Oakland/E**	23
Midi | **Downtown**	20
Millennium | **Downtown**	25
MoMo's | **S Beach**	17
☑ Navio | **Half Moon Bay/S**	24
One Market | **Embarcadero**	23
☑ Pacific's Edge | **Carmel/S**	25
Pakwan | **Hayward/E**	21
Palio d'Asti | **Downtown**	20
Parcel 104 | **Santa Clara/S**	23
Piperade | **Downtown**	25
Plouf | **Downtown**	21
Plumed Horse | **Saratoga/S**	25
Ponzu | **Downtown**	20
Rick & Ann | **Berkeley/E**	21
Risibisi | **Petaluma/N**	22
☑ Ritz-Carlton | **Nob Hill**	27
Roy's | **SoMa**	23
Saison | **Mission**	25
Sanraku | **Downtown**	21
Santé | **Sonoma/N**	23
Scala's Bistro | **Downtown**	23
☑ Scoma's | **Fish. Wharf**	22
☑ Seasons | **Downtown**	26
Sens | **Downtown**	19
Sent Sovi | **Saratoga/S**	25

Menus, photos, voting and more - free at ZAGAT.com

71 St. Peter | **San Jose/S**	20
Z Sierra Mar | **Big Sur/S**	28
Silks | **Downtown**	25
Z Slanted Door | **Embarcadero**	26
South Park | **SoMa**	22
St. Orres | **Gualala/N**	22
Supperclub | **SoMa**	14
Syrah | **Santa Rosa/N**	25
Table 28 | **Boonville/N**	23
Tarpy's | **Monterey/S**	21
Tommy Toy | **Downtown**	24
Ton Kiang | **Outer Rich**	24
Town's End | **Embarcadero**	20
231 Ellsworth | **San Mateo/S**	23
Unicorn | **Downtown**	22
Vik's Chaat | **Berkeley/E**	23
Waterbar | **Embarcadero**	20
Waterfront | **Embarcadero**	18
Zazie | **Cole Valley**	22
Zibibbo | **Palo Alto/S**	19
Zitune | **Los Altos/S**	23
Zucca | **Mtn View/S**	18

QUIET CONVERSATION

Z Acquerello | **Polk Gulch**	28
Alexander's | **Cupertino/S**	26
Applewood Inn | **Guerneville/N**	24
Arcadia | **San Jose/S**	21
Z Auberge/Soleil | **Rutherford/N**	26
Aubergine | **Carmel/S**	25
NEW Baumé | **Palo Alto/S**	28
BayWolf | **Oakland/E**	26
Bella Vista | **Woodside/S**	22
Bushi-tei | **Japantown**	22
Cafe Jacqueline | **N Beach**	25
Campton Place | **Downtown**	25
Casanova | **Carmel/S**	23
Chantilly | **Redwood City/S**	25
Z Chez Panisse | **Berkeley/E**	28
Chez TJ | **Mtn View/S**	22
Z Cyrus | **Healdsburg/N**	28
Duck Club | **multi.**	21
Ecco | **Burlingame/S**	24
Estate | **Sonoma/N**	23
Z Farmhouse Inn | **Forestville/N**	27
Fifth Floor | **SoMa**	25
Five | **Berkeley/E**	22
Flea St. Café | **Menlo Pk/S**	25
Z Fleur de Lys | **Downtown**	27
Forbes Mill | **multi.**	22
Z Gary Danko | **Fish. Wharf**	29
Kyo-Ya | **Downtown**	24
Lalime's | **Berkeley/E**	25
L'Ardoise | **Castro**	23

Z La Toque | **Napa/N**	27
Z Le Papillon | **San Jose/S**	26
Lovejoy's Tea | **Noe Valley**	21
Luce | **SoMa**	21
Madrona | **Healdsburg/N**	26
Z Manresa | **Los Gatos/S**	27
NEW Manzanita | **Truckee/E**	25
Marché | **Menlo Pk/S**	24
Marché/Fleurs | **Ross/N**	24
Z Masa's | **Downtown**	27
Z Meadowood Rest. | **St. Helena/N**	26
Mescolanza | **Outer Rich**	24
Morton's | **San Jose/S**	24
Moss Room | **Inner Rich**	20
Murray Circle | **Sausalito/N**	24
O Chamé | **Berkeley/E**	23
Z Pacific's Edge | **Carmel/S**	25
Plumed Horse | **Saratoga/S**	25
Postino | **Lafayette/E**	21
Quattro | **E Palo Alto/S**	21
Z Quince | **Downtown**	26
NEW Rest. at Ventana | **Big Sur/S**	22
Richmond Rest. | **Inner Rich**	25
Scott's | **Palo Alto/S**	19
Z Seasons | **Downtown**	26
Silks | **Downtown**	25
Solbar | **Calistoga/N**	25
Soule Domain | **Kings Bch/E**	25
St. Orres | **Gualala/N**	22
Terzo | **Cow Hollow**	23
Urban Tavern | **Downtown**	17
Zaré/Fly Trap | **SoMa**	23

RAW BARS

Z Absinthe | **Hayes Valley**	22
Ame | **SoMa**	26
Anchor Oyster | **Castro**	23
Bar Crudo | **W Addition**	25
Bistro Vida | **Menlo Pk/S**	19
Z Bouchon | **Yountville/N**	26
NEW Café des Amis | **Cow Hollow**	–
Café Rouge | **Berkeley/E**	20
Central Market | **Petaluma/N**	25
Z Farallon | **Downtown**	24
NEW Fish Story | **Napa/N**	–
Fog City Diner | **Embarcadero**	19
Foreign Cinema | **Mission**	23
Fresca | **Noe Valley**	22
NEW Georges | **Downtown**	–
Go Fish | **St. Helena/N**	23
Grand Cafe | **Downtown**	20
Grand Pu Bah | **Potrero Hill**	20
NEW Hog & Rocks | **Mission**	–

SPECIAL FEATURES

☑ Hog Island Oyster | **multi.**	25
Lake Chalet | **Oakland/E**	14
Luka's Taproom | **Oakland/E**	20
NEW Mayes | **Polk Gulch**	19
Meritage Martini | **Sonoma/N**	21
Metro | **Lafayette/E**	22
Monti's | **Santa Rosa/N**	21
Nick's Cove | **Marshall/N**	19
Pesce | **Russian Hill**	22
Sam's Chowder | **Half Moon Bay/S**	19
Station House | **Pt Reyes/N**	18
☑ Sushi Ran | **Sausalito/N**	27
☑ Swan Oyster | **Polk Gulch**	27
Waterbar | **Embarcadero**	20
Willi's Seafood | **Healdsburg/N**	24
Woodhse. | **Castro**	20
Yabbies Coastal | **Russian Hill**	22
Yankee Pier | **multi.**	18
Zibibbo | **Palo Alto/S**	19
☑ Zuni Café | **Hayes Valley**	25

ROMANTIC PLACES

☑ Acquerello | **Polk Gulch**	28
☑ Ahwahnee | **Yosemite/E**	19
Albion River Inn | **Albion/N**	24
Alexander's | **Cupertino/S**	26
☑ Amber India | **SoMa**	24
Ana Mandara | **Fish. Wharf**	22
Anton/Michel | **Carmel/S**	25
Applewood Inn | **Guerneville/N**	24
☑ Auberge/Soleil | **Rutherford/N**	26
Aubergine | **Carmel/S**	25
☑ Aziza | **Outer Rich**	26
Barndiva | **Healdsburg/N**	20
NEW Baumé | **Palo Alto/S**	28
Bella Vista | **Woodside/S**	22
☑ Big 4 | **Nob Hill**	23
Bing Crosby's | **Walnut Creek/E**	19
NEW Bistro Central Parc | **W Addition**	–
Bistro/Copains | **Occidental/N**	25
Bistro Elan | **Palo Alto/S**	25
Bistro Vida | **Menlo Pk/S**	19
☑ Bottega | **Yountville/N**	26
☑ Boulevard | **Embarcadero**	27
Brix | **Napa/N**	23
Bushi-tei | **Japantown**	22
Cafe Beaujolais | **Mendocino/N**	24
Cafe Jacqueline | **N Beach**	25
Candybar | **W Addition**	17
NEW Cantinetta Piero | **Yountville/N**	21
Caprice | **Tiburon/N**	21
Casanova | **Carmel/S**	23

Cav Wine Bar | **Hayes Valley**	20
Chantilly | **Redwood City/S**	25
☑ Chapeau! | **Inner Rich**	26
☑ Chez Panisse | **Berkeley/E**	28
Chez Papa | **SoMa**	23
Chez Spencer | **Mission**	25
Chez TJ | **Mtn View/S**	22
Christy Hill | **Tahoe City/E**	20
☑ Coi | **N Beach**	26
Cool Café | **Palo Alto/S**	20
☑ Cyrus | **Healdsburg/N**	28
Deetjen's | **Big Sur/S**	23
Donato | **Redwood City/S**	24
Ducca | **SoMa**	17
Duck Club | **multi.**	21
Ecco | **Burlingame/S**	24
☑ Erna's Elderberry | **Oakhurst/E**	28
Estate | **Sonoma/N**	23
☑ Étoile | **Yountville/N**	24
☑ Farmhouse Inn | **Forestville/N**	27
Fifth Floor | **SoMa**	25
Flea St. Café | **Menlo Pk/S**	25
☑ Fleur de Lys | **Downtown**	27
Forbes Island | **Fish. Wharf**	19
☑ French Laundry | **Yountville/N**	29
Gabriella Café | **Santa Cruz/S**	21
☑ Garden Court | **Downtown**	18
☑ Gary Danko | **Fish. Wharf**	29
Gitane | **Downtown**	21
Harvest Moon | **Sonoma/N**	25
Incanto | **Noe Valley**	24
Indigo | **Civic Ctr**	19
☑ Jardinière | **Civic Ctr**	26
John Ash | **Santa Rosa/N**	22
Katia's Tea | **Inner Rich**	23
Khan Toke | **Outer Rich**	22
La Corneta | **Burlingame/S**	21
NEW La Costanera | **Montara/S**	24
☑ La Folie | **Russian Hill**	28
La Forêt | **San Jose/S**	26
Lalime's | **Berkeley/E**	25
La Mar | **Embarcadero**	24
La Note | **Berkeley/E**	22
La Petite Rive | **Little River/N**	26
L'Ardoise | **Castro**	23
☑ La Toque | **Napa/N**	27
Le Papillon | **San Jose/S**	26
Little River Inn | **Little River/N**	21
Luce | **SoMa**	21
MacCallum | **Mendocino/N**	23
Madera | **Menlo Pk/S**	23
Madrona | **Healdsburg/N**	26
Ma Maison | **Aptos/S**	20
Mantra | **Palo Alto/S**	22

Menus, photos, voting and more – free at ZAGAT.com

NEW Manzanita | **Truckee/E**	25
Marché/Fleurs | **Ross/N**	24
☑ Marinus | **Carmel Valley/S**	27
Martini Hse. | **St. Helena/N**	26
☑ Masa's | **Downtown**	27
Matterhorn Swiss | **Russian Hill**	22
NEW Mayes | **Polk Gulch**	19
☑ Meadowood Rest. | **St. Helena/N**	26
Medjool | **Mission**	19
Moosse Café | **Mendocino/N**	24
Moss Room | **Inner Rich**	20
Murray Circle | **Sausalito/N**	24
Napa Wine Train | **Napa/N**	18
Nick's Cove | **Marshall/N**	19
O Chamé | **Berkeley/E**	23
Olema Inn | **Olema/N**	19
Ozumo | **Oakland/E**	23
☑ Pacific's Edge | **Carmel/S**	25
Pampas | **Palo Alto/S**	21
Peasant/Pear | **Danville/E**	24
Pianeta | **Truckee/E**	21
Picco | **Larkspur/N**	25
☑ Quince | **Downtown**	26
Rest. at Stevenswood | **Little River/N**	24
NEW Rest. at Ventana | **Big Sur/S**	22
Risibisi | **Petaluma/N**	22
☑ Ritz-Carlton | **Nob Hill**	27
River Ranch | **Tahoe City/E**	15
☑ Roy's | **Pebble Bch/S**	25
Sea Salt | **Berkeley/E**	21
Sent Sovi | **Saratoga/S**	25
71 St. Peter | **San Jose/S**	20
Shadowbrook | **Capitola/S**	18
Shokolaat | **Palo Alto/S**	21
☑ Sierra Mar | **Big Sur/S**	28
Silks | **Downtown**	25
Slow Club | **Mission**	22
Solbar | **Calistoga/N**	25
Soule Domain | **Kings Bch/E**	25
Starlight | **Sebastopol/N**	22
St. Michael's | **Palo Alto/S**	22
St. Orres | **Gualala/N**	22
Sunnyside | **Tahoe City/E**	17
Supperclub | **SoMa**	14
Tav./Lark Creek | **Larkspur/N**	19
Terra | **St. Helena/N**	26
Terzo | **Cow Hollow**	23
1300/Fillmore | **W Addition**	23
Twist | **Campbell/S**	20
Venticello | **Nob Hill**	23
Viognier | **San Mateo/S**	23
Wente Vineyards | **Livermore/E**	24
Wild Goose | **Tahoe Vista/E**	-

Wolfdale's | **Tahoe City/E**	25
Woodward's Gdn. | **Mission**	24
Zarzuela | **Russian Hill**	24

SENIOR APPEAL

☑ Acquerello | **Polk Gulch**	28
Alfred's Steak | **Downtown**	22
Alioto's | **Fish. Wharf**	18
Anton/Michel | **Carmel/S**	25
NEW Baker/Banker | **Upper Fillmore**	25
NEW Baumé | **Palo Alto/S**	28
Bella Vista | **Woodside/S**	22
☑ Big 4 | **Nob Hill**	23
Bing Crosby's | **Walnut Creek/E**	19
NEW Bocanova | **Oakland/E**	21
Caprice | **Tiburon/N**	21
Chantilly | **Redwood City/S**	25
Christy Hill | **Tahoe City/E**	20
Cole's Chop | **Napa/N**	24
Cook St. Helena | **St. Helena/N**	25
☑ Cyrus | **Healdsburg/N**	28
Duck Club | **multi.**	21
Epic Roasthse. | **Embarcadero**	21
Estate | **Sonoma/N**	23
Fior d'Italia | **N Beach**	20
☑ Fleur de Lys | **Downtown**	27
Forbes Mill | **multi.**	22
☑ Garden Court | **Downtown**	18
Harris' | **Polk Gulch**	25
Hayes St. Grill | **Hayes Valley**	23
☑ House of Prime | **Polk Gulch**	25
Izzy's Steak | **Marina**	20
Joe DiMaggio | **N Beach**	20
La Ginestra | **Mill Valley/N**	21
Lalime's | **Berkeley/E**	25
LB Steak | **San Jose/S**	22
Le Central Bistro | **Downtown**	20
NEW Manzanita | **Truckee/E**	25
☑ Masa's | **Downtown**	27
☑ Meadowood Rest. | **St. Helena/N**	26
Morton's | **multi.**	24
North Bch. Rest. | **N Beach**	23
Plumed Horse | **Saratoga/S**	25
NEW Rest. at Ventana | **Big Sur/S**	22
Rotunda | **Downtown**	21
Sardine Factory | **Monterey/S**	20
☑ Scoma's | **Fish. Wharf**	22
Sens | **Downtown**	19
Solbar | **Calistoga/N**	25
Soule Domain | **Kings Bch/E**	25
☑ Tadich Grill | **Downtown**	23
Urban Tavern | **Downtown**	17

SPECIAL FEATURES

Vic Stewart	**Walnut Creek/E**	21
Waterbar	**Embarcadero**	20
NEW Wayfare Tav.	**Downtown**	-
Zaré/Fly Trap	**SoMa**	23

SINGLES SCENES

Ace Wasabi's	**Marina**	20
Anchor & Hope	**SoMa**	21
Andalu	**Mission**	20
Balboa Cafe	**multi.**	19
NEW Barbacco	**Downtown**	25
Barlata	**Oakland/E**	21
Barndiva	**Healdsburg/N**	20
Beach Chalet	**Outer Sunset**	14
Beretta	**Mission**	23
Betelnut Pejiu	**Cow Hollow**	23
Bissap Baobab	**Mission**	22
Z Bix	**Downtown**	24
Blowfish Sushi	**Mission**	21
Blue Plate	**Mission**	23
Broken Record	**Excelsior**	22
Butterfly	**Embarcadero**	22
Cafe Bastille	**Downtown**	17
Café Claude	**Downtown**	22
NEW Cannery Row Brew	**Monterey/S**	-
Cascal	**Mtn View/S**	19
Catch	**Castro**	18
Cha Cha Cha	**multi.**	21
Cin-Cin Wine	**Los Gatos/S**	24
NEW Comstock	**N Beach**	-
Cosmopolitan	**SoMa**	19
Cottonwood	**Truckee/E**	21
Davenport Rdhse.	**Davenport/S**	19
Dosa	**Upper Fillmore**	22
Dragonfly	**Truckee/E**	22
E&O Trading	**multi.**	19
Elite Cafe	**Pacific Hts**	19
Emmy's Spaghetti	**Bernal Hts**	19
15 Romolo	**N Beach**	-
5A5 Steak	**Downtown**	22
Flora	**Oakland/E**	22
Foreign Cinema	**Mission**	23
Fritz Fries	**multi.**	17
Gar Woods	**Carnelian Bay/E**	17
NEW Georges	**Downtown**	-
Gitane	**Downtown**	21
Gordon Biersch	**multi.**	15
Grand Pu Bah	**Potrero Hill**	20
Guaymas	**Tiburon/N**	17
Half Moon Brew	**Half Moon Bay/S**	15
NEW Heart	**Mission**	-
Heaven's Dog	**SoMa**	20
NEW Hog & Rocks	**Mission**	-
Home	**Castro**	19
Hopmonk	**Sebastopol/N**	18
NEW Ironside	**S Beach**	17
Jake's/Lake	**Tahoe City/E**	16
Joya	**Palo Alto/S**	20
Junnoon	**Palo Alto/S**	22
Kan Zaman	**Haight-Ashbury**	19
La Trappe	**N Beach**	18
Local Kitchen	**SoMa**	20
Luce	**SoMa**	21
Luna Park	**Mission**	19
Magnolia	**Haight-Ashbury**	20
NEW Marlowe	**SoMa**	-
Martins West	**Redwood City/S**	24
NEW Mayes	**Polk Gulch**	19
Medjool	**Mission**	19
Miss Pearl's	**Oakland/E**	16
MoMo's	**S Beach**	17
Monk's Kettle	**Mission**	20
Moody's Bistro	**Truckee/E**	24
Nettie's Crab	**Cow Hollow**	18
Nihon	**Mission**	21
Orson	**SoMa**	19
Ottimista	**Cow Hollow**	17
Ozumo	**multi.**	23
Poesia	**Castro**	21
Quattro	**E Palo Alto/S**	21
Red Lantern	**Redwood City/S**	18
River Ranch	**Tahoe City/E**	15
Rose Pistola	**N Beach**	21
Serpentine	**Dogpatch**	19
Sino	**San Jose/S**	19
Slow Club	**Mission**	22
NEW Starbelly	**Castro**	20
Sunnyside	**Tahoe City/E**	17
Sushi Groove	**multi.**	22
Ti Couz	**Mission**	21
Tipsy Pig	**Marina**	19
Tokyo Go Go	**Mission**	21
Tommy's Mex.	**Outer Rich**	18
Tres Agaves	**S Beach**	17
Tsunami	**W Addition**	22
2223	**Castro**	21
Umami	**Cow Hollow**	23
Universal Cafe	**Mission**	23
Xanh	**Mtn View/S**	21
Zibibbo	**Palo Alto/S**	19
Z Zuni Café	**Hayes Valley**	25

SLEEPERS

(Good food, but little known)

Bistro Moulin	**Monterey/S**	29
Café Fiore	**S Lake Tahoe/E**	25
Evan's	**S Lake Tahoe/E**	25
4505 Meats	**Embarcadero**	28

Menus, photos, voting and more – free at ZAGAT.com

SPECIAL FEATURES

Burger Joint | **multi.** 18
BurgerMeister | **multi.** 20
Cactus Taqueria | **multi.** 20
Cheesecake Fac. | **multi.** 16
Ebisu | **S San Francisco/S** 23
Z El Tonayense | **multi.** 24
FatApple's | **multi.** 17
Fentons | **Oakland/E** 20
Fog City Diner | **Embarcadero** 19
Fremont Diner | **Sonoma/N** 22
Gar Woods | **Carnelian Bay/E** 17
Goat Hill Pizza | **Potrero Hill** 20
Gott's Roadside | **St. Helena/N** 21
Hard Rock | **Fish. Wharf** 12
Hula's | **multi.** 18
Jake's/Lake | **Tahoe City/E** 16
Jake's Steaks | **Marina** 21
Joe's Cable Car | **Excelsior** 23
La Corneta | **multi.** 21
Lanesplitter | **Oakland/E** 16
Little Chihuahua | **W Addition** 22
MacArthur Pk. | **Palo Alto/S** 17
Max's | **multi.** 17
Mel's Drive-In | **multi.** 14
Mijita | **S Beach** 21
Miller's Deli | **Polk Gulch** 19
Park Chalet | **Outer Sunset** 14
Pasta Pomodoro | **multi.** 17
Patxi's Pizza | **Cow Hollow** 22
Pauline's | **Mission** 22
Piaci | **Ft Bragg/N** 27
NEW Pi Bar | **Mission** 14
Picante Cocina | **Berkeley/E** 21
Pizza Antica | **Lafayette/E** 21
Pizza Nostra | **Potrero Hill** 22
Pizza Pl./Noriega | **Outer Sunset** -
Pizzeria Picco | **Larkspur/N** 25
Plant Cafe | **Marina** 20
Rosso Pizzeria | **Santa Rosa/N** 26
Rutherford Grill | **Rutherford/N** 23
Sardine Factory | **Monterey/S** 20
Shen Hua | **Berkeley/E** 19
NEW SliderBar | **Palo Alto/S** -
Stinking Rose | **N Beach** 18
Sunnyside | **Tahoe City/E** 17
NEW Super Duper | **Castro** -
NEW TacoBar | **Pacific Hts** -
NEW Tacolicious | **multi.** 23
Tonga | **Nob Hill** 14
NEW Trueburger | **Oakland/E** -

THEME RESTAURANTS

Benihana | **multi.** 17
Bing Crosby's | **Walnut Creek/E** 19

Buca di Beppo | **multi.** 15
Hard Rock | **Fish. Wharf** 12
Hula's | **multi.** 18
Joe DiMaggio | **N Beach** 20
Max's | **multi.** 17
Miss Pearl's | **Oakland/E** 16
Napa Wine Train | **Napa/N** 18
Stinking Rose | **N Beach** 18
Supperclub | **SoMa** 14

TRENDY

Ace Wasabi's | **Marina** 20
À Côté | **Oakland/E** 24
Adesso | **Oakland/E** 23
Anchor & Hope | **SoMa** 21
Z A16 | **Marina** 25
Balboa Cafe | **Cow Hollow** 19
Barndiva | **Healdsburg/N** 20
Bar Tartine | **Mission** 23
Beretta | **Mission** 23
Betelnut Pejiu | **Cow Hollow** 23
Bistro Don Giovanni | **Napa/N** 24
Z Bix | **Downtown** 24
Blowfish Sushi | **Mission** 21
Bocadillos | **N Beach** 23
NEW Boot/Shoe | **Oakland/E** 24
Z Bottega | **Yountville/N** 26
Z Bouchon | **Yountville/N** 26
Bungalow 44 | **Mill Valley/N** 22
NEW Café des Amis | **Cow Hollow** -
Café Rouge | **Berkeley/E** 20
Cascal | **Mtn View/S** 19
César | **Berkeley/E** 22
Cha Cha Cha | **multi.** 21
Charanga | **Mission** 23
Chaya | **Embarcadero** 22
Coco500 | **SoMa** 23
NEW Commonwealth | **Mission** -
Corso | **Berkeley/E** 23
NEW Delarosa | **Marina** 22
Z Delfina | **Mission** 26
Doña Tomás | **Oakland/E** 21
Dosa | **multi.** 22
Emmy's Spaghetti | **Bernal Hts** 19
Farina | **Mission** 24
15 Romolo | **N Beach** -
5A5 Steak | **Downtown** 22
Flora | **Oakland/E** 22
Flour + Water | **Mission** 24
Fonda Solana | **Albany/E** 22
Foreign Cinema | **Mission** 23
Front Porch | **Bernal Hts** 19
Garibaldis | **Oakland/E** 22
Gitane | **Downtown** 21

Grand Pu Bah | **Potrero Hill**	20
NEW Heart | **Mission**	-
Heaven's Dog | **SoMa**	20
NEW Hog & Rocks | **Mission**	-
Hopmonk | **Sebastopol/N**	18
Z Jardinière | **Civic Ctr**	26
Joya | **Palo Alto/S**	20
Junnoon | **Palo Alto/S**	22
Lake Chalet | **Oakland/E**	14
Limón | **Mission**	23
Mamacita | **Marina**	22
Mantra | **Palo Alto/S**	22
Maverick | **Mission**	24
Medjool | **Mission**	19
Miss Pearl's | **Oakland/E**	16
NEW Morph | **Outer Rich**	-
Z Mustards | **Yountville/N**	25
Naked Fish | **S Lake Tahoe/E**	23
Nihon | **Mission**	21
Z Nopa | **W Addition**	25
Orson | **SoMa**	19
Osha Thai | **multi.**	20
Ottimista | **Cow Hollow**	17
Ozumo | **multi.**	23
Pauline's | **Mission**	22
Piazza D'Angelo | **Mill Valley/N**	21
NEW Pi Bar | **Mission**	14
Picán | **Oakland/E**	21
Picco | **Larkspur/N**	25
Pizzeria Delfina | **Mission**	25
Pizzeria Picco | **Larkspur/N**	25
Press | **St. Helena/N**	24
Red Lantern | **Redwood City/S**	18
Salt House | **SoMa**	21
Z Sebo | **Hayes Valley**	27
Serpentine | **Dogpatch**	19
Sidebar | **Oakland/E**	20
Sino | **San Jose/S**	19
Z Slanted Door | **Embarcadero**	26
Slow Club | **Mission**	22
NEW Social Kitchen | **Inner Sunset**	-
Spork | **Mission**	20
SPQR | **Pacific Hts**	24
NEW Starbelly | **Castro**	20
Supperclub | **SoMa**	14
Sushi Groove | **multi.**	22
Tamarine | **Palo Alto/S**	25
Terzo | **Cow Hollow**	23
1300/Fillmore | **W Addition**	23
Tipsy Pig | **Marina**	19
Town Hall | **SoMa**	23
Tres Agaves | **S Beach**	17
Tsunami | **W Addition**	22
Umami | **Cow Hollow**	23

Underwood Bar | **Graton/N**	24
Waterbar | **Embarcadero**	20
Wood Tavern | **Oakland/E**	25
Xanh | **Mtn View/S**	21
XYZ | **SoMa**	20
Yoshi's SF | **W Addition**	21
Zibibbo | **Palo Alto/S**	19
Z Zuni Café | **Hayes Valley**	25
ZuZu | **Napa/N**	24

VALET PARKING

Z Absinthe | **Hayes Valley**	22
Z Ahwahnee | **Yosemite/E**	19
Albona Rist. | **N Beach**	23
Amber Bistro | **Danville/E**	22
Ame | **SoMa**	26
Americano | **Embarcadero**	18
Ana Mandara | **Fish. Wharf**	22
Andalu | **Mission**	20
Anzu | **Downtown**	22
Aquarius | **Santa Cruz/S**	23
Arcadia | **San Jose/S**	21
Z Auberge/Soleil | **Rutherford/N**	26
Aubergine | **Carmel/S**	25
Z Aziza | **Outer Rich**	26
NEW Baker/Banker | **Upper Fillmore**	25
Balboa Cafe | **Cow Hollow**	19
NEW Barbacco | **Downtown**	25
Bardessono | **Yountville/N**	21
Baxter's Bistro | **Truckee/E**	-
Benihana | **Burlingame/S**	17
Z Big 4 | **Nob Hill**	23
Bing Crosby's | **Walnut Creek/E**	19
Z Bix | **Downtown**	24
Blowfish Sushi | **San Jose/S**	21
Boccalone | **Embarcadero**	24
Z Boulevard | **Embarcadero**	27
Bridges | **Danville/E**	22
Z Buckeye | **Mill Valley/N**	23
Campton Place | **Downtown**	25
NEW Cantinetta Piero | **Yountville/N**	21
Casa Orinda | **Orinda/E**	16
Cha Am Thai | **SoMa**	19
Chantilly | **Redwood City/S**	25
Chaya | **Embarcadero**	22
Cheesecake Fac. | **Santa Clara/S**	16
Cliff House | **Outer Rich**	19
Club XIX | **Pebble Bch/S**	22
Z Coi | **N Beach**	26
Cole's Chop | **Napa/N**	24
Crustacean | **Polk Gulch**	25
Delancey St. | **Embarcadero**	18
Dio Deka | **Los Gatos/S**	25

Ducca	**SoMa**	17
Duck Club	**Lafayette/E**	21
Elite Cafe	**Pacific Hts**	19
Epic Roasthse.	**Embarcadero**	21
☑ Evvia	**Palo Alto/S**	27
☑ Farallon	**Downtown**	24
Farina	**Mission**	24
Fifth Floor	**SoMa**	25
Fior d'Italia	**N Beach**	20
5A5 Steak	**Downtown**	22
☑ Fleur de Lys	**Downtown**	27
Florio	**Pacific Hts**	19
Foreign Cinema	**Mission**	23
Garibaldis	**multi.**	22
☑ Gary Danko	**Fish. Wharf**	29
Grand Cafe	**Downtown**	20
Harris'	**Polk Gulch**	25
Hayes St. Grill	**Hayes Valley**	23
Home	**Castro**	19
☑ House of Prime	**Polk Gulch**	25
Hunan	**Chinatown**	21
Il Fornaio	**multi.**	19
Insalata's	**San Anselmo/N**	23
☑ Jardinière	**Civic Ctr**	26
Joe DiMaggio	**N Beach**	20
☑ Kokkari	**Downtown**	27
Kuleto's	**Downtown**	21
Kyo-Ya	**Downtown**	24
☑ La Folie	**Russian Hill**	28
La Scene	**Downtown**	21
☑ La Toque	**Napa/N**	27
LB Steak	**San Jose/S**	22
Le Cheval	**Oakland/E**	20
Lion/Compass	**Sunnyvale/S**	20
Luce	**SoMa**	21
MacArthur Pk.	**Palo Alto/S**	17
NEW Manzanita	**Truckee/E**	25
Marinitas	**San Anselmo/N**	18
☑ Marinus	**Carmel Valley/S**	27
Marzano	**Oakland/E**	21
☑ Masa's	**Downtown**	27
Matterhorn Swiss	**Russian Hill**	22
Maykadeh	**N Beach**	23
Medjool	**Mission**	19
NEW Meritage/Claremont	**Berkeley/E**	25
Mexico DF	**Embarcadero**	18
Midi	**Downtown**	20
Millennium	**Downtown**	25
Miss Pearl's	**Oakland/E**	16
MoMo's	**S Beach**	17
Morton's	**multi.**	24
☑ Navio	**Half Moon Bay/S**	24
Nob Hill Café	**Nob Hill**	21
North Bch. Rest.	**N Beach**	23

One Market	**Embarcadero**	23
Ozumo	**Embarcadero**	23
☑ Pacific's Edge	**Carmel/S**	25
Parcel 104	**Santa Clara/S**	23
☑ Perbacco	**Downtown**	25
Picco	**Larkspur/N**	25
Pizzeria Picco	**Larkspur/N**	25
Plumed Horse	**Saratoga/S**	25
Poggio	**Sausalito/N**	23
Postino	**Lafayette/E**	21
Prima	**Walnut Creek/E**	24
NEW Prospect	**SoMa**	-
Quattro	**E Palo Alto/S**	21
☑ Quince	**Downtown**	26
Rest. LuLu/Petite	**SoMa**	21
Rist. Capellini	**San Mateo/S**	18
☑ Ritz-Carlton	**Nob Hill**	27
Rose Pistola	**N Beach**	21
☑ Roy's	**Pebble Bch/S**	25
Ruth's Chris	**multi.**	24
Santé	**Sonoma/N**	23
☑ Scoma's	**Fish. Wharf**	22
Scott's	**Walnut Creek/E**	19
☑ Seasons	**Downtown**	26
☑ Sierra Mar	**Big Sur/S**	28
Silks	**Downtown**	25
☑ Slanted Door	**Embarcadero**	26
Solbar	**Calistoga/N**	25
☑ Spruce	**Presidio Hts**	26
Straits	**Downtown**	20
Sunnyside	**Tahoe City/E**	17
Suppenküche	**Hayes Valley**	22
Supperclub	**SoMa**	14
Tav./Lark Creek	**Larkspur/N**	19
Terzo	**Cow Hollow**	23
Thanh Long	**Outer Sunset**	24
Tokyo Go Go	**Mission**	21
Tommy Toy	**Downtown**	24
Townhouse B&G	**Emeryville/E**	20
Trader Vic's	**Emeryville/E**	17
231 Ellsworth	**San Mateo/S**	23
Ubuntu	**Napa/N**	26
Urban Tavern	**Downtown**	17
NEW Velvet Room	**Downtown**	-
Venticello	**Nob Hill**	23
Vitrine	**SoMa**	21
Waterbar	**Embarcadero**	20
Waterfront	**Embarcadero**	18
NEW Wayfare Tav.	**Downtown**	-
Wente Vineyards	**Livermore/E**	24
Wine Spectator	**St. Helena/N**	24
XYZ	**SoMa**	20
Yankee Pier	**multi.**	18

Zibbibo | Palo Alto/S — 19
Zuni Café | Hayes Valley — 25

VIEWS

Ahwahnee | Yosemite/E — 19
Albion River Inn | Albion/N — 24
Alioto's | Fish. Wharf — 18
Americano | Embarcadero — 18
Angèle | Napa/N — 23
Applewood Inn | Guerneville/N — 24
Aquarius | Santa Cruz/S — 23
Auberge/Soleil | Rutherford/N — 26
Barbara's | Princeton Sea/S — 20
Barndiva | Healdsburg/N — 20
Beach Chalet | Outer Sunset — 14
Bella Vista | Woodside/S — 22
Imperial/Berkeley | Berkeley/E — 20
Big Sur | Big Sur/S — 21
Bistro Boudin | Fish. Wharf — 20
Bistro Don Giovanni | Napa/N — 24
Blackhawk Grille | Danville/E — 21
Boulette Larder | Embarcadero — 25
NEW Brick/Bottle | Corte Madera/N — -
Bridgetender | Tahoe City/E — 18
Brix | Napa/N — 23
Butterfly | Embarcadero — 22
Cafe Beaujolais | Mendocino/N — 24
Cafe Gibraltar | El Granada/S — 27
Caprice | Tiburon/N — 21
Chapter & Moon | Ft Bragg/N — 23
Chaya | Embarcadero — 22
Cheesecake Fac. | Downtown — 16
Chez TJ | Mtn View/S — 22
Christy Hill | Tahoe City/E — 20
Cliff House | Outer Rich — 19
Club XIX | Pebble Bch/S — 22
Cool Café | Palo Alto/S — 20
Cottonwood | Truckee/E — 21
Davenport Rdhse. | Davenport/S — 19
Delancey St. | Embarcadero — 18
Dragonfly | Truckee/E — 22
Drake's | Inverness/N — 20
Duck Club | multi. — 21
Enrico's | N Beach — 16
Eos | Cole Valley — 23
Epic Roasthse. | Embarcadero — 21
Erna's Elderberry | Oakhurst/E — 28
Étoile | Yountville/N — 24
Farmhouse Inn | Forestville/N — 27
Fish | Sausalito/N — 25
Forbes Island | Fish. Wharf — 19
Frascati | Russian Hill — 25
Gar Woods | Carnelian Bay/E — 17

Gordon Biersch | Embarcadero — 15
Greens | Marina — 24
Guaymas | Tiburon/N — 17
Half Moon Brew | Half Moon Bay/S — 15
Hog Island Oyster | Embarcadero — 25
Il Cane Rosso | Embarcadero — 22
Il Fornaio | Carmel/S — 19
Jake's/Lake | Tahoe City/E — 16
John Ash | Santa Rosa/N — 22
Kenwood | Kenwood/N — 21
NEW La Costanera | Montara/S — 24
NEW Lafitte | Embarcadero — -
La Forêt | San Jose/S — 26
La Mar | Embarcadero — 24
La Petite Rive | Little River/N — 26
La Terrasse | Presidio — 18
Ledford Hse. | Albion/N — 24
Lion/Compass | Sunnyvale/S — 20
Little River Inn | Little River/N — 21
Madera | Menlo Pk/S — 23
Mama's on Wash. | N Beach — 25
Marinus | Carmel Valley/S — 27
McCormick/Kuleto | Fish. Wharf — 20
Meadowood Grill | St. Helena/N — 22
Meadowood Rest. | St. Helena/N — 26
Medjool | Mission — 19
Mendo Café | Mendocino/N — 20
Mendo Hotel | Mendocino/N — 19
NEW Meritage/Claremont | Berkeley/E — 25
Mezza Luna/Caffè | Princeton Sea/S — 22
Mijita | Embarcadero — 21
Mistral | Redwood Shores/S — 19
MoMo's | S Beach — 17
Moosse Café | Mendocino/N — 24
Murray Circle | Sausalito/N — 24
Napa General | Napa/N — 19
Napa Wine Train | Napa/N — 18
Navio | Half Moon Bay/S — 24
Nepenthe | Big Sur/S — 17
Nick's Cove | Marshall/N — 19
One Market | Embarcadero — 23
Ozumo | Embarcadero — 23
Pacific's Edge | Carmel/S — 25
Park Chalet | Outer Sunset — 14
Piatti | Mill Valley/N — 19
Picco | Larkspur/N — 25
Piccolo Teatro | Sausalito/N — 22
Press | St. Helena/N — 24
Ravens' | Mendocino/N — 22
Red's Java | Embarcadero — 15

SPECIAL FEATURES

Rest. at Stevenswood | **Little River/N** — 24

NEW Rest. at Ventana | **Big Sur/S** — 22

River Ranch | **Tahoe City/E** — 15

🅩 Rivoli | **Berkeley/E** — 27

Rotunda | **Downtown** — 21

🅩 Roy's | **Pebble Bch/S** — 25

NEW Rustic | **Geyserville/N** — -

Sam's Chowder | **Half Moon Bay/S** — 19

🅩 Scoma's | **multi.** — 22

Scott's | **multi.** — 19

Shadowbrook | **Capitola/S** — 18

🅩 Sierra Mar | **Big Sur/S** — 28

🅩 Slanted Door | **Embarcadero** — 26

St. Orres | **Gualala/N** — 22

Sunnyside | **Tahoe City/E** — 17

Sutro's | **Outer Rich** — 20

Trader Vic's | **multi.** — 17

Venticello | **Nob Hill** — 23

Waterbar | **Embarcadero** — 20

Waterfront | **Embarcadero** — 18

Water St. Bistro | **Petaluma/N** — 24

Wente Vineyards | **Livermore/E** — 24

Wild Goose | **Tahoe Vista/E** — -

Wine Spectator | **St. Helena/N** — 24

Wolfdale's | **Tahoe City/E** — 25

Zazu | **Santa Rosa/N** — 25

VISITORS ON EXPENSE ACCOUNT

🅩 Acquerello | **Polk Gulch** — 28

Alexander's | **Cupertino/S** — 26

🅩 Auberge/Soleil | **Rutherford/N** — 26

Aubergine | **Carmel/S** — 25

NEW Barbacco | **Downtown** — 25

Bardessono | **Yountville/N** — 21

NEW Baumé | **Palo Alto/S** — 28

NEW Benu | **SoMa** — -

🅩 Bottega | **Yountville/N** — 26

🅩 Boulevard | **Embarcadero** — 27

Campton Place | **Downtown** — 25

🅩 Chez Panisse | **Berkeley/E** — 28

Chez TJ | **Mtn View/S** — 22

Club XIX | **Pebble Bch/S** — 22

🅩 Cyrus | **Healdsburg/N** — 28

Deetjen's | **Big Sur/S** — 23

Dry Creek | **Healdsburg/N** — 24

Epic Roasthse. | **Embarcadero** — 21

🅩 Erna's Elderberry | **Oakhurst/E** — 28

🅩 Evvia | **Palo Alto/S** — 27

Fifth Floor | **SoMa** — 25

Flea St. Café | **Menlo Pk/S** — 25

🅩 Fleur de Lys | **Downtown** — 27

Forbes Mill | **Los Gatos/S** — 22

🅩 French Laundry | **Yountville/N** — 29

🅩 Gary Danko | **Fish. Wharf** — 29

🅩 Greens | **Marina** — 24

Harris' | **Polk Gulch** — 25

🅩 Jardinière | **Civic Ctr** — 26

John Ash | **Santa Rosa/N** — 22

🅩 Kaygetsu | **Menlo Pk/S** — 27

🅩 Kokkari | **Downtown** — 27

Kyo-Ya | **Downtown** — 24

🅩 La Folie | **Russian Hill** — 28

La Forêt | **San Jose/S** — 26

🅩 La Toque | **Napa/N** — 27

🅩 Manresa | **Los Gatos/S** — 27

NEW Manzanita | **Truckee/E** — 25

🅩 Marinus | **Carmel Valley/S** — 27

🅩 Masa's | **Downtown** — 27

McCormick/Kuleto | **Fish. Wharf** — 20

🅩 Meadowood Rest. | **St. Helena/N** — 26

Midi | **Downtown** — 20

NEW Morimoto | **Napa/N** — -

Morton's | **Downtown** — 24

Napa Wine Train | **Napa/N** — 18

Oliveto Rest. | **Oakland/E** — 24

Orson | **SoMa** — 19

🅩 Pacific's Edge | **Carmel/S** — 25

Plumed Horse | **Saratoga/S** — 25

Press | **St. Helena/N** — 24

NEW Prospect | **SoMa** — -

NEW Rest. at Ventana | **Big Sur/S** — 22

🅩 Ritz-Carlton | **Nob Hill** — 27

Roy's | **SoMa** — 23

🅩 Roy's | **Pebble Bch/S** — 25

Santé | **Sonoma/N** — 23

🅩 Seasons | **Downtown** — 26

Sent Sovi | **Saratoga/S** — 25

71 St. Peter | **San Jose/S** — 20

🅩 Sierra Mar | **Big Sur/S** — 28

Silks | **Downtown** — 25

Sino | **San Jose/S** — 19

Tommy Toy | **Downtown** — 24

🅩 Village Pub | **Woodside/S** — 26

Waterbar | **Embarcadero** — 20

NEW Wayfare Tav. | **Downtown** — -

WINE BARS

All Seasons | **Calistoga/N** — 23

🅩 A16 | **Marina** — 25

Bar Bambino | **Mission** — 23

Bar Tartine | **Mission** — 23

Bocadillos | **N Beach** — 23

Bounty Hunter | **Napa/N** — 19

Cafe Zoetrope/Mammarella's | **N Beach** — 20

Menus, photos, voting and more - free at ZAGAT.com

WINNING WINE LISTS

SPECIAL FEATURES

Dry Creek | **Healdsburg/N**	24
Eos | **Cole Valley**	23
Epic Roasthse. | **Embarcadero**	21
Z Erna's Elderberry | **Oakhurst/E**	28
Estate | **Sonoma/N**	23
Z Étoile | **Yountville/N**	24
Fandango | **Pacific Grove/S**	22
Z Farallon | **Downtown**	24
Z Farm | **Napa/N**	23
Z Farmhouse Inn | **Forestville/N**	27
NEW Farmstead | **St. Helena/N**	-
Fifth Floor | **SoMa**	25
54 Mint | **SoMa**	22
Fig Cafe/Wine | **Glen Ellen/N**	25
Five | **Berkeley/E**	22
Flea St. Café | **Menlo Pk/S**	25
Z Fleur de Lys | **Downtown**	27
Forbes Mill | **multi.**	22
Z French Laundry | **Yountville/N**	29
Gabriella Café | **Santa Cruz/S**	21
Z Gary Danko | **Fish. Wharf**	29
NEW Georges | **Downtown**	-
Girl & Fig | **Sonoma/N**	24
Gott's Roadside | **Napa/N**	21
Grasing's Coastal | **Carmel/S**	22
Z Greens | **Marina**	24
NEW Heirloom | **Mission**	-
Incanto | **Noe Valley**	24
Indigo | **Civic Ctr**	19
Z Jardinière | **Civic Ctr**	26
John Ash | **Santa Rosa/N**	22
Jole | **Calistoga/N**	25
Kenwood | **Kenwood/N**	21
Z Kokkari | **Downtown**	27
Kuleto's | **Downtown**	21
Z La Folie | **Russian Hill**	28
La Forêt | **San Jose/S**	26
La Mar | **Embarcadero**	24
Lark Creek Steak | **Downtown**	22
LaSalette | **Sonoma/N**	24
Z La Toque | **Napa/N**	27
Lavanda | **Palo Alto/S**	19
LB Steak | **San Jose/S**	23
Ledford Hse. | **Albion/N**	24
Z Le Papillon | **San Jose/S**	26
Liberty Cafe | **Bernal Hts**	22
Local Kitchen | **SoMa**	20
Luce | **SoMa**	21
Luella | **Russian Hill**	22
Madrona | **Healdsburg/N**	26
Z Manresa | **Los Gatos/S**	27
NEW Manzanita | **Truckee/E**	25
Marché | **Menlo Pk/S**	24

Marinitas | **San Anselmo/N**	18
Z Marinus | **Carmel Valley/S**	27
Martini Hse. | **St. Helena/N**	26
Martins West | **Redwood City/S**	24
Z Masa's | **Downtown**	27
Meadowood Grill | **St. Helena/N**	22
Z Meadowood Rest. | **St. Helena/N**	26
Mendo Bistro | **Ft Bragg/N**	24
Millennium | **Downtown**	25
Monk's Kettle | **Mission**	20
Monti's | **Santa Rosa/N**	21
Montrio Bistro | **Monterey/S**	22
Mosaic | **Forestville/N**	25
Moss Room | **Inner Rich**	20
Z Mustards | **Yountville/N**	25
Naomi Sushi | **Menlo Pk/S**	23
Napa Wine Train | **Napa/N**	18
Z Navio | **Half Moon Bay/S**	24
Nick's Cove | **Marshall/N**	19
955 Ukiah | **Mendocino/N**	23
North Bch. Rest. | **N Beach**	23
Oliveto Cafe | **Oakland/E**	23
Oliveto Rest. | **Oakland/E**	24
One Market | **Embarcadero**	23
Ottimista | **Cow Hollow**	17
Oxbow Wine | **Napa/N**	22
Z Pacific's Edge | **Carmel/S**	25
Palio d'Asti | **Downtown**	20
Pampas | **Palo Alto/S**	21
Passionfish | **Pacific Grove/S**	25
Picán | **Oakland/E**	21
Picco | **Larkspur/N**	25
Piperade | **Downtown**	25
Plumed Horse | **Saratoga/S**	25
PlumpJack | **Olympic Valley/E**	23
Poggio | **Sausalito/N**	23
Prima | **Walnut Creek/E**	24
Z Quince | **Downtown**	26
Z Redd | **Yountville/N**	27
NEW Rest. at Ventana | **Big Sur/S**	22
Rest. LuLu/Petite | **SoMa**	21
Rio Grill | **Carmel/S**	22
Ristobar | **Marina**	-
Z Ritz-Carlton | **Nob Hill**	27
Z Rivoli | **Berkeley/E**	27
RN74 | **SoMa**	22
Rose Pistola | **N Beach**	21
Roy's | **SoMa**	23
Z Roy's | **Pebble Bch/S**	25
NEW Rustic | **Geyserville/N**	-
Santé | **Sonoma/N**	23
Santi | **Santa Rosa/N**	24
Sardine Factory | **Monterey/S**	20

Menus, photos, voting and more - free at ZAGAT.com

SPECIAL FEATURES

Menus, photos, voting and more - free at ZAGAT.com

ALPHABETICAL
PAGE INDEX

All places are in San Francisco unless otherwise noted (East of San
Francisco=E; North of San Francisco=N; South of San Francisco=S).

Visit ZAGAT.mobi from your mobile phone

335

Menus, photos, voting and more - free at ZAGAT.com

Wine Vintage Chart

This chart is based on our 0 to 30 scale. The ratings (by U. of South Carolina law professor **Howard Stravitz**) reflect vintage quality and the wine's readiness to drink. A dash means the wine is past its peak or too young to rate. Loire ratings are for dry whites.

Whites	95	96	97	98	99	00	01	02	03	04	05	06	07	08
France:														
Alsace	24	23	23	25	23	25	26	23	21	24	25	24	26	-
Burgundy	27	26	23	21	24	24	24	27	23	26	27	25	25	24
Loire Valley	-	-	-	-	23	24	26	22	24	27	23	23	24	
Champagne	26	27	24	23	25	24	21	26	21	-	-	-	-	-
Sauternes	21	23	25	23	24	24	29	25	24	21	26	23	27	25
California:														
Chardonnay	-	-	-	23	22	25	26	22	26	29	24	27	-	
Sauvignon Blanc	-	-	-	-	-	-	-	25	26	25	27	25	-	
Austria:														
Grüner V./Riesl.	24	21	26	23	25	22	23	25	26	25	24	26	24	22
Germany:	21	26	21	22	24	20	29	25	26	27	28	25	27	25

Reds	95	96	97	98	99	00	01	02	03	04	05	06	07	08
France:														
Bordeaux	26	25	23	25	24	29	26	24	26	24	28	24	23	25
Burgundy	26	27	25	24	27	22	24	27	25	23	28	25	24	-
Rhône	26	22	24	27	26	27	26	-	26	24	27	25	26	-
Beaujolais	-	-	-	-	-	-	-	-	24	-	27	24	25	23
California:														
Cab./Merlot	27	25	28	23	25	-	27	26	25	24	26	23	26	24
Pinot Noir	-	-	-	-	24	23	25	26	25	26	24	23	27	25
Zinfandel	-	-	-	-	-	-	25	23	27	22	22	21	21	25
Oregon:														
Pinot Noir	-	-	-	-	-	-	-	26	24	25	26	26	25	27
Italy:														
Tuscany	24	-	29	24	27	24	27	-	25	27	26	25	24	-
Piedmont	21	27	26	25	26	28	27	-	25	27	26	25	26	-
Spain:														
Rioja	26	24	25	-	25	24	28	-	23	27	26	24	25	-
Ribera del Duero/ Priorat	26	27	25	24	25	24	27	20	24	27	26	24	26	-
Australia:														
Shiraz/Cab.	24	26	25	28	24	24	27	27	25	26	26	24	22	-
Chile:	-	-	24	-	25	23	26	24	25	24	27	25	24	-
Argentina:														
Malbec	-	-	-	-	-	-	-	-	25	26	27	24	-	

ZAGATWINE™

Stay home and paint the town red.

SAVE $100

Enjoy 12 great wines for ONLY $69.99

(*Plus* FREE GIFT)

Order at **zagatwine.com/2161016**

or call **1-800-892-4427** quote code 2161016

ZAGAT

San Francisco Transit Map

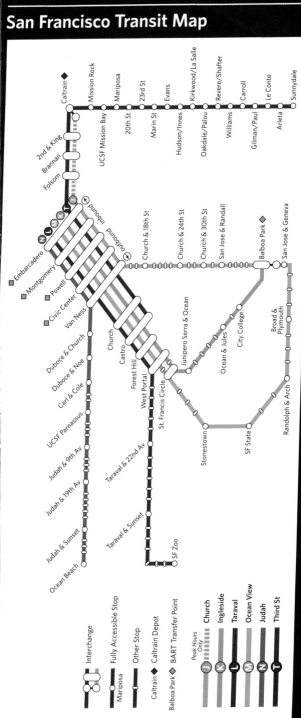

Caltrain · Mission Rock · Mariposa · 20th St · 23rd St · Marin St · Evans · Hudson/Innes · Kirkwood/La Salle · Oakdale/Palou · Revere/Shafter · Williams · Carroll · Gilman/Paul · Le Conte · Arleta · Sunnydale

2nd & King
Brannan
Folsom

UCSF Mission Bay

Embarcadero
Montgomery
Powell
Civic Center
Van Ness

Church & 18th St · Church & 24th St · Church & 30th St · San Jose & Randall · Balboa Park · San Jose & Geneva

Duboce & Church
Duboce & Noe
Carl & Cole
UCSF Parnassus
Judah & 9th Av
Judah & 19th Av
Judah & Sunset
Ocean Beach

Church
Castro
Forest Hill
West Portal
St. Francis Circle

Taraval & 22nd Av
Taraval & Sunset
SF Zoo

Junipero Serra & Ocean
Ocean & Jules
City College
Broad & Plymouth
Randolph & Arch

Stonestown
SF State

Interchange
Fully Accessible Stop
Mariposa
Other Stop
Caltrain Depot — Caltrain
Balboa Park — BART Transfer Point

Peak Hours Only

Church
Ingleside
Taraval
Ocean View
Judah
Third St

Most Popular Restaurants

Map coordinates follow each name. Sections A–G show the City of San Francisco (see adjacent map). Sections H–O show the Greater Bay Area and outlying regions (see reverse side of map).

1 Gary Danko (A-5)

2 Boulevard (C-8)

3 Slanted Door (B-8)

4 French Laundry (J-3)

5 Cyrus (J-2)

6 Chez Panisse (L-3)

7 Zuni Café (E-5)

8 Kokkari Estiatorio (B-7)

9 Chez Panisse Café (L-3)

10 A16 (B-3)

11 Delfina (F-5)

12 Bouchon (J-3)

13 Fleur de Lys (C-6)

14 Acquerello (C-5)

15 Quince (B-7)

16 Yank Sing (C-7, C-8)

17 Tadich Grill (C-7)

18 Ad Hoc (J-3)

19 Perbacco (C-7)

20 Chapeau! (D-2)

21 Absinthe (E-5)

22 Jardinière (D-5)

23 La Folie (B-5)

24 In-N-Out† (A-6)

25 Auberge du Soleil (J-3)

26 Ritz-Carlton Din. Rm. (C-6)

27 Bottega (J-3)

28 Redd (J-3)

29 House of Prime Rib (C-5)

30 Evvia (L-3)

31 Bistro Jeanty (J-3)

32 Mustards Grill (J-3)

33 Aziza (D-1)

34 Buckeye Roadhouse* (K-3)

35 Tartine Bakery (F-5)

36 Spruce (C-3)

37 Chow/Park Chow† (F-5)

38 Manresa (M-4)

39 Scoma's (A-6, L-3)

40 Nopa (E-4)

41 Burma Superstar† (D-2)

42 Farallon (C-6)

43 Amber India† (L-3)

44 Zachary's Pizza† (L-3)

45 Village Pub (L-3)

46 Greens (A-4)

47 Range (G-5)

48 Coi (B-7)

49 Hog Island Oyster (B-8, K-3)

50 Bix (B-7)

---

*Indicates tie with above   † Indicates multiple branches